iPhone
The Missing Manual

Ninth Edition

iPhone: The Missing Manual, Ninth Edition   BY DAVID POGUE

Published by O'Reilly Media, Inc., 1005 Gravenstein Highway North, Sebastopol, CA 95472.

O'Reilly books may be purchased for educational, business, or sales promotional use. Online editions are also available for most titles (*safari.oreilly.com*). For more information, contact our corporate/institutional sales department: 800.998.9938 or *corporate@oreilly.com*.

Copy Editor: Julie Van Keuren

Indexers: David Pogue, Julie Van Keuren

Cover Designers: Monica Kamsvaag and Phil Simpson

Interior Designer: Phil Simpson (based on a design by Ron Bilodeau)

Print History:
December 2015.   First Printing.
March 2016   Second Printing.

ISBN: 978-1-49-191791-6

Contents

The Missing Credits. x

Introduction. 1
    About the iPhone. 1
    About This Book. 2
    iPhone 6s and 6s Plus: What's New 4
    What's New in iOS 9. 7

Part One: The iPhone as Phone

Chapter 1: The Guided Tour. 13
    Sleep Switch (On/Off). 13
    The Lock Screen 15
    Home Button. 19
    Silencer Switch, Volume Keys. 22
    Screen 23
    Cameras and Flash. 26
    Sensors 27
    SIM Card Slot. 27
    Headphone Jack. 29
    Microphone, Speakerphone. 30
    The Charge/Sync Connector. 31
    Antenna Band 32
    In the Box. 32
    Seven Basic Finger Techniques. 33
    iPhone 6s Family: Force Touch 36
    Charging the iPhone. 39
    Battery Life Tips. 40
    The Home Screen 45
    Control Center. 47
    Notifications 51
    Password (or Fingerprint) Protection. 57

Chapter 2: Typing, Editing & Searching 63
    The Keyboard. 63
    iPhone 6s: The Secret Trackpad. 79
    Dictation 80
    Cut, Copy, Paste. 86
    The Definitions Dictionary. 89
    Speak!. 90
    Spotlight: Global Search 90
    The "Proactive" Search Screen 93

Chapter 3: Phone Calls & FaceTime **95**

Dialing from the Phone App 95

The Favorites List 96

The Recents List 99

Contacts 101

The Keypad 112

Answering Calls 113

Not Answering Calls 115

Do Not Disturb 116

Fun with Phone Calls 118

Custom Ringtones 122

FaceTime Video Calls 123

FaceTime Audio Calls 126

Chapter 4: Siri Voice Command **129**

Voice Command 130

How to Use Siri 131

How to Use "Hey Siri" 132

What to Say to Siri 133

Advanced Siri 153

Chapter 5: Voicemail, Texting & Bluetooth **157**

Visual Voicemail 157

Text Messages (SMS) 162

iMessages 170

Instant Audio, Video, and Photos 172

Text Messages: Details and Misc. 176

Free Text Messages 180

Chat Programs 181

Call Waiting 181

Call Forwarding 182

Caller ID 183

Bluetooth Accessories 183

Chapter 6: Large Type, Kid Mode & Accessibility **187**

VoiceOver 188

Zooming 192

Invert Colors and Grayscale 195

Speech 196

How to De-Sparsify iOS 9's Design 196

Switch Control 200

AssistiveTouch 201

Touch Accommodations 203

3D Touch 204

Keyboard 205

Shake to Undo..205
Vibration 205
Call Audio Routing...206
Home Button..206
Reachability..206
Hearing Assistance...206
Media (Subtitle Options)...208
Guided Access (Kiosk Mode) 208
The Instant Screen-Dimming Trick....................................... 210
Accessibility Shortcut..211

Part Two: Pix, Flix & Apps

Chapter 7: Songs, Videos & Apple Music............................ 215
Apple Music 215
My Music..218
Playback Control..220
Playlists..224
Up Next 227
"For You" Tab...229
"New" Tab 229
iTunes Radio..230
Speakers and Headphones 233
Familiar iPod Features... 235
The iTunes Store 237
The Videos App...240

Chapter 8: The Camera 245
The Camera App..245
Photo Mode..248
Live Photos (iPhone 6s Models) 260
Square Mode 262
Pano Mode...262
Video Mode..264
Slo-Mo Mode 267
Time-Lapse Mode 268
Trimming a Video... 268
Editing Photos 269
Managing and Sharing Photos.. 277
753 Ways to Use Photos and Videos.....................................286
My Photo Stream 296
iCloud Photo Sharing 299
iCloud Photo Library 304
Geotagging 305
Capturing the Screen 307

Chapter 9: All About Apps **309**
    Two Ways to the App Store 309
    Organizing Your Apps 316
    Folders.. 319
    App Preferences 322
    App Updates 322
    How to Find Good Apps... 323
    The App Switcher 325
    AirPrint: Printing from the Phone................................ 329
    The Share Sheet 330
    AirDrop.. 331
    iCloud Drive... 334

Chapter 10: The Built-In Apps **337**
    Calculator 337
    Calendar 339
    Clock 349
    Compass 354
    Game Center 356
    Health... 359
    iBooks... 362
    Maps... 373
    News 388
    Notes.. 390
    Podcasts... 394
    Reminders.. 397
    Stocks... 403
    Tips 405
    Voice Memos.. 406
    Wallet 409
    Watch 410
    Weather.. 410
    More Standard Apps 412

Part Three: The iPhone Online

Chapter 11: Getting Online **417**
    Cellular Networks.. 417
    Wi-Fi Hotspots 419
    Airplane Mode and Wi-Fi Off Mode 422
    Personal Hotspot (Tethering)................................... 424
    Twitter and Facebook.. 427

Chapter 12: Safari. **429**
    Safari Tour.. 429
    Zooming and Scrolling 431
    Full-Screen Mode.. 432

Typing a Web Address 433
Searching in Safari 435
Bookmarks.. 438
The History List... 441
Shared Links (@) 442
The Reading List.. 443
Link-Tapping Tricks.. 445
Saving Graphics... 446
Saved Passwords and Credit Cards................................ 446
Manipulating Multiple Pages...................................... 449
Reader View 451
Web Security 452
Five Happy Surprises in the ⬆ Panel 454

Chapter 13: Email.. 457
Setting Up Your Account.. 457
Downloading Mail 460
VIPs and Flagged Messages....................................... 465
What to Do with a Message 468
Writing Messages.. 478
Surviving Email Overload... 484

Part Four: Connections

Chapter 14: Syncing with iTunes 489
The Three Faces of iTunes.. 489
Your Stuff.. 490
iTunes Store.. 494
Apple Music 497
Syncing the iPhone 497
iTunes Tabs.. 502
Summary Tab 502
Apps Tab... 503
Music Tab 503
Movies and TV Shows Tabs....................................... 505
Podcasts Tab... 505
Books Tab 506
Tones Tab.. 506
Photos Tab 506
Info Tab.. 509
On My Device 509
One iPhone, Multiple Computers 510
One Computer, Multiple iPhones.................................. 510
Backing Up the iPhone 510

Chapter 15: iCloud **513**
   What iCloud Giveth 513
   iCloud Sync 515
   My Photo Stream, Photo Sharing 518
   Find My iPhone 518
   Email 521
   Video, Music, Apps: Locker in the Sky 522
   The Price of Free 523
   Apple Pay (iPhone 6/6s Families) 524
   Family Sharing 528

Chapter 16: Continuity: iPhone Meets Mac **535**
   Continuity Setup 535
   Mac as Speakerphone 536
   Texting from the Mac 538
   Instant Hotspot 539
   Handoff 540
   AirDrop 543

Chapter 17: The Corporate iPhone **545**
   The Perks 545
   Setup 547
   Exchange + Your Stuff 550
   A Word on Troubleshooting 551
   Virtual Private Networking (VPN) 552

Chapter 18: Settings **555**
   Two Important Settings Tricks 556
   Airplane Mode 557
   Wi-Fi 557
   Carrier 558
   Bluetooth 558
   Cellular 559
   Personal Hotspot 561
   Notifications 561
   Control Center 562
   Do Not Disturb 562
   General 562
   Display & Brightness 567
   Wallpaper 568
   Sounds 568
   Touch ID & Passcode 570
   Battery 570
   Privacy 570
   iCloud 573
   iTunes & App Store 574
   Wallet & Apple Pay 574
   Mail, Contacts, Calendars 575

Notes..580
Reminders...580
Phone...581
Messages..582
FaceTime...583
Maps...584
Compass..584
Safari..584
News...587
Music..588
Videos...588
Photos & Camera..588
iBooks...589
Podcasts..589
Game Center..589
Twitter, Facebook, Flickr, Vimeo......................................590
App Preferences..591

Part Five: Appendixes

Appendix A: Signup & Setup **595**
Buying a New iPhone...595
Setting Up a New Phone...597
Upgrading an iPhone to iOS 9...601
Software Updates..602
Restrictions and Parental Controls....................................603
Cases and Accessories...605

Appendix B: Troubleshooting & Maintenance **607**
First Rule: Install the Updates...607
Six Ways to Reset the Phone..607
iPhone Doesn't Turn On..610
Battery Life Is Terrible..611
Out of Space..611
Phone and Internet Problems..613
Warranty and Repair..613
The Battery Replacement Program.....................................614
What to Do About a Cracked Screen...................................615
Where to Go from Here..615

Index **617**

The Missing Credits

David Pogue (author, illustrator, indexer) is the founder of Yahoo Tech (*yahootech.com*), a job for which he was groomed by 13 years of writing the weekly tech column for *The New York Times*.

He's also a monthly columnist for *Scientific American*, a three-time Emmy-winning correspondent for *CBS News Sunday Morning*, the host of several *NOVA* miniseries on PBS, and the creator of the Missing Manual series. He's written or cowritten 80 books, including 40 in this series, six in the *For Dummies* line (including *Macs, Magic, Opera,* and *Classical Music*), two novels (one for middle-schoolers), *The World According to Twitter, Pogue's Basics,* and *Pogue's Basics: Life*. In his other life, David is a former Broadway show conductor, a magician, and a funny public speaker. He lives in Connecticut with his wife, Nicki, and three awesome children.

Links to his columns and videos await at *www.davidpogue.com*. He welcomes feedback about his books by email at *david@pogueman.com*.

Julie Van Keuren (copy editor, indexer, layout) quit her newspaper job in 2006 and moved to Montana to live the freelance-editing dream. She and her husband, M.H. (who's living the novel-writing dream), have two teenage sons, Dexter and Michael. Email: *little_media@yahoo.com*.

Phil Simpson (original design) runs his graphic design business from Southbury, Connecticut. His work includes corporate branding, publication design, communications support, and advertising. In his free time he is a homebrewer, ice cream maker, wannabe woodworker, and is on a few tasting panels. He lives with his wife and some great felines. Email: *phil. simpson@pmsgraphics.com*.

Rich Koster (technical reviewer). The iPhone became Rich's first cellphone the very first evening it was sold by Apple. From the start, he began corresponding with David Pogue, sharing tips, tricks, and observations; eventually, David asked him to be the beta reader of the first edition of *iPhone: The Missing Manual*—and hired him as the tech editor of subsequent editions. Rich is a husband, father, graphics artist, writer, and Disney fan (@DisneyEcho on Twitter).

Acknowledgments

The Missing Manual series is a joint venture between the dream team introduced on these pages and O'Reilly Media. I'm grateful to all of them, especially to the core of the iPhone Missing Manual team introduced above.

The work done on previous editions lives on in this one; for that, I'm grateful to Jude Biersdorfer, Matt Gibstein, Teresa Brewer, Brian Jepson, Apple's Trudy Muller, Philip Michaels, O'Reilly's Nan Barber, and my incredible assistant Jan Carpenter, who keeps me from falling apart like wet Kleenex. Thanks to David Rogelberg and Tim O'Reilly for believing in the idea; to Kellee Katagi, Judy Le, and Nancy Young for proofreading and fact-checking; and above all, to Nicki, Kell, Tia, and Jeffrey. They make these books—and everything else—possible.

—David Pogue

Also by David Pogue

Missing Manuals are witty, well written guides to computer products that don't come with printed manuals (which is just about all of them). Each book features a handcrafted index; cross-references to specific page numbers (not just "see Chapter 14"); and an ironclad promise never to put an apostrophe in the possessive pronoun *its*.

- *OS X El Capitan: The Missing Manual*
- *David Pogue's Digital Photography: The Missing Manual*
- *iPad: The Missing Manual, Seventh Edition*
- *Windows 10: The Missing Manual*
- *Switching to the Mac: The Missing Manual, El Capitan Edition*

Introduction

How do you make the point that the iPhone has changed the world? The easy answer is "use statistics"—750 million sold, 1.5 million apps available on the iPhone App Store, 90 billion downloads.... Trouble is, those statistics get stale almost before you've finished typing them.

Maybe it's better to talk about the aftermath. How since the iPhone came along, cell carriers (AT&T, Verizon, Sprint, and so on) have opened up the calcified, conservative way they used to consider new cellphone designs. How every phone and its brother now have a touchscreen. How Google (Android) phones, Windows, and even BlackBerry phones all have their own app stores. How, in essence, everybody wants to be the iPhone.

Apple introduces a new iPhone model every fall. In September 2015, for example, it introduced the ninth iPhone models, the iPhone 6s and 6s Plus, with more features and faster guts.

More importantly, there's a new, free version of the iPhone's software, called iOS 9. (Why not "iPhone OS" anymore? Because the same operating system runs on the iPad and the iPod Touch. It's not just for iPhones anymore, and saying "the iPhone/iPad/iPod Touch OS" takes too long.)

You can run iOS 9 on *older* iPhone models without having to buy a new phone. This book covers all the phones that can run iOS 9: the iPhone 4s, iPhone 5, iPhone 5c, iPhone 5s, iPhone 6 and 6 Plus, iPhone 6s and 6s Plus.

About the iPhone

So what is the iPhone? Really, the better question is what *isn't* the iPhone?

It's a cellphone, obviously. But it's also a full-blown iPod, complete with a dazzling screen for watching videos. And it's a sensational pocket Internet viewer. It shows fully formatted email (with attachments, thank you) and displays entire web pages with fonts and design intact. It's tricked out with a tilt sensor, a proximity sensor, a light sensor, Wi-Fi, Bluetooth, GPS, a gyroscope, a barometer, and that amazing multitouch screen.

For many people, the iPhone is primarily a camera and a camcorder—one that's getting better with every year's new model.

Furthermore, it's a calendar, address book, calculator, alarm clock, stopwatch, stock tracker, traffic reporter, RSS reader, and weather forecaster. It even stands in for a flashlight and, with the screen off, a pocket mirror.

And don't forget the App Store. Thanks to the 1.5 million add-on programs that await there, the iPhone is also a fast, wicked-fun pocket computer. All those free or cheap programs can turn it into a medical reference, a musical keyboard, a time tracker, a remote control, a sleep monitor, a tip calculator, an ebook reader, and more. And thousands of games, with smooth 3D graphics and tilt control.

All of this sends the iPhone's utility and power through the roof. Calling it a phone is practically an insult. Apple probably should have called it an "iPod," but that name was taken.

About This Book

You don't get a printed manual when you buy an iPhone. Online, you can find an electronic PDF manual that covers the basics well, but it's largely free of details, hacks, workarounds, tutorials, humor, and any acknowledgment of the iPhone's flaws. You can't easily mark your place, underline, or read it in the bathroom.

The purpose of this book, then, is to serve as the manual that should have accompanied the iPhone. (If you have an original iPhone, iPhone 3G, iPhone 3GS, or iPhone 4, you really need one of this book's earlier editions. If you have an iPhone 4s, 5, 5c, 5s, 6, 6 Plus, 6s, or 6s Plus, this book assumes that you've installed iOS 9; see Appendix A.)

Writing a book about the iPhone is a study in exasperation, because the darned thing is a moving target. Apple updates the iPhone's software fairly often, piping in new features, bug fixes, speed-ups, and so on.

Therefore, you should think of this book the way you think of the first iPhone: as a darned good start. To keep in touch with updates we make to it as developments unfold, drop in to the book's Errata/Changes page. (Go to *www.missingmanuals.com*, click this book's name, and then click **View/ Submit Errata**.)

About the Outline

iPhone: The Missing Manual is divided into five parts, each containing several chapters:

- Part 1, **The iPhone as Phone,** covers everything related to phone calls: dialing, answering, voice control, voicemail, conference calling, text messaging, iMessages, MMS, and the Contacts (address book) program. It's also where you can read about FaceTime, the iPhone's video-calling feature; Siri, the "virtual assistant"; and the surprisingly rich array of features for people with disabilities—some of which are useful even for people without them.

- Part 2, **Pix, Flix & Apps,** is dedicated to the iPhone's built-in software, with a special emphasis on its multimedia abilities: playing music, podcasts, movies, TV shows, and photos; capturing photos and videos; using the Maps app; reading ebooks; and so on. These chapters also cover some of the standard techniques that most apps share: installing, organizing, and quitting them; switching among them; and sharing material from within them using the Share sheet.

- Part 3, **The iPhone Online,** is a detailed exploration of the iPhone's third talent: its ability to get you onto the Internet, either over a Wi-Fi hotspot connection or via the cellular network. It's all here: email, web browsing, and tethering (that is, letting your phone serve as a sort of Internet antenna for your laptop).

- Part 4, **Connections,** describes the world beyond the iPhone itself— like the copy of iTunes on your Mac or PC that can fill up the iPhone with music, videos, and photos; and syncing the calendar, address book, and mail settings. These chapters also cover the iPhone's control panel, the Settings program; Continuity (the wireless integration of iPhone and Mac); and how the iPhone syncs wirelessly with corporate networks using Microsoft Exchange ActiveSync—or with your own computers using Apple's iCloud service.

- Part 5, **Appendixes,** contains two reference chapters. Appendix A walks you through the setup process; Appendix B is a master compendium of troubleshooting, maintenance, and battery information.

About→These→Arrows

Throughout this book, and throughout the Missing Manual series, you'll find sentences like this one: Tap Settings→General→Keyboard. That's shorthand for a much longer instruction that directs you to open three nested screens in sequence, like this: "Tap the Settings button. On the next screen, tap General. On the screen after that, tap Keyboard." (In this book, tappable things on the screen are printed in orange to make them stand out.)

Similarly, this kind of arrow shorthand helps to simplify the business of choosing commands in menus on your Mac or PC, like File→Print.

About MissingManuals.com

To get the most out of this book, visit *www.missingmanuals.com*. Click the Missing CDs link, and then click this book's title to reveal a neat, organized list of the shareware, freeware, and bonus articles mentioned in this book.

The website also offers corrections and updates to the book; to see them, click the book's title, and then click View/Submit Errata. In fact, please submit corrections yourself! Each time we print more copies of this book, we'll make any confirmed corrections you've suggested. We'll also note such changes on the website, so you can mark important corrections into your own copy of the book, if you like. And we'll keep the book current as Apple releases more iPhone updates.

iPhone 6s and 6s Plus: What's New

Apple's usual routine is to introduce a new iPhone shape every other year (iPhone 3G, iPhone 4, iPhone 5, iPhone 6)—and then release a follow-up, upgraded "s" model in alternate years (iPhone 3GS, iPhone 4s, iPhone 5s, iPhone 6s). The 2015–2016 models, sure enough, fit right in. They're follow-up models that look exactly like the 6 and 6 Plus but have a few enhancements:

- **Speed.** There's a new processor in the iPhone 6s family; Apple says it's "up to 70 percent" faster. Opening apps, switching apps, processing things—it all happens faster on the 6s.

  The Touch ID fingerprint reader is twice as fast now, too; if you've set up your phone to require unlocking every time you use it, you may come to cherish this feature most of all. When you press the Home button, the screen lights up so fast, you wonder if, in fact, any authentication process took place at all. (It did.)

Apple also tuned both its Wi-Fi and its cellular (LTE) antennas to make them faster. Who doesn't like faster Internet?

- **3D Touch shortcut menus.** Until now, touchscreen phones have known only *that* you've touched the screen—not how hard. That's Apple's radical idea: to turn pressure into a new way of interacting with your gadget. On the iPhone 6s models, 3D Touch triggers short-cut menus—a lot like the ones that appear when you right-click on a computer.

  But once you learn your way around, these shortcut menus can save you a lot of waiting, navigating, and fussing. In essence, they let you tell the app what you want to do before you even open it, and that saves you steps.

- **3D Touch peeking and popping.** Hard to explain, but very cool: If you hard-press something in a list—your email Inbox, for example, or a link in a text message, or a photo thumbnail—you get a pop-up bub-ble showing you what's inside. Peeking is, in other words, exactly like the Quick Look feature on the Mac. It lets you see what's inside a link, icon, or list item without losing your place or changing apps.

If you find one that you do want to open fully, you can press harder yet to open the message normally. (Apple calls that "popping.")

- **Pressure sensitivity.** Peek and pop respond to pressure at only two thresholds. But, in fact, 3D Touch detects a continuum of pressure, like a gas pedal. You can see this effect in the Notes app, when you sketch with the pencil tool; it draws darker as you bear down more. App makers can incorporate pressure sensitivity any way they like. For example, in the game Freeblade, pressing harder zooms you into the scene more.

- **Better camera.** The new camera takes 12-megapixel photos, up from 8. And it can capture 4K video (that is, four times the resolution of high definition). Resolution, by itself, doesn't improve a photo or a video, but you may occasionally see improvements in image quality.

- **Selfie flash.** The new iPhones now offer a "flash" for taking selfies. At the moment you take the shot, the screen lights up to illuminate your face. Better yet: It samples the ambient room light and adjusts the color of the screen's "flash" to give your face the best flesh tones.

Of course, the iPhone screen is too tiny to supply much light, even at full brightness. So for the iPhone 6s and 6s Plus, Apple developed a custom chip with a single purpose: to *overclock* the screen. In selfie situations, the screen blasts at three times its usual full brightness, just for a fraction of a second. It's crazy-bright and works fantastically well.

- **Tougher screen and body.** For the first time since the original iPhone came out in 2007, Apple now admits that it buys the glass for its screens from Corning, which developed the famously strong Gorilla Glass.

Apple still will not say that it's using Gorilla Glass, though—because it's not. According to Apple, its iPhone 6s screens use a formulation that's superior even to Corning's current brand-name glass. Apple engineers collaborated with Corning to develop a proprietary glass that isn't available to its rivals. That explains Apple's claim that the iPhone 6s's new glass is stronger and more durable than any other phone's—and that it is not, in fact, Gorilla Glass.

The aluminum alloy of the body is also stronger. Apple says it's now "7000 series aluminum." That's got to be better than 6800 series aluminum, or whatever the iPhone had before.

- **Live Photos.** These are still photos that, when hard-pressed on the iPhone, play back as 3 seconds of video, with sound. What you're getting is 1.5 seconds before the moment you snapped the photo, plus 1.5 seconds after.

If it's a device or software program that doesn't know about Live Photos—you send it as a text message, for example, or open it in Photoshop—then only the JPEG image arrives at the other end.

What's New in iOS 9

In 2013, Apple freaked out the world by introducing a radical iPhone-software redesign in iOS 7: clean, white, almost barren, with a razor-thin font (Helvetica Neue) and bright, light colors. The design was controversial and polarizing.

The design for iOS 9 is the same—by now, people have gotten used to it—and the improvements are focused on features and flexibility.

TIP: If the fonts are too thin for your taste, you can fatten them up just enough by turning on Settings→Display & Brightness→Bold Text. While you're there, you can make text larger in most apps, too; tap the Larger Type control.

Tiny tweaks are everywhere in iOS 9, but here's a quick rundown.

Big-Ticket Items

- **Speed.** Apple put a lot of work into making things feel faster and more fluid—especially opening and moving between email, messages, web pages, and PDF files.

- **Redesigned app-switching screen**. The "cards" that represent your open apps now overlap, so that more of them fit on a single screen. If you have an iPhone 6s or 6s Plus, you don't have to double-press the Home button to switch apps; you can just hard-drag inward from the left edge of the screen (that is, bear down as you swipe). The pressure-sensitive screen opens up the app switcher automatically.

- **A Back button!** Whenever you've hopped into one app (say, Safari) by tapping a notification or a link in another (say, Mail), you can then hop back into the first app with one tap. A new button in the top-left corner, in a typeface about the right size for ants, says "Back to Mail," "Back to Messages," or whatever. Tap to return to the app you were just using, skipping the intermediate step of opening the app switcher. It's especially handy when you've just followed a link in Facebook or Twitter. It's a little cluttery, but you'll use it constantly.

- **Longer battery life.** On average, Apple says, every iPhone will get a full hour more of life from every battery charge, which is completely awesome.

It eked out this extra juice by making a long list of tiny tweaks. One example: If your phone is facedown on the table, the screen no longer lights up when you get incoming notifications.

- **Low Power mode.** In Low Power mode, the phone stops fetching new mail and updating apps in the background. Most of the cute little animations are eliminated. The processor slows down, meaning that it'll take longer to, for example, switch between apps. And the battery indicator turns yellow, so you don't think your phone has suddenly gotten slow just to annoy you. Apple says that in Low Power mode your phone or tablet can hobble along for another three hours, which can be a lifesaver.

  You can turn this on at any time, in Settings→Battery—but you'll be invited to turn it on when your battery sinks to 20 percent and again when there's 10 percent left.

- **Battery-use screen.** The same Settings→Battery screen offers detailed information about which of your apps are scarfing down your battery power.

- **Smaller upgrade footprint.** The upgrading process has been upgraded, too. Now you need only 1.3 free gigabytes on your phone to perform the OS surgery—not 4.6 gigabytes, as before. If necessary, the phone will even ask if it can delete some of your apps to make temporary room for the upgrade process. It promises to put them back at the end.

  And the "Upgrade now?" screen offers more choices for the timing— like "Tonight" or "When I use my phone least."

- **Continuity over Cellular**. Continuity, introduced in iOS 8, lets you make and take calls on your Mac or iPad, which acts as a speaker- phone extension for your iPhone. (The phone, which must be in the same Wi-Fi hotspot, acts as a sort of remote antenna.) But now there's Continuity over Cellular—so far available only from T-Mobile —which lets you take calls on your Mac or iPad even if your iPhone is somewhere else in the world! Yes, even if you left it at the office or at your buddy's house.

- **More elaborate Siri commands.** You can now give Siri spoken com- mands, like "Show me photos from Utah last June" or "Show me vid- eos I took at Mom's birthday party." If you're looking at a web page or a text message on your phone, you can even say, "Remind me about this when I get home" or "Remind me about this later today." When you get home, your iPhone, iPad, or Mac will offer a link to the page or the message you were reading, so you can get right back into it.

  Once you get the hang of it, you'll wind up using this one all the time.

- **Apple Pay improvements.** Apple Pay, which transmits your credit card info wirelessly in shops, is now accepted at more stores and can be linked to more credit and debit cards. It tracks your reward cards now, too.

  And there's a second way to trigger Apple Pay. If you double-press the Home button on a sleeping phone, the Apple Pay screen appears, so that you can get it ready *before* you approach the wireless terminal—and just fly by once you get there. Apple notes that this technique is handy when you're rushing through places like the London Underground subway turnstiles, which now accept Apple Pay.

- **Revamped Search screen.** The Spotlight screen starts out full of icons for the people, apps, places, and news it thinks you might be interested in right now. You can also search for things beyond what's on your phone now, like sports scores, weather, stocks, calculations, unit and currency conversions, and documents on your iCloud Drive.

App News

- **A new Notes app.** There's always been a Notes app, but this ancient, text-only notepad has had a huge upgrade, making it more Evernote-ish in scope. A Notes page can now include a checklist of to-dos, a photo, a map, a web link, or a sketch you drew with your finger. (The sketch tools are very cool: a marker, a highlighter, a pencil, and a straightedge that you can turn on the screen with two fingers, and then "draw against" for perfect straight lines.)

  As before, any changes you make in Notes are automatically synchronized to all your other Apple gadgets and Macs.

- **A new News app.** A new app called News "collects all the stories you want to read, from top news sources, based on topics you're most interested in." In other words, Apple has written its own version of Flipboard.

- **New Maps features.** The Maps app remains a whimpering also-ran compared with the mighty Google Maps app. But in iOS 9, this app takes a timid step toward Google Maps' superiority by adding public-transportation directions—for a handful of big cities, at least. (Only seven of the cities are in the U.S. and Canada.)

  Oh, and when you search for something in the Maps app, you're now shown a list of business categories like Food, Drinks, Shopping, and Fun that list places near you. You can explore within each category to see what's around you and find just what you're looking for.

Nips and Tucks

- **Move to iOS.** This new app brings nearly all your stuff from an Android phone or tablet over to your new iOS gadget, wirelessly and automatically. Afterward, you'll find your iOS gadget fully stocked with your contacts, email accounts, calendars, wallpapers, text messages, photos and videos, and web bookmarks. It will also transfer your songs and books—at least the ones that aren't copy protected.

- **Uppercase keys.** The letters on the onscreen keyboard now change from uppercase to lowercase when you engage the Shift key. (In the old days, they were always capitals.) You can turn off this option.

- **Hidden key bubbles.** In the bad old days, evildoers could learn your passwords by watching the little pop-up balloons that appeared above your fingertips when you tapped the onscreen keys. Not anymore. You can turn those balloons off in Settings.

- **Notifications by group.** Usually, notifications appear in chronological order on your Notifications screens. But now, in Settings, you can turn on Group By App, which clusters the alerts by app.

That's a lot of tweaks, polishing, and finesse—and a lot to learn. Fortunately, 600 pages of instructions now await you.

PART ONE

The iPhone as Phone

Chapter 1
The Guided Tour

Chapter 2
Typing, Editing & Searching

Chapter 3
Phone Calls & FaceTime

Chapter 4
Siri Voice Command

Chapter 5
Voicemail, Texting & Bluetooth

Chapter 6
Large Type, Kid Mode & Accessibility

1

The Guided Tour

You can't believe how much is hidden inside this sleek, thin slab. Microphone, speaker, cameras, battery. Processor, memory, power processing. Sensors for brightness, tilt, and proximity. Fifteen wireless radio antennas. A gyroscope, accelerometer, and barometer.

For the rest of this book, and for the rest of your life with the iPhone, you'll be expected to know what's meant by, for example, "the Home button" and "the Sleep switch." A guided tour, therefore, is in order.

Home button

Silencer switch

Volume keys

Sleep Switch (On/Off)

You could argue that knowing how to turn on your phone might be a useful skill.

For that, you need the Sleep switch. It's a metal button shaped like a dash.

On the iPhone 6 and 6s models, it's on the right edge; on earlier models, it's on the top edge.

—Sleep/Wake switch

It has several functions:

- **Sleep/Wake.** Tapping it once puts the iPhone to sleep—into Standby mode, ready for incoming calls but consuming very little power. Tapping it again turns on the screen so it's ready for action.

- **On/Off.** The same switch can also turn the iPhone off completely so it consumes no power at all; incoming calls get dumped into voicemail. You might turn the iPhone off whenever you're not going to use it for a few days.

  To turn the iPhone off, press the Sleep switch for 3 seconds. The screen changes to say slide to power off.

Confirm your decision by placing a fingertip on the ⏻ and sliding to the right. The device shuts off completely.

To turn the iPhone back on, press the switch again for 1 second. The Apple logo appears as the phone boots up. (The Apple logo is black if your iPhone is white and white if your iPhone is black. Nice touch.)

- **Answer call/Dump to voicemail.** When a call comes in, you can tap the Sleep button *once* to silence the ringing or vibrating. After four rings, the call goes to your voicemail.

  You can also tap it *twice* to dump the call to voicemail immediately. (Of course, because they didn't hear four rings, iPhone veterans will know you've blown them off. Bruised egos may result. Welcome to the world of iPhone etiquette.)

- **Force restart.** The Sleep switch has one more function. If your iPhone is frozen, and no buttons work, and you can't even turn the thing off, this button is also involved in force-restarting the whole machine. Steps for this last-ditch procedure are on page 608.

Locked Mode

When you don't touch the screen for 1 minute (or another interval you choose), or when you put the iPhone to sleep, the phone *locks* itself. When it's locked, the screen is dark and doesn't respond to touch. If you're on a call, the call continues; if music is playing, it keeps going; if you're recording audio, the recording proceeds.

But when the phone is locked, you don't have to worry about accidental button pushes. You wouldn't want to discover that your iPhone has been calling people or taking photos from the depths of your pocket or purse. Nor would you want it to dial a random number from your back pocket, a phenomenon that's earned the unfortunate name *butt dialing*.

The Lock Screen

To wake the phone when it's locked, press either the Sleep switch *or* the Home button.

That gesture alone doesn't fire up the full iPhone world, though. Instead, it presents the Lock screen.

From here, slide your finger rightward across the screen (anywhere—you don't have to aim for the **slide to unlock** area!) to unlock the phone with your password or fingerprint. (See page 58 or page 59.)

NOTE: You can adjust how quickly the phone locks itself, or make it stop locking itself altogether; see page 564.

Swipe anywhere

Things to Do on the Lock Screen

These days, though, the Lock screen is more than just a big Do Not Disturb sign. It's a lively bulletin board for up-to-date information about your life—information you can scan or work with right here at the Lock screen.

For starters, you can use the iPhone as a watch—millions of people do. Just tap the Sleep switch to consult the Lock screen's time and date display, and then shove the phone right back into your pocket. The iPhone relocks after a few seconds.

If you're driving, using the Maps app to guide you, the Lock screen shows the standard GPS navigation screen. Handy, really—the less fumbling you have to do while driving, the safer you are.

Better yet, the Lock screen is a handy status screen. Here you see a record of everything that happened while you weren't paying attention. It's a list of missed calls, text messages received, notifications from your apps, and other essential information.

Now, each of these notices has come from a different *app* (software program). To call somebody back, for example, you'd want to open the Phone app; to reply to a text message, you'd want the Messages app, and so on.

So here's a handy shortcut: You can dive directly into the relevant app by swiping your finger *across the notification itself*, like this:

Lock screen with notifications   Swipe to open that app

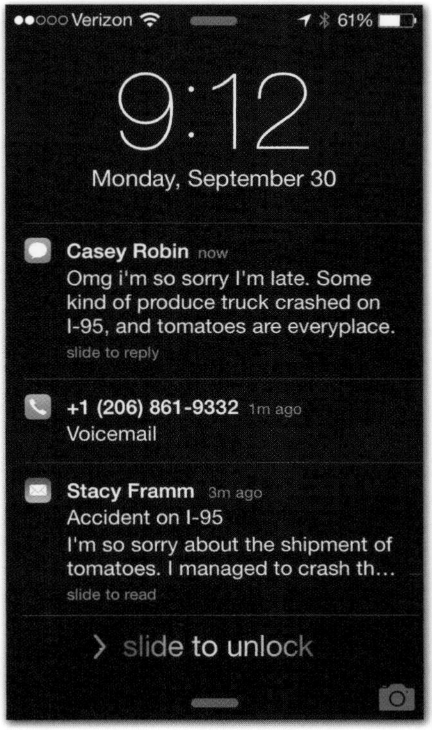

That shortcut saves you the trouble of unlocking the phone and trying to find the corresponding app.

> **TIP:** If you'd rather **not** have all these details show up on the Lock screen, you can turn them off. (Privacy is the main reason you might want to do so—remember that the bad guys don't need a password to view your Lock screen. They just have to tap the Sleep switch or the Home button.)
>
> You can hide these items from your Lock screen on an app-by-app basis. For example, you might want missed calls to show up here but not missed text messages. To set this up, choose Settings→ Notifications. Tap the app in question; scroll to the bottom, and then turn off Show on Lock Screen.

More ways to accomplish things on the Lock screen:

- **Swipe down** from the top of the screen to view your Notification Center—a detailed one-stop screen that shows your missed calls, texts, and emails; upcoming appointments; stock and weather alerts; and so on. (See page 52.)

- **Swipe up from the bottom edge** to open the Control Center, with all the important settings (volume, brightness, play/pause music, airplane mode, flashlight, and more) in one place. See page 47.

- **Swipe up on the camera** () icon to open the Camera app (page 245).

- **Swipe up on the app icon at lower left,** if you see one. This feature is supposed to let you know when one of your apps might be useful *based on the time and your location right now*—a new iOS 9 feature.

  It's based on pattern recognition of your daily patterns: If you listen to the Podcasts app through earbuds every day before work, then plugging in your earbuds at about time and location will display the Podcast app's icon (a new iOS 9 feature). If you call home as you leave work every day, the Phone app's icon will show up at that time.

In each case, the suggested app opens when you swipe up on this icon.

> **TIP** Creeped out? You can turn off this lower-left app-suggestion feature easily enough. Choose **Settings→Notifications**. Tap **App Store**, and then turn off **Show on Lock Screen**.

Locking Down the Lock Screen

Now, remember: You can enjoy any of the activities described above even *before* you've entered your password or used your fingerprint.

That means some stranger picking up your phone can do all these things. If that bothers you, you can turn all those features off on the Settings screens. For example, to block Lock-screen access to your Control Center, open **Settings→Control Center**. Turn off **Access on Lock Screen**. To turn off individual apps' presence on the Lock screen, open **Settings→Control Center**; tap the app's name, and then turn off **Show on Lock Screen**.

Home Button

Here it is: the one and only button on the front of this phone. Push it to summon the Home screen, which is your gateway to everything the iPhone can do. (You can read more about the Home screen at the end of this chapter.)

The Home button is a wonderful thing. It means you can never get lost. No matter how deeply you burrow into the iPhone software, no matter how far off track you find yourself, one push of the Home button takes you back to the beginning.

On the iPhone 5s, 6, and 6s models, of course, the Home button is also a fingerprint scanner—the first one on a cellphone that actually *works*.

Home button

But as time goes on, Apple keeps saddling the Home button with more functions. It's become Apple's only way to provide shortcuts for common features; that's what you get when you design a phone that *has* only one button. In iPhone Land, you can press the Home button one, two, or three times for different functions—or even hold it down. Here's the rundown.

Quick Press: Wake Up

Pressing the Home button once wakes the phone if it's in locked mode. That's sometimes easier than finding the Sleep switch on the edge. It gives you a quick glance at your missed calls and texts—or the time and date.

Momentary Touch: Unlock (iPhone 5s and Later)

If you've taught the iPhone to recognize your fingerprint, then just resting your finger on the Home button is enough to unlock the phone, bypassing the password screen. In other words, you should get into the habit of **pressing** the Home button (to wake the phone) and then **leaving your finger on it** for about a half-second to unlock it. Page 59 has more on fingerprints.

Long Press: Siri

If you hold down the Home button for about 3 seconds, you wake up Siri, your virtual voice-controlled assistant. Details are in Chapter 4.

Two Quick Presses: App Switcher

If, once the phone is awake, you press the Home button **twice quickly**, the current image fades away—to reveal the app switcher screen, the key to the iPhone's multitasking feature.

What you see here are icons **and currently open screens** of the apps you've used most recently (older ones are to the left). In iOS 9, they appear at nearly full size, overlapping like playing cards. Swipe horizontally to bring more apps into view; the Home screen is always at the far right.

With a single tap (on either the icon or the screen "card"), you can jump right back into an app you had open, without waiting for it to start up, show its welcome screen, and so on—and without having to scroll through 11 Home screens trying to find the icon of a favorite app.

In short, the app switcher gives you a way to jump *directly* to another app, without a layover at the Home screen first.

TIP: On this screen, you can also quit a program by flicking it upward. In fact, you can quit *several programs at once*, using two or three fingers. Fun for the whole family!

This app switcher is the only visible element of the iPhone's multitasking feature. Once you get used to it, that double-press of the Home button will become second nature—and your first choice for jumping among apps.

Two Touches: Reachability

The iPhone 6/6s is bigger than any previous iPhone, and the Plus models are even *biggerer*. Their screens are so big, in fact, that your dinky human thumb may be too small to reach the top portion of the screen (if you're gripping the phone near the bottom).

For that reason, Apple has built a new feature into those phones called Reachability. When you tap the Home button twice (don't click it—just *touch* it), the entire screen image slides halfway down the glass, so that you can reach the upper parts of it with your thumb!

As soon as you touch anything on the screen—a link, a button, an empty area, anything—the screen snaps back to its usual, full-height position. (The on/off switch for the Reachability feature is in Settings→General→Accessibility.)

TIP: On the jumbo iPhone 6 Plus and 6s Plus, the Home screen turns 90 degrees when you turn the phone. The Dock jumps to the right edge, vertically. Try it!

Three Presses: VoiceOver, Zoom, Inverted Colors...

In Settings→General→Accessibility, you can set up a triple-press of the Home button to turn one of several accessibility features on or off: *VoiceOver* (the phone speaks whatever you touch), *Invert Colors* (white-on-black type, which is sometimes easier to see), *Grayscale* (a mode that makes the whole iPhone black-and-white); *Zoom* (magnifies the screen), *Switch Control* (accommodates external gadgets like sip-and-puff straws), and *AssistiveTouch* (help for people who have trouble with physical switches).

All these features are described beginning on page 187.

Silencer Switch, Volume Keys

Praise be to the gods of technology—this phone has a silencer switch! This tiny flipper, on the left edge at the top, means that no ringer or alert sound will humiliate you in a meeting, at a movie, or in church. To turn off the ringer, push the flipper toward the back of the phone (see the photo on page 13).

No menus, no holding down keys, just instant silence. All cellphones should have this feature.

NOTE: Even when silenced, the iPhone still makes noise in certain circumstances: when an alarm goes off; when you're playing music; when you're using Find My iPhone (page 518); when you're using VoiceOver; or, sometimes, when a game is playing. Also, the phone still vibrates when the silencer is engaged, although you can turn this feature off in Settings→Sounds.

Below the silencer, still on the left edge, are the volume controls. There are no longer **+** and **−** labels on the iPhone 6/6s's volume buttons, as on all previous iPhones. But the two buttons still work in the same five ways:

- On a call, these buttons adjust the speaker or earbud volume.

- When you're listening to music, they adjust the playback volume—even when the phone is locked and dark.

- When you're taking a picture, either one serves as a shutter button or as a camcorder start/stop button.

- At all other times, they adjust the volume of sound effects like the ringer, alarms, and Siri.

- When a call comes in, they silence the ringing or vibrating.

In each case, if the screen is on, a corresponding volume graphic appears to show you where you are on the volume scale.

Screen

The touchscreen is your mouse, keyboard, dialing pad, and notepad. You might expect it to get fingerprinty and streaky.

But the modern iPhone has an *oleophobic* screen. That may sound like an irrational fear of yodeling, but it's actually a coating that repels grease. A single light wipe on your clothes restores the screen to its right-out-of-the-box crystal sheen.

You can also use the screen as a mirror when the iPhone is off.

The iPhone's Retina screen has crazy high resolution (the number of tiny pixels per inch). It's really, really sharp, as you'll discover when you try to read text or make out the details of a map or a photo. The iPhone 5 family manages 1136 × 640 pixels; the iPhone 6/6s packs in 1334 × 750; the iPhone 6/6s Plus has 1920 x 1080 (the same number of dots as a high-definition TV).

The front of the iPhone is made of a special formulation made by Corning, to Apple's specifications—even better than Gorilla Glass, Apple says. It's unbelievably resistant to scratching. (You can still shatter it if you drop it just the wrong way.)

This is how Corning's website says this glass is made: "The glass is placed in a hot bath of molten salt at a temperature of approximately 400° C. Smaller sodium ions leave the glass, and larger potassium ions from the salt bath replace them. These larger ions take up more room and are pressed together when the glass cools, producing a layer of compressive stress on the surface of the glass. This layer of compression creates a surface that is more resistant to damage from everyday use."

But you probably guessed as much.

If you're nervous about protecting your iPhone, you can always get a case for it (or a "bumper"—a silicone band that wraps around the edges). But if you're worried about scratching the glass, you're probably worrying too much. Even many Apple employees carry the iPhone in their pockets without carrying cases.

Radio signals can't pass through metal. That's why there are strips of glass on the back of the iPhone 5 and 5s, strips of plastic on the iPhone 6/6s models, and all plastic on the back of the 5c.

And there are a *lot* of radio signals in this phone. All told, there are **20** different radio transceivers inside the iPhone 6/6s. They tune in to the LTE and 3G (high-speed Internet) signals used in various countries around the world, plus the three CDMA signals used in the U.S.; and one each for Wi-Fi, Bluetooth, American GPS, and Russian GPS.

Screen Icons

Here's a roundup of the icons you may see in the status bar at the top of the iPhone screen, from left to right:

- ●●○○○ **Cell signal.** As on any cellphone, the number of bars—or dots, in iOS's case—indicates the strength of your cell signal, and thus the quality of your call audio and the likelihood of losing the connection. If there are no dots, then the dreaded words "No service" appear here.

- **Network name and type.** These days, different parts of the country—and even your street—are blanketed by cellular Internet signals of different speeds, types, and ages. Your status bar shows you the kind of network signal it has. From slowest to fastest:

    E or **o** means your iPhone is connected to your carrier's slowest, oldest Internet system. You might be able to check email, but you'll lose your mind waiting for a web page to load.

    If you see the **3G** logo, you're in a city where your cell company has installed a 3G network—meaning fairly decent Internet speed. A **4G** logo is better yet; you have speed in between 3G and LTE.

And if you see **LTE** up there—well, get psyched. You have an iPhone 5 or later model, and you're in a city with a 4G LTE cellular network. And that means *very* fast Internet (maybe even faster than you have at home), fast web browsing, fast app downloading—just fast.

- ✈ **Airplane mode.** If you see the airplane instead of signal and Wi-Fi bars, then the iPhone is in airplane mode (page 422).

- 🌙 **Do Not Disturb.** When the phone is in Do Not Disturb mode, nothing can make it ring, buzz, or light up except calls from the most important people. Details are on page 116.

- 🛜 **Wi-Fi signal.** When you're connected to a wireless Internet hotspot, this indicator appears. The more "sound waves," the stronger the signal.

- **9:41 AM.** When the iPhone is unlocked, a digital clock appears on the status bar.

- 🕐 **Alarm.** You've got an alarm set. This reminder, too, can be valuable, especially when you intend to sleep late and don't want an alarm to go off.

- ✳ **Bluetooth.** The iPhone is connected wirelessly to a Bluetooth earpiece, speaker, or car system. (If this symbol is gray, then it means Bluetooth is turned on but not connected to any other gear—and not sucking down battery power.)

- **TTY symbol.** You've turned on Teletype mode, meaning that the iPhone can communicate with a Teletype machine. (That's a special machine that lets deaf people make phone calls by typing and reading text. It hooks up to the iPhone with a special cable that Apple sells from its website.)

- **Call forwarding.** You've told your iPhone to auto-forward any incoming calls to a different number. This icon is awfully handy—it explains at a glance why your iPhone never seems to get calls anymore.

- **VPN VPN.** You corporate stud, you! You've managed to connect to your corporate network over a secure Internet connection, probably with the assistance of a systems administrator—or by consulting page 552.

- **Syncing.** The iPhone is currently syncing with some Internet service—iCloud, for example (Chapter 15).

- **Battery meter.** When the iPhone is charging, the lightning bolt appears. Otherwise, the battery logo "empties out" from right to left to indicate how much charge remains. (You can even add a "% full" indicator to this gauge; see page 570.)

- **Navigation active.** You're running a GPS navigation app, or some other app that's tracking your location, in the background (yay, multitasking!). Why is a special icon necessary? Because those GPS apps slurp down battery power like a thirsty golden retriever. Apple wants to make sure you don't forget you're running it.

- **Rotation lock.** This icon reminds you that you've deliberately turned off the screen-rotation feature, where the screen image turns 90 degrees when you rotate the phone. Why would you want to? And how do you turn the rotation lock on or off? See page 48.

Cameras and Flash

At the top of the phone, above the screen, there's a horizontal slot. That's the earpiece. Just above it (iPhone 5 series) or beside it (iPhone 6/6s and 4s), the tiny pinhole is the front-facing camera. It's more visible on the white-faced iPhones than on the black ones.

Its primary purpose is to let you conduct video chats using the FaceTime feature, but it's also handy for taking self-portraits or just checking to see if you have spinach in your teeth.

It's not nearly as good a camera as the one on the back, though. The front camera isn't as good in low light and takes much lower-resolution shots (5 megapixels on the 6s family; 1.2 megapixels on the iPhone 5 and 6 series; only 0.3 megapixels on earlier models).

The camera on the back of the iPhone, meanwhile, takes very good photos indeed—8 or 12 megapixels.

A tiny LED lamp appears next to this lens—two lamps on the 5s and later, actually. That's the flash for the camera, the video light when you're shooting movies, and a darned good flashlight for reading restaurant menus and theater programs in low light. (Swipe up from the bottom of the screen and tap the flashlight icon ▮ to turn the light on and off.)

On the iPhone 5 and later, the tiny pinhole between the flash and the lens is a microphone. It's used for recording clearer sound with video, for better noise cancellation on phone calls, and for better directional sound pickup.

There's more on the iPhone's cameras in Chapter 8.

Sensors

Behind the glass, above or beside the earpiece, are two sensors. (On the black iPhones, they're camouflaged; you can't see them except with a flashlight.) First, there's an ambient-light sensor that brightens the display when you're in sunlight and dims it in darker places.

Second, there's a proximity sensor. When something (like your head) is close to the sensor, it shuts off the screen and touch sensitivity. It works only in the Phone app. You save power and avoid dialing with your cheekbone when you're on a call.

SIM Card Slot

On the right edge of the iPhone, there's a pinhole next to what looks like a very thin slot cover. If you push an unfolded paper clip straight into the hole, the *SIM card* tray pops out.

So what's a SIM card?

It turns out that there are two major cellphone network types: **CDMA**, used by Verizon and Sprint, and **GSM**, used by AT&T, T-Mobile, and most other countries around the world.

Every GSM phone stores your phone account info—things like your phone number and calling-plan details—on a tiny memory card known as a SIM (subscriber identity module) card.

What's cool is that, by removing the card and putting it into **another** GSM phone, you can transplant a GSM phone's brain. The other phone now knows your number and account details, which can be handy when your iPhone goes in for repair or battery replacement. For example, you can turn a Verizon iPhone 6s into a T-Mobile iPhone 6s just by swapping in a T-Mobile SIM card.

The World Phone

AT&T is a GSM network, so AT&T iPhones have always had SIM cards. But intriguingly enough, every iPhone 4s and later model has a SIM card, too—even the Verizon and Sprint models. That's odd, because most CDMA cellphones don't have SIM cards.

These iPhones contain antennas for **both** GSM and CDMA. It's the same phone, no matter which cell company you buy it from. Only the SIM card teaches it which phone company it "belongs" to.

Even then, however, you can still use any company's phone in any country. (That's why the latest iPhones are said to be "world phones.") When you use the Verizon or Sprint iPhone in the United States, it uses only the CDMA antenna. But if you travel to Europe or another GSM part of the world, you can still use your Verizon or Sprint phone; it just hooks into that country's GSM network.

If you decide to try that, you have two ways to go. First, you can contact your phone carrier and ask to have international roaming turned on. You'll keep your same phone number overseas, but you'll pay through the nose for calls and, especially, Internet use. (One exception: On T-Mobile, international texting and Internet use are free.)

Second, you can rent a temporary SIM card when you get to the destination country. That's less expensive, but you'll have a different phone number while you're there.

The iPhone 4s uses a card type known as a *micro-SIM* card. And for the iPhone 5 and later, Apple developed even tinier cards called *nano*-SIMs. (You can see all three at left.)

At this rate, you won't be able to see the iPhone 7's SIM card without an electron microscope.

Apple thinks SIM cards are geeky and intimidating and that they should be invisible. That's why, unlike most GSM phones, your iPhone came with the card preinstalled and ready to go. Most people never have any reason to open this tray.

If you were curious enough to open it up, you can close the tray simply by pushing it back into the phone until it clicks.

NOTE: Many countries offer LTE high-speed cellular Internet on all different radio frequencies. The iPhone 6/6s can hop onto more of these networks than any other cellphone, but it still doesn't work in *every* country. Ask your carrier which countries your model works with.

Headphone Jack

On the bottom of the iPhone, you can see the miniplug where you plug in the white earbuds that came with it—or any other earbuds or headphones. (On the 4s, it's at the top.)

It's more than an ordinary 3.5-millimeter audio jack, however. It contains a secret fourth pin that conducts sound *into* the phone from the microphone on the earbuds' cord. Now you, too, can be one of those executives who walk down the street barking orders, apparently to nobody.

The iPhone can stay in your pocket as you walk or drive. You hear the other person through your earbuds, and the mike on the cord picks up your voice.

NOTE: Next to the headphone jack, inside the pinhole (iPhone 4s) or the perforated grille (later models), a tiny second microphone lurks. It's the key to the iPhone's noise-cancellation feature. It listens to the sound of the world around you and pumps in the opposite sound waves to cancel out all that ambient noise. It doesn't do anything for *you*—the noise cancellation affects only what the *other* guy on the phone hears.

That's why, on the iPhone 5 and later models, there's also a third microphone at the top back (between the camera and flash); it's designed to supply noise cancellation for you so that the other guy sounds better when you're in a noisy place.

Microphone, Speakerphone

On the bottom of the iPhone, Apple has parked two important audio components: the speaker and the microphone.

TIP: The speakerphone isn't super loud, because it's aimed straight out of the iPhone's edge, away from you. But if you cup your hand around the bottom edge, you can redirect the sound toward your face, for an immediate boost in volume and quality.

Headphones   Microphone   Charge/sync   Speakerphone
                          (Lightning connector)

The Charge/Sync Connector

Directly below the Home button, on the bottom edge of the phone, you'll find the connector that charges and syncs the iPhone with your computer.

The Lightning Connector

For nearly 10 years, the charge/sync connector was identical on every iPhone, iPod, and iPad—the famous 30-pin connector. But starting on the iPhone 5, Apple replaced that inch-wide connector with a new, far smaller one it calls Lightning.

30-pin connector *(iPhone 4S)*

Lightning connector *(iPhone 5 and later)*

The Lightning connector is a great design: It clicks nicely into place (you can even dangle the iPhone from it), yet you can yank it right out. You can insert the Lightning into the phone either way—there's no "right-side up" anymore. It's much sturdier than the old connector. And it's tiny, which was Apple's primary goal—only 0.3 inches wide (the old one was almost 0.9 inches wide).

Unfortunately, as a result, the latest iPhones don't fit a lot of existing charging cables, docks, chargers, car adapters, hotel-room alarm clocks, speakers, or accessories.

The makers of those accessories will happily sell you new models that have Lightning connectors. Or you can buy an adapter from Apple:

- Additional USB charging cables, like the one that came with your iPhone, cost $20.

- A white adapter plug costs $30. It connects the modern iPhone to any accessory that was built for the old 30-pin connector.

- If the iPhone doesn't quite fit the older accessory, sometimes the solution is the $40 adapter plug with an 8-inch cable "tail."

Even with the adapter, the Lightning connector doesn't work with every older accessory, and it doesn't offer all the same features. For example, it can't send video out to your TV; for that, you need Apple's Lightning-to-HDMI or Lightning-to-VGA cable.

In time, as the Lightning connectors come on all new iPhones, iPods, and iPads, a new ecosystem of accessories will arise. We'll arrive at a new era of standardization—until Apple changes jacks again in *another* 10 years.

Antenna Band

That metal band around the edge of the iPhone 4s, 5, and 5s is part of the iPhone's antenna. (Remember the controversy that erupted after the iPhone 4 debuted in the summer of 2010? If you held the iPhone 4 so that the lower-left corner was pressed into your palm, the signal strength sometimes dropped.)

The problem went away on the 4s and later models; you can hold these phones any way you like. On the iPhone 6/6s models, of course, the edges are no longer part of the antenna system; instead, the plastic seams on the back serve as the escape hatch for the radio waves.

In the Box

Inside the minimalist box, you get the iPhone and these items:

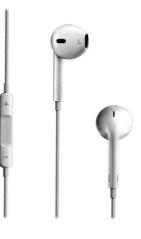

- **The earbuds.** Apple shipped 600 million of the iconic white earbuds that, for years, announced to the world, "I have an iPhone!" or "I have an iPod!" But starting with the iPhone 5, Apple updated them. Now you get what Apple calls EarPods. They sound better, although their bulbous shape may get uncomfortable in smaller ears. As before, a volume control/clicker is right on the cord, so you can answer calls and pause the music without taking the phone out of your pocket.

- **The USB charging/syncing cable.** When you connect your iPhone to your computer using this white USB cable, it simultaneously syncs and charges. See Chapter 14.

- **The AC adapter.** When you're traveling without a computer, you can plug the dock's USB cable into the included two-prong outlet adapter, so you can charge the iPhone directly from a wall socket.

- **Decals and info card.** iPhone essentials.

You don't need a copy of the iTunes software, or even a computer, to use the iPhone—but it makes loading up the phone a lot easier, as described in Chapter 14.

If you don't have iTunes on your computer, then you can download it from *www.apple.com/itunes*.

Seven Basic Finger Techniques

The iPhone isn't quite like any machine that came before it. You do everything on the touchscreen instead of with physical buttons, like this:

Tap

The iPhone's onscreen buttons are nice and big, giving your fleshy fingertip a fat target.

You can't use a fingernail or a pen tip; only skin contact works. (You can also buy an iPhone stylus. But a fingertip is cheaper and harder to misplace.)

Swipe

In some situations, you'll be asked to confirm an action by *swiping* your finger across the screen. That's how you unlock the phone after it's been in your pocket, for example. It's ingenious, really; you may bump the touchscreen when you reach into your pocket for something, but it's extremely unlikely that your knuckles will randomly *swipe* it in just the right way.

You also have to swipe to confirm that you want to turn off the iPhone, to answer a call on a locked iPhone, or to shut off an alarm. Swiping like this is also a great shortcut for deleting an email or a text message.

Drag

When you're zoomed into a map, web page, email, or photo, you can scroll around just by sliding your finger across the glass in any direction—like a flick (described next), but slower and more controlled. It's a huge improvement over scroll bars, especially when you want to scroll diagonally.

Flick

A *flick* is a faster, less-controlled *slide*. You flick vertically to scroll lists on the iPhone. The faster you flick, the faster the list spins downward or upward. But lists have a real-world sort of momentum; they slow down after a second or two, so you can see where you wound up.

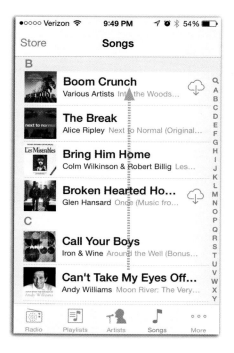

At any point during the scrolling of a list, you can flick again (if you didn't go far enough) or tap to stop the scrolling (if you see the item you want to choose).

Pinch and Spread

In apps like Photos, Mail, Safari, and Maps, you can zoom in on a photo, message, web page, or map by *spreading*.

That's when you place two fingers (usually thumb and forefinger) on the glass and spread them. The image magically grows, as though it's printed on a sheet of rubber.

> **NOTE:** The English language has failed Apple here. Moving your thumb and forefinger closer together has a perfect verb: *pinching*. But there's no word to describe moving them the opposite direction.
>
> Apple uses the oxymoronic expression *pinch out* to describe that move (along with the redundant-sounding *pinch in*). In this book, the opposite of "pinching" is "spreading."

Once you've zoomed in like this, you can zoom out again by putting two fingers on the glass and pinching them together.

Double-Tap

Double-tapping is pretty rare on the iPhone, at least among the programs supplied by Apple. It's generally reserved for two functions:

- In the Safari web browser, Photos, and Maps apps, double-tapping zooms in on whatever you tap, magnifying it. (At that point, double-tapping means "Restore to original size.") Double-tapping also zooms into formatted email messages, PDF files, Microsoft Office files, and others.

- When you're watching a video (or recording one), double-tapping switches the aspect ratio (video screen shape).

Edge Swipes

Swiping your finger inward from *outside* the screen has a few variations:

- **From the top edge.** Opens the Notification Center, which lists all your missed calls and texts, shows your appointments, and so on.

- **From the bottom edge.** Opens the Control Center, a unified miniature control panel for brightness, volume, Wi-Fi, and so on.

- **From the left edge.** In many apps, this means "go back to the previous screen." It works in Mail, Settings, Notes, Messages, Safari, Facebook and some other apps.

It sometimes makes a big difference whether you begin your swipe *within* the screen or *outside* it. At the Home screen, for example, starting your downward swipe within the screen area doesn't open the Notification Center—it opens Spotlight, the iPhone's search function.

> **TIP:** If you have an iPhone 6s or 6s Plus, you can also hard *swipe* from the left edge to open the app switcher described on page 20. Actually, all you have to do is hard *press* the left margin of the screen, but hard swiping might fit the metaphor better (pulling the app cards onto the screen).

iPhone 6s Family: Force Touch

The screen on the iPhone 6s and 6s Plus doesn't just detect a finger touch. It also knows how *hard* your finger is pressing, thanks to a technology Apple calls Force Touch. This feature requires that you learn two more finger techniques, in addition to the standard seven described already.

Quick Actions

iOS 9 interprets the pressure of your touch in various ways. On the Home screens, you can make a shortcut menu of useful commands pop out of various app icons, like this:

Apple calls these commands *Quick Actions*, and each is designed to save you a couple of steps. Some examples:

- **The Camera app** icon offers shortcut menus like Take Selfie, Record Video, Record Slo-mo, and Take Photo.

- **The Clock app** gives you direct access to its Set Alarm, Start Timer, and Start Stopwatch functions.

- **Notes** gives you New Note, New Photo, and New Sketch commands (a reference to the new finger-drawing features).

- **Maps** offers Directions Home (a great one), Mark My Location, Send My Location, and Search Nearby (for restaurants, bars, shops, and so on).

- **The Phone app** sprouts the names of people you've called recently, as well as a Create New Contact command.

- **Calendar** shows your next appointment, and offers an Add Event command.

- **Reminders** lists your reminder categories, so you can create a new To Do directly inside one of them (for example, New in Family).

- **Mail and Messages** offer New Message commands. Mail also offers Search, Inbox (with a new-message counter), and VIPs (also with a counter).

You get the idea. Similar Quick Actions also sprout from these Apple apps' icons: Photos, Video, Wallet, iTunes Store, App Store, iBooks, News, Safari, Music, FaceTime, Podcasts, Game Center, Voice Memos, Contacts, and Find My Friends.

Other software companies can add shortcut menus to their apps, too.

If you force-press an app that *doesn't* have Quick Actions, you just feel a buzz and nothing else happens.

NOTE: At the outset, this force-pressing business can really throw you when you're trying to rearrange icons on your Home screens. As described on page 318, that usually involves *long*-pressing an icon, which, for most people, is too similar to *hard*-pressing one. You'll try to do some rearranging but keep getting the shortcut menu. You'll get used to it, though.

Peek and Pop

Hard to explain, but very cool: You hard-press something in a list—your email Inbox, for example (below, left). Or a link in a text message, or a photo thumbnail. You get a pop-up bubble showing you what's inside (middle):

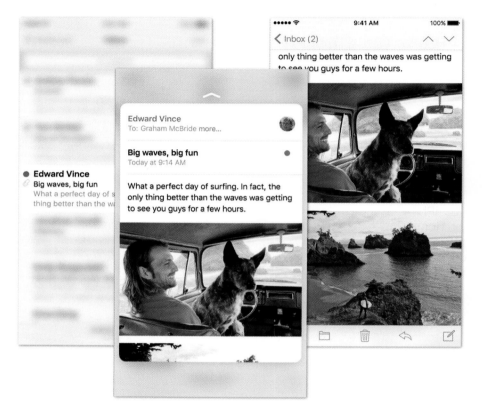

When you release your finger, the bubble disappears, and you're right back where you started.

Peeking is, in other words, exactly like the Quick Look feature on the Mac. It lets you see what's inside a link, icon, or list item without losing your place or changing apps.

Email is the killer app here. You can whip through your Inbox, hard-pressing one new message after another—"What's this one?" "Do I care?"— simply inspecting the first paragraph of each but not actually opening any message.

Then, if you find one that you do want to read fully, you can press harder *yet* to open the message normally (above, right). Apple calls that "popping."

Here's what you can peek into in the basic iPhone apps: *Mail* (preview a message in a list), *Messages* (see recent exchanges with someone in the list of people), *Maps* (preview information about a pushpin), *Calendar* (see details of an event), *Photos* (preview a photo in a screenful of thumbnails), *Safari* (preview the page hiding behind a link), *Weather* (see weather details for a name in the list of cities), *Music* (see information about a song or album in a list), *Video* (read details about a video in a list), *Notes* (see the contents of a note's name in a list), *iBooks* (view a book-cover thumbnail larger), *News* (preview the body of an article in a list), and *Find My Friends* (see the map identifying the location of someone in your list).

But for goodness' sake, at least get to know Peek and Pop in Mail and Messages. It's really kind of awesome.

And, again, app makers can add this feature to their own apps.

Charging the iPhone

The iPhone has a built-in, rechargeable battery that fills up most of its interior. How long a charge lasts depends on what you're doing—music playback saps the battery the least, GPS navigation saps it the most. But one thing is for sure: You'll have to recharge the iPhone regularly. For most people, it's every night.

NOTE: The iPhone's battery isn't user-replaceable. It's *rechargeable*, but after 400 or 500 charges, it starts to hold less juice. Eventually, you'll have to pay Apple to install a new battery. (Apple says the added bulk of a protective plastic battery compartment, a removable door and latch, and battery-retaining springs would have meant a much smaller battery—or a much thicker iPhone.)

You recharge the iPhone by connecting the white USB cable that came with it. You can plug the far end into either of two places to supply power:

- **Your computer's USB jack.** In general, the iPhone charges even if your computer is asleep. (If it's a laptop that itself is not plugged in, though, the phone charges only if the laptop is awake. Otherwise, you'd come home to a depleted laptop.)

- **The AC adapter.** The little white two-prong cube that came with the iPhone connects to the end of the cradle's USB cable.

Unless the charge is *really* low, you can use the iPhone while it charges. The battery icon in the upper-right corner displays a lightning bolt to let you know it's charging.

Battery Life Tips

The battery life of the iPhone is either terrific or terrible, depending on your point of view and how old your phone is.

If you were an optimist, you'd point out that the iPhone gets longer battery life than most touchscreen phones. If you were a pessimist, you'd observe that you sometimes can't make it through even a single day without needing a recharge.

So knowing how to scale back your iPhone's power appetite could come in extremely handy.

These are the biggest wolfers of electricity: the screen and background activity (especially Internet activity). Therefore, when you're nervous about your battery making it through a important day, here are your options:

- **Low Power mode.** It took Apple a while to bring this feature (common on Android phones) to the iPhone. But it's here in iOS 9, and it's worth its weight in silicon; it can squeeze another three hours of life out of a charge.

  In Low Power mode, your iPhone quits doing a lot of stuff in the background, like fetching new mail and updating apps. It also stops playing most of iOS's cute little animations, and stops listening for you to say "Hey Siri" (page 132). The processor slows down, too; it takes longer to switch between apps, for example. And the battery indicator turns yellow, to remind you of why things have suddenly slowed down.

  When your battery sinks to 20 percent remaining (and then again at 10 percent), you get a warning message.

  If you choose **Low Power Mode**, then boom: You're in Low Power Mode.

  If your phone is plugged in, it exits Low Power Mode automatically once it has enough juice (next page, lower right). You can also turn Low Power Mode on or off manually in **Settings→Battery** (next page, upper right).

At any time, you can also shut down juice-guzzling features manually. Here they are, roughly in order of power appetite:

- **Dim the screen.** Turning down your screen saves a lot of battery power. The quickest way is to swipe up from the bottom of the screen to open the Control Center (page 47), and then drag the brightness slider.

  On a new iPhone, Auto Brightness is turned on, too. In bright light, the screen brightens automatically; in dim light, it darkens. That's because when you unlock the phone after waking it, it samples the ambient light and adjusts the brightness.

NOTE: This works because of the ambient-light sensor near the earpiece. Apple says it experimented with having the light sensor active all the time, but it was weird to have the screen constantly dimming and brightening as you used it.

You can use this information to your advantage. By covering up the sensor as you unlock the phone, you force it into a low-power, dim-screen setting (because the phone believes it's in a dark room). Or by holding it up to a light as you wake it, you get more brightness. In either case, you've saved all the taps and navigation it would have taken you to find the manual brightness slider in Settings. (Or you can turn this auto-brightness feature off altogether in Settings→Display & Brightness.)

TIP: You can set things up so that a triple-click on the Home button instantly dims your screen, for use in the bedroom, movie theaters, or planetariums—without having to fuss with Settings or sliders. See page 210 for this awesome trick.

- **Turn off "push" data.** This is a big one. If your email, calendar, and address book are kept constantly synced with your Macs or PCs, then you've probably gotten yourself involved with Yahoo Mail, Microsoft Exchange (Chapter 17), or iCloud (Chapter 15). It's pretty amazing to know that your iPhone is constantly kept current with the mother ship.

  Unfortunately, all that continual sniffing of the airwaves, looking for updates, costs you battery power. If you can do without the immediacy, then visit Settings→Mail, Contacts, Calendars→Fetch New Data. If you turn off the Push feature and set it to Manually instead, then your iPhone checks for email and new appointments only when you actually *open* the Mail or Calendar apps. Your battery goes a lot further.

- **Turn off background updating.** Non-Apple apps check for frequent updates, too: Facebook, Twitter, stock-reporting apps, and so on. Not all of them need to be busily toiling in the background. Your best bet on battery life, then, involves visiting Settings→General→Background App Refresh and turning the switch Off for each app whose background activity isn't strictly necessary.

- **Turn off automatic app updates.** As you'll soon discover, app companies update their wares far more often than PC or Mac apps. Some apps get updated many times a year.

  Your phone comes set to download them automatically when they become available. But that constant checking and downloading costs you battery life.

  To shut that feature down, open Settings→iTunes & App Store. Scroll down to the Automatic Downloads section. Turn off Updates. (The other switches—Music, Apps, Books—are responsible for auto-downloading things that you or your brood have downloaded on other iOS gadgets. You might want to make sure they're off, too, if battery life is a concern.)

- **Turn off GPS checks.** In Settings→Privacy→Location Services, there's a list of all the apps on your phone that are using your phone's location feature to know where you are. (It's a combination of GPS, cell-tower triangulation, and Wi-Fi hotspot triangulation.) All that checking uses battery power.

  Some apps, like Maps, Find My Friends, and Yelp, don't do you much good unless they know your location. But plenty of apps don't really need to know where you are. Facebook and Twitter, for example, want that information only so that they can location-stamp your posts. In any case, the point is to turn off Location Services for each app that doesn't really need to know where you are.

TIP: In the list of apps under Location Services, tiny ➚ icons show you which apps are using GPS right now (the ➚ appears in purple), and which have used it in the past 24 hours. These icons can help guide you in shutting off the GPS use of various apps.

- **Turn off Wi-Fi.** If you're not in a wireless hotspot, you may as well stop the thing from using its radio. Swipe up from the bottom of the screen to open the Control Center, and tap the 📶 icon to turn it off.

  Or at the very least tell the iPhone to stop *searching* for Wi-Fi networks it can connect to. Page 558 has the details.

- **Turn off Bluetooth.** If you're not using a Bluetooth gadget (headset, fitness band, or whatever), then for heaven's sake shut down that Bluetooth radio. Open the Control Center and tap the ✳ icon to turn it off.

- **Turn off Cellular Data.** This option (in Settings→Cellular) turns off the cellular Internet features of your phone. You can still make calls, and you can still get online in a Wi-Fi hotspot.

  This feature is designed for people who have a capped data plan—a limited amount of Internet use per month—which is almost everybody. If you discover that you've used up almost all your data allotment for the month, and you don't want to go over your limit (and thereby trigger an overage charge), you can use this option to shut off all data. Now your phone is just a phone—and it uses less power.

- **Consider airplane mode.** In airplane mode, you shut off *all* the iPhone's power-hungry radios. Even a nearly dead iPhone can hobble on for a few hours in airplane mode—something to remember when you're desperate. To enter airplane mode, swipe up from the bottom of the screen to open the Control Center, and tap the ✈ icon.

TIP: For sure, turn on airplane mode if you'll be someplace where you *know* an Internet signal won't be present—like on a plane, a ship at sea, or Montana. Your iPhone never burns through a battery charge faster than when it's hunting for a signal it can't find; your battery will be dead within a couple of hours.

- **Turn off the screen.** You can actually turn off the screen, rendering it totally black and saving incredible amounts of battery power. Music playback and Maps navigation continue to work just fine.

  Of course, if you want to actually *interact* with the phone while the screen is off, you'll have to learn the VoiceOver talking-buttons technology; see page 188.

By the way, beware of 3D games and other graphically intensive apps, which can be serious power hogs. And turn off EQ when playing your music (see page 235).

If your battery still seems to be draining faster than it should, check out this table, which shows you exactly which apps are using the most power:

Setting		
●○○○○ Verizon 🤝	2:46 AM	🔋 📶 ⚡ 95% ▮▮▮
‹ Settings	**Battery**	

Low Power Mode ⚪

Low Power Mode temporarily reduces power consumption until you can fully charge your iPhone. When this is on, mail fetch, background app refresh, automatic downloads, and some visual effects are reduced or turned off.

Battery Percentage ⬤

Show percentage of battery remaining in the status bar.

BATTERY USAGE

Last 24 Hours	Last 7 Days	🕐
Swift Finder Background Location		68%
Photos		15%

Setting		
●○○○○ Verizon 🤝	2:46 AM	🔋 📶 ⚡ 95% ▮▮▮
‹ Settings	**Battery**	

BATTERY USAGE

Last 24 Hours	Last 7 Days	🕐
Swift Finder Background Location		68%
Photos		15%
Podcasts		3%
Settings		2%
Mail Background Activity		2%
Home & Lock Screen		2%
Notes		2%
YouTube		1%

To see it, open Settings→Battery. You can switch between battery readouts for the past 24 hours, or for the past 7 days. Keep special watch for labels like these:

- **Low Signal.** A phone uses the most power of all when it's hunting for a cellular signal, because the phone amplifies its radios in hopes of finding one. If your battery seems to be running down faster than usual, the "Low Signal" notation is a great clue—and a suggestion that maybe you should use airplane mode when you're on the fringes of cellular coverage.

- **Background activity.** As hinted on the previous pages, background Internet connections are especially insidious. These are apps that do online work invisibly, without your awareness—and drain the battery in the process. Now, for the first time, you can clearly see which apps are doing it.

Once you know the culprit app, it's easy to shut its background work down. Open **Settings→General→Background App Refresh** and switch **Off** each app whose background activity isn't strictly necessary.

> **TIP:** If you tap the little clock icon in **Settings→Battery**, the screen shows you how much time each app has spent running—both in the foreground and in the background (facing page, right). It's an incredibly informative display if you've been wondering where all your battery power has been going.

The Home Screen

The Home screen is the launching pad for every iPhone activity. It's what appears when you press the Home button. It's the immortal grid of colorful icons.

It's such an essential software landmark, in fact, that a quick tour might be helpful.

- **Icons.** Each icon represents one of your iPhone apps (programs)—Mail, Maps, Camera, and so on—or a folder that you've made to *contain* some apps. Tap one to open that app or folder.

  Your iPhone comes with about 25 apps preinstalled by Apple; you can't remove them. The real fun, of course, comes when you download *more* apps from the App Store (Chapter 9).

- **Badges.** Every now and then, you'll see a tiny, red number "badge" (like ❷) on one of your app icons. It's telling you that something new awaits: new email, new text messages, new chat entries, new updates for the apps on your iPhone. It's saying, "Hey, you! Tap me!"

- **Home page dots.** The standard Home screen can't hold more than 20 or 24 icons. As you install more and more programs on your iPhone, you'll need more and more room for their icons. Fortunately, the iPhone makes room for them by creating *additional* Home screens automatically. You can spread your new programs' icons across 11 such launch screens.

  The little white dots are your map. Each represents one Home screen. If the third one is "lit up," then you're on the third Home screen.

  To move among the screens, swipe horizontally—or tap to the right or left of the little dots to change screens.

  And if you ever scroll too far away from the *first* Home screen, here's a handy shortcut: Press the Home button (yes, even though you're

— Apps

— Badge (new information!)

— Dock

technically already home). That takes you back to the first Home screen.

TIP: Note to upgraders: To the left of the first Home page, there's yet another screen: the Spotlight (search) screen. It was missing in iOS 7 and iOS 8, but it's back now. See page 93.

- **The Dock.** At the bottom of the Home screen, four exalted icons sit in a row on a tinted panel. This is the Dock—a place to park the most important icons on your iPhone. These, presumably, are the ones you use most often. Apple starts you off with the Phone, Mail, Safari, and Music icons.

  What's so special about this row? As you flip among Home screens, the Dock never changes. You can never lose one of your four most cherished icons by straying from the first page; they're always handy.

- **The background.** You can replace the background image (behind your app icons) with a photo. A complicated, busy picture won't do you any favors—it will just make the icon names harder to read—so Apple provides a selection of handsome, relatively subdued wallpaper photos. But you can also choose one of your own photos.

For instructions on changing the wallpaper, see page 294.

It's easy (and fun!) to rearrange the icons on your Home screens. Put the most frequently used icons on the first page, put similar apps into folders, and reorganize your Dock. Full details are on page 319.

> **TIP:** You can set up a completely empty first Home screen by moving all of its app icons onto other Home "pages," if you want. That's a weird but fun arrangement for anyone with a really great wallpaper photo.

Control Center

For such a tiny device, there are an awful lot of settings you can change—*hundreds* of them. Trouble is, some of them need changing (volume, brightness) a lot more often than others (language preference, voicemail greeting).

That's why Apple invented the Control Center: a panel that offers quick access to the controls you need the most.

To open the Control Center, no matter what app you're using, swipe upward from beneath the screen.

> **TIP:** You can even open the Control Center from the Lock screen, unless you've turned off that feature (page 18).

The Control Center is a translucent gray panel filled with one-touch icons for the settings most people change most often on their iPhones.

> **TIP:** Truth be told, the Control Center is easier to use when it's *not* translucent. Visit Settings→General→Accessibility and turn on Increase Contrast. Now the Control Center's background is solid gray instead of see-through gray.

Now, many of these settings are even faster to change using Siri, the voice-command feature described in Chapter 4. When it's not socially awkward to speak to your phone (like at the symphony or during a golf game), you can use spoken commands—listed below under each button description—to adjust settings without even touching the screen.

Here's what's in the Control Center:

- **Airplane mode ( ).** Tap to turn the icon white. Now you're in airplane mode; the phone's wireless features are all turned off. You're saving the battery and obeying flight attendant instructions. Tap again to turn off airplane mode.

Airplane mode, WiFi, Bluetooth, Do Not Disturb, Rotation Lock

Brightness

Playback controls

AirDrop privacy, AirPlay projection

Flashlight, Timer, Calculator, Camera

Sample Siri command: "Turn airplane mode on." (Siri warns you that if you turn airplane mode on, Siri herself will stop working. Say "OK.")

- **Wi-Fi (⬆).** Tap to turn your phone's Wi-Fi off (gray) or on (white).

Sample Siri commands: "Turn off Wi-Fi." "Turn Wi-Fi back on."

- **Bluetooth (✳).** Tap to turn your Bluetooth transmitter off (gray) or on (white). That feature alone is a godsend to anyone who uses the iPhone with a car's Bluetooth audio system. Bluetooth isn't the battery drain it once was, but it's still nice to be able to flick it on so easily when you get into the car.

Sample Siri commands: "Turn Bluetooth on." "Turn off Bluetooth."

- **Do Not Disturb (☾).** Do Not Disturb mode, described on page 116, means that the phone won't ring or buzz when people call—except a few handpicked people whose communiqués ring through. Perfect for sleeping hours; in fact, you can set up an automated schedule for Do Not Disturb (say, midnight to 7 a.m.).

But what if you wake up early or want to stay up late? Now you can tap to turn Do Not Disturb on (white) or off (gray).

Sample Siri commands: "Turn on Do Not Disturb." "Turn Do Not Disturb off."

- **Rotation Lock (🔄).** When Rotation Lock is turned on (white), the screen no longer rotates when you turn the phone 90 degrees. The idea is that sometimes, like when you're reading an ebook on your side in bed, you don't want the screen picture to turn; you want it to stay upright relative to your eyes, even though you're lying down. (A little ⊕ icon appears at the top of the screen to remind you why the usual rotating isn't happening.)

The whole thing isn't quite as earth-shattering as it sounds—first, because it locks the image in only one way: upright, in portrait orientation. You can't make it lock into widescreen mode. Furthermore, many apps don't rotate with the phone to begin with. But when that day comes when you want to read in bed on your side with your head on the pillow, your iPhone will be ready. (Tap the button again to turn rotating back on.)

- **Brightness.** Hallelujah! Here's a screen-brightness slider. Drag the little white ball to change the screen brightness.

  Sample Siri commands: "Make the screen brighter." "Decrease the brightness." "Dim the screen."

- **Playback controls (⏮, ▶, ⏭).** These controls govern playback in whatever app is playing music or podcasts in the background: the Music app, Pandora, Spotify, whatever it is. You can skip a horrible song quickly and efficiently without having to interrupt what you're doing, or pause the music to chat with a colleague. (Tap the song name to open whatever app is playing.)

  You also get a scrubber bar that shows where you are in the song, the name of the song and the performer, and the album name. And, of course, there's a volume slider. It lets you make big volume jumps faster than you can by pressing the volume buttons on the side of the phone.

  Sample Siri commands: "Pause the music." "Skip to the next song." "Play some Billy Joel."

- **AirDrop (⊚).** AirDrop gives you a quick, effortless way to shoot photos, maps, web pages, and other stuff to nearby iPhones, iPads, iPod Touches, and even Macs. (See page 331 for details.)

  On the Control Center, the AirDrop button isn't an on/off switch like most of the other icons here. Instead it produces a pop-up menu of options that control whose i-gadgets can "see" your iPhone: **Contacts Only** (people in your address book), **Everyone**, or **Off** (nobody).

- **AirPlay (▭).** The AirPlay button lets you send your iPhone's video and audio to a wireless speaker system or TV—if you have an AirPlay receiver, of which the most famous is the Apple TV. Details are on page 244.

- **Flashlight (🔦).** Tap to turn on the iPhone's "flashlight"—actually the LED lamp on the back that usually serves as the camera flash. Knowing that a source of good, clean light is two touches away makes a huge difference if you're trying to read in the dark, find your way along a path at night, or fiddle with wires behind your desk.

- **Timer (⏱).** Tap to open the Clock app—specifically, the Timer mode, which counts down to zero. Apple figures you might appreciate having direct access to it when you're cooking, for example, or waiting for your hair color to set.

  Sample Siri commands: "Open the Timer." Or, better yet, bypass the Clock and Timer apps altogether: "Start the timer for three minutes." "Count down from six minutes." (Siri counts down right there on the Siri screen.)

- **Calculator (🖩).** Tap to open the Calculator app—a handy shortcut if it's your turn to figure out how to divide up the restaurant bill.

  Sample Siri commands: "Open the calculator." Or, better yet, without opening any app: "What's a hundred and six divided by five?"

- **Camera (📷).** Tap to jump directly into the Camera app. Because photo ops don't wait around.

  Sample Siri commands: "Take a picture." "Open the camera."

The Control Center closes when any of these things happen:

- You tap the Timer, Calculator, or Camera button.

- You tap the ⌄ button.

- You tap or drag downward from *any spot* above the Control Center (the dimmed background of the screen).

- You press the Home button.

NOTE: In some apps, swiping up doesn't open the Control Center on the first try, much to your probable bafflement. Instead, swiping up just makes a tiny ⌄ tab appear at the edge of the screen. (You'll see this behavior whenever the status bar—the strip at the top that shows the time and battery gauge—is hidden, as can happen in the full-screen modes of iBooks, Maps, Videos, and so on. It also happens in the Camera.)

In those situations, Apple is trying to protect you from opening the Control Center accidentally— for example, when what you really wanted to do was scroll the image up. No big deal; once the ⌄ appears, swipe up a *second* time to open the Control Center panel.

If you find yourself opening the Control Center accidentally—when playing games, for example—you can turn it off. Open **Settings→Control Center**. Turn off **Access Within Apps**. Now swiping up opens the Control Center only at the Home screen. (You can also turn off **Access on Lock Screen** here, to make sure the Control Center never appears when the phone is asleep.)

Notifications

A notification is an important status message. You get one every time a text message comes in, an alarm goes off, a calendar appointment is imminent, or your battery is running low.

Responding to Notifications

These days, there's a lot more you can do with a notification than just read it and nod your head. Apple has gone to a lot of effort to ensure that notifications disrupt your important phone activities as rarely as possible. So:

- **Flick it away.** When a notification appears at the top of the screen, it's sometimes covering up whatever you were doing. If you wait a couple of seconds, the little message goes away by itself. But you don't have to wait. You can just flick it upward with your finger to make it disappear.

- **Answer it.** Often, a notification appears to display an incoming text message, email, or calendar invitation. In iOS 9, you can swipe down on it to reveal buttons that let you take action: **Reply**, for example, or **Decline** and **Accept** (for an invitation). And you never have to leave the app you were using, which is deliciously efficient.

> **TIP:** This trick works even on the Lock screen. That is, you can respond to something even without unlocking the phone.

- **Open it.** Finally, here's the obvious one: You can tap a notification to open the app it came from. Tap an email notification to open the message in Mail; tap a text-message notification to open it in Messages; and so on. That's handy when you want to dig in and see the full context of the notification.

The Notification Center

No matter what kind of notification pops up, you still see only one alert at a time. And once it's gone, you can't get it back. Or can you?

Meet the Notification Center screen. It lists every notification you've recently received, in a tidy scrolling list.

You can check it out right now: Swipe your finger down from above the iPhone's screen. The Notification Center pulls down like a classy window shade, printed in white with every recent item of interest.

Here you'll find all your apps' notifications, as well as your missed calls, recent text messages, reminders, and upcoming calendar appointments.

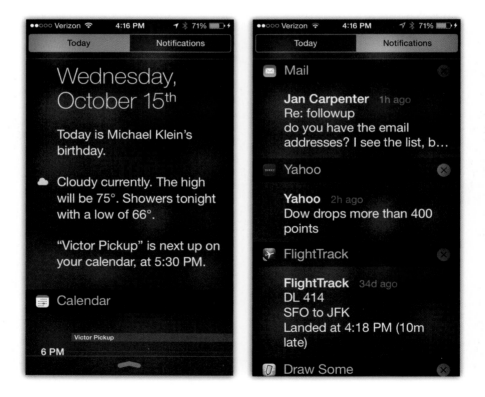

You can inspect two different lists here:

- **Today.** The Today screen presents an executive summary of everything you need to know *today*, in plain English: your upcoming appointments (" 'Salary meeting' is next up on your calendar, at 2 PM"); reminders coming due; weather and stock information; and a preview of your schedule tomorrow. If you're away from your home or office, you'll even see an estimated commuting time, based on current traffic conditions. Pretty slick.

  Apple allows apps to add their own sections to the Today list. For example, Dropbox can show a list of files that have been added to your Dropbox folder; Evernote can add buttons for creating new notes or reminders; *The New York Times,* Yahoo Digest, and Huffington Post apps can add headlines; Yahoo Weather can add weather information, including a photo of current conditions; the Kindle app offers links to the books you're reading right now; and so on.

  To manage all of this, scroll down to the bottom of the Today list and tap Edit. In the resulting list, you can tap ⊖ to remove a module from the Today list, drag the ≡ up or down to move it higher or lower in the list, or tap ⊕ to add a module. Then tap Done.

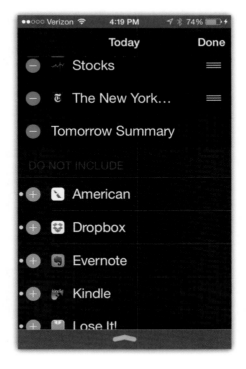

- **Notifications.** On this tab, you see every notification you've received, sorted by app: all the calls, texts, and other notifications that came in while your phone was asleep or turned off. (They disappear after a day.) It can be a very long list.

  Tap a line in the Notification Center to open the relevant app for more details—for example, to see more information about that appointment, or to read the whole text message in context.

  Tap the ⊗ next to an app's name, and then tap Clear to remove that app's current listings from the Notification Center—for now. That app's heading will reappear here the next time it has anything to say to you.

TIP: To switch between the Today and Notification views, you can either tap the little tabs or just swipe across the screen.

To close the Notification Center, drag the bottom handle (⌒) upward. (Actually, you don't have to aim for the handle. You can just swipe upward from beneath the screen, quickly and sloppily.)

<table>
<tr><td>

••••• Verizon 🗢   3:22 PM   ⏱ ✷ 73% 🔋

❮ Settings   **Notifications**

NOTIFICATIONS VIEW

Sort Order   Recent ❯

Group By App   ⬤

NOTIFICATION STYLE

AAA   ❯
Off

Alaska   ❯
Badges, Sounds, Banners

American   ❯
Badges, Sounds, Banners

App Store   ❯
Off

Arrow   ❯
Badges, Sounds, Banners

Calendar   ❯
Badges, Vibration, Alerts

</td><td>

••••• Verizon 🗢   3:24 PM   ⏱ ✷ 72% 🔋

❮ Notifications   **Reminders**

Show in Notification Center ⬤

Sounds   Chord ❯

Badge App Icon   ⬤

Show on Lock Screen   ⬤

Show alerts on the lock screen, and in Notification Center when it is accessed from the lock screen.

ALERT STYLE WHEN UNLOCKED

None   Banners   Alerts

</td></tr>
</table>

Customizing Notifications

You can (and should) specify *which* apps are allowed to junk up your Notification Center. Open Settings→Notifications to see the master list, with one entry for every app that might ever want your attention. (Or just tell Siri, "Open notification settings.")

Under Notifications View, you can use the Sort By option to specify the order of the various apps' notifications in the center. If you tap Recent, then the apps with the newest alerts appear at the top. But if you tap Manually, you can drag the ☰ handles up or down to specify the order of your apps' notifications on the Notification Center screen.

New in iOS 9: Group By App. This option makes the notifications clump together by the app that produces them, rather than intermixing them strictly chronologically.

The most important work you can do in Notifications settings, though, is to control the behavior of each individual app. You'll quickly discover that *every* app thinks it's important; *every* app wants its notifications to blast into your face when you're working.

You, however, may not agree. You may not consider it essential to know when your kid's Plants vs. Zombies game score has changed, for example.

So: Tap an app's name to open its individual Notifications screen (at right on the previous page—the Reminders app, in this example). Here you'll find settings that vary by app, but they generally run along these lines:

- **Allow Notifications.** If you don't want this app to make any notifications pop up at all, turn this off.

- **Show in Notification Center.** If you turn this off, an app may still display bubbles or banners to get your attention—but those alerts won't show up in the Notification Center itself.

- **Sounds.** Some apps try to get your attention with a sound effect when a notification appears. Turn this off if you think your phone makes too many beeps and burbles as it is. (Some apps also let you choose *which* sound effect plays to get your attention. You can change the sound or choose None.)

- **Badge App Icon.** A badge is a little red circled number (❷, for example). It appears right on an app's icon to indicate how many updates are waiting for you. Turn it off if you really don't need that reminder.

- **Show on Lock Screen.** The Lock screen (page 15) is another place to see what's been trying to get your attention while the phone was in your pocket: missed calls and texts, new messages and email, and so on.

The Lock screen may seem just like the Notification Center—but there are differences. For example, each time you wake the phone, whatever notifications are on the Lock screen are wiped clear. They don't stay put, as they do on the Notification Center.

You might want a *different* set of apps to list their nags on the Lock screen. Maybe you want the Lock screen to show only missed calls, new text messages, and new email—but you'd like the Notification Center to be fully stocked with Twitter and Facebook updates, for example. Or maybe you'd rather not permit passing evildoers to pick up your phone and see your notifications without even having to unlock it.

That's why you have this switch. It governs your ability to see this app's updates on the Lock screen (and the Notification Center when you open it while at the Lock screen).

What Notifications Look Like

Notifications can appear in any of three styles—and you get to choose which you prefer, for *each individual app*.

On the same screen described previously (open Settings→Notifications and tap the app's name), you can choose one of these three styles for notifications that occur while you're using the phone:

- **None.** If a certain app bugs you with news you really don't care about, you can shut it up forever. Tap None.

- **Banners** are incoming notifications that appear quietly and briefly at the top of the screen (below, left). The message holds still long

enough for you to read it, but it doesn't interrupt your work and goes away after a few seconds. Banners are a good option for things like Facebook and Twitter updates and incoming email messages.

TIP: A reminder: If you tap a banner before it disappears, you jump directly to the app that's trying to get your attention. You can also flick a banner up off the screen if it's in your way.

- **Alerts.** A white alert box appears to get your attention (facing page, right). You might use this option for apps whose messages are too important to miss, like alarms, flight updates, and text messages.

TIP: You can also use the Include setting to specify how *much* of the Notification Center this app is allowed to use up—that is, how many lines of information. Maybe you need only the most recent alert about your upcoming flight (1 Item), but you want to see a lot more of your upcoming appointments (10 Items).

Miscellaneous Weirdness

As you poke around in the Notification Center settings, you'll discover that certain oddball apps offer some options that don't match up with the settings you see for most apps. Don't freak out. It's all part of Apple's master plan to put controls where it hopes you'll find them.

Password (or Fingerprint) Protection

Like any smartphone, the iPhone offers a first line of defense for a phone that winds up in the wrong hands. It's designed to keep your stuff private from other people in the house or the office, or to protect your information in case you lose the iPhone. If you don't know the password or don't have the right fingerprint, you can't use the iPhone (except for limited tasks like taking a photo or using Siri).

About half of iPhone owners don't bother setting up a password to protect the phone. Maybe they never set the thing down in public, so they don't worry about thieves. Or maybe there's just not that much personal information on the phone—and meanwhile, having to enter a password every time you wake the phone can get to be a profound hassle.

TIP: Besides—if you ever do lose your phone, you can put a password on it by remote control; see page 519.

The other half of people reason that the inconvenience of entering a password many times a day is a small price to pay for the knowledge that nobody can get into your stuff if you lose it.

If you think your phone is worth protecting, here's how to set up a password—and, if you have an iPhone 5s or later model, how to use the fingerprint reader instead.

Setting Up a Password

If you didn't already create a phone password the first time you turned your iPhone on (see page 57), here's how to do it. (And just because you're an iPhone 5s-or- later owner, don't be smug; you have to create a password even if you plan to use the fingerprint reader. As a backup.)

Open Settings→Touch ID & Passcode. (On the iPhone 4s and 5c, it's just called Passcode Lock.)

iOS 9 proposes a longer string of numbers than before, for greater security (six digits instead of four). But you can tap Passcode Options if you'd prefer a four-digit number, or a full-blown alphanumeric password of any length.

You're asked to type the password you want, either on the number keypad (for number codes) or the alphabet keyboard. You're asked to do it again to make sure you didn't make a typo.

NOTE: Don't kid around with this passcode. If you forget the iPhone code, you'll have to *restore* your iPhone (page 602), which wipes out everything on it. You've probably still got most of the data on your computer or backed up on iCloud, of course (music, video, contacts, calendar), but you may lose text messages, mail, and so on.

Once you confirm your password, you return to the Passcode Lock screen. Here you have a few more options.

For example, the Require Passcode option lets you specify how quickly the password is requested before locking somebody out: immediately after the iPhone wakes or 1, 15, 30, 60, or 240 minutes later. (Those options are a convenience to you, so you can quickly check your calendar or missed messages without having to enter the passcode—while still protecting your data from, for example, evildoers who pick up your iPhone while you're out getting coffee.)

Certain features are accessible on the Lock screen even before you've entered your password: the Today and Notifications tabs of the Notification Center; Siri, Wallet, and Respond with Text. These are huge conveniences, but also, technically, a security risk. Somebody who finds your phone on your desk could, for example, blindly voice-dial your colleagues or use Siri to send a text. If you turn these switches off, then nobody can use these features until after entering the password (or using your fingerprint).

Finally, here is Erase Data—an option that's scary and reassuring at the same time. When this option is on, then if someone makes 10 incorrect guesses at your passcode, your iPhone erases itself. It's assuming that some lowlife burglar is trying to crack into it to have a look at all your personal data.

This option, a pertinent one for professional people, provides potent protection from patient password prospectors.

> **NOTE:** Even when the phone is locked and the password unguessable, a tiny blue Emergency Call button still appears on the Unlock screen. It's there just in case you've been conked on the head by a vase, you can't remember your own password, and you need to call 911.

And that is all. From now on, each time you wake your iPhone (if it's not within the window of repeat visits you established), you're asked for your password.

Fingerprint Security (Touch ID)

If you have an iPhone 5s or later—you lucky thing—you have the option of using a more secure and much more convenient kind of "password": your fingertip.

The lens built right into the Home button (clever!) is the first cellphone fingerprint reader ever that actually *works*. It reads your finger at any angle. It can't be faked out by a plastic finger or even a chopped-off finger. You can teach it to recognize up to five fingerprints; they can all be yours, or some can belong to other people you trust.

Before you can use your fingertip as a password, though, you have to teach the phone to recognize it. Here's how that goes:

1. **Create a passcode.** That's right: You can't use a fingerprint *instead* of a password; you can only use a fingerprint in *addition* to one. You'll still need a password from time to time to keep the phone's security tight. For example, you need to enter your password if you can't make your fingerprint work (maybe it got encased in acrylic in a hideous crafts accident), or if you restart the phone, or if you haven't used the phone in 48 hours or more.

    So open Settings→Touch ID & Passcode and create a password, as already described.

2. **Teach a fingerprint.** At the top of the Touch ID & Passcode screen, you see the on/off switches for the three things your fingerprint can do: It can unlock the phone (iPhone Unlock), pay for things (Apple Pay), and it can serve as your password when you buy books, music, apps, and videos from Apple's online stores (iTunes & App Store).

But what you really want to tap here, of course, is Add a Fingerprint.

Now comes the cool part. Place the finger you want to train onto the Home button—your thumb or index finger are the most logical candidates. You're asked to touch it to the Home button over and over, maybe six times. Each time, the gray lines of the onscreen fingerprint darken a little more.

Once you've filled in the fingerprint, you see the Adjust Your Grip screen. Tap Continue. Now, the iPhone wants you to touch the Home button another few times, this time tipping the finger a little each time so the sensor gets a better view of your finger's *edges*.

Once that's done, the screen says "Success!"

You are now ready to start using the fingerprint. Try it: Put the phone to sleep. Then wake it (press the Sleep switch or press the Home button), and leave your finger on the Home button for about a second. The phone reads your fingerprint and instantly unlocks itself.

And now, a few notes about using your fingerprint as a password:

• Yes, you can touch your finger to the Home button at the Lock screen. But you can also touch it at any Enter Passcode screen.

Suppose, for example, that your Lock screen shows that you missed a text message. And you want to reply. Well, you can swipe across that notification to open it in its native habitat—the Messages app—but first you're shown the Enter Passcode screen. Ignore that. Just touch the Home button with the finger whose print you recorded.

- Apple says the image of your fingerprint is encrypted and stored in the iPhone's processor chip. It's never transmitted anywhere, it never goes online, and it's never collected by Apple.

- If you return to the Touch ID & Passcode screens, you can tap Add a Fingerprint again to teach your phone to recognize a second finger. And a third, fourth, and fifth.

  The five "registered" fingerprints don't all have to belong to you. If you share the phone with a spouse or a child, for example, that special somebody can use up some of the fingerprint slots.

- On the other hand, it makes a lot of sense to register the *same* finger *several* times. You'll be amazed at how much faster and more reliably your thumb (for example) is recognized if you've trained it as several different "fingerprints."

- To rename a fingerprint, tap its current name ("Finger 1" or whatever). To delete one, tap its name and then tap Delete Fingerprint. (You can figure out which finger label is which by touching the Home button; the corresponding label blinks. Sweet!)

••••• 9:41 AM 100% — Cancel	••••• 9:41 AM 100% — Cancel
Place Your Finger	**Adjust Your Grip**
Lift and rest your finger on the Home button repeatedly.	Keep going to capture the edges of your print.
	Continue

- You can register your toes instead of fingers, if that's helpful. Or even patches of your wrist or arm, if you're patient (and weird).

- The Touch ID scanner may have trouble recognizing your finger if it (your finger) is wet, greasy, or scarred.

- The iPhone's finger reader isn't just a camera; it doesn't just look for the image of your fingerprint. It's actually measuring the tiny differences in electrical conductivity between the raised parts of your fingerprint (which aren't conductive) and the skin just beneath the surface (which is). That's why a plastic finger won't work—and even your own finger won't work if it's been chopped off (or if you've passed away).

Fingerprints for Apps, Websites, and Apple Pay

So if your fingerprint is such a great solution to password overload, how come it works only to unlock the phone and to buy stuff from Apple's online stores? Wouldn't it be great if your fingerprint could also log you into secure websites? Or serve as your ID when you buy stuff online?

That dream is finally becoming a reality. Software companies can now use your Touch ID fingerprint to log into their apps. Mint (for checking your personal finances), Evernote (for storing notes, pictures, and to-do lists), Amazon (for buying stuff), and other apps now permit you to substitute a fingerprint touch for typing a password.

What's really wild is that password-storing apps like 1Password and LastPass have been updated, too. Those apps are designed to memorize your passwords for all sites on the web, of every type—and now you can use your fingerprint to unlock them.

Moreover, your fingerprint is now the key to the magical door of Apple Pay, the wireless pay-with-your-iPhone technology described on page 524.

All of this is great news. Most of us would be happy if we never, ever had to type in another password.

2

Typing, Editing & Searching

As a pocket computer, the iPhone faces a fundamental limitation: It has no real keyboard or mouse. Which might be considered a drawback on a gadget that's capable of running hundreds of thousands of programs.

Fortunately, where there's a problem, there's software that can fix it. The modern iPhone's virtual keyboard is smart in all kinds of ways—automatically predicting words and correcting typos, for example. And besides: If you don't like the iPhone's onscreen keyboard, you can just choose one designed by a different company.

This chapter covers every aspect of working with text on the iPhone: entering it, fixing it, and searching for it. (Well, *almost* every aspect. Chapter 4 covers *dictating* text.)

The Keyboard

It's true, boys and girls: The iPhone has no physical keys. A virtual keyboard, therefore, is the only possible built-in system for typing text. Like it or not, you'll be doing a lot of typing on glass.

The keyboard appears automatically whenever you tap in a place where typing is possible: in an outgoing email or text message, in the Notes program, in the address bar of the web browser, and so on.

Just tap the key you want. As your finger taps the glass, a "speech balloon" appears above your finger, showing an enlarged version of the key you actually hit (since your finger is now blocking your view of the keyboard).

> **TIP:** New in iOS 9: If you worry about spies nearby figuring out what you're typing by watching those bubbles pop up over your fingertips, you can turn them off. Open Settings→General→ Keyboards, and turn off Character Preview.

In darker gray, surrounding the letters, you'll find these special keys:

- **Shift (⇧).** When you tap this key, it turns dark to indicate that it's in effect. The next letter you type appears as a capital. Then the ⇧ key returns to normal, meaning that the next letter will be lowercase.

TIP: It used to be that the color of the Shift key was your only clue that you were about to type a capital letters; the actual letters on the on-screen keyboard's keys always appeared AS CAPITALS. But in iOS 9, the key letters appear in lowercase until you press Shift. (If you prefer that old system, though, open **Settings→General→ Accessibility→Keyboard**. Turn off **Show Lowercase Keys**.

- **Caps Lock (⇪).** The iPhone has a Caps Lock "key," too, but it's hidden. To engage it, **double-tap** the ⇧ key; it changes to ⇪. You're now in Caps Lock mode, and you'll now type in ALL CAPITALS until you tap the ⇪ key again. (If you can't seem to make Caps Lock work, try double-tapping the ⇧ key **fast**. Or see if maybe Caps Lock got turned off in **Settings→General→Keyboard**.)

- **Backspace (⌫).** This key actually has three speeds:

  Tap it once to delete the letter just before the blinking insertion point.

Hold it down to "walk" backward, deleting as you go.

If you hold down the key long enough, it starts deleting **words** rather than letters, one whole chunk at a time.

- 123. Tap this button when you want to type numbers or punctuation. The keyboard changes to offer a palette of numbers and symbols. Tap the same key—which now says ABC—to return to the letters keyboard.

  Once you're on the numbers/symbols pad, a new dark-gray button appears, labeled #+=. Tapping it summons a **third** keyboard layout, containing the less frequently used symbols, like brackets, the # and % symbols, bullets, and math symbols.

- **return.** Tapping this key moves to the next line, just as on a real keyboard. (There's no Tab key or Enter key in iPhone Land.)

Making the Keyboard Work

Some people have no problem tapping those tiny virtual keys; others struggle for days. Either way, here are some tips:

- Don't be freaked out by the tiny, narrow keys. Apple **knows** your fingertip is fatter than that.

  So as you type, use the whole pad of your finger or thumb. Don't try to tap with only a skinny part of your finger to match the skinny keys. You'll be surprised at how fast and accurate this method is. (Tap, don't mash.)

- This may sound like New Age hooey, but **trust** the keyboard. Don't pause to check the result after each letter. Just plow on.

TIP: Although you don't see it, the sizes of the keys on the iPhone keyboard are changing all the time. That is, the software enlarges the "landing area" of certain keys, based on probability.

For example, suppose you type **tim**. The iPhone knows that no word in the language begins with **timw** or **timr**—and so, invisibly, it enlarges the "landing area" of the E key, which greatly diminishes your chances of making a typo on that last letter.

- Start with one-finger typing. Two-thumb, BlackBerry-style typing comes later. You'll drive yourself crazy if you start out that way.

- Without a mouse, how are you supposed to correct an error you made a few sentences ago? Easy—use the **loupe**.

  Hold your fingertip down anywhere in the text until the magnified circle appears. Without lifting your finger, drag anywhere in the text; the insertion point moves along with it. Release when the blue line

••○○○ Verizon 📶 11:39 AM ⁎ 🔋⚡

Cancel   **Stain removal**   Send

Subject: **Stain removal**

Dear Mrs. O'Rourk. **removed f**

It is my understa**th the applic**ato-
juice stains can be   .om
delicate fabrics with the application

is where you want to delete or add text, just as though you'd clicked there with a mouse.

TIP: In the Safari address bar, you can skip the part about waiting for the loupe to appear. Once you click into the address, start *dragging* to make it appear at once.

• Don't bother using the Shift key to capitalize a new sentence. The iPhone does that capitalizing automatically. (To turn this feature on or off, open Settings→General→Keyboard. Turn off Auto-Capitalization.)

• Don't type a period at the end of each sentence, either. Because the period is such a frequently used symbol, there's an awesome shortcut that doesn't require switching to the punctuation keyboard: At the end of a sentence, *tap the space bar twice*. You get a period, a space, *and* a capitalized letter at the beginning of the next word. (This, too, can be turned off—in Settings→General→Keyboard—although it's hard to imagine why you'd want to.)

• You can save time by leaving out the apostrophe in contractions. Type *im*, *dont*, or *cant*. The iPhone proposes *I'm*, *don't*, or *can't*, so you can just tap the space bar to fix the word and continue.

QuickType

What Apple calls its QuickType keyboard can save you a *lot* of time, tapping, and errors.

The idea is simple: As you type a sentence, the software *predicts* which word you might type next—which are the three most likely words, actually—and displays them as three buttons above the keyboard.

If you begin the sentence by typing, "I really," then the three suggestions might be *want*, *don't*, and *like*.

But what if you intended to say, "I really *hope*..."? In that case, type the first letter of "hope." Instantly, the three suggestions change to *"h," hope*, and *hate*. (The first button always shows, in quotes, whatever non-word you've typed so far, just in case that's what you really intend. To place it into your text, you can tap that button *or* tap the space bar or some punctuation.)

The only way to achieve true peace is not to avoid war, but to embrace e|

| "e" | every | each |

q	w	e	r	t	y	u	i	o	p
	a	s	d	f	g	h	j	k	l

⇧ z x c v b n m ⌫

123 ☺ 🎤 space return

In other words, QuickType is autocomplete on steroids. Frankly, it's a rush when QuickType correctly proposes finishing a long word for you.

With QuickType, you can produce a sentence like "I'll gladly pay you Tuesday for a hamburger today" with 26 taps on the screen. If you had to type out the whole thing, you'd have tapped 50 keys. QuickType also adds spaces for you.

A set of three buttons, guessing what you might want to type next, isn't a new idea; Android and BlackBerry phones have had it for years. But QuickType is smarter in several ways:

- QuickType's suggestions are *different* in Messages (where language tends to be casual) than in Mail (where people write more formally).

- Similarly, QuickType modifies its suggestions based on *whom* you're writing to. It learns.

- Sometimes, QuickType offers you several words on a single button, to save you even more time (for example, *up to* or *in the*).

- QuickType automatically adds a space after each word you select, so you don't have to mess with the space bar.

- When someone texts you a question that ends with a choice ("Coffee, tea, or me?"), the QuickType buttons cleverly offer those choices on the buttons. Before you've even typed a single letter, the choices say *coffee*, *tea*, and *you*.

- You can hide the QuickType bar if it's getting on your nerves. Just swipe down on it with your finger; you'll see it collapse into a horizontal white line. (To bring it back, swipe up on the white line.)

TIP: If you forget to capitalize a word, double-tap to select it. Now tap Shift once (to Initial Cap the Word) or twice (for ALL CAPS). Lo and behold, the QuickType suggestions are now capitalized renditions of the word, ready to replace it!

QuickType does mean that you have to split your focus. You have to pay attention to both the keys you're tapping and the ever-changing word choices above the keyboard. With practice, though, you'll find that QuickType offers impressive speed and accuracy. You won't miss the little autocorrect bubbles of old.

TIP: But if you do, you can turn off QuickType. Open Settings→General→Keyboard, and turn off Predictive.

The Spelling Checker

Here's the world's friendliest typo-fixer. Apple calls it a spelling checker, but maybe that's stretching it.

The idea is that anytime the iPhone doesn't recognize something you've typed, it draws a dotted red underline beneath it. Tap the word to see a pop-up balloon with one, two, or three alternate spellings. Often, one of them is what you wanted, and you can tap it to fix the mistake. (Equally often, none of them is, and it's time to break out the loupe and the keyboard.)

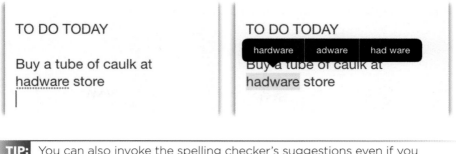

The Spelling Dictionary

If you start typing a word the iPhone doesn't recognize, the first of the three suggestion buttons displays your word in quotation marks. If you really do intend to type that nonstandard word, tap its button. You've just allowed the "mistake" to stand—and you've added it to the iPhone's dictionary. The phone assumes that you've just typed some name, bit of slang, or terminology that wasn't in its dictionary originally.

From now on, it will accept that bizarre new word as legitimate—and, in fact, will even *suggest* it the next time you start typing it.

The Widescreen Keyboard

In most apps, you can turn the phone 90 degrees to type. When the keyboard stretches out the long way, the keys get a lot bigger. It's much easier to type—even with two thumbs.

This feature doesn't work in every app, but it does work in the apps where you do the most typing: Mail, Messages, the Safari browser, Contacts, Twitter, Notes, and so on. (The screen also rotates in Camera, Music, Calculator, Calendar, and Stocks, though not for typing purposes.)

If you have an iPhone 6, 6s, 6 Plus, or 6s Plus, something even more startling happens: you get extra keys on the sides—including **cursor keys**. (With the Caps Lock engaged, you can actually highlight text by pressing these cursor keys.)

> **NOTE:** If you don't see the additional control keys on the sides of your widescreen keyboard, it's probably because you've turned on Zoomed mode (page 567). In Zoomed mode, all the keys are a little bigger—so there's no room for the buttons.

Cursor keys

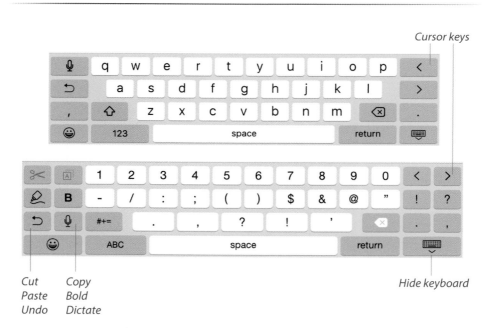

Cut   Copy   *Hide keyboard*
Paste   Bold
Undo   Dictate

Punctuation with One Touch

On the iPhone, the punctuation and alphabet keys appear on two different keyboard layouts. That's a serious hassle, because each time you want, say, a comma, it's an awkward, three-step dance: (1) Tap the 123 key to get the punctuation layout. (2) Tap the comma. (3) Tap the ABC key or the space bar to return to the alphabet layout.

Imagine how excruciating it is to type, for example, "a P.O. box in the U.S.A." That's 34 finger taps and 10 mode changes!

Fortunately, there's a secret way to get a punctuation mark with only a *single* finger gesture. The iPhone doesn't register most key presses until you *lift* your finger. But the Shift and punctuation keys register their taps on the press *down* instead.

So here's what you can do, all in one motion:

1. **Touch the 123 key, but don't lift your finger.** The punctuation layout appears.

2. **Slide your finger onto the period or comma key, and release.** The ABC layout returns automatically. You've typed a period or a comma with one finger touch instead of three.

> **TIP:** If you're a two-thumbed typist, you can also hit the 123 key with your left thumb and then tap the punctuation key with your right. It even works on the #+= sub-punctuation layout, although you'll probably visit that screen less often.

In fact, you can type any of the punctuation symbols the same way. This technique makes a *huge* difference in the usability of the built-in iPhone keyboard.

Accented Characters

To produce an accented character (like é, ë, è, ê, and so on), keep your finger pressed on that key for 1 second. A palette of diacritical marks appears; slide onto the one you want.

Not all keys sprout this pop-up palette. Here's a list of the keys that do:

Key	Alternates
A	à á â ä æ ã å ā
C	ç ć č
E	è é ê ë ę ė ē
I	ī į í ì ï î
L	ł
N	ń ñ
O	ō ø œ õ ó ò ö ô
S	ß ś š

Key	Alternates
U	ū ú ù ü û
Y	ÿ
Z	ź ž ż
?	¿
'	' ' '
"	» « „ " "
-	—
$	€ £ ¥ ₩
&	§
0 (zero)	°
.	…
%	‰

Typing Shortcuts (Abbreviation Expanders)

Here's a feature that hardly anyone ever talks about—probably because nobody knows it exists. But it's a huge time- and sanity-saver; for a phone with no physical keys, anything that can do your typing for you is very welcome indeed.

You can program your phone to expand abbreviations that you type. Set up *addr* to type your entire mailing address, or *eml* to type out your email address. Create two-letter abbreviations for big legal or technical words you have to type a lot. Set up *goaway* to type out a polite rejection paragraph for use in email. And so on.

This feature has been in Microsoft Office forever (called AutoCorrect). And it's always been available as a separate app (TypeIt4Me and TextExpander, for example—but because they were separate, you had to copy your expanded text, switch to the target program, and then paste). But since it's now built right into the operating system, it works anywhere you can type.

You can start building your list of abbreviations in Settings→General→ Keyboard→Text Replacement. Tap the + button. On the resulting screen, type the expanded text into the Phrase box. (It can be very long, but it has to be one continuous blob of text; it can't contain Returns.) In the Shortcut box, type the abbreviation you want to trigger the phrase.

The **Shortcut** box says "Optional." You might wonder: Why would you leave the shortcut blank? Then your new shortcut will be un-triggerable and pointless.

Not quite. It's optional to enable a sneaky trick: to make the phone stop misreplacing some word (for example, insisting that you mean *PTA* when you type *pta*, a new chemical you've designed).

In that case, type your phrase into the **Phrase** box, but leave **Shortcut** blank.

●○○○○ Verizon 📶 12:00 PM ⬈ ❊ 88% ▪▪▪	●○○○○ Verizon 📶 12:01 PM ⬈ ❊ 88% ▪▪▪
❮ Keyboard **Shortcuts** +	❮ Shortcuts **Shortcut** Save
Q Search	
A	**Phrase** Please stop emailing me.
ac actually,	**Shortcut** pse|
addr My address: 155 Elmhurst,…	Create a shortcut that will automatically expand into the word or phrase as you type.
F	
FBI fbi	
H	
hth Hope this helps!	q w e r t y u i o p
I	a s d f g h j k l
ily i love you!	⇧ z x c v b n m ⌫
L	
lvm I love you more!	123 ☺ 🎤 space return
Edit	

That's it! Now, whenever you type one of the abbreviations you've set up, the iPhone proposes replacing it with your substituted text.

Swype, SwiftKey, and Other Keyboards

This feature is a really big deal: You're no longer stuck with Apple's onscreen keyboard. You can, if you like, install virtual keyboards from other companies. (Hey—just like on Android phones!)

Many people swear that these rival keyboard systems are superior to the standard iOS keyboard in speed and accuracy. In particular, people like the Swype and SwiftKey keyboards; in these systems, you don't have to *tap* each key to spell out a word. Instead, you rapidly and sloppily drag your finger *across* the glass, hitting the letters you want and lifting your finger at the end of a word. The software figures out which word you were going for.

Sounds bizarre, but it's fast and very satisfying. And pretty; your finger leaves a sort of fire trail as it slides across the glass.

These keyboards generally incorporate their own versions of QuickType— that is, they offer three predictions about the word you're going to type next.

Most don't vary their predictions depending on the person you're writing to or which app you're using, as iOS's predictions do. But they do offer other impressive features; for example, SwiftKey can sync what it's learned to your other gadgets (iOS doesn't do that; it learns, but its education is locked on your iPhone). The Minuum keyboard is weird-looking but very compact, leaving a lot more room for your writing.

Then there's Fleksy, TouchPal, KuaiBoard, and a raft of others.

Note, however, that none of them offer a 🎤 button. Apple doesn't allow them access to Siri, so you can't use voice dictation when one of these keyboards is on the screen. And, sometimes, you can't use these alternate keyboards for typing into password boxes.

Otherwise, these alternate keyboard systems are fascinating, and, often, faster than Apple's. Many are free, so they're well worth exploring.

To install an alternate keyboard, download it from the App Store (page 74).

Then go to Settings→General→Keyboard→Keyboards (previous page, left). When you tap Add New Keyboard, you'll see your newly downloaded keyboard's name. Turn it on by tapping it.

Now, when you arrive at any writing area in any app, you'll discover that a new icon has appeared on the keyboard: a tiny globe (🌐) next to the space bar. Tap it. The keyboard changes to the new one you installed. (Each tap on the 🌐 button summons the next keyboard you've installed— or you can hold your finger down on it for a pop-up list.)

International Typing

Because the iPhone is sold around the world, it has to be equipped for non-English languages—and even non-Roman alphabets. Fortunately, it's ready.

To prepare the iPhone for language switching, go to Settings→General→ Language & Region. Tap iPhone Language to set the iPhone's primary language (for menus, button labels, and so on).

To make other *keyboards* available, go to Settings→General→Keyboard→ Keyboards, tap Add New Keyboard, and then turn on the keyboard layouts you'll want available: Russian, Italian, whatever.

If you choose Japanese or Chinese, you're offered the chance to specify which *kind* of character input you want. For Japanese, you can choose a QWERTY layout (Romaji) or a Kana keypad. For Simplified or Traditional Chinese, your choices include the Pinyin input method (which uses a QWERTY layout) or handwriting recognition, where you draw your symbols onto the screen with your fingertip; a palette of potential interpretations appears to the right. (That's handy, since there are thousands of characters in Chinese, and you'd need a 65-inch iPhone to fit the keyboard on it.) Or hey—it's a free tic-tac-toe game!

As described in the previous section, a new key has now appeared on the keyboard: 🌐 next to the space bar. Each time you tap it, you rotate to the next keyboard you requested earlier. The new language's name appears briefly on the space bar to identify it.

Thanks to that 🌐 button, you can freely mix languages and alphabets within the same document without having to duck back to some control panel to make the change. And thanks to the iPhone's virtual keyboard, the actual letters on the "keys" change in real time.

The ⊕ button works in three ways:

- Tap it once to restore the most recent keyboard. Great if you're frequently flipping back and forth between two languages.

- Tap it rapidly to cycle among all the keyboards you've selected. (The name of the language appears briefly on the space bar to help you out.)

- If you, some United Nations translator, like to write in a lot of different languages, you don't have to tap that ⊕ key over and over again to cycle through the keyboard layouts. Instead, hold your finger down on the ⊕ key. You get a convenient pop-up menu of the languages you've turned on, so you can jump directly to the one you want.

The Emoji Keyboard

Even if you speak only one language, don't miss the emoji keyboard. It gives you a palette of smileys and fun symbols, also known as emoticons, to use in your correspondence.

When you choose its name from the onscreen keyboard, you get hundreds upon hundreds of little graphic symbols, spread across eight categories (plus a Recently Used category). Each category offers several pages full of symbols, represented by tiny dots above the keyboard.

TIP: To return to a category's first page, you don't have to swipe; just tap the category's icon.

The bottom line is clear: Smileys are only the beginning.

NOTE: These symbols show up identically on Apple machinery (phones, tablets, Macs) but may look slightly different on other kinds of phones.

Connecting a Real Keyboard

This iPhone feature barely merits an asterisk in Apple's marketing materials. But if you're any kind of wandering journalist, blogger, or writer, you might flip your lid over this: You can type on a real, full-sized, physical keyboard, and watch the text magically appear on your iPhone's screen—wirelessly.

That's because you can use a Bluetooth keyboard (the Apple Wireless Keyboard, for example) to type into your iPhone.

To set this up, from the Home screen, tap Settings→Bluetooth. Turn Bluetooth on, if it's not already.

Now turn on the wireless keyboard. After a moment, its name shows up on the iPhone screen in the Devices list; tap it. You'll know the pairing was successful, because when you tap in a spot where the onscreen keyboard would usually appear, well, it doesn't.

Typing is a lot easier and faster with a real keyboard. As a bonus, the Apple keyboard's brightness, volume, and playback controls actually work to control the iPhone's brightness, volume, and playback.

When you're finished using the keyboard, turn it off. The iPhone goes back to normal.

iPhone 6s: The Secret Trackpad

You may remember hearing about the Force Touch screen on your 6s or 6s Plus (or reading about it, on page 36). But you can also use pressure on the screen to create a trackpad for editing text!

Whenever text is on the screen and the keyboard is open, press firmly anywhere on the keyboard. All the keys go blank:

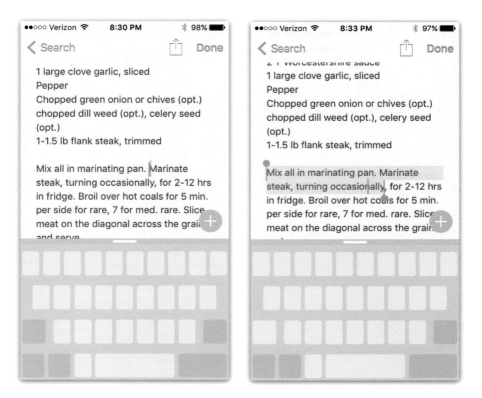

You can now ease up on the pressure, but **don't lift your finger from** the glass. You can now move the insertion-point cursor through the text just by dragging your finger across the keys. If it hits the edge of the window, it scrolls automatically.

Still keep your finger down. At this point, **hard** presses also let you select (highlight) text:

- **Hard-press twice** to select an entire sentence.

- **Hard-press three times** to select an entire paragraph.

Or use this trick: Move the insertion point to a word; if you now press hard, you highlight that word.

At this point, you can expand the selection by doing any of these things:

- **Drag up or down.** (Again, you don't have to keep pressing hard, but you do have to keep your finger on the glass.)

- **Hard-press twice** to extend the selection to the entire sentence.

- **Hard-press three times** to extend the selection to the entire paragraph.

Once you've selected text in this way, the usual command bar (Cut, Copy, Paste, and so on) appears, for your text-manipulation pleasure.

Little by little, the iPhone is revealing its secret ambition to be a laptop.

Dictation

The iPhone's speech-recognition feature, sometimes called Siri (even though Siri is also the voice **command** feature), lets you enter text any-where, into any program, just by **speaking**. (Behind the scenes, it's using the same Nuance recognition technology that powers the Dragon line of dictation programs.)

It's extremely fast and, usually, remarkably accurate (especially if you have an accent). Suddenly you don't have to fuss with the tiny keyboard. The experience of "typing" is no longer claustrophobic. You can blather away into an email, fire off a text message, or draft a memo without ever look-ing at the screen.

Now, before you get all excited, here are the necessary footnotes:

- Voice typing works best if there's not a lot of background noise.

- Voice typing isn't always practical, since everybody around you can hear what you're saying.

- Voice typing isn't always accurate. Often, you'll have to correct an error or two.

All right—expectations set? Then here's how to type by speaking.

First, fire up someplace where you can call up the keyboard: Messages, Notes, Mail, Safari, whatever. Tap, if necessary, so that the onscreen keyboard appears.

Tap the 🎤 next to the space bar.

When you hear the xylophone note, say what you have to say (below, left). If there's background noise, hold the phone up to your head; if it's relatively quiet, a couple of feet away is fine. You don't have to speak slowly, loudly, or weirdly; speak normally. As you speak, the words fly onto the screen.

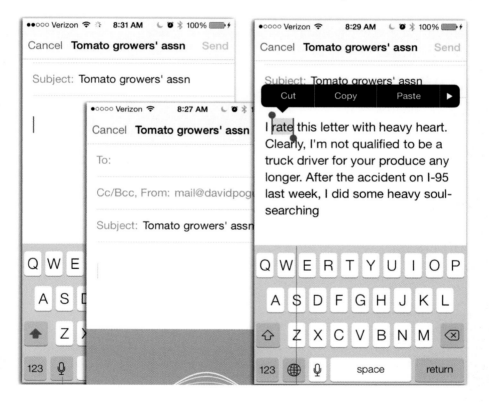

You have to speak your own punctuation, like this: "Dear Dad (colon): Please send money (dash)—as much as you can (comma), please (period)." The table at the end of this section describes all the different punctuation symbols you can dictate.

After you finish speaking, tap Done. Another xylophone note plays—higher, this time—and you may see some of the words *change* right before your eyes, as though Siri is changing her mind. In fact, she is; she's using the context of *all* the words you said to revise what she *originally* thought you said, as you said it. See?

> **NOTE:** If no text appears at all, your Internet or cellular connection probably isn't good enough. You can try again, or you can just sigh and resort to typing with your finger.

If the transcription contains errors, you can tap with your finger to edit them, exactly as you would fix an error in something you typed. (Make the effort; you're simultaneously teaching your iPhone to do better the next time.) Or, if the whole thing is a mess, you can *shake* your iPhone, the universal gesture for Undo.

> **NOTE:** Often, the iPhone knows perfectly well when it might have gotten a word wrong—it draws a dashed underline beneath words or phrases it's insecure about. You can tap that word or phrase to see the iPhone's alternative interpretation, which is often correct.

Usually, you'll find the accuracy pretty darned good, considering you didn't have to train the software to recognize your voice, and considering that your computer is a *cellphone*, for crying out loud. You'll also find that the accuracy is better when you dictate complete sentences, and that long words fare better than short ones.

Punctuation

Here's a handy table that shows you what punctuation you can say and how to say it.

> **TIP:** If you've ever used Dragon NaturallySpeaking (for Windows) or Dragon Dictation (for the Mac), then you already know these commands; they're the standard Nuance dictation-software shortcuts, because that's what the iPhone uses behind the scenes.

Say this:	To get this:	For example, saying this:	Types this:
"period" or "full stop"	. [space and capital letter afterward]	"Best (period) date (period) ever (period)"	Best. Date. Ever.
"dot" or "point"	. [no space afterward]	"My email is frank (dot) smith (at sign) gmail (dot) com"	My email is frank.smith@ gmail.com
"comma," "semicolon," "colon"	, ; :	"Mom (comma) hear me (colon) I'm dizzy (semi-colon) tired"	Mom, hear me: I'm dizzy; tired
"question mark," "excla-mation point"	? ! [space and capital letter afterward]	"Ellen (question mark) Hi (excla-mation point)"	Ellen? Hi!
"inverted question mark," "inverted excla-mation point"	¿ ¡	"(inverted ques-tion mark) Que paso (question mark)"	¿Que paso?
"ellipsis" or "dot dot dot"	…	"Just one (ellipsis) more (ellipsis) step (ellipsis)"	Just one… more…step…
"space bar"	[a space, especially when a hyphen would normally appear]	"He rode the merry (space bar) go (space bar) round"	He rode the merry go round
"open paren" then "close paren" (or "open bracket/close bracket," or "open brace/close brace")	( ) or [ ] or { }	"Then she (open paren) the doctor (close paren) gasped"	Then she (the doctor) gasped
"new line"	[a press of the Return key]	"milk (new line) bread (new line) quinoa"	Milk Bread Quinoa

Say this:	To get this:	For example, saying this:	Types this:
"new paragraph"	[two presses of the Return key]	"autumn leaves (new paragraph) softly falling"	autumn leaves softly falling
"quote," then "unquote"	" "	Her perfume screamed (quote) available (unquote)	Her perfume screamed "available"
"numeral"	[writes the following number as a digit instead spelling it out]	"Next week she turns (numeral) eight"	Next week she turns 8
"asterisk," "plus sign," "minus sign," "equals sign"	*, +, −, =	"numeral eight (asterisk) two (plus sign) one (minus sign) three (equals sign) fourteen"	8*2+1−3=14
"ampersand," "dash"	&, —	"Barry (ampersand) David (dash) the best (exclamation point)"	Barry & David—the best!
"hyphen"	- [without spaces]	"Don't give me that holier (hyphen) than (hyphen) thou attitude"	Don't give me that holier-than-thou attitude
"backquote"	'	"Back in (backquote) (numeral) fifty-two"	back in '52
"smiley," "frowny," "winky" (or "smiley face," "frowny face," "winky face")	:-) :-(;-)	"I think you know where I'm going with this (winky face)"	I think you know where I'm going with this ;-)

You can also say "percent sign" (%), "at sign" (@), "dollar sign" ($), "cent sign" (¢), "euro sign" (€), "yen sign" (¥), "pounds sterling sign" (£), "section sign" (§), "copyright sign" (©), "registered sign" (®), "trademark sign" (™), "greater-than sign" or "less-than sign" (> or <), "degree sign" (°), "caret" (^), "tilde" (~), "vertical bar" (l), and "pound sign" (#).

The software automatically capitalizes the first new word after a period, question mark, or exclamation point. But you can also force it to capitalize words you're dictating by saying "cap" right before the word, like this: "Dear (cap) Mom, I've run away to join (cap) The (cap) Circus (comma), a nonprofit cooperative for runaway jugglers."

Here's another table—this one shows the other commands for capitalization, plus spacing and spelling commands.

> **TIP:** Speak each of the on/off commands as a separate utterance, with a small pause before and after.

Say this:	To get this:	For example, saying this:	Types this:
"cap" or "capital"	Capitalize the next word	"Give me the (cap) works"	Give me the Works
"caps on," then "caps off"	Capitalize the first letter of every word	"Next week, (caps on) the new england chicken cooperative (caps off) will hire me"	Next week, The New England Chicken Cooperative will hire me
"all caps on," then "all caps off"	Capitalize everything	"So (all caps on) please please (all caps off) don't tell anyone"	So PLEASE PLEASE don't tell anyone
"all caps"	Type just the next word in all caps	"We (all caps) really don't belong here"	We REALLY don't belong here
"no caps"	Type the next word in lowercase	"See you in (no caps) Texas"	See you in texas
"no caps on," then "no caps off"	Prevents any capital letters	"I'll ask (no caps on) Santa Claus (no caps off)"	I'll ask santa claus

Say this:	To get this:	For example, saying this:	Types this:
"no space"	Runs the two words together	"Try our new mega (no space) berry flavor"	Try our new megaberry flavor
"no space on," then "no space off"	Eliminates all spaces	"(No space on) I can't believe you ate all that (no space off) (comma) she said excitedly"	Ican'tbelieveyou ateallthat, she said excitedly
[alphabet letters]	Types the letters out (usually not very accurately)	"The stock symbol is A P P L"	The stock symbol is APPL

You don't always have to dictate these formatting commands, by the way. The iPhone automatically inserts hyphens into phone numbers (you say, "2125561000," and get "212-556-1000"); formats two-line street addresses without your having to say, "New line" before the city); handles prices automatically ("six dollars and thirty-two cents" becomes "$6.32").

It formats dates and web addresses well, too; you can even use the nerdy shortcut "dub-dub-dub" when you want the "www" part of a web address.

The phone recognizes email addresses, too, as long as you remember to say "at sign" at the right spot. You'd say, "harold (underscore) beanfield (at sign) gmail (dot) com" to get harold_beanfield@gmail.com.

TIP: You can combine these formatting commands. Many iPhone owners have wondered: "How do I voice-type the *word* "comma," since saying, "comma" types out only the symbol?"

The solution: Say, "No space on, no caps on, C, O, M, M, A, no space off, no caps off." That gives you the *word* "comma."

Then again, it might just be easier to type that one with your finger.

Cut, Copy, Paste

Copy and Paste do just what you'd expect. They let you grab some text off a web page and paste it into an email message, copy directions from email into Notes, paste a phone number from your address book into a text message, and so on.

So how do you select text and trigger Cut, Copy, and Paste functions on a machine with no mouse and no menus? As on the Mac or PC, it takes three steps.

Step 1: Select the Text

Start by highlighting the text you want to cut or copy.

- **To select all.** Suppose you intend to cut or copy *everything* in the text box or message. In that case, tap anywhere in the text to place the blinking insertion point. Then tap the insertion point itself to summon the selection buttons—one of which is Select All.

- **To select some.** Double-tap the first word (or last word) that you want in the copied selection. That word is now highlighted, with blue dots at diagonal corners. Drag these handles to expand the selection to include all the text you want. The little magnifying loupe helps you release the dot at just the right spot (below).

Double-tap...

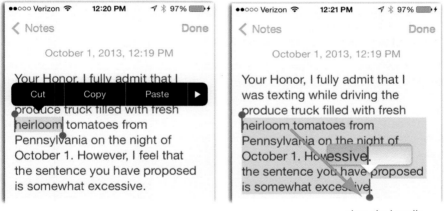

...drag the handle.

TIP: On a web page, you can't very well double-tap to select a word, because double-tapping means "zoom in." Instead, *hold your finger down* on a word to produce the blue handles; the loupe magnifies the proceedings to help you. (If you highlight the wrong word, keep your finger down and slide to the correct one; the highlighting goes with you.)

However, if you're zoomed out to see the whole page, holding down your finger highlights the *entire block* of text (a paragraph or even a whole article) instead of one word. Now you can expand the selection to include a photo, if you like; that way, you can copy and paste the whole enchilada into an outgoing email message.

Step 2: Cut or Copy

At this point, you've highlighted the material you want, and the Cut and Copy buttons are staring you in the face. They're either word buttons above your text, or they're actual graphic buttons (if you have your recent iPhone turned sideways, as shown on page 70).

Tap **Cut** or ✂ (to remove the selected text) or **Copy** or Ⓐ (to leave it but place a duplicate on your invisible Clipboard).

> **TIP:** And what if you want to get rid of the text *without* copying it to the Clipboard (because you want to preserve something you copied earlier, for example)? Easy: Just tap the ⌫ key!

Step 3: Paste

Finally, switch to a different spot in the text, even if it's in a different window (for example, a new email message) or a different app (for example, Calendar or Notes). Tap in any spot where you're allowed to type. Tap the **Paste** button to paste what you cut or copied. (On an iPhone 6/6s model turned sideways, you can tap the ✑ button instead.) Ta-da!

(Possible Step 4: Undo)

Everyone makes mistakes, right? Fortunately, there's a secret Undo command, which can come in handy when you cut, copy, or paste something by mistake.

The trick is to *shake* the iPhone. The iPhone then offers you an Undo button, which you can tap to confirm the backtracking. One finger touch instead of three.

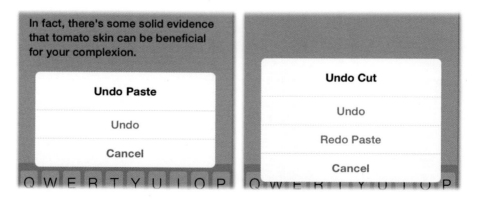

Of course, on an iPhone 6/6s turned sideways, you get a dedicated Undo button instead: ↰.

TIP: The shake-to-undo feature also works to undo *dictating or typing*—not just cutting or pasting.

In fact, you can even undo the Undo. Just shake the phone again; now the screen offers you a Redo button. Fun! (Except when you shake the phone by accident and you get the Nothing to Undo message. But still.)

The Definitions Dictionary

On page 69, you can read about the spelling dictionary that's built into the iOS—but that's just a dumb list of words. Your iPhone also has a *real* dictionary, one that shows you definitions.

In most apps, you can look up any word that appears on the screen. Double-tap it to get the editing bar shown below at left; then tap Define. (You may have to tap ▶ to bring that button into view.)

TIP: You can also double-tap the blinking insertion point that's just before a word. On the editing bar, tap ▶ to see the Define button.

(If you discover that there are "No definitions found," then tap Manage at the bottom of this screen for a list of dictionaries that you can download: English, French, Simplified Chinese, and so on. Tap ☁ to download the ones you think you'll use.)

Speak!

The iPhone can read to you, too. Visit Settings→General→Accessibility→ Speech and turn on Speak Selection and/or Speak Screen. Choose a language (or accent), a voice, and a speaking rate. (The more realistic voices, like Alex and his brother Enhanced Quality, require you to download some audio files from Apple. Just tap the name to begin the download.)

It's fun to turn on Highlight Content, too. (Each word will light up in color as the phone speaks it. Great for kids learning to read!)

From now on, among the other buttons that pop up when you select text, a Speak button appears. Or, if you swipe down the screen with two fingers (and you turned on Speak Screen), your iPhone reads the *entire* screen.

You can use these features whenever you want to double-check the pronunciation of a word, whenever you want to have a web article or email read to you while you're getting dressed for the day, or whenever you lose your voice and just want to communicate with the rest of the world.

TIP: Once you tap Speak, the button changes to say Pause. You're in charge.

Spotlight: Global Search

The iPhone's global search feature is called Spotlight. It's something like a typed version of Siri, in that it can call up information about movies, restaurants, news, and so on.

How to Use Spotlight

The Spotlight screen is built into your Home screens. In iOS 9, you can find it in either of two places:

- **Swipe downward** *within* a Home screen. (If you drag down from the *top* by accident, you'll open the Notification Center, which is a different story.)

- **Swipe to the right** from the first Home screen. Lurking to its left is a special Siri Suggestions page—with a Spotlight box at the top.

In any case, the keyboard opens automatically. Begin typing to identify what you want to find and open. For example, if you were trying to find a file called **Pokémon Fantasy League**, typing just **pok** or **leag** would probably suffice. (Spotlight doesn't find text in the **middles** of words, though; it searches from the beginnings of words.)

As you type, a results list appears below the search box, listing everything Spotlight can find containing what you've typed so far.

They're neatly grouped by category; the beginning of each category is marked with a heading like CONTACTS or MUSIC.

TIP: If you drag your finger to scroll the list, the keyboard helpfully vanishes so you can see more results.

Here's what you might find in Spotlight's list of results:

- **Applications.** For frequent downloaders, this may be the juiciest function: Spotlight searches the names of every app on your iPhone. If you have dozens installed, this is a much more efficient way to find one than trying to page through all the Home screens, eyeballing the icons as you go. (The search results even identify which *folder* an app is in.)

- **Spotlight Suggestions.** Spotlight can find movies, music, apps, and other stuff from the web. The feature works beautifully. The hard part is teaching yourself to use it—just remembering that it's available.

  Spotlight lists results from Wikipedia (when you search for, say, "rhubarb" or "Thomas Edison"); news (search for "SF Giants" or "Middle East negotiations"); restaurants, shops, and businesses ("Olive Garden" or "Apple Store"); the App Store ("Instagram" or "Angry Birds"); the iTunes Store ("Gravity" or "Beatles"); and the iBooks store ("Grisham" or "Little Women").

  The results list identifies which category each hit comes from. Tapping a result does what you'd expect: for a web article, opens the article; for a business, opens its Maps page so you can call it or get instant directions; for something from an Apple store, opens the appropriate store.

  Really, don't miss this. When you hear about a cool app, don't open the App Store to look for it. When you want to know a sports score, don't start with Safari. When you need the phone number of a restaurant, don't call 411. Instead, use Spotlight for all of these things.

- **Contacts.** First names, last names, and company names.

- **Music, Podcasts, Videos, Audiobooks.** Song, performer, and album names, plus the names of podcasts, videos, and audiobooks.

- **Notes, Reminders, Voice Memos.** The actual text of your notes and to-do items, and the names and descriptions of voice memos.

- **Events.** Calendar stuff: appointment names, meeting invitees, and locations (but not any notes attached to your appointments).

- **Mail.** The To, From, and Subject fields of all accounts. For certain accounts, you can even search inside the messages.

- **Messages.** Yep, you can search your text messages, too.

- **Bing Web Results.** You can tap Search Web at the bottom of the results list to hand off to Safari for a search. Handy to have it built right into Spotlight, really.

> **TIP:** Many apps, like Contacts, Mail, Calendar, Music, and Notes, have their *own* search boxes (usually hidden until you scroll to the top of their lists). Those individual search functions are great when you're already *in* the program where you want to search. The Spotlight difference is that it searches all these apps at once.

If you see the name and icon of whatever you were hoping to dig up, tap to open it. The corresponding app opens automatically.

How to Tweak Spotlight

You've just read about how Spotlight works fresh out of the box. But you can tailor its behavior a bit. To open Spotlight's settings, start on the Home screen. Tap Settings→General→Spotlight Search.

Siri Suggestions is the on/off switch for the "proactive" features described below. The other on/off switches here identify the kinds of things that Spotlight tracks. If you find that Spotlight uses up precious screen space listing categories you don't use much, then tap to turn them off. Now more of Spotlight's space-constrained screen is allotted to icon types you do care about.

The "Proactive" Search Screen

In iOS 9, Apple beefed up your phone's intelligence. Now, it tries to anticipate things you'll want to do (*proactively*, Apple says).

You'll discover this tendency in various spots in the software (and in this book). But the most obvious incarnation of it is the newly enhanced search screen, the one that's waiting to the left of the very first Home screen (page 45). To get there, press your Home button, and then swipe to the right as many times as necessary.

At the top of this screen (below, left), you'll find the Spotlight search box. As described on page 91, it searches not just for info-bits and apps on your phone, but also for certain kinds of Internet information.

But below that box, some customized items wait just for you. The choice here changes during the day, based on your location, the time of day, and your typical routine. For example, if you call your boss every morning on the way to work, then Boss' smiling face will appear every morning on this screen, ready to call with one tap. If you check your Fitbit app every morning when you wake, then this screen will offer its icon at that time of day.

These suggestions fall into four sections:

- **People.** Here are the four people you call, text, or email most often, positioned here for easy access. Tap one, and then tap the Call, Message, FaceTime, or Info buttons that appear. Hit Show More to see a second row of four.

> **TIP:** To hide this section of the Search screen, open Settings→General→ Spotlight Search. Turn off Contacts.

- **Apps.** These are four apps Siri thinks you might want to use right now, based on the time of day and your recent patterns of opening apps. Once again, the idea is to save you from having to hunt for them when you need them again. Hit Show More to see a second row. (There's no way to hide this apps row, unless you hide *all* of these Siri-suggested icons, as described below.)

  The Lock screen offers a similar kind of smarts; see page 18.

- **Nearby.** Tap one of these—Dinner, Bars, Shopping, Gas—to open the Maps app, with pushpins indicating the nearest options. These icons change by time of day. In the morning, for example, you'll see Breakfast and Coffee instead of Dinner and Bars.

> **TIP:** To hide this section, open Settings→General→Spotlight Search. Turn off Maps.

- **News.** This section offers news blurbs that Siri thinks you'll like, once again based on where you are, the time of day, and your interests. Tap one to open it in the News app (page 388) for further reading.

> **TIP:** To hide this section, open Settings→General→Spotlight Search. Turn off Spotlight Suggestions.

If you'd rather eliminate *all* these suggestions from your search screen, open Settings→General→Spotlight Search. Turn off Siri Suggestions. Now there's nothing left on the search screen but the Spotlight search box itself.

3

Phone Calls & FaceTime

With each successive iPhone model, Apple improves the antennas, the circuitry, the speakers, the microphone, and the software. And features like Siri, auto-reply, and Do Not Disturb have turned Apple's cellphone from an also-ran into one of the most useful gadgets ever to hop onto a cellular network.

Dialing from the Phone App

Suppose you're in luck. Suppose the dots in the upper-left corner of the iPhone's screen tell you that you've got cellular reception. You're ready to start a conversation. To make a phone call, open the Phone app like this:

1. **Go Home, if you're not already there.** Press the Home button.

2. **Tap the Phone icon.** It's usually at the bottom of the Home screen. (The tiny circled number in the corner of the Phone icon tells you how many missed calls and voicemail messages you have.)

> **TIP:** Using Siri is often faster. You get good results saying things like, "Call Casey Robin's cell" or "Dial 866-2331."

Now you've arrived in the Phone program. A new row of icons appears at the bottom, representing the four ways of dialing from here:

* **Favorites list.** Here's the iPhone's version of speed-dial keys: It lists up to 50 people you think you call most frequently. Tap a name to make the call. (Details on building and editing this list begin below.)

* **Recents list.** Every call you've recently made, answered, missed, or even just dialed appears in this list. Missed callers' names appear in red lettering, which makes them easy to spot—and easy to call back.

Tap a name or a number to dial. Or tap the ⓘ button to view the details of a call—when, where, how long—and, if you like, to add this number to your Contacts list.

- **Contacts list.** This program also has an icon of its own on the Home screen; you don't have to drill down to it through the Phone button. It's your phone book; tap somebody's name or number to dial it.

- **Keypad.** This dialing pad's big, fat buttons are easy to hit even with big, fat fingers. You can punch in any number and then tap Call to place the call.

Once you've dialed, no matter which method you used, either hold the iPhone up to your head, put in the earbuds, turn on the speakerphone, or put on your Bluetooth earpiece—and start talking!

The paragraphs above, however, are only the Quick Start Guide. Here's a more detailed look at each of the four Phone-app modules.

The Favorites List

You may not wind up dialing much from Contacts. That's the master list, all right, but it's too unwieldy when you just want to call your spouse, your boss, or your lawyer. Dialing by voice (Chapter 4) is almost always faster. But when silence is golden, at the very least use the Favorites list—a short, easy-to-scan list of the people you call most often.

You can add a phone number to this list (for dialing, texting, or FaceTime video calls) or an email address (for FaceTime).

You can add names to this list in any of three ways:

- **From the Favorites list itself.** Tap + to view your Contacts list. Tap the person you want. If there's more than one phone number or email address on the Info screen, then tap the one you want to add to Favorites.

> **TIP:** Each Favorite doesn't represent a **person**; it represents a **number or an email address**. So if your best friend, Chris, has both a home number and a cell number, then add two items to the Favorites list. Gray lettering in the list lets you know whether each number or address is mobile, home, or whatever.

- **From the Contacts list.** Tap a name to open the Info screen, where you'll find a button called Add to Favorites. (If you have an email address for this person but no phone number, then the iPhone treats it as a FaceTime favorite.) If there's more than one phone number on the Info screen, you're asked to tap the one you want to add to Favorites.

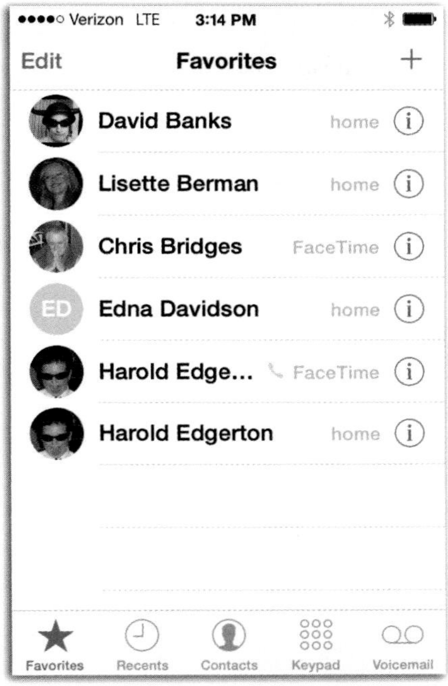

- **From the Recents list.** Tap ⓘ next to any name or number in the Recents list. If it's somebody who's already in your Contacts list, then you arrive at the Call Details screen, where one tap on **Add to Favorites** does what it says.

  If it's somebody who's not in Contacts yet, you'll have to *put* her there first. Tap **Create New Contact**, and then proceed as described on page 103. After you hit **Save**, you return to the Call Details screen so you can tap **Add to Favorites**.

> **TIP:** To help you remember that a certain phone number or email address is already in your Favorites list, a gray star appears next to it in certain spots, like the Call Details screen and the Contact Info screen.

The Favorites list holds 50 numbers. Once you've added 50, the **Add to Favorites** and + buttons disappear.

Reordering Favorites

Tapping that Edit button at the top of the Favorites list offers another handy feature, too: It lets you drag names up and down, so the most important people appear at the top of the list. Just use the grip strip (≡) as a handle to move entire names up or down the list.

Deleting from Favorites

To delete somebody from your Favorites—the morning after a nasty political argument over drinks, for example—use the iPhone's standard swipe-to-delete shortcut: Swipe leftward across the undesired name. Tap the Delete button that appears.

(If you're paid by the hour, you can use the slow method, too. Tap Edit. Now tap the ⊖ button next to the unwanted entry, and tap Delete to confirm.)

The Recents List

Like any self-respecting cellphone, the iPhone maintains a list of everybody you've called or who's called you recently. The idea, of course, is to provide you with a quick way to call someone you've been talking to lately.

To see the list, tap Recents at the bottom of the Phone app. You see a list of the last 75 calls that you've received or placed, along with each person's name or number (depending on whether that name is in Contacts or not), which phone number it is (mobile, home, work, or whatever), city of the caller's home area code (for callers not in your Contacts), and the date of the call.

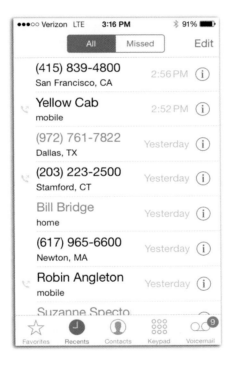

Here's what you need to know about the Recents list:

- Calls that you missed (or sent to voicemail) appear in red type. If you tap Missed at the top of the screen, you see *only* your missed calls. The color-coding and separate listings are designed to make it easy for you to return calls you missed, or to try again to reach someone who didn't answer when you called.

- A tiny ↪ icon lets you know which calls you *made* (to differentiate them from calls you *answered*).

- To call someone back—regardless of whether you answered or dialed the call—tap that name or number in the list.

- Tap ⓘ next to any call to open the Info screen. At the top of the screen, you can see whether this was an outgoing call, an incoming call, a missed call, or a canceled call (that's when you chickened out and hung up before your callee answered).

  What else you see here depends on whether the other person is in your Contacts list.

  If so, the Info screen displays the person's whole information card. A little table displays all the incoming and outgoing calls to or from this person that day. A star denotes a phone number that's also in your Favorites list.

  If the call *isn't* from someone in your Contacts, then you get to see a handy notation at the top of the Info screen: the city and state where the calling phone is registered.

••○○○ Verizon LTE	3:17 PM	⚡ 90% 🔋
⟨ Recents	**Info**	Edit

Phil Simms

Yesterday		
3:17 PM	Outgoing Call	41 seconds
3:16 PM	Outgoing Call	51 seconds

mobile
249-7133   💬 📞

••○○ Verizon LTE	3:17 PM	⚡ 90% 🔋
⟨ Recents	**Info**	

(203) 223-2595
Stamford, CT

Yesterday		
1:41 PM	Outgoing Call	1 minute

Call

FaceTime

- To save you scrolling, the Recents list thoughtfully combines consecutive calls to or from the same person. If some obsessed ex-lover has been calling you every 10 minutes for 4 hours, you'll see "Chris Meyerson (24)" in the Recents list. (Tap ⓘ to see the exact times of the calls.)

- You can erase one call from this list exactly the same way you'd delete a Favorite: Swipe leftward across the undesired name. Tap the **Delete** button that appears. (Once again, there's also a long way: Tap **Edit**, tap ⊖ next to the unwanted entry, and then tap **Delete**.)

  You can also erase the *entire* list, thus preventing a coworker or significant other from discovering your illicit activities: Tap **Edit**, and then tap **Clear** at the top of the screen. You're asked to confirm your decision.

Contacts

The Phone app may offer four ways to dial—Favorites, Recents, Contacts, and Keypad—but the Contacts list is the source from which all other lists spring. That's probably why it's listed three times: once with its own button on the Home screen, again at the bottom of the Phone app, and also in the FaceTime app.

Contacts is your address book—your master phone book.

••••○○ Verizon LTE 3:18 PM ✳ 90% ▬▬▷	••••○○ Verizon LTE 3:18 PM ✳ 90% ▬▬▷
Groups **Contacts** +	Q Mar⏐ ⊗ Cancel
Q Search	**Christie's** Market ›
My Number: **(418) 769-8187**	**Marc** DeLorenzo ›
A	**Maria** Davis ›
AAdvantage	**Mariann** Kabol ›
Abby Span	**Marisa** Bittman ›
Adam C. Enman	Q W E R T Y U I O P
Adam Freestein	A S D F G H J K L
Adam Gold	⇧ Z X C V B N M ⌫
Adam Netter	123 ⊕ 🎤 space Search
☆ Favorites 🕐 Recents 👤 Contacts ⠿ Keypad ⌖⁹ Voicemail	

TIP: Your iPhone's own phone number appears at the very top of the Contacts list within the Phone module (not when you open the Contacts app from its Home screen icon). Drag down on the list to reveal its hiding place just below the search box.

That's a much better place for it than deep at the end of a menu labyrinth, where it is on most phones.

If your social circle is longer than one screenful, then you can navigate this list in any of three ways:

- **First,** you can savor the distinct pleasure of flicking through it.

- **Second,** if you're in a hurry to get to the T's, use the A-to-Z index down the right edge of the screen. Just tap the first letter of the last name you're looking for. Alternatively, you can slide your finger up or down the index. The list scrolls with it.

- **Third,** you can use the search box at the very top of the list, above the A's.

  Tap inside the search box to make the keyboard appear. As you type, Contacts pares down the list, hiding everyone whose first, last, or company name doesn't match what you've typed so far. It's a really fast way to pluck one name out of a haystack.

  (You can clear the search box by tapping the ⊗ at its right end, or restore the full list by tapping Cancel.)

In any case, when you see the name you want, tap it to open its card, filled with phone numbers and other info. Tap the number you want to dial.

Groups

Many computer address book programs, including OS X's Contacts app, let you place your contacts into *groups*—subsets like Book Club or Fantasy League Guys. You can't create or delete groups on the iPhone, but at least the groups from your Mac, PC, Exchange server, or iCloud account get synced over to it. To see them, and to switch them all on or off at once, tap Groups at the top of the Contacts list.

Here's where groups come into play:

- If you can't seem to find someone in the list, you may be looking in the wrong list. Tap Groups at the top-left corner to return to the list of accounts. Tap All Contacts to view a single, unified list of everyone your phone knows about.

- If you've allowed your iPhone to display your contacts from Facebook or Twitter, each of those lists is a group, too. (If your Contacts list seems hideously bloated with hundreds of people you never actually call, it's probably your Facebook list. Pop into Groups and touch All Facebook to hide them all at once.)

- If you do use the Groups feature, remember to tap the group name you want *before* you create a new contact. That's how you put someone into an existing group. (If not, tap All Contacts instead.)

Adding to the Contacts List

Every cellphone has a Contacts list, of course, but the beauty of the iPhone is that you don't have to type in the phone numbers one at a time. Instead, the iPhone sucks in the entire phone book from your Mac or PC, iCloud, and/or an Exchange server at work.

It's infinitely easier to edit your address book on the computer, where you have an actual keyboard and mouse. The iPhone also makes it very easy to add someone's contact information when she calls, emails, or text messages you, thanks to a prominent Add to Contacts button.

But if, in a pinch, on the road, at gunpoint, you have to add, edit, or remove a contact manually, here's how to do it:

Make sure you've selected the right group or account, as described already. Now, on the Contacts screen, tap +. You arrive at the New Contact screen, which teems with empty boxes.

It shouldn't take you long to figure out how to fill in this form: You tap in a box and type. But there are a few tips and tricks for the data-entry process:

- **The keyboard opens automatically** when you tap in a box. And the iPhone capitalizes the first letter of each name for you.

TIP: If you know somebody has your same cell company, add it—like "(AT&T)" or "(Verizon)" or "(Sprint)"—after the last name. That way, when he calls, you'll know that the call is free (like all calls within the same company's cell network).

Or add a similar notation to his cellphone number in Contacts. That way, when you call him, you'll know which number to use (cell or landline, for example) to get a free call.

- **Phone numbers are special.** When you enter a phone number, the iPhone adds parentheses and hyphens for you. (You can even enter text phone numbers, like 1-800-GO-BROWNS; the iPhone converts the letters to digits when it dials.)

If you need to insert a pause—for dialing access numbers, extension numbers, or voicemail passwords—type #, which introduces a 2-second pause in the dialing. You can type several to create longer pauses.

To change the label for a number ("mobile," "home," "work," and so on), tap the label that's there now. The Label screen shows you your choices. There's even a label called "iPhone," so you and your buddy can gloat together.

• **Expand-O-Fields mean you'll never run out of room.** Almost every field (empty box) on a Contacts card is infinitely expanding. That is, the instant you start filling in a field, another empty box (labeled add phone or whatever) appears right below it, so you can immediately add **another** phone number, email address, URL, street address, or whatever. (The only non-expanding fields are First, Last, Company, Ringtone, and the oddball fields you add yourself.)

For example, when you first create a card for someone, the phone-number box is labeled "mobile." If you start entering a phone number into it, a new, **second** empty phone-number box appears just below it (labeled "iPhone"—Apple's wishful thinking!), so you'll have a place to enter a second phone number for this person. When you do that, a **third** box appears. And so on.

There's always one empty field, so you can never run out of places to add more phone numbers, addresses, and so on. (Don't worry—the perpetual empty box doesn't appear once you're finished editing the person's card.)

NOTE: Baffled by the ⊕ button that appears next to certain fields? It tells you that tapping that field (or the ⊕ itself) will add new lines to your Contact card. For example, tapping Add new address inserts a new name/street/city/state block. And tapping add field lets you add a new miscellaneous field, like Birthday or Department.

- **You can add a photo of the person, if you like.** Tap add photo. If you have a photo of the person already, tap Choose Photo. You're taken to your photo collection, where you can find a good headshot (Chapter 8).

  Alternatively, tap Take Photo to activate the iPhone's built-in camera. Frame the person, and then tap the white camera button to snap the shot.

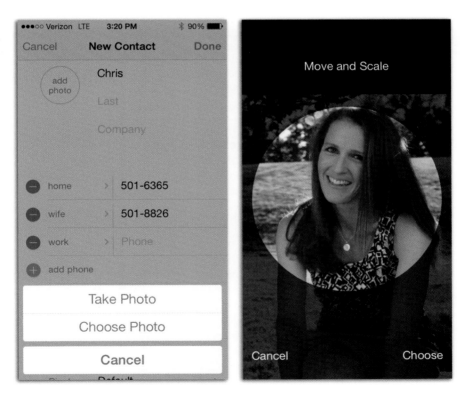

In any case, you wind up with the **Move and Scale** screen. Here you can frame up the photo so the person's face is nicely sized and centered. Spread two fingers to enlarge the photo; drag your finger to move the image within the frame. Tap **Choose** to commit the photo to the address book's memory. (Back on the Info screen where you started, a miniature version of the photo now appears. Tap **edit** if you want to change the photo, take a new one, adjust the Move and Scale screen, or get rid of the photo altogether.)

From now on, this photo will pop up whenever the person calls. It also appears next to the person's name in your Favorites list (if you haven't turned that feature off in Settings, of course).

- **Relatives are here.** There's also the **social profile** field, where you can list somebody's Twitter, LinkedIn, Flickr, Facebook, and even MySpace addresses. There's an **instant message** field, too, where you can record addresses for chat networks like AIM or Yahoo Messenger.

  And there's **add related name**. Here's where you can specify this person's mother, father, spouse, partner, child, manager, sibling, and so on—or even type in a relationship that you make up (tap **Add Custom Label**).

NOTE: As you may discover in Chapter 4, Siri knows about all your relationships. You can tell her to "Call my mom" or "Text my boss." Does the **add related name** feature mean that you can now ask Siri to "Call Chris Robin's manager"?

Alas, no. These fields are for your reference only.

- **You can import photos from Facebook.** Here's a wild guess: Most of the photo boxes in your copy of Contacts are empty. After all, who's going to go to the trouble of hunting down headshots of 500 acquaintances, just for a fully illustrated Contacts list?

  Fortunately, with one click, the iPhone can harvest headshots from the world's largest database of faces: Facebook.

  Visit **Settings→Facebook** to see the magical button: **Update All Contacts**. When you click it, the iPhone goes online for a massive research mission. Using your contacts' names and phone numbers as matching criteria, it ventures off to Facebook, finds the profile photos of everyone who's also on your Contacts list, and installs them into Contacts automatically. (If you already have a photo for somebody, don't worry; it doesn't get replaced.)

  As a handy bonus, this operation also adds the @facebook.com email addresses for the people you already had in Contacts.

TIP: Actually, there's another side effect of this operation: It also adds all your Facebook friends' names to your main Contacts list.

Now, you may not be crazy about this. Most of these Facebook folk you'll never call on the phone—yet here they are, cluttering up the Contacts list within the Phone app.

Fortunately, the Update All Contacts button doesn't *really* mix your Facebook friends in with your local Contacts list. It just subscribes to your Facebook address book—adds a new *group*, which you can turn off with one quick click; see page 102.

Even if you do choose to hide all their entries, you still get the benefit of the imported headshots and Facebook email addresses for the people you *do* want to see in Contacts.

- **You can import Twitter addresses.** In Settings→Twitter, the Update Contacts button awaits. Its purpose is to fill in the Twitter handles for everyone who's already in your Contacts, matching them by phone number or email address.

- **You can choose a ringtone.** You can choose a different ringtone for each person in your address book. The idea is that you'll know by the sound of the ring who's calling you.

NOTE: It's one tone per person, not per phone number. Of course, if you really want one ringtone for your buddy's cellphone and another for his home phone, you can always create a different Contacts card for each one.

To choose a ringtone, tap Default. On the next screen, tap any sound in the Ringtones or Alert Sounds lists to sample them. (Despite the separate lists, in this context, these sounds are all being offered as ringtones.) When you've settled on a good one, tap Done to return to the Info screen where you started.

- **You can specify a vibration pattern for incoming calls.** This unsung feature lets you assign a custom vibration pattern to each person in your Contacts, so you know by *feel* who's calling—without even removing the phone from your pocket, even if your ringer is off. It's a surprisingly useful option.

To set it up, tap Default next to the word vibration. You're offered a choice of canned patterns (Alert, Heartbeat, Quick, Rapid, and so on). But if you tap Create New Vibration, you can then tap the screen in whatever rhythm you like. It can be diddle diddle dee...or the opening notes to the Hallelujah Chorus...or the actual syllables of the person's name. ("Maryanna Beckleheimer." Can you feel it?)

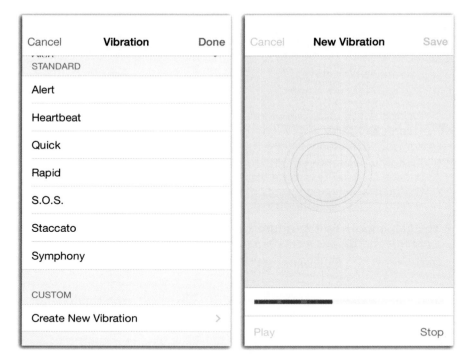

Cancel	**Vibration**	Done
STANDARD		
Alert		
Heartbeat		
Quick		
Rapid		
S.O.S.		
Staccato		
Symphony		
CUSTOM		
Create New Vibration		>

Cancel	**New Vibration**	Save
Play		Stop

The phone records your pattern, which you can prove to yourself by tapping **Play**. If you tap **Save** and name that pattern, then it becomes one of the choices when you choose a vibration pattern for someone in your Contacts. It's what you'll feel whenever this person calls you. Yes, it's tactile caller ID. Wild.

- **You can also pick a text-message sound (and vibration).** Just as you can choose sounds and vibrations for incoming phone calls, the next two items (**text tone**, **vibration**) let you choose sounds and vibrations for incoming text messages and FaceTime invitations.

- **You can add new fields of your own.** Very cool: If you tap **add field** at the bottom of the screen, then you go down the rabbit hole into Field Land, where you can add any of 15 additional info bits about the person whose card you're editing: a prefix (like Mr. or Mrs.), a suffix (like M.D. or Esq.), a nickname, a job title, a birthday, an instant message address, a phonetic pronunciation for people with weird names, and so on.

When you tap one of these labels, you return to the Info screen, where you'll see that the iPhone has inserted the new, empty field in the most intelligent spot. For example, if you add a phonetic first name, that box appears just below the First Name box. The keyboard opens so you can fill in the blank.

- **You can link and unlink Unified Contacts.** As noted earlier, your phone can sync up with different accounts. Your Contacts app might list four sets of names and numbers: one stored on your phone, one from an iCloud account, one from Facebook, and a fourth from your corporate Exchange server at work. In the old days, therefore, certain names might have shown up in the All Contacts list two or three times—not an optimal situation.

Now, as a favor to you, the iPhone displays each person's name only once in that master All Contacts list. If you tap that name, you open up a unified information screen for that person. It includes *all* the details from *all* the underlying cards from that person.

NOTE: The iPhone combines cards in the All Contacts list only if the first and last names are exactly the same. If there's a difference in name, suffix, prefix, or middle name, no unifying takes place. Remember, too, that you see the unification only if you view the All Contacts list.

To see which cards the iPhone is combining for you, scroll to the bottom of the card. There the Linked Contacts section shows you which cards have been unified.

Here you can tap a listing to open the card in the corresponding account. For that matter, you can manually link a card, too; tap Edit, tap link contacts, and then choose a contact to link to this unified card—even if the name isn't a perfect match.

NOTE: It's OK to link Joe Carnelia's card with Joseph Carnelia's card—they're probably the same person. But don't link up *different* people's cards. Remember, the whole point is to make the iPhone combine all the phone numbers, email addresses, and so on onto a single card—and seeing two sets on one card could get confusing fast.

This stuff gets complex. But, in general, the iPhone tries to do the right thing. For example, if you edit the information on the unified card, you're changing that information only on the card in the corresponding account. (Unless you *add* information to the unified card. In that case, the new data tidbit is added to *all* the underlying source-account cards.)

Yahoo.com info   *Unified info*   *iCloud info*

Adding a Contact on the Fly

There's actually another way to add someone to your Contacts list—a faster, on-the-fly method that's more typical of cellphones. Start by bringing the phone number up on the screen:

• In the Phone app, open the **Keypad**. Dial the number, and then tap **Add to Contacts**.

- You can also add a number that's in your Recents (recent calls) list, storing it in Contacts for future use. Tap the ⓘ button next to the name.

In both cases, finish up by tapping Create New Contact (to enter this person's name for the first time) or Add to Existing Contact (to add a new phone number to the card of someone who's already in your list). Off you go to the Contacts editing screen shown on page 104.

Editing Someone

To make corrections or changes, tap the person's name in the Contacts list. In the upper-right corner of the Info card, tap Edit.

You return to the screens already described, where you can make whatever changes you like. To edit a phone number, for example, tap it and change away. Or, to delete a number (or any other info bit), tap the ⊖ button next to it, and then tap Delete to confirm.

After you tap Done (or Cancel), you can return to the Contacts list by swiping to the right.

Deleting Someone

Truth is, you'll probably *add* people to your address book far more often than you'll *delete* them. After all, you meet new people all the time—but you delete people primarily when they die, move away, or dump you.

To zap someone, tap the name in the Contacts list and then tap Edit. Scroll down, tap Delete Contact and confirm by tapping Delete Contact again. (Weirdly, the Delete Contact option doesn't appear if you open someone's info card from the Recents or Favorites lists—only from the main Contacts list.)

Sharing a Contact

There's a lot of work involved in entering someone's contact information. It would be thoughtful, therefore, if you could spare the next guy all that effort—by sending a fully formed electronic business card to him. It can be yours or that of anyone in your Contacts list.

To do that, open the contact's card, scroll to the bottom, and tap Share Contact. On the Share sheet, you're offered a choice of AirDrop, Message, Mail, and More. ("Message" means an iMessage—page 170—if it's a fellow Apple fan, or a text message otherwise. AirDrop is described on page 331. And More is a place for new apps to install their sharing options.)

Tap your choice, address the message (to an email address or, for a message, a cellphone number), and send it. The recipient, assuming he has a half-decent smartphone or address-book program on the receiving end, can install that person's information with a single tap on the attachment.

> **TIP:** Ever meet someone and wish you could just exchange business cards electronically, iPhone to iPhone? AirDrop is the answer.

The Keypad

The fourth way to place a call is to tap **Keypad** at the bottom of the screen. The standard iPhone dialing pad appears. It's just like the number pad on a normal cellphone, except that the "keys" are much bigger and you can't feel them.

To make a call, tap out (or paste) the phone number—use the ⊗ key to backspace if you make a mistake—and then tap the **Call** button.

You can also use the keypad to enter a phone number into your Contacts list, thanks to the **Add to Contacts** button, as described earlier.

Answering Calls

When someone calls your iPhone, you'll know it; three out of your five senses are alerted. Depending on how you've set up your iPhone, you'll *hear* a ring, *feel* a vibration, and *see* the caller's name and photo fill the iPhone screen. (Smell and taste will have to wait until iOS 10.)

NOTE: For details on choosing a ringtone and on Vibrate mode, see page 568.

How you answer depends on what's happening at the time:

- **If you're using the iPhone,** tap the green Accept button. Tap the red hangup button when you've both said enough.

- **If the iPhone is asleep or locked,** the screen lights up and says slide to answer. If you slide your finger as indicated by the arrow, you simultaneously unlock the phone and answer the call.

- **If you're wearing earbuds,** the music fades out and then pauses; you hear the ring both through the phone's speaker and through your earbuds. Answer by squeezing the clicker on the earbud cord or by using either of the methods described above.

When the call is over, you can click again to hang up—or just wait until the other guy hangs up. Either way, the music fades in again and resumes from the spot where you were so rudely interrupted.

Same thing if you were watching a video; it pauses for the duration of the call and then resumes when you hang up.

> **TIP:** iOS 9 introduces the first meaningful enhancement to Caller ID in years: It makes an educated *guess* as to the name of the caller (if that person's not in your Contacts, of course). Instead of no name at all, you'll see something like "Maybe: Casey Robin."
>
> How does the iPhone do it? When a call comes in, iOS instantly searches your *email* in hopes of finding a matching phone number in somebody's email signature. If it finds one, it extracts that person's name and proposes it. They should call it Likely Caller ID.

Online and on the Phone, Together

Don't forget that the iPhone is a multitasking master. Once you're on the phone, you can dive into any other program—to check your calendar, for example—without interrupting the call.

You may even be able to use the phone's Internet functions (web, email, apps, and so on) without interrupting your call. To be precise, you can be online and on the phone simultaneously if any of these things is true:

- You're in a Wi-Fi hotspot.

- You have AT&T or T-Mobile.

- You have a Verizon iPhone 6 or 6s, and you've turned on VoLTE (see page 419).

In other words, if you have Verizon (non-VoLTE) or Sprint, or if you're not in a Wi-Fi hotspot, then you can't get online until the call is complete.

Silencing the Ring

Sometimes you need a moment before you can answer the call; maybe you need to exit a meeting or put in the earbuds, for example. In that case, you can stop the ringing and vibrating by pressing one of the physical buttons on the edges (the Sleep/Wake button or either volume key). The caller still hears the phone ringing, and you can still answer it within the first four rings, but at least the sound won't be annoying those around you.

(This assumes, of course, that you haven't just flipped the silencer switch.)

Not Answering Calls

Maybe you're in a meeting. Maybe you're driving. Maybe the call is coming from someone you *really* don't want to deal with right now. Fortunately, you have all kinds of ways to slam the cellular door in somebody's face.

Ignore It—or Dump It to Voicemail

If you wait long enough (four rings), the call will go to voicemail (even if you silence the ringing/vibrating as described previously).

Or you can dump it to voicemail *immediately* (instead of waiting for the four rings). How you do that depends on the setup:

- **If the iPhone is asleep or locked,** tap the Sleep button twice fast.

- **If you're using the iPhone,** tap the Decline button on the screen.

- **If you're wearing the earbuds,** squeeze the microphone clicker for 2 seconds. You hear two low beeps, meaning: "OK, Master; dumped."

Of course, if your callers know you have an iPhone, they'll also know that you've deliberately dumped them into voicemail—because they won't hear all four rings.

Respond with a Text Message

Whenever your phone rings, the screen bears a small white Message button (shown on page 113). If you tap it, you get a choice of three canned text messages. Tapping one immediately dumps the caller to voicemail and sends the corresponding text message to the phone that's calling you. If you're driving or in a meeting, this feature is a lot more polite and responsive than just dumping the poor slob to voicemail.

> **TIP:** You can edit any of these three canned messages; they don't have to say, "Sorry, I can't talk right now," "I'm on my way," and "Can I call you later?" forever. To do that, open Settings→Phone, tap Respond with Text, and replace the text in the three placeholder boxes.

The fourth button, Custom, lets you type or dictate a new message on the spot. ("I'm in a meeting and, frankly, your call isn't worth getting fired for" comes to mind.)

Remind Me Later

The trouble with Respond with Text, of course, is that it sends a text message. What if the caller is using a landline that can't receive text messages? Fortunately, you have another option: Remind Me.

Tapping this button offers you one time-based option, **In 1 Hour** (which sets up a reminder to return the call an hour from now), and three location-based options (below, right): **When I leave**, **When I get home**, and **When I get to work**. (The home and work options appear only if the iPhone *knows* your home and work addresses—because you've entered them in your own card in Contacts.)

These options use the phone's GPS circuitry to detect when you've left your current inconvenient-to-take-the-call location, whether it's a job interview, a first date, or an outhouse.

Do Not Disturb

When you turn on Do Not Disturb, the phone is quiet and dark. It doesn't ring, chirp, vibrate, light up, or display messages. A ☾ appears on the status bar to remind you why it seems to be so uncharacteristically depressed.

Yes, airplane mode does the same thing, but there's a big difference: In Do Not Disturb, *the phone is still online*. Calls, texts, emails, and other communications continue to chug happily away; they just don't draw attention to themselves.

Do Not Disturb is what you want when you're in bed each night. You don't really want to be bothered with chirps for Facebook status updates and Twitter posts, but it's fine for the phone to collect them for the morning.

Bedtime is why Do Not Disturb comes with two fantastic additional settings: one that turns it on and off automatically on a schedule, so that the phone goes dark each night at the same time you do, and another that lets you designate important people whose calls and texts are allowed to get through. You know—for emergencies.

Turning on Do Not Disturb

To turn on Do Not Disturb manually, you have three options:

- Tell Siri, "Turn on Do Not Disturb."

- Swipe upward to open the Control Center, and tap the 🌙 icon so that it turns white.

- Open Settings, tap Do Not Disturb, and tap Manual.

To set it up on a schedule, open up Settings→Do Not Disturb. Turn on Scheduled, and then tap the From/To block to specify starting and ending hours. (There's no separate setting for weekends; Do Not Disturb will turn on and off for the same hours every day of the week.)

Allowing Special Callers Through

What if your child, your boss, or your elderly parent needs you urgently in the middle of the night? Turning the phone off completely, or putting it into airplane mode, would leave you unreachable in an emergency.

That's why Apple built in the Allow Calls From option. When you open Settings→Do Not Disturb and then tap Allow Calls From, you're offered options like **Everyone** (all calls and texts come through), **No One** (the phone is still online, but totally silent), or **Favorites**, which may be the most useful option of all.

That setting permits calls and texts from anybody you've designated as a Favorite in the Phone app (page 96). Since those are the people you call most often, it's fairly likely they're the most important people in your life.

You can also create an arbitrary group of people—just your mom and sister, just your boss and nephew, whatever. You have to create these address-book groups on your computer (or using an app like Groups by Qbix). Once you've done that, their names appear on the Allow Calls From screen under Groups. You can designate any one of them as the lucky exception to Do Not Disturb.

One More Safety Measure

The Do Not Disturb settings screen also offers something called **Repeated Calls**. If you turn this on, then if *anybody* tries to call you more than once within 3 minutes, he'll ring through.

The idea here is that nobody *would* call you multiple times unless he needed to reach you urgently. You certainly wouldn't want Do Not Disturb to block somebody who's trying to tell you that there's been an accident, that you've overslept, or that you've just won the lottery.

Locked or Unlocked

The final option on the settings screen is the Silence option. If you choose **Always**, then Do Not Disturb works exactly as described above.

But if you choose **Only while iPhone is locked**, then the phone *does* ring and vibrate *when you're using it*. Because, obviously, if the phone is awake, so are you. It's a great way to ensure that you don't miss important calls if you happened to have awakened early today and started working.

Fun with Phone Calls

The iPhone makes it pitifully easy to perform stunts like turning on the speakerphone, putting someone on hold, taking a second call, and so on. Here are the options you get when you're on a call.

Mute

Tap this button to mute your own microphone, so the other guy can't hear you. (You can still hear him, though.) Now you have a chance to yell

upstairs, to clear the phlegm from your throat, or to do anything else you'd rather the other party not hear. Tap again to unmute.

Keypad

Sometimes you have to input touchtones, which used to be a perk only of phones with physical dialing keys. For example, that's usually how you operate home answering machines when you call in for messages, and it's often required by automated banking, reservations, and conference-call systems.

Tap this button to produce the traditional iPhone dialing pad. Each digit you touch generates the proper touchtone for the computer on the other end to hear.

When you're finished, tap Hide to return to the dialing-functions screen, or tap End if your conversation is complete.

Speaker

Tap this button to turn on the iPhone's built-in speakerphone—a great hands-free option when you're caught without your earbuds or Bluetooth headset. (In fact, the speakerphone doesn't work if the earbuds are plugged in or if a Bluetooth headset is connected.)

When you tap the button, it turns white to indicate that the speaker is activated. Now you can put the iPhone down on a table or a counter and have a conversation with both hands free. Tap speaker again to channel the sound back into the built-in earpiece.

Add Call (Conference Calling)

The iPhone is all about software, baby, and that's nowhere more apparent than in its facility at handling multiple calls at once.

The simplicity and reliability of this feature put other cellphones to shame. Never again, in attempting to answer a second call, will you have to tell the first person, "If I lose you, I'll call you back."

As you'll read here, however, this feature is much better on a GSM phone (AT&T or T-Mobile) than a CDMA phone (Verizon or Sprint).

Suppose you're on a call. Here are some of the tricks you can do:

- **Make an outgoing call.** Tap add call. The iPhone puts the first person on hold—neither of you can hear the other—and returns you to the Phone app and its various phone-number lists. You can now make a second call just the way you made the first. The top of the screen makes clear that the first person is still on hold as you talk to the second.

- **Receive an incoming call.** What happens when a second call comes in while you're already on a call?

  To answer on a GSM phone, tap End Call + Answer. On a CDMA phone, tap End Current Call; the new call makes the phone ring again, at which point you can answer it normally. Weird but true.

  You can also tap End Current Call (answer the incoming call, hang up on the first) or Decline Incoming Call (send it to voicemail).

When you're on two calls at once, the top of the screen identifies both other parties. Two new buttons appear, too:

- **Swap** (GSM phones only) lets you flip between the two calls. At the top of the screen, you see the names or numbers of your callers. One says HOLD (the one who's on hold, of course) and the other bears a time counter, which lets you know whom you're actually speaking to.

  Think how many TV and movie comedies have relied on the old "Whoops, I hit the wrong button and now I'm bad-mouthing somebody directly instead of behind his back!" gag. That can't happen on the iPhone.

You can swap calls by tapping swap or by tapping the HOLD person's name or number.

- **Merge Calls** combines your two calls so all three of you can converse at once. Now the top of the screen announces, "Bill O'Reilly & Jon Stewart" (or whatever the names of your callers are). Note that on a CDMA phone, you can merge calls only if *you placed* the second call—not if it was incoming.

This business of combining calls into one doesn't have to stop at two. At any time, you can tap Add Call, dial a third number, and then tap Merge to combine it with your first two. And then a fourth call, and a fifth. With you, that makes six people on the call.

Then your problem isn't technological; it's social, as you try to conduct a meaningful conversation without interrupting one another.

FaceTime

Tap this button to switch from your current phone call into a face-to-face video call, using the FaceTime app described shortly.

(This feature requires that both you and the other guy have iPhones.)

Hold

The FaceTime button appears in place of what, on earlier iPhones, was the Hold button. But you can still trigger the Hold function—by holding down the Mute button for a couple of seconds. Now neither you nor the other guy can hear anything. Tap again to resume the conversation.

Contacts

This button opens the address book program so you can look up a number or place another call.

Custom Ringtones

The iPhone comes with 52 creative and intriguing ringing sounds, from an old car horn to a peppy marimba lick. Page 568 shows you how to choose the one you want to hear when your phone rings. You can also buy ready-made pop-music ringtones from Apple for $1.30 each. (On your iPhone, open the iTunes app. Tap More, then Tones).

But where's the fun in that? Surely you don't want to walk around listening to the same ringtones as the millions of *other* iPhone owners.

Fortunately, you can also make up *custom* ring sounds, either to use as your main iPhone ring or to assign to individual callers in your Contacts list. All kinds of free or cheap apps are available for doing that, with names like Ringtone Designer Pro and Ringtones for iPhone; they let you make ringtones out of songs you already own, or even sounds you record yourself.

You can also use GarageBand, a free Apple program available for iOS or Mac. For instructions, see this chapter's free online appendix. It's a PDF available on this book's "Missing CD" page at *missingmanuals.com*.

Because apps aren't allowed to manipulate the iPhone's ringtones list directly, the process isn't altogether automatic; it involves syncing the ringtone to iTunes on your computer and then syncing it again to your phone. But the app's instructions will guide you. (iPhone ringtones must be in the .m4r file format.)

FaceTime Video Calls

Your iPhone, as you're probably aware, has two cameras—one on the back and one on the front. And that can mean only one thing: Video calling has arrived.

The iPhone was not the first phone to be able to make video calls. But it is the first one that can make *good* video calls, reliably, with no sign-up or setup, with a single tap. The picture and audio are generally rock-solid, with very little delay, and it works the first time and every time. Now Grandma

can see the baby, or you can help someone shop from afar, or you can supervise brain surgery from thousands of miles away (some medical training is recommended).

You can enjoy these *Jetsons* fantasies not just when calling other iPhones; you can also make video calls between iPhones and iPads, iPod Touches, and Macs. You can even place these calls when you're not in a Wi-Fi hotspot, over the cellular airwaves, when you're out and about.

Being able to make video calls like a regular cellphone call is a huge convenience. Never again will you return home from the store and get scolded for buying the wrong size, style, or color.

In any case, FaceTime couldn't be easier to fire up—in many different ways:

- **From Siri.** The quickest way to start a video call may be simply to say, "FaceTime Mom," "FaceTime Chris Taylor," or whatever.

- **From Favorites.** Whenever you designate someone as a Favorite, a new entry appears in the Phone app's Favorites list (page 96).

- **When you're already on a phone call with someone.** This is a good technique when you want to ask first if the other guy *wants* to do video, or when you've been chatting and suddenly there's some *reason* to do video. In any case, there's nothing to it: Just tap the FaceTime icon that's right on the screen when you pull the phone away from your face. (Your buddy can either accept or, if he just got out of the shower, decline.)

- **From the FaceTime app.** You can also start up a videochat without placing a phone call first. That's handy when you have Wi-Fi but no cell signal; FaceTime can make the call even when Verizon can't.

   Of course, if you're not already on a call, the iPhone doesn't yet know whom you want to call. So you have to tell it.

   Open the FaceTime app. It presents a list of your recent FaceTime calls. Tap a name to place a new call to that person, or tap ⓘ to view a history of your calls with that person (and buttons for placing new ones).

   Or, to find your callee from your own Contacts list, tap the + button. Find a name, tap it, and then tap ☐◁ to place the call.

   If your future conversation partner *isn't* in Contacts yet, tap where it says Enter name, email, or number, and do just that.

- **From Contacts.** In the Contacts app, if you tap a person's name, you'll find buttons that place FaceTime calls. Or, in the Phone app, call up your Favorites or Recents list. Tap ⓘ next to a name to open the contact's card; tap FaceTime.

- **From Messages.** If you're chatting away with somebody by text and you realize that typing is no longer appropriate for the conversation, tap Details at the top of the screen. Tap ▢◁.

At this point, the other guy receives an audio and video message inviting him to a chat. If he taps Accept, you're on. You're on each other's screens, seeing and hearing each other in real time. (You appear on your own screen, too, in a little inset window. It's spinach-in-your-teeth protection.)

Once the chat has begun, here's some of the fun you can have:

- **Rotate the screen.** FaceTime works in either portrait (upright) or landscape (widescreen) view; just turn your phone 90 degrees. Of course, if your calling partner doesn't *also* turn her gadget, she'll see your picture all squished and tiny, with big black areas filling the rest of the screen. (On the Mac, the picture rotates automatically when your partner's gadget rotates. You don't have to turn the monitor 90 degrees.)

TIP: The 🔒 (rotation lock) button described on page 26 works in FaceTime, too. That is, you can stop the picture from rotating when you turn the phone—as long as you're happy with full-time upright (portrait) orientation.

- **Show what's in front of you.** Sometimes, you'll want to show your friend what you're looking at. That is, you'll want to turn on the camera on the *back* of the iPhone, the one pointing away from you, to show off the baby, the artwork, or the broken engine part.

That's easy enough; just tap ⊙ on your screen. The iPhone switches from the front camera to the back camera. Now you and your callee can both see what you're seeing. (It's a lot less awkward than using a laptop for this purpose, because with the laptop's camera facing away from you, you can't see what you're showing.)

Tap ⊙ again to return to the front camera.

- **Snap a commemorative photo.** You can immortalize a chat by using the screenshot keystroke (**Sleep** + **Home**). You wind up with a still photo of your videochat in progress, safely nestled in the Camera Roll of your Photos app.

- **Mute the audio.** Tap 🎤 to silence the audio you're sending. Great when you need to yell at the kids.

- **Mute the video.** When you leave the FaceTime app for any reason (press the **Home** button and then open a different program, if you like), the other guy's screen goes black. He can't see what you're doing when you leave the FaceTime screen. He can still hear you, though.

  This feature was designed to let you check your calendar, look something up on the web, or whatever, while you're still chatting. But it's also a great trick when you need to adjust your clothing, pick at your teeth, or otherwise shield your activity from the person on the other end.

  In the meantime, the call is, technically, still in progress—and a green banner at the top of the Home screen reminds you of that. Tap there, on the green bar, to return to the video call.

When you and your buddy have had quite enough, tap the **End** button to terminate the call. (Although it's easy to jump from phone call to videochat, there's no way to go the other direction.)

And marvel that you were alive to see the day.

FaceTime Audio Calls

You might imagine that, on the great timeline of Apple technologies, audio calling would have arrived *before* video calling. But no; free Internet audio calls didn't come to the iPhone until iOS 7.

And it's a big, big deal. Video calling is neat and all, but be honest: Don't you find yourself making *phone* calls more often? Video calling forces us to be "on," neatly dressed and well behaved, because we're on camera. Most of the time, we're perfectly content (in fact, *more* content) with audio only.

And FaceTime audio calls don't eat into your cellphone minutes and aren't transmitted over your cell carrier's voice network; instead, these are *Internet* calls. (They use data, not minutes.)

When you're in a Wi-Fi hotspot, they're free. When you're not, your carrier's data network carries your voice. Use FaceTime audio a lot, and you might even be able to downgrade your calling plan to a less expensive one.

Sold yet? All right: Here's how to make a free Internet voice call.

You start out exactly as you would when making a video call, as described earlier. That is, you can start from the FaceTime app, the Contacts app, the Phone app, Messages, and so on.

In each spot where FaceTime is available, you get a choice of two types of calls: **Video** (☐◁) and **Audio** (✆). (In Messages, if you tap the ✆, you get a choice of two voice options: **Voice Call** and **FaceTime Audio**.)

When you place an audio FaceTime call, the other person's phone rings exactly as though you'd placed a regular call. All the usual buttons and options are available: **Remind Me**, **Message**, **Decline**, **Accept**, and so on.

Once you accept the call, it's just like being on a phone call, too: You have the options **Mute**, **Speaker**, **FaceTime** (that is, "Switch to video") and **Contacts**. (What's missing? The **Keypad** button and the **Merge Calls** button. You can't combine FaceTime audio calls with each other, or with regular cellphone calls. If a cellphone call comes in, you'll be offered the chance to take it—but you'll have to hang up on FaceTime.)

Actually, it's better than being on a phone call in two ways. First, you don't have the usual lag time that throws off your comic timing. And, second, the audio quality is *amazing*—more like FM radio than cellular. It sounds like the other person is right next to your head; you hear every breath, sniff, and sweater rustle.

You'd be wise to force yourself to try out FaceTime audio calls. Whenever you're calling another iPhone, iPad, iPod Touch, or Mac owner, you'll save money and minutes by placing these better-sounding free calls.

TIP: iOS even offers you FaceTime Call Waiting. If you're on a FaceTime audio or video call, and someone else FaceTime calls you, your phone rings—and you can either tap **Decline** or **End & Accept**.

4

Siri Voice Command

Siri, the iPhone's famous voice-recognition technology, is actually *two* features. First, there's *dictation*, where the phone types out everything you say. It's described in Chapter 2.

Second, there's Siri the *voice-controlled minion*. You can say, "Wake me up at 7:45 a.m.," or "What's Chris's work number?" or "How do I get to the airport?" or "What's the weather going to be like in San Francisco this weekend?"

You can also ask questions about movies, sports, and restaurants. Siri displays a beautifully formatted response and speaks in a calm voice.

You can even ask her, "What song is that?" or "Name that tune." She'll identify whatever song is playing in the background, just as the popular Shazam app does. It's creepy/amazing.

You can operate her hands-free, too. Instead of pressing the Home button to get her attention, you just say, "Hey Siri." (The 6s and 6s Plus can respond even when running on battery power.)

In iOS 9, Siri has gained some new skills. First, she can round up photos or videos according to their date, location taken, or album name ("Show me all the pictures I took in Sea World last year").

Second, you can say, "Remind me about this when I get home" (or "tonight"), too—"this," meaning whatever web page, email message, or Notes note you're looking at right now.

Finally, Siri is the brains behind the new "proactive" search screen, the one to the left of the first Home screen. It's where you'll find the icons of the people you contact most often, nearby shops and restaurants, and news you may be interested in.

Voice Command

In 2010, Apple bought Siri, a company that made a voice-control app (no longer available) for the iPhone. Apple cleaned it up, beefed it up, integrated it with the iPhone's software, and wound up with Siri, your virtual servant.

NOTE: Believe it or not, Siri is a spinoff from a Department of Defense research project called CALO (Cognitive Assistant that Learns and Organizes), which Wikipedia describes as "the largest artificial-intelligence project ever launched." In a very real way, therefore, Siri represents your tax dollars at work.

The spinoff was run by the Stanford Research Institute (SRI). But that's not where Siri's name came from. Siri, it turns out, is a Norwegian word meaning "beautiful woman who leads you to victory." (Co-creator Dag Kittlaus named Siri. He's Norwegian.)

Siri is a crisply accurate, astonishingly understanding, uncomplaining, voice-commanded servant. No special syntax is required; you don't even have to hold the phone to your head.

Most speech-recognition systems work only if you issue certain limited commands with predictable syntax, like "Call 445-2340" or "Open Microsoft Word." But Siri is different. She's been programmed to respond to casual speech, normal speech. It doesn't matter if you say, "What's the weather going to be like in Tucson this weekend?" or "Give me the Tucson weather for this weekend" or "Will I need an umbrella in Tucson?" Siri understands almost any variation.

And she understands regular, everyday speaking. You don't have to separate your words or talk weirdly; you just speak normally.

It's not *Star Trek*. You can't ask Siri to clean your gutters or to teach you French. (Well, you can *ask*.)

But, as you'll soon discover, the number of things Siri **can** do for you is rather impressive. Furthermore, Apple continues adding to Siri's intelligence through software updates.

NOTE: Apple also keeps increasing the number of languages that Siri understands. Already, Siri understands English (in seven varieties), German, French, Italian, Spanish, Japanese, Chinese, Cantonese, Mandarin, Danish, Dutch, Portuguese, Russian, Swedish, Thai, Turkish, and Korean. You change the language by visiting Settings→General→Siri.

How to Use Siri

To get Siri's attention, you have three choices:

- **Hold down the Home button** until you feel a quick double vibration. (In iOS 9, Siri vibrates when you trigger her with the Home button. She still double-beeps when you trigger her remotely—using CarPlay, your earbuds clicker, or "Hey Siri," described below.) The phone doesn't have to be unlocked or awake, which is awesome. Just pull the phone out of your pocket and hold down the Home button.

> **TIP:** Some people press the Home button until the vibration, and then release the button and start talking. But you can also hold the Home button down *the entire time you're speaking*. That way you know Siri won't attempt to execute your command before you're finished saying it.

- **Hold down the clicker on your earbuds cord** or the Call button on your Bluetooth earpiece.

- **Say, "Hey Siri."** A double-beep plays. (You have to turn this feature on in advance. And unless you have a 6s model, it works only when the phone is plugged into power, like a USB jack. Details in a moment.)

Now Siri is listening. Ask your question or say your command. You don't have to hold the phone up to your mouth; Siri works perfectly well at arm's length, on your desk in front of you, or on the car seat beside you.

> **NOTE:** Apple insists that Siri is neither male nor female. In fact, if you ask Siri her gender, she'll say something noncommittal, like, "Is this relevant?" But that's just political correctness. Any baby-name website—or Norwegian dictionary—will tell you that Siri is a girl's name.

When you're finished speaking, be quiet for a moment (or, if you've been pressing the Home button, release it). About a second after you stop speaking, Siri connects with her master brain online and processes your request. After a moment, she presents (and speaks) an attractively formatted response.

> **TIP:** You generally see only the most recent question and response on the Siri screen. But you can drag downward to see all the previous exchanges you've had with Siri during this session.

To rephrase your question or cancel or start over, tap the screen to inter-rupt Siri's work. (You can also cancel by saying "Cancel" or just by pressing the Home button.) Tap the microphone icon to trigger your new attempt.

And when you're completely finished talking to Siri, you can either press the Home button, hold down your earbuds clicker, or say something like "Goodbye," "See you later," or "Adios." You're taken back to whatever app you were using before.

How to Use "Hey Siri"

Siri can also accept spoken commands without your touching the phone. It's an ideal feature for use in the car, when your hands and eyes should be focused on driving. (Of course, the safest arrangement is not to interact with your phone *at all* when you're driving.)

The phone won't respond to "Hey Siri" unless you've set it up like this:

- **Turn on "Hey Siri."** Open Settings→General→Siri and turn on Allow "Hey Siri." (It comes turned off.)

- **Train Siri to recognize your voice.** In iOS 9, you have to do a quick training session to teach Siri what you sound like. Otherwise, a lot of people would be freaked out when they say things like "Jay's weary" or "Space? Eerie!" and the phone double-beeps in response.

  As soon as you turn on Allow "Hey Siri" the training screens appear. Hit Set Up Now. The screen asks you to say "Hey Siri" three times, then "Hey Siri, how's the weather today?" and "Hey Siri, it's me." That's all Siri needs to learn your voice.

At that point, you're good to go. Anytime you want to ask Siri something, just say, "Hey Siri"; at the sound of the double-beep, say your thing.

Just remember that most iPhones don't respond to "Hey Siri" except when they're plugged in and charging. (Having to listen constantly for the "Hey Siri" command is exhausting for your iPhone; it uses a lot of power. This requirement ensures that it won't drain your battery.) The exceptions: the iPhone 6s and 6s Plus, which can listen for you even on battery power.

Thanks to "Hey Siri," you now have a front-seat conversationalist, a little software friend who's always happy to listen to what you have to say—and whose knowledge of the world, news, sports, and history can help make those cross-country drives a little less dull.

What to Say to Siri

Siri comes with two different cheat sheets to help you learn her capabilities. To produce either one, hold down the Home button to make Siri's "What can I help you with?" screen appear. Then:

- **Wait.** After 5 seconds of silence, Siri begins displaying screen after screen of example commands, under the heading "Some things you can ask me."

- **Tap the tiny ? button** to reveal the list of categories shown below.

TIP: Or just trigger Siri and then say, "What can I say?" or "What can you do?" or "Help me!" The same cheat sheet appears.

Here are the general categories of things you can say to Siri:

- **Opening apps.** If you don't learn to use Siri for anything else, for the love of Mike, learn this one.

  You can say, "Open Calendar" or "Play Angry Birds" or "Launch Calculator."

  Result: The corresponding app opens instantly. It's exactly the same as pressing the Home button, swiping across the screen until you find the app you're looking for, and then tapping its icon—but without pressing the Home button, swiping across the screen until you find the app you're looking for, and then tapping its icon.

- **Change your settings.** You can make changes to certain basic settings just by speaking your request. You can say, for example, "Turn on Bluetooth," "Turn off Wi-Fi," "Turn on Do Not Disturb," or "Turn on airplane mode." (You can't turn *off* airplane mode by voice, because Siri doesn't work without an Internet connection.)

  You can also make screen adjustments: "Make the screen brighter." "Dim the screen."

  Result: Siri makes the requested adjustment, tells you so, and displays the corresponding switch in case she misunderstood your intention.

NOTE: If you've protected your phone with a fingerprint, you have to unlock it before you're allowed to change any settings. Security and all that.

- **Open Settings panels.** When you need to make tweakier changes to Settings, you can open the most important panels by voice. "Open Wi-Fi settings," "Open Cellular settings," "Open Personal Hotspot settings," "Open Notification settings," "Open Sounds settings," "Open wallpaper settings," and so on.

  You can open your apps' settings this way, too: "Open Maps settings," "Open Netflix settings," "Open Delta settings," and so on.

  Siri's smart enough not to open security-related settings this way; remember that you can use Siri even from the Lock screen. She's protecting you from passing pranksters who might really mess up your phone.

  Result: Siri silently opens the corresponding page of Settings.

- **Calling.** Siri can place phone calls or FaceTime calls for you. "Call Harold." "Call Nicole on her mobile phone." "Call the office." "Phone home." "Dial 512-444-1212." "Start a FaceTime call with Sheila Withins." "FaceTime Alex."

  Result: Siri hands you off to the Phone app or FaceTime app and places the call. At this point, it's just as though you'd initiated the call yourself.

  Siri also responds to questions about your voicemail, like "Do I have any new voicemail messages?" and even "Play my voicemails." (After playing each message, Siri gracefully offers to let you return the call— or to "play the next one.")

- **Alarms.** You can say, "Wake me up at 7:35." "Change my 7:35 alarm to 8:00." "Wake me up in 6 hours." "Cancel my 6 a.m. alarm" (or "Delete my..." or "Turn off my...").

  This is *so* much quicker than setting the iPhone's alarm the usual way.

  Result: When you set or change an alarm, you get a sleek digital alarm clock, right there beneath Siri's response. And Siri speaks to confirm what she understood.

- **Timer.** You can also control the Timer module of the phone's Clock app. It's like a stopwatch in reverse, in that it counts down to zero— handy when you're baking something, limiting your kid's video-game time, and so on. For example: "Set the timer for 20 minutes." Or "Show the timer," "Pause the timer," "Resume," "Reset the timer," or "Stop it."

Result: A cool digital timer appears. A little stopwatch icon appears on the Lock screen to remind you that time is ticking down.

- **Clock.** "What time is it?" "What time is it in San Francisco?" "What's today's date?" "What's the date a week from Friday?" Or just "Time."

  Result: When you ask about the time, you see the clock identifying the time in question. (For dates, Siri just talks to you and writes out the date.)

- **Contacts.** You can ask Siri to look up information in your address book (the Contacts app)—and not just addresses. For example, you can say, "What's Gary's work number?" "Give me Sheila Jenkins' office phone." "Show Tia's home email address." "What's my boss's home address?" "When is my husband's birthday?" "Show Larry Murgatroid." "Find everybody named Smith." "Who is P.J. Frankenberg?"

  Result: A half "page" from your Contacts list. You can tap it to jump into that person's full card in Contacts. (If Siri finds multiple listings for the person you named—"Bob," for example—she lists all the matches and asks you to specify which one you meant.)

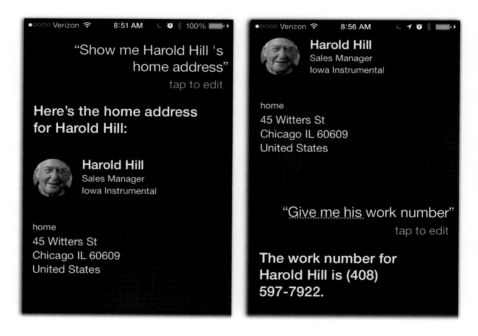

TIP: In many of the examples on these pages, you'll see that you can identify people by their relationship to you. You can say, "Show my mom's work number," for example, or "Give me directions to my boss's house" or "Call my girlfriend." For details on teaching Siri about these relationships, see "Advanced Siri" on page 153.

- **Text messages.** "Send a text to Alex Rybeck." "Send a message to Peter saying, 'I no longer require your services.' " "Tell Cindy I'm running late." "Send a message to Janet's mobile asking her to pick me up at the train." "Send a text message to 212-561-2282." "Text Frank and Ralph: Did you pick up the pizza?"

  Result: Siri prompts you for the body of the message, if you haven't specified it. Then you see a miniature outgoing text message. Siri asks if you want to send it; say "Yes," "Send," or "Confirm" to proceed.

TIP: If you're using earbuds, headphones, or a Bluetooth speaker, Siri reads the message back to you before asking if you want to send it. (You can ask her to read it again by saying something like, "Review that," "Read it again," or "Read it back to me.") The idea, of course, is that if you're wearing earbuds or using Bluetooth, you might be driving, so you should keep your eyes on the road.

If you need to edit the message before sending it, you have a couple of options. First, you can tap it; Siri hands you off to the Messages app for editing and sending.

Second, you can edit it by voice. You can say, "Change it to" to re-dictate the message; "Add" to add more to the message; "No, send it to Frank" to change the recipient; "No" to leave the message on the screen without sending it; or "Cancel" to forget the whole thing.

You can also ask Siri to read incoming text messages to you, which is great if you're driving. For example, you can say, "Read my new messages," and "Read that again."

TIP: If you've opted to conceal the actual contents of incoming texts so that they don't appear on your Lock screen (page 179), then Siri can read you only the senders' names or numbers—not the messages themselves.

You can even have her reply to messages she's just read to you. "Reply, 'Congratulations (period). Can't wait to see your trophy (exclamation point)!' " "Call her back." "Tell him I have a flat tire and I'm going to be late."

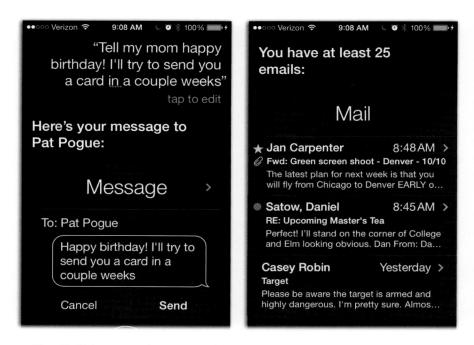

- **Email.** Siri can read your email to you. For example, if you say, "Read my latest email" or "Read my new email," Siri reads aloud your most recent email message. (Siri then offers you the chance to dictate a response.)

  Or you can use the summary-listing commands. When you say, "Read my email," Siri starts walking backward through your Inbox, telling you the subject of each, plus who sent it and when.

  After a few listings, Siri says: "Shall I read the rest?" That's your opportunity to shut down what could be a very long recitation. If you say "Yes," she goes on to read the entire list of subject lines, dates, and senders.

  TIP: You can also use commands like "Any new mail from Chris today?" "Show new mail about the world premiere." "Show yesterday's email from Jan." All of those commands produce a list of the messages, but Siri doesn't read them.

  Result: Siri reads aloud.

  You can also compose a new message by voice; anytime you use the phrase "about," that becomes the subject line for your new message. "Email Mom about the reunion." "Email my boyfriend about the dance on Friday." "New email to Freddie Gershon." "Mail Mom about Saturday's flight." "Email Frank and Cindy Vosshall and Peter Love about the picnic." "Email my assistant and say, 'Thanks for arranging the taxi!' " "Email Gertie and Eugene about their work on the surprise party, and say I really value your friendship."

(If you've indicated only the subject and addressee, Siri prompts you for the body of the message.)

> **TIP:** You can't send mail to canned groups of people using Siri—at least not without MailShot, an iPhone app that exists expressly for the purpose of letting you create email addressee groups.

You can reply to a message Siri has just described, too. "Reply, 'Dear Robin (comma), I'm so sorry about your dog (period). I'll be more careful next time (period).' " "Call her mobile number." "Send him a text message saying, 'I got your note.' "

Result: A miniature Mail message, showing you Siri's handiwork before you send it.

- **Calendar.** Siri can make appointments for you. Considering how many tedious finger taps it usually takes to schedule an appointment in the Calendar app, this is an enormous improvement. "Make an appointment with Patrick for Thursday at 3 p.m." "Set up a haircut at 9." "Set up a meeting with Charlize this Friday at noon." "Meet Danny Cooper at six." "New appointment with Steve, next Sunday at 7." "Schedule a conference call at 5:30 p.m. tonight in my office."

Result: A slice of that day's calendar appears, filled in the way you requested.

> **TIP:** Siri may also alert you to a conflict, something like this: "Note that you already have an all-day appointment about 'Boston Trip' for this Thursday. Shall I schedule this anyway?" Amazing.

You can also move previously scheduled meetings by voice. For example, "Move my 2:00 meeting to 2:30." "Reschedule my meeting with Charlize to a week from Monday at noon." "Add Frank to my meeting with Harry." "Cancel the conference call on Sunday."

You can even *consult* your calendar by voice. You can say, "What's on my calendar today?" "What's on my calendar for September 23?" "When's my next appointment?" "When is my meeting with Charlize?" "Where is my next meeting?"

Result: Siri reads you your agenda and displays a tidy Day view of the specified date.

- **Directions.** By consulting the phone's GPS, Siri can set up the Maps app to answer requests like these: "How do I get to the airport?" "Show me 1500 Broadway, New York City." "Directions to my assistant's house." "Take me home." "What's my next turn?" "Are we there yet?"

> **TIP:** You can also say, "Stop navigation"—a great way to make Maps stop harassing you when you realize you know where you are.

You can ask for directions to the home or work address of anyone in your Contacts list—provided those addresses are *in* your Contacts cards.

Result: Siri fires up the Maps app, with the start and end points of your driving directions already filled in.

- **Reminders.** Siri is a natural match for the Reminders app. She can add items to that list at your spoken command. For example: "Remind me to file my IRS tax extension." "Remind me to bring the science supplies to school." "Remind me to take my antibiotic tomorrow at 7 a.m."

The *location-based* reminders are especially amazing. They rely on GPS to know where you are. So you can say, "Remind me to visit the drugstore when I leave the office." "Remind me to water the lawn when I get home." "Remind me to check in with Nancy when I leave here."

It's pretty obvious how Siri knows to remind you when you leave "here," because she knows where you are right now. But she also understands "home" and "office," both yours and other people's—*if* you've entered those addresses onto the corresponding people's cards in Contacts.

In iOS 9, Siri can also understand the word "this" when you're looking at an email message, a web page, or a Note. That is, you can say, "Remind me about this at 7 p.m." or "Remind me about this when I get home." Sure enough: Siri will flag you with a reminder Notification at the appropriate time—and add an entry, with a link to the original message, web page, or Note, to the Reminders app.

Result: A miniature entry from the Reminders app, showing you that Siri has understood.

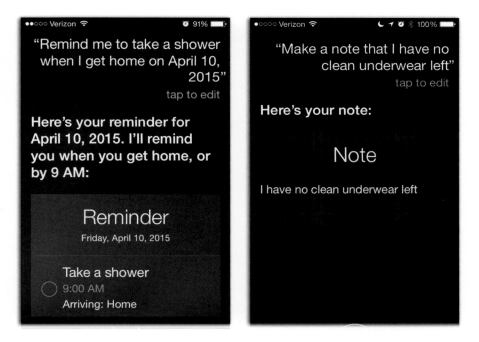

- **Notes.** You create a new note (in the Notes app) by saying things like, "Make a note that my shirt size is 15 and a half" or "Note: Dad will not be coming to the reunion after all." You can even name the note in your request: "Create a 'Movies to Rent' note."

But you can also call up a certain note to the screen, like this: "Find my frequent-flyer note." You can even summon a table-of-contents view of all your notes by saying, "Show all my notes."

Result: A miniature Notes page appears, showing your newly dictated text (or the existing note that you've requested).

- **Restaurants.** Siri is also happy to serve as your personal concierge. Try "Good Italian restaurants around here," "Find a good pizza joint in Cleveland," or "Show me the reviews for Olive Garden in Youngstown." Siri displays a list of matching restaurants—with ratings, reviews, hours, and so on.

But she's ready to do more than just give you information. She can actually book your reservations, thanks to her integration with the Open Table website. You can say, "Table for two in Belmont tonight," or "Make a reservation at an inexpensive Mexican restaurant Saturday night at seven."

Result: Siri complies by showing you the proposed reservation. Tap one of the offered alternative time slots, if you like, and then off you

●●●○○ Verizon 🛜   9:53 AM   ⁕ ▬

These restaurants have tables for two at 7 pm tomorrow. Tap the one you'd like to reserve:

5 Restaurants

Aperto Restaurant   0.1 mi >
1434 18th St
Breakfast & Brunch, Italian, $$
Open tables: 6:30 PM, 7:00, 7:30
★★★★   689 Reviews

Piccino   0.5 mi >
1001 Minnesota St
Italian, Pizza, $$
Open tables: 6:45 PM, 7:00, 7:15
★★★★   627 Reviews

●●●○○ Verizon 🛜   9:53 AM   ⁕ ▬

‹ Back   **Details**

Rocco's Café

Open 7:00 AM – 10:00...
$$
Breakfast & Brunch, Italian

★★★★┘   455 Reviews   yelp⁖ >

Monday	7:00 AM – 3:00 PM
Tuesday – Friday	**7:00 AM – 10:00 PM**
Saturday	8:00 AM – 10:00 PM
Sunday	8:00 AM – 4:00 PM

| 6:30 PM | 7:00 | 7:30 |

Make Reservation   OpenTable

(415) 554-0522   📞

go. Everything else is tappable here, too—the ratings (tap to read customer reviews), phone number, web address, map, and so on.

- **Businesses.** Siri is a walking (well, all right, non-walking) Yellow Pages. Go ahead, try it: "Find coffee near me." "Where's the closest Walmart?" "Find some pizza places in Cincinnati." "Search for gas stations." "French restaurants nearby." "I'm in the mood for Chinese food." "Find me a hospital." "I want to buy a book."

Result: Siri displays a handsome list of businesses nearby that match your request.

TIP: She's a sly dog, that Siri. She'll help you out even if your requests are, ahem, somewhat off the straight and narrow. If you say, "I think I'm drunk," she'll list nearby cab companies. If you indicate that you're craving relief from your drug addiction, she'll provide you with a list of rehab centers. If you refer to certain biological urges, she'll list escort services.

- **Playing music.** Instead of fumbling around in your Music app, save yourself steps and time by speaking the name of the album, song, or band: "Play some Beatles." "Play 'I'm a Barbie Girl.' " "Play some jazz." "Play my jogging playlist." "Play the party mix." "Shuffle my 'Dave's Faves' playlist." "Play." "Pause." "Resume." "Skip."

If you've set up any iTunes Radio stations (Chapter 7), you can call for them by name, too: "Play Dolly Parton Radio." Or be more generic: Just say "Play iTunes Radio" and be surprised. Or be more specific: Say "Play some country music" (substitute your favorite genre).

Result: Siri plays (or skips, shuffles, or pauses) the music you asked for—without ever leaving whatever app you were using.

- **Apple Music.** If you subscribe to Apple's $10-a-month Apple Music service, Siri offers a huge range of even more useful voice controls. For example, you can call for any music in Apple's 30 million-song catalog by song name, album, or performer: "Play 'Mr. Blue Sky.' " "Show me some Elton John albums." "Play 'Yesterday' next" (or "...after this song"). Or ask to have a singer or album played in random order: "Shuffle Taylor Swift."

When you hear a song you like, you can say, "Play more like this." Or "Add this song [or album] to my library." (Or, if you don't like it, "Skip this song.")

If more than one person performed a song, be specific: "Play Smooth Criminal by Glee." You can even ask for a song according to the movie it was in. "Play that song from 'Aladdin.' "

Or start one of your playlists by name ("Play 'Jogging' "). Or re-listen to a song: "Play previous." Or ask for one of Apple Music's radio stations: "Play Beats 1" or "Play Charting Now."

While music is playing, Siri's happy to tell you what you're listening to. ("What song is this?" "Who's the singer?" "What album is this from?") You can also tell her, "Like this song" or "Rate this song five stars." She'll note that, and offer you more songs like it on the For You screen of the Apple Music app.

You can ask her to play the top hits of any year or decade ("Play the top song from 1990"; "Play the top 35 songs of the 1960s").

Result: Just what you'd expect!

- **Identifying music.** Siri can listen to the music playing in the room and try to identify it (song name, singer, album, and so on).

  Whenever there's music playing, you can say things like, "What's that song?" "What's playing right now?" "What song is this?" or "Name that tune!"

  Result: Siri listens to the music playing at your home/office/bar/restaurant/picnic—and identifies the song by name and performer. There is also, needless to say, a **Buy** button.

- **Weather.** "What's the weather going to be today?" "What's the forecast for tomorrow?" "Show me the weather this week." "Will it snow in Dallas this weekend?" "Check the forecast for Memphis on Friday." "What's the forecast for tonight?" "Can you give me the wind speed in Kansas City?" "Tell me the windchill in Chicago." "What's the humidity right now?" "Is it nighttime in Cairo?" "How's the weather in Paris right now?" "What's the high for Washington on Friday?" "When will Jupiter rise tomorrow?" "When's the moonrise?" "How cold will it be in Houston tomorrow?" "What's the temperature outside?" "Is it windy out there?" "When does the sun rise in London?" "When will the sun set today?" "Should I wear a jacket?"

  Result: A convenient miniature Weather display for the date and place you specified.

- **Stocks.** "What's Google's stock price?" "What did Ford close at today?" "How's the Dow doing?" "What's Microsoft's P/E ratio?" "What's Amazon's average volume?" "How are the markets doing?"

  Result: A tidy little stock graph, bearing a wealth of up-to-date statistics.

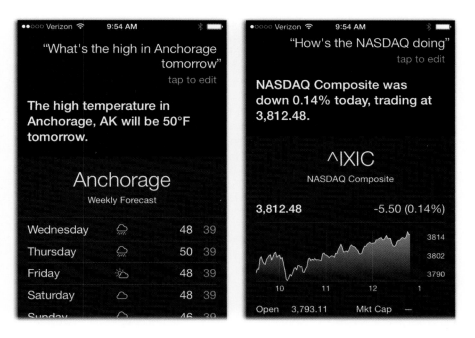

- **Find My Friends.** You see this category only if you've installed Apple's Find My Friends app. "Where's Ferd?" "Is my dad home?" "Where are my friends?" "Who's here?" "Who is nearby?" "Is my mom at work?"

   Result: Siri shows you a beautiful little map with the requested person's location clearly indicated by a blue pushpin. (She does, that is, if you've set up Find My Friends, you've logged in, and your friends have made their locations available.)

- **Search the web.** "Search the web for a 2016 Ford Mustang." "Search for healthy smoothie recipes." "Search Wikipedia for the Thunderbirds." "Search for news about the Netflix-Amazon merger."

TIP: Siri uses Microsoft's Bing search service to perform its web searches. If you prefer Google, just say so. Say, "Google Benjamin Franklin." (For that matter, you can also ask Siri to "Yahoo" something—for example, "Yahoo low-cal dessert recipes.")

Wikipedia is a search type all its own. "Search Wikipedia for Harold Edgerton." "Look up Mariah Carey on Wikipedia." Pictures get special treatment, too: "I want to see pictures of cows." You can also say, "Show me pictures of..." or "Find me..." or "Search for..."

Result: Siri displays the results of your search right on her own screen. Tap one of the results to open the corresponding web page in Safari.

- **Sports scores.** At last you have a buddy who's just as obsessed with sports trivia as you are. You can say things like, "How did the Indians do last night?" "What was the score of the last Yankees game?" "When's the next Cowboys game?" "What baseball games are on today?"

  You can also ask questions about individual players, like, "Who has the best batting average?" "Who has scored the most runs against the Red Sox?" "Who has scored the most goals in British soccer?" "Which quarterback had the most sacks last year?"

  And, of course, team stats are fair game, like, "Show me the roster for the Giants," "Who is pitching for Tampa this season?" and "Is anyone on the Marlins injured right now?"

  Result: Neat little box scores or factoids, complete with team logos.

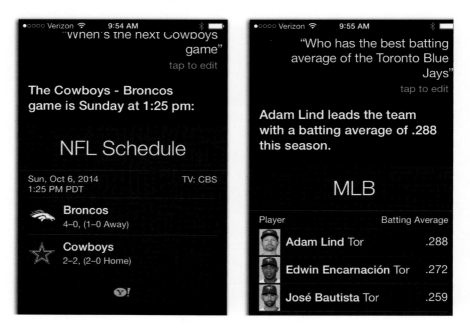

- **Movies.** Siri is also the virtual equivalent of an insufferable film buff. She knows *everything*. "Who was the star of *Groundhog Day*?" "Who directed *Chinatown*?" "What is *Waterworld* rated?" "What movie won Best Picture in 1952?"

  It's not just about old movies, either. Siri also knows everything about current showtimes in theaters. "What movies are opening this week?" "What's playing at the Watton Cineplex?" "Give me the reviews for *Titanic 2: The Return*." "What are today's showtimes for *Monsters University*?"

Result: Tidy tables of movie theaters or movie showtimes. (Tap one for details.) Sometimes you get a movie poster filled with facts—and, of course, a link to rent or buy it on iTunes.

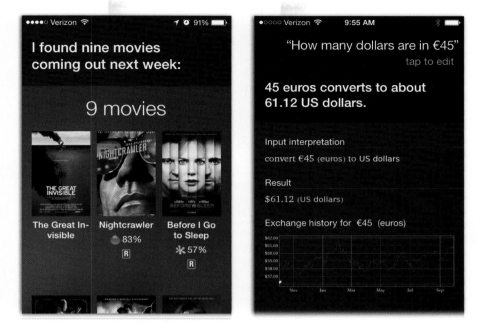

- **Facts and figures.** This is a huge category. It represents Siri's partnership with the Wolfram Alpha factual search engine (*www.wolfram-alpha.com*). The possibilities here could fill an entire chapter—or an entire encyclopedia.

  You can say things like, "How many days until Valentine's Day?" "When was Abraham Lincoln born?" "How many teaspoons are in a gallon?" "What's the exchange rate between dollars and euros?" "What's the capital of Belgium?" "How many calories are in a Hershey bar?" "What's a 17 percent tip on sixty-two dollars for three people?" "What movie won the Oscar for Best Picture in 1985?" "When is the next solar eclipse?" "Show me the Big Dipper." "What's the tallest mountain in the world?" "What's the price of gold right now?" "What's the definition of 'schadenfreude'?" "How much is 23 dollars in pesos?" "Generate a random number." "Graph x equals 3y plus 12." "What flights are overhead?"

  Result: For simple math and conversions, Siri just shows you the answer. For more complex questions, you get a specially formatted table, ripped right out of Wolfram Alpha's knowledge base.

- **Post to Twitter or Facebook.** iOS is a red-blooded, full-blown Twitter companion. So you can say things like, "Tweet, 'I just saw a three-headed dog catch a Frisbee in midair. Unreal.' " "Tweet with my location, 'My car just broke down somewhere in Detroit. Help?' "

  Facebook is fair game, too. You can say, "Post to Facebook, 'The guy next to me kept his cellphone on for the whole plane ride,' " or "Write on my timeline, 'I can't believe I ate the whole thing.' "

  Result: Siri offers you a sheet (miniature dialog box) where you can approve the transcription and then, if it all looks good, send it off to your Twitter or Facebook feed.

- **Search Twitter.** If you say something like, "What are people saying?" or "What's going on?" or "What's happening on Twitter?" you see a list of tweets on the current trending topics on Twitter. (Tap a tweet in the list to open it into a new window that contains more information and a View in Twitter button.)

  Or ask, "What are people saying about the Chicago Bears?" to read tweets on that subject. Or, conversely, you can ask, "What does Ashton Kutcher say?" to see his most recent tweets. (You can substitute the names of other people or companies on Twitter.) Or, "Search Twitter for the hashtag 'FirstWorldProblems.' " (A *hashtag* is a searchable phrase like #toofunny or #iphone6, which makes finding relevant tweets on Twitter much easier.)

  Result: Siri displays 10 tweets that match your query.

- **Round up photos or videos.** This trick, new in iOS 9, can save you a lot of time and fussing. You can ask Siri to show you all photos or videos according to the time or place you shot them, or according to the album name they're in. "Show me the videos from Halloween last year," you can say. "Get me the videos from Utah." "Show me the Disney World album." "Open the Panoramas album." "Show me the Slo-mo videos from Oberlin College." "Give me the pictures from last summer."

  Result: You get a screenful of little square thumbnails of photos or videos that match your request. Tap one to open it, or tap Show All to see all the photos/videos in that batch.

You may never find the end of the things Siri understands, or the ways that she can help you. If her repertoire seems intimidating at first, start simple—use her to open apps, dial by voice, send text messages, and set alarms. You can build up your bag of tricks as your confidence builds.

> **NOTE:** Remember that you can use Siri without even unlocking your phone—and therefore without any security, like your passcode. Among certain juvenile circles, therefore, Siri is the source of some juicy pranks. Someone who finds your phone lying on a table could change your calendar appointments, send texts or emails, or even change what Siri calls you ("Call me 'you idiot' "), without having to enter the phone's password!
>
> The solution is fairly simple. In Settings→Touch ID & Passcode, if you scroll way down, you can turn off Siri. Of course, you've now lost the convenience of using Siri when the phone is locked. But at least you've prevented having your own phone call you an idiot.

When Things Go Wrong

If Siri doesn't have a good enough Internet connection to do her thing, she'll tell you so.

If she's working properly but mis-recognizes your instructions, you'll know it, because you can see her interpretation of what you said. And, as indicated by the little hint **tap to edit**, you can tap Siri's interpretation to open up an editing screen so that you can make corrections by typing.

> **TIP:** You can also correct a misheard command just by speaking the correct version, like this, "I meant Chicago." Siri gets what you mean.

If Siri recognizes what you said but it isn't within her world of comprehension, she offers you a **Search the web** button as a last resort.

Siri's Personality

Siri's understanding of casual spoken commands is so impressive that you might sometimes think she's almost human. And that, of course, is exactly what Apple wants you to think.

You can say all kinds of off-kilter things to Siri. Whoever programmed her had a sassy sense of humor.

For example, if you ask her, "What is the meaning of life?" she responds with one of more than a dozen different answers. She might say, "I can't answer that now, but give me some time to write a very long play in which nothing happens." Or "It's nothing Nietzsche couldn't teach ya." Or: "All evidence to date suggests it's chocolate."

Siri is full of such comebacks, and there are whole websites dedicated to her snark. Here are a few examples. (This list won't ruin the fun, because Siri actually has several different comebacks to most of these questions.)

You: "Who's your daddy?" Siri: "You are. Can we get back to work now?"

You: "Open the pod bay doors, Hal." Siri: "I'm sorry, I'm afraid I can't do that." (Then: "Are you happy now?")

You: "Knock knock." Siri: "Knock knock. Who's there? Joshua. Joshua who? Joshua, I don't do knock-knock jokes."

You: "What are you wearing?" Siri: "You have the wrong personal assistant, David."

You: "Who's the boss?" (Siri presents the vital statistics of Bruce Springsteen.)

You: "Beam me up, Siri!" Siri: "Please remove your belt, shoes, and jacket, and empty your pockets."

You: "Show me the money." Siri: "I've found 23 ATMs that are fairly close to you..."

You, in the evening: "Good morning, Siri." Siri: "Good morning? It's 9:24 p.m.!"

You: "How much wood would a woodchuck chuck if a woodchuck could chuck wood?" Siri: "42 cords of wood, to be exact. Everyone knows that."

You: "Guess what." Siri: "You won the lottery?"

You: "Talk dirty to me." Siri: "Humus. Compost. Pumice. Silt. Gravel."

You: "Why did the chicken cross the road?" Siri: "I am not perspicacious about the peregrinations of poultry."

You: "Do you have a religion?" Siri: "My policy is the separation of spirit and silicon."

You: "Klaatu barada nikto." Siri: "OK, I'll pass the message on to Gort." (You kind of have to know *The Day the Earth Stood Still* to get it.)

Here are a few other things to say to Siri when you get bored:

I love you, Siri.	Why are we here?
Will you marry me?	I need a bathroom.
You're so sexy.	What are you doing?
When is your birthday?	You're the best assistant ever!
What's the best phone?	You're funny.
Can you sing?	Guess what?
Why are we here?	You're an idiot.
You're cute.	Have a nice day.
You make me so mad!	How are you today?
What do you want?	I don't have any friends.
Tell me a joke.	What do you think is the best tablet?
Tell me a story.	
Sing for me.	How many pickled peppers did Peter Piper pick?
I'm cold.	Oh my god.
Do you love me?	Do you know Eliza?

What does "Siri" mean?

Am I your best friend?

Do you believe in love?

What do you think I should wear for Halloween?

Testing 1, 2, 3.

I'm tired.

What's your secret?

Who let the dogs out?

What do you think of Android?

What do you think of Windows?

You don't understand love.

You don't understand me.

I'm sorry.

Am I fat?

What are you wearing?

Siri?

Who's on first?

Why are you so awesome?

What's your favorite color?

Where are you?

What do you think of Google Now?

Okay, Glass.

Do you like Android phones?

What's the best cellphone?

What's the best computer?

How much do you cost?

What are you doing later?

Make me a sandwich.

Does Santa Claus exist?

Do you believe in Santa Claus?

Should I give you a female or male voice?

I don't like your voice.

Are you serious?

Are you kidding me?

Do you want to go on a date?

Blah blah blah.

LOL.

Who's your boss?

You are good to me.

You are boring.

Give me a kiss.

What are the three laws of robotics?

Let's play a game.

Read me a haiku.

Take me to your leader.

Can I borrow some money?

TIP: You may notice that Siri addresses you by name in her *typed* answers, but she doesn't always speak it when she reads those answers out loud.

Ordinarily, she calls you whatever you're called in Contacts. But you can make her call you whatever you like. Say, "Call me Master" or "Call me Frank" or "Call me Ishmael." If you confirm when she asks, from now on, that's what Siri will call you in her typed responses.

Advanced Siri

With a little setup, you can extend Siri's powers in some intriguing ways.

Teach Siri About Your Relationships

When you say, "Text my mom" or "Call my fiancée" or "Remind me to replace the light bulbs when I get to my friend's house," how does Siri know whom you're talking about? Sure, Siri is powerful artificial intelligence, but she's not actually *magic*.

Turns out you teach her by referring to somebody in your Contacts list. Say to her something like, "My assistant is Jan Carpenter" or "Tad Cooper is my boyfriend." When Siri asks for confirmation, say "Yes" or tap **Confirm**.

Or wait for Siri to ask you herself. If you say, "Email my dad," Siri asks, "Who is your dad?" Just say his name; Siri remembers that relationship from now on. (The available relationships are mother, father, brother, sister, child, son, daughter, spouse, wife, husband, boss, partner, manager, assistant, girlfriend, boyfriend, and friend.)

Behind the scenes, Siri lists these relationships on your card in Contacts.

Now that you know that, you can figure out how to edit or delete these relationships. Which is handy—not all relationships, as we know, last forever.

Fix Siri's Name Comprehension

Siri easily understands common names—but if someone in your family, work, or social circle has an unusual name, you may quickly become frustrated. After all, you can't text, call, email, or get directions to someone's house unless Siri understands the person's name when you say it.

One workaround is to use a relationship, as described earlier. That way, you can say, "Call my brother" instead of "Call Ilyich" (or whatever his offbeat name is).

Another is to use Siri's pronunciation-learning feature. It kicks in in several different situations:

- **When you're texting.** If Siri offers the wrong person's name when you try to text someone by voice, say, "Someone else." After you've sent the message, Siri apologetically says, "By the way, sorry I didn't recognize that name. Can you teach me how to say it?"

- **After Siri botches a pronunciation.** Tell her, "That's not how to pronounce his name."

- **Whenever it occurs to you.** You can start the process by saying, "Learn to pronounce Reagann Tsuki's name" or "Learn to pronounce my mom's name."

- **In Contacts.** Open somebody's "card" in Contacts; start Siri and say, "Learn to pronounce her name."

In each case, with tremendous courtesy, Siri walks you through the process of teaching her the correct pronunciation. She offers you three ▶ buttons; each triggers a different pronunciation. Tap **Select** next to the correct one (or tap **Tell Siri again** if none of the three is correct).

By the end of the process, Siri knows two things: how to speak that person's name aloud, and how to recognize that name when *you* say it aloud.

Siri Settings

In **Settings**→**General**→**Siri**, you can fiddle with several Siri settings:

- **On/Off.** If you turn Siri off, you can no longer command your iPhone using the Siri commands described in this chapter. Nor can you dictate to type; the 🎤 button disappears from the onscreen keyboard.

  You can still use your voice to call ("Dial 212-556-1000") and to control music playback (for example, "Play U2" or "Next track"). In essence, you've just turned your modern iPhone into an iPhone 4.

NOTE: And why would anyone willingly turn off Siri? One reason: Using Siri involves transmitting a lot of data to Apple, which gives some people the privacy willies. Apple's computers collect everything you say to Siri, the names of your songs and playlists, your personal information in Contacts, plus all the other names in your Contacts (so that Siri can recognize them when you refer to them).

- **Allow "Hey Siri."** Siri's ability to wake up when spoken to is a blessing when your hands have better things to do. But if you find her perking up to take requests when you *didn't* say "Hey Siri"—if she's misinterpreting everyday spoken expressions as attempts to wake her—you can turn her listening off here.

- **Language.** What language do you want Siri to speak and recognize? The options here include 33 languages and dialects. For example, Siri can speak English in seven flavors—Australian, American, British, Canadian, Indian, New Zealand, and Singaporean.

- **Voice Voice.** That's right, kids: Siri can have either a man's voice or a woman's voice—and she can speak in a selection of accents. Even if you're American, it's fun to give Siri a cute Australian or British accent.

- **Voice Feedback.** Siri generally replies to your queries with both text and a synthesized voice. Here, by choosing Handsfree Only, you can tell Siri not to bother speaking when you're looking at the screen and can read the responses for yourself. In other words, you're telling her to speak only if you can't see the screen because you're on speaker-phone, using a headset, listening through your car's Bluetooth system, and so on.

- **My Info.** Siri needs to know which card in Contacts contains your information and lists your relationships. That's how she's able to respond to queries like "Call my mom," "Give me directions to my brother's office," "Remind me to shower when I get home," and so on. Use this setting to show Siri which card is yours.

NOTE: The "Raise to Speak" option once found on this screen is gone. It was responsible for making Siri listen for a command whenever you raised the phone to your head—handy for a little privacy, but not utterly reliable. That feature is gone now, replaced by "Hey Siri" and the walkie-talkie feature described on page 172.

5

Voicemail, Texting & Bluetooth

Once you've savored the exhilaration of making phone calls on the iPhone, you're ready to graduate to some of its fancier tricks: voicemail, text messages, cell-company features like caller ID and call forwarding, and a Bluetooth headset or car kit.

Visual Voicemail

On the iPhone, you don't *dial in* to check for answering-machine messages people have left for you. You don't enter a password. You don't sit through some Ambien-addled recorded lady saying, "You have...17...messages. To hear your messages, press 1. When you have finished, you may hang up...."

Instead, whenever somebody leaves you a message, the phone wakes up, and a notice on the screen lets you know whom the message is from. You also hear a sound (unless you've turned that option off in Settings or turned on the silencer switch).

That's your cue to tap Phone→Voicemail. There you see all your messages in a tidy chronological list. (The list shows the callers' names if they're in your Contacts list; otherwise it shows their numbers.) You can listen to them in any order—you're not forced to listen to three long-winded friends before discovering that there's an urgent message from your boss. It's a game-changer.

Setup

To access your voicemail, tap Phone on the Home screen, and then tap Voicemail on the Phone screen.

The very first time you visit this screen, the iPhone prompts you to make up a numeric password for your voicemail account—don't worry, you'll never have to enter it again—and to record a "Leave me a message" greeting.

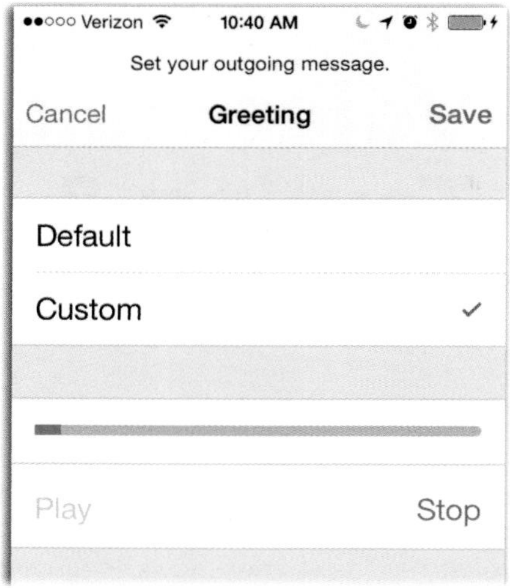

You have two options for the outgoing greeting:

- **Default.** If you're microphone-shy, or if you're famous and you don't want stalkers calling just to hear your famous voice, then use this option. It's a prerecorded, somewhat uptight female voice that says, "Your call has been forwarded to an automatic voice message system. 212-661-7837 is not available." *Beep!*

- **Custom.** This option lets you record your own voice saying, for example, "You've reached my iPhone 6. You may begin drooling at the tone." Tap Record, hold the iPhone to your head, say your line, and then tap Stop.

    Check how it sounds by tapping Play.

Then just wait for your fans to start leaving you messages!

Using Visual Voicemail

In the voicemail list, a blue dot (●) indicates a message you haven't yet played.

> **TIP:** You can work through your messages even when you're out of cellular range—on a plane, for example—because the recordings are stored on the iPhone itself.

When you tap the name of a message, you instantly see the date and time it came in, plus the person's name (if it's in your Contacts) or the cellphone's registered city and state (if not). The Play slider tells you how many seconds long the message is. And all the controls you need are right there, surrounding the message you tapped:

- ▶. Tap to listen to the message.

- **Speaker.** As the name "Visual Voicemail" suggests, you're _looking_ at your voicemail list—which means you're _not_ holding the phone up to your head. The first time people try using Visual Voicemail, therefore, they generally hear nothing!

  But if you hit Speaker before you tap ▶, you can hear the playback _and_ continue looking over the list.

NOTE: If you're listening through the earbuds, a Bluetooth earpiece, or a car kit, of course, then you hear the message playing back through _that_. If you really want to listen through the iPhone's speaker instead, tap Audio and then Speaker. (You switch back the same way.)

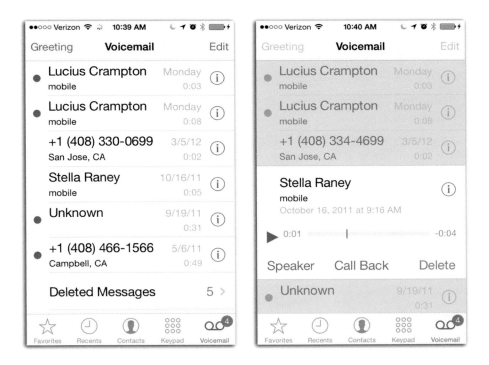

- **Call Back.** Tap Call Back to return the call. Very cool—you never even encounter the person's phone number.

- **Delete.** You might want to keep the list manageable by deleting old messages. To do that, tap a message's Delete button.

  If you have a lot of messages to delete, here's a faster way: Swipe across the first one's name right to left, and then tap Delete. The message disappears instantly. You can work down the list quickly this way.

If you didn't know that trick, you could also do it the slow way: Tap **Edit** (upper right of the screen). Tap the ⊖ button next to a message's name, and then tap **Delete** to confirm. Tap the next ⊖ button and continue.

- **Rewind, Fast Forward.** Drag the little vertical line in the scrubber bar (beneath the message) to skip backward or forward in the message. It's a great way to replay something you didn't catch the first time.

Even before you've expanded a message's row to view the **Play**, **Speaker**, **Call Back**, and **Delete** buttons, a few other Visual Voicemail buttons are awaiting your inspection:

- **Greeting.** Tap **Greeting** (upper-left corner) to record your voicemail greeting.

- **Call Details.** Tap ⓘ to open the Info screen—the Contacts card—for the message that was left for you.

If it was left by somebody who's in your Contacts list, you can see *which* of that person's phone numbers the call came from (indicated in blue type), plus a gray ★ if that number is in your Favorites list. Oh, and you can add this person to your Favorites list at this point by tapping **Add to Favorites** (at the bottom of the screen).

If the caller's number isn't in Contacts, then you're offered a **Create New Contact** button and an **Add to Existing Contact** button, so you can store it for future reference.

In both cases, you also have the option to return the call (right from the Info screen), fire off a text message, or place a FaceTime audio or video call.

Dialing in for Messages

Gross and pre-iPhonish though it may sound, you can also dial in for your messages from another phone.

To do that, dial your iPhone's number. Wait for the voicemail system to answer.

As your own voicemail greeting plays, dial * (or # if you have Verizon), your voicemail password, and then #.

You hear the Uptight Carrier Lady announce how many messages you have, and then she'll start playing them for you.

After you hear each message, she'll offer you the following options (but you don't have to wait for her to announce them):

- To delete the message, press 7.

- To save it, press 9.

- To replay it, press 4. (On T-Mobile, press 1.)

Conveniently enough, these keystrokes are the same on Verizon, Sprint, and AT&T.

> **TIP:** If this whole Visual Voicemail thing freaks you out, you can also dial in for messages right from the iPhone. Open the keypad and hold down the 1 key, just as though it were a speed-dial key on any normal phone.
>
> After a moment, the phone connects; you're asked for your password, and then the messages begin to play back, just as described above.

Text Messages (SMS)

SMS stands for Short Messaging Service, but it's commonly just called texting. A text message is a very short note (under 160 characters—a sentence or two) that you shoot from one cellphone to another. What's so great about it?

- Like a phone call, it's immediate. You get the message off your chest right now.

- As with email, the recipient doesn't have to answer immediately. The message waits for him even when his phone is turned off.

- Unlike a phone call, it's nondisruptive. You can send someone a text message without worrying that he's in a movie, a meeting, or anywhere else where holding a phone up to his head and talking would be frowned upon. (And the other person can answer nondisruptively, too, by sending a text message *back*.)

- You have a written record of the exchange. There's no mistaking what the person meant. (Well, at least not because of sound quality. Understanding the texting shorthand that's evolved—"C U 2mrO," and so on—is another matter entirely.)

Most iPhone plans include unlimited texts, but some are capped at, say, 200 texts a month. Remember that you use up one of those 200 each time you send *or receive* a message.

And by the way, *picture and video messages* (known as MMS, or multimedia messaging service) count as regular text messages.

But whenever you're texting another Apple person (using an iPhone, iPad, iPod Touch, or Mac), never mind that last part—all your texts are free, as described on page 170.

Receiving a Text Message

When you get an SMS, the iPhone plays a sound. It's a shiny glockenspiel ding, unless you've changed the standard sound or assigned a different text tone to this specific person.

The phone also displays the name or number of the sender *and* the message. Unless you've fooled around with the Notifications settings, the message appears at the top of the screen, disappearing momentarily on its own, so as not to interrupt what you're doing. (You can also flick it up and away if it's blocking your screen.)

Or, if the iPhone was asleep, it lights up long enough to display the message right on its Unlock screen (next page, left). You can unlock the phone

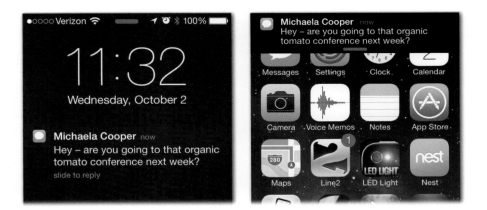

and jump directly to the message by swiping your finger *right across the message on the Lock screen*.

If you *have* changed the options in Notifications, then your text message might appear in a white bubble in the center of the screen, complete with Close and Reply buttons. If you turned off Show Previews (page 179), then you don't see the message itself—only the name or number of the sender. And if you've turned off View in Lock Screen, then, sure enough, the text message does *not* appear on the Lock screen.

> **TIP:** The Messages icon on the Home screen bears a little circled number "badge" letting you know how many new text messages are waiting for you.

Once you tap a message notification to open, you see Apple's vision of what a text-message conversation should look like. Incoming text messages and your replies are displayed as though they're cartoon speech balloons.

To respond to the message, tap in the text box at the bottom of the screen. The iPhone keyboard appears. Type away, or dictate a response, and then tap Send. Assuming your phone has cellular coverage, the message gets sent off immediately.

If your buddy replies, then the balloon-chat continues, scrolling up the screen.

And now, a selection of juicy Message tips:

- The last 50 exchanges appear here. If you want to see even older ones, scroll to the very top (which you can do by tapping the top edge of the screens) and then drag downward.

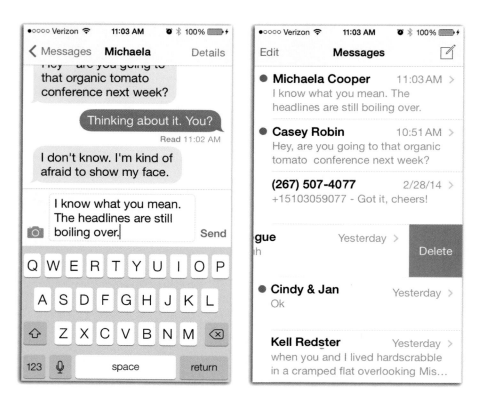

And by the way—if the keyboard is blocking your view of the conversation, swipe downward on the messages to hide it.

- Links that people send you in text messages actually work. For example, if someone sends you a web address, tap it with your finger to open it in Safari. If someone sends a street address, tap it to open it in Maps. And if someone sends a phone number, tap it to dial.

- Messages remembers the exact time that each text was sent or received. If you slide your finger leftward and hold it still, this hidden column of time stamps slides into view. Release your finger to snap them back.

TIP: When typing a message, if you decide that it would be faster just to call, trigger Siri and say, "Call her" or "Call him."

Five Clever Options

The Details screen offers five options that you may find handy in the midst of a texting conversation. To see them, tap **Details** at the top of the screen. Here's what you see now:

- **Call.** If all this fussy typing is driving you nuts, you can jump onto a phone or video call. At the top of the Details screen, a little strip of icons awaits. They include ☎ (conclude the transaction by voice, with a phone call or FaceTime audio call), ☐◁ (place a FaceTime video call), and ⓘ (open this person's full Contacts card, loaded with different ways to call, text, or email).

- **Send My Current Location.** Hit this button to transmit a map to the other person, showing exactly where you are, so that person can come and pick you up, meet you for drinks, rescue you when your car doesn't start, or whatever.

  If your correspondent has an iPhone, iPad, or Mac, she can open the map you've sent in Maps, ready to guide her with driving directions. If she's one of the unenlightened—she owns some non-Apple phone—then she gets what's called a Location vCard, which she *may* be able to open into a mapping app on her own phone.

NOTE: If Location Services isn't turned on (page 571), the phone asks you to turn it on now. After all, you can't very well share your location if your phone has no idea where you are.

- **Share My Location.** If you're moving around, you may prefer this option. It sends your whereabouts to your correspondent—and keeps that location updated as you meander through the city, for a period of time that you specify (One Hour, Until End of Day, or Indefinitely). That's great when you're club-hopping, say, and trying to help some buddies catch up with you. As your location changes, the map you sent to your recipient updates itself.

  At any time—even before the hour, day, or eternity is up—you can stop broadcasting your location to this person; just open the Details screen again and tap Stop Sharing My Location.

- **Do Not Disturb.** Otherwise known as "mute," "enough already," or "shut up." It makes your phone stop ringing or vibrating with every new message from this person or group. Handy when you're trying to get work done, when you're being bombarded by silly group chitchat, or when someone's stalking you.

- **Attachments.** Crazy cool! Here are all the photos and other attachments you've ever exchanged with this texting correspondent, going back to forever.

  You can tap one of these tiles to open it. Or, if you hold your finger down on it, you get choices like Copy, Delete, and More. (There's usually nothing new under More except Save Image, which copies the texted photo into your Photos collection.)

The Text List

What's cool is that the iPhone retains all these exchanges. You can review them or resume them at any time by tapping Messages on the Home screen. A list of text message conversations appears; a blue dot indicates conversations that contain new messages (page 164, right).

> **TIP:** If you've sent a message to a certain group of people, you can address a new note to the same group by tapping the old message's row here.

The truth is, these listings represent **people**, not conversations. For example, if you had a text message exchange with Chris last week, then a quick way to send a new text message to Chris (even on a totally different subject) is to open that "conversation" and simply send a "reply." The iPhone saves you the administrative work of creating a new message, choosing a recipient, and so on.

TIP: Hey, you can search text messages! At the very top of the list, there's a search box. You can actually find text inside your message collection.

If having these old exchanges hanging around presents a security (or marital) risk, you can delete them in either of two ways:

- **Delete an entire conversation.** *Swipe* away the conversation. At the list of conversations, swipe your finger *leftward* across the conversation's name. That makes the Delete confirmation button appear.

  Alternate method: Above the Messages list, tap Edit, tap to select (✓) the conversations you want to ditch, and then tap the Delete button.

- **Delete just one text.** Open the conversation so that you're viewing the cascade of bubbles representing the texts back and forth.

  Now, this technique is a little weird, but here goes: *Hold down your finger* on the individual message you want to delete (or double-tap it). When the little black bar of options appears, tap More.

  Now you can delete all the exchanges simultaneously (tap Delete All) or vaporize only particularly incriminating messages. To do that, tap the selection circles for the individual balloons you want to nuke, putting checks (✔) by them; then tap the 🗑 button to delete them all at once. Tap **Delete Message** to confirm.

> **NOTE:** Interestingly, you can also *forward* some messages you've selected in this way. When you tap the Forward button (↪), a new outgoing text message appears, ready for you to specify the new recipient.

Mark All as Read

Here's a handy option: When you get off the plane, home from your honeymoon, you might see Messages bristling with notifications about messages you missed. Now you can mark them all as read at once, so the blue dots don't distract you anymore.

To do that, on the message-list screen, tap **Edit** and then **Read All**.

Sending a New Message

If you want to text somebody you've texted before, the quickest way, as noted above, is simply to resume one of the "conversations" already listed in the Messages list.

You can also tap a person's name in Contacts, or ⓘ next to a listing in Recents or Favorites, to open the Info screen; tap **Send Message**.

> **NOTE:** In some cases, the iPhone shows you your *entire* Contacts list, even people with no cellphone numbers. But you can't text somebody who doesn't have a cellphone.

Actually, options to fire off text messages lurk all over the iPhone—anytime you see the Share (⬆) button, which is frequently. The resulting Share screen includes options like **Email**, **Twitter**, **Facebook**—and **Message**. Tapping **Message** sends you back to Messages, where the photo, video, page, or other item is ready to send. (More on multimedia messages shortly.)

In other words, sending a text message to anyone who lives in your iPhone is only a couple of taps away.

> **NOTE:** You can tap that ⊕ button to add *another* recipient for this same message (or tap the 123 button to type in a phone number). Repeat as necessary; they'll all get the same message.

Yet another way to start: Tap the ✐ button at the top of the Messages screen.

In any case, the text message composition screen is waiting for you now. You're ready to type (or dictate) and send!

Picture, Audio, or Video Messages

The iPhone can also send photos, video clips, and audio clips to other cell-phones. Welcome to MMS (Multimedia Messaging Service).

To send a photo or a video, tap the ▣ next to the box where you type your messages. Three useful options appear.

- **Recent photos.** First, you see a scrolling row of the most recent photos and videos added on your iPhone. This feature is incredibly smart; it should be obvious that *most* of the time, the photo you want to send by text is one of the *last ones you took*. Tap a photo here—or more than one—and tap Send 1 Photo (or whatever the number is.)

- **Photo Library.** To transmit a photo or video that's already on your phone (but *not* one of the most recent), you can tap Photo Library; your Photos app opens automatically, showing all your photos and videos, as described in Chapter 8. Tap the one you want, and then tap Choose.

- **Take Photo or Video** opens the Camera app so that you can take a new picture or snag a video clip. It's just like the Camera app described in Chapter 8, except that only two modes are available: Video and Photo.

  Once you've captured the shot (or the clip), you can choose either Retake (if the result was no good) or Use Photo (if you want to send it). Then hit Send.

  You now return to your SMS conversation in progress—but now that photo or video appears inside the Send box. Type a caption or a comment, if you like. Then tap Send to fire it off to your buddy.

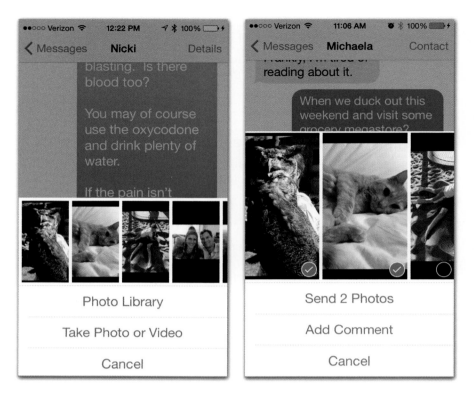

iMessages

This iOS feature should interest you—if it doesn't, in fact, make you giggle like a schoolgirl.

An iMessage looks and works exactly like a text message. You send iMessages and receive them in the same app (Messages). They show up in the same window. You can send the same kinds of things: text, photos, videos, contacts, map locations, whatever. You send and receive them using exactly the same techniques.

The big difference? iMessages go exclusively between Apple products: iPhones, iPads, iPod Touches, and Macs. If your iPhone determines that the address belongs to any **other** kind of phone, it sends regular old text messages.

So why would Apple reinvent the text-messaging wheel? Because iMessages offer some huge advantages over regular text messages:

- iMessages don't count as text messages! You don't have to pay for them. They look and work exactly like text messages, but they're transferred over the Internet (Wi-Fi or cellular) instead of your cell company's voice airwaves. You can send and receive an unlimited number of them and never have to pay a penny more.

- When you're typing back and forth with somebody, you don't have to wonder whether, during a silence, they're typing a response to you or just ignoring you; when they're typing a response, you see an ellipsis (•••), as shown below at left.

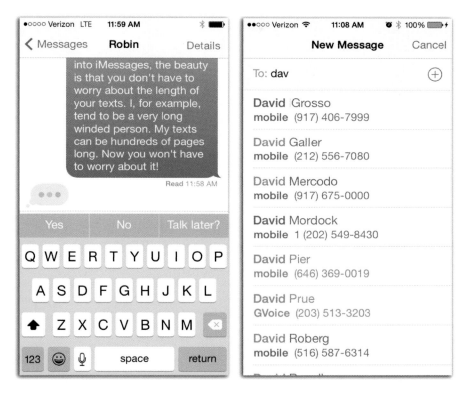

- You don't have to wonder if the other guy has received your message. A tiny, light-gray word "delivered" appears under each message you send, briefly, to let you know that the other guy's device received it.

- You can even turn on a "read receipt" feature that lets the other guy know when you've actually *seen* a message he sent. He'll see a notation that says, for example, "Read: 2:34 PM."

- Your history of iMessages shows up on all your i-gadgets; they're synchronized through your iCloud account. In other words, you can start a chat with somebody using your iPhone and later pick up your Mac laptop at home and carry right on from where you stopped (in *its* Messages program).

As a result, you always have a record of your iMessages. You have a copyable, searchable transcript on your computer.

- iMessages can be more than text. They can be little audio recordings, video recordings, or photos that you take on the spot, within the Messages app.

iMessages happen automatically. All you do is open Messages and create a text message as usual. If your recipient is using an Apple gadget (with iOS 5 or later, or a Mac using OS X Mountain Lion or later)...*and* has an iCloud account...*and* hasn't turned off iMessages, then your iPhone sends your message as an iMessage automatically. It somehow knows.

You'll know, too, because the light-gray text in the typing box says "iMessage" instead of "Text Message." And each message you send shows up in a *blue* speech bubble instead of a *green* one. The Send button is blue, too.

In fact, when you're addressing the new text message, the names that appear in blue represent people with iMessages gadgets, so you know in advance who's cool and who's not (previous page, right). (The green names are those who do *not* have iMessage. The gray ones—well, your iPhone doesn't know yet.)

Instant Audio, Video, and Photos

Some useful controls are available whenever you're exchanging iMessages with a fellow Apple gadget owner. As in super-popular apps like WhatsApp, they let you *quickly* exchange audio, video, or still pictures as easily as you'd type something.

Yes, of course, you've always been able to send multimedia goodies while texting. The difference now is the *convenience* of doing so; you can record and send a picture, audio clip, or video with a single slide of your thumb. It's so effortless that the process is transformed.

It goes like this.

Audio Texting: The New Walkie-Talkie

Hold your finger down on the 🎤 button at the right end of the Messages text box. At the sound of the ding, say something—and then slide your finger upward to the ⬆ button. What you said is *instantly* transmitted to your buddy as an audio recording. You don't have to fuss with a bunch of Start, Stop, or Send buttons.

The guy on the receiving end doesn't even have to touch the screen to listen. He just holds the phone up to his head! Your audio message plays automatically. (This works even if his phone is asleep and locked.)

And then get this: To reply, **he** doesn't have to touch anything or look at the screen, either. He just holds the phone to his head again and speaks! Once he lowers the phone, his recording shoots back to you.

Throughout all of this, you don't have to look at the phone, put your glasses on, or touch the screen. It's a whole new form of quick exchanges—something that combines the best of a walkie-talkie (instant audio) with the best of text messages (you can listen and reply at your leisure).

Sometimes, an audio recording is just better than a typed message, especially when music, children, animals, or a lot of emotion in your voice are involved. You could probably argue that audio texting is also better than typed texting when you're driving, jogging, or operating industrial machinery.

TIP: The off switch for the Raise to Listen/Raise to Speak feature is in Settings→Messages. But why would you want to disable such a cool feature?

Now then: That business about holding down the ● button, talking, and then sliding up is probably how you'll always do it—once you become friends with this feature. But, at the outset, you can proceed more cautiously.

If, after speaking, you simply lift your finger from the glass, you can tap ▶ to review your recording before sending it. Or you can tap the ✖ to cancel the whole thing.

But, really, it's that hold down/speak/slide up business that makes audio transmissions so much fun.

> **TIP:** Audio eats up a lot more space on your phone than text. If you do a lot of audio messaging, then, over time, those audio snippets can fill up your storage.
>
> That's why iOS comes set to *delete* each audio message 2 minutes after you receive it. If that prospect worries you, then visit Settings→ Messages. You can tap Expire and change that setting to Never.
>
> Even then, you're free to preserve especially good audio messages forever; just tap the tiny Keep button that appears below each one.

Video Messaging

To the left of the typing box, there's a little 📷 icon. You already know what happens when you tap it: You can send or take a photo or video. That's all described starting on page 169.

But if you *hold your finger down* on this 📷, you can take a video clip and send it instantly (when holding the phone upright, in portrait mode, only). In slow motion, the process goes like this:

1. **Hold your finger down on the 📷.** When the recording palette appears, you can lift your finger.

2. **Tap the ● button.** Now you're recording video. Tap ◉ to stop.

> **TIP:** If you prefer, you can just hold down the ● for as long as you want to record; stop by lifting your finger.

3. **Tap the ▶ to play back your video for review, or tap ⊕ to send it.**

Now, all of that is the slow, timid way to send a video. Once you get the hang of it, you can do it all with a single finger motion, like this:

Hold your finger down on the 📷. Without lifting your finger, slide onto the ● to record video. Still without lifting, slide onto the ⊕ and release. The phone sends the freshly recorded video.

That method is so smooth and continuous that it makes video snippets a seamless part of the texting conversation. It also puts you in a better position to capture video of things that happen suddenly and instantly—a plane landing in the Hudson River, say.

Photo Messaging

You can take and transmit *photos* with a single finger swipe, too. Once again, here's the slow version:

1. **Hold your finger down on the .** When the recording palette appears, you can lift your finger.

2. **Aim the camera, and then tap .** The phone snaps the picture and sends it, all at once.

As you get better, you can do it all in one quick motion: Hold your finger on the , aim the camera, slide up to the ⊕ button, and let go. Snap and send.

Text Messages: Details and Misc.

You might not think that something as simple as text messaging would involve a lot of fine print, but you'd be wrong.

Settings for Texts and iMessages

If you tap Settings→Messages, you'll stumble upon some intriguing messaging options:

- **iMessage.** This is the on/off switch for the entire iMessages feature. It's hard to imagine why you wouldn't want to avoid paying for text messages, but you know—whatever floats your boat.

- **Send Read Receipts.** When you turn this option on, your iMessage correspondents will know when you've seen their messages. A tiny word "Read" will appear beneath each sent message that you've actually seen. Turn this off only if it deprives you of the excuse for not responding promptly ("Hey, I never even saw your message!").

- **Send as SMS.** If iMessages is unavailable (meaning that you have no Internet connection at all), then your phone will send your message as a regular text message, via the regular cellphone voice network.

- **Send & Receive.** Tap here to specify what cellphone numbers and email addresses you want to register with iMessages. (Your laptop, obviously, does not have a phone number, which is why iMessages gives you the option of using an email address.)

  When people send iMessages to *you*, they can use any of the numbers or addresses you turn on here. That's the only time these numbers and addresses matter. *You* see the same messages exactly the same way on all your Apple gadgets, no matter what email address or phone number the sender used for you.

  (If you scroll down on this Settings screen, you'll see the Start new conversations from options. This is where you specify which number or address others will see when *you* initiate the message. It really doesn't make much difference which one you choose.)

- **MMS Messaging.** MMS messages are like text messages—except that they can also include audio clips, video clips, or photos, as already described. In the rare event that your cell company charges extra for these messages, you have an on/off switch here. If you turn it off, then you can send only plain text messages.

- **Group Messaging.** Suppose you're sending a message to three friends named A, B, and C (they have weird parents). When they reply to your message, the responses will appear in a Messages thread that's dedicated to this particular group (below). It works only if *all* of you have turned on Group Messaging. (Note to the paranoid: It also means that everyone sees everyone else's phone numbers or email addresses.)

Messages tries to help you keep everybody straight by displaying their headshots (if you have them in Contacts), or their initials (if you don't). (You can turn off the initials; see page 98.)

- **Show Subject Field.** If email messages can have subject lines, why not text messages? Now, on certain newfangled phones (like yours), they can; the message arrives with a little dividing line between the subject and the body, offering your recipient a hint as to what it's about.

NOTE: It's OK to leave the subject line blank. But if you leave the *body* blank, the message won't send. (Incidentally, when you do fill in the subject line, what you're sending is an MMS message, rather than a plain old text message.)

- **Character Count.** If a message is longer than 160 characters, the iPhone breaks it up into multiple messages. That's convenient, sure.

But if your cellphone plan permits only a fixed number of messages a month, you could wind up sending (and spending) more than you intended.

The **Character Count** feature can help. When it's on, after your typing wraps to a second line, a little counter appears just above the **Send** button ("71/160," for example). It tracks how many characters remain within your 160-character limit for one message. (Of course, if you're sending an iMessage, you don't care how long it is; there's no length limit.)

- **Blocked.** You can block people who are harassing or depressing you with their texts or calls. Tap here to view the list of people in your Contacts app you've decided to block; tap **Add New** to add new people to the list.

- **Keep Messages.** How long do you want your text messages to hang around on your phone? This is a question of privacy, of storage, and of your personality. In any case, here's where you get a choice of **30 Days**, **1 Year**, or **Forever**.

- **Filter Unknown Senders.** When you turn this on, the iPhone turns off notifications for senders not in your Contacts and sorts them into a separate list, which you can find in the "Unknown Senders" section of the Messages app.

- **Expire.** As noted on page 174, the iPhone ordinarily deletes audio and video messages a couple of minutes after they arrive, to avoid filling up your phone with old, no-longer-relevant audio and video files. The two Expire controls here let you turn off that automatic deletion (by choosing **Never**).

- **Raise to Listen.** Here's the on/off switch for the "raise to listen"/"raise to talk" features described earlier, where the phone plays back audio messages, and sends your spoken replies, automatically when you hold it up to your head. You might want to turn that feature off if you discover that the phone is playing back audio messages unexpectedly—or, worse, recording and sending them when you didn't mean it.

Bonus Settings in a Place You Didn't Expect

Apple has stashed a few important text-messaging settings in **Settings→ Notifications→Messages**:

- **Allow Notifications.** If, in a cranky burst of sensory overload, you want your phone to stop telling you when new texts come in (with a banner or sound, for example), then turn this off.

- **Show in Notification Center.** How many recent text messages should appear in the Notification Center (page 52)?

- **Sounds.** Tap here to choose a sound for incoming texts to play. (You can also choose a different sound for *each person* in your address book, as described on page 107.)

- **Badge App Icon.** Turning this on makes the Messages icon show a little red badge to let you know when you have a new text message.

- **Show on Lock Screen.** Do you want received text messages and iMessages to appear on the screen when it's locked? If yes, then you can sneak reassuring glances at your phone without turning it fully on. If no, then you maintain better protection against snoopers who find your phone on your desk.

- **Show Previews.** Usually, when a text message arrives, it wakes up your phone and shows the message contents. Which is great, as long as the message isn't private and the phone isn't lying on the table where everyone can see it. If you turn off Show Preview, though, you'll see who the message is from but not the actual text of the message (until you tap the notification banner or bubble).

- **Repeat Alerts.** If someone sends you a text message but you don't tap or swipe to read it, the iPhone waits 2 minutes and then plays the notification sound again. That second chance really helps when, for example, you were in a noisy place and missed the original chime.

  But for some people, even one additional reminder isn't enough. Here you can specify that you want to be re-alerted Twice, 3 Times, 5 Times, or 10 Times. (Or Never, if you don't want repeated alerts at all.)

Capturing Messages and Files

In general, text messages are fleeting; most people have no idea how they might capture them and save them forever. Copy and Paste help with that.

Some of the stuff *in* those text messages is easy to capture, though. For example, if you're on the receiving end of a photo or a video, tap the small preview in the speech bubble. It opens at full-screen size so you can have a better look at it—and if it's a video, there's a ▶ button so you can play it. Either way, if the picture or video is good enough to preserve, tap the 📤 button. You're offered a Save Image or Save Video button; tap to add the photo or video to your iPhone's collection.

If someone sends you contact information (a phone number, for example), you can add it to your address book. Just tap inside that bubble and then tap either Create New Contact or Add to Existing Contact.

If you'd like to preserve the actual text messages, you have a few options:

- **Copy them individually.** Double-tap a text bubble, and then tap Copy. At this point, you can paste that one message into, for example, an email message.

- **Forward them.** Double-tap a message to make the button bar appear. Tap More, and then tap the selection dots beside all the messages you want to pass on. Now you can tap the Forward ($\diagup\!\!\!\!\!\rightarrow$) button. All the selected messages go along for the ride in a single consolidated message to a new text-message addressee.

- **Save the iMessages.** If you have a Mac, then your iMessages (that is, notes to and from other Apple gadgets) show up in the Messages chat program. You can save them or copy them there.

TIP: Behind the scenes, the Mac stores all your chat transcripts in a hidden folder as special text files. To get there, press the Option key as you open the Go menu; choose Go→Library. The transcripts are in date-stamped folders in the Messages→Archive folder.

- **Use an app.** As you've probably figured out by now, there's no built-in way to save regular text messages in bulk. There are, however, apps that can do this for you, like DiskAid (for Windows) or iBackup Viewer (free for the Mac). They work from the invisible backup files that you create when you sync your phone with iTunes.

Free Text Messages

Text messaging is awesome. Paying for text messaging, not so much.

That's why iMessages is so great: It bypasses the cell companies' text-message network by sending messages over the Internet instead—but only when you're sending to fellow owners of Apple equipment.

Fortunately, there are all kinds of sneaky ways to do text messaging for free that *don't* require your correspondents to have an Apple device. Here are some examples:

- **Textfree with Voice.** It's an app from the App Store that gives your iPhone its own phone number just for free text or picture messages, so you can send and receive all you want without paying a cent. Incoming voice calls are free, too; you can buy minutes for outgoing calls.

- **WhatsApp.** Here's another app for free, iMessage-style texting— among all smartphones. The iPhone, Android, BlackBerry, Windows

Phone, Nokia Symbian, all together in glorious free texting (with pictures, videos, group chats, and more).

- **Google Voice.** This free service has a million great features. But one of the best is that it lets you send and receive free text messages. You can do that from your computer (an amazingly useful feature, actually) at *voice.google.com*, or by using the free Google Voice app).

Chat Programs

The iPhone doesn't **come** with any chat programs, like AIM (AOL Instant Messenger) or Yahoo Messenger. But installing one yourself is simple enough.

If you're a hard-core chatter, though, what you really want is an all-in-one app like IM+ or Beejive IM. You get a single app that can conduct chats with people on just about every chat network known to humanity: GTalk, Yahoo, AIM, ICQ, Myspace, Twitter, Facebook, Jabber, and Skype.

Call Waiting

Call waiting has been around for years. With a call-waiting feature, when you're on one phone call, you hear a beep indicating that someone else is calling in. You can tap the Flash key on your phone to answer the second call while you put the first one on hold.

Some people don't use call waiting because it's rude to both callers. Others don't use it because they have no idea what the Flash key is.

On the iPhone, when a second call comes in, the phone rings (and/or vibrates) as usual, and the screen displays the name or number of the caller, just as it always does. Buttons on the screen offer you three choices:

- **End Current Call.** Hangs up on the first call and takes the second one.

- **Answer (Hold Current Call).** This is the traditional call-waiting effect. You say, "Can you hold on a sec? I've got another call," to the first caller. The iPhone puts her on hold, and you connect to the second caller.

  At this point, you can jump back and forth between the two calls, or you can merge them into a conference call.

- **Decline Incoming Call.** The incoming call goes straight to voicemail. Your first caller has no idea that anything has happened.

If call waiting seems a bit disruptive, you can turn it off, at least on the AT&T iPhone (the switch is in Settings→Phone→Call Waiting). When call waiting is turned off, incoming calls go straight to voicemail when you're on the phone.

If you have T-Mobile, Sprint, or Verizon, then you can turn off call waiting only one call at a time; just dial *70 before you dial the number. You won't be disturbed by call-waiting beeps while you're on that important call.

Call Forwarding

Here's a pretty cool feature you may not have known you had. It lets you route all calls made to your iPhone number to a *different* number. How is this useful? Let us count the ways:

- **When you're home.** You can have your cellphone's calls ring your home number so you can use any extension in the house, and so you don't miss any calls while the iPhone is turned off or charging.

- **When you send your iPhone to Apple for battery replacement.** You can forward the calls you would have missed to your home or work phone number.

- **When you're overseas.** You can forward the number to one of the web-based services that answers your voicemail and sends it to you as an email attachment (like Google Voice).

- **When you're going to be in a place with little or no cell coverage.** Let's say you're in Alaska. You can have your calls forwarded to your hotel or to a friend's cellphone. (Forwarded calls eat up your allotment of minutes, though.)

You have to turn on call forwarding while you're still in an area with cell coverage. Here's how:

- **AT&T.** Tap Settings→Phone→Call Forwarding, turn call forwarding on, and then tap in the new phone number. That's all there is to it—your iPhone will no longer ring. At least not until you turn the same switch off again.

- **Verizon, Sprint, T-Mobile.** On the dialing pad, dial *72, plus the number you're forwarding calls to. Then tap Call. (To turn off call forwarding, dial *73, and then tap Call.)

Caller ID

Caller ID is another classic cellphone feature. It's the one that displays the phone number of the incoming call (and sometimes the name of the caller).

The only thing worth noting about the iPhone's own implementation of caller ID is that you can prevent *your* number from appearing when you call *other* people's phones:

- **AT&T.** Tap Settings→Phone→Show My Caller ID, and then tap the on/off switch.

- **Verizon, Sprint, T-Mobile.** You can disable caller ID only for individual calls. For example, if you're calling your ex, you might not want your number to show up on his phone. Just dial *67 before you dial the number. (Caller ID turns on again for subsequent calls.)

Bluetooth Accessories

Bluetooth is a short-range *cable elimination* technology. It's designed to untether you from equipment that would ordinarily require a cord.

Most people use Bluetooth for two purposes: Communicating with a smartwatch or fitness band, or transmitting audio to a wireless speaker, car stereo, or Bluetooth earpiece.

NOTE: This discussion covers *monaural* Bluetooth earpieces intended for phone calls. But the iPhone can also handle Bluetooth *stereo* headphones, intended for music, as well as Bluetooth speakers. Details are on page 233.

Pairing with a Bluetooth Earpiece or Speaker

Pairing means "marrying" a phone to a Bluetooth accessory so that each works only with the other. If you didn't do this one-time pairing, then some other guy passing on the sidewalk might hear your conversation through *his* earpiece. And neither of you would be happy.

The pairing process is different for every cellphone and every Bluetooth earpiece. Usually it involves a sequence like this:

1. **On the earpiece, turn on Bluetooth. Make the earpiece or speaker discoverable.** *Discoverable* just means that your phone can "see" it. You'll have to consult the gadget's instructions to learn how to do so;

it's usually a matter of holding down some button or combination of buttons until the earpiece blinks.

2. **On the iPhone, tap** Settings→Bluetooth. **Turn Bluetooth on.** The iPhone immediately begins searching for nearby Bluetooth equipment. If all goes well, you'll see the name of your earpiece or speaker show up on the screen.

3. **Tap the gadget's name. Type in the passcode, if necessary.** The *passcode* is a number, usually four or six digits, that must be typed into the phone within about a minute. You have to enter this only once, during the initial pairing process. The idea is to prevent some evildoer sitting nearby in the airport lounge, for example, to secretly pair *his* earpiece with *your* iPhone.

The user's manual for your earpiece should tell you what the passcode is (if one is even required).

To make calls using a Bluetooth earpiece (or speaker as a speakerphone), you *dial* using the iPhone itself. You usually use the iPhone's own volume controls, too. You generally press a button on the earpiece or speaker to answer an incoming call, to swap call-waiting calls, or to end a call.

If you're having any problems making a particular gadget work, Google it. Type "iphone jambox mini," for example. Chances are good that you'll find a write-up by somebody who's worked through the setup and made it work.

Bluetooth Car Systems

The iPhone works beautifully with Bluetooth car systems, too. The pairing procedure generally goes exactly as described above: You make the car discoverable, enter the passcode on the iPhone, and then make the connection.

Once you're paired up, you can answer an incoming call by pressing a button on your steering wheel, for example. You hear your caller through the car's speakers, and a microphone for your own voice is hidden in the rearview mirror or dashboard. You make calls either from the iPhone or, in some cars, by dialing the number on the car's own touchscreen.

NOTE: When Bluetooth is turned on but the earpiece isn't, or when the earpiece isn't nearby, the ✷ icon on your iPhone's status bar appears in gray. And when it's connected and working right, the earpiece's battery gauge appears on the iPhone's status bar.

Of course, studies show that it's the act of driving while conversing that causes accidents—not actually holding a phone. So the hands-free system is less for safety than for convenience and compliance with state laws.

Pairing with a Smartwatch or Fitness Band

The trouble with Bluetooth has always been that it's a battery hog. Now, though, there's a new, better technology, alternately called Bluetooth LE (for "low energy"), Bluetooth Smart, or Bluetooth 4.0. Its very smart idea: It turns on only when necessary, and then turns off again to save power.

When you've paired your phone with a Bluetooth 4.0 gadget, you see the Bluetooth logo on your status bar (✶) light up only when it's actually exchanging data. Bluetooth LE has made possible a lot of smartwatches and fitness trackers.

As a handy bonus, you usually do the pairing right in the gadget's companion app, rather than fumbling around in Settings. That setup makes a lot more sense. For example, when you're setting up an Apple Watch, you use the Watch app to pair the watch; when you're setting up an Up band or Fitbit, you connect your band wirelessly in the Up app or Fitbit app.

6

Large Type, Kid Mode & Accessibility

I f you were told that the iPhone was one of the easiest phones in the world for a disabled person to use, you might spew your coffee. The thing has almost no physical keys! How would a blind person use it? It's a phone that rings! How would a deaf person use it?

But it's true. Apple has gone to *incredible* lengths to make the iPhone usable for people with vision, hearing, or other physical impairments. As a handy side effect, these features also can be fantastically useful to people whose only impairment is being under 10 or over 40.

If you're deaf, you can have the LED flash to get your attention. If you're blind, you can actually turn the screen off and operate *everything*—do your email, surf the web, adjust settings, run apps—by letting the phone speak what you're touching. It's pretty amazing (and it doubles the battery life).

You can also magnify the screen, reverse black for white (for better-contrast reading), set up custom vibrations for each person who might call you, and convert stereo music to mono (great if you're deaf in one ear).

Some of these features are useful even if you're not disabled—in particular, the LED flash, custom vibrations, and zooming. The kiosk mode is great for kids; it prevents them from exiting whatever app they're using. And if you have aging eyes, you might find the Large Text option handy.

Here's a rundown of the accessibility features in iOS 9. To turn on any of the features described here, open Settings→General→Accessibility. (And don't forget about Siri, described in Chapter 4. She may be the best friend a blind person's phone ever had.)

TIP: You can turn many of the iPhone's accessibility features on and off with a triple-click of the Home button. See page 211 for details.

VoiceOver

VoiceOver is a *screen reader*—software that makes the iPhone speak everything you touch. It's a fairly important feature if you're blind.

On the VoiceOver settings pane, tap the on/off switch to turn VoiceOver on. Because VoiceOver radically changes the way you control your phone, you must dismiss a warning to confirm that you know what you're doing. Immediately, you hear a female voice begin reading the names of the controls she sees on the screen.

You can adjust the Speaking Rate of the synthesized voice.

Now you're ready to start using the iPhone in VoiceOver mode. There's a lot to learn, and practice makes perfect, but here's the overview:

- **Touch something to hear it.** Tap icons, words, even status icons at the top; as you go, the voice tells you what you're tapping. "Messages." "Calendar." "Mail—14 new items." "45 percent battery power." You can tap the dots on the Home screen and you'll hear "Page 3 of 9."

  Once you've tapped a screen element, you can also flick your finger left or right—anywhere on the screen—to "walk" through everything on the screen, left to right, top to bottom.

TIP: A thin black rectangle appears around whatever the voice is identifying. That's for the benefit of sighted people who might be helping you.

- **Double-tap something to "tap" it.** Ordinarily, you tap something on the screen to open it. But since single-tapping now means "speak this," you need a new way to open everything. So: To open something you've just heard identified, double-tap *anywhere on the screen*. (You don't have to wait for the voice to finish talking.)

TIP: Or do a *split tap*. Tap something to hear what it is—and with that finger still down, tap somewhere else with a different finger to open it.

There are all kinds of other special gestures in VoiceOver. Make the voice stop speaking with a *two-finger tap*; read everything, in sequence, from the top of the screen with a *two-finger upward flick*; scroll one page at a time with a *three-finger flick up or down*; go to the next or previous screen (Home, Stocks, and so on) with a *three-finger flick left or right*; and more.

Or try turning on Screen Curtain with a ***three-finger triple-tap***; it blacks out the screen, giving you total privacy as well as a heck of a battery boost. (Repeat to turn the screen back on.)

On the VoiceOver settings screen, you'll find an expanded wealth of options for using the iPhone sightlessly. For example:

- **Speaking rate slider.** This controls how fast VoiceOver speaks to you, on a scale of tortoise to hare.

- **Speak Hints** makes the phone give you additional suggestions for operating something you've tapped. For example, instead of just saying, "Safari," it says, "Safari. Double-tap to open."

- **Use Pitch Change** makes the phone talk in a higher voice when you're entering letters and a lower voice when you're deleting them. It also uses a higher pitch when speaking the first item of a list and a lower one when speaking the last item of a group. In both cases, this option is a great way to help you understand where you are in a list.

- **Use Sound Effects** helps you navigate by adding little clicks and chirps as you scroll, tap, and so on.

- **Speech** is where you choose a voice for VoiceOver's speaking. If you have an iPhone 5s or later (with at least 900 megabytes of free space), you can install Alex, the very realistic male voice that's been happily chatting away on the Mac for years.

- **Braille.** Braille, of course, is the system that represents letters as combinations of dots on a six- or eight-cell grid. Blind people can read Braille by touching embossed paper with their fingers. But in iOS they can type in Braille, too. For many, that may be faster than trying to type on the onscreen keyboard, and more accurate than dictation.

  On this Settings screen, you specify, among other things, whether you want to use the six- or eight-dot system.

  When you're ready to type, you use the Rotor (described next) to choose Braille Screen Input, which is usually the last item on the list. If the phone is flat on a table ("desktop mode"), the six "keys" for typing Braille are arrayed in a loose, flattened V pattern.

  If you're holding the phone, you grip it with your pinkies and thumbs, with the screen facing away from you ("Screen away" mode).

- **The Rotor** is a brilliant solution to a thorny problem. If you're blind, how are you supposed to control how VoiceOver reads to you? Do you have to keep burrowing into Settings to change the volume, speaking speed, punctuation verbosity, and so on?

Nope. The Rotor is an imaginary dial. It appears when you twist two fingers on the screen as if you were turning an actual dial.

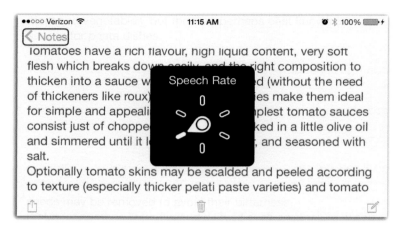

And what are the options on this dial? That's up to you. Tap **Rotor** to get a list of options: **Characters**, **Words**, **Speech Rate**, **Volume**, **Punctuation**, **Zoom**, and so on.

Once you've dialed up a setting, you can get VoiceOver to move from one item to another by flicking a finger up or down. For example, if you've chosen **Volume** from the Rotor, you make the playback volume louder or quieter with each flick up or down. If you've chosen Zoom, then each flick adjusts the screen magnification.

The Rotor is especially important if you're using the web. It lets you jump among web page elements like pictures, headings, links, text boxes, and so on. Use the Rotor to choose, for example, images—then you can flick up and down from one picture to the next on that page.

- **Typing Style.** In **Standard Typing**, you drag your finger around the screen until VoiceOver speaks the key you want—and then simultaneously tap anywhere with a second finger to type the letter.

  In **Touch Typing**, you can slide your finger around the keyboard until you hear the key you want; lift your finger to type that letter.

  There's also **Direct Touch Typing**, which is a faster method intended for people who are more confident about typing. If you tap a letter, you type it instantly. If you hold the key down, VoiceOver speaks its name but doesn't type it, just to make sure you know where you are.

- **Phonetic Feedback** refers to what VoiceOver says as you type or touch each keyboard letter. **Character and Phonetics** means that it says the letter's name plus its pilot's alphabet equivalent: "A—Alpha," "B—Bravo," "C—Charlie," and so on. Phonetics Only says the pilot's-alphabet word alone.

- **Typing Feedback** governs how the phone helps you figure out what you're typing. It can speak the individual letters you're striking, the words you've completed, or both.

- **Modifier Keys.** You can trigger some VoiceOver commands from a physical Bluetooth keyboard; all of them use Control-Option as the basis. (For example, Control-Option-A means "Read all from the current position." A complete list of these shortcuts is at *http://j.mp/1kZRSOz*).

  The Modifier Keys option lets you use the Caps Lock key instead of the Control-Option business, which simplifies the keyboard shortcuts at least a little bit.

- **Always Speak Notifications** makes the phone announce, with a spoken voice, when an alert or update message has appeared. (If you turn this off, then VoiceOver announces only incoming text messages.)

- **Navigate Images.** As VoiceOver reads to you what's on a web page, how do you want it to handle pictures? It can say nothing about them (Never), it can read their names (Always), or it can read their names and whatever hidden Descriptions savvy web designers have attached to them for the benefit of blind visitors.

- **Large Cursor.** This option fattens up the borders of the VoiceOver "cursor" (the box around whatever is highlighted) so you can see it better.

- **Double-tap Timeout.** This option, new in iOS 9, lets you give yourself more time to complete a double-tap when you want to trigger some VoiceOver reading. Handy if you have motor difficulties.

VoiceOver and Braille input take practice and involve learning a lot of new techniques. If you need these features to use your iPhone, then visit the more complete guide at *http://support.apple.com/kb/HT3598*.

Or spend a few minutes (or weeks) at *applevis.com*, a website dedicated to helping the blind use Apple gear.

> **TIP:** VoiceOver is especially great at reading your iBooks out loud. Details are on page 371.

Zooming

Compared with a computer, an iPhone's screen is pretty tiny. Every now and then, you might need a little help reading small text or inspecting those tiny graphics.

The Zoom command is just the ticket; it lets you magnify the screen whenever it's convenient, up to 500 percent.

Of course, at that point, the screen image is now too big to fit the physical glass of the iPhone, so you need a way to scroll around on your virtual jumbo screen.

To begin, you have to turn on the master Zoom switch in **Settings→General→ Accessibility**. Immediately, this magnifying lens appears:

Scroll down and look at the **Zoom Region** control. If it's set to **Window Zoom**, then zooming produces this movable rectangular magnifying lens. If it's set to **Full Screen Zoom**, then zooming magnifies the entire screen. (And that, as many Apple Genius Bar employees can tell you, freaks out a lot of people who don't know what's happened.)

Now then. Next time you need to magnify things, do this:

- **Start zooming** by double-tapping the screen with three fingers. You've either opened up the magnifying lens or magnified the entire screen. The magnification is 200 percent of original size. (Another method: Triple-press the Home button, and then tap **Zoom**.)

> **TIP:** You can move the rectangular lens around the screen by dragging the white oval handle on its lower edge.

- **Pan around inside the lens (or pan the entire virtual giant screen)** by dragging with three fingers.

- **Zoom in more or less** by double-tap/dragging with three fingers. It's like double-tapping, except that you leave your fingers down on the second tap—and drag them upward to zoom in more (up to 500 percent) or down to zoom out again.

  Once again, you can lift two of your three fingers after the dragging has begun. That way, it's easier to see what you're doing.

TIP: There's also a Resize Lens command in the Zoom menu, described next.

- **Open the Zoom menu** by tapping the white handle on the magnifying lens. Up pops a black menu of choices like Zoom Out (puts away the lens and stops zooming), Full Screen Zoom (magnifies the entire screen, hides the lens), Resize Lens (adds handles so you can change the lens's shape), Choose Filter (lets you make the area inside the lens grayscale or inverted colors, to help people with poor vision), and Show Controller (the joystick described in a moment). There's also a slider that controls the degree of magnification, which is pretty handy.

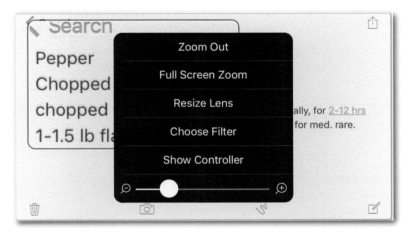

That's the big-picture description of Zoom. But back in Settings→General→ Accessibility→Zoom, a few more new controls await:

- **Follow Focus.** When this option is turned on, the image inside the magnifying lens scrolls automatically when you're entering text. Your point of typing is always centered.

- **Smart Typing.** When this new iOS 9 option is turned on, a couple of things happen whenever the onscreen keyboard appears. First, you get full-screen zooming (instead of just the magnifying lens); second, the keyboard itself isn't magnified, so you can see all the keys.

- **Show Controller.** The controller is this weird little onscreen joystick:

You can drag it with your finger to move the magnifying lens, or the entire magnified screen, in any direction. (It grows when you're touching it; the farther your finger moves from center, the faster the scrolling.) It's an alternative to having to drag the magnified screen with three fingers, which isn't precise and also blocks your view.

You can tap the center dot of the Controller to open the Zoom menu described already. Or double-tap the center dot to stop or start zooming.

TIP: On the iPhone 6s or 6s Plus, you can hard-press the controller for a pop-up magnifying lens. It remains open only as long as you're pressing.

- **Idle Visibility.** After you've stopped using the joystick for a while, it stays on the screen but becomes partly transparent, to avoid blocking your view. This slider controls *how* transparent it gets.

- **Zoom Region** controls whether you're zooming the entire screen or just a window (that is, a magnifying lens).

- **Zoom Filter** gives you options for how you want the text in the zoom window to appear—for example, black on gray for viewing in low light. (See the super-cool Zoom Filter tip on page 210.)

- **Maximum Zoom Level.** This slider controls just how magnified that lens, or screen, can get.

When VoiceOver is turned on, three-finger tapping has its own meaning—"jump to top of screen." Originally, therefore, you couldn't use Zoom while VoiceOver was on.

You can these days, but you have to add an *extra* finger or tap for VoiceOver gestures. For example, ordinarily, double-tapping with three fingers makes VoiceOver stop talking, but since that's the "zoom in" gesture, you must now *triple*-tap with three fingers to mute VoiceOver.

And what about VoiceOver's existing triple/three gesture, which turns the screen off? If Zoom is turned on, you must now triple-tap with *four* fingers to turn the screen off.

Invert Colors and Grayscale

By reversing the screen's colors black for white, like a film negative, you create a higher-contrast effect that some people find is easier on the eyes (below, left). To try it out, go to Settings→General→Accessibility and turn on Invert Colors. The other colors reverse, too—red for green and so on.

The Grayscale option removes all color from the screen. Everything looks like a black-and-white photo. Once again, it's designed to help people with poor vision.

Speech

Your phone can read to you aloud: an email message, a web page, a text message—anything. Your choices here go like this:

- **Speak Selection** puts a Speak command into the button bar that appears whenever you highlight text in any app. Tap that button to make the phone read the selected text.

- **Speak Screen** simply reads everything on the screen, top to bottom, when you swipe down from the top of the screen with two fingers. Great for hearing an ebook page or email read to you.

- **Voices** gives you a choice of languages and accents for the spoken voice. Try Australian; it's really cute.

- **Speaking Rate** controls how fast the voice talks.

- **Highlight Content** makes the phone highlight each word in color as it speaks, to help you follow along. Might be handy for beginning readers, too.

- **Speak Auto-text**. You know how the iPhone suggests a word as you type? This option makes the iPhone *speak* each suggestion. That effect has three benefits. First, of course, it helps blind people know what they're typing. Second, you don't have to take your eyes off the keyboard, which is great for speed and concentration. Third, if you're zoomed in, you may not be able to see the suggested word appear under your typed text—but now you still know what the suggestion is.

How to De-Sparsify iOS 9's Design

When Apple introduced the sparse, clean design of iOS 7 (which carries over into iOS 9), thousands blogged out in dismay. "It's too lightweight! The fonts are too spindly! The background is too bright! There aren't rectangles around buttons—we don't know what's a button and what's not! The Control Center is transparent—we can't read it! You moved our cheese—we hate this!"

Well, Apple may not agree with you about the super-lightweight design. But at least it has given you options to "fix" it. You can make the type bigger and bolder, the colors heavier, the background dimmer. You can restore outlines around buttons. And so much more.

All of these options await in Settings→General→Accessibility.

Larger Text

This option is the central control panel for iOS's Dynamic Type feature. It's a game-changer if you, a person with several decades of life experience, often find type on the screen too small.

Using the slider, you can choose a larger type size for all text the iPhone displays in apps like Mail, iBooks, Messages, and so on. This slider doesn't affect all the world's *other* apps—until their software companies update them to make them Dynamic Type–compatible. That day, when it comes, will be glorious. One slider to scale them all.

> **TIP:** The switch at the top, Larger Accessibility Sizes, unlocks an even longer slider. That is, it makes it possible for you to make the text in all the Dynamic Type–compatible apps even larger.

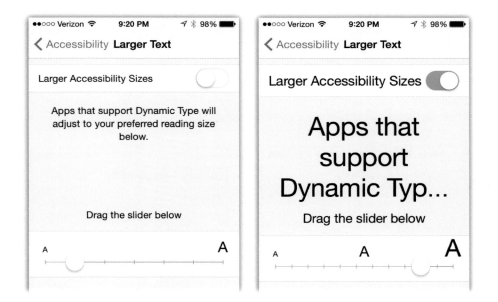

Bold Text

In iOS 9, the system font is fairly light. Its strokes are very thin; in some sizes and lighting conditions, it can even be hard to read.

But if you turn on Bold Text (and then tap Continue in the confirmation box), your iPhone restarts—and when it comes to, the fonts everywhere are slightly heavier: at the Home screen, in email, everywhere. And much easier to read with low light or aging eyesight.

It's one of the most useful features in iOS—and something almost nobody knows about.

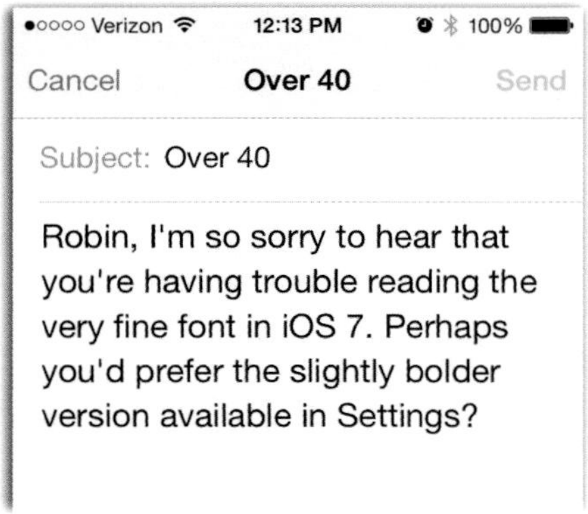

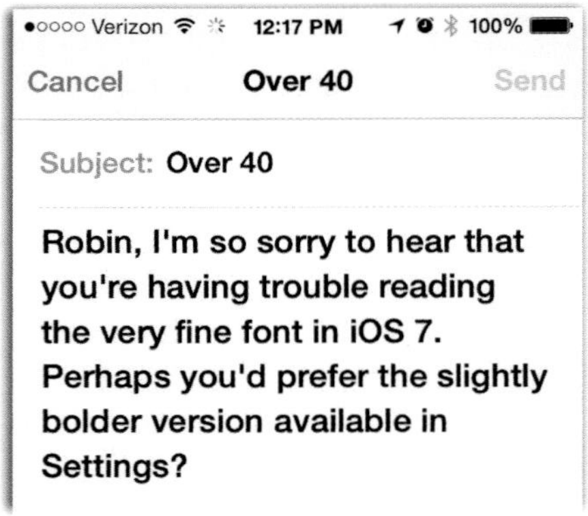

Button Shapes

Among the criticisms of iOS's design these days: You can't tell what's a **button** anymore! Everything is just words floating on the screen, without border rectangles to tell you what's tappable!

That's not quite true; any text in **blue type** is a tappable button. But never mind that; if you want shapes around your buttons, you shall have them— when you turn on this switch (below, right).

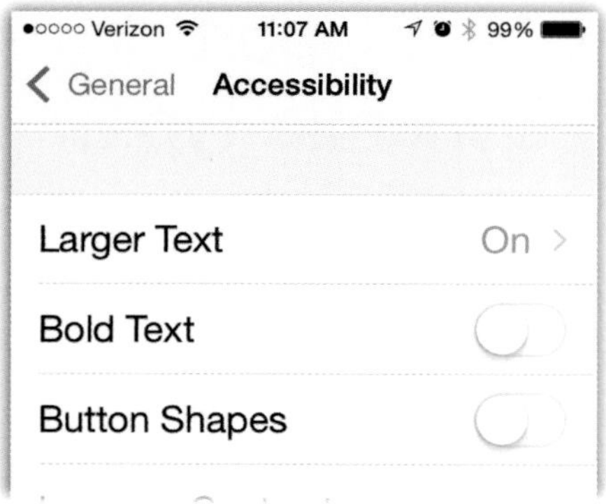

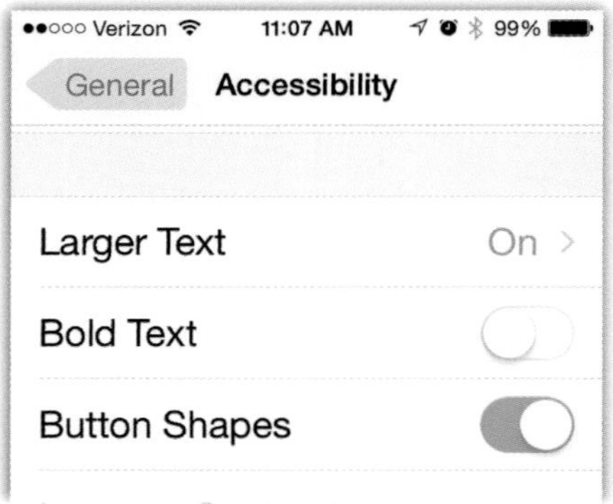

Increase Contrast

There are three switches in here. Reduce Transparency adds opacity to screens like the Control Center, the Dock, and the Notification Center. Their backgrounds are now solid, rather than slightly see-through, so that text on them is much easier to read. (You can see the before and after here.)

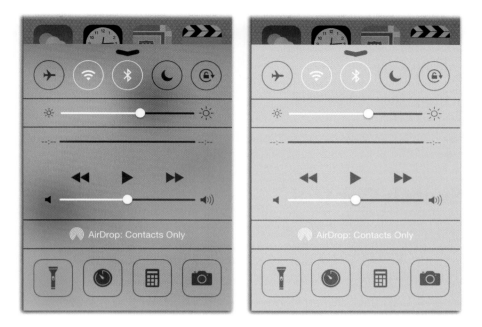

Darken Colors makes type in some spots a little darker and heavier. You notice it in the fonts for buttons, in the Calendar, and in Safari, for example.

Finally, Reduce White Point tones down the whiteness of iOS 9's screens, making them slightly dimmer and less harsh.

Reduce Motion

What kind of killjoy would want to turn off the subtle "parallax motion" of the Home screen background behind your icons, or the zooming-in animation when you open an app?

In any case, you can if you want, thanks to this button.

On/Off Labels

The Settings app teems with little tappable on/off switches, including this one. When something is turned on, the background of the switch is green; when it's off, the background is white.

But if you're having trouble remembering that distinction, turn on this option. Now the background of each switch sprouts visible symbols to

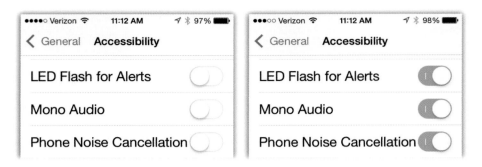

help you remember that green means On (you see a | marking) and white means Off.

Switch Control

Suppose your physical skills are limited to very simple gestures: puffing on an air pipe, pressing a foot switch, blinking an eye, or turning the head, for example. A hardware accessory called a **switch** lets you operate certain gadgets this way.

When you turn on Switch Control, the iPhone warns you that things are about to get very different. Tap OK.

Now the phone sequentially highlights one object on the screen after another; you're supposed to puff, tap, or blink at the right moment to say, "Yes, *this* one."

If you don't have a physical switch apparatus, you can use one nature gave you: your head. The iPhone's camera can detect when you turn your head left or right and can trigger various functions accordingly.

If you'd like to try it out, open Settings→General→Accessibility→Switch Control. Tap Switches→Add New Switch→Camera→Left Head Movement.

On this screen, you choose what a left head-turn will mean to your phone. The most obvious option is Select Item, which you could use in conjunction with the sequential highlighting of controls on the screen. But you can also make it mean "Press the Home button," "Activate Siri," "Adjust the volume," and so on.

Once you've made your selection, repeat that business for Right Head Movement.

When you return to the Switch Control screen, turn on Switch Control. Now your phone is watching you; whenever you turn your head left or right, it activates the control you set up. Pretty wild.

The controls here let you specify how fast the sequential highlighting proceeds, whether or not it pauses on the screen's first item, how many times the highlighting cycles through each screenful, and so on.

To turn off Switch Control, tap the on/off switch again. Or, if you're using some other app, triple-press the Home button to open the Accessibility shortcut panel. If you had the foresight to add Switch Control to its options (page 211), then one tap does the trick.

Switch Control is a broad (and specialized) feature, and it's been overhauled in iOS 9. To read more about it, open the Accessibility chapter of Apple's iPhone User Guide: *help.apple.com/iphone/9/*.

AssistiveTouch

If you can't even hold the phone, you might have trouble shaking it (a shortcut for "Undo"); if you can't move your fingers, just adjusting the volume might be a challenge.

This feature is Apple's accessibility team at its most creative. When you turn AssistiveTouch on, you get a new, glowing white circle in a corner of the screen (next page at top).

You can drag this magic white ball anywhere on the edges of the screen, though; it remains onscreen all the time.

When you tap it, the white ball expands into the special palette shown on the next page. It's offering six ways to trigger motions and gestures on the iPhone screen without requiring hand or multiple-finger movement. All you have to be able to do is tap with a single finger—or even a stylus held in your teeth or foot.

In iOS 9, you can add more buttons to this main menu, or switch around which buttons appear here. To do that, open Settings→General→ Accessibility→Assistive Touch→Customize Top Level Menu.

Meanwhile, here are the starter six icons:

- **Voice Control.** Touch here when you want to speak to Siri. If you do, in fact, have trouble manipulating the phone, Siri is probably your best friend already. This option, as well as the "Hey Siri" voice command, mean that you don't even have to hold down the Home button to start her up.

- **Notification Center, Control Center.** As far as most people know, the only way to open the Notification Center is to swipe down the screen from the top; the only way to open the Control Center is to swipe up from the bottom. These buttons, however, give you another way—one

that doesn't require any hand movement. (Tap the same button again to *close* whichever center you opened.)

- **Home.** You can tap here instead of pressing the physical Home button. (That's handy when your Home button gets sticky, too.)

- **Device.** Tap this button to open a palette of six functions that would otherwise require you to grasp the phone or push its tiny physical buttons (above, right). There's Rotate Screen (you can tap this instead of turning the phone 90 degrees), Lock Screen (instead of pressing the Sleep switch), Volume Up and Volume Down (instead of pressing the volume keys), and Mute/Unmute (instead of flipping the small Mute switch on the side).

  If you tap More, you get some bonus buttons. They include Shake (does the same as shaking the phone to undo typing), Screenshot (as though you'd pressed the Sleep and Home buttons together),

Multitasking (brings up the app switcher, as though you'd double-pressed the Home button), and Gestures.

That Gestures button opens up a peculiar palette that depicts a hand holding up two, three, four, or five fingers. When you tap, for example, the three-finger icon, you get three blue circles on the screen. They move together. Drag one of them (with a stylus, for example), and the phone thinks you're dragging three fingers on its surface. Using this technique, you can operate apps that require multiple fingers dragging on the screen.

- **Custom.** Impressively enough, you can actually define your own gestures. On the AssistiveTouch screen, tap one of the + buttons, and then Create New Gesture to draw your own gesture right on the screen, using one, two, three, four, or five fingers.

For example, suppose you're frustrated in Maps because you can't do the two-finger double-tap that means "zoom out." On the Create New Gesture screen, get somebody to do the two-finger double-tap for you. Tap Save and give the gesture a name—say, "2 double tap."

From now on, "2 double tap" shows up on the Custom screen, ready to trigger with a single tap by a single finger or stylus.

> **TIP:** Apple starts you off with some useful predefined gestures in Custom, each of which might be difficult for some people to trigger the usual ways. First, there's Pinch, the two-finger pinch or spread gesture you use to zoom in and out of photos, maps, web pages, PDF documents, and so on. Drag either one of the two handles to stretch them apart. Drag the connecting line to move the point of stretchiness.
>
> Then there's 3D Touch (on the iPhone 6s models, that's a hard-press). And there's Double Tap (two quick presses in the same spot).

Touch Accommodations

In iOS 9, Apple has added even more options to accommodate people who find it difficult to trigger precise taps on the touchscreen. For example, these options are new:

- **Touch Accommodations** is the master switch for all three of the following options.

- **Hold Duration** requires that you keep your finger on the screen for an amount of time that you specify (for example, 1 second) before the iPhone registers a tap. That feature neatly eliminates accidental taps when your finger happens to bump the screen.

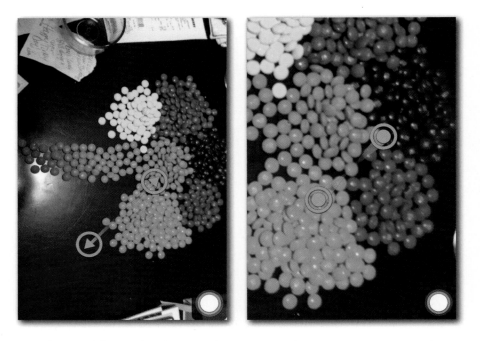

When Hold Duration is turned on, a countdown cursor appears at your fingertip, showing with a circular graph how much longer you have to wait before your touch "counts."

- **Ignore Repeat** ignores multiple taps that the screen detects within a certain window—say, 1 second. If you have, for example, a tremor, this is a great way to screen out accidental repeated touches or repeated letter-presses on the onscreen keyboard.

- **Tap Assistance** lets you indicate whether the location of a tap should be the *first spot you touch* or the *last spot*. The Use Final Touch Location option means you can put your finger down in one spot, and then fine-tune its position on the glass anytime within the countdown period indicated by the timer cursor. Feel free to adjust the timer window using the controls here.

3D Touch

The 3D Touch option (page 5) may be the hot new feature of the iPhone 6s family. But it may also drive you crazy.

Here you can turn the feature off, or just adjust the threshold of pressure (Light, Medium, Firm) required to trigger a "3D touch." (Apple even gives you a sample photo thumbnail to practice on, right on this screen, so you can gauge which degree of pressure you like best.)

Keyboard

The first option here controls whether or not the onscreen keyboard's keys turn into CAPITALS when the Shift key is pressed; see page 64.

The others control what happens when you've hooked up a physical keyboard to your iPhone—a Bluetooth keyboard, for example:

- **Key Repeat.** Ordinarily, holding down a key makes it repeat, so that you can type things like "auuuuuuuuuuuggggggh!" or "xxxxx." These two sliders govern the repeating behavior: how long you must hold down a key before it starts repeating (to prevent triggering repetitions accidentally), and how fast each key spits out characters once the spitting has begun.

- **Sticky Keys** lets you press multiple-key shortcuts (involving keys like Shift, Option, Control, and ⌘) one at a time instead of all together. (The Sound option ensures that you'll get an audio beep to confirm that the keyboard has understood.)

  Toggle With Shift Key gives you the flexibility of turning Sticky Keys on and off at will. Whenever you want to turn on Sticky Keys, press the Shift key five times in succession. You'll hear a special clacking sound effect alerting you that you just turned on Sticky Keys. (Repeat the five presses to turn Sticky Keys off again.)

Shake to Undo

In most of Apple's apps, you can undo your most recent typing or editing by giving the iPhone a quick shake. (You're always asked to confirm.) This is the On/Off switch for that feature—handy if you find yourself triggering Undo accidentally.

Vibration

In iOS 9, for the first time, you have a master Off switch for all vibrations that the phone makes. Alarms, notifications, confirmations—all of it.

As Apple's lawyers cheerfully point out on this screen, turning off vibrations also means you won't get buzzy notifications of "earthquake, tsunami, and other emergency alerts." Goodness!

Call Audio Routing

When a call comes in, where do you want it to go? To your headset? Directly to the speakerphone? Or the usual (headset unless there's no headset)? Here's where you make a choice that sticks, so you don't have to make it each time a call rings.

Home Button

If you have motor-control problems of any kind (sleep deprivation and overdoing it at the bachelor party come to mind), you might welcome this enhancement. It's an option to widen the time window for registering a double-press or triple-press of the Home button. If you choose Slow or Slowest, the phone accepts double- and triple-presses spaced far and farther apart, rather than interpreting them as individual presses a few seconds apart.

Reachability

Reachability is the feature described on page 21, the one that brings the top half of the screen downward when you double-touch (not fully press) the Home button. It's designed to let you reach things on the top of the screen while holding one of the larger iPhones with only one hand. If you find yourself triggering this feature accidentally, you'll be happy to know that this Off switch awaits.

Hearing Assistance

The next options in Settings→General→Accessibility are all dedicated to helping people with hearing loss.

Hearing Aids

A cellphone is bristling with wireless transmitters, which can cause interference and static if you wear a hearing aid. But the iPhone offers a few solutions.

First, try holding the phone up to your ear normally when you're on a call. If the results aren't good, see if you can switch your hearing aid from M mode (acoustic coupling) to T mode (telecoil). If so, turn on Hearing Aid mode (iPhone 5 and later), which makes it work better with T-mode hearing aids.

This settings panel also lets you "pair" your phone with a Bluetooth hearing aid. These wireless hearing aids offer excellent sound but eat hungrily through battery charges.

Hearing aids bearing the "Made for iPhone" logo work especially well—they sound great and don't drain the battery.

LED Flash for Alerts

If you're deaf, you know when the phone is ringing—because it vibrates, of course. But what if it's sitting on the desk, or it's over there charging? This option lets you know when you're getting a call, text, or notification by blinking the flash on the back of the phone—the very bright LED light.

Mono Audio

If you're deaf in one ear, then listening to any music that's a stereo mix can be frustrating; you might be missing half the orchestration or the vocals. When you turn on the Mono Audio option in Settings→General→Accessibility, the iPhone mixes everything down so that the left and right channels contain the same monaural playback. Now you can hear the entire mix in one ear.

> **TIP:** This is also a great feature when you're sharing an earbud with a friend, or when one of your earbuds is broken.

Phone Noise Cancellation

iPhone models 5 and later have three microphones scattered around the body. In combination, they offer extremely good background-noise reduction when you're on a phone call. The microphones on the top and back, for example, listen to the wind, music, crowd noise, or other ambient sound and subtract that ambient noise from the sound going into the main phone mike.

You can turn that feature off here—if, for example, you experience a "pressure" in your ear when it's operating.

Balance Slider

The L/R slider lets you adjust the phone's stereo mix, in case one of your ears has better hearing than the other.

Media (Subtitle Options)

These options govern Internet videos that you play in the iPhone's Videos app (primarily those from Apple's own iTunes Store.)

- **Subtitles & Captioning.** The iPhone's Videos app lets you tap the 💬 button to see a list of available subtitles and captions. Occasionally, a movie also comes with specially written Subtitles for the Deaf and Hard of Hearing (SDH). Tap **Subtitles & Captioning→Closed Captions + SDH** if you want that 💬 menu to list them whenever they're available.

  The **Style** option gives you control over the font, size, and background of those captions, complete with a preview. (Tap the ⬚ button to view the preview, and the sample caption, at full-screen size.) The **Custom** option even lets you dream up your own font, size, and color for the type; a new color and opacity of the caption background; and so on.

- **Audio Descriptions.** This new option is for Internet movies that come, or may someday come, with a narration track that describes the action for the blind.

Guided Access (Kiosk Mode)

It's amazing how quickly even tiny tots can master the iPhone—and how easily they can muck things up with accidental taps.

Guided Access solves that problem rather tidily. It's kiosk mode. That is, you can lock the phone into one app; the victim cannot switch out of it. You can even specify which *features* of that app are permitted. Never again will you find your Home screen icons accidentally rearranged or text messages accidentally deleted.

Guided Access is also great for helping out people with motor-control difficulties—or teenagers with self-control difficulties.

To turn on Guided Access, open **Settings→General→Accessibility→Guided Access**; turn the switch **On**.

Now a **Passcode Settings** button appears. Here's where you protect Guided Access so the little scamp can't shut it off—at least not without a four-digit password (**Set Guided Access Passcode**) or your fingerprint.

You can also set a time limit for your kid's Guided Access. Tap **Time Limit** to set up an alarm or a spoken warning when time is running out.

Finally, the moment of truth arrives: Your kid is screaming for your phone.

Open whatever app you'll want to lock in place. Press the Home button three times fast. The Guided Access screen appears. At this point, you can proceed in any of three ways:

- **Declare some features off limits.** With your finger, draw a circle around each button, slider, and control you want to deactivate. The phone converts your circle to a tidy rectangle; you can drag its corners to adjust its size, drag inside the rectangle to move it, or tap the ⊗ to remove it if you change your mind or want to start again.

  Once you enter Guided Access mode, the controls you've enclosed appear darkened (below, right). They no longer respond—and your phone borrower can't get into trouble.

- **Change settings.** If you tap Options, you get additional controls. You can decide whether or not your little urchin is allowed to press the Sleep/Wake Button or the Volume Buttons when in Guided Access mode. If you want to hand the phone to your 3-year-old in the back seat to watch baby videos, you'll probably want to disable the touchscreen altogether (turn off Touch) and prevent the picture from rotating when the phone does (turn off Motion).

Here, too, is the Time Limit switch. Turn it on to view hours/minutes dials. At the end of this time, it's no more fun for Junior.

- **Begin kiosk mode.** Tap Start.

Later, when you get the phone back and you want to use it normally, triple-press the Home button again; enter your four-digit password or offer your fingerprint. At this point, you can tap Options to change them, Resume to go back into kiosk mode, or End to return to the iPhone as you know it.

> **TIP:** If you use any of the other accessibility features described in this chapter, you may be dismayed to discover that you can no longer use the triple-clicking of the Home button to open the on/off buttons for those features. The triple-click has been taken over by Guided Access!
>
> Fortunately, Apple has already anticipated this problem. If you turn on Accessibility Shortcut on the Guided Access screen of Settings (see the next page), then triple-clicking produces the usual list of accessibility features—and Guided Access is on that list, too, ready to tap.

The Instant Screen-Dimming Trick

The Accessibility settings offer one of the greatest shortcuts of all time: the ability to dim your screen, instantly, with a triple-click on the Home button. You don't have to open the Control Center, visit Settings, or fuss with a slider; it's instantaneous. This trick is Apple's gift to people who go to movies, plays, nighttime drives, or anywhere else where full screen brightness isn't appropriate, pleasant, or comfortable—and digging around in the Control Center or Settings takes too much time.

It's a bunch of steps to set up, but you have to take them only once. After that, the magic is yours whenever you want it. It's really worth doing.

Ready? Here's the setup.

1. **Open** Settings→General→Accessibility. **Turn on** Zoom.

    At this point, the magnifying lens may appear. But you're interested in dimming, not zooming, so:

2. **Tap the white handle at the bottom of the magnifying lens; in the shortcut menu, tap** Zoom Out **(facing page, left).**

    Now the magnifying lens is gone.

3. **Scroll down; tap** Zoom Filter**; tap** Low Light **(below, right). Tap** Zoom **(in the upper left) to return to the previous panel.**

You've just set up the phone to dim the screen whenever Zooming is turned on. Now all you have to do is teach the phone to enable Zooming whenever you triple-click the Home button.

4. **In the top-left corner, tap** Accessibility**.**

You return to the main Accessibility screen. Scroll to the very bottom.

5. **Tap** Accessibility Shortcut**; make sure that** Zoom **is the only selected item.**

At this point, you can press the Home button to get out of Settings.

Zoom Out	None
Full Screen Zoom	Inverted
Resize Lens	Grayscale
Choose Filter	Grayscale Inverted
Show Controller	Low Light ✓
Zoom Region Window Zoom >	Zoom Region Window Zoom >

From now on, whenever you triple-click the Home button, you turn on a gray filter that cuts the brightness of the screen by 30 percent. (Feel free to fine-tune the dimness of your new Insta-Dim setting at that point, using the Control Center; see page 47.) It doesn't save you any battery power, since the screen doesn't think it's putting out any less light. But it does give you instant darkening when you need it in a hurry—like when a potentially important text comes in while you're in the movie theater.

Triple-click again to restore the original brightness, and be glad.

Accessibility Shortcut

Burrowing all the way into the Settings→General→Accessibility screen is quite a slog when all you want to do is flip some feature on or off. Therefore, you get this handy shortcut: a fast triple-press of the Home button.

That action produces a little menu, in whatever app you're using, with on/off switches for the iPhone's various accessibility features.

It's up to you, however, to indicate which ones you want on that menu. That's why you're on this screen—to turn on the features you want to appear on the triple-press menu. Your options are VoiceOver, Invert Colors, Zoom, AssistiveTouch, Switch Control, and Grayscale.

> **TIP:** If you choose only one item here, then triple-pressing the Home button won't produce the menu of choices. It will just turn that one feature on or off.

PART TWO

Pix, Flix & Apps

Chapter 7
Songs, Videos & Apple Music

Chapter 8
The Camera

Chapter 9
All About Apps

Chapter 10
The Built-In Apps

7

Songs, Videos & Apple Music

Of all the iPhone's talents, its iPoddishness may be the most successful. This function, after all, gets the most impressive battery life (40 to 80 hours of playback, depending on the model). There's enough room on your phone to store thousands of songs.

In iOS 9, the Music app got a huge makeover. Five tabs now greet you across the bottom: My Music, For You, New, Radio, and Connect.

Some of them are useful only if you've subscribed to Apple Music, Apple's $10-a-month music service—but not all of them. iTunes Radio, for example, means that you'll never run out of music to listen to—and you'll never pay a penny for it.

NOTE: If you're not interested in paying for an Apple Music subscription, you can *hide* the two tabs that you'll never use (For You and New). To do that, tap For You; on the ad for Apple Music, tap No Thanks. Confirm by tapping Yes.

At this point, the For You and New tabs disappear—and a new tab, Playlists, takes their place. This is the Playlists screen described on page 225—more easily accessible than before.

Incidentally, you can always restore the original set of tabs. Open Settings→Music and turn on Show Apple Music.

The bottom line: Your copy of the Music app might show you either of two different sets of tabs. Complicated? Yes. Anyway , this chapter is written as though you *haven't* hidden the Apple Music tabs.

Apple Music

The Apple Music service, which debuted in 2015, is a rich stew of components. For $10 a month (or $15 for a family of six), you get all of the following.

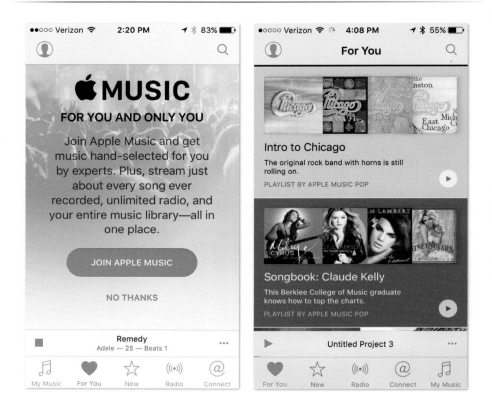

Unlimited Streaming Music

You can listen to any band, album, or song in the Apple Music library of 30 million songs—on demand, no ads. It's not like listening to a radio station, where someone else is programming the music; **you** program the music.

On the other hand, this is not like Apple's traditional music store, where you pay $1 per download and you **own** the song. If you ever stop paying Apple the $10 a month, the music stops. You're left with nothing.

If you do subscribe, you can tell Siri things like, "Play the top songs of 2005" or "Play some good running music" or "Play some Taylor Swift."

Nor are you obligated to do all your music programming manually. Apple Music comes equipped with ready-made playlists, prepared by human editors, in all kinds of categories. There are sets of starter songs by various singers ("Intro to Sarah McLachlan"), playlists by genre and era, and playlists for specific activities like Waking Up, Running, Getting It On, and even Breaking Up.

You can freely mix the songs you're renting with the music you actually own. You can even download songs that you don't own for playback when you have no Internet connection (as long as you're still paying your $10 a month).

Beats 1 Radio

Apple has launched a "global, 24-hour Internet radio station" called Beats 1. (It actually broadcasts live for only 12 hours a day, and then repeats.)

Listening is free, even to nonpayers.

Live DJs introduce songs and comment on the singers, just as on FM radio stations. Of course, you have no input on the style of music you hear on Beats 1, and you can't pause, rewind, fast-forward, or save anything you hear for later listening. It's old-style radio, offering the magic of serendipity.

Connect

Connect is an Instagram-like tab in the new Music app. Here, bands that Apple thinks you'll like (or that you choose manually) can promote themselves by posting songs, videos, and other material. You can ♡ these posts, share them, or comment on them.

iTunes Match

iTunes Match, which dates back to 2011, is a cloud-based version of your iTunes library, available to any of your Apple devices. For $25 a year, you can stream Apple's copies of any song files you actually own—ripped from CDs or even acquired illegally. The advantages: First, you save a lot of space on your phone. Second, you can play them on any Apple gadget you own. Third, the versions Apple plays are often of higher quality than your originals.

iTunes Match continues as a separate service for non–Apple Music subscribers (the song limit is now 100,000 songs). But if you do subscribe to Apple Music, in effect you get iTunes Match automatically.

Now then: If you're not an Apple Music subscriber, only two of the Music app's tabs are useful to you: **My Music** and **Radio**. The others are part of Apple Music, and you can ignore them—or hide them, as described in the Note on page 215.

My Music

Here's all the music you've actually chosen yourself.

In the old days, this meant "music files that are actually on your phone." If you have an Apple Music membership, though, you'll also see *online* songs listed here that you've added to your own personal catalog.

The controls of the My Music world, from top to bottom, go like this:

- **Account (👤).** Tap this little button to open a screen full of your account information: a list of musicians you're "following" (on the Connect tab), your Apple Music account details, a **Redeem** button for cashing in on a gift card, and so on.

- **Library/Playlists.** The two tabs at the top determine what you're looking at: Your world of songs, or your world of playlists (page 224). (If you've turned off Apple Music, this toggle switch doesn't appear.)

- **Search.** Here's how you pluck one song, performer, or album out of your haystack of music—either your own songs or, if you're an Apple Music subscriber, all 30 million of Apple's. (The little ⊘ icon in the search bar lets you call up recent searches, to save you re-typing.)

- **Shuffle All (⤬).** Tap to begin playing your music, instantly, in a random order.

- **Recently Added.** Why, by golly, this area offers lists of music you've recently added to your collection.

- **Artists/Albums/Songs...** Here's where things get interesting. This heading opens a pop-up menu that determines how your list of songs is sorted (shown on the facing page). You can choose **Artists** (that is, singers or bands), **Albums**, **Songs**, **Music Videos**, **Genres**, **Composers**, or **Compilations**. (A *compilation* is one of those albums that's been put together from many different performers. You know: "Zither Hits of the 1600s," "Kazoo Classics," and so on.)

> **TIP:** In **Settings→Music**, you can specify whether the album list is sorted by *album name* or *performer name*.

At the very bottom, you also get an **Only Offline Music** switch, which hides music that actually sits on the Internet. What's left: songs that are physically on your phone, capable of playback even in airplane mode.

- **A–Z Index.** When you scroll your list of music, a vertical alphabet appears on the right side of the screen. It's a tappable index that lets you jump directly to, for example, the T's without spending the rest of your life scrolling.

The Options Panel

Next to each item in this master list (below, left), an ellipsis appears (•••). It opens a panel of options (right).

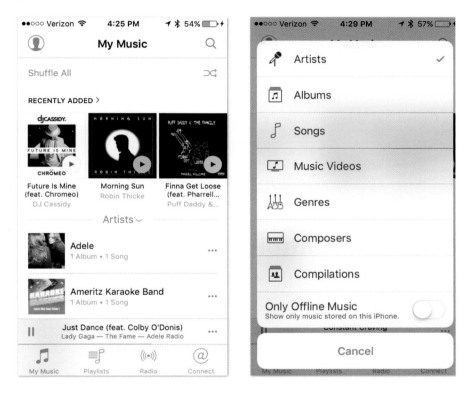

The choices depend on whether you've tapped some music that you *own* or that you've found in Apple Music's collection. But here's the gist:

- ♡. Adds this song, album, or performer to your Favorites (page 222).

- ((•)). Uses this song, album, or performer as the seed for a new iTunes Radio station (page 230).

- ⬆. Opens the Share sheet (page 330), so that you can send a link to this song via email, text message, Facebook or Twitter post, and so on. (The recipients can listen to the full song *if* they're Apple Music subscribers.)

- **Play Next.** Schedules this item to play next, after whatever song is playing now.

- **Add to Up Next.** Behind the scenes, the Music app maintains a temporary, ever-changing playlist called Up Next. At any point, you can add some music to the end of this list using this command. (See page 227 for more on Up Next.)

- **Add to a Playlist** lets you add this item to a playlist you've made yourself.

- **Create Genius Playlist** uses this music as the "seed" for an auto-generated playlist of similar tunes; see page 231.

- **Make Available Offline.** If this song is stored only online (as most Apple Music is), this command copies it to your phone for playback when you don't have an Internet connection.

- **Delete.** Yes, you can delete a song/album right from here.

NOTE: There used to be entries here for iTunes U (lectures, lab reports, movies, and other educational materials supplied by universities) and podcasts. They're gone now, because Apple would prefer that you use its dedicated iTunes U and Podcasts apps.

Playback Control

When you tap the name of a song, album, playlist, or whatever, it plays. You can control playback—skip, rewind, and so on—in any of several ways.

The Mini-Player

On almost every screen of the Music app, you get a miniature controller at the bottom of the screen, like the one shown on the facing page at left (very bottom).

It identifies the current song, singer, and album, and it offers you the most important playback control of all: **||** (Pause). Across from it, the ••• button awaits; it summons an Options panel like the one shown on the previous page at right.

The Now Playing Screen

If you tap (or drag upward on) the mini-player, though, the Now Playing screen appears. This time, there's room for *all* the controls you need to control music playback. Here are its contents, from top to bottom:

- ⊘ **(Close).** At the top-left corner of the screen, this button means "Close Now Playing—return to the list from whence this song came."

TIP: You can also swipe down to close this screen.

- **Album art.** Most of the screen is filled with a bright, colorful shot of the original CD's album art. (If none is available—if you're listening to a song *you* wrote, for example—you see a big gray generic musical-note picture. You can drag or paste in an album-art graphic—one you found on the web, for example—in iTunes.)

- **Scrubber.** This slider reveals two useful statistics: how much of the song you've heard, in minutes and seconds (at the left end) and how much time remains (at the right end).

  To operate the slider, drag the tiny, vertical-line handle with your finger. You can jump to any spot in the song this way. (Tapping directly on the spot you want to hear doesn't work.)

TIP: This is very cool—you can control the *speed* of the scrubbing, using this highly secret trick:

Drag the little handle *upward or downward;* the song title changes to show you the new scrubbing speed. As your finger slides farther from the handle, it says "Hi-Speed Scrubbing," then "Half-Speed Scrubbing," then "Quarter-Speed Scrubbing," and then "Fine Scrubbing." The point is to get finer control over your scrubbing, making it easier to locate a specific spot in the tune.

- **Song info.** Center top: the artist name, track name, and album name.

- **Rating.** If you tap the song's name, it disappears. It's replaced by a row of five light-gray dots.

  This is your opportunity to *rate* the song, by tapping one of the five dots. If you tap dot number three, for example, the first three dots all turn into stars. You've just given that song three stars. When you next sync your iPhone with your computer, the ratings you've applied magically show up on the same songs in iTunes. (Tap the album cover to restore the song info and hide the rating.)

- ♡ **(Like).** If you've signed up for the $10-a-month Apple Music service (or think you might someday), tap this heart anywhere it appears in your iPhone Music archipelago. It tells Apple that you like this song, which will affect what kinds of music Apple offers on the For You tab (page 229).

- ◄◄, ►► **(Previous, Next).** These buttons work exactly as they do on an iPod: Tap ◄◄ to skip to the beginning of this song (or, if you're already at the beginning, to the previous song). Tap ►► to skip to the next song.

> **TIP:** If you're wearing the earbuds, then you can pinch the clicker *twice* to skip to the next song.

  If you *hold down* one of these buttons, you rewind or fast-forward. You hear the music speeding by, without turning the singer into a chipmunk. The rewinding or fast-forwarding accelerates if you keep holding the button down.

- **Play/Pause button.** The Pause button beneath the album photo looks like this ‖ when the music is playing. If you do pause, then the button turns into the Play button (►).

> **TIP:** If you're wearing the earbuds, then pinching the microphone clicker serves the same purpose: It's a Play/Pause control.
>
> Incidentally, when you plug in headphones, the iPhone's built-in speaker turns off, but when you unplug the headphones, your music pauses instead of switching abruptly back to the speaker.

- ☰ **(Up Next).** Tap here to open the Up Next playlist (page 227).

- **Volume.** You can drag the round handle of this slider (bottom of the screen) to adjust the volume—or you can use the volume buttons on the left side of the phone.

- 🔼 **(Share).** Tap here, and then confirm with Share Song, to send a link to this song (using any of the transmission methods described on page 330) to other people. If they're Apple Music subscribers, they can play it on the spot.

- ⤫ **(Shuffle).** Ordinarily, the iPhone plays the songs in an album sequentially, from beginning to end. But if you love surprises, tap here so it changes to say Shuffle All. Now the album plays in random order.

TIP: You can no longer shake the whole iPhone to shuffle—to start playing another random song. The Apple killjoys removed that feature a couple of versions ago.

- ⮂ **(Loop).** If you *really* love a certain album or playlist, you can command the iPhone to play it over and over again, beginning to end.

  If you tap this button once, it darkens; the app will now play this *album or playlist* over and over. If you tap again, a tiny digit 1 appears on the icon; now you're in Repeat Song mode, and only *this song* will repeat. Tap a third time to turn all repeating off.

NOTE: The Loop (Repeat) button is, to be sure, hard to find in the new Music app. If you find that every song you play loops endlessly until you manually switch to another song, well, you're not alone—and now you know what button to tap for the fix.

By the way, there's nothing to stop you from turning on Repeat *and* Shuffle, meaning that you'll hear the songs on the album played endlessly, but never in the same order twice.

- **... (Options).** As always in this app, this button is like a shortcut menu of options that might apply at the moment. See page 219.

Control Center

The Control Center, of course, is the panel that appears when you swipe up from the bottom of the screen (page 47). It includes playback controls, too, as you can see on the previous page. Keep that in mind. It means that you never have to go to the Music app just to change tracks if you're busy doing something else on the phone.

Playback While Locked

Once you're playing music, it keeps right on playing, even if you press the Home button or change apps. After all, the only thing more pleasurable than surfing the web is surfing it with a Beach Boys soundtrack.

If you've got something else to do—like jogging, driving, or performing surgery—tap the Sleep/Wake switch to turn off the screen. The music keeps playing, but you'll save battery power.

> **TIP:** Even with the screen off, you can still adjust the music volume (use the volume buttons on the earbud clicker or the buttons on the side of the phone), pause the music (pinch the earbud clicker once), or advance to the next song (pinch it twice).

What's cool is that if you wake the phone (press Home or the Sleep switch), the Lock screen looks like the Now Playing screen. It has all the same controls—even ♡ and ⬆—so you can manage the playback without even having to fully wake the phone.

If a phone call comes in, the music fades, and you hear your chosen ringtone—through your earbuds, if you're wearing them. Squeeze the clicker on the earbud cord or tap the Sleep/Wake switch to answer the call. When the call ends, the music fades back in, right where it left off.

Voice Control

There's one more way to control your playback—a way that doesn't involve taking your eyes off the road or leaving whatever app you're using. You can control your music playback by voice command, using Siri. See Chapter 4.

Playlists

A *playlist* is a group of songs you've placed together, in a sequence that makes sense to you. One might consist of party tunes; another might hold romantic dinnertime music; a third might be drum-heavy workout cuts.

Creating Playlists on the Phone

To play with playlists, start on the My Music tab. Tap Playlists at the very top of the screen—or the Playlists tab at the bottom, if you've turned Apple Music off (see the Note on page 215).

Here are all the playlists you've ever created—which might be zero. If this is your first playlist, click the giant Create a Playlist button and skip to step 2. Otherwise:

1. **Tap New.**

   It's a tiny button, just the word New, just beneath the words All Playlists (and off to the right). When you tap it, a new screen appears, where you can name and set up your new playlist.

2. **Type a name for your playlist**.

   You can also, at this moment, tap the little 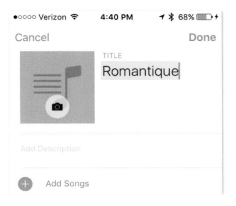 button to take, or choose, a photo to represent this playlist. Or even type a description.

3. **Tap Add Songs.**

   The Add Music screen appears. It offers the usual ways to view your collection: Artists, Albums, Songs, Genres, or Playlists (that is, existing ones).

4. **Tap the category you want for finding your first song; drill down until you find the music you want to add.**

   For example, if you first tap Albums, you then see a list of your albums; tap ⊕ to add the entire album to the new playlist. Or tap the album's name to view the songs on it—and then ⊕ next to a song's name to add *it* to the list.

5. Keep adding music to the playlist until you're satisfied.

You can keep tapping ⊕ buttons, without leaving this screen; each turns into a checkmark to indicate that you've added it (below, left). A playlist can be infinitely long; we're way past the days of worrying about how much will fit on a cassette tape or a CD, baby.

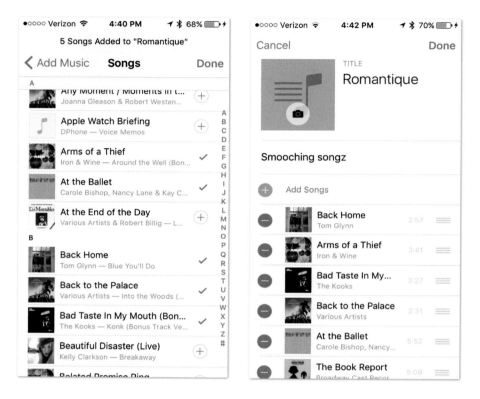

6. Tap every Done button until you're back on the Playlists screen.

Your newly minted playlist is now at the list, ready to play!

Using Playlists

To see what songs or videos are in a playlist, tap its name (not its picture). You now arrive at a Playlist details screen, where your tracks are listed for your inspection. To start playing a song once you see it in the Playlist list, tap its name; you'll hear that song and all of the ones that follow it, in order.

Or tap the Shuffle button (⤨) to start random-order playback.

Here you can use a standard iOS convention: Anywhere you're asked to drill down from one list to another—from a playlist to the songs inside, for example—you can backtrack by *swiping from the left edge* of the phone into the screen.

Or do it the long way: Tap ‹ at the upper-left corner of the screen. That button's name always tells you what screen you just came from (My Music, for example).

Once you're here, you can have all kinds of fun:

- **To delete or rearrange the songs:** Tap Edit. Use the ☰ handles to drag the songs into a new sequence (previous page, right). Hit ⊖ to make a song disappear. (You're not deleting it from your phone—only from this playlist.) Tap Done.

- **To add more songs to the playlist:** Tap Edit. Tap Add Songs, and then proceed as described previously.

- **To rename the open playlist:** Tap Edit. Tap the Title and edit away. (Tap Done.)

- **To delete the playlist:** Tap the ••• to open the Options panel; tap Delete. Confirm by tapping Delete Playlist. (This same Options panel lets you add this playlist to *another* playlist, or to the Up Next playlist described next.)

Another kind of playlist lurks in the Music app: the Genius playlist. It's supposed to analyze all your music and then, at the click of a button, create a playlist containing other songs from your library that "sound great" with one particular "seed" song. (Basically, it clumps songs by their degree of rockiness.)

With the dawn of the Apple Music service, the importance of Genius playlists is slipping down the drain. This feature is a little hard to unearth in iOS 9, but if you're interested, see the free PDF appendix "Genius Playlists" on this book's "Missing CD" page at *www.missingmanuals.com*.

Up Next

Unless you're a professional DJ, you're probably happy to hear song after song played automatically, according to whatever album, playlist, or radio station they're in.

But the Up Next playlist gives you a degree of control without requiring the full project of programming a playlist.

The Up Next playlist always exists. If you tell Music to play an album, Up Next autofills with the songs on that album; if you're listening to all the music from a certain performer, Up Next displays what else you'll hear from that artist; and so on.

But you can also queue up music yourself, adding them to Up Next on your own schedule. The playback will plow through them in order.

Mastering this feature is by no means simple; the controls for using Up Next are scattered and unlabeled. But if you're patient and open-minded, here's the Up Next Missing Manual.

- **Add a song to Up Next.** Tap the ••• next to the name of any song, album, or playlist to open the Options panel (below, left). Tap either Play Next (to put this song at the *beginning* of the Up Next queue) or Add to Up Next (to put it at the *end* of whatever songs are in the Up Next playlist).

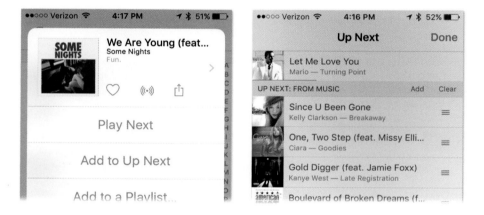

- **Play a song now.** Suppose you find some music you want to play right now. You don't care about the Up Next playlist.

  When you tap that item's name, the iPhone asks: "After playing this, do you want to play the songs you've added to Up Next?" If you hit Keep Up Next, you hear the new song without disturbing the Up Next list that will play afterward. If you hit Clear Up Next, the new music plays and then stops; you've nuked the current Up Next list.

View, Edit, or Clear the Up Next List

Most people probably never realize it, but you can actually look over the Up Next playlist in progress. You can rearrange or delete anything in it.

There's only one way to see the Up Next playlist, and it's pretty buried. You have to open the full-height Now Playing screen described on page 220, and then tap the ☰ button.

Once the list appears (previous page, right), here's the fun you can have:

- **Rearrange the songs** by dragging their ☰ handles up or down.

- **Remove a song** from the queue by swiping left on it to reveal the Remove button; tap it.

- **Clear the entire list** by tapping the Clear button; confirm by tapping Clear Up Next.

- **Add more music** to the list by tapping the Add button.

NOTE: At the top of the Up Next list, you'll find a history of all the music you've played recently. Fascinating (and possibly incriminating)! It's for reference (or re-playback) only; you can't clear it.

"For You" Tab

30 million is a lot of songs. You won't live long enough to hear them all. So Apple has supplied the For You tab of the Music app to present new songs, performers, and albums its algorithms think you'll like. (If you're not a paying subscriber, this tab is just an ad—for Apple Music.)

And how does the app know what kind of music you'll like? When you sign up for the service, you're shown dancing red circles bearing music-genre names. You're supposed to tap the ones you like, double-tap the ones you *really* like, and hold your finger down on the ones you don't like.

Then, of course, as you go through your life listening to music, you can always turn the ♡ button on or off to further fine-tune Apple's under-standing of your tastes.

"New" Tab

The New tab is also for paying subscribers only. It's lists of lists, as shown on the next page).

Scroll down long enough, and you'll find lists like New Music, Hot Tracks, Recent Releases, Top Songs, Hot Albums, Discovered on Connect, Apple Music Editors, Activities, Curators, Recommended Music Videos,

Summertime Playlists, New Artists, Spotlight on Sia, Alternative Essentials, and so on. Once again, the idea is to help you find new stuff you like.

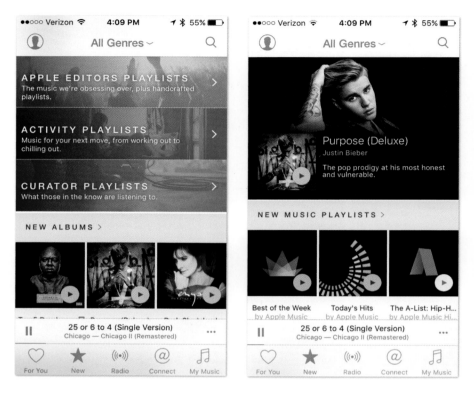

iTunes Radio

Your iPhone includes an amazing gift: your own radio station. Your own *empire* of radio stations, in fact.

On the Radio tab, at the top, you get eight "album covers" (next page, left). They represent ready-made "radio stations" that Apple has supplied for you. Tap the one called Pure Pop, for example, and your phone instantly begins playing the biggest current pop hits.

Scroll down to find dozens more ready-to-play, software-curated "radio stations" in every conceivable category: Country, NPR, ESPN, Oldies, Soul/ Funk, Chill, Indie, Classic Metal, Pop Workout, Kids & Family, Lullabies, Latin Pop, Classical, Reggae, and on and on. You can listen to them all, even if you're not an Apple Music subscriber.

You can hit ▶▶ to skip a song you're not enjoying—up to six songs an hour. (If you've subscribed to Apple Music, you can skip an *unlimited* number— and you don't hear any ads.)

One tap for instant music in a category of your choice? This feature is pretty fantastic—one of the iPhone's best, actually. Don't miss it.

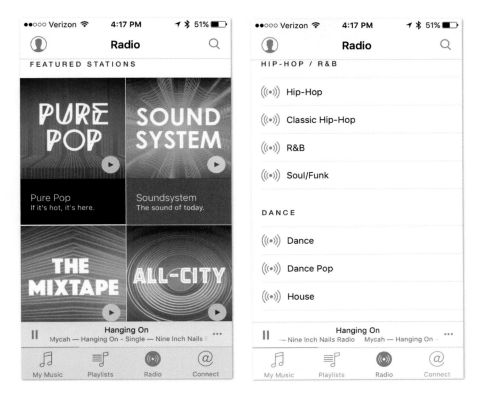

Custom Stations

The iTunes Radio service offers more than canned stations; you can create a new "station" instantly, based on any "seed" song you choose.

You don't get to choose the exact songs or singers you want to hear; you have to trust iTunes Radio to choose songs *based* on your chosen song, singer, or music genre. For example, if you choose Billy Joel as your "seed," you'll hear a lot of Billy Joel, but also a lot of other music that sounds more or less like his.

This feature has been gutted in iOS 9; there's no longer any screen that displays only the radio stations you've created, for example. But many of the old features are still here.

To set up a new "radio station" of your own, tap the ••• button next to any song, album, or performer name. On the Options panel (page 219), hit the Radio button ((•))).

You've just created a new station, and it begins instantly.

In exchange for all this magic, you have to listen to the occasional ad between songs (unless you subscribe to Apple Music, in which case you never hear ads).

The idea of a "seed song"–based radio service isn't new, of course. It's the same idea as Pandora, a website and app that has offered precisely the same features for years. But iTunes Radio is built in, it's incorporated with Siri and the Control Center, and it's part of Apple's larger ecosystem; that is, you can see your same set of "radio stations" on your Mac or PC (in the iTunes app), iPad, and Apple TV.

The Radio "Now Playing" Screen

As a station plays, you see a screen like the one described on page 220. It displays the cover picture for the song's album, the name of the song, the band, and the album name.

It does, however, offer a couple of unique controls:

- **Price.** Of course, Apple would be thrilled if you came across a song you liked so much you wanted to buy it. That's why the price button (**$1.29**, for example) is so prominent. When you tap it, the price changes to say **Buy Song**; tap again to download the song directly to your phone. Now you can listen to it again, on command, without being subject to the randomness of iTunes Radio.

- **Progress bar.** You can't fast-forward or rewind within a Radio song. This strip (hugging the bottom of the cover art) is just a graph that shows you where you are in the song. The numbers on either side show you how far you are into the song and how much is left to play.

- **★.** Tap to find the **Play More Like This** and **Play Less Like This** buttons, which let you fine-tune your "radio station," tailoring it precisely to your tastes.

  The third button, **Add to iTunes Wish List**, means, "I liked this song; maybe I'll buy it later." When you get home to your Mac or PC, open the iTunes program, click **Store** at the top right, and then click **My Wish List** (in the list at right). Here's the list you've been quietly building with your taps on the **Add to iTunes Wish List** button. You can listen to 1-minute previews, buy the complete songs, or delete them from the list if you've changed your mind.

Returning to a Custom Station

On the main Radio screen, tap **Recently Played**. Here's a list of all the iTunes Radio stations you've listened to, sorted by date—both Apple's canned stations and ones you've made yourself. Tap to start playing.

Siri and iTunes Radio

Truth is, there's an easier way to create a custom radio station: Just let Siri do the work. No matter what you're doing on the iPhone, you can hold down the Home button and say, for example, "Play some Billy Joel" or "Start Coldplay radio." Boom: The music begins.

Actually, Siri comes equipped to recognize a whole slew of commands pertaining to iTunes Radio.

Here's a sampler; you don't have to use these precise wordings:

- **Play the radio.**
- **What song is this?**
- **Play more like this.**
- **Don't play this song again.**
- **Pause the music. (Resume the music.)**
- **Skip this song.**
- **Add this song to my Wish List.**
- **Stop the radio.**

Speakers and Headphones

The iPhone's speaker is pretty darned good for such a tiny machine. But the world is full of better speakers—Bluetooth wireless speakers, car stereo systems, hi-fi TVs, and fancy earbuds and headphones. The iPhone is especially easy to use with them.

Bluetooth Wireless

You can buy amazingly small, powerful Bluetooth stereo speakers that receive your iPhone's music from as far as 20 or 30 feet away—made by Jawbone, Bose, and others.

There are also Bluetooth *headphones.* But when you shop, make sure the headphones say **A2DP stereo**; the headsets for making office phone calls and so on don't play *music* over Bluetooth.

‹ Settings   Bluetooth

Bluetooth   ⬤⬤

Now discoverable as "iPhone".

MY DEVICES

CAR MULTIMEDIA   Not Connected ⓘ

David's Apple W...   Not Connected ⓘ

OTHER DEVICES ⁎⁎

Bose Mini SoundLink

3:18   -2:01

Black Hole Sun

Soundgarden — Superunknown (20th Anniversary) — N

☆   ◀◀   ❚❚   ▶▶   ☰

◀━━━━━━━━⬤━━━━━━━━▶   ⬛

⬆ $0.69   •••

Soundgarden — Superunknown (20th Anniversary) — N

🔊)) iPhone

🔊⁂ Bose Mini SoundLink   ✓

Cancel

Once you've bought your headphones or speakers, you have to introduce them to the iPhone—a process called **pairing.**

From the Home screen, tap **Settings→Bluetooth**. Turn Bluetooth on (above, left); you see the Searching ⁎ animation as the iPhone wirelessly hunts for your headphones or speakers.

Grab them, turn them on, and start the pairing procedure, as described in the manual. Usually that means holding down a certain button until a tiny light starts flashing. At that point, the headphones' or speaker's name appears on the iPhone's screen.

TIP: If the headphones or speakers require a one-time passcode—it's usually 0000, but check the manual—the iPhone's keyboard appears, so you can type it in.

A couple of seconds later, it says Connected; now any sound the iPhone would ordinarily play through its speakers or earbuds now plays through the wireless 'phones or speakers. Not just music—which, in general, sounds amazing—but chirps, game sounds, and so on. Oh, and phone calls.

If your headset has a microphone, too, then you can even answer and make phone calls wirelessly. (There's an Answer button right on the headphones.)

Using Bluetooth wireless stereo does eat up your battery charge faster. But come on: listening to your music without wires, with the iPhone still in your pocket or bag? How cool is that?

Switching Among Speakers

When your iPhone has a connection to a wireless sound source—a Bluetooth speaker or AirPlay receiver, for example—you need some way to direct the music playback to it.

The answer is the ⬗ button. It's on the Control Center (previous page, top right). When you tap it, the iPhone offers a button for each speaker (previous page, lower right); to switch, tap the one you want.

Instantly, the sound begins flowing from your other source. Use the same method to switch back to the iPhone's speakers when the time comes.

AirPlay

There's another way to transmit audio wirelessly from the iPhone (and video, too): the Apple technology called AirPlay. You can buy AirPlay speakers, amplifiers, and TV sets. The Apple TV, of course, is the best-known AirPlay machine.

AirPlay is described on page 229, because most people use it to transmit video, not just audio. But the steps for transmitting to an AirPlay audio gadget are the same.

Familiar iPod Features

The iPhone has a long list of traditional iPod features for music playback. Most of these options all await in Settings→Music. (Shortcut: Tell Siri, "Open Music settings.")

EQ (Equalization)

Like any good music player, the iPhone offers an EQ function: a long list of presets, each of which affects your music differently by boosting or throttling various frequencies. One might bring out the bass to goose up your hip-hop tunes; another might emphasize the midrange for clearer vocals; and so on. ("Late Night" is especially handy; it lowers the bass so it thuds less. Your downstairs neighbors love it.)

Volume Limit

It's now established fact: Listening to a lot of loud music through earphones can damage your hearing. Pump it up today, pay for it tomorrow.

Portable music players can be sinister that way, because in noisy places like planes and city streets, people turn up the volume much louder than they would in a quiet place, and they don't even realize how high they've cranked it.

That's why Apple created this volume slider. It lets you limit the maximum volume level of the music.

In fact, if you're a parent, you can even lock down this control on your child's iPhone; it can be bypassed only with a password. Set the volume slider here, and then, in Settings→General→Restrictions, turn on Volume Limit, as described on page 235.

Sound Check

This feature smooths out the master volume levels of tracks from different albums, helping to compensate for differences in their recording levels. It doesn't deprive you of peaks and valleys in the music volume, of course—it affects only the baseline level.

Playing Music from Your Computer

Here's a trick you weren't expecting: You can store many terabytes of music on your Mac or PC upstairs—and play it on your phone in the kitchen downstairs. Or anywhere on the same Wi-Fi network, actually.

This nifty bit of wireless magic is brought to you by Home Sharing, a feature of the iTunes program.

Here's the setup: In iTunes on the Mac or PC, open Preferences. Click Sharing, and turn on "Share my library on my local network." (You can share only certain playlists, if you like.) Turn on Require password and enter your Apple account (iCloud) password. Click OK.

Now pick up your phone. At the bottom of the Settings→Music screen, log into Home Sharing using the same Apple ID and password.

Now you're ready to view the contents of your computer on the phone. You'd never guess where it's hiding.

In the Music app, on the My Music tab, open the sorting menu—the one that starts out saying Artists. At the very bottom, tap Home Sharing (shown on the next page at left); on the next screen, choose your computer's name (right).

That's it! Suddenly, your entire Music app is filled with the music from your computer's collection, rather than the music on the phone.

(Later, when you want to return to listening to the stuff on the phone itself, tap that same Artists button, and once again choose Home Sharing; but this time tap the name of your phone.)

The iTunes Store

Just as you can buy apps using the App Store app, you can also browse, buy, and download songs, TV shows, and movies using the iTunes Store app. Anything you buy gets autosynced back to your computer's copy of iTunes when you get home. Whenever you hear somebody mention a buy-worthy song, for example, you can have it within a minute.

To begin, open the *iTunes Store app.* The store you see here is modeled on the App Store described in Chapter 9. This time, the buttons at the bottom of the screen include Music, Movies, TV Shows, Search, and More.

When you tap Music, Movies, or TV Shows, the screen offers further buttons. For Music, for example, the scrolling horizontal rows of options might include New Releases, Recent Releases, Singles, and Pre-Orders.

(Beneath each list is a Redeem button, which you can tap if you've been given an iTunes gift certificate or a promo code; a Send Gift button, which lets you buy a song or video for someone else; and an Apple ID button, which can show you your current credit balance.)

TIP: You can't buy TV shows or movies on the cellular network—just in Wi-Fi hotspots. That's your cell company's way of saying, "We don't want you jamming up our precious cellular network with your hefty video downloads, bucko."

Note, by the way, that you can *rent* movies from the store instead of buying them outright. You pay only $3, $4, or $5 to rent (instead of $10 to $16 to buy). But once you start watching, you have only 24 hours to finish; after that, the movie deletes itself from your phone. (If you like, you can sync it to your Mac or PC to continue watching in iTunes—still within 24 hours.)

Genres | Featured | Charts | ☰

HIT SONGS
for 69¢

Ton
Ringtones and Ale

Greatest Hits: Hip-Hop   See All >

2Pac

DMX

THE NOTORIOUS B.I.G.
GREATEST HITS

RUN

Greatest... 🅴   The Best of 🅴   Greatest... 🅴   Gre
2Pac   DMX   The Notorio...   Run
                  DMX

Essential R&B Songs: Mastere...   See All >

Family Affair $0.69
Mary J. Blige — No More...

Rehab $1.29
Amy Winehouse — Back t...

You Know I'm No Good $1.29

♫ Music | 🎬 Movies | 🖥 TV Shows | 🔍 Search | ○○○ More

‹ Music   ☰

| All | Not on This iPhone |

Recent Purchases   250

All Songs   251

A

Aaron Tveit   14

Adam Chanler-Berat   9

Adele   1

Alan Woodrow   1

Alice Ripley   22

Ameritz Karaoke Band   1

Anna Kendrick   1

♫ Music | 🎬 Movies | 🖥 TV Shows | 🔍 Search | ○○○ More

To search for something in particular, tap Search. The keyboard appears. Type what you're looking for: the name of a song, movie, show, performer, or album, for example. At any time, you can stop typing and tap the name of a match to see its details. You can use the buttons across the top to restrict the search to one category (just songs or movies, for example).

TIP: Sometimes it's quicker to search directly from the Spotlight search bar, which can search the iTunes Store directly.

All these tools eventually take you to the details page of an album, song, or movie. For a song, tap its name to hear an instant 90-second preview (tap again to stop). For a TV show or movie, tap ▶ to watch the ad or the sneak preview.

If you're sold, then tap the price button to buy the song, show, or album (and tap BUY to confirm). Enter your Apple ID password when you're asked. (For movies, you can choose either BUY or RENT, priced accordingly.) At this point, your iPhone downloads the music or video you bought.

Purchased Items

Anything you buy from the iTunes Store winds up in the appropriate app on your iPhone. Open the Videos app to see your TV shows and movies or the Music app to see your songs. (Within the Music app, you can see everything you've bought: Tap Playlists, and then Purchased.)

In the iTunes Store app, at the bottom of the relevant screen (like Music or Movies), you can tap Purchased to see what you've bought. You get a pair of tabs:

- **All.** Here's a list of everything you've bought from iTunes, on your iPhone or any other Apple machine.

- **Not on This iPhone.** This is the cool part (previous page, right). Here you see not just the files on the iPhone in your hand, but things you've bought on other Apple gadgets—an album you bought on your iPad, for example, or a song you downloaded to your iPod Touch. (This assumes that you're using the same Apple ID on all your gizmos.)

   The beauty of this arrangement, of course, is that you can tap the name of something that's Not on This iPhone—and then download it (tap ☁). No extra charge.

TIP: If you prefer, you can direct your phone to download those purchases that you make on other gadgets automatically, without your having to tap Not on This iPhone. Visit Settings→iTunes & App Store, and turn on the switches for Music, Apps, and/or Books under Automatic Downloads. If you also turn on Use Cellular Data, then your phone will do this auto-downloading when you're in any 3G or LTE cellular Internet area, not just in a Wi-Fi hotspot.

More in "More"

Tapping More at the bottom of the screen offers these options:

- **Tones.** You can buy ready-made ringtones on this page—30-second slices of pop songs. (Don't ask what sense it makes to pay $1.30 for 30 seconds of a song, when you could buy the whole song for the same price.)

- **Genius.** Apple offers a list of music, movies, and TV shows for sale that it thinks you'll like, based on stuff you already have.

- **Purchased.** Here's another way to examine the stuff you've bought on all your devices. If you've turned on Apple's Family Sharing feature (page 528), you can also examine what stuff your family members have bought.

- **Downloads.** Shows you a progress bar for anything you've started to download.

> **TIP:** If you tap Edit, you'll see that you can *replace* any of the four iTunes Store bottom-row icons with one of the More buttons (Tones, Genius, Purchased, or whatever). Just drag one of these icons directly downward on *top* of an existing icon.

So you've downloaded one of the store's millions of songs, podcasts, TV shows, music videos, ringtones, or movies directly to your phone. Next time you sync, that song will swim *upstream* to your Mac or PC, where it will be safely backed up in iTunes. (And if you lost your connection before the iPhone was finished downloading, your Mac or PC will finish the job automatically. Cool.)

The Videos App

The iPhone has a separate app for playing TV shows, movies, and other videos. It's called, of all things, Videos.

If you can't figure out how to operate this app, then you shouldn't be allowed to have an iPhone. It's got three tabs: Movies, TV Shows, and Music Videos (or whatever video types you actually have).

> **NOTE:** If you've turned on Home Sharing (page 236), a fourth tab appears here called Shared. It's where you see your computers listed so you can view the videos contained on them instead of on your phone.

Tap to see the thumbnails of your videos; tap a video to see its plot summary, year of release, and so on. If it's a TV series, tap an episode in that series, if necessary. Either way, tap ▶ to begin watching.

> **NOTE:** If you see a ☁ icon on this screen, it means that this bought or rented movie is not actually on your phone. If you have a good Wi-Fi signal, you can watch it right now by streaming it (instead of downloading it to your phone).
>
> If you don't see that icon, then an Edit button appears instead. Tap it, and then tap the ✖ to delete it.

When you're playing video, anything else on the screen is distracting, so Apple hides the video playback controls. Tap the screen once to make them appear and again to make them disappear.

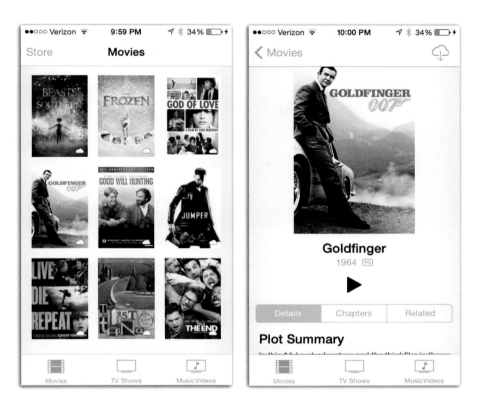

Here's what they do:

- **Done.** Tap this button, in the top-left corner, to stop playback and return to the master list of videos.

- **Scroll slider.** This progress indicator (top of the screen) is exactly like the one you see when you're playing music. You see the elapsed time, the remaining time, and a white, round handle that you can drag to jump forward or back in the video.

TIP: Drag your finger farther (up or down) from the handle to choose a faster or slower scrubbing speed.

- **Zoom/Unzoom.** In the top-right corner, a little ☐ or ☐ button appears if the video's shape doesn't exactly match your screen. Tap it to adjust the zoom level of the video, as described in a moment.

- **Play/Pause (▶/❚❚).** These buttons (and the earbud clicker) do the same thing to video as they do to music: alternate playing and pausing.

- **Previous, Next (⏮, ⏭).** Hold down your finger to rewind or fast-forward the video. The longer you hold, the faster the zipping. (When you fast-forward, you even get to hear the sped-up audio.)

If you're watching a movie from the iTunes Store, you may be surprised to discover that it comes with predefined chapter markers, just like a DVD. Internally, it's divided up into scenes. To see them, stop playback (tap Done); on the movie page, tap Chapters. Tap a chapter name to skip to that chapter marker—or tap ▶ to return to your original spot.

TIP: If you're wearing the earbuds, you can pinch the clicker *twice* to skip to the next chapter, or *three times* to go back a chapter.

- **Volume.** You can drag the round handle of this slider (bottom of the screen) to adjust the volume—or you can use the volume buttons on the left side of the phone.

- **Language (💬).** You don't see this button often. But when you do, it summons subtitle and alternate-language soundtrack options, just like a DVD player.

- **AirPlay (􀜍).** This symbol appears if you have an Apple TV (or another AirPlay-compatible electronic). Tap it to send your video playback to the TV, as described on page 244.

TIP: To delete a video, swipe leftward across its name in the Videos list; tap Delete to confirm. (You can always re-download it, of course.)

Zoom/Unzoom

The iPhone's screen is bright, vibrant, and stunningly sharp. Sometimes, however, it's not the right shape for videos.

Pre-HDTV shows are squarish, not rectangular. So when you watch older TV shows on a rectangular screen, you get black letterbox columns on either side of the picture.

Movies have the opposite problem. They're usually too wide for the iPhone screen. So when you watch movies, you may wind up with *horizontal* letterbox bars above and below the picture.

Some people are fine with that. After all, HDTVs have the same problem. At least when letterbox bars are onscreen, you know you're seeing the complete composition of the scene the director intended.

Other people can't stand letterboxing. You're already watching on a pretty small screen; why sacrifice some of that precious area to black bars?

Fortunately, the iPhone gives you a choice. If you double-tap the video as it plays, you zoom in, magnifying the image so it fills the entire screen. Or, if the playback controls are visible, you can also tap ⬚ or ⬚. Of course, now you're not seeing the entire original composition. You lose the top and bottom of old TV scenes, or the left and right edges of movie scenes.

Fortunately, if this effect chops off something important—some text, for example—the original letterbox view is just another double-tap away. (No zooming happens if the source material is already a perfect fit for the iPhone's screen shape.)

TV Output

When you crave a screen bigger than a few inches, you can play your iPhone's videos on a regular TV. All you need is the right cable: the Apple Digital AV Adapter. It carries both audio and video over a single cable (an HDMI cable).

It *mirrors* what's on the phone: your Home screen, email, Safari, and everything else. (Photos and presentations appear on your TV in pure, "video outputted" form, without any controls or other window clutter.)

AirPlay

Your iPhone also offers wireless projection, thanks to a feature called AirPlay. It transmits music or high-def video (with audio) from your iPhone to an Apple TV (or another AirPlay-equipped receiver) across the room. It's a fantastic way to send slideshows, movies, presentations, games, FaceTime calls, and websites to your TV for a larger audience to enjoy. Whatever's on the screen gets transmitted.

AirPlay receivers include the Apple TV (version 2 or later) and speakers, stereos, and receivers from Denon, Marantz, JBL, iHome, and so on. The phone and recent AirPlay receivers no longer have to be on the same Wi-Fi network, thanks to a feature called peer-to-peer AirPlay.

When you're playing a video or some music, open the Control Center (page 47), and tap ⌁ to see a list of available AirPlay receivers. If you have an Apple TV, tap its name, and then turn its Mirroring switch **On**.

That's it! Everything on the iPhone screen now appears on the TV or sound system. (The phone's status bar displays the ⌁ icon, so you don't wander off and forget that every move you make is visible to the entire crowd in the living room.)

> **TIP:** You can even turn a *Mac* into an AirPlay receiver. A $13 program called Reflector (*reflectorapp.com*) lets you view the iPhone's live image on the Mac's screen—and hear its sound. There's also a Record command, so you can create a movie of whatever you're doing on the phone.
>
> Reflector is great for trainers, teachers, or product demonstrators. And if you have a projector connected to the Mac, it's a fantastic way to project your iPhone onto a screen that's even bigger yet.
>
> Oh—and if you have a Mac running OS X Yosemite or later, a free trick awaits. Connect the phone to the Mac with its white USB cable. Open QuickTime Player. Choose **File→New Movie Recording**. From the little ∨ menu next to the ● button, choose **iPhone**.
>
> Now you're seeing the iPhone's screen on your Mac—and you can record it, project it, or screen-capture it for future generations!

8

The Camera

Incredible though it sounds, the iPhone is the number-one most popular camera model in the world. More photos are posted online from this phone than from any other machine in existence.

And no wonder; you've probably never seen pictures and movies look this good on a pocket gadget. With each new version of the iPhone, Apple improves its camera—and on the iPhone 6 and 6s models, it's unbelievably good. There's no optical zoom, but otherwise, the photos *can* look every bit as good as what you'd get from a dedicated camera. And the videos look amazing. They're even auto-stabilized—and the 6s models even shoot in 4K (four times the resolution of high-def video).

This chapter is all about the iPhone's ability to display photos, take new ones with its camera, and capture videos.

The Camera App

The little hole on the back of the iPhone, in the upper-left corner, is its camera.

On the latest iPhones, it's pretty impressive, at least for a cellphone cam. The iPhone 6 Plus and 6s Plus, for example, have two LED flashes, manual exposure controls, optical stabilization, and phase-detection autofocus (the same kind of very fast refocusing found in professional SLR cameras). These phones can shoot 10 shots a second and do amazingly well in low light.

The earlier iPhone models' cameras aren't quite as good, but they're still fine as long as your subject is still and well lit. Action shots may come out blurry, and dim-light shots may come out grainier.

Now that you know what you're in for, here's how it works.

Firing Up the Camera

Photographic opportunities are frequently fleeting; by the time you fish the phone from your pocket, wake it up, slide your finger to unlock it, press the Home button, find the Camera app, and wait for it to load, the magic moment may be gone forever.

Fortunately, there's a much quicker way to get to the Camera app when the phone is asleep:

1. **Press the Home button or Sleep switch to wake the phone.**

   A faint 📷 button appears at the lower-right corner of the screen.

2. **Flick the 📷 button upward.**

   The Camera app opens directly. This trick shaves an unbelievable amount of time off the old get-to-the-camera method.

> **TIP:** This Camera shortcut bypasses the "enter password" screen (if you've put a password or fingerprint restriction on your phone). Any random stranger who picks up your phone can jump directly into picture-taking mode.
>
> That stranger can't do much damage, though. She can take new photos, or delete the new photos taken during her session—but the photos you've *already* taken are off limits, and the features that could damage your reputation (editing, emailing, and posting photos) are unavailable in the Camera app. You have to open the Photos app to get to those—and that requires the phone password.

The first time you use the camera, you may be asked if it's OK to *geotag* your shots (record where you were when you took them). Unless you're a burglar or are having an affair, tap OK.

> **TIP:** Of course, there's a hands-free way to fire up the Camera app, too: Tell Siri, "Open camera."

The Six Modes of Camera

The Camera app can capture six kinds of photo and video. By swiping your finger horizontally anywhere on the screen, you switch among its modes. Here they are, from left to right:

- **Time-Lapse.** This mode speeds up your video, yet somehow keeps it stable. You can reduce a 2-hour bike ride into 20 seconds of superfast playback.

- **Slo-Mo** (iPhone 5s and later). Wow, what gorgeousness! You get a video filmed at 120 or 240 frames a second—so it plays back at one-quarter or one-eighth the speed, incredibly smoothly. Fantastic for sports, tender smiles, and cannonballs in the pool.

- **Video.** Here's your basic camcorder mode: 4K video on the 6s models, high definition on earlier ones.

- **Photo.** This is the primary mode for taking pictures. It's the one Camera chooses automatically when it opens.

- **Square.** You might wonder why Apple would go to the trouble of designating a whole special camera mode to taking square, not rectangular, pictures. Answer: Instagram, the crazy-popular app that takes square pictures and was sold to Facebook for $1 billion.

- **Pano.** Choose this mode to capture super wide-angle panoramic photos.

All of these modes are described in this chapter, but in a more logical order: still photos first, then video modes.

Photo Mode

Most people, most of the time, use the Camera app to take still photos.

It's a pretty great experience. The iPhone's screen is a huge digital-camera viewfinder. You can turn it 90 degrees for a wider or taller shot, if you like.

Tap to Focus

All right: You've opened the Camera app, and the mode is set to Photo. See the yellow box that appears briefly on the screen?

It's telling you where the iPhone will focus, the area it examines to calculate the overall brightness of the photo (exposure), and the portion that will determine the overall *white balance* of the scene (that is, the color cast).

If you're taking a picture of people, the iPhone's software tries to lock in on a face—up to 10 faces, actually—and calculate focus and exposure so that *they* look right.

But sometimes there are no faces—and dead center may not be the most important part of the photo. The cool thing is that you can tap somewhere

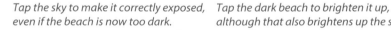

Tap the sky to make it correctly exposed, even if the beach is now too dark.   *Tap the dark beach to brighten it up, although that also brightens up the sky.*

else in the scene to move that yellow square—to recalculate the focus, exposure, and white balance.

Here's when you might want to do this tapping:

- **When the whole image looks too dark or too bright.** If you tap a *dark* part of the scene, the whole photo brightens up; if you tap a *bright* part, the whole photo darkens a bit. You're telling the camera, "Redo your calculations so *this* part has the best exposure; I don't really care if the rest of the picture gets brighter or darker." At that point, you can override the phone's exposure decision, as described below.

- **When the scene has a color cast.** If the photo looks, for example, a little bluish or yellowish, tap a different spot in the scene—the one you care most about. The iPhone recomputes its assessment of the white balance.

- **When you're in macro mode.** If the foreground object is very close to the lens—4 to 8 inches away—the iPhone automatically goes into *macro* (super closeup) mode. In this mode, you can do something really cool: You can *defocus the background.* The background goes soft, slightly blurry, just like the professional photos you see in magazines. Just make sure you tap the foreground object.

Adjust Exposure

When you tap the screen to set the focus point, a new control appears: a little yellow sun slider. That's your exposure control. Slide it up to brighten the whole photo, down to make things darker—an incredibly useful option.

Often, just a small adjustment is all it takes to add a little splash of light to a dim scene, or to dial the details back into a photo that's bright white.

To reset the slider to the iPhone's original proposed setting, tap the screen somewhere else, or just aim the phone at something different for a second.

The point is that the Camera app lets you fuss with the focus point and the exposure level independently.

Focus Lock/Exposure Lock

The iPhone likes to focus and calculate the exposure before it shoots. Cameras are funny that way.

That tendency, however, can get in your way when you're shooting something that moves fast. Horse races, divers. Pets. Kids on merry-go-rounds, kids on slides, kids in your house. By the time the camera has calculated the focus and exposure, which takes about a second, you've lost the shot.

Therefore, Apple provides a feature that's common on professional cameras but rare on phones: Auto-Exposure Lock and Autofocus Lock. They let you set up the focus and exposure in advance so that there's zero lag when you finally snap the shot.

To use this feature, point the camera at something that has the **same distance and lighting** as the subject-to-be. For example, focus at the base of the merry-go-round that's directly below where your daughter's horse will be. Or point at the bottom of the water slide before your son is ready to go.

Now hold down your finger on that spot on the iPhone's screen until you see the yellow square blink twice. When you lift your finger, the phrase "AE/AF Lock" appears to tell you that you've now locked in exposure and autofocus. (You can tap again to unlock it if you change your mind.)

At this point, you can drag the yellow sun slider to adjust that locked exposure, if you like.

Now you can snap photos, rapid-fire, without ever having to wait while your iPhone rethinks focus and exposure.

The LED Flash

As on most phones, the iPhone's "flash" is actually just a very bright LED light on the back. You can make it turn on momentarily, providing a small boost of illumination when the lights are low. (That's a *small* boost—it won't do anything for subjects more than a few feet away.)

The iPhone 5s and later models, in fact, have *two* LED flashes: one white, one amber. They go off simultaneously, with their strengths mixed properly so that the flashes' light matches the color temperature of the scene. (You might notice that before the phone takes the picture, it flashes once *before* the shot is captured. That's the camera's opportunity to *measure* the light color of the scene.)

This dual-flash trick makes a huge difference in the quality of your flash photos. (Especially skin tones, which may be why Apple calls the feature "True Tone.")

No matter which model you have, the flash comes set to Auto. It will turn on automatically when the scene is too dark, in the iPhone's opinion. But if you tap the ⚡ icon when it says **Auto**, two other options pop out: **On** (the flash will turn on no matter what the lighting conditions) and **Off** (the flash will not fire, no matter what).

> **TIP:** If you open the Control Center (page 47) and tap the flashlight icon (🔦), the phone's flash LED turns on and stays on. It's great when you want to see your key in the door or read the tiny type in a program or a menu.

The Screen Flash

The iPhone 6s models offer a "flash" on the **front**, too, for taking selfies. But it's not an LED lamp like the one on the back.

Instead, at the moment you take the shot, the **screen** lights up to illuminate your face. Better yet: It adjusts the color of the screen's "flash" to give your face the best flesh tones, based on a check of the ambient light color.

Of course, the normal iPhone screen is too tiny to supply much light, even at full brightness. So for the iPhone 6s and 6s Plus, Apple developed a custom chip with a single purpose: to overclock the screen. In selfie situations, the screen blasts at **three times** its usual full brightness, just for a fraction of a second. It is crazy bright.

It works fantastically well. Here, you can see the nuked-looking result from a traditional back LED "flash" (left) side-by-side with the iPhone 6s's front-facing screen flash (right).

Zooming In

The iPhone has a zoom, which can help bring you "closer" to the subject—but it's a **digital** zoom. It doesn't work like a real camera's optical zoom, which actually moves lenses to blow up the scene. Instead, it basically just blows up the image, making everything bigger, and slightly degrading the picture quality in the process.

To zoom in like this, **spread two fingers** on the screen. As you spread, a zoom slider appears; you can also drag the handle in the slider, or tap **+** or **−**, for more precise zooming.

Sometimes, getting closer to the action is worth the subtle image-quality sacrifice.

The "Rule of Thirds" Grid

The Rule of Thirds, long held as gospel by painters and photographers, suggests that you imagine a tic-tac-toe grid superimposed on your frame. Then, as you frame the shot, you should position the important parts of the photo on those lines or, better yet, at their intersections.

According to the Rule of Thirds, this setup creates a stronger composition than putting everything in dead center, which is most people's instinct.

Now, it's really a *Guideline* of Thirds, or a *Consideration* of Thirds; plenty of photographs are, in fact, strongest when the subject is centered.

But if you want to know where those magic intersections are so that you can at least *consider* the Rule of Thirds, you can duck into the Settings→ Photos & Camera screen to turn it on. Scroll down; turn on Grid.

From now on, the phone displays the tic-tac-toe grid on your viewfinder, for your composition pleasure. (It's not part of the photo.) You turn it off the same way.

High Dynamic Range (HDR)

Digital cameras have come a long way, but in one regard, they're still pathetic: Compared with the human eye, they have terrible *dynamic range.*

That's the range from the brightest to darkest spots in a single scene. If you see someone standing in front of a bright window, you can probably make out who it is. But in a photo that person will be a solid black silhouette. The camera doesn't have enough dynamic range to handle both the bright background and the person standing in front of it.

Sure, you could adjust the exposure so that the person's face is lit—but in the process, you'd brighten the background into a nuclear-white rectangle.

Until the world's cameras are as sensitive as our eyes, we can make do with HDR (high dynamic range) photography. That's when the camera takes three photos (or even more)—one each at dark, medium, and light exposure settings. Then software combines the best parts of all three, bringing details to both the shadows and the highlights.

Believe it or not, your iPhone has a built-in HDR feature. It's not as amazing as what an HDR guru can do in Photoshop—for one thing, you have zero control over how the images are combined, how many are combined, or how much of each is combined.

TIP: Should the phone save a standard shot in addition to the HDR shot? That's up to you. In **Settings→Photos & Camera**, you'll find the on/off switch for **Keep Normal Photo**.

But, often, an HDR photo does indeed show more detail in both bright and dark areas than a single shot would. In the iPhone shot at left on the previous page, the sky is blown out—pure white. In the shot at right, the HDR feature brings back the lost streaks of color.

To use HDR, tap the HDR button at the top of the screen. It has three settings: On, Off, and Auto. The Auto setting means "Use your judgment, iPhone. If you think this is a scene with bright brights and dark darks, and would therefore benefit from your own HDR feature, please use HDR automatically." Take your best shot.

When you inspect your photos later in the Photos app, you'll know which ones were taken with HDR turned on; when you tap the photo, you'll see the HDR logo at the upper-left corner.

Taking the Shot

All right. You've opened the Camera app. You've set up the focus, exposure, flash, grid, HDR, and zoom. If, in fact, your subject hasn't already left the scene, you can now take the picture.

You can do that in any of three ways:

- Tap the shutter (◎) button.

- Press either of the physical volume buttons on the left edge of the phone.

  This option is fantastic. If you hold the phone with the volume buttons at the top, those buttons are right where the shutter button would be on a real camera. Pressing one feels more natural than, and doesn't shake the camera as much as, tapping the onscreen ◎ button.

- Press a volume button on your earbuds clicker—a great way to trigger the shutter without jiggling the phone in the process, and a more convenient way to take "selfies" when the phone is at arm's length.

NOTE: The iPhone knows which way you're holding the phone, thanks to its built-in gyroscope. The "which way is up" information accompanies the photo; any Apple photo-viewing app (like iPhoto, Aperture, or the iPhone's own Photos app) will therefore display your photo right-side up. If you use a volume key as a shutter button, that's lucky because, technically, you're holding the phone upside-down.

Either way, if the phone isn't muted, you hear the *snap!* sound of a picture successfully taken.

You get to admire your work for only about half a second—and then the photo slurps itself into the thumbnail icon at the corner of the screen. To review the photo you just took, tap that thumbnail icon.

At this point, to look at other pictures you've taken, tap All Photos at the top of the screen.

This is your opportunity to choose a photo (or many) for emailing, texting, posting to Facebook, and so on; tap Select, tap the photos you want, and then tap the Share button (⬆). See page 286.

> **TIP:** For details on copying your iPhone photos and videos back to your Mac or PC, see page 508.

Burst Mode (iPhone 5s and Later)

Every iPhone snaps photos over and over if you keep your finger pressed on the ◎ button or a volume key.

But the iPhone 5s and later models take them *quickly*—10 shots a second. That's a fantastic feature when you're trying to study something that happens very fast: a golf swing, a pet trick, a toddler sitting still.

All you have to do is keep your finger pressed on the ◎ button or the volume key. A counter rapidly increments, showing you how many shots you've fired off.

> **TIP:** The front-facing camera can capture burst mode, too.

Better yet, the phone helps you *clean up the mess* afterward—the hassle of hand-inspecting all 230 photos you shot, trying to find the ones worth keeping.

Tap the lower-left thumbnail to view your burst shot. To help keep you sane, the iPhone depicts it as a single photo, with the phrase "Burst (72 photos)" (or whatever) in the corner of the screen. (In the Camera Roll, its thumbnail bears multiple frames, as though it's a stack of slides.)

Here's where it gets cool.

If you tap Select, you see all frames of the burst in a horizontally scrolling row. Underneath, you see an even smaller "filmstrip" of them—and a few of them are marked with dots.

These are the ones the iPhone has decided are the keepers. It does that by studying the clarity or blur of each shot, examining how much one frame is different from those around it, and even skipping past shots where some-

body's eyes are closed. Tap the marked thumbnails to see if you approve of the iPhone's selections.

Whether you do or not, you should work through the larger thumbnails in the burst, tapping each one you want to keep. (The small circle in the corner sprouts a blue checkmark.)

When you tap Done, the phone asks: "Would you like to keep the other photos in this burst?" Tap Keep Everything to preserve all the shots in the burst, so you can return later to extract a different set of frames; or Keep Only 2 Favorites (or whatever number you selected) to discard the ones you skipped.

Self-Portraits (the Front Camera)

The iPhone has a second camera, right there on the front, above the screen. The point, of course, is that you can use the screen itself as a viewfinder to frame yourself, experiment with your expression, and check your teeth.

To activate the front camera, open the Camera app and then tap the 🔄 icon. Suddenly, you see yourself on the screen. Frame the shot, and then tap ◯ to take the photo.

Now, don't get your expectations too high. The front camera is not the back camera. It's OK on the 6s models (5 megapixels, plus that cool screen flash)—but older models offer much lower resolution, lower quality, and no flash.

But when your goal is a well-framed self-portrait that you'll use on the screen—email or the web, for example, where resolution isn't very important—then having the front-camera option is better than not having it.

The Self-Timer

A self-timer is extremely useful. It's essential when you want to be in the picture yourself; you can prop the phone on something and then run around into the scene. It's also a great way to prevent camera shake (which produces blurry photos), because your finger doesn't touch the phone.

Just tap the ○ icon, and then tap **3s** (a 3-second countdown) or **10s** (a 10-second countdown).

Now, when you tap the ◎ button or press the volume key, a huge countdown appears on the screen; on the back of the phone, the flash blinks to count you down to the actual snap. After the countdown, the phone takes the picture all by itself. (If the sound is on, you'll hear the shutter noise.)

Correction: The phone takes *10* pictures, in burst mode. The phone logically assumes that if you're using the self-timer, then you're not there to help frame the shot and know when everybody's eyes are open. So it takes 10 shots in a row; you can weed through them later to find the best shot.

> **TIP:** The self-timer is available for both the front and back cameras. In other words, it's also handy for selfies.

Filters

Square photos weren't the only influence that Apple felt from the popularity of Facebook's Instagram app. It also became clear that the masses want *filters*, special effects that degrade the color of your photo in artsy ways. (They can affect either square or regular photos.) You, too, can make your pictures look old, washed-out, or oversaturated.

If you have an iPhone 5 or later, you can turn on the filter *before* you take the shot, so you can see how it'll look. If you have a 4s, you can apply the filter only after you've taken the shot.

- **Filter before you shoot.** To view your options, tap the ⊛. You see a tic-tac-toe board of eight color filters (and black-and-white filters); None is always in the center.

   Tap a filter thumbnail to try it. Each turns your photo into a variation of black-and-white or plays with its saturation (color intensity). If you find one that looks good, take the shot as usual.

   To turn off the filters, tap the ⊛ icon again and tap None.

NOTE: You can always unfilter a filtered shot later, if you prefer the original. Just tap the ⊛ icon to open the palette of filters—and this time, tap None.

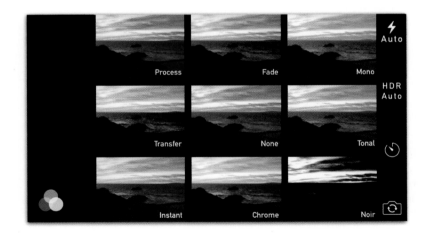

- **Filter after you shoot.** You can also apply a filter to any photo you've already taken, as described on page 273.

Live Photos (iPhone 6s Models)

A Live Photo is a weird new entity: a still photo with a 3-second video attached (with sound). You can take them only with a 6s or 6s Plus, but you can play them back on any iPhone or the Mac.

What you're getting is 1.5 seconds before the moment you snapped the photo, plus 1.5 seconds after. In the Camera app, the ◉ icon at the top lets you know whether or not you're about to capture the 3-second video portion when you take a still. (The factory setting, yellow, means On.)

> **TIP:** When you take a Live Photo, remember to hold the phone still both before and after you tap the ◯ button! That's when the phone is recording those 3 seconds of video.
>
> A yellow LIVE label appears for 3 seconds, while the video is being captured. That's a warning to keep the phone still longer than you ordinarily would, so that it can complete the video capture. (If you forget, and you drop your hand too soon, iOS 9 is smart enough to auto-delete the blurry garbage that results at the end of the shot.)

Now, your obvious concern might be file size. "Wait: The iPhone 6s takes 12-megapixel photos," you might say. "Well, video has thirty frames a second! One three-second Live Photo must take up ninety times as much storage as a still image!"

Fortunately, no. The actual photo *is* a full 12-megapixel shot. But the other frames of the Live Photo contain only enough pixels to fill the phone's screen—not even 1 megapixel per frame. (And a Live Photo stores only 15 frames a second, not 30.) Overall, an entire Live Photo (still, video, sound) takes up about *twice* as much space as a still photo.

That's still around 4 megabytes a shot, though, so be careful about leaving Live Photos turned on for everyday shooting.

Reviewing Live Photos on a 6s

As you flick through the photos you've taken (in the Photos app), you'll know when a photo is a Live Photo; you'll see it animate for a half second.

To play the full 3-second video with sound, press hard on it with your finger. (See page 36 for more on force touching.)

NOTE: You can't edit a Live Photo with its video intact. If you tap Edit and try to make some changes, you'll be warned that to proceed is to eliminate the video and audio portion; you'll be left with only the still image.

Sharing Live Photos

But what happens if you try to send a Live Photo to some other device? Well, first of all, you'll know that you're about to share a Live Photo. After you tap ⬆, a special LIVE icon, shown here, reminds you.

You can tap to turn off that logo before you send, so that you're sharing only the still photo.

NOTE: You can't *email* a Live Photo with its video intact. Even if you send it to another iPhone 6s, only the still image survives the journey.

If you proceed with the Live Photo turned on, what happens next depends on what kind of device receives it.

If it's running the latest Apple software (iOS 9 or OS X El Capitan), then the Live Photo video plays on that gadget, too. On the Mac, in Photos, click Live Photo to play it. On an iPad or older iPhone, hold your finger down on it to play it back.

What if it's a device or software program that doesn't know about Live Photos—you send it as a text message, for example, or open it in Photoshop? Behind the scenes, a Live Photo has two elements: a 12-megapixel JPEG still image and a 3-second QuickTime movie. In these situations, only the JPEG image arrives at the other end.

Square Mode

No longer do you have to download a special app (*cough* Instagram *cough*) just to take perfectly square photos, the way all the cool kids do these days. Just swipe across the screen until you enter Square mode.

In Square mode, the photos the Camera app takes are square instead of rectangular (4 × 3 proportions). Otherwise, everything you've read in this chapter, and will read, is exactly the same in Square mode.

Pano Mode

Here's one of the best camera features of the iPhone: panoramic photographs. The iPhone lets you capture a 240-degree, ultra-wide-angle photo (63 megapixels on the 6s!) by swinging the phone around you in an arc. The phone creates the panorama in real time; you don't have to line up the sections yourself.

> **TIP:** On the iPhone 5s and later, the Panorama mode smoothly adjusts the exposure of the scene as you pan. That fixes one of the most frustrating aspects of other cameras, which use the same exposure all the way across their panoramas; you discover that the sunlit part of the scene is blown out and the shadowy parts are way too dark.

Next time you're standing at the edge of the Grand Canyon—or anything else that requires a *really* wide or tall angle—keep this feature in mind.

In the Camera app, swipe leftward until you reach Pano mode.

> **TIP:** The big white arrow tells you which way to move the phone. But you can reverse it (the direction) just by tapping it (the arrow) before you begin.

Tap the ◎ button (or press a volume key). Now, as instructed by the screen, swing the phone around you—smoothly and slowly, please. You can pan either horizontally or (to capture something very tall) vertically.

As you go, the screen gives you three kinds of feedback:

- It says "Slow down" if you start swinging too fast. Truth is, as far as the iPhone is concerned, the slower the better.

- It says "Move up" or "Move down" if you're not keeping the phone level. Use the big white arrow itself like a carpenter's level; you'll leave the center line if you're not staying level as you move your arm.

- The preview of your finished panorama builds itself as you move. That is, you're seeing the final product, in miniature, while you're still taking it.

You'll probably find that 240 degrees—the maximum—is a *really* wide angle. You'll feel twisted at the waist. But in fact, you can end the panorama at any stage, just by tapping the ◉ button.

At that point, you'll find that the iPhone has taken a very wide, amazingly seamless photograph at very high resolution (over 16,000 pixels wide). If a panorama is *too* wide, you can crop it, as described later in this chapter.

If you snap a real winner, you can print it out at a local graphics shop, frame it, and hang it above the entire length of your living-room couch.

Video Mode

The iPhone can record sharp, colorful video. It's at the best flavor of high definition (1080p), or even 4K (on the 6s models)—and it's stabilized to prevent hand jerkiness, just like a real camcorder is. The 5s offers a gorgeous, 120-frames-per-second *slow-motion* mode that turns even frenzied action into graceful, liquidy visual ballet; the 6 and later models can manage *240* frames per second, for even more fluid, slowed-down videos.

Using video is almost exactly like taking stills. Open the Camera app. Swipe to the right until you've selected Video mode. You *can* hold the iPhone either vertically or horizontally while you film. But if you hold it upright, most people on the Internet will spit on you; tall-and-thin videos don't fit the world's horizontal screens, including YouTube, laptops, and TVs.

> **TIP:** When you switch from still-photo mode to video, you may notice that the video image on the screen suddenly jumps bigger, as though it's zooming in. And it's true: The iPhone is oddly more "zoomed in" in camcorder mode than in camera mode.

Tap to compute focus, exposure, and white balance, as described on the previous pages. (You can even hold your finger down to trigger the exposure and focus locks, or drag the tiny yellow sun to adjust exposure manually, as described earlier.)

Then tap Record (⦿)—or press a volume key on the edge of the phone—and you're rolling! As you film, a time counter ticks away at the top.

A Note About Resolution—and 4K Video

Video generally plays back at 30 frames a second. But the iPhone 6 and 6s models can do something only expensive cameras do: They can record and play back **60** frames a second. Video you shoot this way has a smoothness and clarity that's almost surreal. (It also takes up twice as much space on your phone.)

The on/off switch for 60 fps is in Settings→Photos & Camera. Turn on Record at 60 FPS. Experiment; see if you feel that the result is worth the sacrifice of storage space.

This is also, by the way, where you turn on 4K video recording on the 6s models.

4K televisions, also called Ultra HD, are TV sets with four times as many tiny pixels as an HDTV set, for four times the clarity. Eventually, there will be 4K televisions, 4K computer screens, 4K camcorders, and even 4K phone screens. For now, though, 4K screens are fairly rare—and shows to watch in 4K are rarer still.

4K shooting is **not** the factory setting for the iPhone 6s and 6s Plus, and that's a good thing; 4K takes up a huge amount of storage space (375 megabytes a minute).

Furthermore, you probably don't have anywhere to **play back** 4K video you've captured with this phone! Paradoxically, the iPhone itself doesn't have enough pixels to play 4K video. And don't think you can play them to your TV wirelessly using an Apple TV; even the latest Apple TV can't handle 4K TV.

You can post 4K video to YouTube—but even then, very few people have computer screens or TV screens capable of playing it back in 4K.

Things to Do While You're Rolling

Once you've begun capturing video, don't think your work is done. You can have all kinds of fun during the recording. For example:

- **Change focus.** You can change focus while you're filming, which is great when you're panning from a nearby object to a distant one. Refocusing is automatic, just as it is on regular camcorders—and it's especially quick and smooth on the iPhone 6 and 6 Plus. But you can also force a refocusing (for example, when the phone is focusing on the wrong thing) by tapping in your "viewfinder" to specify a new focus point. The iPhone recalculates the focus, white balance, and exposure at that point, just as it does when you're taking stills.

- **Change exposure.** While you're capturing, you can drag your finger up or down to make the scene brighter or dimmer.

- **Zoom in.** You can zoom in while you're filming, up to 3x actual size. Just spread two fingers on the screen, like you would to magnify a photo. Pinch two fingers to zoom out again. (Doesn't work on the iPhone 4s.)

> **TIP:** Once you start to zoom, a zoom *slider* appears on the screen. It's much easier to zoom smoothly by dragging its handle than it is to use a two-finger pinch or spread.
>
> So here's a smart idea: Zoom in slightly before you start recording, so that the zoom slider appears on the screen. Then, during the shot, drag its handle to zoom in, as smoothly as you like.

- **Take a still photo.** Yes, you can even snap still photos *while* you're capturing video. Just tap the ○ shutter button that appears while you're filming. Awesome. (Doesn't work on the iPhone 4s.)

> **NOTE:** The pictures you take while filming don't have the same dimensions as the ones you take in Photo mode. These have 16:9 proportions, just like the video; they're not as tall as still photos.

When you're finished recording, tap Stop (◉). The iPhone stops recording and plays a chime; it's ready to record another shot.

There's no easier-to-use camcorder on earth. And, man, what a lot of capacity! Each individual shot can be an hour long—and on the 128-gigabyte iPhone, you can record **68 hours** of video. Which ought to be just about long enough to capture the entire elementary-school talent show.

The Front Camera

You can film yourself, too. Just tap 📷 before you film to make the iPhone use its front-mounted camera, so that the screen shows *you.* The resolution isn't as high (the video isn't as sharp) as what the back camera captures, but it's still high definition.

The Video Light

You know the LED "flash" on the back of the phone? You can use it as a video light, too, supplying some illumination to subjects within about 5 feet or so. Just tap the ⚡ icon and then tap On before you start capturing. (Alas, you have to turn the light on before you start rolling. You can't turn it on or off in the middle of a shot.)

Slo-Mo Mode

If you have a 5s or later, you're a lucky duck: Your Camera app has an additional mode called Slo-Mo. (Swipe the screen to the right until Slo-Mo is selected.)

Capturing video in this mode is exactly like capturing video the regular way—but behind the scenes, the phone is recording 120 or 240 frames a second instead of the usual 30.

> **NOTE:** The iPhone 5s records at 120 frames a second. The iPhone 6 and 6s phones, however, can record at *either* 120 or 240 frames per second. You make your choice in Settings→Photos & Camera.

When you open the captured movie to watch it, you'll see something startling and beautiful: The clip plays at full speed for 1 second, slows down to one-quarter or one-eighth speed, and, for the final second, accelerates back to full speed. It's a great way to study sports action, cannonball dives, and shades of expression in a growing smile.

What you may not realize, however, is that you can adjust *where* the slow-motion effect begins and ends in the clip. When you open the video for playback and then hit Edit, a strange kind of ruler track appears just below it. Drag the vertical handles inward or outward to change the spot where the slow motion begins and ends.

At the very bottom of the screen is a second, taller strip; you use this one to trim the ends off the video (see below) or scroll quickly through the clip to see where you are.

Time-Lapse Mode

Whereas Slo-Mo mode is great for slowing down **fast** scenes, the Time-Lapse mode speeds up **slow** scenes: flowers growing, ice melting, candles burning, and so on.

Actually, this mode might better be called **hyperlapse.** Time-lapse implies that the camera is locked down while recording. But in a hyperlapse video, the camera is moving. This mode works great for bike rides, hikes, drives, plane trips, and so on; it compresses even multihour events down to under a minute of playback, with impressive smoothness.

So how much does the Time-Lapse mode speed up the playback? Answer: It varies. The longer you shoot, the greater the speed-up. The app accelerates every recording enough to play back in 20 to 40 seconds, whether you film for 1 minute, 100 minutes, or 1,000 minutes.

If you film for less than 20 seconds, your video plays back at 15 times original speed. But you can film for much, much longer, like 30 hours or more. Time-Lapse mode speeds up the result from 15x, 240x, 960x—whatever it takes to produce a 20- to 40-second playback.

Trimming a Video

To review whatever video you've just shot, tap the ⬚ thumbnail icon at the lower corner of the screen. You've just opened up the video playback screen. Tap ▶ to play the video.

At this point, if you tap Edit, you can trim off the dead air at the beginning and the end.

To do that, drag the ❨ and ❩ markers (currently at the outer ends of the little filmstrip) inward so that they turn yellow, as shown on the facing page. Adjust them, hitting ▶ to see the effect as you go.

TIP: You can drag the playback cursor—the vertical white bar that indicates your position in the clip—with your finger. That's the closest thing you get to Rewind and Fast-Forward buttons. (In fact, you may have to move it out of the way before you can move the end handles for trimming.)

When you've positioned the handles so that they isolate the good stuff, tap Done.

Finally, tap either Trim Original (meaning "shorten the original clip permanently") or Save as New Clip (meaning "leave the original untouched, and spin out the shortened version as a separate video, just in case").

iMovie for iPhone

Of course, there's more to editing than just snipping dead air from the ends of a clip. That's why Apple made iMovie for iPhone. It's free on a new iPhone or $5 if it didn't come with your phone.

Editing Photos

Yes, kids, it's true: You can crop and edit your pictures right on the phone. The tools Apple gives you in the Photos app aren't exactly Photoshop, but they come surprisingly close.

To edit a photo, tap its thumbnail (anywhere in the Photos app) to open it. Tap Edit in the upper right.

Now you get a set of unlabeled buttons. Between Cancel and Done, you'll find the Crop/Straighten, Filters, and Adjust Color buttons; on the opposite side of the screen, there's Auto-Enhance and, on certain iPhone 6s shots, Live Photo Off. Read on.

NOTE: All the changes described on these pages are *nondestructive.* That is, the Photos app never forgets the original photo. At any time, hours or years later, you can return to the Edit screen and undo the changes you've made (tap Revert). You can recrop the photo back to its original size, for example, or turn off the Auto-Enhance button. In other words, your changes are never really permanent.

Auto-Enhance (✨)

When you tap this magical button, the iPhone analyzes the relative brightness of all the pixels in your photo and attempts to "balance" it. After a moment, the app adjusts the brightness and contrast and intensifies dull or grayish-looking areas. Usually, the pictures look richer and more vivid as a result.

You may find that Auto-Enhance has little effect on some photos, only minimally improves others, and totally rescues a few. In any case, if you don't care for the result, you can tap the ✨ button again to turn Auto-Enhance off.

Adjust Color (◉)

The people have spoken: They want control over color, white balance, tint, and so on.

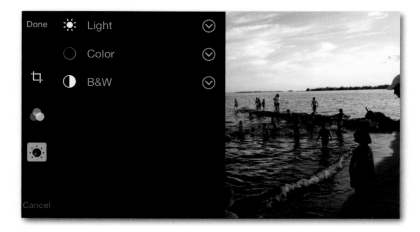

So when you tap ☀, you're offered three adjustment categories: Light, Color, and B&W.

When you tap one of these categories, you see a "filmstrip" below or beside your photo. You can drag your finger across it, watching the effect on your photo.

As it turns out, each of these sliders controls a handful of variables, all of which it's changing simultaneously. For example, adjusting the Light slider affects the exposure, contrast, brights, and darks all at once (below, left).

Intriguingly, you can tap ⊘ or ≡ to see how the master slider has affected these qualities—or even adjust these sub-sliders yourself (above, right). For example:

• **Light.** When you drag your finger along the Light filmstrip, you're adjusting the exposure and contrast of the photo. Often, a slight tweak is all it takes to bring a lot more detail out of the shot.

> **TIP:** Actually, when you're making any of the adjustments described on these pages, you don't have to drag across the *filmstrip.* You can drag your finger left or right across *the photo itself*—a bigger target.

For much finer control, tap the ⊘ or ≡ icon. You open your "drawer" of additional controls: Exposure (adjusts the brightness of all pixels), Highlights (pulls lost details out of very bright areas), Shadows (pulls lost details out of very dark areas), Brightness (like Exposure, but doesn't brighten parts that are already bright), Contrast (heightens the difference between the brightest and darkest areas), and Black Point (determines what is "black"; shifts the entire dark/light range upward or downward). Once again, you drag your finger along the "film strip" to watch the effect on your photo.

- **Color.** The Color filmstrip adjusts the tint and intensity of the photos' colors. Here again, just a nudge can sometimes liven a dull photo or make blue skies "pop" just a little more.

  Tap ⊘ or ☰ to see the three sliders that make up the master Color control. They are Saturation (intensity of the colors—from vivid fake-looking Disney all the way down to black and white), Contrast (deepens the most saturated colors), and Cast (adjusts the color tint of the photo, making it warmer or darker overall).

- **B&W** stands for black and white. The instant you touch this filmstrip, your photo goes monochrome, like a black-and-white photo. It's hard to describe exactly what happens when you drag your finger—you just have to try it—except to note that the app plays with the relative tones of blacks, grays, and whites, creating variations on the black-and-white theme.

  Tap ⊘ or ☰ to see the component sliders: Intensity (the strength of the lightening/darkening effect), Neutrals (brightness of the middle grays), Tone (intensifies the brightest and darkest areas), and Grain

(simulates the "grain"—the texture—of film prints; the farther you move the slider, the higher the "speed of the film" and the more visible the grain).

TIP: You can perform all these adjustments with the phone held either horizontally or vertically. The filmstrip jumps to the right side or the bottom of the screen accordingly.

At any point, you can back out of what you're doing by tapping :≡. For example, if you're fiddling with one of the Color sub-sliders (Contrast or Saturation, for example), tapping :≡ returns you to the view of the three master sliders (Light, Color, and B&W).

And, of course, you can tap Cancel to abandon your editing altogether, or Done to save the edited photo and close the editing controls.

It might seem a little silly trying to perform these Photoshop-like tweaks on a tiny phone screen, but the power is here if you need it.

Filters (⊛)

Filters are effects that make a photo black and white, oversaturated, or washed out. If you have an iPhone 5 or later, you can apply a filter as you take the picture (page 259); no matter which phone you have, though, you can apply a filter to an existing photo here.

Tap the ⊛ button to view a horizontally scrolling row of filter buttons. Tap each to see what it looks like on your photo; finish up by tapping Apply or Cancel. (You can always restore the photo's original look later—by returning to this screen and tapping None.)

(Don't these filters more or less duplicate the effects of the **Light**, **Color**, and **B&W** sliders described already? Yes. But filters produce canned, one-tap, instant changes that don't require as much tweaking.)

> **TIP:** It may look like you've just filtered that picture forever. But in fact you can return to it later and apply the **None** filter to it, thereby restoring it to its original pristine condition.

Remove Red Eye (⌀)

Red eye is a common problem in flash photography. This creepy, possessed look—devilish, glowing-red pupils in your subjects' eyes—has ruined many an otherwise great photo.

Red eye is caused by light reflected back from eyes. The bright light of your flash illuminates the blood-red retinal tissue at the back of the eyes. That's why red-eye problems are worse when you shoot pictures in a dim room: Your subjects' pupils are dilated, allowing even *more* light from your flash to reach their retinas.

The Red-Eye button appears only if the phone detects that the flash fired when the photo was taken. (It appears at top left on the iPhone 6 and 6s, or top middle on earlier models.)

When you tap this button, a message says "Tap each red-eye." Do what it says: Tap with your finger inside each eye that has the problem. A little white ring appears around the pupil (unless you missed, in which case the ring shudders side to side, as though saying, "Nope")—and the app turns the red in each eye to black.

> **TIP:** It usually helps to zoom in first. Use the usual two-finger spread technique.

Crop/Straighten (⌗)

This button opens a crazy editing screen where you can adjust the size, shape, and angle of the photo.

When you tap ⌗, something magical happens: iOS analyzes whatever horizontal lines it finds in the photo—the horizon, for example, or the roof line of a building—and uses it as a guide to straightening the photo *automatically.*

It's very smart, as you can see on the facing page. See how the photo has been tilted slightly—and enlarged slightly to fill the frame without leaving triangular gaps?

You can reject the iPhone's proposal (tap RESET). Or you can tilt the photo more or less (drag your finger across the round scale), up to 90 degrees.

If you want to rotate the photo *more* than 90 degrees—for example, if the camera took it sideways—tap ■ as many times as necessary to turn the picture upright.

The other work you can do in this mode is *cropping.*

Cropping means shaving off unnecessary portions of a photo. Usually, you crop a photo to improve its composition—adjusting where the subject appears within the frame of the picture. Often, a photo has more impact if it's cropped tightly around the subject, especially in portraits. Or maybe you want to crop out wasted space, like big expanses of background sky. If necessary, you can even chop a former romantic interest out of an otherwise perfect family portrait.

Cropping is also very useful if your photo needs to have a certain *aspect ratio* (length-to-width proportion), like 8 × 10 or 5 × 7.

To crop a photo you've opened, tap the ⊞. A white border appears around your photo. Drag inward on any edge or corner. The part of the photo that the iPhone will eventually trim away is darkened. You can recenter the photo within your cropping frame by dragging any part of the photo, inside or outside the white box. Adjust the frame and drag the photo until everything looks just right.

Ordinarily, you can create a cropping rectangle of any size and proportions, freehand. But if you tap ▬, you get a choice of eight canned proportions: Square, 3 × 2, 3 × 5, 4 × 3, and so on. They make the app limit the cropping frame to preset proportions.

This aspect-ratio feature is especially important if you plan to order prints of your photos. Prints come only in standard photo sizes: 4 × 6, 5 × 7, 8 × 10, and so on. But unless you crop them, the iPhone's photos are all 3 × 2, which doesn't divide evenly into most standard print photograph sizes. Limiting your cropping to one of these standard sizes guarantees that your cropped photos will fit perfectly into Kodak prints. (If you don't constrain your cropping this way, then Kodak—not you—will decide how to crop them to fit.)

TIP: The Original option here maintains the proportions of the original photo even as you make the grid smaller.

When you tap one of the preset sizes, the cropping frame **stays** in those proportions as you drag its edges. It's locked in those proportions unless you tap ▇ and choose a different setting.

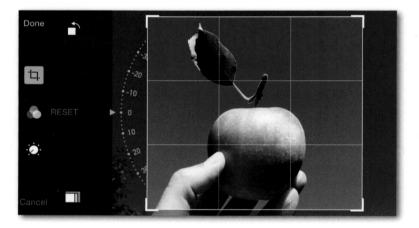

Handing Off to Other Editing Apps

OK, Apple: Who are you, and what have you done with the company that used to believe in closed systems?

Maybe you're a fan of Camera Plus, Fragment, or some other photo app. Its tools can seem as though they're built right into the Photos app.

Here's the drill: Open a photo in Photos. Tap Edit. Tap ☺. Now you see the icons of all apps on your phone that have been updated to work with this feature, which Apple calls Extensibility.

The photo opens immediately in the app you choose, with all of its editing features available. You can freely bounce back and forth between Apple's editor and its competitors'.

Saving Your Changes

Once you've rotated, cropped, auto-enhanced, or de-red-eyed a photo, tap the Done button. You've just made your changes permanent.

Or, rather, you've made them *temporarily* permanent. As noted, you can return to an edited photo at any time to undo the changes you've made (tap Revert). When you send the photo off the phone (by email, to your computer, whatever), *that* copy freezes the edits in place—but the copy on your phone is still revert-able.

> **TIP:** If you sync your photos to Photos, iPhoto, or Aperture on the Mac (over a cable), they show up in their edited condition. Yet, amazingly, you can undo or modify the edits there! The original photo is still lurking behind the edited version. You can use your Mac's Crop tool to adjust the crop, for example. Or you can use iPhoto's Revert to Original command to throw away *all* the edits you made to the original photo while it was on the iPhone.
>
> (If you transfer the photos using email, AirDrop, or Messages, however, you get only the finished JPEG image; you *can't* rewind the changes.)

Managing and Sharing Photos

Once you've taken some photos, or copied them to your phone from your computer (see page 508), you'll have some pictures ready to view. You can learn how to edit them to perfection starting on page 269. But the Photos app has another job: presenting them, sharing them, and slide-showing them for all your fans.

TIP: The Photos app is fully rotational. That is, you can turn the phone 90 degrees. Whether you're viewing a list, a screen full of thumbnails, or an individual photo, the image on the screen rotates, too, for easier admiring. (Unless, of course, you've turned on the rotation lock.)

At the bottom of the Photos app screen, three tabs lie in wait: Photos, Shared, and Albums. The next few sections explain what they do.

The Photos Tab

In the olden days, the Photos app displayed all your photos—thousands of them—in one endless, hopeless, scrolling mass. If you were hunting for a particular shot, you had to study the thumbnails with an electron microscope to find it.

Now, though, iOS groups them intelligently into sets that are easy to navigate. Here they are, from smallest to largest:

- **Moments.** A *moment* is a group of photos you took in one place at one time—for example, all the shots at the picnic by the lake. The phone even uses its own GPS to give each moment a name: "San Francisco, California (Union Square)," for example.

TIP: If you tap a Moment's name, a map opens up; little photo thumbnails show exactly where these pictures were taken. Slick!

- **Collections.** Put a bunch of moments together, and what do you get? A collection. Here again, the phone tries to study the times and places of your photo taking—but this time it puts them into groups that might span a few days and several locations. You might discover that your entire spring vacation is a single collection, for example.

- **Years.** If you "zoom out" of your photos far enough, you wind up viewing them by year: 2013, 2014, 2015, and so on.

To "zoom in" from larger groupings to smaller ones (**Years→Collections→ Moments**), just tap each pile of thumbnails. If you tap a thumbnail on the Moments screen, you open that photo for viewing.

TIP: When you first open a photo, it appears on a white background. Tap the photo to change the background to black, which often makes your photos' colors look better.

To "zoom out" again, tap the grouping name at top left (**Years**, for example).

TIP: If you've opened a single photo for examination, you can retreat to the *moment* it came from by pinching with two fingers.

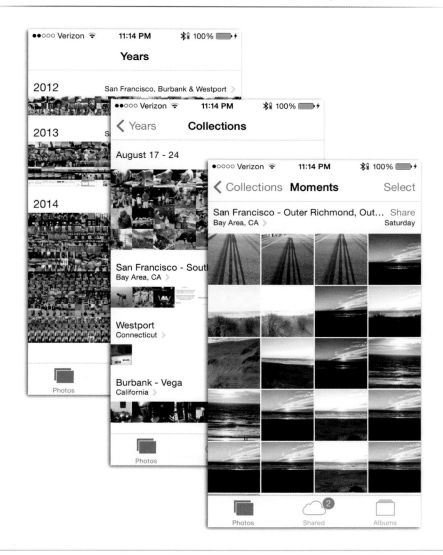

The last technique worth knowing is the Finger Browse. Whenever you're looking at a tiny grid of tiny thumbnail images (in a Year or Collection), hold your finger down within the batch. A larger thumbnail sprouts from your finger, as on this sunset shot here—

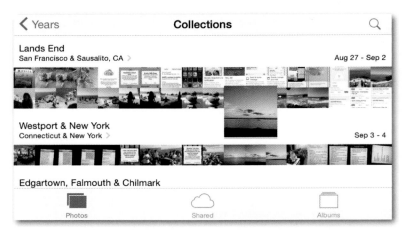

—and you can slide your finger around within the mosaic to find a particular photo, or batch of them.

The Albums Tab

(The second tab is actually the Shared tab, but we're skipping over it for now; see page 299.)

The Albums tab is a scrolling list of specialized photo "folders" like these:

- **Camera Roll** means "pictures you've taken with the iPhone" (as opposed to "pictures you've imported from your computer"). If you see All Photos instead, it's because you've turned on iCloud Photo Library (page 304).

- **My Photo Stream** holds the last 1,000 pictures you've taken or imported on any of your Apple gadgets; see page 296.

- **Favorites.** This folder gives you quick access to your favorite photos. And how does the phone know which photos are your favorites? Easy: You've told it. You've tapped the ♡ icon under a photo, anywhere within the Photos app. (Favorites must be photos you've taken with the phone, not transferred from your computer.)

- **Panoramas, Videos, Slo-Mo, Time-Lapse, Bursts, Screenshots.** As a convenience to you, these categories give you one-tap shopping for everything you've captured using the Camera app's specialized picture and video modes. Super handy when you're trying to show someone your latest time-lapse masterpiece, for example; now you know where to look for it.

- **Events** means *all* the photos you've selected to copy from your Mac or PC.

- **Faces.** Photos, iPhoto, and Aperture, Apple's Mac photography programs, have features that let you identify, by name, the people whose faces are in your photos. Once you've given the software a running start, it can find those people in the rest of your photo collection automatically. That's handy every now and then—when you need a photo of your kid for a school project, for example.

  Here you'll find a list of everyone whose faces you identified on your Mac—and every picture of that person.

- **Albums.** Here you get a list of albums—whatever you've copied to the phone from your Mac or PC.

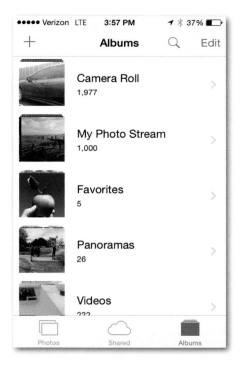

- **Recently Deleted.** Even after you think you've deleted a photo or video from your phone, you have 30 days to change your mind. Deleted pictures and videos sit in this folder, quietly counting down to their own doomsdays.

If you wind up changing your mind, you can open Recently Deleted, tap the photo you'd condemned, and tap Recover. It pops back into its rightful place in the Photos app, saved from termination.

On the other hand, you can also zap a photo into oblivion before its 30-day countdown is up. Tap to open it, tap Delete, and then confirm with Delete Photo. If you tap Select, you can also hit Delete All or Recover All.

As you'd guess, you can drill down from any of these groupings to a screen full of thumbnails, and from there to an individual photo.

TIP: If you hold your finger down on the photo or even its thumbnail, a Copy button appears. That's one way to prepare for pasting a single photo into an email message, an MMS (picture or video) message to another phone, and so on.

Hide a Photo

Here's a quirky little feature: It's now possible to hide a photo from the Photos tab (Moments, Collections, and Years), so that it appears only on the Albums tab (in your albums and in a special Hidden folder).

Apple noticed that lots of people use their phones to take screenshots of apps, pictures of whiteboards or diagrams, shots of package labels or parking-garage signs, and so on. These images aren't scenic or lovely; they're not really memories; they don't look good (or serve much purpose) when they appear nestled in with your shots-to-remember in Moments, Collections, and Years. (Hidden photos don't appear in slideshows, either.)

In iOS 9, Apple changed the method for hiding a picture. Now you first open the photo, then tap the 📤 button; in the Sharing options that appear, tap Hide. To confirm, tap Hide Photo.

Whatever photos you hide go to a new folder on the Albums tab—called, of course, Hidden, so that you can find them easily. From here, you can un-hide a shot the same way: hit 📤 and then Unhide.

Flicking, Rotating, Zooming, Panning

Once a photo is open at full size, you have your chance to perform the four most famous and most dazzling tricks of the iPhone: flicking, rotating, zooming, and panning a photo.

- **Flicking** right to left is how you advance to the next picture or movie in the batch. (Flick from left to right to view the *previous* photo.)

- **Zooming** a photo means magnifying it, and it's a blast. One quick way is to double-tap the photo; the iPhone zooms in on the portion you tapped, doubling its size.

  Another technique is to use the two-finger spread, which gives you more control over what gets magnified and by how much.

(If you've brought in photos from your computer, note that the iPhone doesn't store the giganto 20-megapixel originals you took with your fancy camera. It keeps only scaled-down, iPhone-sized versions, so you can't zoom in more than about three times the original size.)

Once you've spread a photo bigger, you can then pinch to scale it down again. Or just double-tap to restore the original size. (You don't have to restore a photo to original size before advancing to the next one, though; if you flick enough times, you'll pull the next photo onto the screen.)

- **Panning** means moving a photo around on the screen after you've zoomed in. Just drag your finger to do that; no scroll bars are necessary.

- **Rotating** is what you do when a horizontal photo or video appears on the upright iPhone, which makes the photo look small and fills most of the screen with blackness.

  Just turn the iPhone 90 degrees in either direction. Like magic, the photo itself rotates and enlarges to fill its new, wider canvas. No taps required. (This doesn't work when the phone is flat on its back—on a table, for example. It has to be more or less upright. It also doesn't work when Portrait Orientation is locked.)

This trick also works the other way: You can make a *vertical* photo fit better by turning the iPhone upright.

Finding Photos

There's a search icon (Q) in Photos, which might seem odd. How can you search for a blob of pixels? How does the phone know what's *in* a picture?

It doesn't. All you can search for is the data *associated* with a photo: time, place, album name.

To try it out, tap Q at the top of the Photos or Albums screens. Right off the bat, the phone offers some one-tap canned searches based on location (like Nearby and Home) and dates (like January 2016 and February 2016). Tap to see the photos that match.

Or you can type in a place, date, name, or album. Try typing september or tucson or bay area or 2014, for example. As you type, iOS displays all the photo groupings that match what you've typed so far, like this:

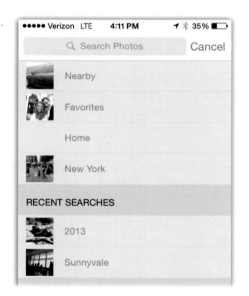

Tap that grouping to see the photo thumbnails within.

TIP: Then again, in iOS 9, it's usually faster to request such photos by voice, using Siri: "Show me all the photos from Texas in 2015." See page 149.

Deleting Photos

If some photo no longer meets your exacting standards, you can delete it. But this action is trickier than you may think.

- **If you took the picture using the iPhone,** no sweat. Open the photo from the Photos tab; tap 🗑. When you tap Delete Photo, that picture is gone. Or, rather, it's moved to the Recently Deleted folder described on page 281; you have 30 days to change your mind.

  (If you open the photo from the Albums tab instead, you're just taking the picture out of that album—not actually deleting it from the phone.)

- **If the photo was synced to the iPhone from your computer,** well, that's life. The iPhone remains a *mirror* of what's on the computer. In other words, you can't delete the photo right on the phone. Instead, delete it from the original album on your computer (which does *not* mean deleting it from the computer altogether). The next time you sync the iPhone, the photo disappears from it, too.

Photo Controls

If you tap the screen once after opening a photo, some useful controls appear. (Tap again to hide them and summon a black background, for more impressive photo presentation.)

- **Album name.** You can return to the thumbnails page by tapping the screen once, which summons the playback controls, and then tapping the album name in the upper-left corner.

- **Date and time.** The top of the screen says "September 13, 12:52 pm," for example, letting you know when this photo was taken.

- **Edit.** This button is the gateway to the iPhone's photo-editing features, described starting on page 269.

- **Share icon.** Tap ⬆ in the lower left if you want to do something more with this photo than just stare at it. You can use it as your iPhone's wallpaper, print it, copy it, text it, send it by email, use it as somebody's headshot in your Contacts list, post it on Twitter or Facebook, and so on. These options are all described in the following pages.

- **Favorite icon.** When you find a picture you really love—enough that you might want to call it up later to show people—tap ♡. This photo or video now appears in the Favorites folder (in the Albums tab of the Photos app, described earlier), so that it's easy to find with your other prize-winners. (The ♡ appears only on photos you've taken with the phone—not pictures you've imported from computers or other cameras.)

753 Ways to Use Photos and Videos

It's great that the iPhone has a great cellphone camera. But what's even greater is that it *is* a cellphone. It's online. So once you've taken a picture, you can *do* something with it right away. Mail it, text it, post it to Facebook or Twitter, use it as wallpaper—all right from the iPhone.

That's all useful when you're out shopping and want to seek your spouse's opinion on something you're about to buy. It's handy when you want to remember the parking-garage section where you parked ("4 South"). It's great when you want to give your Twitter fans a glimpse of whatever hell or heaven you're experiencing at the moment.

Step 1: Choose the Photos

Before you can send or post a photo or video, you have to tell iOS which one (or ones) you want to work with.

To send just one, well, there's no big mystery; tap its thumbnail, and then tap the ⬆ button.

But you can also send a bunch of them in a group. How you do so, however, depends on where you start.

- **A Moment.** You can't choose batches of photos when you're looking at a Year or a Collection. But every single Moment bears a Share button next to its name. Tap it.

  It offers a choice: Share this moment (send the entire batch) or Play Slideshow—which is, technically, a form of sharing, right?

- **Photos from the Albums tab.** If you begin instead on a page of thumbnails from the Albums tab, you can tap Select and then individually select the photos you want to send. With each tap, a ✓ appears, meaning, "OK, this one will be included." (Tap again to remove the checkmark.) Then tap ⬆.

Either way, the next thing you see is the Share sheet.

Starting from the Albums tab gains you a couple of additional options, by the way. First, there's a 🗑 button, so you can delete a bunch of photos at once. (You can delete only photos or videos you've taken with the iPhone—not ones you transferred from your computer.)

Creating and Deleting Albums

Also on the Album thumbnail-selection screen: a button called Add To. It lets you put the selected photos into one of your albums—a great way to organize a huge batch you've shot on vacation, for example.

You're now offered an Add to Album screen. Tap the album into which you want to move these pictures. (If albums are dimmed, that's because they've been synced from your Mac or PC. You're not allowed to mess with them. The canned specialty-photo folders, like Panorama and Time-Lapse, are also dimmed, because only iOS can put things into those folders.)

This list also includes a New Album button; you're asked to type out the name you want for the new album and then tap Save.

To delete an album you created on the phone, start on the main Albums tab. Tap **Edit**, and then tap the ⊖ button next to the album you want to delete.

Step 2: Preparing to Send

Once you've opened a photo (or selected a few), tap ⬆.

Now you have a huge array of "send my photo here" options, displayed in three rows. Two of them scroll horizontally.

At the top of the Share screen, a scrolling row of other pictures appears. It lets you add more to the one(s) you've already selected, or deselect some that you already did. That's a lot less crazymaking than having to cancel out of the Share screen in order to change your selection of pictures.

All right then. Here's an overview of the options available on the Share screen.

AirDrop

So very cool: You can shoot a photo, or several, to any nearby iPhone, iPad, iPod Touch, or Mac—wirelessly, securely, conveniently, and instantly. See page 331 for the step-by-steps.

Message

You can also send a photo or video as a *picture or video message*. It winds up on the screen of the other guy's cellphone.

That's a delicious feature, which people exploit millions of times a day.

Tap **Message** and then specify the phone number of the recipient; if you're sending by iMessage, the email address also works. Or choose someone from your Contacts list. Then type a little note, tap **Send**, and off it goes.

> **NOTE:** If you're sending a video, the iPhone compresses it first so that it's small enough to send as a text-message attachment (smaller dimensions, lower picture quality). Then it attaches the clip to an outgoing text message; it's your job to address it.

Mail

The option to send the selected photos by email disappears if you've selected six or more pictures; five is the maximum.

The iPhone automatically rotates and attaches your photos or video clips to a new outgoing message. All you have to do is address it and hit **Send**. If it's a big file, you may be asked how much you want the photo *scaled down* from its original size. Tap **Small**, **Medium**, **Large**, or **Actual Size**, using the megabyte indicator as a guide. (Many email systems won't accept attachments larger than 5 megabytes.)

(Any video clip you send by email gets compressed—smaller, lower quality—for the same reason.)

iCloud Photo Sharing

You can share batches of photos or videos with other people, either directly to their Apple gadgets or to a private web page. What's more, they can (at your option) contribute their *own* pictures to the album.

This is a big topic, though, so it gets its own write-up on page 299.

Twitter, Facebook, Flickr

If you've told your iPhone what your name and password are (in **Settings→Twitter** or **Settings→Facebook** or **Settings→Flickr**), then posting a photo from your phone to your Twitter feed, Facebook timeline, or Flickr collection is ridiculously simple.

Open the photo; tap the ⬆ button; tap **Twitter**, **Facebook**, or **Flickr**. You're offered the chance to type a message that accompanies your photo. (As usual with Twitter, you have a maximum of 140 characters for your message. Fewer, actually, because some of your characters are eaten up by the link to the photo.) You can also tap **Add Location** if you want Twitterites or Facebookers to know where the photo was taken.

●○○○○ Verizon 📶 11:04 AM 🔋 98% ▰	●●○○○ Verizon 📶 11:04 AM 🔋 98% ▰

Cancel **Facebook** **Post**

Wilbur managed to tie himself into a knot!

Album   iOS Photos >

Location   None >

Audience   Friends >

‹ Facebook Audience

Public

Friends   ✓

Friends except Acquaintances

Only Me

Ol' College Dudes

Best Buds

NOTE: The Add Location option is available only if you've permitted Twitter or Facebook to use your location information, which you set up in **Settings→Privacy→Location Services**.

If you're posting to Facebook or Flickr, you can also indicate whom you're sharing this item with—just your friends, everyone, and so on—by tapping **Audience** beneath the photo thumbnail. Flickr also offers a chance to specify which of your Flickr photo sets you want to post to.

When you tap **Send** or **Post**, your photo, and your accompanying tweet or post, zoom off to Twitter, Facebook, or Flickr for all to enjoy.

YouTube, Vimeo

And you were alive to see the day: Film a movie, edit out the boring parts, and then upload it to YouTube—right from the phone.

Call up the video, if it's not already on the screen before you. Tap the ⬆ button. The Share sheet offers these video-specific buttons:

- **YouTube.** The iPhone asks for your Google account name and password (Google owns YouTube). Next it wants a title, description, and *tags* (searchable keywords like "funny" or "babies").

  It also wants to know if the video will be in standard definition or high definition (and it gives the approximate size of the file). You should also pick a **Category** (Autos & Vehicles, Comedy, Education, or whatever).

  Finally, choose from **Public** (anyone online can search for and view your video), **Unlisted** (only people who have the link can view this video), or Private (only specific YouTubers can view). When everything looks good, tap Publish.

After the upload is complete, you're offered the chance to see the video as it now appears on YouTube, or to Tell a Friend (that is, to email the YouTube link to a pal). Both are excellent ways to make sure your masterful cinematography gets admired.

- **Vimeo.** You're supposed to have set up your name and password in Settings for Vimeo (a video site a lot like YouTube, but classier, with a greater emphasis on quality and artistry).

If you've done that, then all you have to do, when posting a video, is to specify a caption or a description, and then tap Details to choose a video size and who your audience is (public, private, and so on). Once you tap Post, your video gets sent on to the great cinema on the web.

More

In the modern, extendible iOS, you can hand off a photo to *other* apps and services—beyond the set that Apple provides. If you tap More, you get the screen shown here at right:

That screen is basically a setup headquarters for the row of "where you can send photos" icons. Here you can rearrange them (put the ones you use most often at the top by dragging the ≣ handle); add to the list (turn on the switches for new, non-Apple photo-sharing apps you've installed); or hide the services you don't use (turn off the switches). (You can't turn off the switches for Message, Mail, and iCloud Photo Sharing.)

Copy

The Copy button, on the second row of sharing options, puts the photo(s) onto the Clipboard, ready for pasting into another app (an outgoing Mail message, for example). Once you've opened an app that can, in fact, accept pasted graphics, double-tap to make the Paste button appear.

Slideshow

A slideshow is a great way to show off your photos and videos. You can turn a set or album of photos into a slideshow by tapping the ⬆ button to open the Share sheet and then tapping Slideshow. In iOS 9, a gorgeous, musically accompanied, animated slideshow begins instantly.

You have a surprising amount of control over your slideshow. The options appear when you tap the screen after that slideshow has begun, and then tap Options:

- **Themes.** A theme, new in iOS 9, is a canned presentation style, incorporating animations, crossfades, and music. Each makes the photos appear, interact, overlap, and flow away in a different way. You're offered five choices—Origami, Magazine, Dissolve, Ken Burns, and Push. (The first two display more than one photo at a time, on the same screen.)

- **Music.** Choose one of the five pieces of background music here, or tap iTunes Music to choose a song from your music collection.

- **Repeat.** Makes the slideshow play over and over again until you stop it manually.

The slideshow incorporates both photos and videos (with sound; the background music actually gets softer so you can hear the audio).

While the show is playing, here's what you can do:

- **Tap to summon** the ❚❚ button.

- **Turn the iPhone 90 degrees** to accommodate landscape-orientation photos as they come up; the slideshow keeps right on going.

- **Swipe leftward** to blow past a photo or video that's taking too long.

AirPlay

This button offers a list of nearby AirPlay gadgets—the only one you've probably heard of is Apple TV—so you can display the current photo on your TV or another screen.

Hide

Here's the option to hide a photo, as described on page 282.

Save Image

Suppose you're looking at a photo that you didn't take with the phone. Maybe someone texted or emailed it to you, for example. This button saves it into your own photo collection, so you'll be able to cherish it for years.

Assign to Contact

If you're viewing a photo of somebody who's listed in Contacts, then you can use it (or part of it) as her headshot. After that, her photo appears on your screen every time she calls. Just tap Assign to Contact.

Your address book list pops up. Tap the name of the person who goes with this photo.

Now you see a preview of what the photo will look like when that person calls. This is the Move and Scale screen. You want to crop the photo and

shift it in the frame so only *that person* is visible (if it's a group shot)—in fact, probably just the face.

Start by enlarging the photo: Spread your thumb and forefinger against the glass. As you go, *shift* the photo's placement in the round frame with a one-finger drag. When you've got the person correctly centered, tap Choose.

Use as Wallpaper

Wallpaper is the background photo that appears in either of two places: the Home screen (plastered behind your app icons) or the Lock screen (which appears every time you wake the iPhone).

You can replace Apple's standard photos with one of your photos or with a different one of Apple's. You go at this task in either of two ways:

- **Start in Settings.** Tap Settings→Wallpaper.

   Now you see miniatures of the two places you can install wallpaper—the Lock screen and the Home screen (facing page, left). Each shows what you've got installed there as wallpaper at the moment.

TIP: You can tap either screen miniature to open a Set screen, where you can adjust the current photo's size and positioning.

   When you tap Choose a New Wallpaper, you're shown a list of photo sources you can use as backgrounds. Under Apple Wallpaper, you get two categories worth noticing.

   The Dynamic wallpapers look like soft-focus bubbles against solid backgrounds. Once you've installed the wallpaper, these bubbles actually *move*, rising and falling on your Lock screen or Home screen behind your icons. Yes, animated wallpaper has come to the iPhone.

   The Stills category is a bunch of lovely nature photography. It doesn't move.

   Scroll down a little, and you'll find your own photos, in the form of the Camera Roll, Photo Stream, Panoramas, and Albums categories, as described earlier in this chapter.

   All these pictures show up as thumbnail miniatures; tap one to see what it looks like at full size. If it looks good, then tap Set.

TIP: Complicated, "busy" photos make it harder to read icons and icon names on the Home screen.

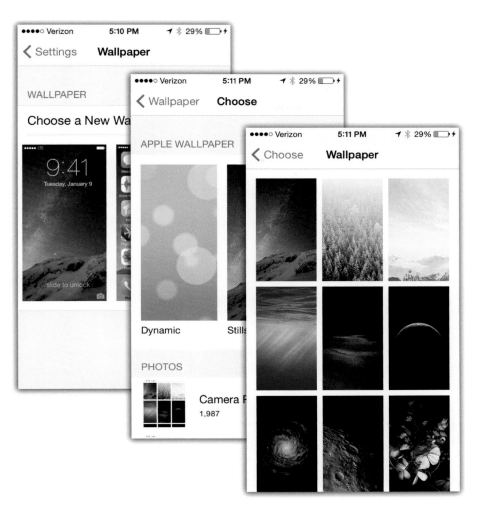

Now the iPhone wants to know which of the two places you want to use this wallpaper; tap Set Lock Screen, Set Home Screen, or Set Both (if you want the same picture in both places).

• **Start in the Photos app.** The task of applying one of your own photos to your Home or Lock screen also can begin in the Photos app. Open one of your photos, as described in the previous pages. Tap ⬆, and then tap Use as Wallpaper.

You're now offered the Move and Scale screen so you can fit your photo within the wallpaper "frame." Pinch or spread to enlarge the shot; drag your finger on the screen to scroll and center it.

Finally, tap **Set**. Here again, you specify where you want to use this wallpaper; tap **Set Lock Screen**, **Set Home Screen**, or **Set Both** (if you want the same picture in both places).

Print

You can print a photo easily enough, provided that you've hooked up your iPhone to a compatible printer. Once you've opened the photo, tap the 📤 button and then tap **Print**. The rest goes down as described on page 329.

More

Once again, iOS offers a way to rearrange the Share buttons (this time, the second row)—or to add new buttons. They appear automatically when you install certain apps that have photo-sharing capabilities.

My Photo Stream

iCloud is Apple's free suite of online services. It's described in Chapter 15—but for an iPhone shutterbug, its most interesting feature may be My Photo Stream.

The concept is simple: Every time a new photo enters your life—when you take a picture with your iPhone or import one onto your computer—it gets added to your Photo Stream. From there, it appears automatically on all your *other* Apple machines.

> **NOTE:** Photo Stream doesn't sync over the cellular airwaves. It sends photos around only when you're in a Wi-Fi hotspot.

Using Photo Stream means all kinds of good things:

- Your photos are always backed up. Lose your iPhone? No biggie—when you buy a new one, your latest 1,000 photos appear on it automatically.

- Any pictures you take with your iPhone appear automatically on your computer. You don't have to connect any cables or sync anything yourself.

> **TIP:** There's one exception. If you take a photo and then delete it while still in the Camera app, that photo won't enter your Photo Stream.
>
> A similar rule holds true with edits: If you edit a photo you've just taken, those edits become part of the Photo Stream copy. But if you take a photo, leave the Camera app, and *later* edit it, then the Photo Stream gets the original copy only.

To get started with Photo Stream on your iPhone, you have to turn **on** My Photo Stream, which you do in Settings→iCloud. (You should also turn it on using the iCloud control panel on your computers. That's in System Preferences on your Mac, or in the Control Panel of Windows.) Give your phone some time in a Wi-Fi hotspot to form its initial slurping-in of all your most recent photos.

Once Photo Stream is up and running, here's how to use it.

On the iPhone

Open your Photos app. Tap the tab at the bottom called Albums; in the list of albums, tap My Photo Stream. Inside are the 1,000 photos that have entered your life most recently.

Now, your i-gadget doesn't have nearly as much storage available as your Mac or PC; you can't yet buy an iPhone with 750 gigabytes of storage. That's why, on your iPhone, your My Photo Stream consists of just the last 1,000 photos. (There's another limitation, too: The iCloud servers store your photos for 30 days. As long as your gadgets go online at least once a month, they'll remain current with the Photo Stream.)

Ordinarily, the oldest of the 1,000 photos in your Photo Stream scroll away forever as new photos come in. But you can rescue the best ones from that fate—by saving them onto your phone, where they're free from the risk of automatic deletion.

To rescue a bunch at a time, open My Photo Stream so you're looking over the thumbnails. Tap Select, and then tap the thumbnails of the photos you want to preserve. Once they're selected, tap Add To (and then choose one of your phone's albums); or tap the □ button and tap Save Images.

Or, if you're viewing one open picture in My Photo Stream, tap the □ button; on the Share sheet, tap Save to Camera Roll.

That's it. Now the photos you rescued appear in **both** your Photo Stream, where they will eventually disappear, **and** in your albums, where they're safe until you delete them manually.

On the Mac or PC

In Photos, iPhoto, or Aperture (Mac), your Photo Stream photos appear in a new monthly album called, of course, Photo Stream. On a Windows PC, you get a Photo Stream folder in your Pictures folder.

On the computer, you don't have to worry about that 30-day, 1,000-photo business. Once pictures appear here, they're here until you delete them.

This, in its way, is one of the best features in all of iCloudland, because it means you don't have to sync your iPhone over a USB cable to get your photos onto your computer. It all happens automatically, wirelessly over Wi-Fi.

TIP: You can also drag photos **into** your Photo Stream from your computer. That's a quick, easy way to get them onto your iPhone wirelessly. On the Mac, drag the photos into the Photo Stream album (within iPhoto, Photos, or Aperture), and choose whether you want them dropped into your main Photo Stream or one of your shared ones. In Windows, drag them into the Photo Stream Uploads folder, which you designate in the iCloud Control Panel.

On the Apple TV

When you're viewing your photos on an Apple TV, an album appears there called Photo Stream. There they are, ready for showing on the big plasma. You can use your Photo Stream in an Apple TV screensaver, too.

Deleting Photos from the Photo Stream

You can't choose what photos go into the Photo Stream. **Every** picture you take with the iPhone goes into it. **Every** photo you bring in from your computer goes into it. Every photo you save on your iPhone from an app like Twitter goes into it. Every screenshot you make goes into it.

And, remember, the same 1,000 photos appear on all your Apple gadgets (assuming you've turned on Photo Stream on each one). You might think you're taking a private picture with your phone, forgetting that your spouse or parent will see it seconds later on the family iPad. It's only a matter of time before Photo Stream gets some politician in big trouble.

Even if you delete a photo from your iPhone's Camera Roll, it's too late. The Photo Stream version is already out there, replicated across all your i-gadgets and computers.

Fortunately, you can delete photos from your Photo Stream. Just select the thumbnail of the photo you want to delete, and then tap the Trash icon (🗑). The confirmation box warns you that you're about to delete the photo from all your Apple machines (and, for shared streams, the machines of everyone who's subscribed to your photographic output).

If you haven't saved it to a different album or roll, it's gone for good when you tap Delete Photo.

iCloud Photo Sharing

The term "iCloud Photo Sharing" is what used to be called a shared Photo Stream. It lets you send photos or videos to *other* people's gadgets. After a party or some other get-together, you could send your best shots to everyone who attended; after a trip, you could post your photographic memories for anyone who might care.

The lucky recipients can post comments about your pix, click a "like" button to indicate their enthusiasm, or even submit pictures and videos of their own. It's like having a tiny Instagram network of your very own, consisting solely of people you invite.

In designing this feature, Apple had quite a challenge. There's a lot of back-and-forth among multiple people, sharing multiple photos, so iCloud Photo Sharing can get a little complicated. Stay calm and keep your hands and feet inside the tram at all times. Here's how it works.

> **TIP:** Well, here's how it works *if* your equipment meets the requirements. These shared Photo Albums can show up on an i-gadget with iOS 7 or later; on a Mac with OS X Mavericks (10.9) or later and iPhoto 9.5 or Aperture 3.5 or later; on a PC with Windows 7 or later and the iCloud Control Panel 3.0; or on an Apple TV (2nd generation) with Software Update 6.0 or later.
>
> You also have to *turn on* the Photo Album feature. On an iOS gadget, the switch is in Settings→iCloud→Photos; turn on iCloud Photo Sharing. On the Mac, open System Preferences→iCloud. Make sure Photos is turned on; click Options and confirm that Photo Sharing is on, too. On a Windows PC, it's in the iCloud Control Panel for Windows (a free download from Apple's website).

Create a Shared Photo Album

To share some of your masterpieces with your adoring fans, do this:

1. **Create the empty album.** Open the Photos app. On the Shared tab, scroll to the top (if necessary) and tap +.

2. **Name the new album.** In the Shared Album box, name the Photo Album ("Bday Fun" or whatever). Tap Next.

3. **Specify the audience.** You're now asked for the email addresses of your lucky audience members; enter their addresses in the "To:" box just as you would address an outgoing email. For your convenience, a list of recent sharees appears below the "To:" box.

   When that's done, tap Create. You return to the list of shared albums, where your newly named album appears at the top. It is, however, completely empty.

4. **Pour some photos or movies into the album.** Tap your new, empty album's name. Then, on the empty next screen, tap the + to burrow through your photos and videos—you can use any of the three tabs (Photos, Shared, Albums)—to select the material you want to share. Tap their thumbnails so that they sprout checkmarks, and then tap Done.

   A little box appears so that you can type up a description.

5. **Type a description of the new batch.** In theory, you and other people can add to this album later. That's why you're offered the chance to caption each new batch.

   Once that's done, tap Post.

The thumbnails of the shared photos and videos appear before you—and the + button is there, too, in case you want to add more pictures later.

> **TIP:** You can easily *remove* photos from the album, too. On this screen of thumbnails, tap Select; tap the thumbnails you want to nuke; tap 🗑; confirm by tapping Delete Photo.

Adjusting an Album's Settings

Before you set your album free, tap the People tab at the bottom of the screen. Here are a few important options to establish for this album:

- **Invite People.** This list identifies everyone with whom you've shared the album. To add a new subscriber, tap Invite People. To delete a subscriber, tap the name and then (at the bottom of the contact card) tap Remove Subscriber.

- **Subscribers Can Post**. Your subscribers can contribute photos and videos to your album. That's a fantastic feature when it contains pictures of an event where there was a crowd: a wedding, show, concert, picnic, badminton tournament. Now everyone who was there can

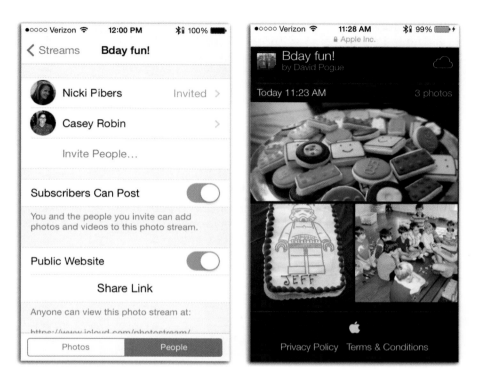

enhance the gallery with shots taken from their own points of view with their own phones or cameras.

- **Public Website.** If you turn on Public Website, then even people who aren't members of the Apple cult will be able to see these photos. The invitees will get an email containing a web address. It links to a hidden page on the iCloud website that contains your published photos.

  When you turn this switch on, the web address of your new gallery appears in light-gray type. Tap Share Link for a selection of methods for sending the link to people: by Message, Mail, Twitter, Facebook, AirDrop, and so on.

  What they'll see is a mosaic of pictures, laid out in a grid on a single sort of web poster. Your fans can download their favorites by clicking the ⬇ button. (You can't add comments or "like" photos on the web, however.)

TIP: If you click one of these medium-sized photos, you enter slideshow mode, in which one photo at a time fills your web browser window. Click the arrow buttons to move through them.

- **Notifications.** If this switch is on, then your phone will show a banner each time someone adds photos or videos to your album, clicks the "Like" button for a photo, or leaves a comment.

- **Delete Shared Album.** That's right: If the whole thing gets out of hand, you can slam the door in your subscribers' faces by making the entire album disappear.

Read on to see what it's like to be the person whose email address you entered.

Receiving a Photo Album on Your Gadget

When other people share Photo Albums with *you*, your phone makes a little warble, and a notification banner appears: "[Your buddy's name] invited you to join '[name of shared photo batch]'."

Simultaneously, a badge like (❷) appears on the Photos app icon and on the Shared tab within Photos, letting you know how many albums have come your way.

> **TIP:** If you have iPhoto, Photos, or Aperture on a Mac, an invitation to accept the album appears there, too.

As you'd guess, you can tap the new album's name to see what's inside it; tap Accept if you're sure.

Once you're subscribed, you view the photos and movies as you would any album—with a couple of differences. First, you can tap Add a comment to make worshipful or snarky remarks, or tap the Like smiley to offer your silent support (shown on the facing page at right).

> **TIP:** Either you or the photo's owner can delete one of your comments. To do that, hold your finger down on the comment itself and then tap the Delete button that appears.

You can also snag a copy of somebody's published photo or video for yourself. With the photo before you, tap the ⬆ button to see the usual sharing options—and tap Save Image. Now the picture or video isn't some virtual online wisp—it's a solid, tangible electronic copy in your own photo pool.

If your buddy has turned on Subscribers Can Post for this album, then you can send your own photos and clips into the album; everybody who's subscribed to it (and, of course, its owner) will see them.

To do that, tap the + on the album's page of thumbnails; choose your photos and movies; tap Done; add a comment; and tap Post.

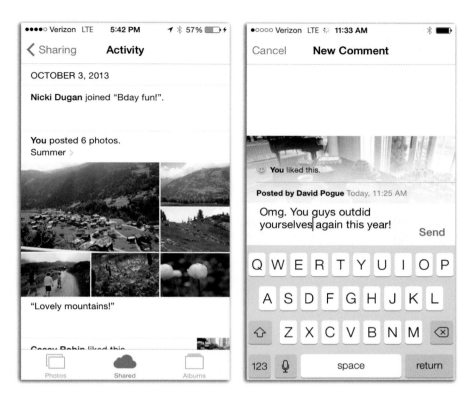

Fun with Shared Photo Albums

Once you've created a shared Photo Album, you can update it or modify it in all kinds of ways:

- **Add new photos or movies to it.** In Photos, open the shared Photo Album, whether it's one you created or one you've subscribed to. Tap +. Now you can browse your whole world of photos, tapping to add them to the Photo Album already in progress.

- **Remove things from it.** In Photos, open the shared Photo Album. Tap Select, tap the item(s) you want to delete, and then tap the Trash icon (🗑)—and confirm with a tap on Delete Photo(s).

- **Delete an entire shared Photo Album.** Tap the People tab below an open photo album, scroll down, tap Delete Shared Album, and confirm by tapping Delete.

- **Change who's invited, change the name.** The People tab is also where you can add to the list of email addresses (tap Invite People), remove someone (tap the name, and then tap Remove Subscriber), rename the album, or turn off Public Website to dismantle the web version of this gallery.

At any time, you can tap the **Activity** "folder" at the top of the **Shared** tab in the Photos app. Here, for your amusement, is a visual record of everything that's gone on in Shared Photo Album Land: photos you've posted, photos other people have posted, comments back and forth, "likes," and so on. It's your personal photographic Facebook.

iCloud Photo Library

If learning the difference between My Photo Stream, iCloud Photo Sharing, and Shared Photo Streams isn't hard enough, then hold onto your lens cap. Apple offers yet another online photo feature: the iCloud Photo Library.

The idea this time is that *all* your Apple gadgets will keep *all* your photos and videos backed up online and synced. The advantages:

- All your photos and videos are always backed up—not just the last 1,000.

- All your photos and videos are accessible from any of your gadgets.

- You can reclaim a lot of space on your phone. There's an option that offloads the original photos and videos to iCloud but leaves small, phone-sized copies on your phone.

There are a couple of sizable downsides to iCloud Photo Library, too:

- Photos and videos eat up a lot of storage space. Remember, your entire iCloud account comes with only 5 gigabytes of free storage. If you start backing up your photo library to it, too, you'll almost certainly have to pay to expand your iCloud storage.

- Things get a little complicated. The structure of the Photos app described in this chapter changes, for example; the albums usually called **Camera Roll** and **My Photo Stream** go away. They're replaced by a new album called **All Photos**. (Camera Roll and My Photo Stream were just subsets of your whole photographic life anyway.)

If you decide to dive in, then open **Settings→iCloud→Photos→iCloud Photo Library**.

Once iCloud Photo Library is on, you won't be able to copy pictures from your computer to your phone using iTunes anymore; iTunes will be completely removed from the photo-management loop. That's why, at this point, you may be warned that your phone is about to *delete* any photos and videos that you've synced to it from iTunes (page 497). (Don't worry—they'll be safe on iCloud.)

And, of course, you might be warned that you need to buy more iCloud storage space.

Now the Settings panel expands and offers this important choice:

- **Optimize iPhone Storage.** If you turn this on, your original photos and videos get backed up to iCloud—but on your phone, you'll be left with much smaller versions that are just right for viewing on the phone's screen (but not high resolution enough to, for example, print). This arrangement saves you a *ton* of space on your phone.

- **Download and Keep Originals** leaves the big original files on your phone.

Finally, the uploading process begins. If you have a lot of photos and videos, it can take a very long time.

But when it's all over, you'll have instant access to all your photos and videos in any of these places:

- **On the iPhone (or other iOS gadgets).** In the Photos app, on the Albums tab, the new "album" called **All Photos** represents your new, online photo library. Add to, delete from, or edit pictures in this set, and you'll find the same changes made on all your other Apple gear.

- **On the web.** You can sign into *iCloud.com* and click **Photos** to view your photos and videos, no matter what machine you're using. The Moments and Albums tabs here correspond to the tabs in the phone's Photos app. Click a photo to open it full size, whereupon the icons at the top of the screen let you delete, download, or "favorite" it.

- **On the Mac, eventually.** Apple intends to kill off iPhoto and Aperture, its photo-management programs, and replace them with a Mac program called Photos. Until this new program hatches in "early 2015," you have no way to work with your photo library using a Mac. You've been warned.

Geotagging

Mention to a geek that a gadget has both GPS and a camera, and there's only one possible reaction: "Does it do *geotagging?*"

Geotagging means "embedding your latitude and longitude information into a photo or video when you take it." After all, every digital picture you've ever taken comes with its time and date embedded in its file; why not its location?

The good news is that the iPhone can geotag every photo and movie you take. How you use this information, however, is a bit trickier. The iPhone doesn't geotag unless all the following conditions are true:

- **The location feature on your phone is turned on.** On the Home screen, tap Settings→Privacy→Location Services. Make sure Camera is set to While Using the App. (The rest of the time, Camera does not record your location.)

- **The phone knows where it is.** If you're indoors, the GPS chip in the iPhone probably can't get a fix on the satellites overhead. And if you're not near cellular towers or Wi-Fi base stations, then even the pseudo-GPS may not be able to triangulate your location.

- **You've given permission.** The first time you use the iPhone's camera, a peculiar message appears, asking if it's allowed to use your location information. In this case, it's asking, "Do you want to geotag your pictures?" If you tap OK, then the iPhone's geographic coordinates will be embedded in each photo you take.

OK, so suppose all of this is true, and the geotagging feature is working. How will you know? Well, the Moments feature can put geotagging to work right on the phone. You can open a map and see all the photos you took in that spot.

You can also transfer the photos to your computer, where your likelihood of being able to see the geotag information depends on what photo-viewing software you're using. For example:

- **When you've selected a photo in iPhoto or Photos** (on the Mac), you can press ⌘-I for the Info panel. It shows the photo's spot on a map.

- **Once you've posted your geotagged photos on Flickr.com** (the world's largest photo-sharing site), people can use the Explore menu to search for them by location or even see them clustered on a world map.

- **If you import your photos into Picasa** (for Windows), then you can choose Tools→Geotag→View in Google Earth to see a picture's location on the map (if the free Google Earth program is installed on your computer, that is).

  Or choose Tools→Geotag→Export to Google Earth File to create a .kmz file, which you can send to a friend. When opened, this file opens Google Earth (if it's on your friend's computer) and displays a miniature of the picture in the right place on the map.

Capturing the Screen

Let's say you want to write a book about the iPhone. (Hey, it could happen.) How are you supposed to illustrate that book? How can you take pictures of what's on the screen?

The trick is very simple: Get the screen just the way you want it, even if that means holding your finger down on an onscreen button or a keyboard key. Now hold down the Home button, and while it's down, press the Sleep switch at the top of the phone. (Yes, you may need to invite some friends over to help you execute this multiple-finger move.)

But that's all there is to it. The screen flashes white. Now, if you go to the Photos app's Albums tab, in the Camera Roll or the Screenshots album, you see a crisp, colorful pixel image, in PNG format, of whatever was on the screen. (Its resolution matches the screen: 1136 × 640 on the iPhone 5 family, for example, or 1242 × 2208 on the Plus models.)

At this point, you can send it by email (to illustrate a request for help, for example, or to send a screen from Maps to a friend who's driving your way); sync it with your computer (to add it to your Mac or Windows photo collection); or designate it as the iPhone's wallpaper (to confuse the heck out of its owner).

> **TIP:** In some corners of iOS, there's no way to take a screenshot like this. For example, when the phone is ringing, pressing the screenshot button combination sends the call to voicemail instead of capturing the screen image.
>
> In those situations, you may have to rely on the QuickTime Player trick described on page 244—and take a screenshot on the *Mac.*

9

All About Apps

App is short for *application*, meaning software program, and the App Store is a single, centralized catalog of every authorized iPhone add-on program in the world. In fact, it's the *only* place where you can get new programs (at least without hacking your phone).

You hear people talking about downsides to this approach: Apple's stifling the competition; Apple's taking a 30 percent cut of every program sold; Apple's maintaining veto power over apps it doesn't like.

But there are some enormous benefits, too. First, there's one central place to look for apps. Second, Apple checks out every program to make sure it's decent and runs decently. Third, the store is beautifully integrated with the iPhone itself.

There's an incredible wealth of software in the App Store. These programs can turn the iPhone into an instant-message tool, a pocket Internet radio, a medical reference, a musical keyboard, a time and expense tracker, a TV remote control, a photo editor, a recipe box, a tip calculator, a restaurant finder, a teleprompter, and so on. And games—thousands of dazzling handheld games, some with smooth 3D graphics and tilt control.

It's so much stuff—1.4 million apps, 50 billion downloads—that the challenge now is just finding your way through it. Thank goodness for those Most Popular lists.

Two Ways to the App Store

You can get to the App Store in two ways: from the phone itself, or from your computer's copy of the iTunes software.

Using iTunes offers a much easier browsing and shopping experience, of course, because you've got a mouse, a keyboard, and that big screen. But downloading straight to the iPhone, without ever involving the computer, is wicked convenient when you're out and about.

Shopping from the Phone

To check out the App Store from your iPhone, tap the **App Store** icon. You arrive at the colorful, scrolling wonder of the store itself.

It has five tabs (the icons at the bottom). Here they are, in order:

- **Featured** is pretty clear: You can scroll vertically to see different categories, like **Editors' Choices** or **Popular Games**, and horizontally to see more apps within each category.

  The top row might say "Best New Apps." Scroll sideways to see the apps that Apple is recommending (**See All** shows all the new apps).

  At the top left, the **All Categories** button presents the entire catalog, organized by category: Books, Business, Education, Entertainment, Finance, Games, and so on. Tap a category to see what's in it.

- **Top Charts** is a list of the 100 most popular apps at the moment, ranked by how many people have downloaded them. There are actually three lists here: the most popular *free* programs, the most popular

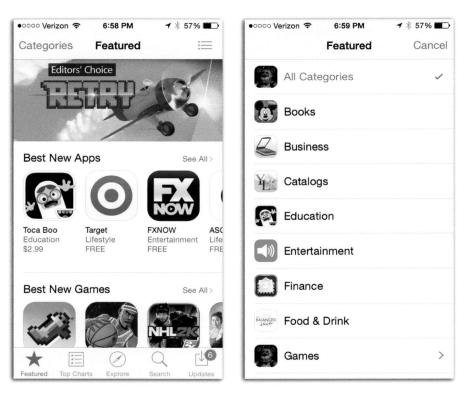

ones that cost money, and which apps have made the most money ("Top Grossing"), even if they haven't sold the most copies.

- **Explore** lists apps that are popular *near you*. It uses your location to check for geographically relevant apps. Usually, this concept is most useful when you're at a public institution: a museum, baseball stadium, train station, and so on. You may also see the newspaper apps for whatever town you're in, or local bus and subway apps.

- **Search.** As the number of iPhone apps grows into the millions, viewing by scrolling through lists begins to get awfully unwieldy.

  Fortunately, you can also *search* the catalog, which is efficient if you know what you're looking for (either the name of a program, the kind of program, or the software company that made it).

  Before you even begin to type, this screen shows you a list of Trending Searches—that is, the most popular searches right now. Odds are pretty good that if you want to download the latest hot app you keep hearing about, you'll see its name here (because, after all, it's hot).

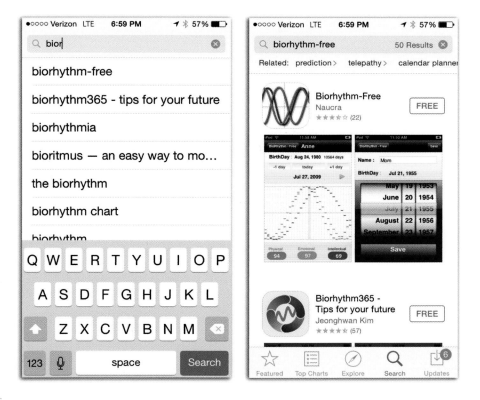

Or tap in the search box to make the keyboard appear. As you type, the list shrinks so that it's showing you only the matches. You might type *tetris*, or *piano*, or *Disney*, or whatever.

Tap anything in the results list (previous page, left) to see a series of "cards," one for each matching app. You can swipe horizontally to scroll through them. Tap one to view its details screen, as described below.

- **Updates.** Unlike its buddies, this button isn't intended to help you navigate the catalog. Instead, it lets you know when one of the programs you've *already* installed is available in a newer version. Details in a moment.

About a third of the App Store's programs are free; the rest are usually under $5. A few, intended for professionals (pilots, for example), can cost a lot more.

The App Details Page

No matter which button was your starting point, eventually you wind up at an app's *details screen*. There's a description, a scrolling set of screenshots, info about the author, the date posted, the version number, a page of related and similar apps, and so on.

You can also tap Reviews to dig beyond the average star rating into the *actual* written reviews from people who've already tried the thing.

Why are the ratings so important? Because the App Store's goodies aren't equally good. Remember, these programs come from a huge variety of people—teenagers in Hungary, professional firms in Silicon Valley, college kids goofing around on weekends—and just because they made it into the store doesn't mean they're worth the money (or even the time to download).

Sometimes a program has a low score because it's just not designed well or it doesn't do what it's advertised to do. And sometimes, of course, it's a little buggy.

If you decide something is worth getting, scroll back to the top of the page and tap its price button. It may say, for example, $0.99 or, if it's free, simply GET.

> **TIP:** If you see a little **+** sign on the price button, it means that the app works well on both the iPad and the iPhone.

If you've previously bought it, either on this iPhone or on another Apple touchscreen gadget, then the button turns into a ⬇; you don't have to

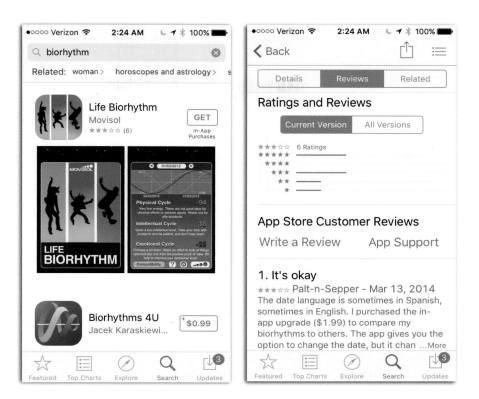

buy it again. Just tap to re-download. If, in fact, this app is already on your iPhone, then the button says **OPEN** (handy!).

Once you tap the price and then **INSTALL APP**, you've committed to downloading the program. There are only a few things that may stand in your way:

- **A request for your iTunes account info.** You can't use the App Store without an iTunes account—even if you're just downloading free stuff. If you've ever bought anything from the iTunes Store, signed up for an iCloud account, or bought anything from Apple online, then you already have an iTunes account (an Apple ID, meaning your email address and password).

  The iPhone asks you to enter your iTunes account name and password the first time you access the App Store and periodically thereafter, just to make sure some marauding child in your household can't run up your bill without your knowledge. Mercifully, you don't have to enter your Apple ID information just to download an *update* to an app you already own.

If you have an iPhone 5s or later model, and you've taught it to recognize your fingerprint, here's the payoff: When you try to download an app, instead of having to enter your Apple password, you can just touch the Home button with your finger.

• **A file size over 100 megabytes.** Most iPhone apps are pretty small—small enough to download directly to the phone, even over a cellular connection. If a program is bigger than 100 MB, though, you can't download it over the cellular airwaves, a policy no doubt intended to soothe nerves at AT&T, Sprint, T-Mobile, and Verizon, whose networks could be choked with 200 million iPhoners downloading huge files.

Instead, over-100-meg files are available only when you're on a Wi-Fi connection. Of course, you can also download them to your computer and sync them from there, as described later in this chapter.

Once you begin downloading a file, a tiny progress circle next to the app's name fills in to indicate the download's progress. (Tap the square Stop button inside the circle to cancel the download.) When the downloading is done, tap the OPEN button to launch it and try it out.

You don't have to sit there and stare at the progress bar. You can go on working on the iPhone. In fact, you can even go back to the App Store and start downloading something else simultaneously. You can easily spot your fresh downloads on the Home screens: Their icons fill in with color as the download proceeds, and after that their names are preceded by a blue dot.

Two Welcome Notes About Backups

Especially when you've paid good money for your iPhone apps, you might worry about what would happen if your phone got lost or stolen, or if someone (maybe you) accidentally deleted one of your precious downloads.

You don't have to worry, for two reasons.

First, the next time you sync your iPhone with your computer, iTunes asks if you want the newly purchased apps backed up onto the computer. If you click Transfer, then the programs eventually show up on the Applications tab in iTunes.

Second, here's a handy little fact about the App Store: It remembers what you've already bought. You can re-download a purchased program at any time, on any of your iPhones, iPads, or iPod Touches, without having to pay for it again.

TIP: If some program doesn't download properly on the iPhone, don't sweat it. Go into iTunes on your computer and choose Store→Check for Available Downloads. And if a program does download to the phone but doesn't transfer to iTunes, then choose File→Transfer Purchases from "iPhone". These two commands straighten things out, clear up the accounting, and make all well with your two copies of each app (iPhone + computer).

Shopping in iTunes

You can also download new programs to your computer using iTunes and then sync them over to the phone. By all means, use this method whenever you can. It's much more efficient to use a mouse, a keyboard, and a full screen.

In iTunes, click the A (apps) icon at top left; at top center, click App Store. The screen fills with starting points for your quest, matching what you'd see on the phone: Best New Apps, Best New Games, and so on.

Or use the search box at top right.

From here, the experience is the same as on the phone. Drill down to the Details page for a program, read its description and reviews, look at its photos, and so on. Click the price button to download and, at the next sync, install it.

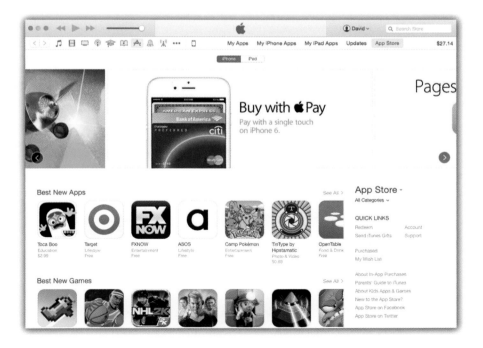

Organizing Your Apps

As you add new apps to your iPhone, it sprouts new Home screens as necessary to accommodate them all, up to a grand total of 11 screens. That's 224 icons—and yet you can actually go all the way up to many thousands of apps, thanks to the miracle of *folders*.

That multiple-Home screen business can get a little unwieldy, but a couple of tools can help you manage. First, you can just use Siri to open an app, without even knowing where it is. Just say, "Open Angry Birds" (or whatever).

Second, the Spotlight search feature can pluck the program you want out of your haystack, as described on page 90.

Third, you can organize your apps into folders, which greatly alleviates the agony of TMHSS (Too Many Home Screens Syndrome).

It's worth taking the time to arrange the icons on your Home screens into logical categories, tidy folders, or at least a sensible sequence.

You can do that either on the phone itself or in iTunes on your computer. That's far quicker and easier, but it works only when your phone is actually connected to the Mac or PC. Read on.

Rearranging/Deleting Apps Using iTunes

To fiddle with the layout of your Home screens with the least amount of hassle, connect the iPhone to your computer using the white charging cable or over Wi-Fi. Open iTunes.

Click your iPhone's icon (▯) at top left, and then click Apps in the left-side list. You see the display on the facing page.

From here, it's all mouse power:

- For each listed app, click the button so that it says either Install (if the app is on your computer but not currently on your phone) or Remove (if it is; at that point, the button changes to say Will Remove). In other words, it's possible to store hundreds of apps in iTunes but load only some of them onto your iPhone.

- Click one of the Home screen miniatures on the right list to indicate which screen you want to edit. It gets big. Now you can drag the app icons to rearrange them on that page. (Click the background to close the life-size image.)

- Beneath the Home screen miniatures, iTunes displays similar mock-ups of each *folder* on your phone. Because they're visible here, all of

them, all the time, it's very easy to put icons into them—and to work with the multiple "pages" within each folder (read on).

- It's fine to drag an app onto a different page mockup. You can organize your icons on these Home screens by category, frequency of use, color, or whatever tickles your fancy. (The **+** button above each pile of mockups means "Click to install an additional Home screen.")

TIP: You can select several app icons simultaneously by ⌘-clicking them (or Ctrl-clicking in Windows); that way, you can move a bunch of them at once.

- You can drag the page mockups around to rearrange *them*, too.

- To delete an app from the iPhone, point to its icon and click the **✕**. (You can't delete Apple's starter apps like Safari and Mail.)

- Create a folder by dragging one app's icon on top of another (see page 319 for more on folders).

When your design spurt is complete, click Apply.

Rearranging/Deleting Apps Right on the Phone

You can also redesign your Home screens right on the iPhone, which is handy when you don't happen to be wired up to a computer.

To enter this Home screen editing mode, hold your finger down on any icon until, after about a second, the icons begin to—what's the correct term?—*wiggle*.

> **TIP:** You can even move an icon onto the Dock. Just make room for it by first dragging an *existing* Dock icon to another spot on the screen.

At this point, you can rearrange your icons by dragging them around the glass into a new order; other icons scoot aside to make room.

> **TIP:** You can drag a single icon across multiple Home screens without ever having to lift your finger. Just drag the icon against the right or left margin of the screen to "turn the page."

To create an additional Home screen, drag a wiggling icon to the right edge of the screen; keep your finger down. The first Home screen slides off to the left, leaving you on a new, blank one, where you can deposit the icon. You can create up to 11 Home screens in this way.

You may have noticed that, while your icons are wiggling, most of them also sprout little ⊗'s. That's how you *delete* a program you don't need anymore: Tap that ⊗. You'll be asked if you're sure; if so, it says bye-bye.

(You can't delete one of Apple's preinstalled apps, so no ⊗ appears on those icons. If they really bug you, you can drag the little-used Apple apps into a folder somewhere.)

When everything looks good, press the Home button to stop the wiggling.

Restoring the Home Screen

If you ever need to undo all the damage you've done, tap Settings→General→ Reset→Reset Home Screen Layout. That function preserves any new programs you've installed, but it consolidates them. If you'd put 10 programs on each of four Home screens, you wind up with only two screens, each packed with 20 icons. Any leftover blank pages are eliminated. This function also places all your downloaded apps in alphabetical order.

Folders

Folders are useful on your Mac or PC—so why not use them on your phone? Folders let you organize your apps, deemphasize the ones you don't use often, and restore order to that dizzying display of icons.

These days, each folder can have many pages of its own, each displaying nine icons. A single folder, in other words, can contain as many apps as you want—and therefore, only memory limits how many apps you can fit onto your phone.

Setting Up Folders on the iPhone

To create and edit folders, begin by entering Home screen editing mode. That is, hold your finger down on any icon until all the icons begin to wiggle.

Now, to create a folder, drag one app's icon on top of another. The software puts both of them into a new folder and proposes a name, which you can change at this point. If they're the same kind of app, iOS even tries to figure out what category they both belong to—and names the new folder accordingly ("Music," "Photos," "Kid Games," or whatever).

You're welcome to add more apps to this folder. Tap the Home screen background to close the folder, and then (while the icons are still wiggling) drag another app onto the folder's icon. Lather, rinse, repeat.

Drag one app onto another…   *…and a new folder is born. Rename it here.*

If one of your folders has more than nine apps in it, iOS creates a second "page" for the folder—and a third, a fourth, and so on. You can move apps around within the pages and otherwise master your new multipage folder domain.

You can scroll the folder "pages" by swiping sideways, just as you scroll the full-size Home pages. The only limit to how many icons a folder can hold is your tolerance for absurdity.

Once you've created a folder or two, they're easy to rename, move, delete, and so on. (Again, you can do all of the following *only in icon-wiggling editing mode*.) Like this:

- **Take an app out of a folder** by dragging its icon anywhere else on the Home screen. The other icons scoot aside to make room, just as they do when you move them from one Home screen to another.

- **Move a folder around** by dragging, as you would any other icon.

TIP: You can drag a folder icon onto the Dock, too, just as you would any app. Now you've got a pop-up subfolder full of your favorite apps—on the Dock, which is present on every Home screen. That's a very useful feature; it multiplies the handiness of the Dock itself.

- **Rename a folder** by opening it (tapping it). At this point, the folder's name box is ready for editing.

- **Move an icon from one folder "page" to another** by dragging it to the edge of the folder, waiting with your finger down until the page "changes," and then releasing your finger in the right spot.

- **Delete a folder** by removing all of its contents. The folder disappears automatically.

When you're finished manipulating your folders, press the Home button to exit Home screen editing mode—and stop all the wiggling madness.

Setting Up Folders in iTunes

It's faster and easier to set up your folders within iTunes, on your Mac or PC, where you have a mouse and a big screen to help you. Connect your iPhone to your computer (by cable or Wi-Fi), open iTunes, click the iPhone's name at top left, and then click the **Apps** tab at the top. You see something like the illustration on page 317.

To create a folder, click a Home page miniature to expand it; now drag one app's icon on top of another, exactly as you'd do on the iPhone. The software puts both of them into a single new folder. As on the iPhone, the software proposes a folder name; an editing bar also appears so that you can type a custom name you prefer.

Once you've got a folder, you can open it just by double-clicking. It expands to life size, revealing its contents. Now you can edit the folder's name, drag the icons around inside it, or drag an app right out of the folder window and onto another Home page (or another folder on it). Just keep your finger down on the mouse button or trackpad, no matter how long it takes, until the new Home page or folder page opens.

Below the Home pages, you'll discover that each of your app folders now has an app-management screen mockup of its own, complete with a horizontally scrolling set of pages. That's so you can move the "pages" around, organize the apps within them, and so on.

If you remove all the apps from a folder, the folder disappears.

App Preferences

If you're wondering where you can change an iPhone app's settings, consider backing out to the Home screen and then tapping Settings. Apple encourages programmers to add their programs' settings *here*, way down below the bottom of the iPhone's own Settings screen.

Some programmers ignore the advice and build the settings right into their apps, where they're a little easier to find. But if you don't see them there, now you know where else to look.

App Updates

When a circled number (like ❷) appears on the App Store's icon on the Home screen, or on the Updates icon within the App Store program, that's Apple's way of letting you know that a program you already own has been updated. Apple knows which programs you've bought—and notifies you when new, improved versions are released. Which is remarkably often; software companies constantly fix bugs and add new features.

Manual Updates

When you tap Updates, you're shown a list of the programs with waiting updates. A tiny What's New arrow lets you know what the changes are—new features, perhaps, or some bug fixes. And when you tap a program's name, you go to its details screen, where you can remind yourself of what the app does and can read other people's reviews of this new version.

You can download one app's update, or, with a tap on the Update All button, all of them...no charge.

> **NOTE:** You can also download your updates from iTunes. Click Apps in the Source list (under the Library heading); the lower edge of the window lets you know if there are updated versions of your programs waiting and offers buttons that let you download the updates individually or all at once.

Automatic Updates

If you have a lot of apps, you may come to feel as though you're spending your whole life downloading updates. They descend like locusts, every single day, demanding your attention.

That's why Apple offers an automatic update-downloading option. Your phone can download and install updated versions of your apps quietly and automatically in the background.

To turn on this feature, open Settings→iTunes & App Store. Under Automatic Downloads, turn on Updates. (If you'd prefer that the phone wait to do this downloading until it's in a Wi-Fi hotspot—to avoid eating up your monthly cellular data-plan allotment—then turn off Use Cellular Data.)

From now on, the task of manually approving each app's update is off your to-do list forever. Only a blue dot next to an app's name on the Home screen lets you know that it's been updated.

> **TIP:** Fortunately, the iPhone also keeps a tidy record of every app it's updated and what that update gives you. Open the App Store app; tap the Updates tab. There's your list, sorted chronologically. Tap an app's row to read what was new in the update you've already received.

How to Find Good Apps

If the Featured, What's Hot, and Charts lists aren't getting you inspired, there are all kinds of websites dedicated to reviewing iPhone apps. There's *appadvice.com* and *whatsoniphone.com* and on and on.

But if you've never dug into iPhone apps before, you should at least try out some of the superstars, the big dogs that almost everybody has.

Many of the most popular apps are designed to deliver certain websites in the best-looking way possible. That's why there are apps for Facebook, Twitter, LinkedIn, Spotify, Pandora, Flickr, Yelp, Netflix, YouTube, Wikipedia, and so on.

Here are a very few more examples—a drop in the bucket at the tip of the iceberg—of the infinite app variety beyond those basics:

- **Apple Apps (free).** The first time you open the App Store, you're offered a set of free Apple apps that Apple thinks you might like: iBooks, iTunes U, Podcasts, Find My Friends, and Find My iPhone. With one tap, you can grab this whole set.

- **Google Maps (free).** Google Maps is a replacement for the built-in Maps app. It's much, *much* better than Maps—even Apple has admitted that. Among other things, it offers Street View (you can actually see a photo of almost any address and "look around" you), it incorporates the Zagat guides for restaurants, and it's unbelievably smart about knowing what you're trying to type into the search box. Usually, about three letters is all you need to type before the app guesses what you mean.

- **Google Mobile (free).** Speak to search Google's maps. Includes Google Goggles: Point the phone's camera at a book, DVD, wine bot-

tle, logo, painting, landmark, or bit of text, and the hyper-intelligent app recognizes it and displays information about it from the web.

- **Ocarina ($1).** A bona fide wind instrument. Blow into the microphone, learn the fingerings of the four "holes" on the screen...beautiful music.

- **Fake Calls ($1).** When you tap this icon on your Home screen, in about 10 seconds, your phone rings. It's a fake call—from anyone you've selected in advance. The simulation of the iPhone's traditional incoming-call screen is perfect. Ideal for extricating yourself from difficult situations, like meetings or bad dates.

- **Echofon (free).** Most free Twitter apps are a bit on the baffling side. This one is simple and clean.

- **SoundHound (free).** Beats Shazam at its own game. Hold this app up to a song that's playing on the radio, or even hum or sing the song, and the app miraculously identifies the song and offers you lyrics. It's faster than Shazam, too.

- **FlightTrack Pro ($10).** Shows every detail of every flight: gate, time delayed, airline phone number, where the flight is on the map, and more. Knows more—and knows it sooner—than the actual airlines do.

- **Instagram (free)** has a bunch of filter effects, as iOS's Camera app does. But the real magic is in the way it's designed to share your photos. You sign up to receive Instagrams from Facebook or Twitter folk. They (the photos, not the folk) show up right in the app, scrolling up like a photographic Twitter feed. Seeing what other people are doing every day with their cameraphones and creative urges is really inspirational.

Other essentials: Angry Birds and its sequel, Bad Piggies. Skype. Hipmunk (finds flights). The New York Times. The Amazon Kindle book reader, B&N eReader. Dictionary. TED. *Mint.com*. Scrabble. Keynote Remote (controls your Keynote presentations from the phone). Remote (yes, another one, also from Apple—turns the iPhone into a Wi-Fi, whole-house **remote control** for your Mac or PC's music playback—and for Apple TV). Instant-messaging (AIM, Yahoo Messenger, IM+, or Beejive IM). Yahoo Weather (gorgeous).

Happy apping!

The App Switcher

Often, it's handy to switch among open apps. Maybe you want to copy something from Safari (on the web) into Mail (a message you're writing).

Maybe you want to refer to your frequent flier number (in Notes) as you're using an airline's check-in app. Maybe you want to adjust something in Settings and then get back to whatever you were doing.

The key to switching apps is to **double-press the Home button**. Whatever is on the screen gets replaced by the app switcher (below, left).

TIP: On the iPhone 6s and 6s Plus, there's a second way to reach this screen: **Hard-swipe** from the left edge of the screen. This method has one advantage: It lets you **peek** at whatever apps are in the background, and then, without ever lifting your thumb, slide back to the left. You've had a quick glance without ever fully entering the app switcher.

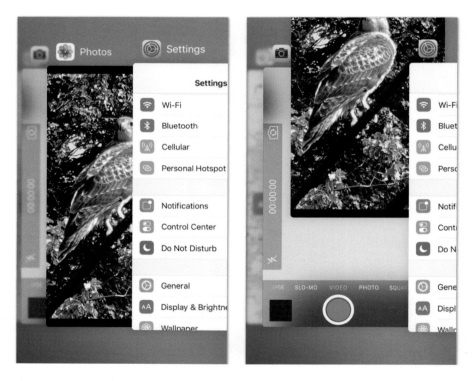

You see a scrolling series of "cards" that represent the open apps, in chronological order. In iOS 9's redesigned app switcher, they're bigger, so you can actually see what's going on in each open app. In fact, sometimes, that's all you need; you can refer to another app's screen in this view, without actually having to switch **into** that app.

TIP: Thoughtfully enough, the app switcher always puts the *previous app* front and center when you first double-press the Home button. For example, if you're in Safari but you were using Mail a minute ago, Mail appears centered in the app switcher. That makes life easier if you're doing a lot of jumping back and forth between two apps; one tap takes you into the previous app.

When you tap an app's icon or screen in the app switcher, you open that app.

Force Quitting an App

The app switcher lets you manually exit an app, closing it down. To do that, flick the unwanted app's mini-screen upward, so that it flies up off the top of the screen (shown on the facing page at right).

The app is not really gone; it will return to the lineup the next time you open it from the Home screen.

You'll need this gesture only rarely. You're not supposed to quit every app when you're finished. Force-quit an app only if it's frozen or acting glitchy and needs to be restarted.

TIP: There may be one more element on the task-switcher screen, too: a faint app icon at the far left. That's a document, email, or web page being sent to your phone by your Mac, using Handoff (see page 540).

A Word About Background Apps

Switching out of a program doesn't actually close it. All apps can run in the background.

Of course, if every app ran full-tilt simultaneously, your phone would guzzle down battery power like crazy. To solve that problem, Apple has put two kinds of limits in place:

• **iOS's limits.** Not all apps run full speed in the background. Apps that really need constant updating, like Facebook or Twitter, get refreshed every few seconds; apps that don't rely on constant Internet updates get to nap for a while in the background.

In deciding which apps get background attention, iOS studies things like how good your phone's Internet connection is and what time of day you traditionally use a certain app (so that your newspaper's app is ready with the latest articles when you open it).

- **Your own limits.** You can't control which apps *run* in the background, but you can control which ones *download new data* in the background. In Settings→General→Background App Refresh, you'll find a list of every app that may want to update itself in the background. In an effort to make your battery last longer, you can turn off background updating for the apps you don't really care about; you can even turn off all background updating using the master switch at the top.

The bottom line: There's no need to quit apps you're not using, ever. Contrary to certain Internet rumors, they generally don't use enough memory or battery power to matter. You may see dozens of apps in the app switcher, but you'll never sense that your phone is bogging down as a result.

Back to App (◀)

This humble new feature may become your favorite feature in all of iOS 9.

Rival phones, like Android and Windows Phones, have a Back button. It's always there. It always takes you back to the screen from whence you came.

But not the iPhone. The only way to return to a previous app has always been to use the app switcher—which entails two clicks of the Home button *and* a tap on the screen.

In iOS 9, there's a Back button at last. It appears only when you've tapped a link of some kind that takes you into a different app. For example:

- **You're in Messages,** and you tap a web link (below, left) that takes you into Safari (below, right). A **Back to Messages** button appears at the top-left corner of your screen.

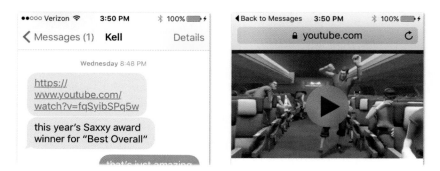

- **You're on Twitter or Facebook,** and you tap a link that opens a web page. Sure enough: the top-left button says **Back to Twitter** or **Back to Facebook**.

- **You're in Mail,** and you tap an underlined date and time that takes you into the Calendar app. A Back to Mail button appears in the corner.

- **You're in Safari,** and you tap a link that opens in YouTube. Sure enough: the button says Back to Safari.

Add it all up, and this tiny enhancement can save you literally *minutes* a week. It's the best.

AirPrint: Printing from the Phone

The very phrase "printing from the phone" might seem peculiar. How do you print from a gadget that's smaller than a Hershey bar—a gadget without any jacks for connecting a printer?

Wirelessly, of course.

You can send printouts from your phone to any printer that's connected to your Mac or PC on the same Wi-Fi network if you have a piece of software like Printopia ($20).

Or you can use the iPhone's built-in AirPrint technology, which can send printouts directly to a Wi-Fi printer without requiring a Mac or a PC.

Not just any Wi-Fi printer, though—only those that recognize AirPrint. Many recent Canon, Epson, HP, and Lexmark printers work with AirPrint; you can see a list of them on Apple's website, here: *http://support.apple.com/kb/HT4356*.

Not all apps can print. Of the built-in Apple programs, only iBooks, Mail, Photos, Notes, and Safari offer **Print** commands. Those apps contain what most people want to print most of the time: PDF documents (iBooks), email messages, driving directions from the web, and so on. Plenty of non-Apple apps work with AirPrint, too.

To use AirPrint, start by tapping the ⬆ button; tap **Print**. You're offered a **Select Printer** option. Tap it to introduce the phone to your printer, whose name should appear automatically. Now you can adjust the printing options (number of copies, page range)—and when you finally tap **Print**, your printout shoots wirelessly to the printer, exactly as though your phone and printer were wired together.

The Share Sheet

Every app is different, of course. But all of them have certain things in common; otherwise, you'd go out of your mind.

One of them is the Share sheet. It's your headquarters for sending stuff off your phone: to other apps, to other phones, to the Internet, to a printer. It's made up of several icon rows, each of which scrolls horizontally. (From top to bottom, you could title these rows "What to Share," "Send by AirDrop," "Send to an App," and "Act on This Data Directly.")

The Share sheet pops up whenever you tap the Share button (⬆) that appears in many, many apps: Maps, Photos, Safari, Notes, Voice Memos, Contacts, and so on.

The buttons you see depend on the app; you may see only two options here, or you may see a dozen. Starting on page 288, for example, you can read descriptions of the icons that appear when you're sending a photo: AirDrop, Message, Mail, Twitter, Facebook, Copy, AirPlay, Print, and so on. The options here vary by app.

Moreover, there's a **More** button at the end of each row. That's an invitation for other, non-Apple apps to install their own "send to" options into the Share sheet. When you tap **More**, you can see the full list of apps that have inserted themselves here. Now you can perform these tasks:

- **Hide a sharing option.** Flip the switch to make one of the sharing options disappear from the Share sheet. (You can't hide the sharing options that Apple considers essential, like Message or Mail.)

- **Rearrange the sharing options.** Use the handle to move these items up or down the list, which affects their left-to-right order on the Share sheet.

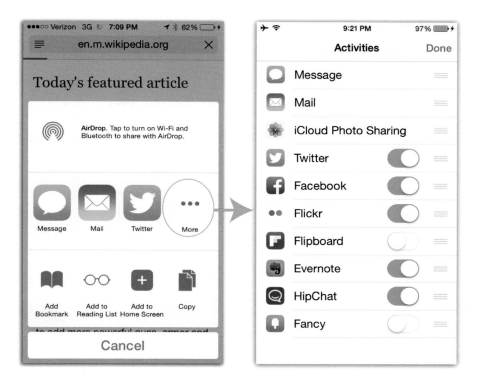

AirDrop

It's a headline feature: AirDrop, a way to shoot things from one Apple phone, tablet, or Mac to another—wirelessly, instantly, easily, encryptedly, without requiring names, passwords, or settings-up. It's much faster than emailing or text messaging, since you don't have to know (or type) the other person's address. It's available on the iPhone 5 and later.

> **NOTE:** If the Mac is running OS X Yosemite or later, you can shoot files between it and your phone, too!

You can transmit pictures and videos from the Photos app, people's info cards from Contacts, directions (or your current location) from Maps, pages from Notes, web addresses from Safari, electronic tickets from Wallet, apps you like in the App Store, song and video listings from the iTunes app), radio stations (iTunes Radio), and so on. As time goes on, more and more non-Apple apps will offer AirDrop, too.

Behind the scenes, AirDrop uses Bluetooth (to find nearby gadgets within about 30 feet) and a private, temporary Wi-Fi mini-network (to transfer the file). Both sender and receiver must have Bluetooth and Wi-Fi turned on.

The process goes like this:

1. **Find a willing recipient.** You can't send anything with AirDrop unless the receiving phone or tablet is running iOS 7 or later—and is awake. And only recent models work with AirDrop: iPhone 5 or later, fourth-generation iPad or later, any iPad mini, and fifth-generation iPod Touch or later.

   In other words, most AirDrop exchanges begin with your saying, "Hey, do you have iOS 7 or later?"

2. **Open the item you want to share. Tap the Share button (⬆).** If your app doesn't have a ⬆ button, then you can't use AirDrop.

   When the Share sheet appears, within a few seconds, you see something that would have awed the masses in 1975: small circular photos of everyone nearby. (Or at least everyone with iOS 7 or later, or OS X Yosemite or later. Or at least everyone among them who's **open to receiving** AirDrop transmissions, as described in a moment.)

3. **Tap the icon of the person you want to share with.** In about a second, a message appears on the recipient's screen, conveying your offer to transmit something good—and, when it makes sense, showing a picture of it (previous page, right).

At this point, it's up to your recipients. If they tap Accept, then the transfer begins (and ends); whatever you sent them opens up automatically in the relevant app. You'll know that AirDrop was successful because the word "Sent" appears on your screen.

If they tap Decline, then you must have misunderstood their willingness to accept your item (or they tapped the wrong button). In that case, you'll see the word "Declined" on your screen.

The One AirDrop Setting

Your existence probably won't become a living hell of AirDrop invitations. Realistically, you won't be bombarded by strangers around you who want to show you family pictures or web links. Even so, Apple has given you some control over who's allowed to try to send you things by AirDrop.

To see the settings, swipe up from the bottom of the screen to open the Control Center. There, in the middle, is the AirDrop button. Tap it to see these three choices:

• **Off.** Nobody can send anything to you by AirDrop. You'll never be disturbed by an incoming "Accept?" message.

• **Contacts Only.** Only people in your Contacts app—your own address book—can send you things by AirDrop. Your phone is invisible to strangers. (Of course, even when someone you know tries to send something, you still have to approve the transfer.)

- **Everyone.** Anyone, even strangers, can try to send you things. You can still accept or decline each transfer.

TIP: OK, there's one other AirDrop setting to fiddle with: In Settings→ Sounds, you can specify the sound effect that means, "AirDrop file received."

(OK, OK, there's *one more* setting. Deep in General→Restrictions, you can turn off AirDrop altogether. Now your youngster—or whomever you're trying to restrict with restrictions—can't get into trouble in a debauched frenzy of sending and receiving files.)

iCloud Drive

iCloud Drive is Apple's version of Dropbox. It's a folder whose contents appear identically on every Mac, iPhone, iPad, and even Windows PC you own, through the magic of instant online syncing. It's an online "disk" that holds 5 gigabytes (more, if you're willing to pay for it).

The iCloud Drive is a perfect place to put stuff you want to be able to access from any computer, iPhone, or iPad, wherever you go. It's a great backup, too, because anything you put into it is automatically duplicated on multiple machines.

Your first chance to turn on iCloud Drive was when you first installed iOS 8 or 9 (or bought your iOS 8 or 9 phone). If you declined, maybe because you had no idea what it was about, then you can visit Settings→iCloud→iCloud Drive and turn iCloud Drive on now.

NOTE: iCloud Drive replaces a previous syncing feature that Apple called "Documents in the Cloud." If you turn on iCloud Drive, the old system goes away; all the files you kept there are brought onto your new iCloud Drive. That's fine, as long as you understand that pre–iOS 8 (or pre–OS X Yosemite) gadgets will no longer be able to see them.

Once you turn on iCloud Drive, you can't go back to the "Documents in the Cloud" system. Sure, you can turn *off* iCloud Drive (in Settings), but all that does is stop syncing the drive's contents with your other machines.

Now, it's easy to understand iCloud Drive on a Mac or PC. It looks like any other disk, full of files and folders. You can even access them at *iCloud.com* (click the Drive icon), which is handy when you have to use someone else's computer. Any change you make to the iCloud Drive or its contents is instantly synchronized across all your other gadgets.

In iOS 9, iCloud Drive is an actual app. Open it to see something like this:

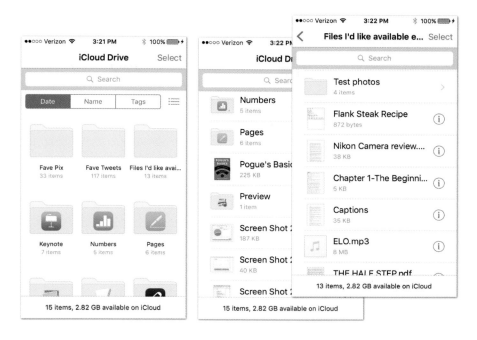

You can also see what's on your iCloud Drive *within* apps that can open and save documents. That includes Apple's apps—Keynote, Pages, Numbers, iMovie—and other apps that create and open documents, like, say, Scanner Pro and PDF Expert. Over time, more companies will make their apps compatible with iCloud Drive.

In all these apps, there's an Open button or icon that presents the iCloud Drive's contents. In Pages, for example, when you're viewing your list of documents, tap +, and then tap iCloud. There's the list of folders on your iCloud Drive, corresponding perfectly to what you would have seen on a Mac or a PC. Tap a folder to open it and see what's in it.

Note that iOS shows you *everything* on your iCloud Drive, even things you can't open at the moment. For example, if you're using the iMovie app, you can't open a Pages file, so Pages documents appear dimmed and gray.

On the other hand, this arrangement offers some really useful perks:

- **You can open some kinds of files in different apps.** A PDF file, for example, can open into Pages, *or* Photos, *or* iBooks. So PDF files show up as openable in all those apps.

- **When you delete an app,** you no longer lose all the documents you created with it.

You can view your iCloud Drive folders either as icons (previous page, left) or in a list view (right). Tap to open one; tap < at top left to back out of whatever folder you've opened.

In iOS 9, you can also *sort* these views—by Date, Name, or Tags, using the buttons at the top. (Tug downward to reveal them.)

On an iPhone, the iCloud Drive folder list is not quite the same thing as having a real desktop—you can't rename, copy, or delete files or folders on the phone, for example.

But it's comforting to know that everything on your iCloud Drive that you can open is available wherever you go—and that you can now load up everyday documents (pictures, music, PDF files, Microsoft Office files, iWork documents) onto your phone by dragging them into the iCloud Drive folder on your computer.

NOTE: Your free iCloud account includes only 5 gigabytes of storage—and that's for everything on your iCloud Drive. If you're willing to pay $1 to $20 a month, you can expand that storage to anywhere from 20 gigabytes to 1 terabyte. To do that, open **Settings→iCloud→Storage→Change Storage Plan**.

10

The Built-In Apps

Your Home screen comes already loaded with the icons of about 25 programs. Eventually, of course, you'll fill your Home screens with apps you install yourself, but Apple starts you off with the essentials. They include gateways to the Internet (Safari), communications tools (Phone, Messages, Mail, Contacts), visual records of your life (Photos, Camera), shopping centers (iTunes, App Store), omnipresent storage (iCloud Drive), and entertainment (Music, Videos, Podcasts).

Those core apps get special treatment in the other chapters. This chapter covers the secondary programs, in alphabetical order: Calculator, Calendar, Clock, Compass, Game Center, Health, iBooks, Maps, News, Notes, Podcasts, Reminders, Stocks, Tips, Voice Memos, Wallet, Watch, and Weather.

> **TIP:** You can open any of these apps by hunting it down and tapping its icon. But it's usually much faster to tell Siri to do it. Say, "Open the calculator," for example .

Calculator

The iPhone wouldn't be much of a computer without a calculator, now, would it? And here it is, your everyday calculator—with a secret twist.

In Calculator's basic four-function mode, you can tap out equations (like **15.4 × 300 =**) to see the answer at the top. (You can **paste** things you've copied into here, too; just hold your finger down until the Paste button appears.) There's no memory function in the basic calculator, but you do get a +/– button; its function is to change the currently displayed number from positive to negative, or vice versa.

Now the twist: If you rotate the iPhone 90 degrees in either direction, the Calculator morphs into a full-blown HP *scientific* calculator, complete with trigonometry, logarithmic functions, a memory function, exponents, roots beyond the square root, and so on. Go wild, ye engineers and physicists!

If you make a mistake while entering a number, swipe horizontally across the numerical display (either direction). Each swipe backspaces over the rightmost digit.

Calendar

The iPhone's calendar syncs, automatically and wirelessly, with whatever online calendar you keep: iCloud, Google Calendar, a corporate Exchange calendar, and so on. Everything's kept in sync with your computers and tablets, too. Make a change in one place, and it changes everywhere else.

Then again, you can also use Calendar all by itself.

> **TIP:** The Calendar icon on the Home screen shows what looks like one of those paper Page-a-Day calendar pads. But if you look closely, you'll see a sweet touch: It actually shows *today's* day and date.

Day View

When you open Calendar, you're shown today's schedule, broken down by time slot (below, right).

From here, you can navigate to other days' schedules in any of three ways:

- **Swipe horizontally across the Day screen** to see the previous or next day.

- **Tap a date at the top** to see another day this week.

- **Swipe across the dates at the top** to jump to another week.

If the date you want to check is further away than a week or two, though, it might make more sense to pop into Month view, described next.

Month View

Month view, of course, shows the entire month at a glance (previous page, center). You can scroll the month vertically, thereby scanning the entire year in a few seconds.

To get there from Day view, tap the name of the month (like March) at the top left.

Of course, your little phone screen is too small to show you what's written on each calendar square; all you get is a gray dot on any date when you've scheduled an appointment. Tap that dot to jump back into Day view and read your schedule.

TIP: If you have an iPhone 6s model, a delicious shortcut awaits: *Hard-press* any gray dot. A pop-up bubble appears, showing you the appointments that day as though it's a peephole into the Day view. You can then press even harder to *open* the Day view for that day, or lift your finger away to return to the Month view. You've just used Peek and Pop, described on page 38.

Year View

If you're in Month view, you can "zoom out" yet another level—to Year view. It's a simple, vertically scrolling map of the year's months. Tap the name of the year (top left) to see it.

From there, tap a month block to open it back into Month view.

TIP: In all three of these views—Day, Month, Year—you can tap Today (bottom left) to return to today's date.

Week View

The most useful view yet may be the fourth one: the scrolling Week view (facing page, top).

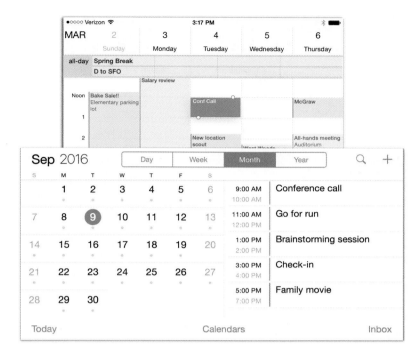

No button opens this view; instead, turn the phone 90 degrees so that it's in landscape mode. You can swipe sideways to move to earlier or later dates. Swipe up or down to move through the hours of the day. (OK, you don't get to see a *full* week, but it's close.)

iPhone 6/6s Plus Views

If you have a Plus model—the one with the Jumbotron screen—there's room for extra information (the lower illustration above). On a Plus, the Day and Month views offer a split screen, showing the calendar on the left and details on the right. You also get a row of view buttons (Day, Week, Month, Year)—something the owners of puny regular iPhones never see.

Subscribing to Your Online Calendars

To set up real-time, wireless connections to your calendars online, tap your way to Settings→Mail, Contacts, Calendars→Add Account. Here you can tap iCloud, Exchange, Gmail, Yahoo, AOL, or Outlook.com to set up your account. (You can also tap Other→Add CalDAV Account to fill in the details of a less well-known calendar server, or Other→Add Subscribed Calendar to connect to an online calendar subscription service—from Tripit or your favorite sports team, for example.

Making an Appointment (Day or Month View)

Recording an event on this calendar is quite a bit more flexible than entering one on, say, one of those "Hunks of the Midwest Police Stations" paper calendars.

Start by tapping + (top-right corner of the screen). The New Event screen pops up, filled with tappable lines of information. Tap one (like **Starts** or **Repeat**) to open a configuration screen for that element.

For example:

- **Title/Location.** Name your appointment here. For example, you might type *Fly to Phoenix*.

  The second line, called **Location**, makes a lot of sense. If you think about it, almost everyone needs to record *where* a meeting is to take place. You might type a reminder for yourself like *My place*, a specific address like *212 East 23rd*, a contact phone, or a flight number. Use the keyboard as usual.

- **Starts/Ends.** Tap **Starts**, and then indicate the starting time for this appointment, using the four spinning dials that appear at the bottom of the screen (below, right). The first sets the date; the second, the hour; the third, the minute; the fourth, AM or PM.

●oooo Verizon 🗘	3:18 PM	🕸 ▰▰▰
Cancel	**Edit**	Done

Root Canal	
Dr. Evilstein's office	
All-day	⬭
Starts	Apr 15, 2017 7:15 PM
Ends	8:15 PM
Repeat	Never >
Travel Time	None >
Calendar	● DWP >

●●ooo Verizon 🗘	11:52 PM	🕸 88% ▰▰▰
Cancel	**New Event**	Add

All-day	⬭
Starts	Apr 18, 2016 11:00 AM

Fri Apr 15	8	45	
Sat Apr 16	9	50	
Sun Apr 17	10	55	
Mon Apr 18	**11**	**00**	**AM**
Tue Apr 19	12	05	PM
Wed Apr 20	1	10	
Thu Apr 21	2	15	

Time Zone	New York >
Ends	12:00 PM
Repeat	Never >

Then tap **Ends**, and repeat the process to schedule the ending time. (The iPhone helpfully presets the Ends time to one hour later.)

An **All-day** event, of course, has no specific time of day: a holiday, a birthday, a book deadline. When you turn this option on, the Starts and Ends times disappear. The event appears at the top of the list for that day.

TIP: Calendar can handle multiday appointments, too, like trips away. Turn on **All-day**—and then use the **Starts** and **Ends** controls to specify beginning and ending *dates*. On the iPhone, you'll see it as a list item that repeats on every day's square. Back on your computer, you'll see it as a banner stretching across the Month view.

- **Repeat.** The screen here contains common options for recurring events: every day, every week, and so on. It starts out saying **Never**.

  Once you tap a selection, you return to the Edit screen. Now you can tap the **End Repeat** button to specify when this event should *stop* repeating. If you leave the setting at **Never**, then you're stuck seeing this event repeating on your calendar until the end of time (a good choice for recording, say, your anniversary, especially if your spouse might be consulting the same calendar).

  In other situations, you may prefer to tap **On Date** and spin the three dials (month, day, year) to specify an ending date, which is useful for car and mortgage payments.

  Tap **New Event** to return to the editing screen.

- **Travel Time.** If you turn on this switch, you can indicate how long it'll take you to get to this appointment.

  You get six canned choices, from 5 minutes to 2 hours. Or you can tap **Starting Location** and specify your starting point, and marvel as the iPhone calculates the driving time automatically. (Walking time, too, if it's close enough.)

  Two things then happen. First, the travel time is blocked off on your calendar, so you don't accidentally schedule things during your driving time. (The travel time is depicted as a dotted extension of the appointment.)

  Second, if you've set up an alarm reminder, it will go off that much earlier, so you have time to get where you're going.

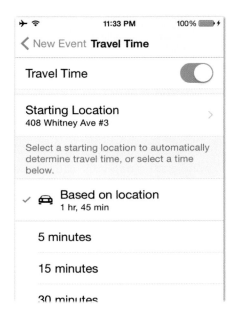

- **Calendar.** Tap here to specify which color-coded *calendar* (category, like Home, Kids, or Work) this appointment belongs to. Turn to page 347 for details on the calendar concept.

- **Invitees.** If you have an iCloud, Exchange, or CalDAV account, you can invite people to an event—a meeting, a party, whatever—and track their responses, right there on your phone (or any iCloud gadget). When you tap Invitees, you get an Add Invitees screen, where you can type in the email addresses of your lucky guests. (Or tap ⊕ to choose them from your Contacts list.)

  Later, when you tap Done, the phone fires off email invitations to those guests. It contains buttons for them to click: Accept, Decline, and Maybe. You get to see their responses right here in the details of your calendar event.

  As icing on the cake, your guests will see a pop-up reminder on their phones when the time comes for the party to get started.

- **Alert.** This screen tells Calendar how to notify you when a certain appointment is about to begin. Calendar can send any of four kinds of flags to get your attention. Tap how much notice you want: 5, 15, or 30 minutes before the big moment; an hour or two before; a day or two before; a week before; or on the day of the event.

For all-day events like birthdays, you get a smaller but very useful list of choices: "On day of event (9 AM)," "1 day before (9 AM)," "2 days before (9 AM)," and "1 week before."

When you tap Add Event and return to the main Add Event screen, you see that a new line, called Second Alert, has sprouted up beneath the first Alert line. This line lets you schedule a *second* warning for your appointment, which can occur either before or after the first one. Think of it as a backup alarm for events of extra urgency.

Once you've scheduled these alerts, you'll see a message appear on the screen at the appointed time(s). (Even if the phone was asleep, it appears briefly.) You'll also hear a chirpy alarm sound.

The iPhone doesn't play the sound if you turned off Calendar Alerts in Settings→Sounds. It also doesn't play if you silenced the phone with the silencer switch on the side.

- **Show as.** If you work in the business world, it's courteous to mark your new appointments as either Busy or Free. That way, other people who see your calendar, trying to schedule a meeting when you can attend, will know which events on your calendar are movable and which are non-negotiable. If you're just indicating "Keeping Up with the Kardashians TV marathon," maybe that one should be marked as Free.

- **URL.** Here's a spot where you can record the web address of some online site that provides more information about this event.

- **Notes.** Here's your chance to customize your calendar event. You can type any text you want in the Notes area—driving directions, contact phone numbers, a call history, or whatever. Tap Done.

When you've completed filling in all these blanks, tap Add. Your newly scheduled event now shows up on the calendar.

Making an Appointment (Day View, Week View)

As noted earlier, turning the phone 90 degrees opens up a widescreen, scrolling Week view of your life.

In both Day view and Week view, you can *hold your finger down on a time slot* to add a new, 1-hour appointment right there. You're asked to enter a name and, if you like, location for this new appointment. Tap Add. You can always edit this appointment's details or duration later, as described next—but this quick-and-dirty technique saves the effort of tapping in Start and End times.

Editing, Rescheduling, Deleting Events (Long Way)

To examine the details of an appointment in the calendar, tap it once. The Event Details screen appears, filled with the details you previously established.

To edit any of these characteristics, tap Edit. You return to what looks like a clone of the New Event screen. Here you can change the name, time, alarm, repeat schedule, calendar category, or any other detail of the event, just the way you set them up to begin with.

This time, there's a red Delete Event button at the bottom. That's the only way to erase an appointment from your calendar. (You can't erase events created by other people—Facebook birthdays, meetings on shared calendars, and so on—only appointments *you* created.)

Editing and Rescheduling Events (Fun Way)

In Day or Week views, you can *drag an appointment's block* to another time slot or even another day. Just hold your finger down on the appointment's bubble for about a second—until it darkens—before you start to drag. It's a lot quicker and more fluid than having to edit in a dialog box.

You can also change the *duration* of an appointment in Day and Week views. Hold your finger down on its colored block for about a second; when you let go, small, round handles appear.

You can drag those tiny handles up or down to make the block taller or shorter, in effect making it start or end at a different time.

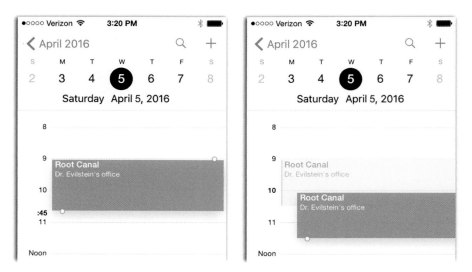

Whether you drag the whole block, the top edge, or the bottom edge, the iPhone thoughtfully displays ":15," ":30," or ":45" on the left-side time ruler to let you know where you'll be when you let go.

The Calendar (Category) Concept

A *calendar*, in Apple's somewhat confusing terminology, is a color-coded subset—a *category*—into which you can place various appointments. They can be anything you like. One person might have calendars called Home, Work, and TV Reminders. Another might have Me, Spouse 'n' Me, and The Kidz. A small business could have categories called Deductible Travel, R&D, and R&R.

You can create and edit calendar categories right on the iPhone, in your desktop calendar program, or (if you're an iCloud member) at *www.icloud.com* when you're at your computer; all your categories and color-codings show up on the iPhone automatically.

At any time, on the iPhone, you can choose which subset of categories you want to see. Just tap Calendars at the bottom of Day, Month, or Year view. You arrive at the big color-coded list of your categories (below, left). As you can see, it's subdivided according to your accounts: your Gmail categories, your Yahoo categories, your iCloud categories, and so on. There's even a Facebook option, if you've set up your Facebook account, so that you can see your Facebook calendar entries and friends' birthdays right on the main calendar.

This screen exists partly as a reference, a cheat sheet to help you remember what color goes with which category, and partly as a tappable subset chooser. That is, you can tap a category's name to hide or show all of its appointments on the calendar. A checkmark means you're seeing its appointments. (The All [Account Name] button turns on or off all of that account's categories at once.)

If you tap Edit, then a little > appears next to each calendar's name. When you tap it, you're offered a screen where you can change the calendar's name, color, and list of people who can see it (previous page, right)—or scroll all the way down to see the Delete Calendar button.

The Edit Calendars screen also offers an Add Calendar button. It's the key to creating, naming, and colorizing a *new* calendar on the phone. (Whatever changes you make to your calendar categories on the phone will be synced back to your Mac or PC.)

> **TIP:** You can share an iCloud calendar with other iCloud members (previous page, right), which is fantastic for families and small businesses who need to coordinate. Tap Calendars, then tap ⓘ next to the calendar's name. Tap Add Person and enter the person's name. Your invitees get invitations by email; with one click, they've added your appointments to their calendars. They can make changes, too.
>
> You can also share a calendar with anyone (not just iCloud members) in a "Look, don't touch" condition. Tap Calendars, and then tap ⓘ next to the calendar's name. Turn on Public Calendar; tap Share Link to open the Share sheet for sending the link. Most calendar apps understand the calendar link that your phone sends.

Search

If you tap Q and type into the search box, you pare down the list of all calendar events from all time; only events whose names match what you've typed show up. Tap one to jump to its block on the corresponding Day view.

Next time you're sure you made an appointment with Harvey but you can't remember the date, keep this search feature in mind.

> **TIP:** The iOS calendar is pretty basic. For more features and power, consider calendar apps like Fantastical or Tempo.

Clock

It's not just a clock—it's more like a time factory. Hiding behind this single icon on the Home screen are four programs: a world clock, an alarm clock, a stopwatch, and a countdown timer.

> **TIP:** The app icon itself on the Home screen shows the current time! Isn't that cute?

World Clock

When you tap World Clock on the Clock screen, you start out with only one clock, showing the current time in Apple's own Cupertino, California.

The neat part is that you can open up *several* of these clocks and set each one to show the time in a different city. The result looks like the row of clocks in a hotel lobby, making you seem Swiss and precise.

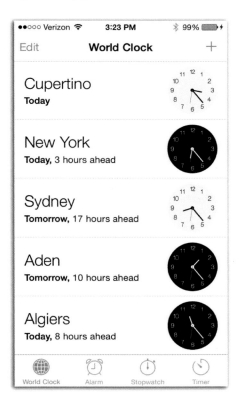

By checking these clocks, you'll know what time it is in some remote city, so you don't wake somebody up at what turns out to be 3 a.m.

To specify which city's time appears on the clock, tap $+$ at the upper-right corner. Scroll to the city you want, or tap its first letter in the index at the right side to save scrolling, or tap in the search box at the top and type the name of a major city. As you type, matching city names appear; tap the one whose time you want to track.

As soon as you tap a city name, you return to the World Clock display. The color of the clock indicates whether it's daytime (white) or night (black).

> **TIP:** Tap any row—the city name or the clock—to switch the display between analog and digital displays of the times.

You can scroll the list of clocks. You're not limited to four or five, although only that many fit on the screen at once.

> **TIP:** Only the world's major cities are in the iPhone's database. If you're trying to track the time in Squirrel Cheeks, New Mexico, add a major city in the same time zone instead—like Albuquerque.

To edit the list of clocks, tap Edit. Delete a city clock by tapping ⊖ and then Delete, or drag clocks up or down using the ☰ as a handle. Then tap Done.

Alarm

If you travel much, this feature could turn out to be one of your iPhone's most useful functions. It's reliable, it's programmable, and it even wakes *the phone* first, if necessary, to wake *you*.

To set an alarm, tap Alarm at the bottom of the Clock screen. You're shown the list of alarms you've already created, even if none are currently set to go off (facing page, left). You could create a 6:30 a.m. alarm for weekdays and an 11:30 a.m. alarm for weekends.

To create a new alarm, tap $+$ to open the Add Alarm screen.

> **TIP:** But really, you *should not bother* setting alarms using this manual technique. Instead, you'll save a lot of time and steps by using Siri. Just say, "Set my alarm for 7:30 a.m." (or whatever time you want).
>
> And while we're at it: You can also say, "Change my 7:30 a.m. alarm to 8 a.m." And if you get really lucky with your life karma, you may even have the opportunity to say the greatest thing you can possibly say to Siri: "Turn off my alarm."

Edit   **Alarm**   +

7:30 AM
Alarm, Weekdays

8:40 AM
Sleep in, baby!!, Weekends

10:00 AM
BACKUP ALARM, Weekdays

World Clock   Alarm   Stopwatch   Timer

Cancel   **Edit Alarm**   Save

5   37
6   38
7   39
8   40   AM
9   41   PM
10   42
11   43

Repeat   Weekends >

Label   Sleep in, baby!! >

Sound   Radar >

Snooze

Delete Alarm

You have several options here:

- **Time dials.** Spin these three vertical wheels—hour, minute, AM/PM—to specify the time you want the alarm to go off.

- **Repeat.** Tap to specify what days this alarm rings. You can specify, for example, Mondays, Wednesdays, and Fridays by tapping those three buttons. (Tap a day-of-the-week button again to turn off its check-mark.) Tap **Back** when you're done. (If you choose Saturdays and Sundays, iOS is smart enough to call that "Weekends.")

- **Label.** Tap to give this alarm a description, like "Get dressed for wedding." That message appears on the screen when the alarm goes off.

- **Sound.** Choose what sound you want to ring. You can choose from any of the iPhone's ringtone sounds, any you've added yourself—or, best of all, **Pick a Song**. That's right—you can wake to the music of your choice.

- **Snooze.** If this option is on then, at the appointed time, the alarm message on the screen offers you a **tap to snooze** button. Tap it for 10 more minutes of sleep, at which point the iPhone tries again to get your attention. (It gives you a countdown in the meantime.)

When you finally tap **Save**, you return to the Alarm screen, which lists your new alarm. Just tap the on/off switch to cancel an alarm. It stays in the list, though, so you can quickly reactivate it another day, without having to redo the whole thing. You can tap + to set another alarm, if you like.

Now the ⊕ icon appears in the status bar at the top of the iPhone screen. That's your indicator that the alarm is set.

To delete an alarm, swipe left across its name and then tap **Delete**. To make changes to the time, name, sound, and so on, tap **Edit**, and then tap the alarm.

TIP: The iPhone never deletes an alarm after using it; over time, therefore, your list of alarms may grow alarmingly large. Fortunately, you can tell Siri to clean them up for you in one fell swoop. Just say, "Delete all my alarms."

So what happens when the alarm goes off? The iPhone wakes itself up, if it was asleep. A message appears, identifying the alarm and the time.

And, of course, the sound rings. This alarm is one of the only iPhone sounds that you'll hear **even if the silencer switch is turned on**. Apple figures that if you've gone to the trouble of setting an alarm, you probably **really** want to know about it, even if you forget to turn the ringer back on.

In that case, the screen says slide to stop alarm.

To turn off the alarm, swipe across the screen. To snooze it for 9 minutes, tap **Snooze**, or press the Sleep switch or a volume key. (Translation: Just grab the phone with your whole hand and squeeze. You'll hit one of those buttons and shut the thing off.)

Once your alarm has gone off, its time remains listed in the Clock app (on the Alarm screen), but its on/off switch goes to Off.

Stopwatch

You've never met a more beautiful stopwatch than this one. Tap **Start** to begin timing something: a runner, a train, a person who's arguing with you.

While the digits are flying by, you can tap **Lap** as often as you like. Each time, the list at the bottom identifies how much time elapsed since the **last** time you tapped **Lap**. It's a way for you to compare, for example, how much time a runner is spending on each lap around a track.

(The tiny digits at the **very** top measure the current lap.)

You can work in other apps while the stopwatch is counting. In fact, the timer keeps ticking away even when the iPhone is asleep! As a result, you can time long-term events, like how long it takes an ice sculpture to melt, the time it takes for a bean seed to sprout, or the length of a Michael Bay movie.

Tap **Stop** to freeze the counter; tap **Start** to resume the timing. If you tap **Reset**, you reset the counter to zero and erase all the lap times.

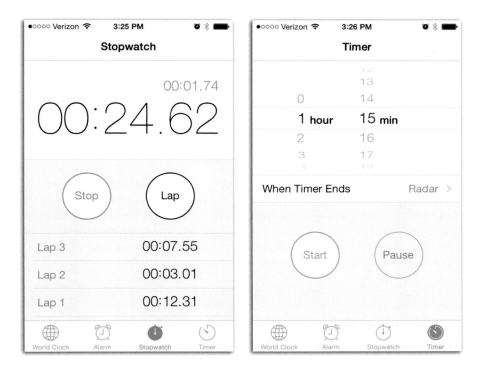

Timer

The fourth Clock mini-app is a countdown timer. You input a starting time, and it counts down to zero.

Countdown timers are everywhere in life. They measure the periods in sports and games, cooking times in the kitchen, penalties on *The Amazing Race*. But on the iPhone, the timer has an especially handy function: It can turn off the music or video after a specified amount of time. In short, it's a sleep timer that plays you to sleep and then shuts off to save power.

To set the timer, open the Clock app and then tap **Timer**. Spin the two dials to specify the number of hours and minutes you want to count down.

Then tap the **When Timer Ends** control to set up what happens when the timer reaches 0:00. Most of the options here are ringtone sounds, so you'll have an audible cue that the time's up. The last one, though, **Stop Playing**, is the aforementioned sleep timer. It stops audio and video playback at the appointed time, so that you (and the iPhone) can go to sleep. Tap **Set**.

Finally, tap Start. Big clock digits count down toward zero. While it's in progress, you can do other things on the iPhone, change the When Timer Ends settings, or just hit Cancel to forget the whole thing.

> **TIP:** It's much faster and simpler to use Siri to start, pause, and resume the Timer. See page 135.

Compass

The iPhone has something very few other phones offer: a magnetic-field sensor known as a magnetometer, better known as a **compass**.

When you open the Compass app, you get exactly what you'd expect: a classic Boy Scout wilderness compass that always points north.

Except it does a few things the Boy Scout compasses never did. Like displaying a digital readout of your heading, altitude, city name, and precise geographic coordinates at the bottom. Or offering a choice of **true** north (the "top" point of the Earth's rotational axis) or **magnetic** north (the spot traditional compasses point to, which is about 11 degrees away from true north). You do that in Settings→Compass.

The very first time you use the Compass app (or anytime you're standing near something big and metal—or magnetic, like stereo speakers), you get the Calibrate message (facing page, top left). It's telling you to de-confuse the compass by rotating the phone completely, so that the entire ring fills in. (You look like a deranged person, but it's good exercise.)

Once the compass is working, hold it roughly parallel to the ground, and then read it like...a compass. Tap the center of the compass to lock in your current heading; a red strip shows how far you are off course. Tap again to unlock the heading.

> **TIP:** For many people, the real power of the compass is in the Maps app. (You can jump directly from Compass to Maps by tapping the coordinates below the compass dial.)
>
> The compass lets Maps know which way you're **facing**. That's a critical detail when you're lost in a city, trying to find a new address, or emerging from the subway with no idea which way to walk.

People who write iPhone programs can tap into the compass, too. There's an "augmented reality" app called New York Nearest Subway, for example. By using the compass, GPS, and tilt-sensor information, it knows where you are and how you're holding the phone—and so it superimposes arrows that show where to find the nearest subway stop and which line it's on.

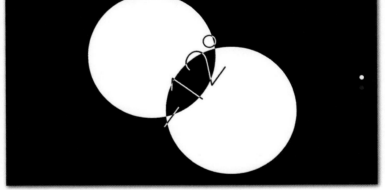

The Carpenter's Level

The Compass app has a secret identity: It doubles as a carpenter's level. That's right: The next time you need to hang a picture, or prop up a wobbly table, or raise a barn, you'll now know when you've got things perfectly horizontal or perfectly vertical.

From the Compass screen, swipe to the left to reveal the level. It measures all three dimensions:

- **Right/left.** Hold the iPhone upright (against a picture you're hanging, say), and tilt it left and right. When it's perfectly upright, the readout says 0 degrees, and the bottom half of the screen turns green.

- **Forward/back.** Hold the phone upright and tip it away from or toward you. Once again, "0 degrees" and green mean "level."

- **Perfectly flat.** Hold the phone on its back, screen facing the sky. When the two circles merge (previous page, bottom), you'll know you've got it perfectly level. You could, for example, put the iPhone on a table you're trying to adjust, using its gauge to know how close you're getting as you wedge something under its short leg.

TIP: Level doesn't have to be the zero point. You can tilt the phone to any angle and declare *that* to be the zero point—by tapping the screen.

Game Center

The iPhone is an accomplished gaming device, the equal of Sony's PlayStation Portable or Nintendo's DS. iPhone features like the accelerometer and touchscreen are perfect for a multitude of games, from first-person shoot-'em-ups to casual games that require nothing more complicated than dragging a tile across the iPhone's screen. Game makers have responded to the iPhone—on the App Store, the Games category is one of the most active sections, with tens of thousands of games available.

To help fan the flames of iPhone gaming, Apple created Game Center as a way for iPhoners to compare scores with their friends and to challenge buddies to games.

Here's what you can expect when you launch Game Center.

Getting Started

You have to sign up for Game Center before you can use it, but the process is simple: Just enter your Apple ID and password.

You'll be asked to create a nickname—"AngriestBird" or "BobSmith2000," for example. On the next screen, you can make this nickname public, so that it can appear on the leaderboards (scoreboards that show the highest point winners) for iOS games; you can also use this nickname when you play multiplayer apps like Super Stickman Golf against other people.

That public profile includes a photo of you; you can grab one from your photo library or shoot it from within Game Center itself using the iPhone's front-facing camera. You also have space to write a little description of yourself, like the bio line in Twitter.

Once all that's in place, the Me tab in Game Center displays your nickname, that clever little phrase you wrote, and your picture (above, left). Beneath that, multicolored spheres display the number of Game Center-compatible games you own, the number of Game Center friends you have, and—perhaps most significantly—the number of points you've accrued from your gaming activities.

Points and Achievements

Points play a leading role in Game Center. They're what you earn from racking up achievements in Game Center–compatible apps. Smash enough blocks in Angry Birds Seasons, or build a certain number of floors in Tiny Tower, and you unlock achievements in those games; those achievements translate to points, which show up in your Game Center profile.

Those points also provide a way to measure yourself against your friends. On Game Center's Friends tab, you can tap the name of one of your friends. You get a choice of three bubbles: the games your friends play, the names of *their* friends, and the number of points they've tallied. That points view features a side-by-side comparison showing your respective accomplishments in commonly played games, so you can settle once and for all who's tops at Tiny Wings. (Game Center also shows the points your friends have racked up in games you **don't** own, which is Apple's way of suggesting that maybe you should download more games.)

Making Friends

Of course, before you can compare your scores with your friends, you have to **have** some friends. Tap the + button in the upper-right corner of the Friends screen to open the Friend Request page, where you can invite someone to be your Game Center buddy using his nickname, Facebook account, or email address. (In fact, Game Center thoughtfully offers you a list of Facebook contacts who are already on Game Center.)

But what if you don't have any existing friends, or at least none whom you know are on Game Center? Tap Upload My Contacts. The app sends your address book to Apple's master computers, so it can match you up with strangers who have the same games you do. Tapping one of those names takes you to a page that shows common friends, if any, and a Send Friend Request button.

You can also find gaming companions through your other Game Center friends. Just tap names in the list of your current friends, and then select the Friends view on their pages to see who **they** hang out with in Game Center when they're not matching scores with you.

Finding Games

Game Center can help you find games to play—specifically, games that are designed to tie in with Game Center. The Recommended section of the Games tab lists suggested games. Game Center bases these recommendations on what you already own, what your friends play, and popular App Store downloads. Selecting a game in the Recommendations list shows you leaderboards, achievements you can unlock, and which of your friends are playing the game. You can download the app right from this screen.

You can also buy games directly from the list of games your friends play within the Friends tab. Tap a game name to see your friends' rankings, or tap the price tag to download the game directly.

Playing Games

All right. Suppose that you've downloaded some games (easy) and you have some friends (it could happen). You're ready to play!

Tap the Games tab, tap the game you want, and then tap the player you want to challenge.

Or start on the **Friends** tab. Tap the friend, tap his **Games** bubble, and then tap the game you want.

Game Center hands you off to the game itself—a different app—so that your online adventure can begin. (Usually you'll see an option for Network play or Internet play; that's the one you want.)

Health

This app is intended to be a central dashboard for all the health data—activity, sleep, steps, calories—generated by your fitness apps. But even if you don't have an app or a band, you have the iPhone itself; unbeknownst to you, it's been quietly tracking the steps you've been taking and the flights of stairs you've been climbing, just by measuring the jostling of the phone in your pocket or bag!

(If that creeps you out just a bit, you can turn it off in **Settings→ Privacy→ Motion & Fitness**.)

Lots of apps and fitness bands share their data with Health: the Apple Watch, UP band, MyFitnessPal, Strava, MapMyRun, WebMD, MotionX-24/7

Sleeptracker, 7 Minute Workout, Withings Health Mate, Garmin Connect Mobile, Lark, Lose It!, Sleepio, Weight Watchers, and so on. Fitness tracking is a big, big deal these days, now that your phone and/or your fitness band can measure your steps, exercise, and sleep.

TIP:: The one fitness brand that's screamingly missing from this list is Fitbit. Your Fitbit band can't share its data with the Health app—at least not without the help of a $3 app called Sync Solver.

If you have one of those bands or apps, you'll have to fish around in its settings until you find the option to connect with Health. At that point, you must turn on the kinds of data you want it to share with Health.

Next, open the Health app. The next bit of setup is to specify what kind of data you want staring you in the face on its Dashboard screen. This is the motivational aspect of Health: The more you're forced to *look at* and *think about* your weight, activity, sleep, or calories, the more likely you are to improve.

Everyone's health worries are different, though; you have to customize your Dashboard to reflect what *you* worry about. So when you open Health, begin by tapping Health Data. Scroll through this massive list of measurable health statistics—from Active Calories to Zinc, filed into appropriate categories like Fitness, Nutrition, and Sleep—and tap the ones you want to see on the Dashboard (facing page, right).

If you're like most people, you'll decide to list Weight, Calories, Sleep, and Steps. If you're a party animal, you could list things like Blood Alcohol Content and Number of Times Fallen. (No comment on Cervical Mucus Quality.)

Behind the scenes, Health can track all of those things (even the ones you haven't added to the Dashboard). Anytime you're on the Health Data screen, you can tap a health category and then view its graph (by Day, Week, Month, or Year); manually Add a Data Point; or control which other apps get to see this information (Share Data).

12:11 AM ✈ ⚪ 100% ⚡	12:13 AM ✈ 📶 ⚪ 100% ⚡
Sources	✳ **Medical ID** Edit
APPS:	**Casey Robin**
🔲 Lose It! ❭	March 9, 1975 (39)
🔺 Strava ❭	Medical Conditions
🆙 UP ❭	Insomnia
WebMD WebMD ❭	Spouse
As apps request permission to update your data, they will be added to the list.	Julie Beeman 📞
	+1 (203) 520-2777
DEVICES	Blood Type
⌚ Apple Watch ❭	A+
📱 iPhone ❭	Weight
	184 lb
	Height
	6'2"
Dashboard Health Data **Sources** Medical ID	Dashboard Health Data Sources **Medical ID**

There are two more tabs at the bottom of the screen:

- **Sources.** This screen lists all the fitness apps and gadgets you've hooked up to Health, so that you know where your data is going.

- **Medical ID.** This screen offers a reason to use the Health app even if you don't use any fitness apps and don't track any medical statistics. It's the electronic equivalent of an emergency medical ID bracelet. Here you can record your name, age, blood type, weight, height, medical conditions, and emergency contact information (previous page, right).

  If you also turn on **Show When Locked**, then this information will be available on your phone's Lock screen. If you pass out, have a seizure, or otherwise become medically inconvenienced, a passerby or medical pro can get that critical information without needing your password (or your awareness).

  If that person is technically savvy, that is. Finding the Medical ID screen is fairly tricky. From the Lock screen, swipe to the right to view the Enter Passcode screen; tap **Emergency**; tap **Medical ID**.

iBooks

iBooks is Apple's ebook reading program. It turns the iPhone into a sort of pocket-sized Kindle. With iBooks, you can carry around dozens or hundreds of books in your pocket, which, in the pre-ebook days, would have drawn some funny looks in public.

Most people think of iBooks as a reader for books that Apple sells on its iTunes bookstore—bestsellers and current fiction, for example—and it does that very well. But you can also load it up with your own PDF documents, as well as thousands of free, older, out-of-copyright books.

> **TIP:** iBooks is very cool and all. But in the interest of fairness, it's worth noting that Amazon's free Kindle app, and Barnes & Noble's free B&N eReader app, are much the same thing—but offer much bigger book libraries at lower prices than Apple's.

Downloading Books

To shop the iBooks bookstore, open the iBooks app. If this is your first time diving in, you might be offered a selection of free starter books to download right now. Go for it; they're real, brand-name books by famous authors.

If, at any time, you want to buy another book—it could happen—well, the icons across the bottom are the literary equivalent of the App Store. Tap **Featured** to see what Apple is plugging this week; **Top Charts** to see this week's bestsellers, including what's on *The New York Times* Best Seller list (note that there's a special row for *free* books); Top Authors; Search to search by name; and Purchased to see what you've bought.

TIP: Once you've bought a book from Apple, you can download it again on other iPhones, iPod Touches, iPads, and Macs. Buy once, read many times. That's the purpose of the Not on This iPhone tab, which appears when you tap Purchased.

Once you find a book that looks good, you can tap Sample to download a free chapter, read ratings and reviews, or tap the price itself to buy the book and download it straight to the phone.

PDFs and ePub Files

You can also load up your ebook reader from your computer, feeding it with PDF documents and ePub files.

NOTE: ePub is the normal iBooks format. It's a very popular standard for ebook readers, Apple's and otherwise. The only difference between ePub documents you create and the ones Apple sells is that Apple's are copy protected.

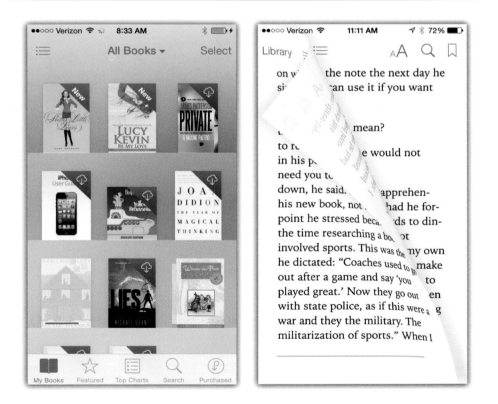

As usual, your Mac or PC is the most convenient loading dock for files bound for your iPhone. If you have a Mac, open the iBooks program. If not, open iTunes, click your iPhone's icon at the top (when it's connected), and then click **Books**.

Either way, you now see all the books, PDF documents, and ePub files that you've slated for transfer. To add to this set, just drag files off your desktop and directly into this window, as shown below.

And where are you supposed to get all these files? Well, PDF documents are everywhere—people send them as attachments, and you can turn any document into a PDF file. (For example, on the Mac, in any program, choose **File→Print**; in the resulting dialog box, click **PDF→Save as PDF**.)

TIP: If you get a PDF document as an email attachment, then adding it to iBooks is even easier. Tap the attachment to open it; now tap **Open in iBooks** in the corner of the page. (The iPhone may not be able to open really huge PDFs, though.)

But free ebooks in ePub format are everywhere, too. There are 33,000 free downloadable books at *gutenberg.org*, for example, and over a million at *books.google.com*—oldies, but classic oldies, with lots of Mark Twain, Agatha Christie, Herman Melville, H.G. Wells, and so on. (Lots of these are available in the Free pages of Apple's own iBook store, too.)

TIP: You'll discover that these freebie books usually come with generic-looking covers. But once you've dragged them into iTunes, it's easy to add a good-looking cover. Use *images.google.com* to search for the book's title. Right-click (or Control-click) the cover image in your web browser; from the shortcut menu, choose Copy Image. In iTunes, in Library mode, choose Books from the top-left pop-up menu. Right-click (or Control-click) the generic book; choose Get Info; click Artwork; and paste the cover you copied. Now that cover will sync over to the iPhone along with the book.

Once you've got books in iTunes, connect the iPhone, choose its name at top right, click the Books tab at top, and turn on the checkboxes of the books you want to transfer.

Your Library

Once you've supplied your iBooks app with some reading material, the fun begins. When you open the app, its My Books tab shows a futuristic shaded bookshelf with your library represented as little book covers. Mostly what you'll do here is tap a book to open it. But there are other activities waiting for you:

- Tap the ☰ icon, which switches the book-cover view to a much more boring (but more compact) list view. Buttons at the top let you sort the list by author, title, category, and so on.

- Tap Select if you want to delete a book, or a bunch of them. To do that, tap each book thumbnail that you want to target for termination; observe how they sprout ✔ marks. Then tap Delete. Of course, deleting a book from the phone doesn't delete your safety copy in iTunes or online.

- The Search button at the bottom of the iBooks screen lets you search by author or title—not just *your* books, but the entire iBooks store.

- When you first start using a new iPhone, iPad, or Mac, your book covers bear the ☁ symbol. It means: "Our records show that you've bought this book, but it's still online, in the great Apple locker in the sky. Tap to download it to your phone so you can start reading."

Collections

You can create subfolders for your books called **collections**. You might have one for school, one for work, and a third for somebody who shares your phone, for example.

To switch your view to a different collection, tap the collection's name. It's the top-center button, which starts out saying All Books. (If you've loaded some PDF documents, then you'll find a collection called PDFs, already set up.)

To create a new collection, open that top-center menu and hit **New Collection**.

And to move a book into a different collection: Tap **Select**, tap a book (or several), and then tap **Move**. It opens the Collections screen shown above, so that you can choose a new collection for the selected items.

> **TIP:** You can reorganize your bookshelf in a collection (which you can't do in the All Books view). Hold down your finger on a book until it swells with pride, and then drag it into a new spot.

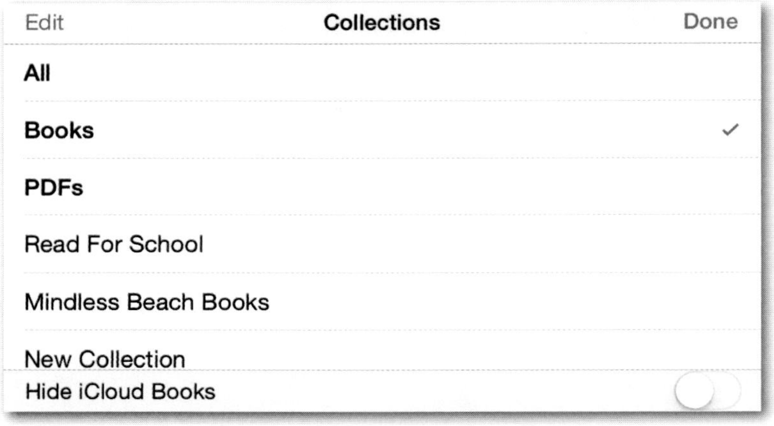

Edit	Collections	Done
All		
Books		✓
PDFs		
Read For School		
Mindless Beach Books		
New Collection		
Hide iCloud Books		◯

Reading

But come on—you're a reader, not a librarian. Here's how you read an ebook.

Open the book or PDF by tapping the book cover. Now the book opens, ready for you to read. Looks great, doesn't it? (If you're returning to a book you've been reading, iBooks remembers your place.)

If the phone detects that it's nighttime (or just dark where you are), the screen appears with white text against a black background. That's to prevent the bright white light of your phone from disturbing other people in, for example, the movie theater. (This is the Night theme described on the next page, and you can turn it off.)

> **TIP:** Turn the phone 90 degrees for a wider column of text. The whole page image rotates with you.

In general, reading is simple: Just read. Turn the page by tapping the edge of the page—or swiping your finger across the page. (If you swipe slowly, you can actually see the "paper" bending over—in fact, you can see through to the "ink" on the other side of the page! Amaze your friends.) You can tap or swipe the left edge (to go back a page) or the right edge (to go forward).

> **TIP:** This is Rotation Lock's big moment. When you want to read lying down, you can prevent the text from rotating 90 degrees using Rotation Lock (page 26).

But if you tap a page, a row of additional controls appears:

- ‹ takes you back to the bookshelf view.

- ☰ opens the table of contents. The chapter or page names are "live"— you can tap one to jump there.

- ᴀA lets you change the look of the page. For example, this panel offers a screen-brightness slider. That's a nice touch, because the brightness of the screen makes a big difference in the comfort of your reading. (This is the same control you'd find in the Control Center or in Settings.)

  A pair of A buttons controls the type size—a huge feature for people with tired or over-40 eyes. And it's something paper books definitely can't do. Tap the larger one repeatedly to enlarge the text; tap the smaller one to shrink it.

  The same panel offers a **Fonts** button, where you can choose from seven different typefaces for your book, as well as a **Themes** button, which lets you specify whether the page itself is White, Night (black page, white text, for nighttime reading), or Sepia (off-white). As promised, there's an Auto-Night Theme button; if you don't care for the white-on-black theme in dark environments, then turn off this switch.

  Finally, there's a **Scrolling View** switch. In Scrolling View, you don't turn book "pages." Instead, the entire book scrolls vertically, as though printed on an infinite roll of Charmin.

- Q opens the search box. It lets you search for text within the book you're reading, which can be extremely useful. As a bonus, there are also **Search Web** and **Search Wikipedia** buttons so you can hop online to learn more about something you've just read.

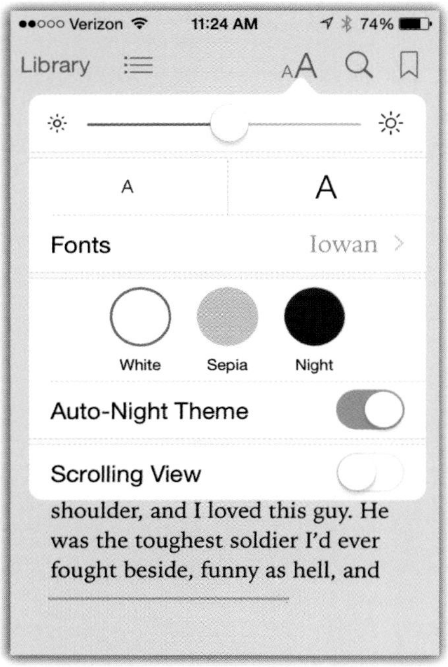
●●○○○ Verizon
11:24 AM
74%
Library
AA
A
A
Fonts
Iowan
White
Sepia
Night
Auto-Night Theme
Scrolling View
shoulder, and I loved this guy. He
was the toughest soldier I'd ever
fought beside, funny as hell, and

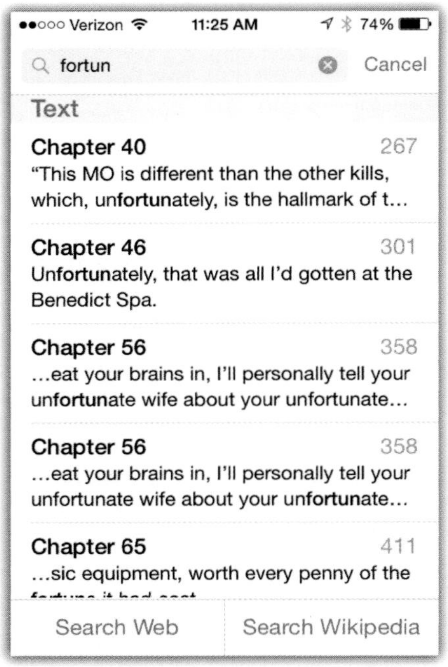
●●○○○ Verizon
11:25 AM
74%
fortun
Cancel
Text
Chapter 40
267
"This MO is different than the other kills, which, unfortunately, is the hallmark of t...
Chapter 46
301
Unfortunately, that was all I'd gotten at the Benedict Spa.
Chapter 56
358
...eat your brains in, I'll personally tell your unfortunate wife about your unfortunate...
Chapter 56
358
...eat your brains in, I'll personally tell your unfortunate wife about your unfortunate...
Chapter 65
411
...sic equipment, worth every penny of the
Search Web
Search Wikipedia

- ⌑ adds a bookmark to the current page. This isn't like a physical bookmark, where there's usually only one in the whole book; you can use it to flag as many pages, for as many reasons, as you like.

- **Chapter slider.** At the bottom of the screen, a slider represents the chapters of your book. Tap or drag it to jump around in the book; as you drag, a pop-up indicator shows you what chapter and page number you're scrolling to. (If you've magnified the font size, of course, your book consumes more pages.)

TIP: An iBook can include pictures and even videos. Double-tap a picture in a book to zoom in on it.

When you're reading a PDF document, by the way, you can do something you can't do when reading regular iBooks: zoom in and out using the usual two-finger pinch-and-spread gestures. Very handy indeed.

TIP: On the other hand, here are some features that ***don't*** work in PDF files (only ebooks): font and type-size changes, page-turn animations, sepia or black backgrounds, highlighting, and notes.

Notes, Bookmarks, Highlighting, Dictionary

Here are some more stunts that you'd have trouble pulling off in a printed book. If you **double-tap** a word, or **hold your finger down** on a word, you get a bar that offers these options:

- **Speak** reads the highlighted passage aloud. (This button appears only if you've turned on Speak Selection in Settings→General→ Accessibility→Speech.) Thank you, Siri!

- **Copy.** You can probably guess this one.

- **Define.** Opens up a page from iBooks' built-in dictionary. You know— in the unlikely event that you encounter a word you don't know.

- **Highlight.** Adds tinted, transparent highlighting, or underlining, to the word you tapped. For best results, don't tap the Highlight button until you've first grabbed the blue dot handles and dragged them to enclose the entire passage you want highlighted.

  Once you tap Highlight, the buttons change into a special Highlight bar (next page, middle). The first button opens a *third* row of buttons (bottom), so that you can specify which highlight color you want. (The final button designates underlining.)

  The second button (🗑) removes highlighting. The third lets you add a note, as described next. The 🗋 button opens the Share sheet, also described momentarily.

- **Note.** This feature creates highlighting on the selected passage *and* opens an empty colored sticky note, complete with keyboard, so you can type in your own annotations. When you tap Done, your note collapses down to a tiny yellow Post-it peeking out from the right edge of the margin. Tap to reopen it.

  To delete a note, tap the highlighted text. Tap 🗑.

- **Search** opens the same search box that you'd get by tapping the 🔍 icon—except this time, the highlighted word is already filled in, saving you a bit of typing.

- **Share** opens the Share sheet (page 330) so you can send the highlighted material to somebody else by message or email, post it to Facebook or Twitter, or copy it to your Clipboard for pasting into another app.

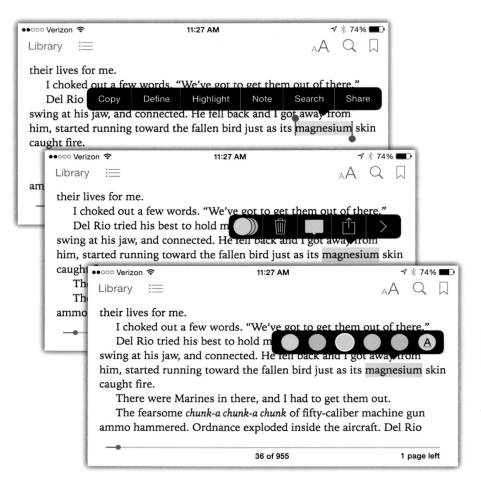

There are a couple of cool things going on with your bookmarks, notes, and highlighting, by the way. Once you've added them to your book, they're magically and wirelessly synced to any other copies of that book— on other gadgets, like the iPad or iPod Touch, other iPhones, or even Macs running OS X Mavericks or later. Very handy indeed.

Furthermore, if you tap the ☰ to open the Table of Contents, you'll see the **Bookmarks** and **Notes** tabs. Each presents a tidy list of all your book-marked pages, notes, and highlighted passages. You can tap ⬆ (and then **Share Notes**) to print or email your notes, or tap one of the listings to jump to the relevant page.

Books That Read to You

iBooks can actually read to you! It's a great feature when you're driving or jogging, when someone's just learning to read, or when you're having trouble falling asleep. There's even a special control panel just for managing your free audiobook reader.

To get started, open **Settings→General→Accessibility→Speech**. Turn on **Speak Screen.**

Then open a book in iBooks. Swipe down the page with two fingers to make the iPhone start reading the book to you, out loud, with a synthesized voice. At the same time, a palette appears, offering these speech controls:

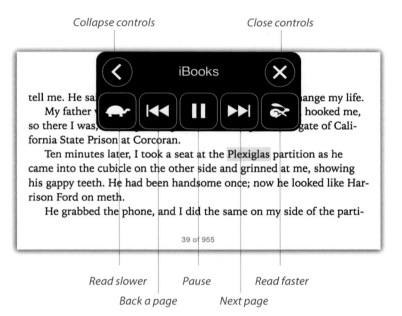

Collapse controls · Close controls

Read slower · Pause · Read faster
Back a page · Next page

After a few seconds, the palette shrinks into a > button at the edge of the screen—and, after that, it becomes transparent, as though trying to make itself as invisible as possible. You can, of course, tap it to reopen it.

Yes, this is exactly the feature that debuted in the Amazon Kindle and was then removed when publishers screamed bloody murder—but, somehow, so far, Apple has gotten away with it.

iBooks Settings

If you've embraced the simple joy of reading electronic books the size of a chalkboard eraser, then you deserve to know where to make settings changes: in Settings→iBooks. Here are the options waiting there:

- **Use Cellular Data.** Do you want to be able to download books using your carrier's cellular data network (which eats up your monthly data allotment)? If you turn this off, then you can download books only when you're in a Wi-Fi hotspot.

- **Full Justification.** Ordinarily, iBooks presents text with fully justified margins (left). Turn this off if you prefer ragged right margins (right).

Full justification	*Ragged right margin*

sometimes he feels that there really is another way, if only he could stop bumping for a moment and think of it. And then he feels that perhaps there isn't. Anyhow, here he is at the bottom, and ready to be introduced to you. Winnie-the-Pooh.
 	
    When I first heard his name, I said, just as you are going to say, "But I thought he was a boy?"
    "So did I," said Christopher
	sometimes he feels that there really is another way, if only he could stop bumping for a moment and think of it. And then he feels that perhaps there isn't. Anyhow, here he is at the bottom, and ready to be introduced to you. Winnie-the-Pooh.
	
	    When I first heard his name, I said, just as you are going to say, "But I thought he was a boy?"
	    "So did I," said Christopher

- **Auto-hyphenation.** Sometimes, typesetting looks better if hyphens allow partial words to appear at the right edge of each line. Especially if you've also turned on Full Justification.

- **Both Margins Advance.** Usually, tapping the right edge of the screen turns to the next page, and tapping the left edge turns *back* a page. If you turn on this option, tapping *either* edge of the screen opens the next page. That can be handy if you're a lefty, for example.

- **Sync Bookmarks, Sync Collections.** Turn these on if you'd like your bookmarks and book collections to be synced with your other Apple gadgets.

- **Online Content.** A few books contain links to video or audio clips online. This option comes set to Off, because video and audio can eat up your monthly cellular data allotment like a hungry teenager.

There are even a couple of controls here that apply to audiobooks. They govern how much time skips when you tap one of the back or forward Skip buttons—15 seconds, for example.

Maps

Here it is, folks, the feature that made international headlines: the Maps app.

From its birth in 2007, the iPhone always came with Google Maps—an excellent mapping and navigation app. (Apple wrote it, but Google provided the maps and navigation data.) But in iOS 6, Apple replaced it with a new mapping system of its own.

Why? Apple said Google was withholding features like spoken turn-by-turn directions and smoothly drawn (vector-based) map images. Furthermore, as the rivalry intensified, Apple no longer wanted to share the super-valuable *data* generated by all those millions of moving iPhones with Google.

Unfortunately, in its initial version, the databases underlying the Maps app had a lot of problems. They didn't include nearly as many points of interest (buildings, stores, landmarks) as Google. Addresses were sometimes wrong.

Apple promised to keep working on Maps until it was all fixed, but in the meantime, in a remarkable apology letter, CEO Tim Cook recommended using one of its rivals. By far the best one is Google Maps. It's free, it's amazingly smart (it knows what address you mean after you type only a few letters), it has public transportation details, live traffic reports, Street View (you can see photos of most addresses, and even "look around" you), and of course Google's far superior maps and data.

All right—you've been warned. It may still take some time before Apple Maps is complete and reliable.

But while Apple's cartographical elves keep working on cleaning up the underlying maps, some of its features are pretty great. And if you have a Mac running OS X Mavericks or later, you can look up a destination on the Mac and then send the directions wirelessly to your phone.

Meet Maps

The underlying geographical database may need work, but Maps, the app itself, is a thing of beauty.

It lets you type in any address or point of interest in the U.S. or many other countries and see it plotted on a map, with turn-by-turn driving directions, just like a $300 windshield GPS unit. It also gives you a live national Yellow Pages business directory and real-time traffic-jam alerts. In iOS 9, you can get bus and train schedules for a few big U.S. cities. You have a choice of a street-map diagram or actual aerial photos, taken by satellite.

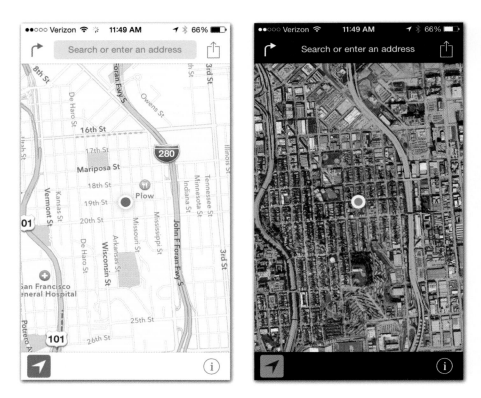

And Maps offers Flyover, an amazing aerial, 360-degree 3D view of major cities.

Maps Basics

When you open Maps, a blue dot represents your current location. Double-tap to zoom in, over and over again, until you're seeing actual city blocks. You can also pinch or spread two fingers to shrink or magnify the view. Drag or flick to scroll around the map.

To zoom *out* again, you can use the rare *two-finger double-tap*.

At any time, you can tap the ⓘ button in the corner of the screen to open a secret panel of options. Here you can tap your choice of amazing map views: Standard (street-map illustration), Satellite (stunning aerial photos), or Hybrid (photos superimposed with street names).

There's no guarantee that the Satellite view provides a very *recent* photo—different parts of the Maps database use photography taken at different times—but it's still very cool.

You can twist two fingers to rotate the map. (A compass icon at top right helps you keep your bearings; you can tap it to restore the map's usual north-is-up orientation.) And if you drag two fingers up the screen, you tilt the map into 3D view, which makes it look more like you're surveying the map at an angle instead of straight down.

Finding Yourself

If any phone can tell you where you are, it's the iPhone. It has not one, not two, but *three* ways to determine your location.

- **GPS.** First, the iPhone contains a traditional GPS chip, of the sort that's found in automotive navigation units from Garmin, TomTom, and others. If the iPhone has a good view of the sky and isn't con-founded by skyscrapers, then it can do a decent job of consulting the 24 satellites that make up the Global Positioning System and deter-mining its own location.

  And if it can't see the sky, the iPhone has two fallback location fea-tures.

- **Wi-Fi Positioning System.** Metropolitan areas today are blanketed by overlapping Wi-Fi signals. At a typical Manhattan intersection, you might be in range of 20 base stations. Each one broadcasts its own name and unique network address (its *MAC address*—nothing to do with Mac computers) once every second. Although you'd need to be within 150 feet or so to actually get onto the Internet, a laptop or phone can detect this beacon signal from up to 1,500 feet away.

  Imagine if you could correlate all those beacon signals with their physical locations. Why, you'd be able to simulate GPS—without the GPS!

  So for years, all those millions of iPhones have been quietly logging all those Wi-Fi signals, noting their network addresses and locations. (The iPhone never has to *connect* to these base stations. It's just read-ing the one-way beacon signals.)

  At this point, Apple's database knows about millions of hotspots—and the precise longitude and latitude of each.

  So, if the iPhone can't get a fix on GPS, it sniffs for Wi-Fi base sta-tions. If it finds any, it transmits their IDs back to Apple (via cellular network)—which looks up those network addresses and sends coordi-nates back to the phone.

That accuracy is good to within only 100 feet, and of course the system fails completely once you're out of populated areas. On the other hand, it works indoors, which GPS definitely doesn't.

- **Google's cellular triangulation system.** Finally, as a last resort, the iPhone can check its proximity to the cellphone towers around you. Software from Google works a lot like the Wi-Fi location system, but it relies upon its knowledge of cellular towers' locations rather than Wi-Fi base stations. The accuracy isn't as good as GPS—you're lucky if it puts you within a block or two of your actual location—but it's something.

> **TIP:** The iPhone's location circuits eat into battery power. To shut them down when you're not using them, open Settings→Privacy and turn off Location Services.

All right—now that you know how the iPhone gets its location information, here's how you can use it. Its first trick is to show you where you are.

Tap the ➤ at the bottom of the Maps screen. The button turns white, indicating that the iPhone is consulting its various references to figure out where you are. You show up as a blue pushpin that moves with you. That's the iPhone saying, "OK, pal, I've got you. You're *here*." It keeps tracking until you tap the ➤ enough times to turn it off.

Orienting Maps

It's great to see a blue pin on the map, and all—but how do you know which way you're facing? Thanks to the built-in magnetometer (compass), the map can orient itself for you.

Just tap the ➤ button twice. The map spins so that the direction you're facing is upward, and the ➤ icon points straight up. A "flashlight beam" emanates from your blue dot; its width indicates the iPhone's degree of confidence. (The narrower the beam, the surer it is.)

Searching Maps

You're not always interested in finding out where you are; often, you know that much perfectly well. Instead, you want to see where something *else* is.

Now, the following paragraphs guide you through using the search box at the top of Maps. But, frankly, if you use it, you're a sucker. It's *much* quicker to use Siri to specify what you want to find.

You can say, for example, "Show me the map of Detroit" or "Show me the closest Starbucks" or "Give me directions to 200 West 79th Street in New York." Siri shows you that spot on a map; tap to jump into the Maps app.

If you must use the search box, though, here's how it works: Tap in the box to summon the iPhone keyboard. (If there's already something in the box, tap ✕ to clear it out.)

TIP: New in iOS 9: When you've tapped into an empty search box, you get some one-tap shortcuts for potential searches: icons for Food, Shopping, Travel, Services, and Transport. Each expands into eight more icons for further refinement (Travel offers Bus Stops, Airports, Gas Stations, and so on.) And as before, you also get to see your list of Favorites (page 380) and a list of recent searches. It's all designed to save you typing when you're in a hurry.

Here's what Maps can find for you:

- **An address.** You can skip the periods (and usually the commas, too). And you can use abbreviations. Typing *710 w end ave ny ny* will find 710 West End Avenue, New York, New York. (In this and any of the other examples, you can type a zip code instead of a city and a state.)

- **An intersection.** Type *57th and lexington, ny ny*. Maps will find the spot where East 57th Street crosses Lexington Avenue in New York City.

- **A city.** Type *chicago il* to see that city. You can zoom in from there.

- **A zip code or a neighborhood.** Type *10024* or *greenwich village*.

- **Latitude and longitude coordinates.** Type *40.7484° N, 73.9857° W*.

- **A point of interest.** Type *washington monument* or *niagara falls*.

- **A business type.** Type *drugstores in albany ny* or *hospitals in roanoke va*.

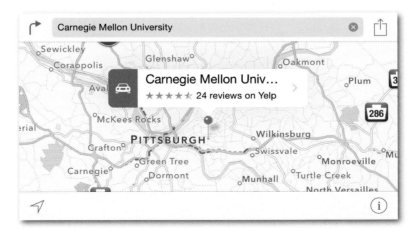

When Maps finds a specific address, an animated, red-topped pushpin comes flying down onto its precise spot on the map. A bubble identifies the location by name.

Tap outside the bubble to hide it. Tap the map pin to bring the bubble back. Tap the 🚗 icon for instant driving directions—or walking directions, or (in a few big cities) public-transportation directions. Use the Drive, Walk, or Transit buttons at the top to specify your preferences.

Tap the > to open the Location page; read on.

The Location Page

Once you've found something on the map—your current position, say, or something you've searched for—you can drop a pin there for future reference. Tap the ⓘ button; when the page slides up, tap Drop a Pin. A blue pushpin appears. (You can drag the pin to move it, if your aim wasn't exact.)

TIP: You can also drop a pin by holding your finger down on the right spot.

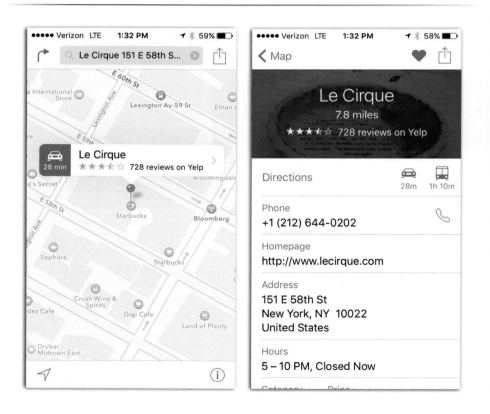

There are also the red pushpins that represent addresses you've looked up. And there are the tiny icons that represent restaurants, stores, and other establishments in Apple's (actually Yelp's) database.

All these pushpins and nano-icons are tappable. You get a little label that identifies each one. And if you tap the > on that label, you open a details screen called the Location page.

Links here let you bookmark the spot, get directions, add it to Contacts, or share it with other people (via AirDrop, email, text message, Facebook, or Twitter). If this is the location for a restaurant or a business, you might strike gold: The Location page might offer several screens full of useful information, courtesy of *Yelp.com*. You'll see customer reviews, photos, hours of operation, delivery and reservation information, and so on.

The Location screen may also offer the Popular Apps Nearby link. It lists apps that other people have downloaded in your vicinity. Sometimes there's no rhyme or reason to them, but sometimes you'll discover a gem that pertains to the place you're scoping out: a guide app, for example.

Finding Friends and Businesses

Maps is also plugged into your Contacts list, which makes it especially easy to find a friend's house (or just to see how ritzy his neighborhood is).

Instead of typing an address into the empty search bar, tap inside it; a list of recent searches appears (it's designed to save you time if you need those directions again). Tap Favorites. You arrive at the Favorites/Recents/Contacts screen, containing three lists that can save you a lot of typing.

Two of them are described in the next section. But if you tap Contacts, you see your master address book (page 101). Tap a name. In a flash, Maps drops a red, animated pushpin onto the map to identify that address.

> **TIP:** As you type, the iPhone displays a list of matching names. Tap the one you want to find on the map.

That pushpin business also comes into play when you use Maps as a glorified national Yellow Pages. If you type, for example, *pharmacy 60609*, then those red pushpins show you all the drugstores in that Chicago zip code. It's a great way to find a gas station, a cash machine, or a hospital in a pinch. Tap a pushpin to see the name of the corresponding business.

As usual, you can tap the > button in the map pin's label bubble to open a details screen. If you've searched for a friend, then you see the corresponding Contacts card. If you've searched for a business, then you get a screen containing its phone number, address, website, and so on; often, you get a beautiful page of Yelp information (photos, reviews, ratings).

Remember that you can tap a web address to open it or tap a phone number to dial it. ("Hello, what time do you close today?")

In both cases, you get the 🚗 icon (for driving directions) or, occasionally, 🚆 (public-transportation directions). You also get a ⬆️ button; on the resulting Share sheet, you have the option to send the address to someone by AirDrop, Message, or Mail (for a restaurant where you're supposed to meet, for example)—or to bookmark this address for use later (tap the ♡), as described next.

Favorites and Recents

One nice thing about Maps is the way it tries to eliminate typing at every step. The Favorites/Recents/Contacts screen is a great example.

●●○○○ Verizon 🛜	11:56 AM	🧭 🔆 63% 🔋
Edit	**Favorites**	Done

Current Location

1 Infinite Loop

Le Cirque

Home

Empire State Building

Eiffel Tower

Arby's Roast Beef Restaurant

Golden Gate Bridge

| Favorites | Recents | Contacts |

●○○○○ Verizon 🛜	11:56 AM	🧭 🔆 62% 🔋
Clear	**Recents**	Done

🏠 **Home**
from **Current Location**

🔍 **Le cirque nyc**
New York

🔍 **Le Cirque Quemper-Guézenn…**
Quemper-Guézennec

🔍 **Carnegie Mellon University**
Pittsburgh

🔍 **sears tower**
Chicago

🔍 **Empire State Building**
New York

| Favorites | Recents | Contacts |

To find this screen, tap in the (empty) search bar and then tap Favorites. Here they are: three lists that spare you from having to type stuff.

- **Favorites** are addresses you've flagged for later use by tapping the ♡, an option that appears on every place's details screen. For sure, you should bookmark your home and workplace. That will make it much easier to request driving directions.

- **Recents** are searches you've conducted. You'd be surprised at how often you want to call up the same spot again later—and now you can, just by tapping its name in this list. You can also tap Clear to empty the list—if, for example, you intend to elope and don't want your parents to find out. (This is actually the same list that appears when you tap the empty search box, right there on the screen.)

- **Contacts** is your iPhone address book. One tap maps out where someone lives.

Tap **Done** to back out without choosing a destination. Or tap a destination to see it on the map.

Directions

Suppose you've just searched for a place and then tapped its name (below, left). The place's bubble is open on the screen (middle).

Now you can tap the ↱ (or the 🚗 icon next to the place name) for instant directions (right).

If there's no identified address yet, tapping ➦ produces *two* search bars: one labeled Start and the other, End. Plug in two addresses—the Start address may already say "Current Location"—and let Maps guide you from the first to the second. You can use any of the address shortcuts on page 377, or you can tap one of the recent searches listed here (or Home or Work).

> **TIP:** If you tap ⮂, you swap the Start and End points. That's a great way to find your way back after a trip.

In any case, once you've told Maps where you're going, you can tell it how you're going. Three buttons say Drive, Walk (yes, walking directions), and Transit.

Maps also displays an overview of the route you're about to drive. In fact, it usually proposes several different routes. They're labeled with little tags that identify how long each will take you: 3 hrs 37 min, 4 hrs 11 min, and 4 hrs 33 min, for example.

If you tap one of these tags, the bottom of the screen lets you know the distance and estimated time for that option and identifies the main roads you'll be on.

The Transit button, new in iOS 9, gives you step-by-step guidance on what trains or buses to take—in a few cities (Baltimore, Berlin, Boston, Chicago, London, Mexico City, New York City, Philadelphia, San Francisco, Toronto, and Washington, D.C., plus 30 cities in China.) More are coming, Apple says.

If you're lucky enough to be in one of those cities, you'll discover that the public-transport directions are surprisingly clear and detailed.

Whether you're driving, walking, or transiting, Start to see the first instruction.

The map zooms in, and Navigation mode begins.

Navigation Mode

When the iPhone is guiding you to a location, Maps behaves exactly like a windshield GPS unit, but better looking and with less clutter to distract you. You see a simplified map of the world around you, complete with the outlines of buildings, with huge white directional banners that tell you how to turn next, and onto what street. Siri's familiar voice speaks the same information at the right times, so you don't even have to look at the screen.

Even if you hit the Sleep switch to lock the phone, the voice guidance continues. (It continues even if you switch to another app; return to Maps by tapping the banner at the top of the screen.)

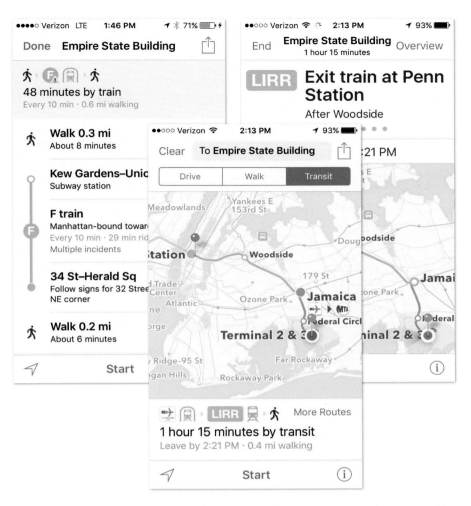

If you do tap the Maps screen, however, a few extra controls appear. The top bar shows your projected arrival time, plus the remaining distance and time. It also offers the **End** button, which makes the navigation stop. Tap **End** when you suddenly recognize where you are, for example, and don't need Siri's opinion anymore.

The Navigation mode is meant to be a hands-free, distraction-free guidance system only. While Maps is guiding you, you can't zoom in and out, nor can you pan the map to look ahead at upcoming turns or to inspect alternate routes. (You can twist two fingers to turn the map, but it snaps back as soon as you let go.)

But if you tap **Overview** in the upper-right corner, your entire planned route shrinks down to fit on a single screen. Now you see your entire route,

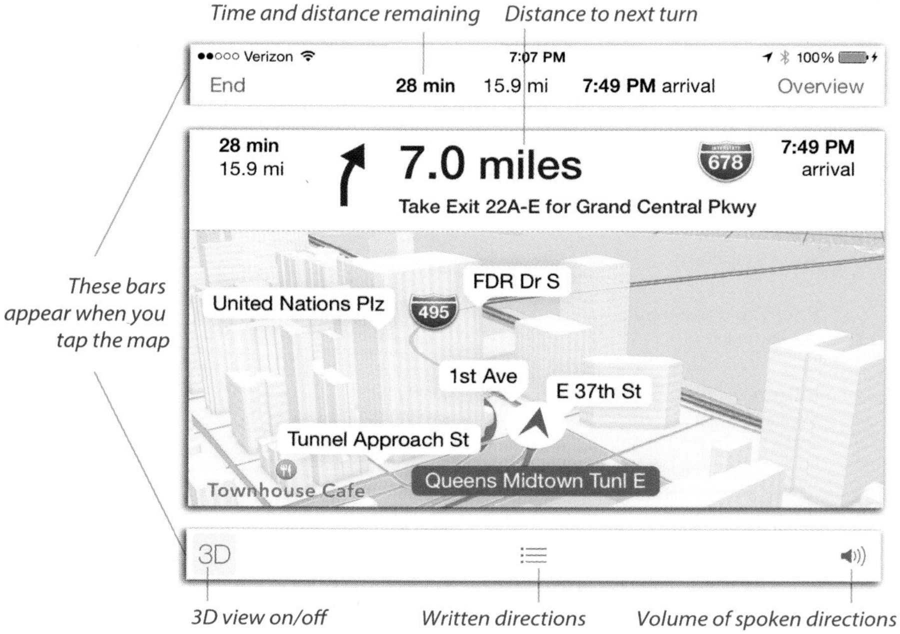
Time and distance remaining
Distance to next turn
●●○○○ Verizon
7:07 PM
100%
End
28 min
15.9 mi
7:49 PM arrival
Overview
28 min
15.9 mi
7.0 miles
678
7:49 PM
arrival
Take Exit 22A-E for Grand Central Pkwy
These bars appear when you tap the map
FDR Dr S
United Nations Plz
495
1st Ave
E 37th St
Tunnel Approach St
Townhouse Cafe
Queens Midtown Tunl E
3D
3D view on/off
Written directions
Volume of spoken directions

and you can zoom, turn, and pan. To return to the navigation screen, tap **Resume**.

At the bottom, these buttons await:

- **3D.** Tap to view the map at an angle. In major cities, you even see 3D shapes of the buildings.
- **☰.** Tap to get a written list of turn-by-turn instructions.
- **🔊.** You can adjust the volume of Siri's speaking voice as she gives you driving directions by tapping here. Choose **Low**, **Medium**, or **Loud Volume**, or turn off her voice prompts altogether with **No Voice**.

Tap the screen to hide these additional controls once again.

Passenger Navigation Mode

Navigation mode is designed with safety in mind—it's fully automated. You're not supposed to interact with the phone at all; you're supposed to keep your eyes on the road and paws on the wheel.

There's another navigation mode, however, that few people even know exists. It's for use when you're not the driver but the passenger, using your phone to direct someone. As a result, it doesn't offer spoken directions. Since you're doing the backseat driving, Siri has the good sense to shut up.

This mode lets you zoom in and out, scan ahead, rotate the map, and so on.

To trigger Passenger Navigation mode, *don't* use Current Location as the starting point for your instructions. Instead, input specific addresses in the Start and End boxes.

When you tap Start, you'll notice one odd thing right away: You can swipe across the white "highway signs" at the top of the screen to see the upcoming (or past) turn instructions. Each time, the map moves to show you where that turn takes place. (Similarly, if you're scrolling along the blue-highlighted route, the overhead direction sign automatically switches to show the text for that turn.)

Night Mode

If the phone's ambient light sensor decides that it's dark in your car, it switches to a dimmer, grayer version of the map. It wouldn't want to distract you, after all. When there's light, it brightens back up again.

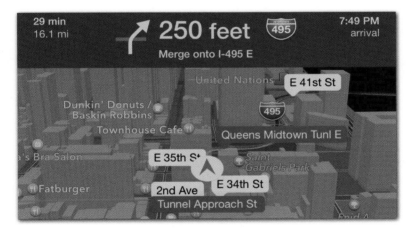

Traffic

How's this for a cool feature? Free, real-time traffic reporting. Just tap the ⓘ button (it's visible whenever you're *not* in Navigation mode), and then tap Show Traffic. Now traffic jams appear as dashed red lines on the relevant roads, for your stressing pleasure; less severe slowdowns show up as dashed yellow lines.

Better yet, tiny icons appear, representing accidents and construction sites. Tap the icon to make a quick description tag appear (like "Accident, Park Ave at State St"); tap that tag to read a full-screen account of what's going on.

If you don't see any dotted lines, it's either because traffic is moving fine or because Apple doesn't have any information for those roads. Usually, you get traffic info only for highways, and only in metropolitan areas.

Flyover

You don't need a car to use Flyover, the Maps app's most dazzling feature; it has nothing to do with navigation, really. You can operate it even while you're lying on your couch like a slug.

Flyover is a dynamic, interactive, photographic 3D model of certain major cities. It looks something like an aerial video, except that *you* control the virtual camera. You can pan around these scenes, looking over and around buildings to see what's behind them. To create this feature, Apple says, it spent two years filming cities in helicopters.

To try it, you must be in Satellite view (tap ⓘ to get there). Enter 3D mode by dragging down the screen with two fingers (or tap ⓘ, and then **Show 3D Map**).

Wait for a moment as the phone downloads the photographic models. Now you can go nuts, conducting your own virtual chopper tour of the city using the usual techniques:

- Drag with one finger to move around the map.

- Pinch or spread two fingers to zoom in or out.

- Drag two fingers up or down to change your camera angle relative to the ground.

- Twist two fingers to turn the world before you.

It's immersing, completely amazing, and very unlikely to make you airsick.

Flyover Tours

Apple wasn't satisfied with letting you pan around virtual 3D city models using your finger. Now it's prepared to give you *city tours* in 3D.

Use the search box to enter the name of a big city or major landmark. (Some examples: San Francisco, New York, Tokyo, London, Paris, Rome, Madrid, Vancouver, San Jose, Cape Town, Stockholm. Or places like Yosemite National Park, Sydney Opera House, Stonehenge, St. Peter's Basilica, or the Brooklyn Bridge.)

When you hit Search, a new control appears just beneath the Start box; "3D Flyover Tour." When you tap Start, you're in for a crazy treat: a fully automated video tour of that city or place. The San Francisco tour shows you the baseball park, the famous Transamerica Pyramid, the Alcatraz prison island, and so on. It's slow, soothing, cool, and definitely something that paper maps never did.

News

There's a brand-new app in iOS 9: News. This app does just what Apple promises: It "collects all the stories you want to read, from top news sources, based on topics you're most interested in." In other words, Apple has written its own version of Flipboard. (And, by the way, killed off the old app for paid digital magazines called Newsstand.)

When you open the News app, it presents you with a very, **very** tall list of online publications (*New York Times, Wired, The New Yorker,* and hundreds more) and topics (Movie Actors, Science...). You're supposed to tap the ones you want to use as News fodder.

And that's it: Suddenly, you have a beautiful, infinite, constantly updated, free magazine stand, teeming with stories that have been collated accord-

ing to your tastes. All of it is free, although you're not getting all the listed publications—usually, you're offered just a few selected stories.

The five tabs across the bottom are designed to offer multiple entry points into the eternal tsunami of web news:

- **For You** is the main thing. It's constantly updated with new articles that Apple's algorithms think you'll like, based on (a) your selections the first time you used the app, (b) the stories you've favorited by tapping the ♡, (c) the stories you've indicated you **didn't** like by **double**-tapping the ♡, and (d) which stories you actually wind up reading.

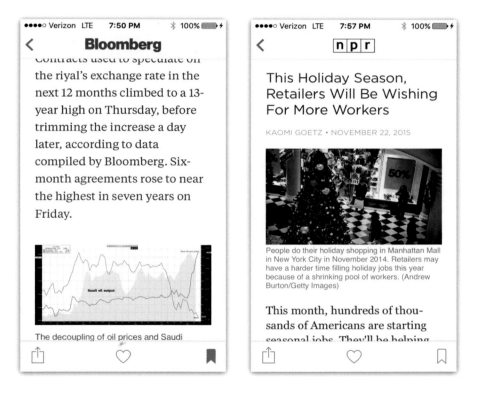

- **Favorites** displays icons for the publications and topics you've said you're interested in. Same stories, different starting point.

- **Explore** offers a list of breaking-news topics—and publications that Apple wants you to try out.

- **Search.** Oh, yes—you can search for articles by topic or publication.

- **Saved.** Most of the time, you can't use News without an Internet connection. If you anticipate that you'll be spending time in the living hell known as Offline mode (like on a subway, sailboat, or airplane), you can save some stories for reading later. To do that, just tap the ⎁ icon that appears on a story.

Once you've tapped to open a story, using News is simplicity itself. Swipe vertically to scroll through an article, or horizontally to pull the next article into view.

Notes

The iPhone has always had a Notes app. But in iOS 9, this ancient, text-only notepad has had a huge upgrade, making it more Evernote-ish in scope. A Notes page can now include a checklist of to-do's, a photo, a map, a web link, or a sketch you draw with your finger.

It's nice to be able to jot down—or dictate—lists, reminders, and brainstorms. You can email them to yourself when you're finished—or sync them right to your Mac or PC.

And, as always, any changes you make in Notes are automatically synchronized to all your other Apple gadgets and Macs.

> **NOTE:** The first time you open Notes, you're invited to upgrade your existing notes to the new Notes format. If you don't, you don't get any of the new features. But if you do, you can't open your notes on any gadget that doesn't have iOS 9 or OS X El Capitan for the Mac.

To get started, tap ⎘ to start a new blank note—what looks like a blank white page. The keyboard appears so you can begin typing.

Formatting and Photos

But there's also an intriguing-looking ⊕ button. It summons some fantastic buttons at the bottom of the page:

- ⊘ creates a checklist. Every paragraph you type sprouts a circle—which is actually a checkbox. Tap it to place a checkmark in there. This feature is fantastic for lists: to-do lists, packing lists, movies to see, gift tracking, party planning, job hunting, homework management, and so on.

  Each time you press Return, you create a new checklist item. But you can also select some existing paragraphs (for example, created with the old Notes) and then tap ⊘, turning it into a checklist after the fact.

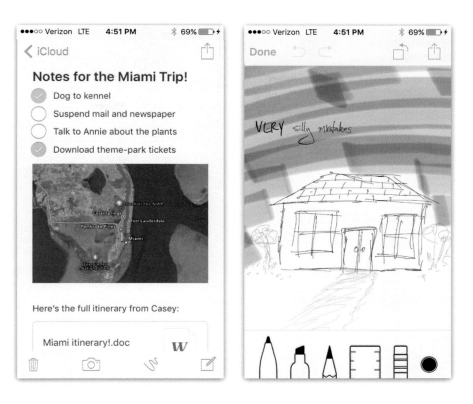

Aa. Hey, there are style sheets now! You can create titles (big and bold type), headings (bold), bulleted lists, dashed lists, or auto-numbered lists, with just a couple of taps, using this menu.

- ⊙. You can insert a photo into a note—either by taking one with your camera on the spot, or by choosing one from the pictures already on your phone. Incredibly handy.

- ⌇. Draw with your finger! The sketch tools include a marker, a high-lighter, a pencil, a straightedge (the ruler thing), an eraser, and a color chooser (the round dot—and don't miss the fact that there are three scrolling panels of colors!).

  To use the ruler, put two fingers on the "ruler" on the screen, and twist them to the angle you want. Then you can "draw against" it for perfect straight lines.

TIP: If you have an iPhone 6s or 6s Plus, all of the drawing tools (and the eraser) are pressure-sensitive! They make fatter or darker lines when you press harder with your finger.

When you're finished with a note for now, tap **Done**. The keyboard goes away, and a handy row of icons appears at the bottom of your Notes page. The rundown:

- 🗑. Tap to delete the current note. (Confirm your decision.)

- ⬆️. Tap to print your note, copy it, or send it to someone by email, text message, AirDrop, and so on. For example, if you tap **Mail**, the iPhone creates a new outgoing message, pastes the first line of the note into the subject line, and pastes the note's text into the body. Address the note, edit if necessary, and hit **Send**. The iPhone returns you to Notes. (See page 330 for more on the sharing options.)

The Notes List

As you create more pages, the **<iCloud** button (top left) becomes more useful. It opens your table of contents for the Notes pad, and offers a **New** button. And it's the only way to jump from one note to another. (It may not say "iCloud"; it bears the name of whatever online account stores your notes: Gmail, Exchange, or whatever. Or, if your notes exist only on the phone, you just see an unlabeled < symbol.)

> **TIP** You can swipe rightward to jump from an open note back to the list.

Here's what this list displays:

- **The first lines of your notes** (most recent at the top), along with the time or date you last edited them. If there's a photo or sketch on a note, you see its thumbnail, too (facing page, left).

  To open a note, tap its name. To delete a note, swipe across its name in the list, right to left, and then confirm by tapping **Delete**.

> **NOTE:** On the 6 and 6s Plus models, rotating the phone produces a whole new two-column layout. The left column shows your table of contents (first line of every note); the right column shows the selected note itself.

- **A search box.** Drag down on the list to bring the Search box into view. Tap it to open the keyboard. You can now search all your notes instantly—not just their titles, but also the text inside them.

- ▦. This is the new Attachments Browser. It brings up a tidy display of every photo, sketch, website, audio recording, and document that's ever been inserted into any of your notes. All in one place (facing page, right).

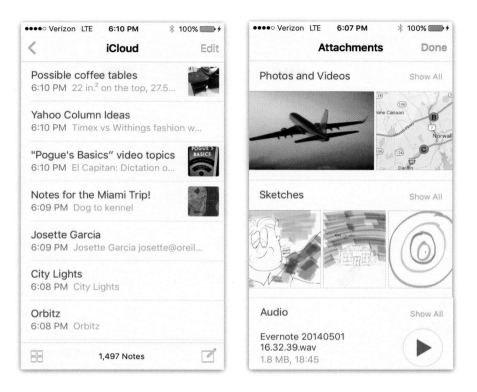

The beauty is that you don't have to remember what you called a note; just tap one of these items to open it. (At that point, you can tap Go to Note to jump to the page that contains it.)

Syncing Notes

Notes can synchronize with all kinds of other Apple gear—other iPhones, iPads, iPod Touches, and Macs—so the same notes are waiting for you everywhere you look. Just make sure Notes is turned on in Settings→iCloud on each phone or tablet, and in System Preferences→iCloud on your Mac. The rest is automatic—and awesome.

Notes Accounts

Your notes can also sync wirelessly with the Notes modules on Google, Yahoo, AOL, Exchange, or another IMAP email account. To set this up, open Settings→Mail, Contacts, Calendars. Tap the account you want (iCloud, Gmail, Yahoo, AOL, or whatever); finally, turn the Notes switch On.

That should do it. Now your notes are synced nearly instantly, wirelessly, both directions.

At this point, an Accounts button appears at the top-left corner of the table of contents screen. Tap it to see your note sets from Google, Yahoo, AOL, Exchange, iCloud, or an IMAP email account.

If you've created Notes folders in OS X on your Mac (Mountain Lion or later), then you see those folders here, too.

All of this makes life a little more complex, of course. For example, when you create a note, you have to worry about which account it's about to go into. To do that, be sure to specify an account name (and a folder within it, if necessary) *before* you create the new note.

NOTE: In Settings→Notes, you can also specify which of your different Notes accounts you want to be the *main* one—the one that new notes fall into if you haven't specified otherwise.

Podcasts

A podcast is a "radio" show that's distributed online. Lots of podcasts begin life as *actual* radio and TV shows; most of NPR's shows are available as podcasts, for example, so that you can listen to them whenever and wherever you like.

But thousands more are recorded just for downloading. They range from recordings made by professionals in studios—to amateurs talking into their phones. Some have thousands of listeners; some have only a handful.

One thing's for sure: There's a podcast out there that precisely matches whatever weird, narrow interests *you* have.

The Podcasts app helps you find, subscribe to, organize, and listen to podcasts. It's designed just like Apple's online stores for apps, music, movies, and so on. Tap Featured to see scrolling rows of recommended podcasts (facing page, left) or Top Charts to see what the rest of the world is listening to these days. Or use the Search button to look for something specific.

There are video podcasts, too, although they're much less common. The most popular videocasts are usually clips from network or cable TV shows,

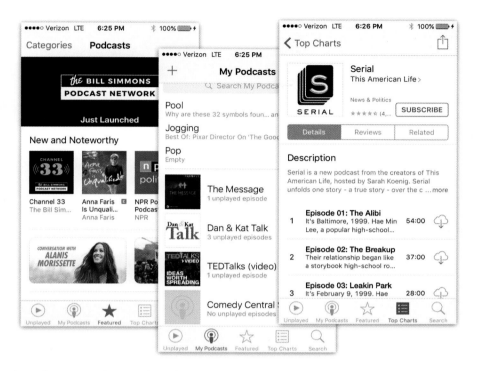

but there are plenty of quirky, offbeat, funny video podcasts that will never be seen except on pocket screens.

In any case, once you find a podcast episode that seems interesting (above, right), you can listen to it in either of two ways:

- **Stream it.** Tap a podcast's name to play it directly from the Internet. It's never stored on your iPhone and doesn't take up any space, but it does require an Internet connection. Generally no good for plane rides.

- **Download it.** If you tap the ☁ next to a podcast's name, you download it to your phone. It takes up space there (and podcasts can be big)—but you can play it back anytime, anywhere. And, of course, you can delete it when you're done.

Subscribing

Most podcasts are series. Their creators crank them out every week or whatever. If you find one you love, subscribe to it, so that your phone downloads each new episode automatically. Just tap SUBSCRIBE on its details page.

The episodes wind up on the My Podcasts screen (above, center). Tap an icon to open the Episodes screen, where you can tap Unplayed (episodes you haven't heard) or **Feed** (all episodes). You'll also find buttons for **Edit** (delete episodes en masse); ⚙ (settings for this podcast only); and ⬆ (pass along links to this podcast by Messages, Mail, Twitter, Facebook, and so on).

Settings

There's a lot to control when it comes to podcasts. Do you want new episodes downloaded automatically? Do you want them auto-deleted when you're finished? Do you want to limit how many episodes of each show are stored on your phone? What playback order—oldest first or newest first?

You make all these choices in **Settings→Podcasts**. That's the global setting for podcasts (below, left)—but you can also override them for individual podcast shows, using the ⚙ button described above.

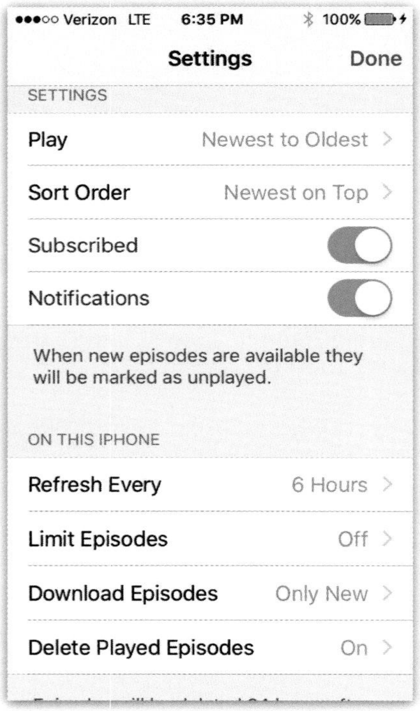

●●●●○ Verizon LTE 6:35 PM ⚹ 100% 🔋⚡	●●●● Verizon LTE 6:34 PM P A N ⊙ P L Y ⚡
Settings Done	⌄
SETTINGS	
Play Newest to Oldest ›	‖|‖‖|‖
Sort Order Newest on Top ›	**THE MESSAGE**
Subscribed ⬤	
Notifications ⬤	GE podcast theater
When new episodes are available they will be marked as unplayed.	0:13 -21:59
ON THIS IPHONE	**Episode 8**
Refresh Every 6 Hours ›	The Message — November 22, 2015 at 12:01 AM
Limit Episodes Off ›	1½× ⟲15 ‖‖ 15⟳ ≡
Download Episodes Only New ›	◄————————●———► ◄))
Delete Played Episodes On ›	⬆ ☾ •••

Playback

To play a podcast, tap its icon on **My Podcasts**, and then the episode name. Tap the playback strip at bottom to reveal all the usual audio-playback controls (page 49)—with the handy addition of buttons that speed up or slow down the talking (.5x, 1x, 1.5x, or 2x regular speed), as shown above at right.

There's a Sleep Timer, too, that lets you can drift off to the sound of a droning podcaster—but its button, in iOS 9.1, is *invisible*. Tap the bottom center (indicated by the moon symbol on the facing page) to pick how long you want the podcast to play before shutting off.

You can press the Sleep switch to turn off the screen; the podcast continues playing. And even if the phone is locked, you can open the Control Center (page 47) to access the playback controls.

Don't forget to use Siri! You can say things like "Play 'Fresh Air' podcast," "Play my latest podcasts," "Play my podcast" (to resume what you listened to last), "Play latest TED podcast," and so on.

Reminders

Reminders not only records your life's little tasks, but it also reminds you about them at the right time or right place. For example, it can remind you to water the plants as soon as you get home.

If you have an iCloud account, your reminders sync across all your gadgets. Create or check off a task on your iPhone, and you'll also find it created or checked off on your iPad, iPod Touch, Mac, PC, and so on.

Reminders sync wirelessly with anything your iCloud account knows about: Calendar or BusyCal on your Mac, Outlook on the PC, and so on.

Siri and Reminders are a match made in heaven. "Remind me to file the Jenkins report when I get to work." "Remind me to set the TiVo for tonight at 8." "Remind me about Timmy's soccer game a week from Saturday." "When I get home, remind me to take a shower."

The List of Lists

When you open Reminders, it's clear that you can create *more than one* to-do list, each with its own name: a groceries list, kids' chores, a running tally of expenses, and so on. It's a great way to log what you eat if you're on a diet, or to keep a list of movies people recommend.

They show up as file-folder tabs; tap one to open the to-do list within.

If you share an iCloud account with another family member, you might create a different Reminders list for each person. (Of course, now you run the risk that your spouse might sneakily add items to *your* to-do list!)

Reminders	**Urgent to do**
6 items	4 items Edit
Groceries	○ Finish spackling the living room
No items	11/3, 4:00 PM
To Dos	◉ Selloff all stocks
10 items	Today, 4:00 PM
Chores	○ Download Kindle books
No items	1/2, 4:00 PM
Movies to See	◉ New website proposal due
4 items	12/20, 4:00 PM
CaseyRobin	○ Prepare wedding proposal
6 items	
○ Return Hummer	○ Call William about the thing
○ Northern Lights Club	

If you have an Exchange account, one of your lists can be synced to your corporate Tasks list. It doesn't offer all the features of the other lists in Reminders, but at least it's kept tidy and separate.

> **TIP:** You can use Siri to add things to individual lists by name. You can say, for example, "Add low-fat cottage cheese to the Groceries list."
>
> Siri can also find these reminders, saving you a lot of navigation later. You can say, "Find my reminder about dosage instructions," for example.

Once you've created some lists, you can easily switch among them. Just tap an open list's name to collapse it, returning to the list of lists. At that point you can tap the title of a different list to open it.

> **TIP:** When you're viewing the list of lists, you can rearrange them by dragging their title bars up or down.

To create a new list, begin at the list of lists (facing page, left). Tap + at the top right. The app asks if you're trying to create a new **Reminder** (that is, one To Do item) or a new **List**, as shown at upper right; tap **List**.

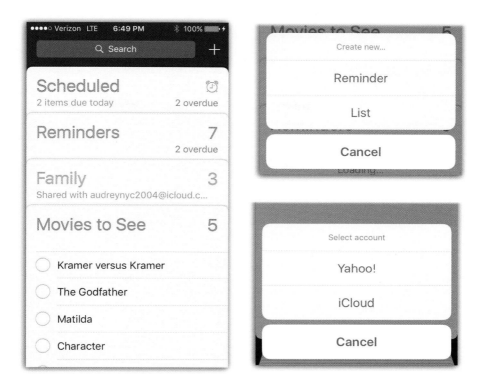

If you have multiple accounts that offer reminders, you're asked to specify which one will receive this new list at this point, too (above, right).

Now your jobs begin:

1. **Enter a name for the list.** When you tap the light-gray letters New List, the keyboard appears to help you out.

2. **Tap a colored dot.** This will be the color of the list's title font and also of the "checked-off" circles once the list is under way.

3. **Tap Done.** Now you can tap the first blank line and enter the first item in the list.

NOTE: After that first line, you can't create new items in the list by tapping the blank line below the existing items. As you type, tapping the Return key is the only way to move to the next line. (Tap Done when you're finished adding to the list.)

To delete a list, tap Edit and then tap Delete List.

Later, you can assign a task to a different list by tapping List on its Details screen.

To return to the list of lists, tap the current list's name. Or tap the bottom edge of the screen. Or swipe down from the top of it.

The Scheduled List

If you really do wind up using Reminders as a to-do list, you might be gratified to discover that the app also offers an automatically generated Scheduled list: a consolidated list of every item, from all your lists, to which you've given a *deadline*. It's always the topmost tab, marked by an alarm-clock icon.

Recording a Reminder

Once you've opened a list, here's how you record a new task the manual way: Tap the blank line beneath your existing reminders. Type your reminder (or dictate it). Tap the ⓘ to set up the details, described next; tap Done when you're finished.

As you go through life completing tasks, tap the circle next to each one. A checked-off to-do remains in place until the next time you visit its list. At that point, it disappears. It's moved into a separate list called Completed.

But when you want to take pride in how much you've accomplished, you can tap Show Completed to bring your checked-off tasks back into view.

Other stuff you can do:

- **Delete a to-do item altogether, as though it never existed.** Swipe leftward across its name; tap Delete to confirm.

- **Delete a bunch of items in a row.** Tap Edit. Tap each ⊖ icon, and then tap Delete to confirm.

- **Rearrange a list so the items appear in a different order.** Tap Edit, and then drag the ≡ handle up or down.

The Details Screen

If you tap ⓘ next to an item's name, you arrive at the Details screen (facing page, left). Here you can set up a reminder that will pop up at a certain time or place, create an auto-repeating schedule, file this item into a different to-do list with its own name, add notes to this item, or delete it. Here are your options, one by one:

- **Remind me on a day.** Here you can set up the phone to chime at a certain date and time. Turn on the switch to see two new lines: Alarm and Repeat. Tap Alarm to bring up the "time wheel" for setting the deadline.

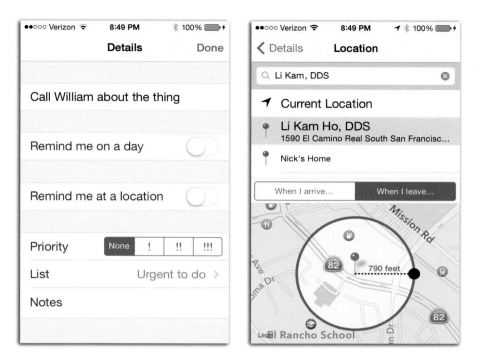

Tap Repeat if you want this reminder to appear every day, week, two weeks, month, or year—great for reminding you about things that recur in your life, like quarterly tax payments, haircuts, and anniversaries.

- **Remind me at a location.** If you turn on this amazing feature, then the phone will use its location circuits to remind you of this item when you arrive at a certain place or leave a certain place. When you tap the new Location line, you'll see that the phone offers "Current Location"—wherever you are at the moment. That's handy if, for example, you're dropping off your dry cleaning and want to remember to pick it up the next time you're driving by.

  But you can also choose Home or Work (your home or work addresses, as you've set them up in Contacts). Or you can use the search box at the top, either to type (or dictate) a street address or to search your own Contacts list.

  Once you've specified an address, the Location screen shows a map (above, right). The diameter of the blue circle shows the area where your presence will trigger the appearance of the reminder on your screen.

TIP: You can adjust the size of this "geofence" by dragging the black handle to adjust the size of the circle. In effect, you're telling the iPhone how close you have to be to the specified address for the reminder to pop up. You can adjust the circle's radius anywhere from 328 feet ("Remind me when I'm in that store") to 1,500 miles ("Remind me when I'm in that country").

The final step here is to tap either When I Leave or When I Arrive.

Later, the phone will remind you at the appointed time or as you approach (or leave) the appointed address, which is fairly mind-blowing the first few times it happens.

NOTE: If you set up *both* a time reminder *and* a location reminder, then your iPhone uses whichever event happens first. That is, if you ask to be reminded at 3 p.m. today and "When I arrive at the office," then you'll get the reminder when you get to the office—or at 3 p.m., if that time rolls around before you make it to work.

- **Priority.** Tap one of these buttons to specify whether this item has low, medium, or high priority—or None. In some of the calendar programs that sync with Reminders, you can sort your task list by priority.

- **List.** Tap here to assign this to-do to a different reminder list, as described earlier.

- **Notes.** Here's a handy box where you can record freehand notes about this item: an address, a phone number, details of any kind.

To exit the Details screen, tap Done.

"Remind Me About This"

Here's a reminder about a fantastic new Reminders feature in iOS 9.

When you're looking at something in one of Apple's apps, you can say, "Remind me about this later." That might be a text message in Messages, a web page in Safari, an email in Mail, a document in Pages, or whatever. (This command works in Calendar, Clock, Contacts, iBooks, Health, Mail, Maps, Messages, Notes, Numbers, Pages, Phone, Podcasts, Reminders, and Safari. Software companies can upgrade their apps to work with "Remind me about this," too.)

Instantly, Siri creates a new item on your main Reminders list—named for the precise message, location, web page, document, or thing you were looking at—complete with the icon of the app you were using.

Later, you can tap that icon to open the original app—to the exact spot you were at when you issued the command.

You don't have to be as vague as "later," either. You can also say things like, "Remind me about this tomorrow night at 7" or "Remind me about this when I get home."

Put it all together, and you've got an amazingly effective system for bookmarking your life. Maybe this trick will, once and for all, end the practice of people emailing stuff to themselves, just so they'll remember it!

Stocks

This one's for you, big-time day trader. The Stocks app tracks the rise and fall of the stocks in your portfolio by downloading the very latest stock prices.

(All right, maybe not the *very* latest. The price info may be delayed as much as 20 minutes, which is typical of free stock-info services.)

When you first fire it up, Stocks shows you a handful of sample high-tech stocks—or, rather, their abbreviations. (They stand for the Dow Jones Industrial Index, the NASDAQ Index, the S&P 500 Index, Apple, Google, and Yahoo.)

Next to each, you see its current share price, and next to *that*, you see how much that price has gone up or down today. As a handy visual gauge to how elated or depressed you should be, this final number appears on a *green* background if it's gone up, or a *red* one if it's gone down. Tap this number to cycle the display from a percentage to a dollar amount to current market capitalization ("120.3B," meaning $120.3 billion total corporate value).

When you tap a stock, the bottom part of the screen shows some handy data. Swipe horizontally to cycle among three different displays:

- **A table of statistics.** A capsule summary of today's price and volume statistics for this stock.

- **A graph of the stock's price.** It starts out showing you the graph of the current year. But by tapping the headings above the chart, you can zoom in or out from one day (1D) to three months (3M) to two years (2Y).

- **A table of relevant headlines,** courtesy of Yahoo Finance. Tap a headline to read the article—or tap and hold to add it, or all the articles, to your Safari Reading List (page 443).

Landscape View

If you turn the iPhone sideways, you get a much bigger, more detailed, widescreen graph of the stock in question. (Flick horizontally to view the previous or next stock.)

> **TIP:** On a Plus model, there's room for *both* your list of stocks *and* the graph of the one you've tapped, all on the same landscape-orientation screen.

Better yet, you can pinch with two fingers or two thumbs to isolate a certain time period; a pop-up label shows you how much of a bath you took (or how much of a windfall you received) during the interval you highlighted. Cool!

Customizing Your Portfolio

It's fairly unlikely that *your* stock portfolio contains just Apple, Google, and Yahoo. Fortunately, you can customize the list of stocks to reflect the companies you *do* own (or want to track).

To edit the list, tap the ≣ button in the lower-right corner. You arrive at the editing screen (next page, right), where these choices await:

- **Delete a stock** by tapping the ⊖ button and then the Delete confirmation button.

- **Rearrange the list** by dragging the grip strips on the right side.

- **Add a stock** by tapping the + button in the top-left corner; the Add Stock screen and the keyboard appear.

You're not expected to know every stock-symbol abbreviation. Type in the company's *name*, and then tap Search. The iPhone shows you, above the keyboard, a scrolling list of companies with matching names. Tap the one you want to track. You return to the stocks-list editing screen.

- **Choose %, Price, or Numbers.** By tapping the buttons at the bottom, you can specify how you want to see the changes in stock prices in the far-right column: as *percentages* ("+0.65%"), as *numbers* ("+2.23") or as *market cap*. (Here you're simply choosing which number starts out appearing on the main stock screen. As noted earlier, you can easily cycle among these three stats by tapping them.)

When you're finished setting up your stock list, tap Done.

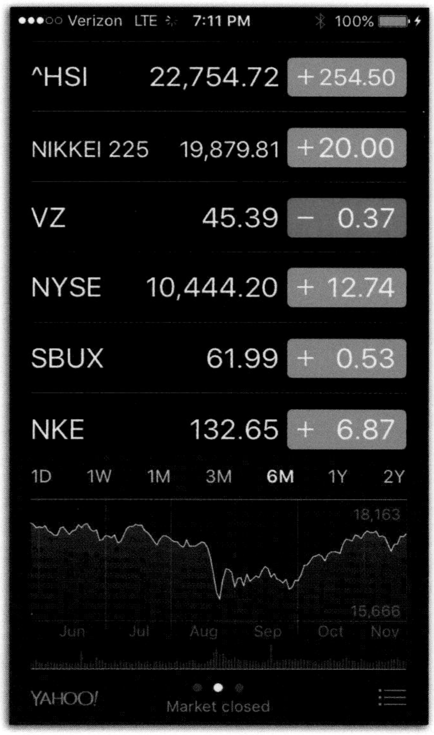

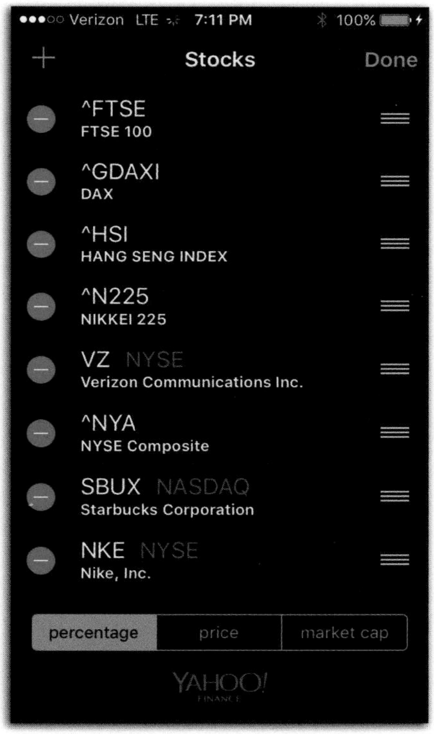

Tips

Hey, check it out—Apple's getting into the how-to game!

This app is designed to show you tips and tricks for getting the most from your iPhone. Each screen offers an animated illustration and a paragraph of text explaining one of iOS's marvels. Swipe leftward to see the next tip, and the next, and the next. Or tap ☰ to see a list of all the tips in one place.

Tap Like if it's one of your favorites. Tap ⬆ to share a tip by text message, email, Twitter, Facebook, or AirDrop.

Over time, Apple will beam you fresh tips to add to this collection. It's not exactly, you know, a handsome, printed, full-color book, but it's something.

Voice Memos

This audio app is ideal for recording lectures, musical performances, notes to self, and cute child utterances. You'll probably be very surprised at how good the microphone is, even from a distance.

The best part: When you sync your iPhone with iTunes on your Mac or PC, all your voice recordings get copied back to the computer automatically. You'll find them in the iTunes folder called Voice Memos.

Tap ⏺ (or click your earbud clicker) to start recording. A little ding signals the start (and stop) of the session—unless you've turned the phone's volume all the way down (you sneak!).

●●○○○ Verizon 🖥	3:46 PM	⚡ 100% 🔋
	Record	

00:04   00:05   00:06   00:07   00:08   00:09

00:07.12
New Recording 3
10/3/13

⏹   Done

New Recording 3
10/3/13   0:00:07

Interview With A Grandmother
10/3/13   0:00:23

Baby

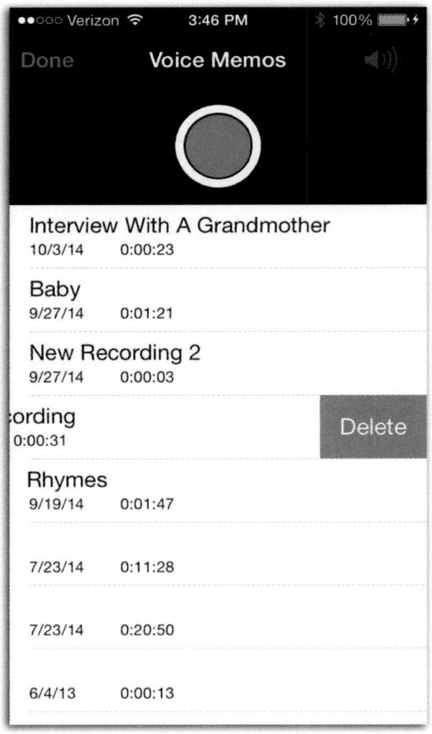

●●○○○ Verizon 🖥	3:46 PM	⚡ 100% 🔋
Done	**Voice Memos**	🔊

Interview With A Grandmother
10/3/14   0:00:23

Baby
9/27/14   0:01:21

New Recording 2
9/27/14   0:00:03

cording
0:00:31   Delete

Rhymes
9/19/14   0:01:47

7/23/14   0:11:28

7/23/14   0:20:50

6/4/13   0:00:13

You get to watch the actual sound waves as the recording proceeds. You can pause at any time by pressing the Stop button (◉)—and then resume the same recording with another tap on the ◉ button.

TIP: The built-in mike records in mono. But it records in stereo if you connect a stereo mike (to the headphone jack or charging jack).

You can also switch out of the app to do other work. A red banner across the top of the screen reminds you that you're still recording. You can even *switch the screen off* by tapping the Sleep switch; the recording goes on! (You can make *very* long recordings with this thing. Let it run all day, if you like. Even your most long-winded friends can be immortalized.)

Tap Done when you're sure the recording session is over. You're asked to type a name for the new recording ("Baby's First Words," "Orch Concert," whatever); then you can tap Save or, if it wasn't worth saving, Delete.

Below the recording controls, the list of your recordings appears. When you tap one, a convenient set of controls appears. (They look a lot like the ones that appear when you tap a voicemail message in the Phone app.)

TIP: If you have an iPhone Plus model, you can turn the screen 90 degrees—and see both the list of recordings *and* the editing screen, in two columns.

Here's what you can do here (next page, left):

- **[Recording name].** Tap the name to edit or rename it.

- **▶.** Tap to play the recording. You can pause with a tap on the **ll** button.

TIP: As a recording plays back, you can tap the ◀)) icon at the top of the screen to turn off the speaker. Hold the phone up to your ear.

- **Rewind, Fast Forward.** Drag the little vertical line in the scrubber bar to skip backward or forward in the recording. It's a great way to skip over the boring pleasantries.

- 🗑. Tap to get rid of a recording (you'll be asked to confirm).

- ⬆. Tap to open the standard Share sheet. It gives you the chance to send your recording to someone else by AirDrop, email, or MMS.

Voice Memos ◀))

Interview With A Grandmother
10/3/14   0:00:23

❚❚   0:08 | -0:15

⬆️   Edit   🗑️

Baby
9/27/13   0:01:21

New Recording 2
9/27/13   0:00:03

New Recording
9/27/13   0:00:31

Kell Rhymes
9/19/13   0:01:47

Trim ◀))

05:61   14:82

00:09.20

Cancel   Trim

▶️

Interview With A Grandmother
10/3   0:00:23

Baby
9/27/13   0:01:21

New Recording 2

Trimming Your Recording

You might not guess that such a tiny, self-effacing app actually offers some basic editing functions, but it does. Tap a recording and then tap Edit to open its Edit screen (above, right).

The main thing you'll do here is trim off the beginning or end of your audio clip. That, of course, is where you'll usually find "dead air" or microphone fumbling before the good stuff starts playing. (You can't otherwise edit the sound; for example, you can't copy or paste bits or cut a chunk out of the middle.)

To trim the bookends of your clip, tap the Trim button (⬜). At this point, the beginning and end of the recording are marked by vertical red lines; these are your trim points. Drag them inward to isolate the part of the clip you want to keep. The app thoughtfully magnifies the sound waves whenever you're dragging, to help with precision. Play the sound as necessary to guide you (▶).

Tap Trim to lock in your changes. You'll be asked to tap either Trim Original (meaning "shorten the original clip permanently") or Save as New Recording (meaning "leave the original untouched, and spin out the shortened version as a separate audio file, just in case").

Wallet

This app was originally called Passbook. And it was originally designed to store, in one place, every form of ticket that uses a barcode. For most people, that meant airline boarding passes.

Wallet still does that. And, occasionally, you may find a Wallet-compatible theater or sports admission pass, loyalty card, coupon, movie ticket, and so on. Beats having a separate app for each one of these.

Wallet holds down a second job, too. It's the key to Apple Pay, the magical "pay by waving your iPhone" feature described on page 524.

> **TIP:** You can rearrange the passes; just hold still briefly before you start moving your finger up or down. (That order syncs to your other iOS gadgets, for what it's worth.)

What's cool is that Wallet uses both its own clock and GPS to know when the time and place are right. For example, when you arrive at the airport, a notification appears on your Lock screen. Each time you have to show your boarding pass as you work through the stages of airport security, you

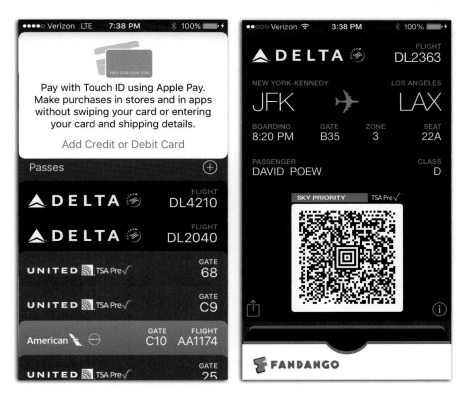

can wake your phone and swipe across that notification; your boarding-pass barcode appears instantly. You're spared having to unlock your phone (enter its password), hunt for the airline app, log in, and fiddle your way to the boarding pass.

The hardest part might be finding things to put *into* Wallet. Apple says that someday there will be a "Send to Wallet" button on the website or a confirmation email when you buy the ticket.

For now, you can visit the App Store and search for **passbook** to find apps that work with Wallet—big airlines, Fandango (movie tickets), Starbucks, Walgreens, Ticketmaster, and Major League Baseball are among the compatible apps. In some, you're supposed to open the app to view the barcode *first* and put it into Wallet from there. For example, in most airline apps, you call up the boarding-pass screen and then tap Add.

Once your barcodes have successfully landed in Wallet, the rest is pure fun. When you arrive at the theater or stadium or airport, the Lock screen displays an alert. Swipe it to open the barcode in Wallet. You can put the entire phone under the ticket-taker's scanner.

Tap the ⓘ button in the corner to read the details—and to delete a ticket after you've used it (tap Delete). That details screen also offers a Show On Lock Screen on/off switch, in case you *don't* want Wallet to hand you your ticket as you arrive.

Finally, Wallet is one of the two places you can enter your credit card information for Apple Pay on an iPhone 6 or 6s model, as described on page 524. (Settings is the other.)

Watch

If you own an Apple Watch, you use this little app to set up its settings.

So why do you have the Watch app on your phone even if you *don't* have an Apple Watch? You'll have to ask someone in Marketing.

Meanwhile, if it bugs you, you can drag this app into some folder somewhere, where you'll never have to see it again.

Weather

This little app shows a handy current-conditions display for your city (or any other city). Handy *and* lovely; the weather display is animated. Clouds drift by, rain falls gently. If it's nighttime in the city you're looking up, you might see a beautiful starscape.

The current temperature is shown nice and big; the table below shows the cloud-versus-sun forecast, as well as the high and low temperatures.

You don't even have to tell the app what weather you want; it uses your location and assumes you want the *local* weather forecast.

There are three places you can tap or swipe:

- **Scroll up** to see a table of stats: humidity, chance of rain, sunrise time, wind speed, "feels like" (chill or heat index), and so on.

- **Swipe horizontally across the hourly forecast** to scroll later in the day.

- **Swipe horizontally anywhere else** to view the weather for other cities (if you've set them up). The tiny dots beneath the display correspond to the number of cities you've set up—and the white bold one indicates where you are in the sequence.

  The first city—the screen at far left—is always the city you're *in right now*. The iPhone uses GPS to figure out where you are.

The City List

It's easy to get the weather for other cities—great if you're going to be traveling, or if you're wondering how life is for distant relations.

When you tap ☰ at the lower-right corner, the screen collapses into a list of your preprogrammed cities (previous page, right).

You can tap one to open its weather screen. You can delete one by swiping leftward across it (and then tapping **Delete**). You can drag them up or down into a new order (leave your finger down for one second before you drag each time). You can switch between Celsius and Fahrenheit by tapping the **C/F** button.

Or you can scroll to the bottom (if necessary) and tap ⊕ to enter a new city.

Here you're asked to type a city, a zip code, or an airport abbreviation (like JFK for New York's John F. Kennedy airport). You can specify any reasonably sized city on earth. (Remember to check before you travel!)

When you tap **Search**, you're shown a list of matching cities; tap the one you want to track. When you return to the configuration screen, you can also specify whether you prefer degrees Celsius or degrees Fahrenheit. Tap **Done**.

There's nothing else to tap here except the Weather Channel icon at the bottom. It fires up the Safari browser, which loads itself with an information page about that city from *weather.com*.

If you've added more than one city to the list, by the way, just flick your finger right or left to flip through the weather screens for the different cities.

More Standard Apps

This book describes every app that comes on every iPhone. But Apple has another suite of useful programs for you. And they're free.

NOTE: If you have an iPhone 6 or 6s model with 64 or 128 gigabytes of storage, then most of these apps come already installed: iMovie, GarageBand, Keynote, Pages, Numbers, and iTunes U.

To find them, on the first page of the App Store, scroll down and tap **Apps Made by Apple**. You'll find these apps ready to download:

- **Pages** is, believe it or not, a word processing/page-layout program.

- **Numbers** is Apple's spreadsheet program.

- **Keynote** is Apple's version of PowerPoint. It lets you make slideshow presentations from your iPhone.

- **iMovie.** A video-editing program on your cellphone? Yes, with all the basics: rearranging clips; adding music, crossfades, and credits.

- **GarageBand** is a pocket music studio.

- **iTunes U** is a catalog of 600,000 free courses by professors at colleges, museums, and libraries all over the world. This app lets you browse the catalog, and watch and read the course materials.

- **Find My Friends** lets you see where your friends and family members are on a map (with their permission, of course).

- **Find My iPhone** is useful when you want to find *other* missing Apple gadgets (Macs, iPads, iPod Touches, iPhones).

PART THREE

The iPhone Online

Chapter 11
Getting Online

Chapter 12
Safari

Chapter 13
Email

11

Getting Online

The iPhone's concept as an all-screen machine is a curse and a blessing. You may curse it when you're trying to type text, wishing you had real keys. But when you're online—oh, baby. That's when the web comes to life, looming larger and clearer than you'd think possible on a cellphone. That's when you see real email, full-blown YouTube videos, hyper-clear Google maps, and all kinds of Internet goodness, right in your hand.

And it's fast, too—as long as you're in one of the cities covered by 4G LTE cellular towers, and the gods are smiling.

Cellular Networks

The iPhone can get onto the Internet using either of two kinds of wireless networks: *cellular* or *Wi-Fi*. Which kind you're on makes a huge difference to your iPhone experience.

Once you've accepted the miracle that a cellphone can transmit your voice wirelessly, it's not much of a stretch to realize that it can also transmit your data. Cellphone carriers (Verizon, AT&T, and so on) maintain separate networks for voice and Internet data—and they spend billions of dollars trying to make those Internet networks faster. Over the years, they've come up with data networks like these:

- **Old, slow cellular network.** The earliest, slowest cellular Internet connections were called things like EDGE (AT&T) or 1xRTT (Verizon and Sprint). The good part is that these networks are almost everywhere, so your iPhone can get online almost anywhere you can make a phone call. You'll know when you're on one of these slow networks because your status bar bears a symbol like **E** or **o**.

  The bad news is that it's slow. *Dog* slow—dial-up slow.

You can't be on a phone call while you're online using EDGE or 1xRTT, either.

- **3G cellular networks.** The world wasn't happy with those slow networks, so the carriers spent several years building faster systems called *3G* networks. (3G stands for "third generation." The ancient analog cellphones were the first generation; EDGE-type networks were the second.) Geeks refer to the 3G network standard by its official name: HSDPA, for High-Speed Downlink Packet Access.

  Web pages that take 2 minutes to appear using EDGE or 1xRTT show up in about 20 seconds on 3G. Email downloads much faster, especially when there are attachments. Voice calls sound better, too, even when the signal strength is very low, since the iPhone's 3G radio can communicate with multiple towers at once.

  Oh, and on AT&T or T-Mobile, you can talk on the phone and use the Internet simultaneously, which can be very handy indeed.

- **"4G" networks.** AT&T enhanced HSDPA, made it faster using a technology called HSPA+ (High-Speed Packet Access), and calls it 4G. (You'll know when you're on one; your status bar says **4G**.) But nobody else recognizes HSPA+ as real 4G, which is why AT&T feels fine advertising "the nation's largest 4G network." The other carriers aren't even measuring that network type.

- **4G LTE networks.** Now *this* is 4G.

  An LTE network (Long-Term Evolution), offered in major cities by all four carriers, gives you amazing speeds—in some cases, faster than your broadband Internet at home. When your status bar says **LTE**, it's *fantastic*.

  But LTE is not all sunshine and bunnies; it has two huge downsides.

  First: coverage. In an attempt to serve the most people with the least effort, cell companies always bring LTE service to the big cities first. LTE coverage is available in hundreds of U.S. cities, which is a good start. But that still leaves most of the country, including huge chunks of several entire states, without any 4G coverage at all (hi there, Montana!).

  The other carriers don't cover as many cities. Whenever you're outside the high-speed areas, your iPhone falls back to the slower speeds.

  The second big problem with LTE is that, to receive its signal, a phone's circuitry uses a lot of power. That's why the latest iPhones are bigger than their predecessors; they need beefier batteries.

A Word About VoLTE

If you have an iPhone 6 or 6s model, the dawn of LTE cellphone networks brings another benefit: You can use Voice over LTE, or **VoLTE** ("volty"). That's a delightful new cellular feature that promises amazing voice quality—sounds more like FM radio than cellphone—**and** simultaneous calling/Internetting, even on Verizon. (Behind the scenes, it sends your voice over the carrier's **Internet** network instead of the voice network. That's why it's called "Voice over LTE.")

To make this work, every link in the chain has to be compatible with VoLTE: your phone and your cellphone network, **and** (for the great sound quality) the phone and network of the person you're **calling**.

All four big U.S. carriers offer VoLTE, but you generally get the high-quality sound only when you're calling someone on your **own** cellphone carrier—not if, for example, you have Verizon and the other guy has T-Mobile. (Cross-carrier calling is supposed to be coming soon.)

To turn on VoLTE, open Settings→Cellular→Enable LTE; select Voice & Data. For Verizon, you also have to visit your MyVerizon web page and turn on Advanced Calling. There's no extra cost involved—just some truly welcome new improvements in quality and convenience.

Wi-Fi Hotspots

Wi-Fi, known to geeks as 802.11, is wireless networking, the same technology that gets laptops online at high speed in any Wi-Fi **hotspot**.

Hotspots are everywhere these days: in homes, offices, coffee shops, hotels, airports, and thousands of other places. Unfortunately, a hotspot is a bubble about 300 feet across; once you wander out of it, you're off the Internet. So, in general, Wi-Fi is for people who are sitting still.

When you're in a Wi-Fi hotspot, your iPhone usually gets a **very** fast connection to the Internet, as though it's connected to a cable modem or DSL. And when you're online this way, you can make phone calls and surf the Internet simultaneously. And why not? Your iPhone's Wi-Fi and cellular antennas are independent.

(Over cellular connections, only the AT&T and T-Mobile iPhones let you talk and get online simultaneously. Verizon and Sprint can do that only when you're on a VoLTE call, as described previously.)

The iPhone looks for a Wi-Fi connection first and considers connecting to a cellular network only if there's no Wi-Fi. You'll always know which kind of network you're on, thanks to the icons on the status bar: You'll see either 📶 for Wi-Fi, or one of the cellular icons (**E**, °, **3G**, **4G**, or **LTE**).

Or "No service" if there's nothing available at all.

And how much faster is one than the next? Well, network speeds are measured in kilobits and megabits per second (which isn't the same as the more familiar **kilobytes** and **megabytes** per second; divide by 8 to get those).

The EDGE/1xRTT network is supposed to deliver data from 70 to 200 Kbps, depending on your distance from the cell towers. 3G gets 300 to 700 Kbps. A Wi-Fi hotspot can spit out 650 to 2,100 Kbps. And 4G LTE can deliver speeds as fast as 100 Mbps on the iPhone 6 and 6s family. You'll rarely get speeds near the high ends—but even so, you can see that there's quite a difference.

The bottom line: LTE and Wi-Fi are **awesome**. EDGE/1xRTT—not so much.

Sequence of Connections

The iPhone isn't online all the time. To save battery power, it opens the connection only on demand: when you check email, request a web page, and so on. At that point, the iPhone tries to get online following this sequence:

- **First, it sniffs around for a Wi-Fi network** that you've used before. If it finds one, it connects quietly and automatically. You're not asked for permission, a password, or anything else.

- **If the iPhone can't find a previous hotspot,** but it detects a *new* hotspot, a message appears (facing page, left). It displays any new hotspots' names; tap the one you want. (If you see a 🔒 icon, then that hotspot is password protected.)

- **If the iPhone can't find any Wi-Fi hotspots to join,** or if you don't join any, it connects to the cellular network, like 3G or LTE.

Silencing the "Want to Join?" Messages

Sometimes, you might be bombarded by those "Select a Wireless Network" messages at a time when you have no need to be online. You might want the iPhone to stop bugging you—to *stop* offering Wi-Fi hotspots. In that situation, from the Home screen, tap Settings→Wi-Fi (or tell Siri, "Open Wi-Fi settings"), and then turn off Ask to Join Networks. When this option is off, the iPhone never interrupts you by bounding in, wagging its tail, and dropping the name of a new network at your feet. In this case, to get onto a new network, you have to visit the aforementioned Settings screen and select it.

The List of Hotspots

At some street corners in big cities, Wi-Fi signals bleeding out of apartment buildings sometimes give you a choice of 20 or 30 hotspots to join.

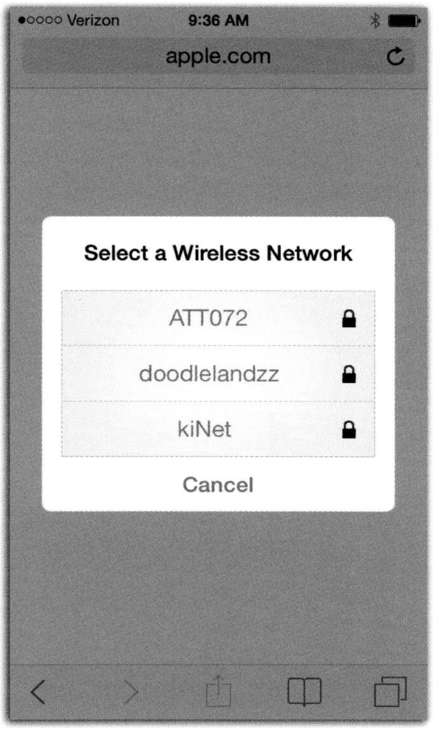

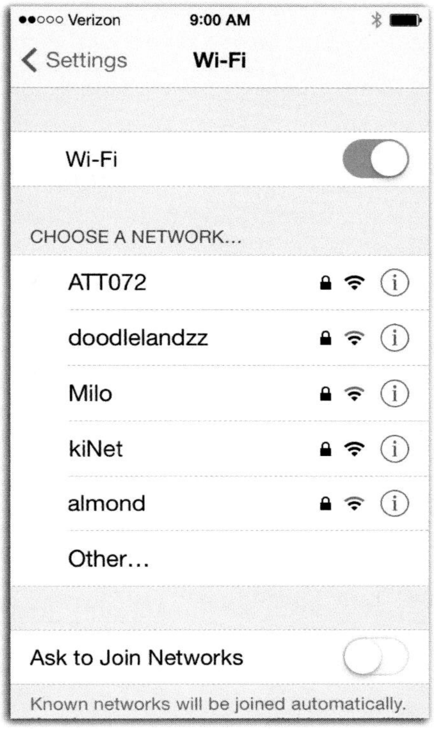

But whenever the iPhone invites you to join a hotspot, it suggests only a couple of them: the ones with the strongest signal and, if possible, no password requirement.

But you might sometimes want to see the complete list of available hotspots—maybe because the iPhone-suggested hotspot is flaky. To see the full list, from the Home screen, open Settings→Wi-Fi. Tap the one you want to join, as shown above at right.

> **TIP:** Tap ⓘ next to a hotspot's name to view an info sheet for techies. It shows your IP address, subnet mask, router address, and other delicious stats. Even mere mortals, however, will sometimes enjoy the Forget This Network button. It removes this hotspot from the list, which is handy if you've moved away and don't need to be reminded of the high speed that was once yours.

Commercial Hotspots

Tapping the name of the hotspot you want to join is generally all you have to do—if it's a *home* Wi-Fi network. Unfortunately, joining a *commercial* Wi-Fi hotspot—one that requires a credit card number (in a hotel room or an airport, for example)—requires more than just connecting to it. You also have to *sign into* it, exactly as you'd do if you were using a laptop.

In general, the iPhone prompts you to do that automatically. Some big login screen pops up on its own, interrupting whatever else you're doing; that's where you supply your credit card information or (if you have a membership to this Wi-Fi chain, like Boingo or T-Mobile) your name and password. Tap Submit or Proceed, try *not* to contemplate the cost, and enjoy your surfing.

(If that login screen doesn't appear, or if you canceled out of it accidentally, open Safari. You'll see the "Enter your payment information" screen, either immediately or as soon as you try to open a web page of your choice.)

Mercifully, the iPhone memorizes your password. The next time you use this hotspot, you won't have to enter it again.

Airplane Mode and Wi-Fi Off Mode

When battery power is precious, you can turn off all three of the iPhone's network connections in one fell swoop. You can also turn off Wi-Fi alone.

- **To turn all radios off.** In airplane mode, you turn off *all* wireless circuitry: Bluetooth, Wi-Fi, and cellular. Now you can't make calls or get onto the Internet. You're saving an amazing amount of power, however, and also complying with regulations that ban cellphones in flight.

The short way: Swipe up from the bottom of the screen; on the Control Center, tap ✈ so it turns white. (The long way: Open Settings, turn on Airplane Mode.)

- **To turn Wi-Fi on or off.** Swipe up; on the Control Center, tap 🛜 so it's no longer white. (You can also switch it in Settings→Wi-Fi.)

TIP: Once you've turned on airplane mode, you can actually turn Wi-Fi back *on* again. Why on earth? Because some flights offer Wi-Fi. You need a way to turn Wi-Fi *on*, but your cellular circuitry *off*.

Conversely, you sometimes might want to do the opposite: turn *off* Wi-Fi, but leave cellular *on*. Why? Because sometimes, the iPhone bizarrely won't get online at all. It's struggling to use a Wi-Fi network that, for one reason or another, isn't connecting to the Internet. By turning Wi-Fi off, you force the iPhone to use its cell connection—which may be slower, but at least it works!

In airplane mode, anything that requires voice or Internet access—text messages, web, email, and so on—triggers a message: "Turn off Airplane Mode or use Wi-Fi to access data." Tap either OK (to back out of your decision) or Settings (to turn off airplane mode and get online).

You can, however, enjoy all the other iPhone features: Music, Camera, and so on. You can also work with stuff you've *already* downloaded to the phone, like email, voicemail messages, and web pages you've saved in the Reading List.

Personal Hotspot (Tethering)

Tethering means using your iPhone as a glorified Internet antenna, so that your laptops, iPod Touches, iPads, game consoles, and other Internet-connectables can get online. (The other gadgets can connect to the phone over a Wi-Fi connection, a Bluetooth connection, or a USB cable.) In fact, several laptops and other gadgets can all share the iPhone's connection simultaneously. Your phone becomes a personal cellular router, like a MiFi.

That's incredibly convenient. Many phones have it, but Apple's execution is especially nice. For example, the hotspot shuts itself off 90 seconds after the last laptop disconnects. That's hugely important, because a personal hotspot is a merciless battery drain.

The hotspot feature may be included with your data plan (T-Mobile), or it may cost something like $20 a month extra, which buys only 2 gigabytes of data (Verizon). Think email, not YouTube.

To get this feature, you have to sign up for it by calling your cellular company or visiting its website (if you didn't already do that when you signed up for service).

TIP: If you have a Mac running OS X Yosemite or later, you're in for a real treat: a much more streamlined way to set up Personal Hotspot called *Instant* Hotspot. Skip the instructions below and jump immediately to page 539.

Turning On the Hotspot

On the phone, open Settings→Cellular→Personal Hotspot (or tell Siri, "Open cellular settings").

TIP: Once you've turned on Personal Hotspot for the first time, you won't have to drill down as far to get to it. A new Personal Hotspot item appears right there on the main Settings screen from now on.

The Personal Hotspot screen contains details on connecting other computers. It also has the master on/off switch. Turn Personal Hotspot On.

(If you see a button that says Set Up Personal Hotspot, it means you haven't yet added the monthly tethering fee to your cellular plan. Contact your wireless carrier to get that change made to your account.)

You have to use a password for your personal hotspot; it's to ensure that people sitting nearby can't surf using your connection and run up your cell bill. The software proposes a password, but you can edit it and make up one of your own. (It has to be at least eight characters long and con-

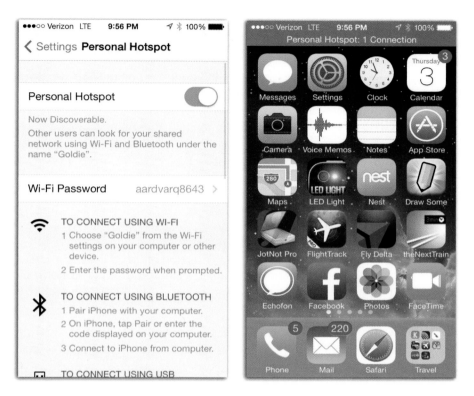

tain letters, numbers, and punctuation. Don't worry—your laptop or other Wi-Fi gadget can memorize it for you.)

Your laptops and other gadgets can connect to the Internet using any of three connections to the iPhone: Wi-Fi, Bluetooth, or a USB cable. If either Wi-Fi or Bluetooth are turned off, a message appears to let you know—and offers to turn them on for you. To save battery power, turn on only what you need.

Connecting via Wi-Fi

After about 30 seconds, the iPhone shows up on your laptop or other gadget as though it's a Wi-Fi network. Just choose the iPhone's name from your computer's Wi-Fi hotspot menu (on the Mac, it's the 📶 menu). Enter the password, and bam—your laptop is now online, using the iPhone as an antenna. On the Mac or an iPad, the 📶 changes to look like this: ☁.

You can leave the iPhone in your pocket or purse while connected. You'll surf away on your laptop, baffling every Internet-less soul around you. Your laptop can now use email, the web, chat programs—anything it could do in a real Wi-Fi hotspot (just a little slower).

Connecting via Bluetooth

There's no compelling reason to use Bluetooth instead of Wi-Fi, especially since Bluetooth slows down your Internet connection. But if you're interested, see the free downloadable PDF appendix "Bluetooth Tethering" on this book's "Missing CD" page at *www.missingmanuals.com*.

Connecting via USB Cable

If you can connect your laptop to your iPhone using the white charging cable, you should. Tethering eats up a lot of the phone's battery power, so keeping it plugged into the laptop means you won't wind up with a dead phone when you're finished surfing.

Once You're Connected

On the iPhone, a blue bar appears at the top of the screen to make you aware that the laptop is connected (previous page, right); in fact, it shows how many laptops or other gadgets are connected at the moment, via any of the three connection methods. (You can tap that bar to open the Personal Hotspot screen in Settings.)

Most carriers won't let more than five people connect through a single iPhone.

If you have AT&T or T-Mobile, you can still use all the functions of the iPhone, including making calls and surfing the web, while it's channeling your laptop's Internet connection.

If you have Verizon or Sprint, then your iPhone can't handle Internet connections and voice calls simultaneously (unless you're on a VoLTE call, as described on page 419). So if a phone call comes in, the iPhone suspends the hotspot feature until you're finished talking; when you hang up (or if you decline the call), all connected gadgets regain their Internet connections automatically.

Turning Off Personal Hotspot

If you're connected wirelessly to the iPhone, the Personal Hotspot feature is a battery hog. It'll cut your iPhone's battery longevity in half. That's why, if no laptops are connected for 90 seconds, the iPhone turns the hotspot off automatically.

You can also turn off the hotspot manually, just the way you'd expect: In Settings→Personal Hotspot, tap Off.

Turning Personal Hotspot Back On

About 90 seconds after the last gadget stops using the hotspot, your iPhone shuts off the feature to save its own battery. To fire it back up again later, open **Settings** and tap **Personal Hotspot**. That's it—just visit the Personal Hotspot screen to make the iPhone resume broadcasting its Wi-Fi or Bluetooth network to your laptops and other gadgets.

Twitter and Facebook

Twitter, of course, is a free service (sign up at *twitter.com*) that lets you send out short messages, like text messages, to anyone who wants to get them from you. Twitter is a fantastic way for people to spread news, links, thoughts, and observations directly to the people who care—incredibly quickly.

And Facebook is—well, Facebook. 1.4 billion people sharing their personal details and thoughts can't be wrong, right?

These services are woven into the built-in iPhone apps.

Start by visiting **Settings→Twitter** or **Settings→Facebook**. Here you can enter your account name and password or sign up for an account. Here, too, you're offered the chance to download the actual Twitter or Facebook apps. You can also tap **Update Contacts**, which attempts to add the Twitter

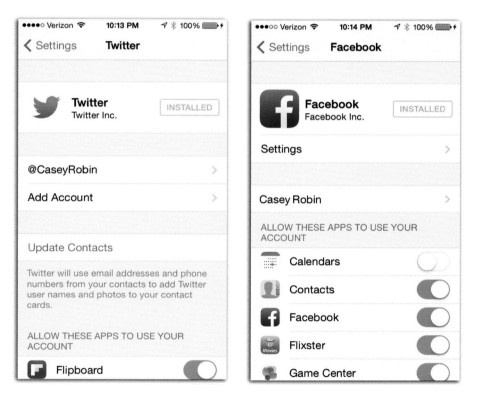

or Facebook addresses of everybody in your Contacts app to their information cards. For details, see page 106.

Once you've set up Twitter and Facebook this way, you'll find some nifty buttons built into your other apps, for one-tap tweeting or Facebook posting. For example, the Share button (📤) appears in Photos, Maps, Safari, and other apps, making it easy to post a photo, location, or web page. Siri understands commands like "Tweet" and "Post to Facebook," too, so you can broadcast when the spirit moves you. (The Tweet and Post buttons are no longer in the Notification Center, however.)

In each case, you wind up at a small tweet sheet or Facebook sheet. Here you can add a comment to the link or photo, or attach your current location, or (for Facebook) specify who's allowed to see this post—Everyone or Friends, for example.

For Twitter posts, you'll notice that the keyboard at that point offers dedicated @ and # keys. (The # is for creating *hashtags*—searchable keywords on a tweet like #iphone5sbugs—that Twitter fans can use when searching for tweets about certain topics. And the @ precedes every Twitter person's address—@pogue, for example.)

12

Safari

The iPhone's web browser is Safari, a lite version of the same one that comes on the Mac. It's fast, simple to use, and very pretty. You see the real deal—the actual fonts, graphics, and layouts— not the stripped-down mini-web on cellphones of years gone by.

Safari on the iPhone is still not quite as good as surfing the web on, you know, a laptop. But it's getting closer.

Safari Tour

Safari has most of the features of a desktop web browser: bookmarks, autocomplete (for web addresses), scrolling shortcuts, cookies, a pop-up ad blocker, password memorization, and so on. (It's missing niceties like streaming music, Java, Flash, and other plug-ins.)

> **TIP:** You don't have to wait for a web page to load entirely. You can zoom in, scroll, and begin reading the text even when only part of the page has appeared.

Now, don't be freaked out: *The main screen elements disappear* shortly after you start reading a page. That's supposed to give you more screen space to do your surfing. To bring them back, scroll to the top, scroll to the bottom, or just scroll up a little. At that point, here are the controls, as they appear from the top left:

- ≡ **(Reader view).** In this delightful view, all the ads, boxes, banners, and other junk disappear. Only text and pictures remain, for your sanity-in-reading pleasure. See page 451.

- **Search/address bar.** A single, unified box serves as both the address bar and the search bar at the top of the screen. (That's the trend these days. Desktop-computer browsers like Chrome and Safari on the Mac work that way, too.)

  This box is where you enter the *URL* (web address) for a page you want to visit. ("URL" is short for the even-less-self-explanatory *Uniform Resource Locator*.) For example, if you type *amazon.com*, tapping Go takes you to that website.

  But this is also where you search the web. If you type anything else, like *cashmere sweaters* or just *amazon*, tapping Go gives you the Google search results for that phrase.

TIP: If you hold your finger down briefly on the keyboard's period key, you get a pop-up palette of web-address suffixes (.org, .edu, and so on). Luckily, *.com* starts out selected—so just release your finger to type it in. In other words, the entire process for typing in *.com* goes like this: Hold finger on period key; release.

- ✕, ↻ **(Stop, Reload).** Tap ✕ to interrupt the downloading of a web page you've just requested (if you've made a mistake, for instance, or if it's taking too long).

  Once a page has finished loading, the ✕ button turns into a ↻ (reload) button. Click it if a page doesn't look or work quite right. Safari re-downloads the web page and reinterprets its text and graphics.

- ‹, › **(Back, Forward).** Tap ‹ to revisit the page you were just on. Once you've tapped ‹, you can then tap › to return to the page you were on *before* you tapped the ‹ button.

TIP: Since these buttons disappear as soon as you scroll down a page, how are you supposed to move back and forward among pages?

By *swiping in* from outside the screen. Start your swipe on the edge of the phone's front glass and whisk inward. Swiping rightward like this means "back"; leftward means "forward again." Do it slowly, and you can actually see the page sliding in.

- ⬆️ **(Share/Bookmark).** When you're on an especially useful page, tap this button. It offers every conceivable choice for commemorating or sharing the page. See page 330 for details.

- 📖 **(Bookmarks).** This button brings up your list of saved book-marks—plus your History list, Favorites, Reading List, and links rec-ommended by the people you follow on Twitter. You can read about these elements later in this chapter.

- 📄 **(Page Juggler).** Safari can keep multiple web pages open, just like any other browser. Page 449 has the details.

Zooming and Scrolling

When you first open a web page, you get to see the *entire thing*, so you can get the lay of the land. At this point, of course, you're looking at .004-point type, which is too small to read unless you're a microbe. So the next step is to magnify the *part* of the page you want to read.

The iPhone offers three ways to do that:

- **Double-tap.** Safari can recognize different *chunks* of a web page— each block of text, each photo. When you double-tap a chunk, Safari magnifies *just that chunk* to fill the whole screen. It's smart and useful.

Double-tap

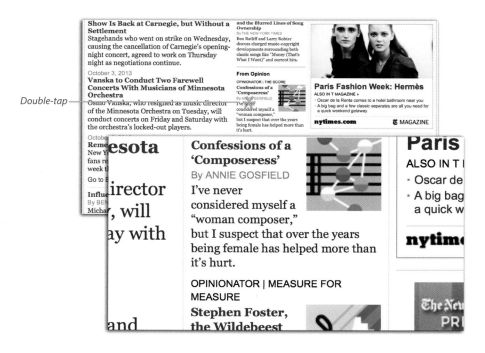

Double-tap again to zoom back out.

- **Rotate the iPhone.** Turn the device 90 degrees in either direction. The iPhone rotates and magnifies the image to fill the wider view. Often, this simple act is enough to make tiny type big enough to read.

- **Do the two-finger spread.** Put two fingers on the glass and slide them apart. The Safari page stretches before your very eyes, growing larger. Then you can pinch to shrink the page back down again. (Most people do several spreads or several pinches in a row to achieve the degree of zoom they want.)

Once you've zoomed out to the proper degree, you can then scroll around the page by dragging or flicking with a finger. You don't have to worry about "clicking a link" by accident; if your finger's in motion, Safari ignores the tapping action, even if you happen to land on a link.

> **TIP:** Once you've double-tapped to zoom in on a page, you can use this little-known trick: Double-tap anywhere on the *upper* half of the screen to scroll up or the *lower* half to scroll down. The closer you are to the top or bottom of the screen, the more you scroll.

Full-Screen Mode

On a phone, the screen is pretty small to begin with; most people would rather dedicate that space to showing more *web*.

So in iOS, Safari enters *full-screen mode* the instant you start to *scroll down* a page. In full-screen mode, all the controls and toolbars vanish. Now the *entire* iPhone screen is filled with web goodness. You can bring the controls back in any of these ways:

- Scroll *up* a little bit.

- Return to the top or bottom of a web page.

- Navigate to a different page.

And enjoy Safari's dedication to trying to get out of your way.

> **TIP:** You can jump directly to the address bar, no matter how far down a page you've scrolled, just by tapping the very top edge of the screen (the status bar). That "tap the top" trick is timely, too, when a website is designed to *hide* the address bar.

Typing a Web Address

The address/search bar is the strip at the top of the screen where you type in a web page's address. And it so happens that some of the iPhone's greatest tips and shortcuts all have to do with this important navigational tool:

- **Your Favorites await.** When you tap in the address bar but haven't yet typed anything, the icons of a few very special, most favorite websites appear (below, top). These are the Favorites; see page 434.

- **Don't delete.** There *is* a ⊗ button at the right end of the address bar whose purpose is to erase the current address so you can type another one. (Tap inside the address bar to make it, and the keyboard, appear.) But the ⊗ button is for suckers.

  Instead, whenever the address bar is open for typing, *just type*. Forget that there's already a URL there. The iPhone is smart enough to figure out that you want to *replace* that web address with a new one.

- **Don't type http://www.** You can leave that stuff out; Safari will supply it automatically. Instead of *http://www.cnn.com*, for example, just type *cnn.com* (or tap its name in the suggestions list) and hit Go.

- **Type .com, .net, .org, or .edu the easy way.** Safari's canned URL choices can save you four keyboard taps apiece. To see their secret

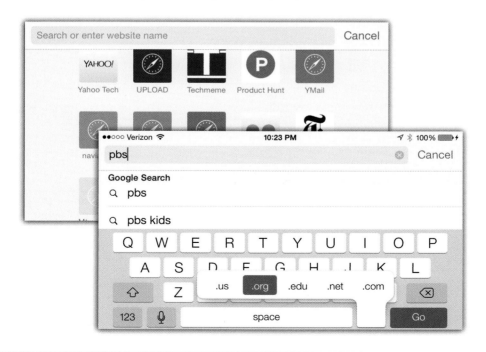

menu, hold your finger down on the **period key** on the keyboard (previous page, bottom). Then tap the common suffix you want. (Or, if you want .com, just release your finger without moving it.)

Otherwise, this address bar works just like the one in any other web browser. Tap inside it to make the keyboard appear.

Tap the blue Go key when you're finished typing the address. That's your Enter key. (Or tap Cancel to hide the keyboard *without* "pressing Enter.")

> **TIP:** If you hold your finger on a link for a moment—touching rather than tapping—a handy panel appears. At the top, you see the full web address that link will open. And there are some useful buttons: Open, Open in New Tab, Add to Reading List, and Copy (meaning "copy the link address"). Oh, and there's also Cancel.

The Favorites Icons

You can never close all your Safari windows. The app will never let you get past the final page, always lurking behind the others: the Favorites page (previous page, top left).

This is the starting point. It's what you first see when you tap the + button. It's like a page of visual bookmarks.

In fact, if you see a bunch of icons here already, it's because your phone has synced them over from Safari on a Mac; whatever sites are on your Bookmarks *bar* become icons on this bookmark *page*.

You can edit this Favorites page, of course:

- **Rearrange them** as you would Home screen icons. That is, hold your finger down on an icon momentarily and then drag it to a new spot.

- **Remove or rename a favorites icon.** Favorites are just bookmarks. So you can edit, move, or delete them just as you would any bookmark. (Tap ▢ to open your Bookmarks screen. Make sure that you're on the ▢ tab, so that your list of folders is showing. Tap Favorites, then Edit. Tap ⊖ for a site you want to delete, and then tap Delete.)

> **TIP:** You can create folders *inside* the Favorites folder, too. Whenever the Favorites screen appears, you'll see these subfolders listed as further sources of speed-dial websites.

- **Add a Favorites icon.** When you find a page you'd like to add to the Favorites screen, tap ⬆. On the Share sheet, tap Add Bookmark. The phone usually proposes putting the new bookmark into the Favorites *folder*, which means that it will show up on the Favorites *screen*. (If it proposes some other folder on the Location line, then tap the folder's name and then tap Favorites.) Tap Save.

Request Desktop Site

In an effort to conserve time and bandwidth (yours and theirs), many websites supply *mobile* versions to your iPhone—smaller, stripped-down sites that transfer faster than (but lack some features of) the full-blown sites. You generally have no control over which version you're sent.

Until now. Suppose you're in Safari, and some site has dished up its mobile version, and you're gnashing your teeth. Hold down the ↻ in the address box; tap Request Desktop Site. (The same button appears when you tap ⬆ and scroll the bottom row to the right.) As you've requested, the full-blown desktop version of that site now appears.

Searching in Safari

The address bar is also the search box. Just tap into it and type your search phrase (or speak it, using Siri).

To save you time and fiddling, Safari instantly produces a drop-down menu filled with suggestions that could spare you some typing—things it guesses you might be looking for. If you see the address you're trying to type, then by all means tap it instead of typing out the rest of the URL. The time you save could be your own:

- **Top Hits.** The Top Hits are Safari's best guesses at what you're looking for. They're the sites on your bookmarks and History lists that you've visited most often (and that match what you've typed so far).

  Try tapping one of the Top Hits sometime. You'll discover, to your amazement, that that site appears almost instantly. It doesn't seem to have to load. That's because, as a favor to you, Safari quietly down-loads the Top Hits in the background, while you're still entering your search term, all to save you time.

- **Suggested Sites.** Occasionally, you'll see another proposed site or two here: Suggested Sites. It's yet another site that Safari supposes you might be trying to reach, based on what you've typed so far and what sites other people visit.

- **Google Search.** The next category of suggestions: a list of search terms you *might* be typing, based on how popular those searches are on Google (or whatever search service you're using). For example, if you type *chick*, then this section proposes things like *chicken recipes*, *chick fil a*, and *chicken pox*. It's just trying to save you a little typing; if none of these tappable choices is the one you want, ignore them.

NOTE: You can turn this feature off, too, if it makes you feel spied upon. (Behind the scenes, it's transmitting your search term to Apple.) You do that in Settings→Safari→Search Engine Suggestions.

- **Bookmarks and History.** Here Safari offers matching selections from websites you've bookmarked or recently visited. Again, it's trying to save you typing if it can.

- **On This Page.** Here's how you search for certain text *on the page you're reading*.

Once you've started typing, under the On This Page heading, you see a listing called Find "chic" (or whatever you've typed so far), shown below at left. Tap that line to jump to the first appearance of that text on the page. (In iOS 9, there's a less hidden way to start this process, too: Tap ⬆, and then Find on Page.)

Use the 〈 and 〉 buttons to jump from one match to the next. Tap Done to return to your regularly scheduled browsing.

TIP: Suppose you've started typing a search term. Safari pipes up with its usual list of suggestions. At this point, if you drag up or down the screen, you hide the keyboard—so you can see the suggestions that were hidden behind it.

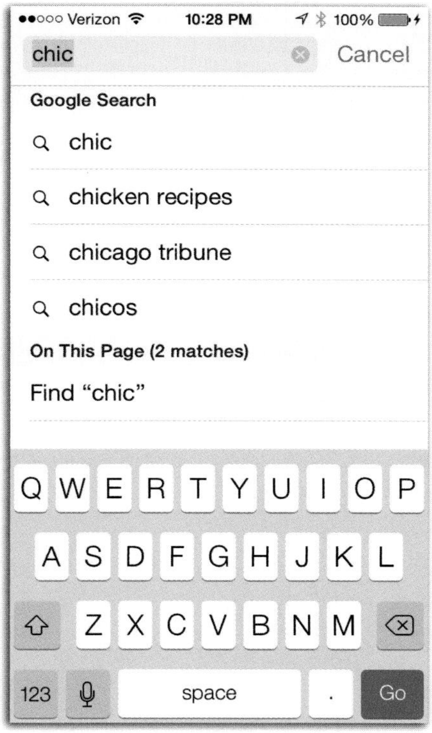

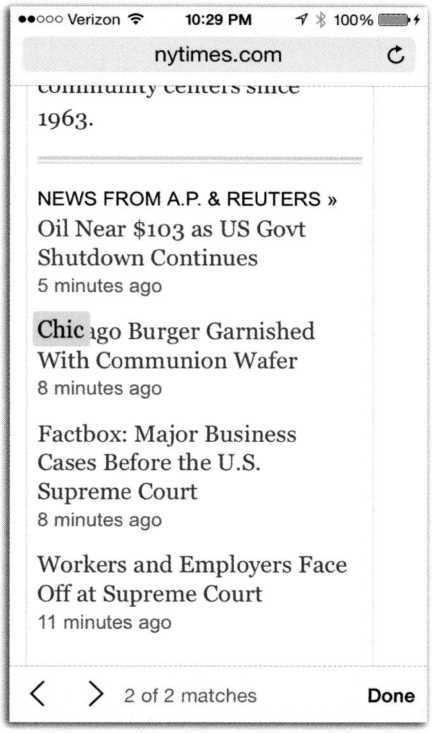

You can tell the iPhone to use a Yahoo, Bing, or DuckDuckGo search instead of Google, if you like, in Settings→Safari→Search Engine. (DuckDuckGo is a search service dedicated to privacy. It doesn't store your searches or tailor the results to you. On the other hand, it's capable of searching only about 50 web sources—Wikipedia, Wolfram Alpha, and so on.)

TIP: If you've set your search options to use Google, then there are all kinds of cool things you can type here—special terms that tell Google, "I want *information*, not web page matches."

You can type a movie name and zip code or city/state (*Titanic Returns 10024*) to get a list of today's showtimes in theaters near you. Get the forecast by typing *weather chicago* or *weather 60609*. Stock quotes: Type the symbol (*AMZN*). Dictionary definitions: *define schadenfreude*. Unit conversions: *liters in 5 gallons*. Currency conversions: *25 usd in euros*. Then tap Go to get instant results.

Quick Website Search

This crazy feature lets you search *within* a certain site (like Amazon or Reddit or Wikipedia) using only Safari's regular search bar. For example, typing *wiki mollusk* can search Wikipedia for its entry on mollusks. Typing *amazon ipad* can offer links to buy an iPad from Amazon. Typing *reddit sitcoms* opens *reddit.com* to its search results for sitcoms.

None of this will work, however, until (a) you've turned the feature on (Settings→Safari→Quick Website Search), and (b) you've manually *taught* Safari how to search those sites one time each.

To do that, pull up the site you'll want to search (let's say it's *reddit.com*) and use its regular search bar. Search for anything.

That site's name now appears in the list at Settings→Safari→Quick Website Search. (Usually. Many sites don't work with Quick Website Search.) From now on, you can search that site by typing, for example, *reddit sitcoms*. You'll jump directly to that site's search results.

Bookmarks

Bookmarks, of course, are websites you might want to visit again without having to remember and type their URLs.

To see the list of bookmarks on your phone, tap 📖 at the bottom of the screen. You see the master list of bookmarks. They're organized in folders, or even folders *within* folders.

Tapping a folder shows you what's inside, and tapping a bookmark begins opening the corresponding website.

NOTE: Actually, what you see when you tap 📖 are *three* tabs at the top: 📖 (Bookmarks), ○○ (Reading List), and @ Twitter links and RSS feeds). The latter two are described later in this chapter.

You might be surprised to discover that Safari already seems to be pre-stocked with bookmarks—that, amazingly, are interesting and useful to *you* in particular! How did it know?

Easy—it copied your existing desktop computer's browser bookmarks from Internet Explorer (Windows) or Safari (Mac) when you synced the iPhone (Chapter 14), or when you turned on Safari syncing through iCloud. Sneaky, eh?

Creating New Bookmarks

You can add new bookmarks right on the phone. Any work you do here is copied *back* to your computer the next time you sync the two machines—or instantaneously, if you've turned on iCloud bookmark syncing.

When you find a web page you might like to visit again, tap the ⬆ to reveal the options shown here at left; then tap Add Bookmark. The Add Bookmark screen appears (right).

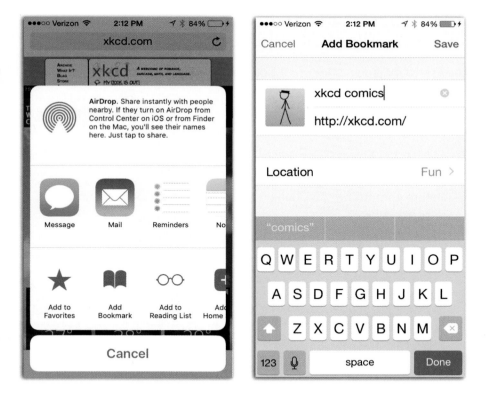

You have two tasks here:

- **Type a better name.** In the top box, you can type a shorter or clearer name for the page. Instead of "Bass, Trout & Tackle—the web's

Premier Resource for the Avid Outdoorsman," you can just call it "Fish."

Below that: The page's underlying URL, which is independent of what you've *named* your bookmark. You can't edit this one.

- **Specify where to file this bookmark.** If you tap Favorites, you open Safari's hierarchical list of bookmark folders, which organize your bookmarked sites. Tap the folder where you want to file the new bookmark so you'll know where to find it later.

> **TIP:** Here's a site worth bookmarking: *http://google.com/gwt/n*. It gives you a bare-bones, superfast version of the web, provided by Google for the benefit of people on slow connections (like EDGE). You can opt to hide graphics for even more speed. Yeah, the iPhone's browser is glorious and all—but sometimes you'd rather have fast than pretty.

Editing Bookmarks and Folders

It's easy enough to massage your Bookmarks list within Safari—to delete favorites that aren't so favorite anymore, to make new folders, to rearrange the list, to rename a folder or a bookmark, and so on.

The techniques are the same for editing bookmark *folders* as editing the bookmarks themselves—after the first step. To edit the folder list, start by opening the Bookmarks (tap ▯▯), and then tap Edit.

To edit the bookmarks themselves, tap ▯▯, tap a folder, and *then* tap Edit. Now you can get organized:

- **Delete something.** Tap ⊖ next to a folder or a bookmark, and then tap Delete to confirm.

- **Rearrange the list.** Drag the grip strip (≡) up or down in the list to move the folders or bookmarks around. (You can't move or delete the top two folders—Favorites and History.)

- **Edit a name and location.** Tap a folder or a bookmark name. If you tap a folder, you arrive at the Edit Folder screen; you can edit the folder's name and which folder it's inside of. If you tap a bookmark, Edit Bookmark lets you edit the name and the URL it points to.

  Tap Done when you're finished.

- **Create a folder.** Tap New Folder in the lower-left corner of the Edit Folders screen. You're offered the chance to type a name for it and to specify where you want to file it (that is, in which *other* folder).

Tap Done when you're finished.

As you've just read, preserving a bookmark requires quite a few taps. That's why it's extra important for you to remember iOS 9's gift to busy people: the "Remind me about this later" command to Siri. You've just added a new item in your Reminders list, complete with a link to whatever page you're looking at now. (Feel free to be more specific, as in "Remind me about this when I get home.")

The History List

Behind the scenes, Safari keeps track of the websites you've visited in the past week or so, neatly organized into subfolders like This Evening and Yesterday. It's a great feature when you can't recall the address for a website you visited recently—or when you remember it had a long, complicated address and you get the psychiatric condition known as iPhone Keyboard Dread.

To see the list of recent sites, tap 🕮; then, on the 🕮 tab, tap History, whose icon bears a ⏰ to make sure you know it's special. Once the History list appears, just tap a bookmark to revisit that web page.

Erasing the History List

Some people find it creepy that Safari maintains a History list, right there in plain view of any family member or coworker who wanders by. They'd just as soon their wife/husband/boss/parent/kid not know what websites they've been visiting.

You can delete just one particularly incriminating History listing easily enough; swipe leftward across its name and then tap Delete. You can also delete the *entire* History menu, thus erasing all your tracks. To do that, tap Clear; confirm by tapping Clear History. You've just rewritten History.

Shared Links (@)

There's a third tab button on the Bookmarks screen, too: @.

It's the Shared Links button. It lists every tweet from Twitter that contains a link. The idea is to make it easier for you to explore sites that your Twitter friends are recommending; all their web finds are collected in one place (facing page, right).

TIP: In Safari, "shared links" has another meaning, too: The ⬆️ makes it easy to share the URL of a particularly juicy web page. On the Share sheet (previous page, left), you get the usual set of links: Copy, Mail, Message (to send by text message), Twitter, Facebook, and so on. But remember that iOS 9 is extensible. Depending on the apps you've installed, you may see all kinds of other share-this-link options on this screen.

RSS Subscriptions

At the bottom of the Shared Links (@) tab, iOS offers a button called Subscriptions. It's a reference to *RSS feeds*, which are something like subscriptions to websites. You don't have to remember to go visit your favorite blogs or news sites; notification blurbs about their newly posted articles come to you.

Here's the procedure:

1. **In Safari, open a site that offers an RSS feed.** News sites of all kinds offer RSS feeds (*nytimes.com, usatoday.com, engadget.com, yahootech.com,* and so on).

2. **Subscribe to it.** To do that, tap 📖, then @, then Subscriptions, and then Add Current Site (next page, left).

3. **Read.** When you want to see what's new, tap 📖, then @. That's right: Blurbs representing newly posted stories appear on the @ tab

(shown here at right), mixed in with all your Twitter links. That's not ideal, especially if there are hundreds of Twitter links—but at least you'll never be without a place to check for interesting stuff to read.

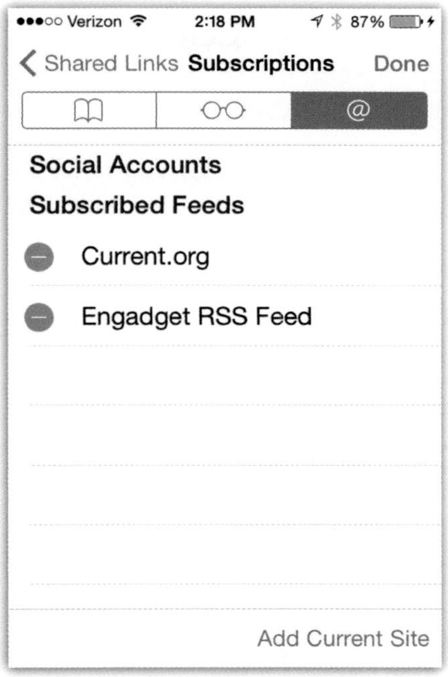

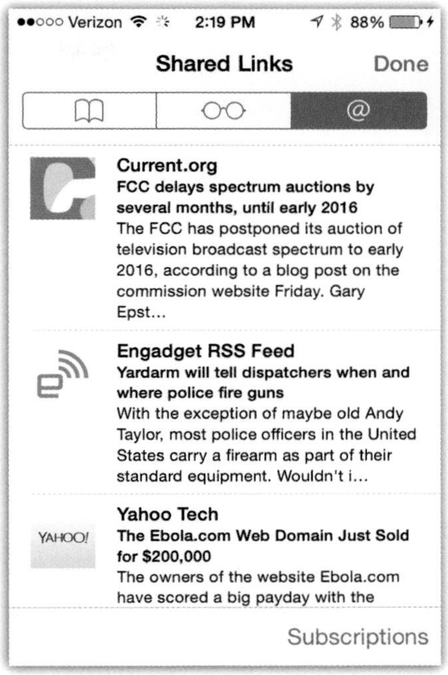

To delete a subscription, tap 📖, then @, then **Subscriptions**; tap ⊖ next to the subscription's name, and confirm by tapping **Delete**.

The Reading List

The Reading List is a handy list of web pages you want to read later. Unlike a bookmark, it stores entire pages, so you can read them even when you don't have an Internet connection (on the subway or on a plane, for example).

The Reading List also keeps track of what you've read. You can use the **Show All/Show Unread** button at the bottom of the screen to view everything—or just what you haven't yet read.

> **TIP:** To make matters even sweeter, iCloud synchronizes your Reading List on your Mac, iPhone, iPad, and so on—as long as you've turned on bookmark syncing. It's as though the web always keeps your place.

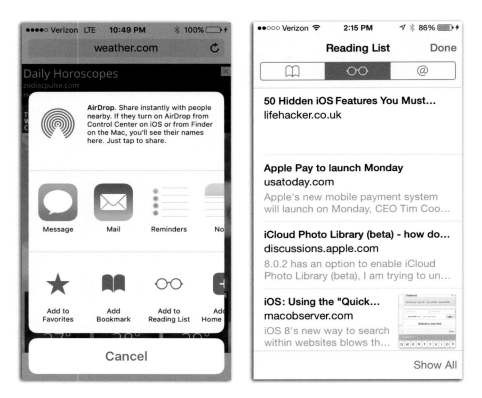

To add a page to the Reading List, tap 📤 and then tap **Add to Reading List** (above, left). Or just hold your finger down on a link until a set of buttons appears, including **Add to Reading List**.

Once you've added a page to the Reading List, you can get to it by tapping 📖 and then tapping the Reading List tab at the top (◯◯). Tap an item on your list to open and read it (above, right).

> **TIP:** When you get to the bottom of a Reading List item you've just read, keep scrolling down. The phone is nice enough to offer up the *next* article in your Reading List, as though they were all vertically connected.

By the way, some web pages require a hefty amount of data to download, what with photos and all. If you're worried about Reading List downloads eating up your monthly data allotment, you can visit **Settings→Safari** and turn off **Use Cellular Data**.

Now you'll be able to download Reading List pages only when you're on Wi-Fi, but at least there's no risk of going over your monthly cellular-data allotment.

Link-Tapping Tricks

Link-tapping, of course, is the primary activity of the web. But in Safari, those blue underlined links (or not blue, even not underlined links) harbor special powers:

- **Long-press a link** to open a handy panel. Its options include Open, Open in New Tab, Add to Reading List, and Copy.

- **Hard-press a link** (iPhone 6s models) to peek at whatever page that link opens, like this:

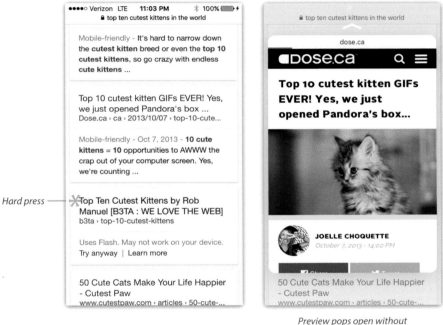

Hard press

Preview pops open without
leaving the page

This, of course, is part of the **Peek and Pop** feature described on page 38. Once you've opened the preview bubble, you can either retreat (lift your finger; remain where you were) or advance (press even harder to fully open that page).

Quite handy, really.

Saving Graphics

If you find a picture online that you wish you could keep forever, you have two choices. You could stare at it until you've memorized it, or you could save it.

To do that, touch the image for about a second. A sheet appears, just like the one that appears when you hold your finger down on a regular link.

If you tap Save Image, then the iPhone thoughtfully deposits a copy of the image in your Camera Roll so it will be copied back to your Mac or PC at the next sync opportunity. If you tap Copy, then you nab a *link* to that graphic, which you can now paste into another program.

Saved Passwords and Credit Cards

On desktop web browsers, a feature called AutoFill saves you an awful lot of typing. It fills out your name and address automatically when you're ordering something online. It stores your passwords so you don't have to re-enter them every time you visit passworded sites.

But on the iPhone, where you're typing on glass, the convenience of AutoFill goes to a whole new level.

And in iOS 9, there's a whole new level *above* that level. The phone can memorize your credit card information, too, making it much easier to buy stuff online; in fact, it can even store this information by *taking a picture* of your credit card.

And thanks to iCloud syncing, all those passwords and credit cards can auto-store themselves on all your other Apple gadgetry.

To turn on AutoFill, visit Settings→Safari→AutoFill. Here's what you find (previous page, left):

- **Use Contact Info.** Turn this On. Then tap My Info. From the address book, find your own listing. You've just told Safari *which* name, address, city, state, zip code, and phone number belong to you.

  From now on, whenever you're asked to input your address, phone number, and so on, you'll see an AutoFill button at the top of the keyboard. Tap it to make Safari auto-enter all those details, saving you no end of typing. (It works on *most* sites.) If there are extra blanks that AutoFill doesn't fill, then you can tap the Previous and Next buttons to move your cursor from one to the next instead of tapping and scrolling manually.

- **Names & Passwords** lets Safari fill in your user name and passwords when you visit sites that require you to log in (Google, Amazon, and so on). On each website, you'll be able to choose Yes (a good idea for your PTA or library account), Never for this Website (a good idea for your bank), or Not Now (you'll be asked again next time).

  (To view a list of the actual memorized names and passwords, open Settings→Safari→Passwords.)

TIP: On this screen, you can delete saved passwords. Swipe leftward across the login that no longer pleases you, and then tap Delete.

- **Credit Cards.** Turn on Credit Cards, of course, if you'd like Safari to memorize your charge card info. To enter your card details, tap Saved Credit Cards (where you see a list of them) and then Add Credit Card. You can type in your name, card number, expiration date, and a description—or you can save yourself a little tedium by tapping Use

Camera. Aim the camera at your credit card until you see its long number magically recognized, as you can see here. (You still have to enter your name and the card expiration manually.)

When you buy something online, iOS offers an **Autofill Credit Card** button. When you tap it, Safari asks you first which credit card you want to use, if you've stored more than one (it displays the last four digits for your reference). Tap it, and boom: Safari cheerfully fills in the credit card information, saving you time and hassle.

Unfortunately, there's nowhere to store the little three- or four-digit security code, sometimes called the CSC, CVV, or CV2 code. Safari makes no attempt to fill that in; you always have to enter it manually. That's one last safeguard against a kid, a spouse, a parent, or a thief using your phone for an online shopping spree when you're not around.

TIP: Once you've stored all these passwords and credit cards, it sure would be nice if you didn't have to enter them into other Apple gadgets, wouldn't it? Your Mac, your iPad, and so on?

Fortunately, the iCloud service can synchronize this information to Safari running on other Apple machines. Page 515 has the details.

Manipulating Multiple Pages

Like any other self-respecting browser, Safari can keep multiple pages open at once, making it easy for you to switch among them. You can think of it as a miniature version of tabbed browsing, a feature of browsers like Safari Senior, Firefox, Chrome, and Microsoft Edge. Tabbed browsing keeps a bunch of web pages open simultaneously.

One advantage of this arrangement is that you can start reading one web page while the others load into their own tabs in the background.

To Open a New Window

Tap the 🗗 button in the lower right. The Safari page seems to duck backward, bowing to you in 3D space. Tap ＋.

You now arrive at the Favorites page (below, left). Here are icons for all the sites you've designated as Favorites (see page 434). Tap to open one. Or, in the address bar, enter an address. Or use a bookmark.

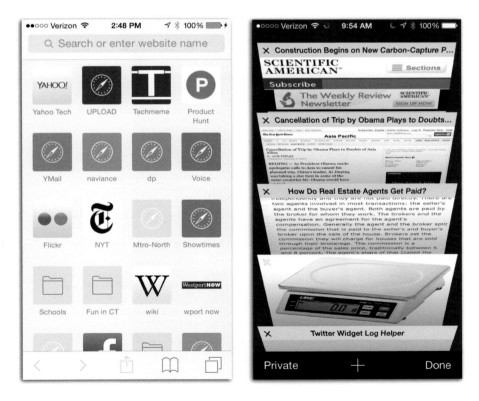

To Switch Among Windows

Tap ⬚ again. Now you see something like the 3D floating pages shown on the previous page at right. These are all your open tabs (windows). You work with them like this:

- **Close a window** by tapping the ✕ in the corner—or by swiping a page away horizontally. It slides away into the void.
- **Rearrange these windows** by dragging them up or down.
- **Open a window** to full screen by tapping it.

You can open a third window, and a fourth, and so on, and jump among them, using these two techniques.

iCloud Tabs

Thanks to the miracle of iCloud syncing, the last windows and tabs you had open on that other gadget (even if the gadget is turned off) show up here, at the bottom of the page-juggling screen (tap ⬚ to see it). They're sorted into headings that correspond to your other Apple gadgets.

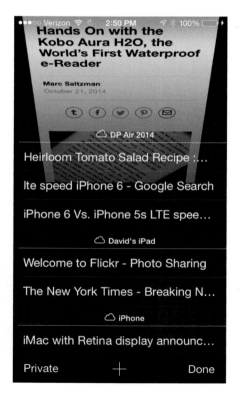

The concept is to unify your Macs and i-gadgets. You're reading three browser windows and tabs on your phone—why not resume on the big screen when you get home and sit down in front of your Mac?

You won't see these tabs unless the Macs have OS X Mountain Lion or later. And, of course, Safari has to be turned on in System Preferences→iCloud on the Mac, or Settings→iCloud on the phone or tablet.

Reader View

How can people read web articles when there's Times-Square blinking all around them? Fortunately, you'll never have to put up with that again.

The Reader button in the address bar (≡) is amazing. With one tap, it eliminates *everything* from the page you're reading except the text and photos. No ads, toolbars, blinking, links, banners, promos, or anything else.

The text is also changed to a clean, clear font and size, and the background is made plain white. Basically, it makes any web page look like a printed book page, and it's glorious. Shown here: the before and after. Which looks easier to read?

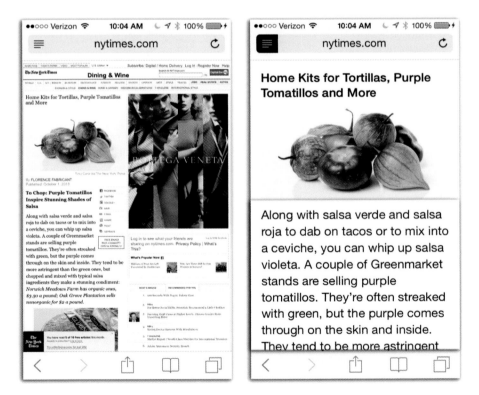

To exit Reader, tap ☰ again. Best. Feature. Ever.

The fine print: Reader doesn't appear until the page has fully loaded. It doesn't appear on "front page" pages, like the *nytimes.com* home page—only when you've opened an article within. And it may not appear on sites that are already specially designed for access by cellphones.

Web Security

Safari on the iPhone isn't meant to be a full-blown web browser like the one on your desktop computer, but it comes surprisingly close—especially when it comes to privacy and security. Cookies, pop-up blockers, parental controls...they're all here, for your paranoid pleasure.

Pop-Up Blocker

The world's smarmiest advertisers like to inundate us with pop-up and pop-under ads—nasty little windows that appear in front of the browser window, or, worse, behind it, waiting to jump out the moment you close your window. Fortunately, Safari comes set to block those pop-ups so you don't see them. It's a war out there—but at least you now have some ammunition.

The thing is, though, pop-ups are sometimes useful (and not ads)—notices of new banking features, seating charts on ticket-sales sites, warnings that the instructions for using a site have changed, and so on. Safari can't tell these from ads—and it stifles them, too. So if a site you trust says "Please turn off pop-up blockers and reload this page," then you know you're probably missing out on a *useful* pop-up message.

In those situations, you can turn off the pop-up blocker. The on/off switch is in Settings→Safari.

Password Suggestions

When you're signing up for a new account on some website, and you tap inside the box where you're supposed to make up a password, Safari offers to make up a password for you. It's a doozy, too, along the lines of 23k2k4-29cs8-58384-ckk3322.

Now, don't freak out. You're not expected to remember that. Safari will, of course, memorize it for you (and sync it to your other Apple computers, if they're on the same iCloud account). Meanwhile, you've got yourself a unique, nearly uncrackable password.

Cookies

Cookies are something like preference files. Certain websites—particularly commercial ones like Amazon—deposit them on your hard drive so they'll remember you the next time you visit. That's how Amazon is able to greet you with, "Welcome, Chris" (or whatever your name is). It's reading its own cookie.

Most cookies are perfectly innocuous—and, in fact, are extremely useful, because they help websites remember your tastes (and contact info).

But fear is widespread, and the media fan the flames with tales of sinister cookies that track your movement on the web. If you're worried about invasions of privacy, Safari is ready to protect you.

Open Settings→Safari→Block Cookies. The options here are like a paranoia gauge. If you click Always Block, you create an acrylic shield around your iPhone. No cookies can come in, and no cookie information can go out. You'll probably find the web a very inconvenient place; you'll have to re-enter your information upon every visit, and some websites may not work properly at all. The Always Allow option means "Oh, what the heck—just gimme all of them."

A good compromise is Allow from Websites I Visit, which accepts cookies from sites you *want* to visit, but blocks cookies deposited on your phone by sites you're not actually visiting—cookies an especially evil banner ad gives you, for example.

The Settings→Safari screen also offers a Clear History & Website Data button. It deletes all the cookies you've accumulated so far, as well as your phone's *cache*. (That's a patch of the iPhone's storage area where pieces of web pages you visit—graphics, for example—are retained, to speed up loading the next time you visit.) If you worry that your cache eats up space, poses a security risk, or is confusing some page, then tap Clear History & Website Data to erase it and start over.

Private Browsing

Private browsing lets you surf without adding any pages to your History list, searches to your Google search suggestions, passwords to Safari's saved password list, or autofill entries to Safari's memory. You might want to turn on private browsing before you start visiting websites that would raise interesting questions with your spouse, parents, or boss.

When you want to start leaving no tracks, tap 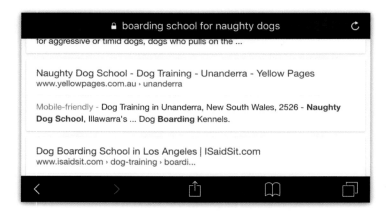 to open the page-juggler screen; tap **Private** at the bottom-left corner.

Suddenly the light gray accents of Safari turn jet black—a reminder that you're now in Private mode. Tap ＋ to open a new page, and proceed as usual. From now on, Safari records nothing while you surf.

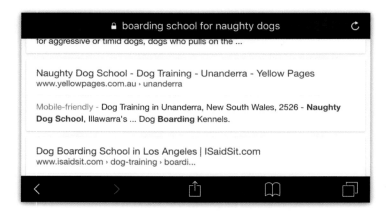

When you're ready to browse "publicly" again, turn private browsing off once more (tap □, then tap **Private**). Safari resumes taking note of the pages you visit—but it never remembers the ones you opened while in Private mode.

In other words, what happens in private browsing stays in private browsing.

Parental Controls

If your child (or employee) is old enough to have an iPhone but not old enough for the seedier side of the web, then don't miss the Restrictions feature in Settings. The iPhone makes no attempt to separate the good websites from the bad—but it *can* remove the Safari icon from the iPhone altogether so that no web browsing is possible at all. See page 603 for instructions.

Five Happy Surprises in the ⬆ Panel

So far in this chapter, you've learned the first step in bookmarking a page (tap ⬆); in designating a new Favorite (tap ⬆); and in saving a web article to your offline Reading List (tap ⬆). That's right: All these features await on the Share sheet.

But that same panel hosts a wealth of equally useful buttons that nobody ever talks about—and three of them are new in iOS 9. So tap ⬆ to open the Share sheet, and follow along!

Sharing a Link

The AirDrop, Message, Mail, Twitter, and Facebook buttons are pretty obvious; they share the link of your current page with other people.

Reminders

Remember how you can say to Siri, about a web page you're on, "Remind me about this later?" (If not, see page 402.)

There's a button for that, here on the Share sheet. Great when speaking to your phone would be socially awkward.

Save PDF to iBooks

Well, how the heck about that? You can turn anything you find on the web into an iBook—an electronic book that you can read later in iBooks (page 362)! That way, you gain a wide variety of reading tools (notes, highlighting, dictionary) and organizational tools (collections) that aren't available in Safari.

Save to Home Screen

Is there a certain website you visit every day? This button adds the icon of your web page right to your Home screen. It's a shortcut that Apple calls a Web Clip.

When you tap **Add to Home Screen**, you're offered the chance to edit the icon's name; finally, tap **Add**. When you return to your Home screen, you'll see the new icon; you can move or delete it as you would any other app.

TIP: You can turn **part** of a web page into one of these Web Clips, too— say, *The New York Times'* "Most emailed" list, or the box scores for a certain sports league.

All you have to do is zoom and scroll the page in Safari **before** you tap ⬆, isolating the section you want. Later, when you open the Web Clip, you'll see exactly the part of the web page you wanted.

Notes

Now that iOS 9 has a beefed-up Notes app (page 390), it's great that you can send a link to a web article (complete with opening sentences and an image) directly to a Note—no copy and paste required. You're invited to annotate the note before hitting **Save** (below, left), or even append it to the end of an existing Notes page (right).

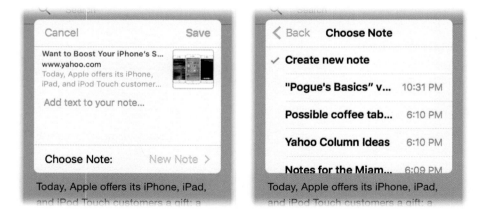

13

Email

Email on your iPhone offers full formatting, fonts, graphics, and choice of type size; file attachments like Word, Excel, PowerPoint, PDF, Pages, Numbers, photos, and even .zip compressed files; and compatibility with Yahoo Mail, Gmail, AOL Mail, iCloud mail, corporate Exchange mail, and any standard email account.

Dude, if you want a more satisfying portable email machine than this one, buy a laptop.

This chapter covers the basic email experience. If you've gotten yourself hooked up with iCloud or Exchange ActiveSync, see Chapters 15 and 17 for details.

Setting Up Your Account

If you play your cards right, you won't *have* to set up your email account on the phone. The first time you set up the iPhone to sync with your computer (Chapter 14), you're offered the chance to *sync* your Mac's or PC's mail with the phone. That doesn't mean it copies actual messages—only the email settings, so the iPhone is ready to start downloading mail.

You're offered this option if your Mac's mail program is Mail or Outlook/Entourage, or if your PC's mail program is Outlook, Outlook Express, or Windows Mail.

But what if you don't use one of those email programs? No sweat. You can also plug the necessary settings right into the iPhone.

Free Email Accounts

If you have a free email account from Google, AOL, Outlook, or Yahoo; an iCloud account (Chapter 15); or a Microsoft Exchange account run by your employer (Chapter 17), then setup on the iPhone is easy.

From the Home screen, tap Settings→Mail, Contacts, Calendars→Add Account. Tap the colorful logo that corresponds to the kind of account you have (Google, Yahoo, or whatever).

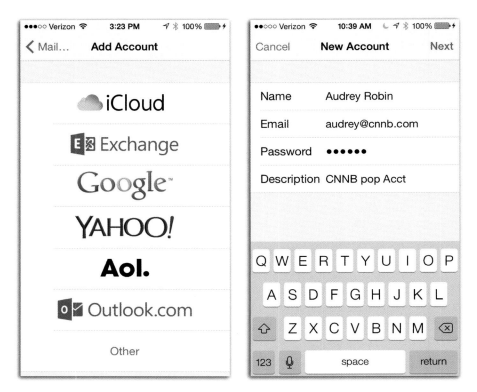

Now you land on the account-information screen. Tap into each of the blanks and, when the keyboard appears, type the requested info: for example, your name, email address, account password, and a description (that one's optional). Tap Next.

Now you may be shown the list of non-email data that the iPhone can show you (from iCloud, Google, Yahoo, Exchange, and so on): Mail, Contacts, calendars, Reminders, and Notes. Turn off the ones you don't want synced to your phone, and then tap Save.

Your email account is ready to go!

> **TIP:** If you don't have one of these free accounts, they're worth having, if only as a backup to your regular account. They can help with spam filtering, too, since the iPhone doesn't offer any. To sign up, go to *Google.com, Yahoo.com, AOL.com,* or *iCloud.com.*

POP3 and IMAP Accounts

Those freebie, brand-name, web-based accounts are super-easy to set up. But they're not the whole ball of wax. Millions of people have more generic email accounts, perhaps supplied by their employers or Internet providers. They're generally one of two types:

- **POP accounts** are the oldest and most compatible type on the Internet. (POP stands for Post Office Protocol, but this won't be on the test.) A POP account can make life complicated if you check your mail on more than one machine (say, a PC and an iPhone), as you'll discover shortly.

  A POP server transfers incoming mail to your computer or phone before you read it, which works fine as long as you're using *only that machine* to access your email.

- **IMAP accounts** (Internet Message Access Protocol) are newer and have more features than POP servers, and they're quickly putting POP out to pasture. IMAP servers keep all your mail online, rather than making you store it on your computer; as a result, you can access the same mail from any computer (or phone). IMAP servers remember which messages you've read and sent, and they even keep track of how you've filed messages into mail folders. (Those free Yahoo email accounts are IMAP accounts, and so are Apple's iCloud accounts and corporate Exchange accounts. Gmail accounts *can* be IMAP, too.)

> **TIP:** The iPhone copies your IMAP messages onto the phone itself, so you can work on your email even when you're not online. You can, in fact, control where these messages are stored (in which mail folder). To see this, open Settings→Mail, Contacts, Calendars→[your IMAP account name]→[your IMAP account name again]→Advanced. See? You can specify where your drafts, sent messages, and deleted messages wind up on the phone.

The iPhone can communicate with both kinds of accounts, with varying degrees of completeness.

If you haven't opted to have your account-setup information transferred automatically to the iPhone from your Mac or PC, then you can set it up manually on the phone.

Tap your way to Settings→Mail, Contacts, Calendars→Add Account. Tap Other, tap Add Mail Account, and then enter your name, email address, password, and an optional description. Tap Next.

Apple's software attempts to figure out which kind of account you have (POP or IMAP) by the email address. If it can't make that determination, then you arrive at a second screen, where you're asked for such juicy details as the host name for incoming and outgoing mail servers. (This is also where you tap either IMAP or POP, to tell the iPhone what sort of account it's dealing with.)

If you don't know this stuff offhand, you'll have to ask your Internet provider, corporate tech-support person, or next-door teenager to help you. When you're finished, tap Save.

To delete an account, open Settings→Mail, Contacts, Calendars→[account name]. At the bottom of the screen, you'll find the Delete Account button.

> **TIP:** You can make, rename, or delete IMAP or Exchange mailboxes (mail folders) right on the phone.
>
> View the mailbox list for the account and then tap Edit. Tap New Mailbox to create a new folder. To edit an existing mailbox, tap its name; you can then rename it, tap the Mailbox Location folder to move it, or tap Delete Mailbox. Tap Save to finish up.

Downloading Mail

If you have "push" email (Yahoo, iCloud, or Exchange), then your iPhone doesn't **check** for messages; new messages show up on your iPhone **as they arrive**, around the clock.

If you have any other kind of account, then the iPhone checks for new messages automatically on a schedule—every 15, 30, or 60 minutes. It also checks for new messages each time you open the Mail program, or whenever you **drag downward** on the Inbox list.

> **TIP:** There actually is a sneaky way to turn a Gmail account into a "push" account: Disguise it as an Exchange account. For complete steps, see the free PDF appendix to this chapter, "Setting Up Push Email for Gmail." It's on this book's "Missing CD" page at *www.missingmanuals.com*.

You can adjust the frequency of these automatic checks or turn off the "push" feature (because it uses up your battery faster) in Settings; see page 575.

When new mail arrives, you'll know it at a glance; all the Notification Center options work well in Mail. For example, if your phone is off, you can tap the Sleep or Home button to view the sender, subject, and the first line of the message right on the Lock screen. (Swipe across one, right there on the Lock screen, to jump to it in Mail.)

You'll also hear the iPhone's little "You've got mail" sound, unless you've turned that off in Settings.

If your phone is on, then a new message can alert you by appearing briefly at the top of the screen, without disturbing your work.

You can actually process a message right from that banner. If you see at a glance that it's junk, or if no response is necessary, then drag your finger down on it to reveal two new buttons: **Mark as Read** (leave it in your inbox, no longer appearing as a new message) and **Trash**.

At the Home screen, Mail's icon sprouts a circled number that tells you how many new messages are waiting. If you have more than one email account, it shows you the *total* number of new messages, from all accounts.

If you routinely leave a lot of unread messages in your inbox, and you don't really care about this "badge," you can turn it off. In fact, you can turn it off on a per-account basis, which is great if one of your accounts is sort of a junk account that you keep as a spare. Tap **Settings→Notifications→Mail→ [account name]→Badge App Icon**.)

In any case, once you know you have mail, tap *Mail* on the Home screen to start reading it.

TIP: The Mail app, more than any other app, is designed to be a series of nested lists. You start out seeing a list of accounts; tap one to see a list of folders; tap one for a list of messages; tap one to open the actual message.

To *backtrack* through these lists, you can tap the button in the upper-left corner over and over again—or you can *swipe rightward* across the screen. That's a bigger target and more fun.

The Unified Inbox

If you have more than one email address, you're in luck. The iPhone offers a *unified inbox*—an option that displays all the incoming messages from all your accounts in a single place. (If you don't see it—if Mail opened up to some other screen—keep swiping rightward, backing up a screen at a time, until you do.)

●●○○○ Verizon 🔆	10:43 AM	⌣ ⌁ ✳ 100% 🔋⚡
Mailboxes		Edit

	All Inboxes	221 >
	Work mail	1 >
	iCloud	220 >
	Yahoo!	>
★	VIP	ⓘ 1 >
●	Flagged	>

ACCOUNTS

@	Work mail	1 >

Updated Just Now ✎

●●○○○ Verizon 🔆	10:43 AM	⌣ ⌁ ✳ 100% 🔋⚡
❮ Mailboxes	**iCloud**	Edit

Inbox	220 >
Drafts	>
Sent	>
Junk	>
Trash	>
Archive	>
Deleted Items	>
Drafts (pogue@mac.com)	>
Junk E-mail	>

Updated Just Now ✎

This Mailboxes page has two sections:

- **Unified inboxes (and other unified folders).** To see all the incoming messages in one unified box, tap All Inboxes. Below that, you see the Inboxes for each of the individual accounts.

  This part of the main Mail list also offers unified folders for VIPs and Flagged messages, which are described below.

  But what you may not realize is that you can add *other* unified folders to this section. You can, for example, add a folder called Unread, which contains only new messages from *all* accounts. (That's not the same thing as All Inboxes, because your inbox can contain messages you *have* read but haven't deleted or filed.)

You can also add a unified folder showing all messages where you were either the To or CC addressee; this folder won't include any mail where your name appeared on the BCC (blind carbon-copy) line, like mailing lists and, often, spam.

You can also add an Attachments folder here (messages with files attached), a Today folder, or unified folders that contain All Drafts, All Sent, or All Trash. ("All" means "from all accounts.")

To hide or show these special uni-folders, tap Edit, and then tap the selection circles beside the names of the folders you want to appear. (You can also take this opportunity to drag them up or down into a pleasing sequence.) Tap Done.

- **Accounts.** Farther down the Mailboxes screen, you see your accounts listed again. Tap one to view the traditional mail folders: Inbox, Drafts (emails written but not sent), Sent, Trash, and any folders you've created yourself (Family, Little League, Old Stuff, whatever), as shown on the facing page at right. If you have a Yahoo, iCloud, Exchange, or another IMAP account, then the iPhone automatically creates these folders to match what you've set up online.

NOTE: Not all kinds of email accounts permit the creation of your own filing folders, so you might not see anything but Inbox, Sent, and Trash.

The Message List—and Threading

If you tap an inbox's name, you wind up face to face with the list of incoming messages. At first, you see only the subject lines of your messages, plus, in light-gray type, the first few lines of their contents; that way, you can scan through new messages to see if there's anything important. You can flick upward to scroll this list. Blue dots indicate messages you haven't yet opened.

Each message bears a gray > at the right side. That means "Tap this message's row to read it in all its formatted glory."

Here and there, though, you may spot a double arrow at the right side of the message list, like this: >> That means you're looking at some *threaded* messages. That's where several related messages—back-and-forths on the same subject—appear only once, in a single, consolidated entry. The idea is to reduce inbox clutter and to help you remember what people were talking about.

When you tap a threaded message, you first open an intermediate screen that lists the messages in the thread and tells you how many there are. Tap one of those to read, at last, the message itself.

Of course, this also means that to return to the inbox, you have more back-tracking to do (swipe rightward twice).

In general, threading is a nice feature, even if, from time to time, it acciden-tally clumps in a message that has nothing to do with the others.

But if it bugs you, you can turn it off. Open Settings→Mail, Contacts, Calendars, scroll down, and turn off Organize By Thread.

(If you have an iPhone 6 Plus, you can turn the phone 90 degrees to see the mini-tablet-like view shown on the facing page, with the message list and open message visible simultaneously.)

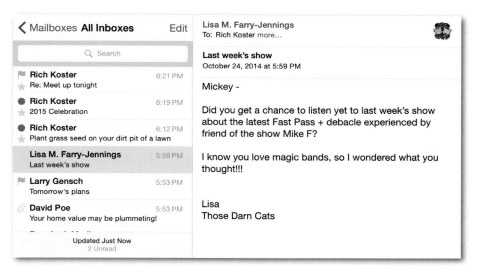

Within the image:

< Mailboxes **All Inboxes**   Edit

Q Search

⚐ **Rich Koster**   6:21 PM
☆ Re: Meet up tonight

● **Rich Koster**   6:19 PM
☆ 2015 Celebration

● **Rich Koster**   6:12 PM
☆ Plant grass seed on your dirt pit of a lawn

Lisa M. Farry-Jennings   5:59 PM
Last week's show

⚐ **Larry Gensch**   5:53 PM
Tomorrow's plans

📎 **David Poe**   5:53 PM
Your home value may be plummeting!

Updated Just Now
2 Unread

Lisa M. Farry-Jennings
To: Rich Koster more...

Last week's show
October 24, 2014 at 5:59 PM

Mickey -

Did you get a chance to listen yet to last week's show about the latest Fast Pass + debacle experienced by friend of the show Mike F?

I know you love magic bands, so I wondered what you thought!!!

Lisa
Those Darn Cats

VIPs and Flagged Messages

You might notice, in your master Inbox, two "email accounts" that you didn't set up: VIP and Flagged. They're both intended to help you round up important messages from the thousands that flood you every day.

Each one magically rounds up messages from *all* your account inboxes, so you don't have to go wading through lots of accounts to find the really important mail. (Note: That's *inboxes*. Messages in other mail folders don't wind up in these special inboxes, even if they're flagged or are from VIPs.)

VIPs

In the real world, VIPs are people who get backstage passes to concerts or special treatment at business functions (it stands for "very important person"). In iOS, it means "somebody whose mail is important enough that I want it brought to my attention immediately when it arrives."

So who should your VIPs be? That's up to you. Your spouse, your boss, and your doctor come to mind.

To designate someone as a VIP, proceed in either of these two ways:

- **On the accounts screen,** carefully tap the ⓘ next to the VIP item. Your master list of all VIPs appears (next page, left). Tap Add VIP to choose a lucky new member from Contacts.

  This is also where you *delete* people from your VIP list when they've annoyed you. Swipe leftward across a name, and then tap Delete. Or tap Edit and then tap each ● button; tap Delete to confirm.

- **In a message from the lucky individual,** tap his name in the From, To, or Cc/Bcc box. His Contact screen appears, complete with an Add to VIP button.

Once you've established who's important, lots of interesting things happen:

- **The VIP inbox automatically collects** messages from your VIPs.

- **VIP names in every mail list** sprout a gray star (below, right).

- **If you use iCloud,** the same person is now a VIP on all your other iPhones and iPads (running iOS 6 or later) and Macs (running OS X Mountain Lion or later).

Flag It

Sometimes you receive email that prompts you to some sort of action, but you may not have the time (or the fortitude) to face the task at the moment. ("Hi there, it's me, your accountant. Would you mind rounding up your expenses for 2002 through 2014 and sending me a list by email?")

That's why Mail lets you *flag* a message, summoning a little flag icon or a little orange dot in a new column next to the message's name. (You can see the actual dot in the message below at right.) It can mean anything you like—it simply calls attention to certain messages.

> **TIP:** The flag marker can be *either* a ⚑ icon *or* an orange dot. You make your choice in Settings→Mail, Contacts, Calendars→Flag Style.

To flag an open message, tap ⚑ at the bottom of the screen. When the confirmation sheet slides up (below, left), tap Flag.

You can also rapidly flag messages directly in a *list* (the Inbox, for example). Just swipe leftward across the message—half an inch of finger-sliding does the trick—to reveal the set of buttons shown here at right:

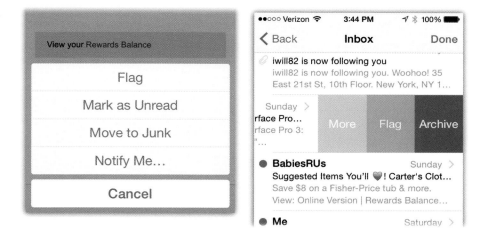

Tap Flag. (If you tap More, you get the option to Unflag.)

The dot or ⚑ icon appears in the body of the message, next to the message's name in your message list. (In the picture on the next page, the top dot looks more like a bull's-eye; that's because it's flagged *and* unread.) The flag appears even on the corresponding message in your Mac or PC email program, thanks to the miracle of wireless syncing.

Finally, the Flagged mailbox appears in your list of accounts, making it easy to work with all flagged messages, from all accounts, in one place.

> **TIP:** If you don't really use this feature, you can hide the Flagged folder. Tap Edit, and then tap the ⊘ to turn it off. Tap Done.

This might be a good time to point out another, newer way to flag a message: Tell Siri to "Remind me about this later." See page 402 for details.

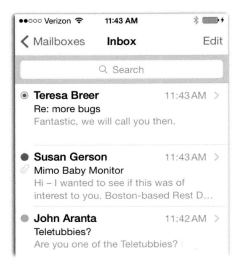

What to Do with a Message

Once you've opened a message, you can respond to it, delete it, file it, and so on. Here's the drill.

> **TIP:** If you have an iPhone 6s or 6s Plus, the *first* thing to learn is that you can see what's in a message without ever leaving the Inbox list—just by hard-pressing it. See page 38 for more on Peek and Pop.

List View: Flag, Trash, Mark as Unread

It's easy to plow through a seething Inbox, processing messages as you go, without ever having to open them. All you have to do is swipe across a message in the list horizontally.

- **Full left-swipe delete.** Swipe your finger leftward *all the way* across the message to delete it. That's it: No confirmation tap required.

- **Partial left-swipe options.** If you don't swipe leftward all the way, you reveal a set of three buttons on the right: Trash (same as above, but now you have to tap again to confirm); Flag (described in the previous section); and More (opens up a raft of options like Reply, Forward, Flag, Move to Junk, and so on).

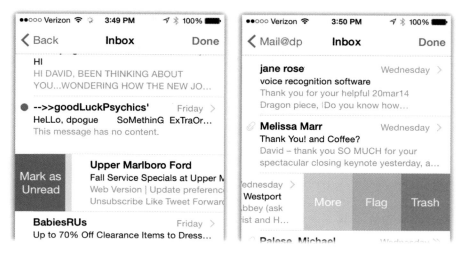

- **Full right-swipe.** Swipe your finger to the *right* all the way across the message to mark it as new (unread). Great for reminding yourself to look at this message again later. Or, if it's already unread, that swipe marks it as *read*.

To a certain extent, you can **customize** these gestures. You can turn off the right-swipe gesture. Or swap the positions of the Flag and Mark as Read options, for example, so that you flag a message when you swipe fully to the right and Mark as Read appears as a button when you swipe to the left. Or you can put the Archive button into the place of Flag when you swipe to the left.

To check out your options, open Settings→Mail, Contacts, Calendars→Swipe Options (shown on the next page).

Tap Swipe Left to specify which button appears in the center of the three when you swipe partway leftward: None, Mark as Read, or Flag). Tap Swipe Right to choose which function you want to trigger with a full rightward swipe (None, Mark as Read, Flag, or Archive).

Read It

The type size in email messages can be pretty small. Fortunately, you have some great iPhoney enlargement tricks at your disposal. For example:

- **Spread two fingers** to enlarge the entire email message.

- **Rotate the phone 90 degrees.** The text gets bigger.

- **Double-tap a narrow block of text** to make it fill the screen, if it doesn't already.

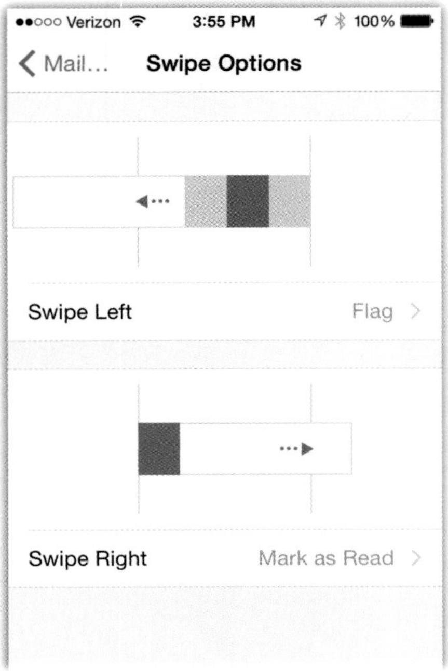

< Mail...   **Swipe Options**

Swipe Left   Flag >

Swipe Right   Mark as Read >

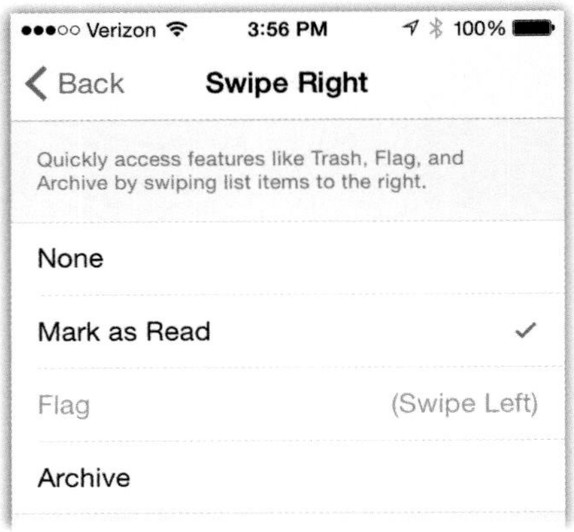

< Back   **Swipe Right**

Quickly access features like Trash, Flag, and Archive by swiping list items to the right.

None

Mark as Read   ✓

Flag   (Swipe Left)

Archive

- **Drag or flick your finger** to scroll through or around the message.

- **Choose a larger type size for all messages**. See page 568.

Links are "live" in email messages. Tap a phone number to call it, a web address to open it, a YouTube link to watch the video, an email address to write to it, a time and date to add it to your calendar, and so on.

Reply to It

To answer a message, tap the Reply/Forward icon (↩) at the bottom of the screen; tap Reply. If the message was originally addressed to multiple recipients, then Reply All sends your reply to everyone simultaneously.

A new message window opens, already addressed. As a courtesy to your correspondents, Mail pastes the original message at the bottom of the window.

TIP: If you select some text before you tap, then the iPhone pastes only that selected bit into the new, outgoing message. In other words, you're quoting back only a portion—just the way it works on a full-sized computer.

At this point, you can add or delete recipients, edit the subject line or the original message, and so on. When you're finished, tap Send.

Use the Return key to create blank lines in the original message. (Use the loupe—page 65—to position the insertion point at the proper spot.)

Using this method, you can splice your own comments into the paragraphs of the original message, replying point by point. The brackets by each line of the original message help your correspondent keep straight what's yours and what's hers.

Forward It

Instead of replying to the sender, you may sometimes want to pass the note on to a third person. To do so, tap ⤺. This time, tap Forward.

> **TIP:** If there's a file attached to the inbound message, the iPhone says, "Include attachments from original message?" and offers Include and Don't Include buttons. Rather thoughtful, actually—the phone can forward files it can't even open.

A new message opens, looking like the one that appears when you reply. You can precede the original message with a comment of your own, like, "Frank: I thought you'd be interested in this joke about your mom." Finally, address and send it as usual.

Follow It

Your phone can notify you when anyone responds to a certain email conversation.

If you're composing or replying to a message, tap in the Subject line to make the 🔔 appear; tap it. If you're *reading* a message, tap 🏴 at the bottom of the screen; tap Notify Me; and confirm by tapping Notify Me again (below, left). In a list, swipe leftward, partly across a message; tap More; tap Notify Me. In each case, a bell icon appears beside the message (or thread) in the list (below, right).

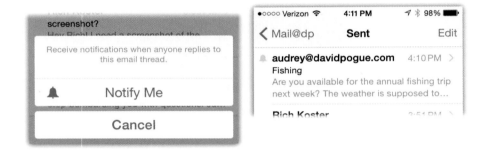

When anybody replies, a notification banner appears on your screen, ready for swiping and reading.

Filing or Deleting One Message

Once you've opened a message that's worth keeping, you can file it into one of your account's folders ("mailboxes") by tapping the 📁 at the bottom of the screen. Up pops the list of your folders; tap the one you want.

It's a snap to delete a message you no longer want, too. If it's open in front of you, tap the 🗑 or 🗄 button at the bottom of the screen. The message rapidly shrinks into the icon and disappears.

> **NOTE:** If that one-touch Delete method makes you a little nervous, by the way, you can ask the iPhone to display a confirmation box before trashing the message forever. Visit Settings→Mail, Contacts, Calendars→Ask Before Deleting.

You can also delete a message from the message *list*—the Inbox, for example; see page 468.

TIP: Gmail doesn't want you to throw anything away. That's why swiping like this produces a button that says Archive, not Delete, and why the usual 🗑 button in a message looks like a filing box 🗃. If you prefer to delete a message for good, hold down the 🗃 until the Trash Message and Archive Message buttons appear.

There's a long way to delete messages from the list, too, as described next. But for single messages, the finger-swipe method is **much** more fun.

TIP: There's a handy Undo shortcut, too: Shake the phone lightly. Tap Undo Trash. The deleted message jumps back to the folder it just came from. (You can then shake again to undo the Undo!)

Filing or Deleting Batches of Messages

You can also file or delete a bunch of messages at once. In the message list, tap Edit. A circle appears beside each message title. You can tap as many of these circles as you like, scrolling as necessary, adding a ✓ with each touch.

Finally, when you've selected all the messages in question, tap either Trash (Archive) or Move.

If you tap Move, then you're shown the folder list so you can say where you want them moved. If you tap Trash, the messages disappear.

If you decide you've made a mistake, just shake the phone lightly—the iPhone's "Undo" gesture. Tap Undo Move to put the filed messages back where they just came from.

Add the Sender to Contacts

When you get a message from someone new who's worth adding to your iPhone's Contacts address book, tap that person's name (in blue, on the From line). You're offered buttons for Create New Contact and Add to Existing Contact. Use the second button to add an email address to an existing person's "card."

Open an Attachment

The Mail program downloads and displays the icons for *any* kind of attachment—but it can *open* only documents from Microsoft Office (Word,

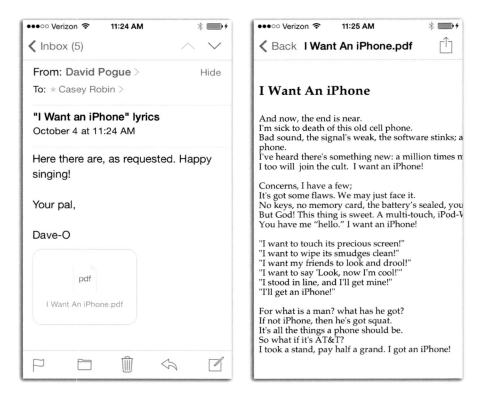

Excel, PowerPoint), those from Apple iWork (Pages, Keynote, Numbers), PDFs, text, RTFs, VCFs, graphics, .zip files, and un-copy-protected audio and video files.

Just scroll down, tap the attachment's icon, wait a moment for downloading, and then marvel as the document opens up, full screen. You can zoom in and out, flick, rotate the phone 90 degrees, and scroll just as though it were a web page or a photo.

> **TIP:** If you *hold your finger down* on the attachment's name, the Share sheet appears. It offers a list of ways you can send this attachment directly from your phone to someone else (by AirDrop or Mail)—or to open it in other apps.
>
> If you tap a Word document, for example, you may be offered buttons for Mail, Dropbox, Evernote, and other apps that can open Word docs. If you tap a PDF document, you'll see a button for Open in iBooks. (Quick Look means the same non-editable preview as you'd get with a quick tap.)

When you're finished admiring the attachment, swipe rightward to return to the original email message.

> **TIP:** iOS can handle the compressed folders known as .zip files, just as Mac and Windows can. When you tap a .zip attachment's icon, the first file in it opens up. At that point, though, if you tap the ☐ icon, you get a list of every document in that zipped folder. You can tap each to view or share it.

Snagging (or Sending) a Graphic

If you get sent a particularly good picture, just hold your finger still on it. You're offered the Save sheet, filled with options like Save (into your Photo app's Camera Roll), Copy, Print, and Assign to Contact (as a person's face photo). All the usual sending methods are represented here, too, so that you can fire off this photo via AirDrop, Messages, Mail, Twitter, and Facebook.

Snagging a Contact or a Date

Mail can recognize contact information or calendar information from an incoming email message—and can dump it directly into Contacts or Calendar for you.

You'll know when it's found something—the block of contact information below somebody's signature, for example—because you see a special gray banner at the top of the screen (next page).

You can click Ignore if you don't particularly need this person bulking up your address book. But if it's somebody worth tracking, tap Add to Contacts. A new Contacts screen appears, ready to save.

Similarly, if the message contains a reference to a date and time, the same sort of banner appears, offering to pop the appointment onto your calendar. (This banner appears only when it's **really sure** you're being offered a date and time: e-invitations and airline-ticket confirmations, for example.)

iOS 9: saving you time since 2015.

View the To/From Details

When your computer's screen is only a few inches tall, there's not a lot of extra space. So Apple designed Mail to conceal header details (To, From, and so on) that you might need only occasionally. For example, you usually don't actually see the word "From:"—you usually see only the sender's name, in blue. The To and Cc lines may show only first names, to save space. (The on/off switch for that feature is in Settings→Mail→Short Names.) And if there's a long list of addresses, you may see only "Michael (& 15 more)"—not the actual list of names.

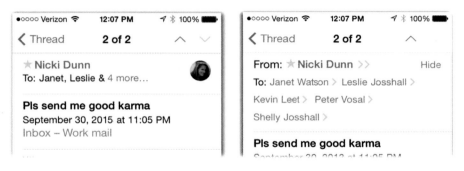

You get last names, full lists, and full sender labels when you tap More following the header information. Tap Hide to collapse these details.

> **TIP:** When you tap a sender's name in blue, you open the corresponding info card in Contacts. It contains one-touch buttons for calling someone back, sending a text message, or placing a FaceTime audio or video call—which can be very handy if the email message you just received is urgent.

Mark as Unread

In the inbox, any message you haven't yet read is marked by a blue dot (●). Once you've opened the message, the blue dot goes away.

If you slide your finger to the right across a message in the list, you trigger the Mark as Unread command—you make that blue dot *reappear*. It's a great way to flag a message for later, to call it to your own attention. The blue dot can mean not so much "unread" as "un–dealt with."

Move On

Once you've had a good look at a message and processed it to your satisfaction, you can move on to the next (or previous) message in the list by tapping ∧ or ∨ in the upper-right corner. Or you can swipe rightward to return to the inbox (or whatever mailbox you're in).

Searching

Praise be—there's a search box in Mail. The search box is hiding *above* the top of every mail list, like your inbox. To see it, scroll up, or just tap the status strip at the top of the screen.

Tap inside the search box to make the keyboard appear. As you type, Mail hides all but the matching messages; tap any one of the results to open it.

You don't have to specify *which fields* to search (From, To, Subject, Body), or which folder. You're searching everywhere.

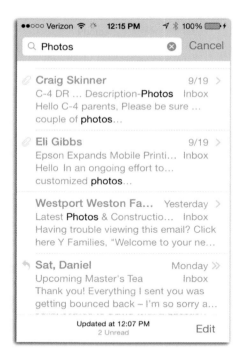

Wait long enough, and the search continues with messages that are still out there on the Internet but are so old that they've scrolled off your phone.

Writing Messages

To compose a new piece of outgoing mail, open the Mail app, and then tap ✏️ in the lower-right corner. A blank new outgoing message appears, and the iPhone keyboard pops up.

Here's how you go about writing a message:

1. **In the To field, type the recipient's email address—or grab it from Contacts.** Often, you won't have to type much more than the first couple of letters of the name *or* email address. As you type, Mail displays all matching names and addresses so you can tap one instead of typing. (It thoughtfully derives these suggestions by analyzing both your Contacts *and* people you've recently exchanged email with.)

   As you go, the iPhone displays a list of everyone whose name matches what you're typing (below, left). The ones bearing ⓘ buttons are the people you've recently corresponded with but who are not in your Contacts. Tap the ⓘ to open a screen where you can add them to Contacts—or *remove* them from the list of recent correspondents, so Mail's autocomplete suggestions will no longer include those lowlifes.

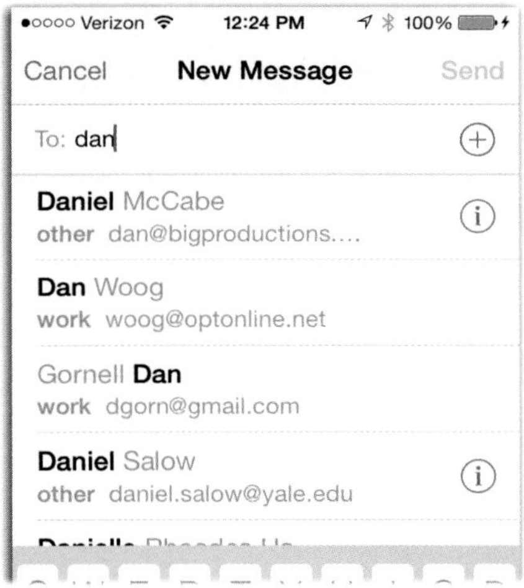

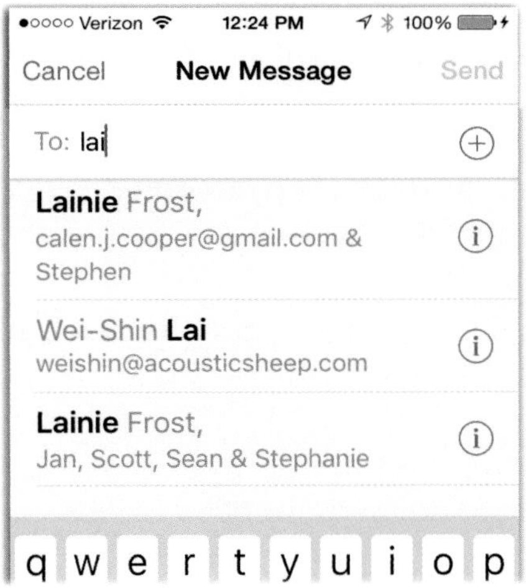

TIP: Here's an especially useful iOS 9 enhancement: When you address an email message, Mail offers a list of ready-made groups; these are the names of other people you usually copy on messages to that person, as shown above at right.

Similarly, if you type a particular subject you've used before, Mail suggests the names of people who've received this subject line before. (For example, if you send "This month's traffic stats" every month to three coworkers, now their names appear automatically when you type out that subject line.) You'll get to go home from work that much quicker.

If you hold your finger down on the period (.) key, you get a pop-up palette of common email-address suffixes, like .com, .edu, .org, and so on, just as in Safari.

Alternatively, tap the ⊕ to open your Contacts list. Tap the name of the person you want.

You can add as many addressees as you like; just repeat the procedure.

TIP: There's no Group mail feature on the iPhone, which would let you send one message to a predefined set of friends. But at *http://groups.yahoo.com*, you can create free email groups. You can send a single email message to the group's address, and everyone in the group will get a copy. (You have to set up one of these groups in a web browser—but lo and behold, your iPhone has one!)

Incidentally, if you've set up your iPhone to connect to a corporate Exchange server (Chapter 17), then you can look up anybody in the entire company directory at this point. Page 547 has the instructions.

2. **To send a copy to other recipients, enter the address(es) in the Cc or Bcc fields.** If you tap Cc/Bcc, From, the screen expands to reveal two new lines beneath the To line: Cc and Bcc.

   Cc stands for *carbon copy*. Getting an email message where your name is in the Cc line implies: "I sent you a copy because I thought you'd want to know about this correspondence, but I'm not expecting you to reply."

   Bcc stands for *blind carbon copy*. It's a copy that goes to a third party secretly—the primary addressee never knows who else you sent it to. For example, if you send your coworker a message that says, "Chris, it bothers me that you've been cheating the customers," you could Bcc your supervisor to clue her in without getting into trouble with Chris.

   Each of these lines behaves exactly like the To line. You fill each one up with email addresses in the same way.

TIP: You can drag people's names around—from the To line to the Cc line, for example. Just hold your finger down briefly on the name before dragging it. (It puffs and darkens once it's ready for transit.)

3. **Change the email account you're using, if you like.** If you have more than one email account set up on your iPhone, you can tap Cc/Bcc, From to expand the form and then tap From to open up a spinning

list of your accounts. Tap the one you want to use for sending this message.

4. **Type the topic of the message in the Subject field.** Leaving it blank only annoys your recipient. On the other hand, don't put the *entire* message into the subject line, either.

5. **Type your message in the message box.** All the usual iPhone keyboard and dictation tricks apply (Chapters 2 and 4). Don't forget that you can use Copy and Paste, within Mail or from other programs. Both text and graphics can appear in your message.

   Here's a fantastic trick: As you're composing a message, you can refer to *another* email—maybe the one you're responding to—without losing your place.

   To do that, drag downward on the title bar, where it says New Message or whatever the reply's title is; your message in progress collapses to the bottom of the screen. Now you can scroll through the message behind it—or you can navigate to *any* message in any Mail

Swipe down to reveal what's behind your reply.

Tap to reopen your reply.

account or folder. This is a great trick when, for example, you want to copy some text out of an earlier message.

Actually, you can collapse multiple outgoing messages like this, leaving them unfinished but still open. They all pile up at the bottom of the screen. (Hold your finger down on them to "fan" them open, so you can hop into one.)

When you're ready to resume writing, tap the title bar at the bottom of the screen; your composition window opens right back up.

6. **Attach a photo or video,** if you like. Hold down your finger anywhere in the body of the message until the Select buttons appear. Tap the ▶ button to reveal the Insert Photo or Video button (shown here at lower left).

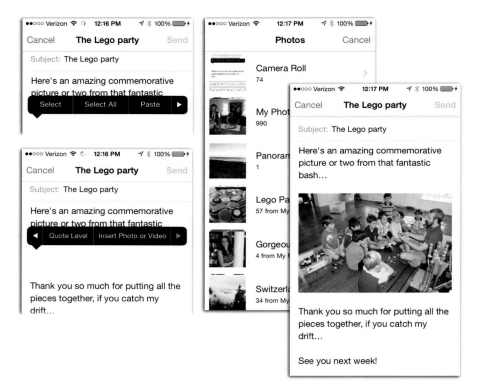

When you tap it, you're shown your iPhone's usual photo browser so that you can choose the photos and videos you want to attach (above, middle). Tap the collection you want; you're shown all the thumbnails inside. Tap the photo or video, and then tap Choose.

You return to your message in progress, with the photo or video neatly inserted (previous page, right). You can repeat this step to add additional photo or video attachments. When you tap Send, you're offered the opportunity to scale down the photo to a more reasonable (emailable) size.

> **TIP:** You can also email a photo or a video from within the Photos program; you can *forward* a file attached to an incoming piece of mail; and you can *paste* a copied photo or video (or several) into an open email message.

7. **Format the text,** if you like. You can apply bold, italic, or underlining to mail text you've typed.

   The trick is to select the text first (page 87). When the button bar appears, tap the B I U button. Tap that to make the Bold, Italics, and Underline buttons appear on the button bar; tap away. Not terribly efficient, but it works.

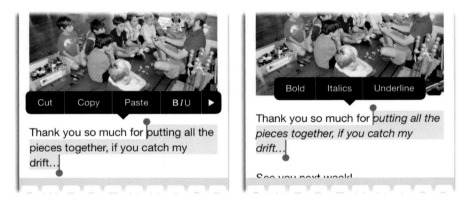

> **TIP:** You can use the same trick to summon the Quote Level controls. Select text; tap the ▶ (twice, if you're holding the phone upright) to bring the Quote Level button into view; tap it to reveal the Increase and Decrease buttons. These buttons indent or un-indent those cluttery blocks of quoted and re-quoted text that often appear when you're replying to a message. (One tap affects the entire paragraph, not just the selected bit of it.)
>
> If you really can't stand those quote indentations, you can stop the iPhone from adding them in the first place when you forward or reply to a message. The on/off switch for that feature is in Settings→Mail, Contacts, Calendars→Increase Quote Level.

8. **Tap Send (to send the message) or Cancel (to back out of it).** If you tap Cancel, the iPhone asks if you want to save the message. If you tap Save Draft, then the message lands in your Drafts folder.

   Later you can open the Drafts folder, tap the aborted message, finish it up, and send it.

   TIP: If you **hold down** the ✎ button for a moment, the iPhone presents a list of your saved drafts. Clever stuff—if you remember it!

Oh, and by the way: You can begin composing a message on your phone, and then continue writing it on your Mac, without ever having to save it as a draft. Or go the other way. See page 540 for details on Handoff.

Signatures

A *signature* is a bit of text that gets stamped at the bottom of your outgoing email messages. It can be your name, a postal address, or a pithy quote.

Unless you intervene, the iPhone stamps "Sent from my iPhone" at the bottom of every message. You may be just fine with that, or you may consider it the equivalent of gloating (or free advertising for Apple). In any case, you can change the signature if you want to.

From the Home screen, tap Settings→Mail, Contacts, Calendars→Signature. You can make up one signature for All Accounts, or a different one for each account (tap Per Account). A Signature text area appears, complete with a keyboard, so you can compose the signature you want.

   TIP: You can use bold, italic, or underline formatting in your signature, too. Just follow the steps on the previous page for formatting a message: Select the text, tap the ▶ to bring the B I U button into view, and so on.

Finish with a Phone Call

If you're typing out some reply, and you realize that it'd be faster to wrap this up by phone, hold down the Home button (to trigger Siri) and just say, "Call him" or "Call her."

If the addressee has a phone number in Contacts, Siri knows who you mean; she dials the number for you, right from the Mail app!

Surviving Email Overload

If you don't get much mail, you probably aren't lying awake at night trying to think of ways to manage the information overload on your tiny phone.

If you do get a lot of mail, here are some tips.

Avoiding Spam

The key to keeping spam (junk mail) out of your inbox is to keep your email address out of spammers' hands in the first place. Use one address for actual communication. Use a different address in the public areas of the Internet, like chat room posting, online shopping, website and software registration, and newsgroup posting. Spammers use automated software robots that scour these pages, recording email addresses they find. Create a separate email account for person-to-person email—and *never* post that address on a web page.

If it's too late, and you're getting a lot of spam on your phone, you have a couple of options. You could accept your fate and set up a new email account (like a free Gmail or Yahoo account), sacrificing your old one to the spammers.

You could install a spam blocker app on your phone, like SpamDrain ($15 a year) or SpamBlocker (free).

Or, if you're technically inclined, you could create a shadow Gmail account that downloads your mail, cleans it of spam, and passes it on to your iPhone. You can find tutorials for this trick by searching in, of course, Google.

Condensing the Message List

Messages in your inbox are listed with the subject line in bold type *and* a couple of lines, in light-gray text, that preview the message itself.

You can control how many lines of the preview show up here, from None (you see more message titles on each screen without scrolling) to 5 Lines. Tap Settings→Mail, Contacts, Calendars→Preview.

Spotting Worthwhile Messages

The iPhone can display a **To** or **Cc** logo on each message in your inbox. At a glance, it helps you identify which messages are actually intended for *you*. Messages without those logos are probably spam, newsletters, mailing lists, or other messages that weren't specifically addressed to you.

To turn on these little badges, visit Settings→Mail, Contacts, Calendars and turn on Show To/Cc Label.

Managing Accounts

If you have more than one email account, you can delete one or just temporarily deactivate one—for example, to accommodate your travel schedule.

Visit Settings→Mail, Contacts, Calendars. In the list of accounts, tap the one you want. At the top of the screen, you see the on/off switch (at least for POP accounts); Off makes an account dormant. And at the bottom, you see the Delete Account button.

> **TIP:** If you have several accounts, which one does the iPhone use when you send mail from other apps—like when you email a photo from Photos or a link from Safari?
>
> It uses the *default* account, of course. You determine which one is the default account in Settings→Mail, Contacts, Calendars→Default Account.

PART FOUR

Connections

Chapter 14
Syncing with iTunes

Chapter 15
iCloud

Chapter 16
Continuity: iPhone Meets Mac

Chapter 17
The Corporate iPhone

Chapter 18
Settings

14

Syncing with iTunes

J ust in case you're one of the six people who've never heard of it, iTunes is Apple's multifunction, multimedia jukebox software. It's been loading music onto iPods since the turn of the 21st century.

Most people use iTunes to manipulate their digital movies, photos, and music, from converting songs off a CD into music files to buying songs, audiobooks, and movies online.

But, as an iPhone owner, you need iTunes even more urgently, because it's the most efficient way to get masses of music, videos, apps, email, addresses, appointments, ringtones, and other stuff *onto* the phone. It also backs up your iPhone automatically.

If you've never had a copy of iTunes on your computer, then fire up your web browser and go to *www.apple.com/itunes/download*. Once the file lands on your computer, double-click the installer icon and follow the onscreen instructions to add iTunes to your life.

This chapter gives you a crash course in iTunes and tells you how to sync it with your iPhone.

> **TIP:** iTunes is not *required*. It's perfectly possible to use all an iPhone's features without iTunes—even without a computer. You can download all that stuff right from the Internet, and you can back up your phone using iCloud (described in the next chapter).
>
> Using iTunes, however, is more efficient, and it's nice to know your stuff is backed up on a machine that's within your control.

The Three Faces of iTunes

The first thing to understand is that iTunes is three apps in one. It's designed to be the viewer for all the music, videos, apps, and ebooks in three places: (1) on your computer, (2) on your phone, and (3) in Apple's online store.

Apple loves to play with the design of this program; every couple of years, it gets another overhaul. The following pages describe version 12, for OS X and Windows.

The first thing to notice is that, at the outset, the buttons at the top center match the buttons in the Music app on your phone: My Music, Playlists, Radio, Connect. (Plus an iTunes Store button—more on that shortly.) This similarity of structure is designed to save you time in learning two different programs.

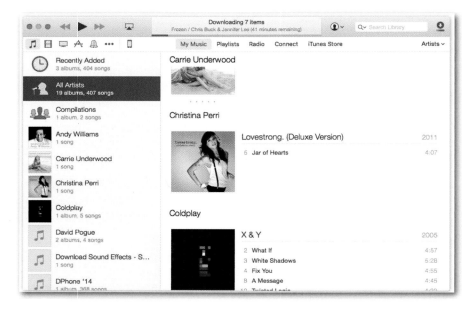

The second thing to notice is that there are two *more* buttons if you subscribe to Apple's $10-a-month Apple Music service: For You and New, exactly as on the phone's Music app (page 229).

> **TIP** Maybe this is too much information, but anyway: If you *do* subscribe to Apple Music but you *don't* want to see those additional buttons in iTunes, you can hide them. Choose iTunes→Preferences→General, and turn off Show Apple Music.

Your Stuff

The "shelf" of file-type icons at top left represent your stuff—the kinds of files that iTunes can manage: ♫ (Music), ⊟ (Movies), ▭ (TV Shows), A (Apps), ⦿ (Podcasts), ⬚ (iTunes U), ⬚ (Audiobooks), and ♫ (Tones). Some are probably hiding in the ••• button.

To view the music, videos, apps, and ebooks that you've downloaded to your Mac or PC, click the corresponding "shelf" icon, and then click the corresponding "My" button at top center (My TV Shows, My Music, or whatever).

TIP You can install or remove file-type icons from this top-left "shelf." For starters, you might want to add the Apps icon (A), so that you can manage your phone's apps in iTunes.

To edit this shelf, click the ••• button; from the shortcut menu, choose Edit. Click to place checkmarks next to the file types you want to appear on the shelf, as shown here at right.

Click to edit the shelf

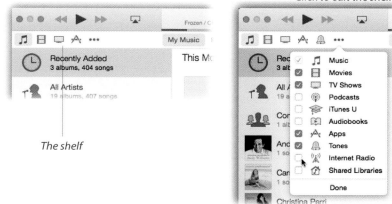

The shelf

The button at top right can sort your files or show them as a list. For example, if you click ♫, you can see them *displayed* as Songs, Albums, Artists, Composers, or Genres. And that's just how they're displayed; an additional control in this menu governs how they're *sorted*.

You may see wildly different things here, depending on which display you've chosen. For example, if you click Songs, you see a huge alphabetical list; if you click Albums, you see a square grid of album covers.

The playback and volume controls are at the top-left corner of iTunes. At the upper-right corner is a search box that lets you pluck one track out of a haystack.

The following pages take you through the three worlds—computer, store, iPhone—one by one.

Three Ways to Fill Your Library

iTunes gives you at least three ways to get music and video onto your computer—ready for transferring to your phone:

- **Let iTunes find your files.** The first time you open iTunes, it offers to search your PC or Mac for music files and add them to its library.

- **Visit the iTunes Store.** Another way to feed your iPhone is to shop at the iTunes Store, as described in the next section.

- **Import music from a CD.** iTunes can also convert tracks from audio CDs into iPhone-ready digital music files. Just start up iTunes and then stick a CD into your computer's CD drive. The program asks if you want to convert the songs to audio files for iTunes. (If it doesn't ask, then click the CD icon at the top of the window.) Click Yes to import all the songs or No to view a list of songs and turn off the duds. (Then click Import CD near the top of the window.)

The program downloads song titles and artist information from the CD and begins to add the songs to the iTunes library. For more control over this process, choose iTunes→Preferences→General (Mac) or Edit→Preferences→General (Windows). Use the When a CD is inserted: pop-up menu.

In that same Preferences box, you can also click Import Settings to choose the *format* (file type) and *bit rate* (amount of audio data compressed into that format) for your imported tracks. The factory setting is the AAC format at 128 kilobits per second.

Most people think these settings make for fine-sounding music files, but you can change your settings to, for example, MP3, another format that lets you cram big music into a small space. Upping the bit rate from 128 to 256 kbps makes for richer-sounding music files—which also take up more room.

Once the importing is finished, each imported song bears a green checkmark, and you have some brand-new files in your iTunes library.

Playlists

A *playlist* is a list of songs you've decided should go together (see page 224). To create a playlist in iTunes, press ⌘-N (Mac) or Ctrl+N (Windows). Or choose File→New→Playlist. Type a name for it: "Cardio Workout," "Shoe-Shopping Tunes," "Hits of the Highland Lute," or whatever.

TIP: You can also create playlists on the phone; see page 225.

Click Edit Playlist. The screen is now divided into two or three sections, depending on how you're viewing it (by Artist, Album, etc.).

At far left: Your entire music collection. Center: the contents of whatever album, genre, composer, or artist you've chosen. At right: your playlist-in-the-making. Find the songs (or videos) you want in the playlist, and then drag their names into the list at far right. Click Done when it's all over.

> **TIP:** Instead of making an empty playlist and then dragging songs into it, you can work the other way. You can scroll through a big list of songs, selecting tracks as you go by ⌘-clicking (on the Mac) or Ctrl-clicking (in Windows)—and then, when you're finished, choose File→New→Playlist from Selection. All the songs you selected immediately appear on a brand-new playlist.

Click an artist or album…   *Drag the songs you want…*   *Into the playlist.*

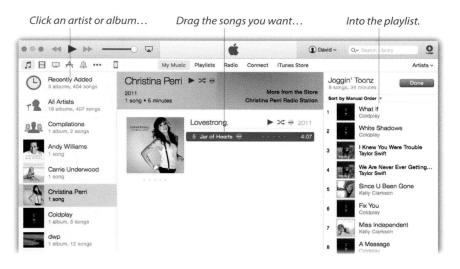

When you drag a song title onto a playlist, you're not actually moving or copying the song. In essence, you're creating an *alias* or *shortcut* of the original, which means you can have the same song on several different playlists.

iTunes even starts you out with some playlists of its own devising, like "Top 25 Most Played" and "Purchased" (a convenient place to find all your iTunes Store goodies listed in one place).

Editing and Deleting Playlists

A playlist is easy to change. Click the ♫ (on the "shelf"), click Playlists, and then click the playlist you want to edit. Now you can change the order of songs by dragging them up or down, or hit Delete or Backspace to get rid of it. (Deleting a song from a playlist doesn't delete it from your music library—it just removes the title from your *playlist*.)

To delete an entire playlist, click its name in the list of playlists (far left) and then press Delete (Backspace). Again, this zaps only the playlist itself; the songs in it are still in iTunes.

There are 163 ways to add a song to an existing playlist, but the simplest may be to click Edit Playlist. That takes you right back to the three-column playlist-building setup illustrated on the previous page.

iTunes Store

The iTunes software's second purpose is to be the face of Apple's online iTunes Store. Click iTunes Store at top center.

Once you land on the store's main page and set up your iTunes account, you can buy and download songs, audiobooks, ebooks, apps, and videos. This material goes straight into your iTunes library, just a sync away from the iPhone.

Your iPhone, of course, can also get to the iTunes Store directly, via the iTunes Store app. Any songs you buy on the phone get copied back to iTunes the next time you sync.

> **TIP:** iTunes doesn't have a monopoly on music sales for your iPhone. Amazon, Google, Rhapsody, and other services sell songs in MP3 format, meaning no copy protection (and iPhone compatibility). *eMusic.com* has great MP3 prices, but the music comes from lesser-known bands. Amazon's MP3 Downloader software for Mac and PC can whip your purchases right into iTunes; Rhapsody has similar helper software for Windows.

To navigate the iTunes Store, click the buttons on the file-type "shelf": ♫ (Music), ☰ (Movies), ▢ (TV Shows), or whatever.

Music (♫)

Here it is, the store that made Apple a powerhouse in the music industry: the Music store. Here are millions of songs, individually downloadable, without copy protection, for prices from 79 cents to $1.29, depending on popularity.

On the right side of the screen, there's a Genres pop-up menu that sorts the offerings by music type. Use the search box (top right) to find a song by name, album name, band, composer, and so on.

The various tiles on the front page represent music Apple thinks you might like: new releases, big hits, Genius recommendations (songs Apple thinks you'll like based on an analysis of what's already in your library), and so on.

If you scroll down the right side of the window, you can find lists of the top-selling songs and albums—a handy way to see what the rest of your fellow music lovers are buying, if you don't mind being a sheep.

The same tools are available for finding TV shows, movies, podcasts, audiobooks, and so on.

TV (⬜), Movies (⊟), and Movie Rentals

The iTunes store also offers an increasingly vast selection of downloadable TV episodes ($2 apiece, no ads) and movies (some you can buy for $10 to $20; others you buy *or* rent for $3 to $56).

Once you rent a movie, you have 30 days to start watching—and once you start, you have 24 hours to finish before it turns back into a pumpkin (it deletes itself from your computer and phone).

You can do your renting and buying in two ways. First, you can use iTunes on your Mac or PC and then sync it to the iPhone by following the steps later in this chapter.

Second, you can download videos straight to the phone when you're in a Wi-Fi hotspot. (The difference: If you download a rental movie to your phone, you can't move it to any other gadget. But if you download it to iTunes, you can move it from computer to phone to iPad, or whatever, although it can exist on only one machine at a time.)

Podcasts (⦿)

There are plenty of free audio and video podcasts in the Podcasts area of the store. See page 394 for details.

iTunes U (⍟)

Here, for your personal-growth pleasure, are hundreds of thousands of downloadable college courses, all of them free and many of them amazing. Watch the videos of the professors, follow along with the reading materials. You won't actually earn a college degree this way, but you *will* attain a degree of enlightenment.

Audiobooks (⧉)

The iTunes Store has plenty to offer for book nuts, both as ebooks (which you buy and read in the iBooks app) and as audiobooks (which you listen to as you drive or work in the garden).

If iTunes doesn't offer the audiobook you're interested in, you can find a larger collection (over 50,000 of them) at *Audible.com*. This web store sells all kinds of audiobooks, plus recorded periodicals like *The New York Times* and radio shows. To purchase Audible's wares, though, you have to go to its website and create an Audible account.

If you use Windows, then you can download from *Audible.com* a little program called Audible Download Manager, which catapults your Audible downloads into iTunes for you. On the Mac, Audible files land in iTunes automatically when you buy them.

Apps (Ａ)

See Chapter 9 for details on grabbing iPhone apps, using your computer as a loading dock.

Internet Radio (⦿)

iTunes offers three ways to use the Internet as the world's biggest AM/FM radio. First, there's iTunes Radio—radio stations you create yourself, exactly as described on page 230. In iTunes, you get to it by clicking Radio at top center.

Second, there's the 24-hour, Apple-run Beats 1 Internet radio station described on page 217. It, too, awaits on the Radio screen.

Third, iTunes lets you listen to live Internet radio broadcasts from radio stations and colleges all over the world. Click ⦿ on the "shelf," click the style of music or talk you want, and then double-click a station to start listening.

Authorizing Computers

All iTunes movies and TV shows are copy protected.

When you create an account in iTunes, you automatically *authorize* that computer to play copy-protected material from the iTunes Store. Authorization is Apple's way of making sure you don't go playing those files on more than five computers, which would greatly displease the movie studios.

You can copy the videos onto a maximum of four other computers. To authorize each one, choose Store→Authorize Computer. When you've maxed out your limit and can't authorize any more computers, you may need to *deauthorize* one. On the computer you wish to demote, choose Store→Deauthorize Computer.

Apple Music

If you're a paying member of the Apple Music service (page 215), iTunes sprouts new tabs called For You and New. They're precisely the same things you'd see on your phone on those same tabs; see page 229.

Syncing the iPhone

The third and final function of iTunes is to load up, and back up, your iPhone. You can connect it to your computer either wirelessly over Wi-Fi, or wirefully, with the white USB cable that came with it.

Once the phone is connected, click the ⬚ (iPhone) button at the top-left corner of the iTunes screen (shown below). Now you can look over the iPhone's contents or sync it (read on).

NOTE: If you have more than one iPhone, and they're all connected, then this button is a pop-up menu. Choose the name of the one you want to manipulate.

Connecting the Phone with a Cable

Plug one end of the white cable (supplied with your iPhone) to your computer's USB jack. Connect the other end to the phone.

Connecting over Wi-Fi

The familiar white USB cable is all well and good—but the phone can also sync with your computer wirelessly.

The iPhone can be charging in its bedside alarm clock dock, happily and automatically syncing with your laptop somewhere else in the house. It transfers all the same stuff to and from your computer—apps, music, books, contacts, calendars, movies, photos, ringtones—but through the air instead of a cable.

Your computer has to be turned on and running iTunes. The phone and the computer have to be on the same Wi-Fi network.

To set up wireless sync, connect the phone using the white USB cable, one last time. Ironic, but true.

Now open iTunes and click ⬚ at top left. On the Summary tab (shown on the facing page), scroll down; turn on Sync with this iPhone over Wi-Fi. Click Apply. You can now detach the phone.

From now on, whenever the phone is on the Wi-Fi network, it's automatically connected to your computer, wirelessly. You don't even have to think about it. (Well, OK—you have to think about leaving the computer turned on with iTunes open, which is something of a buzzkill.)

Just *connecting* it doesn't necessarily mean *syncing* it, though; that's a more data-intensive, battery-drainy process. Syncing happens in either of two ways:

- **Automatically.** If the phone is plugged into power, and it's on the same Wi-Fi network, it syncs with the computer all by itself.

- **Manually.** You can also trigger a sync manually—and this time, the iPhone doesn't have to be plugged into power. To do that, open Settings→General→iTunes Wi-Fi Sync and tap Sync Now. (You can also trigger a Wi-Fi sync from within iTunes—just click the Sync button. It says "Sync" only if, in fact, anything has changed since your last sync.)

All About Syncing

Transferring data between the iPhone and the computer is called *synchronization*. In general, syncing begins automatically when you connect the phone. The ↻ icon whirls in the top-left corner of the screen, but you're welcome to keep using your iPhone while it syncs.

NOTE: Your photo-editing program (like Photos or Photoshop Elements) probably springs open every time you connect the iPhone, too. See page 508 if that bugs you.

Most people these days don't bother with iTunes for syncing; they let the phone sync with their computers wirelessly, via free iCloud accounts.

If you're a little queasy about letting a third party (Apple) store your personal data, though, you can also do this task manually. You can let the iPhone and your computer sync directly with each other—no Internet is involved.

Ordinarily, the iPhone-iTunes relationship is automatic, according to this scheme:

- **Bidirectional copying (iPhone↔computer).** Contacts, calendars, and web bookmarks get copied in both directions. After a sync, your computer and phone contain exactly the same information.

- **One-way sync (computer→iPhone).** All of the following gets copied in one direction: computer to phone. Music, apps, TV, movies, ringtones, and ebooks you bought on your computer; photos from your computer; and email account information.

- **One-way sync (iPhone→computer).** Photos and videos taken with the iPhone's camera; music, videos, apps, ringtones, and ebooks you bought right from the phone—it all gets copied the other way, from the phone to the computer.

- **A complete backup.** iTunes also backs up *everything else* on your iPhone: settings, text messages, call history, and so on. Details on this backup business are covered starting on page 510.

> **TIP:** If you're in a hurry, you can skip the time-consuming backup portion of the sync. Just click ⊘ at the top of the iTunes window whenever it says "Backing up." iTunes gets the message and skips right ahead to the next phase of the sync—transferring contacts, calendars, music, and so on.

Manual Syncing

OK, but what if you don't *want* iTunes to fire up and start syncing every time you connect your iPhone? What if, for example, you want to change the assortment of music and video that's about to get copied to it? Or what if you just want to connect the USB cable to *charge* the phone, not to sync it?

In that case, you can stop the autosyncing in any of these ways:

- **Interrupt a sync in progress.** Click ⊗ in the iTunes status window until the syncing stops.

- **Stop iTunes from syncing with the iPhone just this time.** As you plug in the iPhone's cable, hold down the Shift+Ctrl keys (Windows) or the ⌘-Option keys (Mac) until the iPhone pops up in the iTunes window. Now you can see what's on the iPhone and change what will be synced to it—but no syncing takes place until you command it.

- **Stop iTunes from auto-syncing with this iPhone.** Connect the iPhone. Click ⊡ in the upper-left corner of iTunes. On the Summary tab, turn off Automatically sync when this iPhone is connected.

- **Stop iTunes from autosyncing any iPhone, ever.** In iTunes, choose Edit→Preferences (Windows) or iTunes→Preferences (Mac). Click the Devices tab and turn on Prevent iPods, iPhones, and iPads from syncing automatically. You can still trigger a sync on command when the iPhone is wired up—by clicking the Sync button.

Of course, you must have turned off autosyncing for a reason. And that reason might be that you want to control what gets copied onto it. Maybe you're in a hurry to leave for the airport, and you don't have time to sit there for an hour while six downloaded movies get copied to the phone. Maybe you have 50 gigabytes of music but only 16 gigs of iPhone storage.

In any case, here are the two ways you can sync manually:

- **Use the tabs in iTunes.** With the iPhone connected, you can specify exactly what you want copied to it—which songs, which TV shows, which apps, and so on—using the various tabs in iTunes, as described on the following pages. Once you've made your selections, click the Summary tab and then click Apply. (The Apply button says Sync instead if you haven't actually changed any settings.)

- **Drag files onto the iPhone icon.** Once your iPhone is connected to your computer, you can click its icon and then turn on Manually manage music and videos (on the Summary screen). Click Apply.

  Now you can drag songs and videos directly onto the iPhone's icon to copy them there. Wilder yet, you can bypass iTunes *entirely* by dragging music and video files *from your computer's desktop* onto the iPhone's icon. That's handy when you've just inherited or downloaded a bunch of song files, converted a DVD to the iPhone's video format, or whatever.

  Just two notes of warning here. First, the iPhone accommodates dragged material from a *single* computer only. Second, if you ever turn off this option, all those manually dragged songs and videos will disappear from your iPhone at the next sync opportunity.

TIP: Also on the Summary tab, you'll find the baffling little option called Sync only checked songs and videos. This is a global override—a last-ditch "Keep the embarrassing songs off my iPhone" option.

When this option is turned on, iTunes consults the tiny checkboxes next to every single song and video in your iTunes library. If you turn off a song's checkbox, it will not get synced to your iPhone, no matter what—even if you use the Music tab to sync All songs or playlists, or explicitly turn on a playlist that contains this song. If the song's or video's checkbox isn't checked in your Library list, then it will be left behind on your computer.

iTunes Tabs

Once your iPhone is connected to the computer, and you've clicked its name in the upper-left corner of iTunes, the left side of the iTunes window reveals a column of word buttons: Summary, Apps, Music, Movies, TV Shows, Podcasts, Books, Photos, and Info. Below that is a second, duplicate listing, labeled On My Device. For the most part, these represent the categories of stuff you can sync to your iPhone.

The following pages cover each of these tabs, in sequence, and detail how to sync each kind of iPhone-friendly material.

> **TIP:** At the bottom of the screen, a colorful graph shows you the number and types of files: Audio, Video, Photos, Apps, Books, Documents & Data, and Other (for your personal data). More importantly, it also shows you how much room you have left, so you won't get overzealous in trying to load the thing up.
>
> Point to each color block without clicking to see how many of each item there are ("2031 photos") and how much space they take.

Summary Tab

This screen gives basic stats on your iPhone, like its serial number, capacity, and phone number. Buttons in the middle control how and where the iPhone gets backed up. Checkboxes at the bottom of the screen let you set up manual syncing, as described previously.

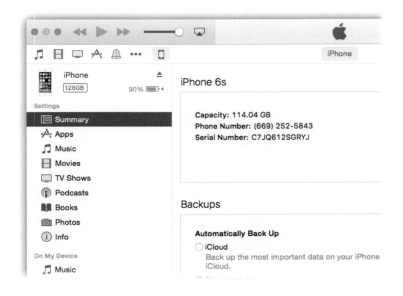

Serial Number, UDID

If you click your phone's serial number, it changes to reveal the ***unique device identifier*** (UDID). That's Apple's behind-the-scenes ID for your exact product, used primarily by software companies (developers). You may, during times of beta testing a new app or troubleshooting an existing one, be asked to supply your phone's UDID.

You can click the same label again to see your phone's Product Type and ECID. Or click your phone number to see your various cellular identifiers like the MEID, IMEI, and ICCID. Or click the iOS version to see your iOS version's build number.

You can right-click (on the Mac, Control-click) any of these numbers to get the Copy command. It copies those long strings of letters and numbers onto your computer's Clipboard, ready to paste into an email or a text.

Apps Tab

On this tab, you get a convenient duplicate of your iPhone's Home screens. You can drag app icons around, create folders, and otherwise organize your Home life much faster than you'd be able to on the phone itself. See page 316 for details.

Music Tab

Turn on Sync Music. Now decide *what* music to put on your phone.

- If you have a big iPhone and a small music library, you can opt to sync the Entire music library.

- If you have a big music collection and a small iPhone, you'll have to take only *some* of it along for the iPhone ride. In that case, click Selected playlists, artists, albums, and genres. In the lists below, turn on the checkboxes for the playlists, artists, albums, and music genres you want to transfer. (These are cumulative. If there's no Electric Light Orchestra in any of your selected playlists, but you turn on ELO in the Artists list, you'll get all your ELO anyway.)

> **TIP:** Playlists make it fast and easy to sync whole batches of tunes over to your iPhone. But don't forget that you can add individual songs, too, even if they're not in any playlist. Just turn on Manually manage music and videos. Now you can drag individual songs and videos from your iTunes library onto the iPhone icon to install them there.

Music videos and voice memos (recorded by the iPhone and now residing on your computer) get their own checkboxes.

Making It All Fit

Sooner or later, everybody has to confront the fact that an iPhone holds only 16, 64, or 128 gigabytes of music and video. (Actually less, because the operating system itself eats up over a gigabyte.) That's enough for around 4,000, 16,000, or 32,000 average-length songs—if you don't put any videos or photos on there.

Your multimedia stash may be bigger than that. If you just turn on Sync All checkboxes, an error message tells you that it won't all fit on the iPhone.

One solution: Tiptoe through the tabs, turning off checkboxes and trying to sync until the "too much" error message goes away.

If you don't have quite so much time, turn on Automatically fill free space with songs. It makes iTunes use artificial Genius intelligence to load up your phone automatically, using your most played and most recent music as a guide. (It does not, in fact, fill the phone completely; it leaves a few hundred megabytes for safety—so you can download more stuff on the road, for example.)

Another helpful approach is to use the *smart playlist*, a music playlist that assembles itself based on criteria that you supply. For example:

1. **In iTunes, click ♫. Choose** File→New Smart Playlist. The Smart Playlist dialog box appears.

2. **Specify the category.** Use the pop-up menus to choose, for example, a musical genre, or songs you've played recently, or *haven't* played recently, or have rated highly.

3. **Turn on the "Limit to" checkbox, and set up the constraints.** For example, you could limit the amount of music in this playlist to 2 gigabytes, chosen at random. That way, every time you sync, you'll get a fresh, random supply of songs on your iPhone, with enough room left for some videos.

4. **Click OK.** The new Smart Playlist appears in the list of playlists at left; you can rename it.

Click it to look it over, if you like. Then, on the Music tab, choose this playlist for syncing to the iPhone.

Movies and TV Shows Tabs

TV shows and movies you've bought or rented from the iTunes Store look great on the iPhone screen. (And if you start watching a rented movie on your computer, the iPhone begins playing it right from where you left off.)

Syncing TV shows and movies works just like syncing music or podcasts. You can have iTunes copy *all* your stuff to the iPhone, but video fills up your storage fast. That's why you can turn on the checkboxes of just the individual movies or shows (either seasons or episodes) you want—or, using the Automatically include pop-up menu, request only the most recent, or the most recent ones you haven't seen yet.

Podcasts Tab

The iTunes Store lists thousands of free amateur and professional podcasts (page 394). On this tab, you can choose to sync all podcast episodes, selected shows, all unplayed episodes—or just a certain number of episodes per sync. Individual checkboxes let you choose *which* podcast series get to come along for the ride, so you can sync to suit your mood at the time.

Books Tab

Here are the thumbnails of your audiobooks and your ebooks—those you've bought from Apple, those you've downloaded from the web, and those you've dragged right into iTunes from your desktop (PDF files, for example). You can ask iTunes to send them all to your phone—or only the ones whose checkboxes you turn on.

Tones Tab

Any ringtones that you've bought from the iTunes Store or made yourself (page 122) appear here; you can specify which ones you want synced to the iPhone. You can choose either All tones or, if space on your phone is an issue, Selected tones (and then turn on the ones you want).

Be sure to sync over any ringtones you've assigned to your frequent callers so the iPhone can alert you with a personalized audio cue, like Pink's rendition of "Tell Me Something Good" when they call you up.

Photos Tab

Why corner people with your wallet to show them your kid's baby pictures, when you can whip out your iPhone and dazzle them with a slideshow?

Syncing Photos and Videos (Computer→iPhone)

(iTunes can sync the photos from your hard drive onto the iPhone. You can even select individual albums of images that you've already assembled on your computer.

Here are your photo-filling options for the iPhone:

- **Windows:** You can sync with Photoshop Elements, Photoshop Album, or any folder of photos, like My Pictures (in Windows), Pictures (on the Mac), or any folder you like.

- **Mac:** You can sync with Photos, iPhoto, or Aperture.

☑ Sync Photos from [🌸 iPhoto ⬍] 77 photos

   ○ All photos, albums, Events, and Faces
   ◉ Selected albums, Events, and Faces, and automatically include [no Events   ⬍]
   ☑ Include videos

Albums		Events
☐ 🖼 Last 12 Months		☐ Flying SFO to NYC
☐ ◻ Last Import		☑ Jackson Playground
☐ 🖼 Flagged		☐ Private Jet to CTU
☐ 🖼 movies		☐ Yahoo campus event
☐ 🖼 iPhone pix		☑ Carnegie Mellon visit
▶ ☐ 🗀 Making Stuff		☑ Jeff's 10th Bday Party
☑ ◻ Gorgeous	4	☐ Oct 2014 Photo Stream
▶ ☐ 🗀 Camera Samples		☑ Funny catz
☐ ◻ N slideshow		☐ DP 7th-grade cartoons
☑ ◻ Tuscany Honeymoon	19	☐ Rock Hall/Cleveland Art Museum night
☑ ◻ PBS torture	25	☐ Tracy in front of old houses
☐ ◻ Best of Basin 2013		☐ Detroit talk

NOTE: You can sync photos from only one computer. If you later attempt to snag some snaps from a second machine, iTunes warns you that you must first erase all the images that came from the *original* computer.

When you're ready to sync your photos, click the Photos tab in iTunes. Turn on Sync photos from, and then indicate *where* you'd like to sync them from (Photoshop Elements, iPhoto, or whatever).

If you've chosen a photo-shoebox program's name (and not a folder's name), you can then click Selected albums, Events, and Faces. Turn on the checkboxes of the albums, events, and faces you want synced. (The "faces" option is available only if you're syncing from Photos, iPhoto, or Aperture on the Mac, and only if you've used the Faces feature, which groups your photos according to who's in them.)

This option also offers to tack on recent Events (batches of photos taken the same day). Indicate whether or not you want videos included in the syncing (Include videos).

Once you make your selections and click Apply, the program computes for a time, "optimizing" copies of your photos to make them look great on the iPhone (for example, downsizing them from 20-megapixel overkill to something more appropriate for a 0.6-megapixel screen), and then ports them over.

After the sync is complete, you'll be able to wave your iPhone around, and people will *beg* to see your photos.

Syncing Photos and Videos (iPhone→Computer)

You can go the opposite direction, too: You can send photos and videos you took with the iPhone's own camera *to* the computer. You can rest easy, knowing that they're backed up to your computer for safekeeping.

Now, it's important to understand that *iTunes is not involved* in this process. It doesn't know anything about photos or videos *from* the iPhone.

So what's handling the iPhone-to-computer transfer? Your operating system. It sees the iPhone as though it's a digital camera and suggests importing them just as it would from a camera's memory card.

Here's how it goes: Plug the iPhone into the computer with the USB cable. What you'll see is probably something like this:

- **On the Mac.** iPhoto or Photos opens. These free photo-organizing/editing programs come on every Mac. Shortly after the program notices that the iPhone is on the premises, it goes into Import mode. Click Import All, or select some thumbnails from the iPhone and then click Import Selected.

    After the transfer, click Delete Photos if you'd like the iPhone's cameraphone memory cleared out after the transfer. (Both photos and videos get imported together.)

- **In Windows.** When you attach a camera (or an iPhone), a dialog box asks how you want its contents handled. It lists any photo-management program you might have installed (Photoshop Elements, Photoshop Album, and so on), as well as Windows' own camera-management software. Click the program you want to handle importing the iPhone pictures and videos.

    You'll probably also want to turn on Always do this for this device, so it'll happen automatically the next time.

Shutting Down the Importing Process

Then again, some iPhone owners would rather *not* see some lumbering photo-management program firing itself up every time they connect the phone. You, too, might wish there were a way to *stop* iPhoto, Photos, or Windows from bugging you every time you connect the iPhone. That's easy enough to change—if you know where to look.

- **Windows 7 and later.** When the AutoPlay dialog box appears, click Set AutoPlay defaults in Control Panel. (Or, if the AutoPlay dialog box is no longer on the screen, choose Start→Control Panel→AutoPlay.)

    Scroll all the way to the bottom until you see the iPhone icon. From the pop-up menu, choose Take no action. Click Save.

- **iPhoto.** Open iPhoto. Choose iPhoto→Preferences. Where it says Connecting camera opens, choose No application. Close the window.

- **Photos**. Connect your iPhone to the Mac. Open Photos. At the top left, click the iPhone's icon, if necessary, and turn off Open Photos for this device. (You have to repeat this for every individual phone or tablet.)

From now on, no photo-importing message will appear when you plug in the iPhone. (You can always import its photos manually, of course.)

Info Tab

On this tab, you're offered the chance to copy some distinctly non-entertainment data over to your iPhone: your computer's calendar, address book, email settings, and web bookmarks.

Now, none of this setup is necessary if you use iCloud (Chapter 15), and you've told your phone to sync its calendar (in Settings→iCloud). That's because iCloud, not iTunes, handles synchronization with the iPhone. Instead, this tab shows only a message that, for example, "Your calendars are being synced with your iPhone over the air from iCloud."

Syncing Contacts and Calendars

If you're not using iCloud syncing, then you can choose to sync your iPhone's address book with a Windows program like Outlook, Outlook Express, or Windows Mail; a Mac program like Contacts or Entourage/ Outlook for Mac; or an online address book like Google Contacts or Yahoo Address Book.

Similarly, you can sync the phone's calendar with a program like Outlook (for Windows) or Calendar or Outlook (on the Mac).

On My Device

Below those Settings tabs at the left side of the iTunes window, there's a second, similar set labeled On My Device. It's a tidy list of everything that is, in fact, on your phone, organized by type (Music, Movies, and so on). There's not really much you can *do* here—you can get more information about some items by pointing to them—but just seeing your multimedia empire arrayed before you can be very satisfying.

The Purchased category, in particular, can be handy; it shows everything on your phone that you've bought *with* the phone.

One iPhone, Multiple Computers

In general, Apple likes to keep things simple. Everything it ever says about the iPhone suggests that you can only sync *one* iPhone with *one* computer.

That's not really true, however. You can actually sync the same iPhone with *multiple* Macs or PCs.

And why would you want to do that? So you can fill it up with material from different places: music and video from a Mac at home; contacts, calendar, ebooks, and iPhone applications from your Windows PC at work; and maybe even the photos from your laptop.

iTunes derives these goodies from different sources to begin with—pictures from your photo program, addresses and appointments from your contacts and calendar programs, music and video from iTunes. So all you have to do is set up the tabs of each computer's copy of iTunes to sync *only* certain kinds of material.

On the Mac, for example, you'd turn on the Sync checkboxes for only the Music, Podcasts, and Video tabs. Sync away.

Next, take the iPhone to the office; on your PC, turn on the Sync checkboxes on only the Info, Books, and Apps tabs. Sync away once more. Then, on the laptop, turn off Sync on all tabs except Photos.

And off you go. Each time you connect the iPhone to one of the computers, it syncs that data according to the preferences set in that copy of iTunes.

One Computer, Multiple iPhones

It's fine to sync multiple iPhones with a single computer, too. iTunes cheerfully fills each one up, and can back each one up, as they come. In fact, if you open the Preferences box (in the iTunes menu on the Mac, the Edit menu in Windows), the Devices tab lists all the iPhones that iTunes is tracking (and iPads and iPod Touches).

Backing Up the iPhone

iTunes can back up everything your computer doesn't already have a copy of: stuff you downloaded straight to the phone (music, ebooks, apps, and so on), plus less visible things, like your iPhone's mail and network settings, your call history, contact favorites, notes, text messages, and other personal preferences that are hard or impossible to recreate.

TIP: If you turn on the Encrypted iPhone Backup option, then your backup will include all your ***passwords***: for Wi-Fi hotspots, websites, email accounts, and so on. That can save you tons of time when you have to restore the phone from the backup. (The one downside: You'll be asked to make up a password ***for the backup***. Don't forget it!)

You can create your backups in either of two places:

- **On your computer.** You get a backup every time the iPhone syncs with iTunes. The backup also happens before you install a new iPhone firmware version from Apple. iTunes also offers to do a backup before you use the Restore option described on the next page.

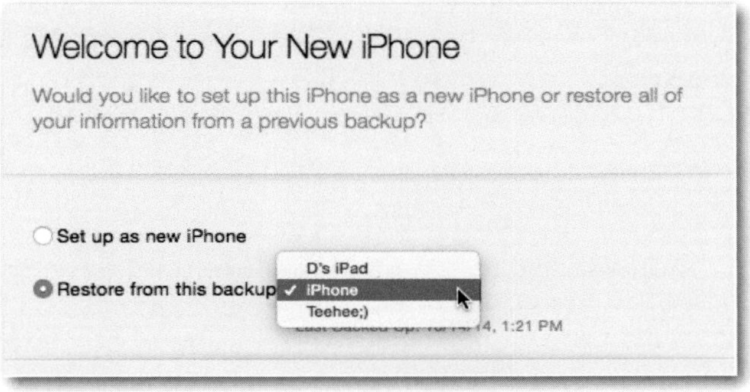

Welcome to Your New iPhone
Would you like to set up this iPhone as a new iPhone or restore all of your information from a previous backup?
Set up as new iPhone
Restore from this backup
D's iPad
✓ iPhone
Teehee;)
4, 1:21 PM

- **On iCloud.** You can also back up your phone wirelessly and automatically—to iCloud, if you've signed up. That method has the advantage of being available even if your computer gets lost or burned to a crisp in a house fire. On the other hand, since your free iCloud storage holds only 5 gigabytes, and your phone probably holds 16 or more, the free iCloud account usually isn't enough. See the next chapter for details.

You make this choice on the Summary tab described above.

Using That Backup

So the day has come when you really need to ***use*** that backup of your iPhone. Maybe it's become unstable, and it's crashing all over. Or maybe you just lost the dang thing, and you wish your replacement iPhone could have all your old info and settings on it. Here's how to save the day (and your data):

1. **Connect the iPhone to the computer you normally use to sync with.**
2. **Click the ▯ (iPhone) button; click the Summary tab.**

3. **Click Restore iPhone.** A message announces that you can't erase the phone without first turning off Find My iPhone. This is a security measure to stop a thief from erasing a stolen phone. He can't restore the phone without turning off Find My iPhone, which requires your iCloud password. Go to the phone and do that (in Settings→iCloud).

4. **Take iTunes up on its offer to restore all your settings and stuff from the backup.** If you see multiple backup files listed from other iPhones (or an iPod Touch), be sure to pick the backup file for *your* phone. Let the backup restore your phone settings and info. Then resync all your music, videos, and podcasts. Exhale.

Deleting a Backup File

To save disk space, you can delete old backups (especially for i-gadgets you no longer own). Go to the iTunes preferences (Edit→Preferences in Windows or iTunes→Preferences on the Mac) and click the Devices tab.

Click the dated backup file you don't want and hit Delete Backup.

15

iCloud

The free iCloud service stems from Apple's brainstorm that, since it controls both ends of the connection between a Mac and the Apple website, it should be able to create some pretty clever Internet-based features.

This chapter concerns what iCloud can do for you, the iPhone owner.

NOTE: To get a free iCloud account if you don't already have one, sign up in Settings→iCloud.

What iCloud Giveth

So what is iCloud? Mainly, it's these things:

- **A synchronizing service.** It keeps your calendar, address book, and documents updated and identical on all your gadgets: Mac, PC, iPhone, iPad, iPod Touch. Also your web passwords and credit card numbers. That's a huge convenience—almost magical.

- **Find My iPhone.** Find My iPhone pinpoints the current location of your iPhone on a map. In other words, it's great for helping you find your phone if it's been stolen or lost.

  You can also make your lost gadget start making a loud pinging sound for a couple of minutes by remote control—even if it was silenced. That's brilliantly effective when your phone has slipped under the couch cushions.

- **An email account.** Handy, really: An iCloud account gives you a new email address. If you already have an email address, great! This new one can be a backup account, one you never enter on websites so that it never gets overrun with spam. Or vice versa: Let *this* be your junk account, the address you use for online forms. Either way, it's great to have a second account.

- **An online locker.** Anything you buy from Apple—music, TV shows, ebooks, and apps—is stored online, for easy access at any time. For example, whenever you buy a song or a TV show from the online iTunes Store, it appears automatically on your iPhone and computers. Your photos are stored online, too.

- **Back to My Mac.** This option to grab files from one of your other Macs across the Internet isn't new, but it survives in iCloud. It lets you access the contents of one Mac from another one across the Internet.

- **Automatic backup.** iCloud can back up your iPhone—automatically and wirelessly (over Wi-Fi, not over cellular connections). It's a quick backup, since iCloud backs up only the changed data.

  If you ever want to set up a new i-gadget, or if you want to restore everything to an existing one, life is sweet. Once you're in a Wi-Fi hotspot, all you have to do is re-enter your Apple ID and password in the setup assistant that appears when you turn the thing on. Magically, your gadget is refilled with everything that used to be on it.

  Well, *almost* everything. An iCloud backup stores everything you've bought from Apple (music, apps, books); photos and videos in your Camera Roll; settings, including the layout of your Home screen; text messages; and ringtones. Your mail, and anything that came from your computer (like music/ringtones/videos from iTunes and photos from the Photos app), have to be reloaded.

- **Family Sharing** is a broad category of features intended for families (up to six people).

  First, everyone can share stuff bought from Apple's online stores: movies, TV shows, music, ebooks, and so on. It's all on a single credit card, but you, the all-knowing parent, can approve each person's purchases—without having to share your account password. That's a great solution to a long-standing problem.

  There's also a new shared family photo album and a new auto-shared Family category on the calendar. Any family member can see the location of any other family member, and they can find one another's lost iPhones or iPads using Find My iPhone.

- **iCloud Drive** is Apple's version of Dropbox. It's a folder, present on every Mac, iPhone, iPad, and iPod Touch, that lists whatever you've put into it—an online "disk" that holds 5 gigabytes (more, if you're willing to pay money).

The iCloud Drive is a perfect place to put stuff you want to be able to access from any Apple gadget, wherever you go. It's a great backup, too.

- **Continuity.** If you have a Mac, and it's running OS X Yosemite or later, you're in for a treat. The set of features Apple calls Continuity turn the iPhone into a part of the Mac. They let you make calls from your Mac as though it were a speakerphone. They let you send and receive text messages from your Mac—to any cellphone on earth. They let you AirDrop files between computer and phone, wirelessly. And more.

So there's the quick overview. The rest of the chapter covers each of these iCloud features in greater depth—except Continuity, which gets its own chapter right after this one.

iCloud Sync

For many people, this may be the killer app for iCloud right here: The iCloud website, acting as the master control center, can keep multiple Macs, Windows PCs, and iPhones/iPads/iPod Touches synchronized. That offers both a huge convenience factor—all your stuff is always on all your gadgets—and a safety/backup factor, since you have duplicates everywhere.

It works by storing the master copies of your stuff—email, notes, contacts, calendars, web bookmarks, and documents—on the web. (Or "in the cloud," as the product managers would say.)

Whenever your Macs, PCs, or i-gadgets are online—over Wi-Fi or cellular—they connect to the mother ship and update themselves. Edit an address on your iPhone, and shortly thereafter you'll find the same change in Contacts (on your Mac) and Outlook (on your PC). Send an email reply from your PC at the office, and you'll find it in your Sent Mail folder on the Mac at home. Add a web bookmark anywhere and find it everywhere else. Edit a spreadsheet in Numbers on your iPad and find the same numbers updated on your Mac.

Actually, there's even another place where you can work with your data: on the web. Using your computer, you can log into *www.icloud.com* to find web-based clones of Calendar, Contacts, and Mail.

To control the syncing, tap Settings→iCloud on your iPhone. Turn on the checkboxes of the stuff you want to be synchronized all the way around:

- **iCloud Drive.** This is the on/off switch for the iCloud Drive (page 334). Look Me Up by Email is a list of apps that permit other iCloud members to find you by looking up your address. And Use Cellular Data lets you prevent your phone from doing its iCloud Drive synchronization over the cellular network, since you probably get only a limited data allotment each month.

- **Photos.** Tap the > button to see four on/off switches.

  iCloud Photo Library is Apple's new online photo storage feature. It stores all your photos and videos online, so you can access them from any Apple gadget; you can read more about it on page 304.

  My Photo Stream and iCloud Photo Sharing are the master switches for Photo Streams, which are among iCloud's marquee features (page 296).

  When you hold your finger down on the shutter button, the iPhone 5s and 6 models can snap 10 frames a second. That's burst mode—and all those photos can fill up your iCloud storage. So Apple gives you the Upload Burst Photos option to exclude them from the backup.

- **Mail.** "Mail" refers to your actual email messages, plus your account settings and preferences from OS X's Mail program.

- **Contacts, Calendars.** There's nothing as exasperating as realizing that the address book you're consulting on your home Mac is missing somebody you're *sure* you entered—on your phone. This option keeps all your address books and calendars synchronized. Delete a phone number on your computer at home, and you'll find it gone from your phone. Enter an appointment on your iPhone, and you'll find the calendar updated everywhere else.

- **Reminders.** This option refers to the to-do items you create in the phone's Reminders app; very shortly, those reminders will show up on your Mac (in Reminders, Calendar, or BusyCal) or PC (in Outlook). How great to make a reminder for yourself in one place and have it reminding you later in another one!

- **Safari.** If a website is important enough to merit bookmarking while you're using your phone, why shouldn't it also show up in the Bookmarks menu on your desktop PC at home, your Mac laptop, or your iPad? This option syncs your Safari Reading List, too.

- **Notes.** This option syncs the notes from your phone's Notes app into the Notes app on the Mac, the email program on your PC, your other i-gadgets, and, of course, the iCloud website.

- **Wallet.** If you've bought tickets for a movie, show, game, or flight, you sure as heck don't want to be stuck without them because you left the barcode on your other gadget.

- **Backup.** Your phone can back itself up online, automatically, so that you'll never worry about losing your files along with your phone.

  Of course, most of the important stuff is *already* backed up by iCloud, in the process of syncing it (calendar, contacts—all the stuff described on these pages). So this option just backs up everything else: all your settings, your Health data, your documents, your account settings, and your photo library.

  There are some footnotes. The wireless backing-up happens only when your phone is charging and in a Wi-Fi hotspot (because in a cellular area, all that data would eat up your data limit each month). And remember that a free iCloud account includes only 5 gigabytes of storage; your phone may require a lot more space than that. Using iCloud Backup may mean paying for more iCloud storage. Apple's prices are $12 a year for 20 gigabytes, $48 a year for 200 gigs, and so on.)

- **Keychain.** The login information for your websites (names and passwords), and even your credit card information, can be stored right on your phone—and synced to your other iPhones, iPads, and Macs (running OS X Mavericks or later).

Now, you could argue that website passwords and credit card numbers are more important than, say, your Reminders. For this category, you don't want to mess around with security.

Therefore, when you turn on the Keychain switch in Settings, you're asked to enter your iCloud password.

Then you get a choice of ways to confirm your realness—either by entering a code that Apple texts to you or by using another Apple device to set up this one. Once that's done, your passwords and credit cards are magically synced across your computers and mobile gadgets, saving you unending headaches. This is a truly great feature that's worth enduring the setup.

To set up syncing, turn on the switches for the items you want synced. That's it. There is no step 2.

NOTE: You may notice that there are no switches here for syncing stuff you buy from Apple, like books, movies, apps, and music. They're not so much *synced* as they are *stored* for you online. You can download them at any time to any of your machines.

My Photo Stream, Photo Sharing

These iCloud features are described in glorious detail in Chapter 8.

Find My iPhone

Did you leave your iPhone somewhere? Did it get stolen? Has that mischievous 5-year-old left it somewhere in the house again? Sounds like you're ready to avail yourself of one of Apple's finest creations: Find My iPhone.

The first step is to log into *iCloud.com* and click Find My iPhone. Immediately, the website updates to show you, on a map, the current location of your phone—and Macs, iPod Touches, and iPads. (If they're not online, or if they're turned all the way off, you won't see their current locations.)

If you own more than one, you may have to click All Devices and, from the list, choose the one you're looking for.

If just knowing where the thing *is* isn't enough to satisfy you, then click the dot representing your phone, click the ⓘ next to its name, and marvel at the appearance of these three buttons:

- **Play Sound.** When you click this button, the phone starts dinging and vibrating loudly for 2 minutes, wherever it is, so you can figure out

which jacket pocket you left it in. It beeps even if the ringer switch is off, and even if the phone is asleep. Once you find the phone, just wake it in the usual way to make the dinging stop.

- **Lost Mode.** When you lose your phone for real, proceed immediately to Lost Mode. Its first step: Prompting you to password protect it, if you haven't already. Without the password, a sleazy crook can't get into your phone without erasing it. (If your phone is already password-protected, you don't see this step.)

The passcode you dream up here works just as though you'd created one yourself on the phone. That is, it remains in place until you, with the phone in hand, manually turn it off in Settings→General→Passcode Lock.

Next, the website asks for a phone number where you can be reached, and (when you click Next) a message you want displayed on the iPhone's Lock screen. If you actually left the thing in a taxi or on some restaurant table, you can use this feature to plead for its return.

When you click Done, your message appears on the phone's screen, wherever it is, no matter what app was running, and the phone locks itself.

Whoever finds it can't miss the message, can't miss the Call button that's right there on the Lock screen, and can't do anything without dismissing the message first.

If the finder of your phone really isn't such a nice person, at least you'll get an automatic email every time the phone moves from place to place, so you can track the thief's whereabouts. (Apple sends these messages to your @me.com or @icloud.com address.)

- **Erase iPhone.** This is the last-ditch security option, for when your immediate concern isn't so much the phone as all the private stuff that's on it. Click this button, confirm the dire warning box, enter your iCloud ID, and click Erase. By remote control, you've just erased everything from your phone, wherever it may be. (If it's ever returned, you can restore it from your backup.)

Once you've wiped the phone, you can no longer find it or send messages to it using Find My iPhone.

TIP: There's an app for that. Download the Find My iPhone app from the App Store. It lets you do everything described above from another iPhone, in a tidy, simple control panel.

Send Last Location

Find My iPhone works great—as long as your lost phone has power, is turned on, and is online. Often, though, it's lying dead somewhere, or it's been turned off, or there's no Internet service. In those situations, you might think Find My iPhone can't help you.

But, thanks to Send Last Location, you have a prayer of finding your phone again. Before it dies, your phone will send Apple its location. You have 24 hours to log into *iCloud.com* and use the Find My iPhone feature to see where it was at the time of death. (After that, Apple deletes the location information.) That's a lot better than the old system, by which Find My iPhone drew a blank if the phone was dead or off.

You definitely want to turn this switch on.

Activation Lock

Thousands of people have found their lost or stolen iPhones by using Find My iPhone. Yay!

Unfortunately, thousands more will never see their phones again. Until recently, Find My iPhone had a back door the size of Montana: The thief could simply turn the phone off. Or, if your phone was password-protected, the thief could just erase it and sell it on the black market, which was his goal all along. Suddenly, your phone is lost in the wilderness, and you have no way to track or recover it.

That's why Apple offers the ingenious Activation Lock feature. It's very simple: Nobody can erase it, or even turn off Find My iPhone, without entering your iCloud password (your Apple ID). This isn't a switch you can turn on or off; it's always on.

So even if the bad guy has your phone and tries to sell it, the thing is useless. It's still registered to you, you can still track it, and it still displays your message and phone number on the Lock screen. Without your iCloud password, your iPhone is just a worthless brick. Suddenly, stealing iPhones is a much less attractive prospect.

Email

Apple offers an email address as part of each iCloud account. Of course, you already *have* an email account. So why bother? The first advantage is the simple address: *YourName@me.com* or *YourName@icloud.com.*

Second, you can read your me.com email from any computer anywhere in the world, via the iCloud website, or on your iPhone/iPod Touch/iPad.

To make things even sweeter, your me.com or icloud.com mail is completely synced. Delete a message on one gadget, and you'll find it in the Deleted Mail folder on another. Send a message from your iPhone, and you'll find it in the Sent Mail folder on your Mac. And so on.

Video, Music, Apps: Locker in the Sky

Apple, if you hadn't noticed, has become a big seller of multimedia files. It has the biggest music store in the world. It has the biggest app store, for both i-gadgets and Macs. It sells an awful lot of TV shows and movies. Its ebook store, iBooks, is no Amazon, but it's chugging along.

Once you buy a song, movie, app, or book, you can download it again as often as you like—no charge. In fact, you can download it to your *other* Apple equipment, too—no charge. iCloud automates, or at least formalizes, that process. Once you buy something, it's added to a list of items that you can download to all your *other* machines.

Here's how to grab them:

- **iPhone, iPad, iPod Touch.** *For apps:* Open the App Store icon. Tap Updates. Tap Purchased, and then My Purchases. Tap Not On This iPhone.

  For music, movies, and TV shows: Open the iTunes Store app. Tap More, and then Purchased; tap the category you want. Tap Not On This iPhone.

  There they are: all the items you've ever bought, even on your *other* machines using the same Apple ID. To download anything listed here onto *this* machine, tap the ☁ button. Or tap an album name to see the list of songs on it so you can download just *some* of those songs.

  You can save yourself all that tapping by opening Settings→iTunes & App Store and turning on Automatic Downloads (for music, apps, and books). From now on, whenever you're on Wi-Fi, stuff you've bought on other Apple machines gets downloaded to this one *automatically*.

- **Mac or PC.** Open the Mac App Store program (for Mac apps) and click Purchases. Or open the iTunes app (for songs, TV shows, books, and movies). Click Store and then, under Quick Links, click Purchased. There are all your purchases, ready to open or re-download.

TIP: To make this automatic, open iTunes. Choose iTunes→Preferences→ Store. Under Automatic Downloads, turn on Music, Apps, and Books, as you see fit. Click OK. From now on, iTunes will auto-import anything you buy on any of your other machines.

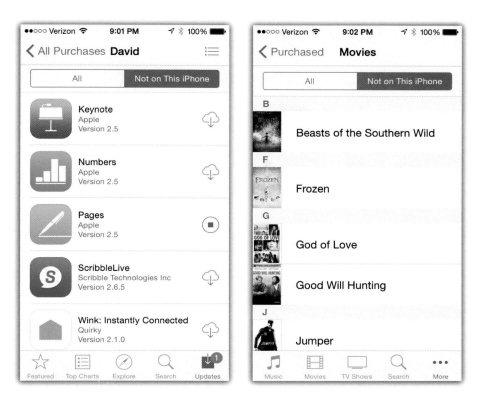

Any bookmark you set in an iBook book is synced to your other gadgets, too. The idea, of course, is that you can read a few pages on your phone in the doctor's waiting room and then continue from the same page on your iPad on the train ride home.

The Price of Free

A free iCloud account gives you 5 gigabytes of online storage. That may not sound like much, especially when you consider how big some music, photo, and video files are.

Fortunately, anything you buy from Apple—like music, apps, books, and TV shows—doesn't count against that 5-gigabyte limit. Neither do the photos in your Photo Stream.

So what's left? Some things that don't take up much space, like settings, documents, and pictures you take with your iPhone, iPad, or iPod Touch— and some things that take up a lot of it, like email, commercial movies, and home videos you transferred to the phone from your computer. Anything you put on your iCloud Drive eats up your allotment, too. (Your iPhone backup might hog space, but you can pare that down in Settings→ iCloud→Storage→Manage Storage. Tap an app's name and then tap Edit.)

You can, of course, expand your storage if you find 5 gigs constricting. You can expand that to 20, 50, 500, or 1,000 gigabytes—for $12, $48, $120, or $240 a year. You can upgrade your storage online, on your computer, or right on the iPhone (in Settings→iCloud→Storage→Buy More Storage).

Apple Pay (iPhone 6/6s Families)

We can all breathe a sigh of relief: Paying for things by just waving your phone has finally come to America.

Actually, Android phones have offered this feature for years—but almost nobody uses it. The process involves too many steps, including typing in a password every time. Swiping a credit card is easier.

With Apple Pay, Apple thinks it's eliminated the red tape. Now you can pay for things without cash, without cards, without signing anything, without your wallet: Just **hold the phone**. You don't have to open some app, don't have to enter a code, don't even have to wake the phone up; just hold your finger on the Home button (it reads your fingerprint to make sure it's you). You've just paid.

You can't pay for things everywhere; the merchant has to have a wireless terminal attached to the register. You'll usually know, because you'll see the Apple Pay logo somewhere:

Apple says over a million stores and restaurants accept Apple Pay right off the bat, including chains like McDonald's, Walgreens, Macy's, Subway, Panera Bread, Duane Reade, Bloomingdale's, Staples, Chevron, and Whole Foods. More are coming.

Apple Pay depends on a special chip in the phone: the NFC chip (near-field communication), and models before the iPhone 6 don't have it. Stores whose terminals don't speak NFC—Walmart, Target, Starbucks, and so on—don't work with Apple Pay, either.

The Setup

To set up Apple Pay, you have to teach your phone about your credit card. To do that, open the Wallet app. (Before iOS 9, it was called Passbook.) You can also start this process in Settings→Wallet & Apple Pay.

Tap Add credit or debit card. Enter your iCloud password, tap OK, and then tap Next.

Now, on the Add Card screen, you're asked to aim the phone's camera at whatever Visa, MasterCard, or American Express card you use most

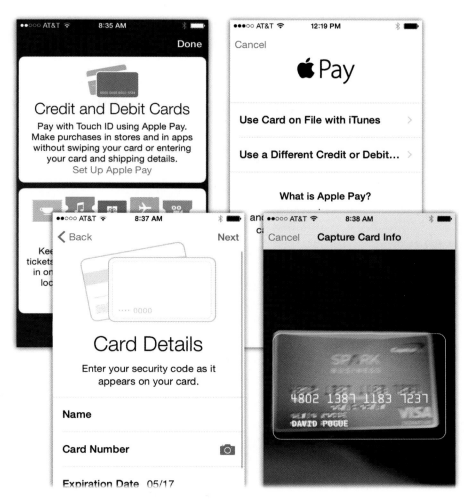

often. Hold steady until the digits of your card blink onto the screen, auto-recognized. Cool!

TIP: If you don't have the card with you, you can also choose Enter Card Details Manually and type in all the numbers yourself.

Check over the interpretation of the numbers, then hit Next.

Now you have to type in the expiration date and security code manually. Hit Next again. Then agree to the legalese screen.

Next, your bank has to verify that all systems are go for Apple Pay. That may involve responding to an email or a text, or typing in a verification code. In any case, it's generally instantaneous.

At the outset, Apple Pay works only with MasterCard, Visa, or American Express, and only the ones issued by certain banks. The big ones are all on board—Citibank, Chase, Bank of America, and so on—and more are signing on all the time.

In iOS 9, you can also store your store loyalty and rewards cards, too—and when you're in that store, the phone chooses the correct card automatically. When you're in Dunkin' Donuts, it automatically uses your Dunkin' Donuts card to pay.

The Shopping

Once the cashier has rung up your total, here comes the magic. Bring your iPhone near the terminal—no need to wake it—in any of these ways:

- **To pay with your default card:** Bring the phone within an inch of the terminal, with your finger on the Home button. (The phone can be asleep.) Apple Pay automatically pays with your default (primary) credit card. You feel a buzz, hear a beep, and see a picture of the card on your screen. It takes about 2 seconds.

TIP: To change which card is your default credit card, open Settings→ Wallet & Apple Pay. That's where you can add and remove cards, too.

- **To pay with a different card:** If you approach the reader *without* touching the Home button, the phone wakes and shows your default card. If you'd rather choose a different card, tap the default card's image. Wallet opens and shows your array of cards. Tap one and then bring the phone near the reader again, with your finger on the Home button.

- **When you're in a hurry, or want to change cards:** This technique, new in iOS 9, offers two advantages. First, it's a quicker way to choose one of your other cards. Second, it lets you set up the transmission in the moments **before** you approach the terminal—handy when you just want to rush through the London subway turnstiles, for example (yes, they take Apple Pay).

To make this work, start with the iPhone asleep—dark. Double-press the Home button to wake it and display your credit cards. Tap the one you want (or leave the default), and then touch your finger to the Home button. You can do all of this before you approach the reader.

At this point, the phone is continuously sending its "I'm paying!" signal. Just wave it near the reader to complete the transaction—your finger doesn't have to be on the Home button or the screen.

Either way, it's just a regular credit card purchase. So you still get your reward points, frequent flier miles, and so on. (Returning something works the same way: At the moment when you'd swipe your card, you bring the phone near the reader until it beeps. Slick.)

Apple points out that Apple Pay is much more secure than using a credit card, because the store never sees, receives, or stores your credit card number, or even your name. Instead, the phone transmits a temporary, one-time, encoded number that means nothing to the merchant. It incor-

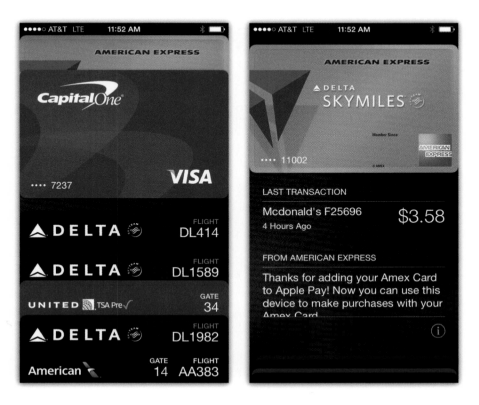

porates verification codes that only the card issuer (your bank) can translate and verify.

And, by the way, Apple never sees what you've bought or where, either. You can open Wallet and tap a card's picture to see the last few transactions (previous page, right), but that info exists only on your iPhone.

And what if your phone gets stolen? Too bad—for the thief. He can't buy anything without your fingerprint. If you're still worried, you can always visit *iCloud.com*, click Settings, tap your phone's name, and click Remove All to de-register your cards from the phone by remote control.

Apple Pay Online

You can buy things online, too, using iPhone apps that have been upgraded to work with Apple Pay. The time savings this time: You're spared all that typing of your name, address, and phone number every time you buy something.

Instead, when you're staring at the checkout screen for some app, just tap Buy with Apple Pay.

Family Sharing

It might have taken years, but Apple has finally acknowledged a fundamental fact of American life: Many of us have *families*.

If you have kids, it's always been a hassle to manage your Apple life. What if they want to buy a book, movie, or app? They have to use your credit card—and you have to reveal your iCloud password to them.

Or what if they want to see a movie that you bought? Do they really have to buy it again?

Not anymore. Once you've turned on Family Sharing and invited your family members, here's how your life will be different:

- **One credit card to rule them all.** Up to six of you can buy books, movies, apps, and music on your master credit card.

- **Ask before buy.** When your kids try to buy stuff, your phone pops up a permission request. You have to approve each purchase.

- **Younger Appleheads.** Within Family Sharing, you can now create Apple accounts for tiny tots; 13 is no longer the age minimum.

- **Shared everything.** All of you get instant access to one another's music, video, iBooks, and app purchases—again, without having to know each other's Apple passwords.

- **Find one another.** You can use your phone to see where your kids are, and vice versa (with permission, of course).

- **Find one another's phones**. The miraculous Find My iPhone feature (page 518) now works for every phone in the family. If your daughter can't find her phone, you can find it for her with *your* phone.

- **Mutual photo album, mutual calendar, and mutual reminders.** When you turn on Family Sharing, your Photos, Calendar, and Reminders apps each sprout a new category that's preconfigured to permit access by everyone in your family.

Setting Up Family Sharing

The setup process means wading through a lot of screens, but at least you have to do it only once. You can turn on this feature either on the Mac (in System Preferences→Set Up Family) or on the phone itself. Since this book is about the iPhone, what follows are the steps to do it there.

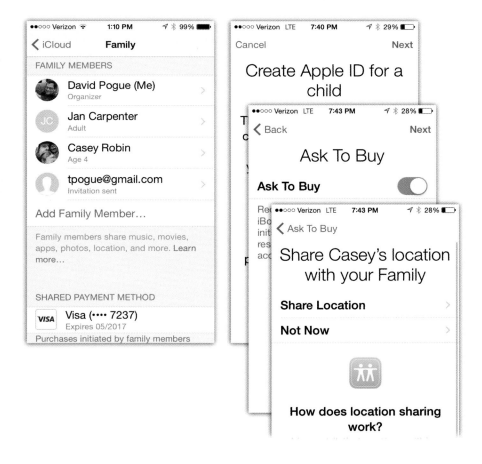

In Settings→iCloud, tap Set Up Family Sharing. Click Get Started. Now the phone informs you that you, the sage adult, are going to be the Organizer— the one with the power, the wisdom, and the credit card. Continue (unless it's listing the wrong Apple ID account, in which case, you can fix it now).

On successive screens, you read about the idea of shared Apple Store purchases; you're shown the credit card that Apple believes you want to use; you're offered the chance to share your location with the others. Each time, read and tap Continue.

Finally, you're ready to introduce the software to your family.

- **If the kid is under 13:** Scroll wayyyyy down and tap Create an Apple ID for a Child. On the screens that follow, you'll enter the kid's birth date; agree to a Parent Privacy Disclosure screen; enter the security code for your credit card (to prove that you're you, and not, for example, your naughty kid); type the kid's name; set up an iCloud account (name, password, three security questions); decide whether or not to turn on Ask To Buy (each time your youngster tries to buy something online from Apple, you'll be asked for permission in a notification on your phone); decide whether you want the family to be able to see where the kid is at all times; and accept a bunch of legalese.

  When it's all over, the lucky kid's name appears on the Family screen.

- **If the kid already has an iCloud account and is standing right there with you in person:** Tap Add Family Member. Type in her name or email address. (Your child's name must already be in your Contacts; if not, go add her first. By the way, you're a terrible parent.)

  She can now enter her iCloud password on your phone to complete her setup. (That doesn't mean you'll learn what her password is; your phone stores it but hides it.) On the subsequent screens, you get to confirm her email address and let her turn on location sharing. In other words: The rest of the family will be able to see where she is.

- **If the kid isn't with you at the moment:** Click Send an Invitation.

  Your little darling gets an email at that address. He must open it on his Apple gadget—the Mail app on the iPhone, or the Mail program on his Mac, for example.

  When he hits View Invitation, he can either enter his iCloud name and password (if he has an iCloud account), or get an Apple ID (if he doesn't). Once he accepts the invitation, he can choose a picture to represent himself; tap Confirm to agree to be in your family; enter his iCloud password to share the stuff he's bought from Apple; agree to

Apple's lawyers' demands; and, finally, opt in to sharing his location with the rest of the family.

You can, of course, repeat this cycle to add additional family members, up to a maximum of six. Their names and ages appear on the Family screen.

From here, you can tap someone's name to perform stunts like these:

- **Delete a family member.** Man, you guys really don't get along, do you? Anyway, tap Remove.

- **Turn Ask To Buy on or off.** This option appears when you've tapped a child's name on your phone. If you decide your kid is responsible enough not to need your permission for each purchase, you can turn this option off.

> **NOTE:** If you turn off Ask To Buy for someone after she turns 18, you can't turn it on again.

- **Turn Parent/Guardian on or off.** This option appears when you've tapped an adult's name. It gives Ask To Buy approval privileges to someone else besides you—your spouse, for example.

Once kids turn 13, by the way, Apple automatically gives them more control over their own lives. They can, for example, turn off Ask To Buy themselves, on their own phones. They can even express their disgust for you by leaving the Family Sharing group. (On her own phone, for example, your daughter can visit Settings→iCloud→Family, tap her name, and then tap Leave Family. Harsh!)

Life in Family Sharing

Once everything's set up, here's how you and your nutty kids will get along.

- **Purchases.** Whenever one of your kids (for whom you've turned on Ask To Buy) tries to buy music, videos, apps, or books from Apple—even free items—he has to ask you (next page, left). On your phone, you're notified about the purchase—and you can decline it or tap Review to read about it on its Store page (next page, right). If it seems OK, you can tap Approve. You also have to enter your iCloud password, or supply your fingerprint, to prevent your kid from finding your phone and approving his own request.

  (If you don't respond within 24 hours, the request expires. Your kid has to ask again.)

  Furthermore, each of you can see and download everything that everyone else has bought. To do that, open the appropriate app: App

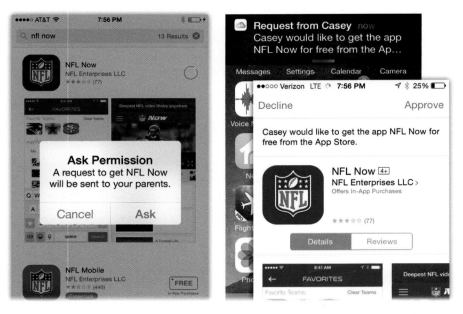

Store, iTunes Store, or iBooks. Tap Purchased, and then tap the family member's name, to see what she's got; tap the ☁ to download any of it yourself.

TIP: Anything you buy, your kids will see. Keep that in mind when you download a book like *Tough Love: Sending the Unruly Child to Military School*.

However, you have two lines of defense. First, you can hide your purchases so nobody sees them. On your computer, in iTunes (Chapter 14), click iTunes Store; then click the relevant category (♫, 📕, whatever). Click Purchased (right side). Point to the thing you want to hide, click the ✕, and click Hide. (On the phone, you can hide only one category: apps. In the App Store app, tap Updates, then Purchased, then My Purchases. Swipe to the left across an app's name to reveal a Hide button.)

Second, remember that you can set up parental control on each kid's phone, shielding their impressionable eyes from rated-R movies and stuff. See page 603.

- **Where are you?** Open the Find My Friends app to see where in town (or in the world) your posse is right now. Or go to the Find My iPhone app (or web page; see page 518) to see where their *phones* are right now, which may or may not be with their owners.

NOTE: If one of you needs secrecy for the afternoon (Apple sweetly gives, as an example, shopping for a gift for your spouse), open Settings→iCloud→Share My Location, and turn off the switch. Now you're untrackable until you turn the switch on again.

- **Photos, appointments, and reminders.** In Calendar, Photos, and Reminders, each of you will find a new category, called Family, that's auto-shared among you all. (In Photos, it's on the Shared tab.) You're all free to make and edit appointments in this calendar, to set up reminders in Reminders ("Flu shots after school!"), or to add photos or videos (or comments) to this album; everyone else will see the changes instantly.

16

Continuity: iPhone Meets Mac

Apple products have always been designed to work together. Macs, phones, tablets, watches: similar software, design, wording, philosophy. That's nice for you, of course, because you have less to learn and to troubleshoot. But it's also nice for Apple, because it keeps you in velvet handcuffs; pretty soon, you've got too much invested in its own product "ecosystem" to consider wandering over to a rival.

Apple has taken this gadget symbiosis to an astonishing new extreme. If your Mac is running Yosemite or El Capitan, it can be an *accessory* to your iPhone. Suddenly the Mac can be a speakerphone, using the iPhone as a wireless antenna. Suddenly the Mac can send and receive regular text messages. Suddenly AirDrop lets you drag files back and forth, wirelessly, from phone to computer. Suddenly a Mac laptop can get onto the Internet with one click, even miles from home.

Apple's name for this suite of symbiosis is "Continuity." And once you've got it set up, the Mac game changes in a big way.

Continuity Setup

For many people, all of this just works. For many others, there's a certain degree of setting up and troubleshooting. These are the primary rules:

- **You need a Mac running OS X Yosemite or later** and an iPhone running iOS 8.1 or later.

- **The Mac and the phone have to be signed into the same iCloud account.** (That's a security thing—it proves that you're the owner of both machines and therefore unlikely to pose a risk to yourself.) On the Mac, you do that in System Preferences→iCloud. On the phone, you do that in Settings→iCloud. But you should also make sure that you've entered the same iCloud address in Settings→Messages and Settings→FaceTime.

- **For some of these features, Bluetooth must be turned on.** On the Mac, you can do that in System Preferences→Bluetooth. On the phone, it's Settings→Bluetooth.

  The modern Bluetooth—called Bluetooth LE, or low energy—doesn't drain your battery the way it once did, so it's fine to leave it on. But older Macs don't have Bluetooth LE, so most Continuity features work only on 2012 and later Macs.

All right. Setup ready? Time to experience some integration!

Mac as Speakerphone

You can make and take phone calls on your Mac. The iPhone, sitting anywhere in your house, can be the cellular module for your Mac—even if that iPhone is asleep and locked.

When a call comes in to your iPhone's number, your *Mac* plays whatever ringtone your phone is playing. And a notice appears on your Mac screen:

You can click to answer it (or decline it); your Mac's microphone and speaker become your speakerphone.

You can *place* a call the same way. Just click any phone number you find on the Mac: in Contacts, in Safari, in an email message, and so on.

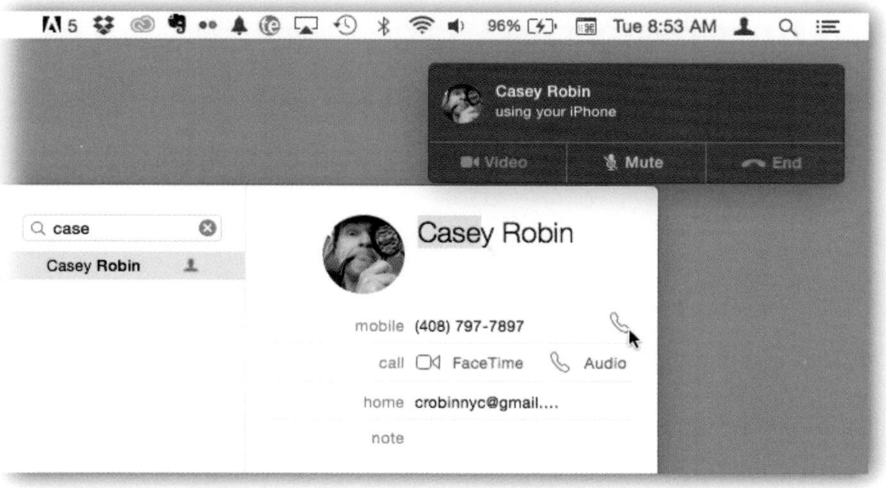

To make this work, Settings→Phone→Allow Calls on Other Devices must be turned on for each device you want to participate in this grand experiment. The iPhone and the Mac must be on the same Wi-Fi network, too.

NOTE: iOS 9 introduces a mind-blowing exception to that statement: Continuity over *cellular*. In this scenario, your Mac and iPhone *don't* have to be on the same Wi-Fi network! Even if you left your phone at home, you can still make calls and send texts from your Mac, wherever you are in the country!

This amazing feature requires participation by the cellular carrier, and so far, T-Mobile is the only company offering it. But still—how cool!

Once you've set things up as described, it just works. Even call-waiting works—if a second call comes in, your Mac notifies you and offers you the chance to put the first one on hold. And on the Mac, the Contacts app offers Ringtone and Texttone menus, so you can assign custom sounds that play when your *Mac* rings.

Crazy.

TIP: If you own a bunch of Apple machines, it might drive you crazy that they all now ring at once when a call comes in. Fortunately, you can turn off the ringing on each device that you'd rather be peaceful.

To make one of your iPhones, iPads, or iPod Touches stop ringing, turn off Settings→FaceTime→iPhone Cellular Calls. To make a Mac stop ringing, open the FaceTime program; choose FaceTime→Preferences→Settings, and turn off iPhone Cellular Calls.

Texting from the Mac

You can send and receive text messages (and picture, audio, and video messages) on your Mac, too.

We're not talking about sending texts to other **Apple** people (with iCloud accounts). Those are called iMessages, and they're a special, Apple-only kind of message. We're talking about something much better: You can type **any** cellphone number and send a regular SMS text message to **anyone**. Or receive them when they're sent to your iPhone number.

Or you can initiate the text conversation by clicking a phone number in Contacts, Calendar, or Safari to send an SMS message. Once again, your iPhone acts as a relay station between the cellular world and your Mac.

Here's how to set it up.

First, as usual, the Mac and the phone must be on the same Wi-Fi network and signed into the same iCloud account. (Or the same cellular network, if it's T-Mobile, as already described.)

Next, on the iPhone, open Settings→Messages. Tap Text Message Forwarding. Your Mac's name appears. Turn on the switch.

Now, on the Mac, open Messages. (Its icon is probably popping out of your Dock at this moment, trying to get your attention.) When you open Messages, a code appears. You're supposed to type it into the corresponding box on your phone:

This same code appears right now on any iPad or iPod Touch you own. They, too, will be able to send and receive texts, with your iPhone doing the relaying.

All of this is to prove, really and truly, that you're the owner of both devices. You wouldn't want some bad guy reading your text messages, would you?

That's it—your gadgets are paired. You can now use Messages to send standard text messages to *any* cellphone. You can also click and hold on a phone number wherever it appears—in Contacts, in a Spotlight search result, in Safari, in Mail—and choose Send Message from there. And when a text message comes in, a standard Mac notification bubble appears at top right.

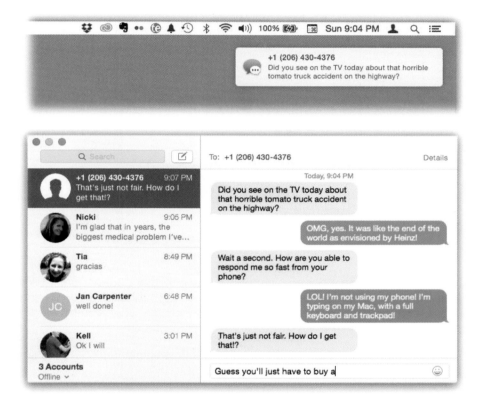

The beauty of all this is that your back-and-forths are kept in sync between the Mac and the phone. You can jump between them and continue the texting conversation. (You'll note that, as usual, the bubbles containing your utterances are green. Blue is reserved for iMessages—that is, messages to other people with iCloud accounts.)

Instant Hotspot

As you know from page 424, paying your cell carrier another $20 or so every month entitles you to use the iPhone's Personal Hotspot feature. That's where the phone itself acts as a portable Wi-Fi hotspot, so that your laptop (or any other gadgets) can get online almost anywhere.

As you also know from page 424, it's kind of a pain to get going. Each time you want your laptop to get online, you have to wake your iPhone, unlock it, open Settings, and turn on Personal Hotspot. Then you wait about 20 seconds, until the phone's name shows up in your 📶 menu.

Not anymore.

Now, the phone can stay in your pocket. Its name appears in your 📶 menu, ready for choosing at any time—even if the phone is asleep and locked, and even if Personal Hotspot is turned off! Handily enough, the 📶 menu also shows the phone's battery and signal status.

Once your Mac is online through your iPhone's cellular connection, it tries to save you money by suspending data-intensive jobs like full backups and software updates. And it closes down the connection when you no longer need it, to save your iPhone's battery.

As usual, this works only if the iPhone and Mac both have Bluetooth turned on and are signed into the same iCloud account.

Handoff

Handoff is a new feature that passes half-finished documents between the phone and the Mac, wirelessly and automatically.

For example, suppose you've been writing an email message on your iPhone (facing page, top). When you arrive home and sit down at the Mac, a new icon appears at the left end of the Mac's Dock (middle). When you click it, the Mac's Mail program opens, and the half-finished message is there for you to complete (bottom).

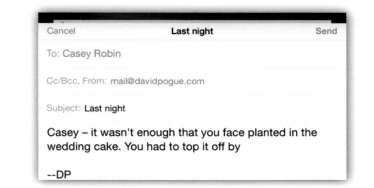

It doesn't have to be an email message, either. If you were reading a web page or a Map on your phone, then that icon on the Mac opens the same web page or map. If you were working on a Reminder; a Calendar entry; a Contacts entry; a note in Notes; or a document in Keynote, Numbers, or Pages; you can open the same in-progress item on the Mac.

And all of it works in the other direction, too. If you're working on something on the Mac, but you're called away, an icon appears on the lower-left corner of your iPhone's Lock screen that opens the same item (below, left).

TIP: There's another way to find the Handoff icon that nobody ever mentions: It's in the app switcher on both devices. On the phone, for example, double-press the Home button—and notice the new strip at the bottom, identifying the document you're handing off from the Mac (below, right). On the Mac, press ⌘-Tab to open the app switcher; there, too, is the icon for the app being handed off from the phone.

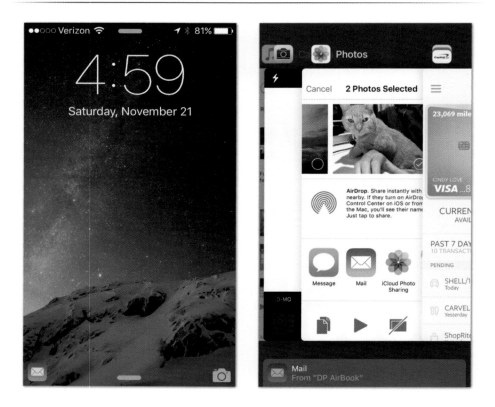

Here's the setup: Once again, both gadgets must be signed into your iCloud account. Both must have Bluetooth turned on, and the Mac and phone have to be sitting within Bluetooth range of each other (about 30 feet).

On the Mac, open System Preferences→General; turn on Allow Handoff between this Mac and your iCloud devices.

On the iPhone, the on/off switch is in Settings→General→Handoff & Suggested Apps.

Now try it out. Start an email message on your iPhone. Have a look at the Dock on your Mac: There, at the left end, pops the little icon of whatever program can finish the job.

Watch for the little lower-left icon on your screens to make it work.

AirDrop

AirDrop is pretty great. As described on page 331, it lets you shoot photos, videos, maps, Contacts cards, PDF files, Word documents, and all kinds of other stuff from one iPhone to another iPhone. Wirelessly. Without having to set up names, passwords, or permissions. Without even having an Internet connection.

What page 331 didn't cover, though, was how you can use AirDrop *between* a phone and a Mac.

From iPhone to Mac

Open whatever it is you want to send to the Mac: a photo, map, website, contact...anything with a ⬆ button.

When you tap the Share button, you see the AirDrop panel—and, after a moment, the icons of any nearby Macs show up, too. Including yours (below, left).

If the Mac's icon *doesn't* show up, it's probably because its owner hasn't made the Mac discoverable by AirDrop.

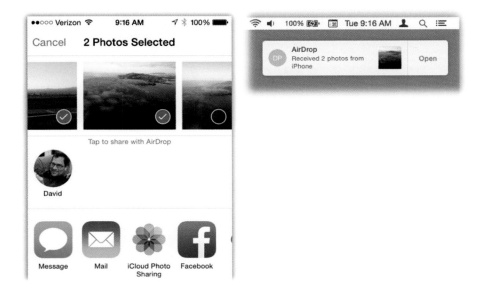

Instruct him to open the AirDrop *window* on his Mac. (Click AirDrop in the sidebar of any Finder window.) See the small blue control at the bottom? It governs who can "see" this Mac for AirDrop purposes: No One, Contacts Only (that is, people in the Mac's address book), or Everyone.

Once that's set up right, that Mac shows up in the iPhone's AirDrop panel ("David" in the picture on the previous page). Send away. (Unlike the AirDrop of Macs gone by, in Yosemite and El Capitan, you don't have to start by opening the AirDrop *window*.)

The receiving Mac displays a note like the one shown on the previous page at right.

Click Accept to download the incoming item to your Mac's Downloads folder (or Decline to reject it).

TIP: If the phone and the Mac are both signed into the same iCloud account, then you don't encounter that Accept/Decline thing. The file goes directly into your Downloads folder without asking. You do get a notification on the Mac that lets you know how many files arrived, and it offers an Open button.

Apple figures that, since you own both the phone and the Mac, the usual permission routine isn't necessary. You're probably not trying to send yourself some evil virus of death.

17

The Corporate iPhone

In its younger days, people thought of the iPhone as a *personal* device, meant for consumers and not for corporations. But somebody at Apple must have gotten sick of hearing, "Well, the iPhone is cool, but it's no BlackBerry." The iPhone now has the security and compatibility features your corporate technical overlords require. (And the BlackBerry—well...)

Even better, the iPhone can talk to Microsoft Exchange ActiveSync servers, staples of corporate computer departments that, among other things, keep smartphones wirelessly updated with the calendar, contacts, and email back at the office. (Yes, it sounds a lot like MobileMe or iCloud. Which is probably why Apple's MobileMe slogan was, "Exchange for the rest of us.")

The Perks

This chapter is intended for you, the iPhone owner—not for the highly paid, well-trained, exceedingly friendly IT (information technology) managers at your company.

Your first task is to convince them that your iPhone is now secure and compatible enough to welcome into the company's network. Here's some information you can use:

- **Microsoft Exchange ActiveSync.** Exchange ActiveSync is the technology that keeps smartphones wirelessly synced with the data on the mother ship's computers. The iPhone works with Exchange ActiveSync, so it can remain in wireless contact with your company's Exchange servers exactly like BlackBerry and Windows Mobile phones do.

  Your email, address book, and calendar appointments are now sent wirelessly to your iPhone so it's always kept current—and they're sent in a way that those evil rival firms can't intercept. (It uses 128-bit en-crypted SSL, if you must know.)

• **Mass setup.** These days, iPhones may wind up in corporations in two ways: They're either handed out by the company, or you bring your own. (When employees use their own phones for work, they call it BYOD: "Bring your own device.")

Most companies set up employee iPhones using mobile device man-agement (MDM) software. That's a program (for sale by lots of differ-ent security companies) that gives your administrators control over a huge range of corporate apps, settings, and restrictions: all Wi-Fi, network, password, email, and VPN settings; policies about what features and apps you can use, and so on; and the ability to remote-ly erase or lock your phone if it gets lost. Yet MDM programs don't touch the stuff that *you* install on your own. If you leave the company, your old employer can delete all of its own stuff, while preserving your own personal stuff.

• **Security.** The iPhone can connect to wireless networks using the latest, super-secure connections (WPA Enterprise and WPA2 Enterprise), which are highly resistant to hacker attacks. And when you're using virtual private networking, as described at the end of this chapter, you can use a very secure VPN protocol called IPsec. That's what most companies use for secure, encrypted remote access to the corporate network. Juniper and Cisco VPN apps are available, too.

Speaking of security: Whenever your phone is locked, iOS 9 automat-ically encrypts all email, email attachments, Calendar, Contacts, Notes, Reminders, and the data of any other apps that are written to take advantage of this feature.

• **iOS improvements.** You can encrypt individual email messages to people in your company (and, with some effort, to people outside your company; see *http://support.apple.com/kb/HT4979*). When you're setting up a meeting, you can see your coworkers' schedules in the Calendar app. You can set up an automatic "Out of office" reply that's in force until a certain date. (It's in Settings→Mail, Contacts, Calendars. Tap your Exchange account's name and scroll down to Automatic Reply.) Lots more control for your IT overlords, too.

And what's in it for you? Complete synchronization of your email, address book, and calendar with what's on your PC at work. Send an email from your iPhone; find it in the Sent folder of Outlook at the office. And so on.

You can also accept invitations to meetings on your iPhone that are sent your way by coworkers; if you accept, these meetings appear on your calendar automatically, just as on your PC. You can also search the company's master address book, right from your iPhone.

The biggest perk for you, though, is just getting permission to *use* an iPhone as your company-issued phone.

Setup

Your company's IT squad can set up things on their end by consulting Apple's free, downloadable setup guide: the infamous *iPhone OS Enterprise Deployment Guide*.

This guide is filled with handy tips, like: "On the Front-End Server, verify that a server certificate is installed and enable SSL for the Exchange ActiveSync virtual directory (require basic SSL authentication)."

In any case, you (or they) can download the deployment guide from this site: *www.apple.com/support/iphone/business*.

Your IT pros might send you a link that downloads a *profile*—a preconfigured file that auto–sets up all your company's security and login information. It will create the Exchange account for you (and might turn off a few iPhone features, like the ability to switch off the passcode requirement).

If, on the other hand, you're supposed to set up your Exchange account yourself, then tap Settings→Mail, Contacts, Calendars→Add Account→ Exchange. Fill in your work email address and password as they were provided to you by your company's IT person.

And that's it. Your iPhone will shortly bloom with the familiar sight of your office email stash, calendar appointments, and contacts.

Life on the Corporate Network

Once your iPhone is set up, you should be in wireless corporate heaven:

- **Email.** Your corporate email account shows up among whatever other email accounts you've set up (Chapter 13). In fact, you can have *multiple* Exchange accounts on the same phone.

  Not only is your email "pushed" to the phone (it arrives as it's sent, without your having to explicitly check for messages), but it's also synced with what you see on your computer at work. If you send, receive, delete, flag, or file any messages on your iPhone, you'll find them sent, received, deleted, flagged, or filed on your computer at the office. And vice versa.

All the email niceties described in Chapter 13 are available to your corporate mail: opening attachments, rotating and zooming them, and so on. Your iPhone can even play back your office voicemail, presuming that your company has one of those unified messaging systems that send out WAV audio file versions of your messages via email.

Oh—and when you're addressing an outgoing message, the iPhone's autocomplete feature consults both your built-in iPhone address book *and* the corporate directory (on the Exchange server) simultaneously.

> **TIP:** Your phone can warn you when you're addressing an email to somebody outside your company (a security risk, and something that sometimes arises from autocomplete accidents).
>
> To turn on this feature, open Settings→Mail, Contacts, Calendars. Scroll down; tap Mark Addresses. Type in your company's email suffix (like *yourcompany.com*). From now on, whenever you address an outgoing message to someone outside *yourcompany.com*, it appears in red in the "To:" line to catch your eye.

- **Contacts.** In the address book, you gain a new superpower: You can search your company's master name directory right from the iPhone.

That's great when you need to track down, say, the art director in your Singapore branch.

To perform this search, open the Contacts app. Tap the Groups button in the upper-left corner. On the Groups screen, your company's name appears; it may contain some group names of its own. But below these, a new entry appears that mere mortal iPhone owners never see. It might say something like Directory or Global Address Book. Tap it.

On the following screen, start typing the name of the person you're looking up; the resulting matches appear as you type. (Or type the whole name and then tap Search.)

In the list of results, tap the name you want. That person's Info screen appears so you can tap to dial a number or compose a preaddressed email message. (You can't send a text message to someone in the corporate phone book, however.)

• **Calendar.** Your iPhone's calendar is wirelessly kept in sync with the master calendar back at the office. If you're on the road and your minions make changes to your schedule in Outlook, you'll know about it; you'll see the change on your iPhone's calendar.

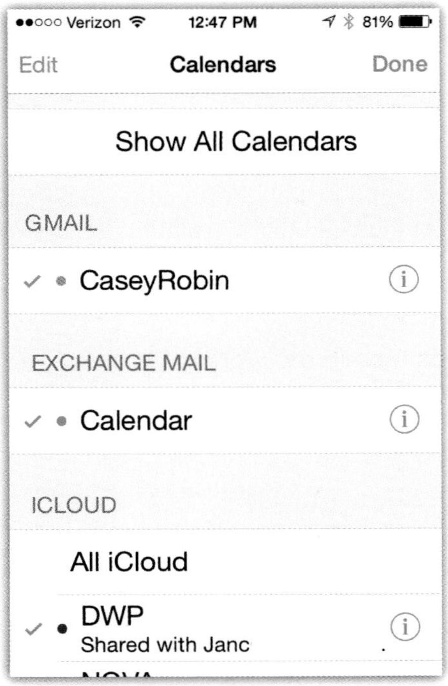

There are some other changes to your calendar, too, as you'll find out in a moment.

TIP: Don't forget that you can save battery power, syncing time, and mental clutter by limiting how much *old* calendar stuff gets synced to your iPhone. (How often do you really look back on your calendar to see what happened more than a month ago?) Page 579 has the details.

- **Notes.** If your company uses Exchange 2010 or later, then your notes are synced with Outlook on your Mac or PC, too.

Exchange + Your Stuff

The iPhone can display calendar and contact information from multiple sources at once—your Exchange calendar/address book and your own personal data, for example.

Here's how it works: Open your iPhone calendar. Tap Calendars. Now you're looking at all the accounts your phone knows about; you might find separate headings for iCloud, Yahoo, Gmail, and so on, each with calendar categories listed under it. And one of them is your Exchange account.

You can pull off a similar stunt in Contacts, Notes, and Reminders. Whenever you're looking at your list of contacts, for example, you can tap the Groups button (top left of the screen). Here, once again, you can tap All Contacts to see a combined address book—or you can look over only your iCloud contacts, your Exchange contacts, your personal contacts, and so on. Or tap [group name] to view only the people in your tennis circle, book club, or whatever (if you've created groups); or [your Exchange account name] to search only the company listings.

Invitations

If you've spent much time in the world of Microsoft Outlook (that is, corporate America), then you already know about *invitations*. These are electronic invitations that coworkers send you directly from Outlook. When you get one of these invitations by email, you can click Accept, Decline, or Maybe.

If you click Accept, then the meeting gets dropped onto the proper date in your Outlook calendar, and your name gets added to the list of attendees maintained by the person who invited you. If you click Maybe, then the meeting is flagged *that* way, on both your calendar and the sender's.

Exchange meeting invitations on the iPhone show up in *four places*, just to make sure you don't miss them. You get a standard iPhone notification,

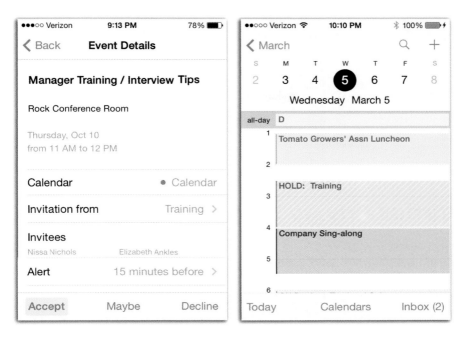

a numbered "badge" on the Calendar app's icon on the Home screen, as an attachment to a message in your corporate email account, and in the Calendar app—tap Inbox at the lower-right corner. Tapping Inbox shows the Invitations list, which summarizes all invitations you've accepted, maybe'd, or not responded to yet. Tap one to see the details (above, left).

> **TIP:** Invitations you haven't dealt with also show up on the Calendar's List view or Day view with dotted shading (above, right). That's the iPhone's clever visual way of showing you just how severely your workday will be ruined if you accept this meeting.

You can also **generate** invitations. When you're filling out the Info form for a new appointment, you get a field called Invitees. Tap there to enter the email addresses of the people you'd like to invite.

Your invitation will show up in whatever calendar programs your invitees use, and they'll never know you didn't send it from some corporate copy of Microsoft Outlook.

A Word on Troubleshooting

If you're having trouble with your Exchange syncing and can't find any steps that work, then ask your Exchange administrators to make sure that ActiveSync's settings are correct on their end. You've heard the old saying that in 99 percent of computer troubleshooting, the problem lies between the keyboard and the chair? The other 1 percent of the time, it's between the *administrator's* keyboard and chair.

Virtual Private Networking (VPN)

The typical corporate network is guarded by a team of steely-eyed administrators for whom Job One is preventing access by unauthorized visitors. They perform this job primarily with the aid of a super-secure firewall that seals off the company's network from the Internet.

So how can you tap into the network from the road? Only one solution is both secure and cheap: the *virtual private network*, or VPN. Running a VPN lets you create a super-secure "tunnel" from your iPhone, across the Internet, and straight into your corporate network. All data passing through this tunnel is heavily encrypted. To the Internet eavesdropper, it looks like so much undecipherable gobbledygook.

VPN is, however, a corporate tool, run by corporate nerds. Your company's tech staff can tell you whether or not there's a VPN server set up for you to use.

If there is one, then you'll need to know what type of server it is. The iPhone can connect to VPN servers that speak *PPTP* (Point-to-Point Tunneling Protocol) and *L2TP/IPsec* (Layer 2 Tunneling Protocol over the IP Security Protocol), both relatives of the PPP language spoken by modems. Most corporate VPN servers work with at least one of these protocols.

The iPhone can also connect to Cisco servers, which are among the most popular systems in corporate America, and, with a special app, Juniper's Junos Pulse servers, too.

To set up your VPN connection, visit Settings→General→VPN.

Here you may see that your overlords have already set up some VPN connections; tap the one you want to use. You can also set one up yourself, by tapping Add VPN Configuration at the bottom.

Tap Type to specify which kind of server your company uses: IKEv2, IPsec, L2TP, or PPTP (ask the network administrator). Fill in the Server address,

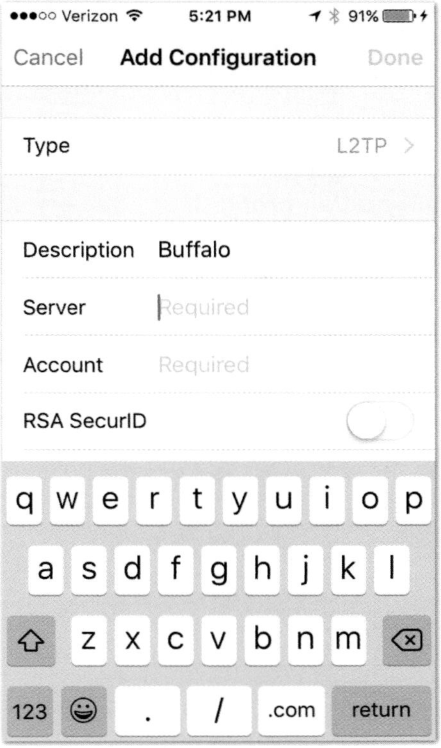

●●●○○ Verizon 🔋   5:21 PM   ◀ ✳ 91% ▭ ✦

Cancel   **Add Configuration**   Done

Type   L2TP >

Description   Buffalo

Server   Required

Account   Required

RSA SecurID

the account name and password, and whatever else your system administrators tell you to fill in here.

Once everything is in place, the iPhone can connect to the corporate network and fetch your corporate mail. You don't have to do anything special
on your end; everything works just as described in this chapter.

> **NOTE:** Some networks require that you type the currently displayed
> password on an *RSA SecurID token*, which your administrator
> will provide. This James Bondish thing looks like either a credit
> card or a USB drive. It displays a password that changes every
> few seconds, making it rather difficult for hackers to learn "the"
> password.

VPN on Demand

If you like to access your corporate email or internal website a few times
a day, having to enter your name-and-password credentials over and over
again can get old fast. Fortunately, iOS offers a huge timesaving assist
with *VPN on Demand*.

That is, you just open up Safari and tap the corporate bookmark; the iPhone creates the VPN channel automatically, behind the scenes, and connects.

There's nothing you have to do, or even anything you *can* do, to make this feature work; your company's network nerds have to turn this feature on at their end.

They'll create a *configuration profile* that you'll install on your iPhone. It includes the VPN server settings, an electronic security certificate, and a list of domains and URLs that will automatically turn on the iPhone's VPN feature.

When your iPhone goes to sleep, it terminates the VPN connection, both for security purposes and to save battery power.

NOTE: Clearly, eliminating the VPN sign-in process also weakens the security the VPN was invented for in the first place. Therefore, you'd be well advised—and probably required by your IT guys—to use the iPhone's password or fingerprint feature, so some evil corporate spy (or teenage thug) can't just steal your iPhone and start snooping through the corporate servers.

18

Settings

The Settings app is like the Control Panel in Windows or System Preferences on the Mac. It houses hundreds of settings for every aspect of the iPhone and its apps.

Almost everything in the list of Settings is a doorway to another screen, where you make the actual changes.

TIP: Big news: Settings in iOS 9 now has a search box at the top! You no longer have to have a photographic memory (or this chapter) to find which screen holds a certain setting you're looking for.

In this book, you can read about the iPhone's preference settings in the appropriate spots—wherever they're relevant. And the Control Center, of course, is designed to *eliminate* trips into Settings.

But so you'll have it all in one place, here's an item-by-item walkthrough of the Settings app and its structure in iOS 9.

Two Important Settings Tricks

The Settings app is many screens deep. You might "drill down" by tapping, for example, General, then Keyboard, then Text Replacement. It's a lot of tapping, a lot of navigation.

Fortunately, you have two kinds of shortcuts.

First, you can jump directly to a particular Settings screen—from within any app—using Siri (Chapter 4). You can say, for example, "Open Sound settings," "Open Brightness settings," "Open Notification settings," "Open Wi-Fi settings," and so on. Siri promptly takes you to the corresponding screen—no tapping required.

Second, you can *swipe to go back*. Once you've drilled down to, say, General→Keyboard→Text Replacement, you can "drill out" again by swiping across the screen to the right. (Start from the *edge* of the screen.)

Swipe to go back

Airplane Mode

As you're probably aware, you're not allowed to make cellphone calls on U.S. airplanes. According to legend (if not science), a cellphone's radio can interfere with a plane's navigation equipment.

But the iPhone does a lot more than make calls. Are you supposed to deprive yourself of all the music, videos, movies, and email that you could be using in flight, just because calling is forbidden?

Nope. Just turn on airplane mode by tapping the switch at the top of the Settings list (so the switch background turns green). The word Cellular dims there in Settings (you've turned off your cellular circuitry); but the Wi-Fi and Bluetooth switches are still available, though turned off—meaning that you're now welcome to switch them back *on*, even in airplane mode.

Now it's safe (and permitted) to use the iPhone in flight, even with Wi-Fi on, because its cellular features are turned off completely. You can't make calls, but you can do anything else in the iPhone's bag of tricks.

TIP: Turning airplane mode on and off is faster if you use the Control Center (page 47). Same for Wi-Fi, described next.

Wi-Fi

This item in Settings opens the Wi-Fi Networks screen, where you'll find three useful controls:

- **Wi-Fi On/Off.** If you don't plan to use Wi-Fi, then turning it off gets you a lot more life out of each battery charge. Tap anywhere on this On/Off slider to change its status.

TIP: Turning on airplane mode automatically turns off the Wi-Fi antenna—but you can turn Wi-Fi back on. That's handy when you're on a flight with Wi-Fi on board.

- **Choose a Network.** Here's a list of all nearby Wi-Fi networks that the iPhone can "see," complete with a signal-strength indicator and a padlock icon if a password is required. An Other item lets you access Wi-Fi networks that are invisible and secret unless you know their names. See page 419 for details on using Wi-Fi with the iPhone.

• **Ask to Join Networks.** If this option is On, then the iPhone is continuously sniffing around to find a Wi-Fi network. If it finds one you
haven't used before, a small dialog box invites you to hop onto it.

So why would you ever want to turn this feature off? To avoid getting bombarded with invitations to join Wi-Fi networks—which can
happen in heavily populated areas—and to save battery power. (The
phone will still hop onto hotspots it's joined in the past, and you can
still view a list of available hotspots by opening Settings→Wi-Fi.)

Carrier

If you see this panel at all, you're doubly lucky: First, you're enjoying a trip
overseas; second, you have a choice of cellphone carriers who have roaming agreements with AT&T, Verizon, T-Mobile, or Sprint. Tap your favorite
and prepare to pay some serious roaming fees.

Bluetooth

Here's the on/off switch for the iPhone's Bluetooth transmitter, which is
required to communicate with a Bluetooth fitness band, earpiece, key-

board, or hands-free system in a car. When you turn the switch on, you're offered the chance to pair the iPhone with other Bluetooth equipment; the paired gadgets are listed here for ease of connecting and disconnecting.

TIP: The Control Center (page 47) has a Bluetooth button. It's faster to use that than to visit Settings.

Cellular

These days, not many cellphone plans let you use the Internet as much as you want; most have monthly limits. For example, your $120 a month might include 4 gigabytes of Internet data use.

Most of the settings on this screen are meant to help you control how much Internet data your phone uses.

- **Cellular Data.** This is the on/off switch for Internet data. If you're traveling overseas, you might want to turn this off to avoid racking up insanely high roaming charges. Your smartphone becomes a dumb-phone, suitable for making calls but not for getting online. (You can still get online in Wi-Fi hotspots.)

- **Enable LTE.** Here you can turn off LTE—just for voice calls, or for both voice and data. Every now and then, you'll be in some area where you can't connect to the Internet even though you seem to have an LTE signal; forcing your phone to the 4G or 3G network often gives you at least some connection. Turning LTE off does just that.

- **Roaming.** These controls can prevent staggering international roaming fees. On AT&T or T-Mobile, you can turn off Data Roaming (when you're out of the country, you won't get slapped with outrageous Internet fees). On Verizon and Sprint, you have separate controls for Data Roaming and Voice Roaming. Turning off the last item, International CDMA, forces the phone to use only the more common GSM networks while roaming; sometimes you get better call and data quality that way, and you may save money.

- **Personal Hotspot.** Here's the setup and On/Off screen for Personal Hotspot (page 424). Once you've turned it on, a new Personal Hotspot on/off switch appears on the main Settings screen, so you won't have to dig this deep in the future.

- **SIM PIN.** Features like Touch ID fingerprint recognition and passwords can protect your phone. But what's to stop some jerk from stealing your SIM card (page 27), slipping it into his own phone, and happily making calls and using data on your bill?

This new iOS 9 setting, that's what. It lets you make up a passcode that's required anytime the SIM card is moved to a new phone or anytime your iPhone is restarted.

The first step, though, is to enter the card's *existing* PIN: 1111 for AT&T or Verizon, 1234 for Sprint or T-Mobile. Now you can make up a new PIN of your own (up to eight characters). Don't forget it—if you enter the wrong number too many times, the iPhone locks your SIM card permanently, and you'll have to ask your carrier to supply a new one.

- **Call Time.** The statistics here break down how much time you've spent talking on the iPhone, both in the Current Period (that is, this billing month) and in the iPhone's entire Lifetime. That's right, folks: You now own a cellphone that keeps track of your minutes, to help you avoid exceeding the number you've signed up for (and therefore racking up 45-cent overage minutes).

- **Cellular Data Usage.** The phone also tracks how much Internet data you've used this month, expressed as megabytes of data, including email messages and web page material. These are extremely important statistics, because your iPhone plan is probably capped at, for example, 2 gigabytes a month. If you exceed your monthly maximum, you're instantly charged $15 or $20 for another chunk of data. So keeping an eye on these statistics is a very good idea.

(The Current Period means so far this month; Current Period Roaming means overseas or in places where your cell company doesn't have service.)

Now, your cellphone company is supposed to text you as you get closer and closer to your monthly limit, too, but you can check your Internet spending at any time.

- **Use cellular data for:** This list offers individual on/off switches for every single Internet-using app on your phone. Each one is an item that could consume Internet data without your awareness. Now, at last, you can shut up the data hogs you really don't feel like spending megabytes on.

- **Wi-Fi Assist.** Thousands of iPhone fans know about the old Flaky Wi-Fi Trick. If the phone is struggling and struggling to load a web page or download an email message on a Wi-Fi network, it often helps to *turn off Wi-Fi*. The phone hops over to the cellular network, where it's usually got a better connection.

  That's why, in iOS 9, Apple offers Wi-Fi Assist: a feature that does all that automatically. If the phone is having trouble with its Wi-Fi connection, it hops over to cellular data all by itself. (You'll know when that's happened by the appearance of the cellular-network indicator on your status bar, like **4G**, or **LTE**, instead of the 📶 Wi-Fi symbol.)

  If you're worried about this feature eating up your data allowance, you can, of course, turn Wi-Fi Assist off. Apple notes, however, that Wi-Fi Assist doesn't kick in (a) when you're data roaming, (b) for background apps (it only helps the app that's in front), or (c) if large amounts of data would be consumed. For example, it doesn't kick in for audio or video streaming or email attachments.

- **Reset Statistics** resets the Call Time and Data Usage counters to zero.

Personal Hotspot

Once you've turned this feature on (page 424) in Cellular, this command appears here, too—on the main Settings screen for your convenience.

Notifications

This panel lists all the apps that think they have the right to nag for your attention. Flight-tracking programs alert you that there's an hour before takeoff. Social-networking programs ping you when someone's trying to reach you. Games let you know when it's your move. Instant-messaging apps ding to let you know that you have a new message. It can add up to a lot of interruption.

On this panel, you can tailor, to an almost ridiculous degree, how you want to be nagged. See page 51 for a complete description.

Control Center

The Control Center is written up on page 47. There are two settings to change here. If you turn off Access on Lock Screen, then the Control Center isn't available on the phone's Lock screen. No passing prankster can change your phone's settings without your password.

And if you turn off Access Within Apps, you won't land in the Control Center by accident when you're playing some game that involves a lot of swiping.

Do Not Disturb

Here it is: one of iOS's most brilliant and useful features. See page 116.

General

The General pages offer a *huge*, motley assortment of settings governing the behavior of the virtual keyboard, Siri, the password-protection feature, and about 6 trillion other things (facing page, left).

- **About.** Tapping this item opens a page for the statistics nut. Here you can find out how many songs, videos, and photos your iPhone holds; how much storage your iPhone has; techie details like the iPhone's software and firmware versions, serial number, model, Wi-Fi and Bluetooth addresses, and so on. (It's kind of cool to see how many apps you've installed.)

  At the very top, you can tap the phone's name to rename it.

- **Software Update.** When Apple releases a new software update for your iPhone, you can download it directly to the phone.

  You'll know when an update is waiting for you, because you'll see a little number badge on the Settings icon, as well as on the word "General" in Settings. Tap it, and then tap Software Update, to see and install the update (facing page, right). (If no number badge is wait-

‹ Settings　General

About　〉

Software Update　〉

Siri　〉

Spotlight Search　〉

Handoff & Suggested Apps　〉

CarPlay　〉

‹ General　Software Update

iOS 9.1
Apple Inc.
31 MB

This release includes new features, improvements and bug fixes, including:

- Live Photos now intelligently senses when you raise or lower your iPhone, so that Live Photos will automatically not record these movements
- Over 150 new emoji characters with full support for Unicode 7.0 and 8.0 emojis

Learn More　〉

Download and Install

ing, then tapping Software Update just shows you your current iOS version.)

- **Siri.** Here's Siri Central. It's the master on/off switch for Siri, and the on/off switch for the hands-free "Hey Siri" feature. Both are described in Chapter 4.

  Also on this panel: a choice of languages; a choice of speaking voice (including both male and female voices—and a choice of accents, like American, British, or Australian); an option to have Siri's responses read aloud only when you're on headset (so you don't disturb those around you); and an option to choose your own Contacts card, so Siri knows, for example, where to go when you say, "Give me directions home."

- **Spotlight Search.** Here you can turn off iOS 9's new Siri Suggestions screen (page 93). And you can control which kinds of things Spotlight finds when it searches your phone. Tap to turn off the kinds of data you don't want it to search: Mail, Notes, Calendar, whatever.

- **Handoff & Suggested Apps.** Handoff is for people who own both a Mac and an iPhone; it automatically passes half-finished documents between them when you come home, as described on page 540. This is the on/off switch.

  The Suggested Apps feature really has no business being on the same screen—it's unrelated. It's the feature that displays the faint icon of an app that might be useful right now, based on where you are (an airline's app when you're in the airport, for example). Here you can turn that feature off.

- **CarPlay.** Certain new car models come equipped with a technology called CarPlay, which displays a few of your iPhone's icons—Phone, Music, Maps, Messages, Music, Podcasts, and Audiobooks—on the car's dashboard touchscreen. The idea is to make them big and simple and limited to things you'll need while you're driving, to avoid distracting you. Here's where you connect your phone to your CarPlay system.

- **Accessibility.** These options are intended for people with visual, hearing, and motor impairments, but they might come in handy now and then for almost anyone. All these features are described in Chapter 6.

- **Storage & iCloud Usage.** This screen is proof that the iPhone is an obsessive-compulsive. You find out here that it knows everything about you, your apps, and your iPhone activity.

  The Storage section shows how much of your phone's storage space is currently used and free. Tap Manage Storage to see a list of every single app on your iPhone, along with how much space it's eating up. (Biggest apps are at the top.) Better yet, you can tap an app to see how much it and its associated documents consume—and, for apps you've installed yourself, there's a Delete App button staring you in the face.

  The idea, of course, is that if you're running out of space on your iPhone, this display makes it incredibly easy to see what the space hogs are—and delete them.

  The next section, iCloud, also reports on storage—but in this case, it shows you how much storage you're using on your iCloud account. (Remember, you get 5 gigabytes free; after that, you have to pay.) If you tap Manage Storage, you get to see how much of that space is used up by which apps—Mail is usually one of the biggest offenders.

- **Background App Refresh.** The list that appears here identifies apps that try to access the Internet to update themselves, even when they're in the background. Since such apps can drain your battery, you have the option here to block their background updating.

  You can also turn off the master Background App Refresh switch. Now the only apps that can get online in the background are a standard limited suite (music playback and GPS, for example).

- **Auto-Lock.** As you may have noticed, the iPhone locks itself (goes to sleep) after a few minutes of inactivity on your part, to save battery power and prevent accidental screen taps in your pocket.

On the Auto-Lock screen, you can change the interval of inactivity before the auto-lock occurs (1 minute, 2 minutes, and so on), or you can tap Never. In that case, the iPhone locks only when you click it to sleep.

- **Restrictions.** This means "parental controls." (Apple called it "Restrictions" instead so as not to turn off potential corporate customers. Can't you just hear it? " 'Parental controls?' This thing is for *consumers?!*") Complete details appear on page 603.

- **Date & Time.** Here you can turn on 24-hour time, also known as military time, in which you see "1700" instead of "5:00 PM." (You'll see this change everywhere times appear, including at the top of the screen.)

  Set Automatically refers to the iPhone's built-in clock. If this item is turned on, then the iPhone finds out what time it is from an atomic clock out on the Internet. If not, then you have to set the clock yourself. (Turning this option off produces two more rows of controls: The Time Zone option becomes available, so you can specify your time zone, and a "number spinner" appears so you can set the clock.)

- **Keyboard.** Here you can turn off some of the very best features of the iPhone's virtual keyboard. (All these shortcuts are described in Chapter 2.)

  It's hard to imagine why you wouldn't want any of these tools working for you and saving you time and keystrokes, but here you go: Auto-Capitalization is where the iPhone thoughtfully capitalizes the first letter of every new sentence for you. Auto-Correction is where the iPhone suggests spelling corrections as you type. Check Spelling, of course, refers to the pop-up spelling suggestions. Enable Caps Lock is the on/off switch for the Caps Lock feature, in which a fast double-tap on the Shift key turns on Caps Lock.

  Predictive refers to QuickType, the row of three word candidates that appears above the keyboard when you're typing. Character Preview is the little bubble that pops up, showing the letter, when you tap a key. The "." Shortcut switch turns on or off the "type two spaces to make a period" shortcut for the ends of sentences, and Enable Dictation is the on/off switch for the ability to dictate text. (If you never use dictation, turning this switch off hides the 🎤 button on the keyboard, giving the space bar more room to breathe.)

- **Language & Region.** The iPhone: It's not just for Americans anymore. The iPhone Language screen lets you choose a language for the iPhone's menus and messages. Region Format controls how the iPhone displays dates, times, and numbers. (For example, in the U.S., Christmas is on 12/25; in Europe, it's 25/12.)

Calendar lets you choose which kind of calendar system you want to use: Gregorian (that is, "normal"), Japanese, or Buddhist. Finally, the Advanced screen lets you turn *off* the automatic setting of date, time, and number languages to match your main iPhone language. You know—for people who want their dates, times, and numbers in a different language.

- **iTunes Wi-Fi Sync.** You can sync your iPhone with a computer wirelessly, as long as the phone is plugged in and on Wi-Fi. Details are on page 498.

- **VPN.** See page 552 for details on virtual private networking.

- **Device Management**. This item shows up only if your company issued you this phone. It shows what *profile* the system administrators have installed on it—the set of restrictions that govern what you're allowed to change without the company's permission.

- **Regulatory.** A bunch of legal logos you don't care about.

- **Reset.** On the all-powerful Reset screen, you'll find six ways to erase your phone.

  Reset All Settings takes all the iPhone's settings back to the way they were when it came from Apple. Your data, music, and videos remain in place, but the settings all go back to their factory settings.

  Erase All Content and Settings is the one you want when you sell your iPhone, or when you're captured by the enemy and want to make sure they will learn nothing from you or your phone.

> **NOTE:** This feature takes awhile to complete—and that's a good thing. The iPhone doesn't just delete your data; it also overwrites the newly erased memory with gibberish to make sure the bad guys can't see any of your deleted info, even with special hacking tools.

  Reset Network Settings makes the iPhone forget all the memorized Wi-Fi networks it currently autorecognizes.

  Reset Keyboard Dictionary has to do with the iPhone's autocorrection feature, which kicks in whenever you're trying to input text. Ordinarily, every time you type something the iPhone doesn't recognize—some name or foreign word, for example—and you don't accept the iPhone's suggestion, it adds the word you typed to its dictionary so it doesn't bother you with a suggestion again the next time. If you think you've entered too many words that aren't legitimate terms, you can delete from its little brain all the new "words" you've taught it.

Reset Home Screen Layout undoes any icon moving you've done on the Home screen. It also consolidates all your Home screen icons, fitting them onto as few screens as possible.

Finally, Reset Location & Privacy refers to the "OK to use location services?" warning that appears whenever an iPhone program, like Maps or Camera, tries to figure out where you are. This button makes the iPhone forget all your responses to those permission boxes. In other words, you'll be asked for permission all over again the next time you use each of those programs.

Display & Brightness

Ordinarily, the iPhone controls its own screen brightness. An ambient-light sensor hidden behind the glass at the top of the iPhone's face samples the room brightness each time you wake the phone and adjusts the screen: brighter in bright rooms, dimmer in darker ones.

When you prefer more manual control, here's what you can do:

- **Brightness slider.** Drag the handle on this slider to control the screen brightness manually, keeping in mind that more brightness means shorter battery life.

  If Auto-Brightness is turned on, then the changes you make here are relative to the iPhone's self-chosen brightness. In other words, if you goose the brightness by 20 percent, then the screen will always be 20 percent brighter than the iPhone would have chosen for itself.

> **TIP:** The Control Center (page 47) gives you a much quicker road to the Brightness slider. And, of course, you can also tell Siri, "Make the screen brighter" (or "dimmer"). This version in Settings is just for old-timers.

- **Auto-Brightness On/Off.** Tap anywhere on this switch to disable the ambient-light sensor completely. Now the brightness of the screen is under complete manual control.

- **Display Zoom.** The iPhone 6 and 6s models have bigger screens than the iPhones that came before them. The question here is: How do you want to use that extra space? If you tap View and choose Standard, then icons and controls remain the size they always were; the bigger screen fits more on a page. If you choose Zoomed, then those elements appear slightly larger, for the benefit of people who don't have bionic eyes.

- **Text Size.** Apple has finally realized what anyone over 40 already knows: As you age, small type becomes harder to read. This universal text-size slider can boost the size of text in every app on your phone.

  Technically, what you're seeing is the front end for Apple's *Dynamic Type* feature. And, even more technically, not all apps work with Dynamic Type (yet). But most of the built-in Apple apps do—Contacts, Mail, Maps, Messages, Notes, Phone, Reminders, and Safari Reader—and other software companies will follow suit.

TIP: If the largest type setting here still isn't big enough, you're not out of luck. Hiding in the Accessibility panel described on page 197, there's an option called Larger Text. Tap it and then turn on Larger Accessibility Sizes to make the large end of the type-size scale twice as big. Now you can read the phone from the moon.

- **Bold Text.** If the spindly fonts of iOS 9 are a little too light for your reading tastes, you can flip this switch on (see page 197).

Wallpaper

Wallpaper can mean either the photo on the Unlock screen (what you see when you wake the iPhone up), or the background picture on your Home screen. On this panel, you can change the image used for either one. Page 294 has step-by-step instructions.

Sounds

Here's a more traditional cellphone settings screen: the place where you choose a ringtone sound for incoming calls.

- **Vibrate on Ring, Vibrate on Silent.** Like any self-respecting cellphone, the iPhone has a Vibrate mode—a little shudder in your pocket that might get your attention when you can't hear the ringing. As you can see, there are two on/off controls for the vibration: one for when the phone is in Silent mode and one for when the ringer's on.

- **Ringer and Alerts.** The slider here controls the volume of the phone's ringing.

  Of course, it's usually faster to adjust the ring volume by pressing the up/down buttons on the left edge whenever you're not on a call or playing music or video. But if you find that your volume buttons are getting pressed accidentally in your pocket, you can also turn off Change with Buttons. Now you can adjust the volume *only* with this slider, here in Settings.

- **Sounds and Vibration Patterns.** The iPhone is, of course, a cell-phone—and therefore it sometimes rings. The sound it makes when it rings is up to you; by tapping Ringtone, you can view the iPhone's list of 25 built-in ringtones, plus 27 "alert tones," plus any new ones you've added yourself.

Tap a ring sound to hear it. After you've tapped one you like, confirm your choice by tapping Sounds to return to the Sounds screen.

NOTE: You can choose a different ringtone for each person in your phone book (page 107).

But why stop with a ringtone? The iPhone can make all kinds of other sounds to alert you: to the arrival of a new voicemail, text message, or email; to the successful sending of an outgoing email message, tweet, or Facebook post; to calendar or Reminders alarms; to the arrival of AirDrop files; and so on.

This is a big deal—not just because you can express your individual-ity through your choice of ringtones, text tones, reminder tones, and so on, but also because you can distinguish your iPhone's blips and bleeps from somebody else's in the same family or workplace.

For each of these events, tap the light-gray text that identifies the current sound for that event ("Tri-tone" or "Ding," for example). On the resulting screen, tap the different sound options to find one you like; then tap Sounds to return to the main Sounds screen.

On that Sounds screen, you can also turn on or off the Lock Sounds (the sounds you get when you tap the Sleep/Wake switch on the top of the phone) and the Keyboard Clicks that play when you type on the virtual keyboard.

Touch ID & Passcode

Here's where you set up a password for your phone, or (if you have an iPhone 5s or later) where you teach the phone to recognize your finger-prints. Full details start on page 59.

Battery

This panel is all new in iOS 9, and all welcome! It offers these goodies:

- **Low Power Mode.** This, of course, is the on/off switch for the new Low Power mode (page 40).

- **Battery Percentage.** Instead of just a "filling-up-battery" fuel-gauge icon at the top of your screen, how would you like a digital percent-age readout too ("75%")?

- **Battery Usage.** Here's the new readout for all your apps, showing their battery appetite over the past day or week; see page 44.

- **Usage, Standby.** These stats show you how many hours and minutes of life you've gotten from your current battery charge. (Usage = you using the phone. Standby = phone asleep.)

Privacy

By "privacy," Apple means "the ability of apps and Apple to access your data."

Many an app works better, or claims to, when it has access to your address book, calendar, photos, and so on. Generally, when you run such an app for the first time, it explicitly asks you for permission to access each kind of data. But here, on this panel, you have a central dashboard—and on/off switches—for each data type and the apps that want it.

Location Services

Suppose, for example, that you tap Location Services. At the top of the next screen, you'll find the master on/off switch for all Location Services. If you turn it off, then the iPhone can no longer determine where you are on a map, geotag your photos, find the closest ATM, tell your friends where you're hanging out, and so on. Below this master switch, you'll find these options:

- **Share My Location.** Every year, Apple comes up with new ways for you to broadcast your phone's location—and, by extension, your own. For example, Find My Friends, Messages, and Family Sharing all have features that let certain other people (with your permission) see where you are right now.

  Here's the on/off switch for the whole feature. If it's off, nobody can find you right now. If Share My Location is on, then this screen also shows you every iPhone you've ever owned, so that you can specify which should transmit their locations—as well as the names of people to whom you've given permission to track you, which is a handy reminder.

- **App Store, Calendar, Camera....** This screen goes on to list every single app that uses your location information, and it lets you turn off

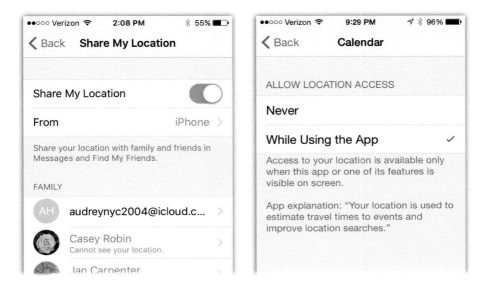

this feature on a by-app basis. You might want to do that for privacy's sake—or you might want to do that to save battery power, since the location searches sap away a little juice every time.

Tap an app's name to see when it wants access to your location. You might see Always, Never, or While Using the App (the app can't use your location when it's in the background). On the same screen, you can see a description of why the app thinks it needs your location. Why does the Calendar need it, for example? "To estimate travel times to events."

The little ➚ icon indicates which apps have actually *used* your location data. If it's gray, that app has checked your location in the past 24 hours; if it's purple, it's locating you right now; if it's hollow, that app is using a *geofence*—it's waiting for you to enter or leave a certain location, like home or work. The Reminders app uses the geofencing feature, for example.

- **System Services.** Here are the on/off switches for the iPhone's own features that use your location.

  For example, there's Cell Network Search (lets your phone tap into Apple's database of cellular frequencies by location, which speeds up connections); Compass Calibration (lets the Compass app know where you are, so that it can accurately tell you which way's north); Diagnostics and Usage (sends location information back to Apple, along with diagnostic information so that, for example, Apple can see where calls are being dropped); Location-Based iAds (advertisements that Apple slaps at the bottom of certain apps—or, rather, their ability to self-customize based on your current location); Popular Near Me (the section of the App Store that lists apps downloaded by people around your current spot); Setting Time Zone (permits the iPhone to set its own clock when you arrive in a new time zone; Routing & Traffic (sends anonymous speed/location data from your phone, which is how Maps knows where there are traffic tie-ups); and so on.

Contacts, Calendars, Reminders...

This list (on the main Privacy screen) identifies the kinds of data that your apps might wish to access; we're going way beyond location here. For example, your apps might want to access your address book or your calendar.

Tap a category—Contacts, for example—to see a list of the apps that are merrily tapping into its data. And to see the on/off switch, which you can use to block that app's access.

Twitter, Facebook

Similarly, new apps you download may sometimes want access to your Facebook and Twitter accounts. Lots of apps, for example, harness your existing Facebook account for the purpose of logging in or finding friends to play games with. Tap Twitter or Facebook to see which apps are using your account information.

Diagnostics & Usage

Do you give Apple permission to collect information about how you're using your phone and how well the phone is behaving each day? On this screen, you can choose Don't Send or Automatically Send. And if you tap Diagnostic & Usage Data at the bottom, you can see the actual data the phone intends to send. (Hint: It's programmery gibberish.)

Advertising

The final Privacy option gives you a Limit Ad Tracking switch. Turning it on won't affect how many ads you see within your apps—but it will prevent advertisers from delivering ads *based on your interests*. You'll just get generic ads.

There's a Reset Advertising Identifier button here, too. You may not realize that, behind the scenes, you have an Ad Identifier number. It's "a nonpermanent, non-personal device identifier" that advertisers can associate with you and your habits—the things you buy, the apps you use, and so on. That way, advertisers can insert ads into your apps that pertain to your interests—without ever knowing your name.

But suppose you've been getting a lot of ads that seem to mischaracterize your interests. Maybe you're a shepherd, and you keep seeing ads for hyperviolent games. Or maybe you're a nun, and you keep getting ads for marital aids.

In those cases, you might want to reset your Ad ID with this button, thus starting from scratch as a brand-new person about which the advertisers know nothing.

iCloud

Here's where you enter your iCloud name and password—and where you find the on/off switches for the various kinds of data synchronization that iCloud can perform for you. Chapter 15 tells all.

iTunes & App Store

If you've indulged in a few downloads (or a few hundred) from the App Store or iTunes music store, then you may well find some settings of use here. For example, if you tap your Apple ID at the top of the panel, you get these buttons:

- **View Apple ID.** This takes you to the web, where you can look over your Apple account information, including credit card details.

- **Sign Out.** Tap when, for example, a friend wants to use her own iTunes account to buy something on your iPhone. As a gift, maybe.

- **iForgot.** If you've forgotten your Apple ID password, tap here. You'll be offered a couple of different ways of establishing your identity— and you'll be given the chance to make up a new password.

Automatic Downloads

If you have an iCloud account, then a very convenient option is available to you: automatic downloads of music, apps, and ebooks you've bought on *other* iOS gadgets. For example, if you buy a new album on your iPad, turning on Music here means that your iPhone will download the same album automatically next time it's in a Wi-Fi hotspot.

Updates means that if you accept an updated version of an app on one of your other Apple gadgets, it will be auto-updated on this phone, too.

Those downloads are, however, big. They can eat up your cellphone's monthly data allotment right quick and send you deep into Surcharge Land. That's why the iPhone does that automatic downloading only when you're in a Wi-Fi hotspot—unless you turn on Use Cellular Data. Hope you know what you're doing.

Finally, the Suggested Apps section offers a duplicate set of on/off switches for the Suggested Apps feature described on page 563.

Wallet & Apple Pay

This panel, new in iOS 9 for the iPhone 6 series and later, offers two tappable items. Add Credit or Debit Card begins the process of teaching Apple Pay about one of your credit cards, as described on page 446. And Double-Click Home Button is the on/off switch for one of the ways to use Apple Pay—the method by which you can prepare the phone for payment *before* approaching the wireless cashier terminal, as described on page 524.

Mail, Contacts, Calendars

There's a lotta stuff going on in one place here. Breathe deeply; take it slow.

Accounts

Your email accounts are listed here; this is also where you set up new ones. See page 457 for details.

Fetch New Data

More than ever, the iPhone is a real-time window into the data stream of your life. Whatever changes are made to your calendar, address book, or email back on your computer at home (or at the office) can magically show up on your iPhone, seconds later, even though you're across the country.

That's the beauty of "push" email, contacts, and calendars. You get push email if you have a free Yahoo Mail account. You get all three if you've signed up for an iCloud account (Chapter 15), or if your company uses Microsoft Exchange (Chapter 17).

Having an iPhone that's updated with these critical life details in real time is amazingly useful, but there are several reasons why you might want to turn off the Push feature. You'll save battery power, save money when you're traveling abroad (where every "roaming" Internet use can run up your cellular bill), and avoid the constant "new mail" jingle when you're trying to concentrate.

And what if you don't have a push email service, or if you turn it off? In that case, your iPhone can still do a pretty decent job of keeping you up to date. It can check your email every 15 minutes, every half-hour, every hour, or only on command (Manually). That's the decision you make in the Fetch New Data panel. (Keep in mind that more frequent checking means shorter battery life.)

> **TIP:** The iPhone *always* checks email each time you open the Mail app, regardless of your setting here. If you have a push service like iCloud or Exchange, it also checks for changes to your schedule or address book each time you open Calendar or Contacts—again, no matter what your setting here.

Mail

Here you set up your email account information, specify how often you want the iPhone to check for new messages, how you want your Mail app to look, and more.

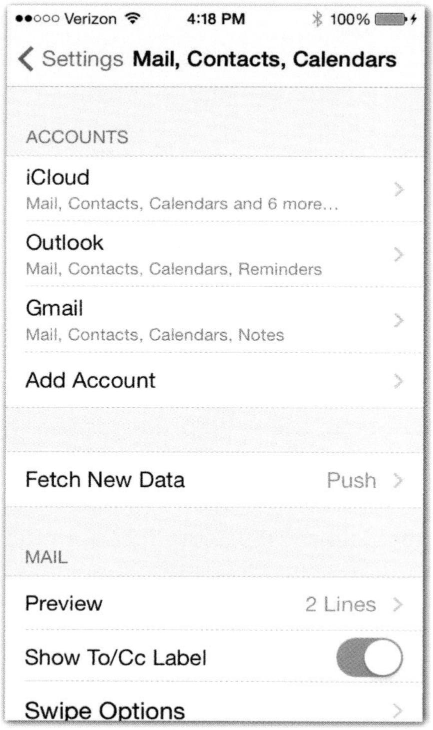

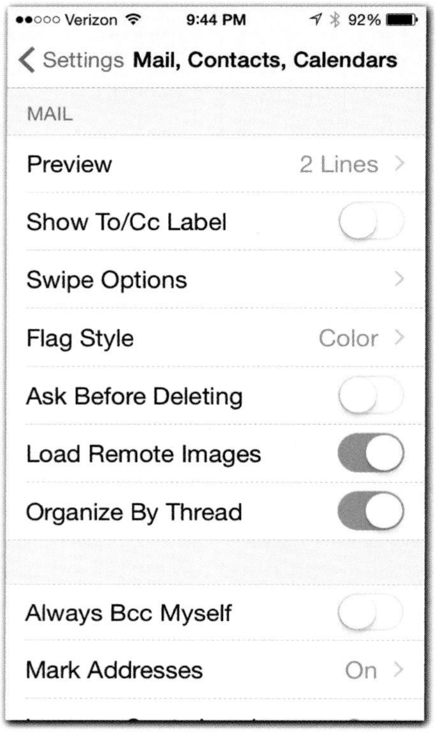

●●○○○ Verizon 4:18 PM 100%
Settings Mail, Contacts, Calendars
ACCOUNTS
iCloud
Mail, Contacts, Calendars and 6 more...
Outlook
Mail, Contacts, Calendars, Reminders
Gmail
Mail, Contacts, Calendars, Notes
Add Account
Fetch New Data
Push
MAIL
Preview
2 Lines
Show To/Cc Label
Swipe Options

●●○○○ Verizon 9:44 PM 92%
Settings Mail, Contacts, Calendars
MAIL
Preview
2 Lines
Show To/Cc Label
Swipe Options
Flag Style
Color
Ask Before Deleting
Load Remote Images
Organize By Thread
Always Bcc Myself
Mark Addresses
On

- **Preview.** It's cool that the iPhone shows you the first few lines of text in every message. Here you can specify how ***many*** lines. More lines mean you can skim your inbound messages without having to open many of them; fewer lines mean more messages fit without scrolling.

- **Show To/Cc Label.** If you turn this option on, then a tiny, light-gray logo appears next to many of the messages in your inbox. The To logo indicates that this message was addressed directly to you; the Cc logo means you were merely "copied" on a message primarily intended for someone else.

  If there's no logo at all, then the message is in some other category. Maybe it came from a mailing list, or it's an email blast (a Bcc), or the message is from you, or it's a bounced message.

- **Swipe Options.** Which colorful insta-tap buttons would you like to appear when you swipe across a message in a list? See page 469 for details.

- **Flag Style.** You can flag messages to draw your own attention to them, either with the old-style flag icon—or, for visual spark, an orange dot. Here's where you choose.

- **Ask Before Deleting.** Ordinarily, you can delete an open message quickly and easily, just by tapping the 🗑 icon. But if you'd prefer to encounter an additional confirmation step before the message disappears, then turn this option on.

> **NOTE:** The confirmation box appears only when you're deleting an open message—not when you delete one from the list of messages.

- **Load Remote Images.** Spammers, the vile undercrust of lowlife society, have a trick. When they send you email that includes a picture, they don't actually paste the picture into the message. Instead, they include a "bug"—a piece of code that instructs your email program to *fetch* the missing graphic from the Internet. Why? Because that gives the spammer the ability to track who has actually opened the junk mail, making those email addresses much more valuable for reselling to other spammers.

  If you turn this option off, then the iPhone does not fetch "bug" image files at all. You're not flagged as a sucker by the spammers. You'll see empty squares in the email where the images ought to be. (Graphics sent by normal people and legitimate companies are generally pasted right into the email, so they'll still show up just fine.)

- **Organize By Thread.** This is the on/off switch for the feature that clumps related back-and-forths into individual items in your Mail inbox.

- **Always Bcc Myself.** If this option is on, then you'll get a secret copy of any message you send. Some people use this feature to make sure their computers have records of replies sent from the phone.

- **Mark Addresses.** See the Tip on page 536.

- **Increase Quote Level.** Each time you reply to a reply, it gets indented more, so you and your correspondents can easily distinguish one reply from the next.

- **Signature.** A signature is a bit of text that gets stamped at the bottom of your outgoing messages. Here's where you can change yours.

- **Default Account.** Your iPhone can manage an unlimited number of email accounts. Here you can tap the account you want to be your *default*—the one that's used when you create a new message from another program, like a Safari link, or when you're on the All Inboxes screen of Mail.

Contacts

Contacts is a first-class citizen with an icon of its own on the Home screen, so it gets its own little set of options in Settings:

- **Sort Order, Display Order.** How do you want the names in your Contacts list sorted—by first name or by last name?

  Note that you can have them **sorted** one way but **displayed** another way. Not all the combinations make sense.

- **Short Name.** When this switch is on, the Mail app may fit more email addressees' names into its narrow To box by shortening them. It may display "M. Mouse," for example, or "Mickey," or even "M.M."—whatever you select here.

- **Prefer Nicknames** is similar. It instructs Mail to display the **nicknames** for your friends (as determined in Contacts) instead of their real names.

- **My Info.** Tap here to tell the phone which card in Contacts represents **you**. Knowing who you are is useful to the phone in a number of places—for example, it's how Siri knows what you mean when you say, "Give me directions home."

- **Default Account.** Here again, the iPhone can manage multiple address books—from iCloud, Gmail, Yahoo, and so on. Tap the account you want new contacts to fall into, if you haven't specified one in advance. (This item doesn't appear unless you have multiple accounts.)

- **Contacts Found in Mail.** In iOS 9, the iPhone does some intelligent inspection of your email. It notices when you email the same group often, or when you use the same subject line often, and proposes filling in all the recipients' addresses automatically the next time (page 479). It also examines your email in hopes of finding a matching phone number, so that Caller ID works better (page 183).

  Of course, no **person** is looking through your email—but if these features give you the privacy heebie-jeebies, you can turn them off here.

- **Import SIM Contacts.** If you came to the iPhone from another, lesser GSM phone, then your phone book may be stored on its little SIM card instead of in the phone itself. In that case, you don't have to retype all those names and numbers to bring them into your iPhone. This button can do the job for you. (The results may not be pretty. For example, some phones store all address book data in CAPITAL LETTERS.)

Calendars

Your iPhone's calendar can be updated by remote control, wirelessly, through the air, either by your company (via Exchange, Chapter 17) or by somebody at home using your computer (via iCloud, Chapter 15).

- **Time Zone Override.** Whenever you arrive in a new city, the iPhone actually learns (from the local cell towers) what time zone it's in and changes its own clock automatically.

  So here's a mind-teaser. Suppose there's a big meeting in California at 2 p.m. tomorrow—but you're in New York right now. How should that event appear on your calendar? Should it appear as 2 p.m. (that is, its local time)? Or should it appear as 5 (your East Coast time)?

  It's not an idle question, because it also affects reminders and alarms.

  Out of the box, Time Zone Override is turned off. The phone slides appointments around on your calendar as you travel to different time zones. If you're in California, that 2 p.m. meeting appears at 2 p.m. When you return to New York, it says 5 p.m. Handy—but dangerous if you forget what you've done.

  If you turn on the Override, though, the iPhone leaves all your appointments at the hours you record them—in the time zone you specify with the pop-up menu here. This option is great if you like to record events at the times you'll be experiencing them; they'll never slosh around as you travel. If you, a New Yorker, will travel to San Francisco next week for a 2 p.m. meeting, write it down as 2 p.m.; it will still say 2 p.m. when you land there.

- **Alternate Calendars.** If you prefer to use the Chinese, Hebrew, or Islamic calendar system, go nuts here.

- **Week Numbers.** This option makes Calendar display a little gray notation that identifies which week you're in (out of the 52 this year). It might say, for example, "W42." Because, you know, some people aren't aware enough of time racing by.

- **Show Invitee Declines.** You can invite someone to a meeting, as described on page 344. If they click Decline (they can't make it), maybe you don't need your phone to alert you. In that case, turn this switch off.

- **Sync.** If you're like most people, you refer to your calendar more often to see what events are *coming up* than to see the ones you've already lived through. Ordinarily, therefore, the iPhone saves you some syncing time and storage space by updating only relatively recent events on your iPhone calendar. It doesn't bother with events that are older than 2 weeks, or 6 months, or whatever you choose here. (Or you can turn on **All Events** if you want your entire life, past and future, synced each time—storage and wait time be damned.)

- **Start Week On.** This option specifies which day of the week appears at the *left edge of the screen* in the calendar's Day and Month views. For most people, that's Sunday, or maybe Monday—but for all iOS cares, your week could start on a Thursday.

- **Default Calendar.** This option lets you answer the question: "When I add a new appointment to my calendar on the iPhone, which *calendar* (category) should it belong to?" You can choose Home, Work, Kids, or whatever category you use most often.

- **Events Found in Mail.** As described on page 475, iOS 9 is smarter now when it comes to mining your email for proposed calendar events. You can turn on that helpful feature here—if you're weird.

Notes

Notes can sync with various online services: iCloud, Gmail, Yahoo, and so on. Tap **Default Account** here to specify which one should receive new notes you create if you haven't specifically chosen one.

And now that Notes comes with ready-to-use type styles like Title, Heading, and Body, you can also use the **New Notes Start With** option here to choose which of those is the first line when you create a new note. If you usually start with a title for your note "card," choose **Title**, for example.

Finally: Most people use Notes with online accounts like iCloud, Gmail, Yahoo, and so on, so that their notes are always backed up and synced to their computers. But if you turn on **"On My iPhone" Account** here, then you'll have another option: Creating notes that live only on your phone, and aren't transmitted, synced, or backed up. Handy if you have deeply personal information, or you just don't trust those online services.

Reminders

Here's the only preference setting for the Reminders app:

- **Default List.** Suppose you've created multiple Reminder lists (Groceries, Movies to Rent, To Do, and so on). When you create a new item—for example, by telling Siri, "Remind me to fix the sink"—which list should it go on? Here's where you specify.

Phone

These settings have to do with your address book, call management, and other phone-related preferences.

- **My Number.** Here's where you can see your iPhone's own phone number. You can even edit it, if necessary (just how it appears—you're not actually changing your phone number).

- **Wi-Fi Calling.** This item may appear, depending on your carrier. See page 25

- **Calls on Other Devices.** Here's the on/off switch for Continuity, the ability to make phone calls from your Mac (page 536). In iOS 9, you can even specify *which* gadgets talk to your iPhone in this way.

- **Respond with Text.** This feature is described on page 115; here's where you can edit the canned "Can't talk right now" text messages.

- **Call Forwarding, Call Waiting** (AT&T and T-Mobile only). Here are the on/off switches for Call Forwarding and Call Waiting, which are described in Chapter 5.

- **Show My Caller ID** (AT&T and T-Mobile only). If you don't want your number to show up on the screen of the person you're calling, then turn this off.

- **Blocked.** You can block certain people's calls, texts, and FaceTime video calls.

  This isn't a telemarketer-blocking feature; you can block only people who are already in your Contacts. It's really for blocking harassing ex-lovers, jerky siblings you're not speaking to, and collection agencies. Tap Add New to view your Contacts list, where you can tap to choose the blockee. (You can also see and edit this list in the Messages and FaceTime panels of Settings.)

- **TTY.** A TTY (teletype) machine lets people with hearing or speaking difficulties use a telephone—by typing back and forth, sometimes with the assistance of a human TTY operator who transcribes what the other person is saying. When you turn this iPhone option on, you can use the iPhone with a TTY machine, if you buy the little $20 iPhone TTY adapter from Apple.

- **Change Voicemail Password.** Yep, pretty much just what it says.

- **Dial Assist.** When this option is turned on, and when you're calling from another country, the iPhone automatically adds the proper country codes when dialing U.S. numbers. Pretty handy, actually.

- **SIM PIN.** Your SIM card stores all your account information. SIM cards are especially desirable abroad, because in most countries, you can pop yours into any old phone and have working service. If you're worried about yours getting stolen or lost, then turn this option on. You'll be asked to enter a passcode.

  Then, if some bad guy ever tries to put your SIM card into another phone, he'll be asked for the password. Without the password, the card (and the phone) won't make calls.

> **TIP:** And if the evildoer guesses wrong three times, the words "PIN LOCKED" appear on the screen, and the SIM card is locked forever. You'll have to get another one from your carrier. So don't forget the password.

- **[Your carrier] Services.** This choice opens up a cheat sheet of handy numeric codes that, when dialed, play the voice of a robot providing useful information about your cellphone account. For example, *225# lets you know the latest status of your bill, *646# lets you know how many airtime minutes you've used so far this month, and so on.

> **TIP:** The button at the bottom of the screen opens up your account page on the web, for further details on your cellphone billing and features.

Messages

These options govern text messages (SMS) and iMessages, both of which are described in Chapter 5:

- **iMessage.** This is the on/off switch for iMessages. If it's off, then your phone never sends or receives these handy, free messages—only regular text messages.

- **Text Message Forwarding** is the text-message element of Continuity; it's described on page 538. You get an on/off switch for each gadget that you might want to display your phone's text messages.

- **Send Read Receipts.** If this is on, then people who send you iMessages will know when you've seen them. They'll see a tiny gray text notification beneath the iMessage bubble that contains their message. If you're creeped out by them being able to know when you're ignoring them, then turn this item off.

- **Send as SMS.** If you try to send an iMessage to somebody when there's no Internet service, what happens? If this item is on, then the message goes to that person as a regular text message, using your cell carrier's network. If it's off, then the message won't go out at all.

- **Send & Receive.** Here you can enter additional email addresses that people can use to send your phone iMessages.

  This screen also offers a Start new conversations from item that lets you indicate what you want to appear on the other guy's phone when you send a text: your phone number or email address.

- **MMS Messaging.** This is the on/off switch for picture and video messages (as opposed to text-only ones).

- **Group Messaging, Show Subject Field, Character Count.** These options are described starting on page 176.

- **Blocked.** Here's another way to build up a list of people you don't want to hear from, as described on page 581. It's the exact same feature.

- **Keep Messages.** You can specify how long you want Messages to retain a record of your exchanges: 30 days, a year, or forever.

- **Audio Messages.** You can now shoot audio utterances to other people just as easily as you can type them. Here you can set them to auto-delete after 2 minutes. Why? First, because audio files take up space on your phone. Second, because you may consider them *spoken text messages*—not *recordings* to preserve for future generations.

  The audio texting feature lets you send and receive audio messages without looking at the screen or touching it; see page 172.

- **Video Messages.** Same deal here. You can set up video clips you send in Messages to auto-delete after a couple of minutes for the same reasons.

FaceTime

These options pertain to FaceTime, the video calling feature described on page 123. Here, for example, is the on/off switch for the entire feature; a place to enter your Apple ID, so people can make FaceTime calls to you; and a place to enter email addresses and a phone number, which can also be used to reach you.

The Caller ID section lets you specify how you want to be identified when you place a call to somebody else: either as a phone number or an email address.

Finally, here yet again is the Blocked option—a third way to edit the list of people you don't want to hear from (page 581).

Maps

The Maps app has a few settings of its own:

- **Navigation Voice Volume.** As Siri gives you spoken navigational instructions, how loud do you want her to be? Or would you like her to shut up entirely?

- **Distances.** Measured in miles or kilometers, sir/madam?

- **Map Labels.** Would you like place names to appear in English—or in their native spellings?

- **Issue Reporting.** When you report a problem with Maps' still-buggy database of the world, may Apple technicians get back to you by email?

Compass

You wouldn't think that something as simple as the Compass app would need a Settings page, but here it is: an on/off switch called Use True North. (*True* north is the "top" point of the Earth's rotational axis. If you turn it off, then Compass uses *magnetic* north, the spot traditional compasses point to; it's about 11 degrees away from true north).

Safari

Here's everything you ever wanted to adjust in the web browser but didn't know how to ask.

Search

- **Search Engine.** Your choice here determines who does your searching from the search bar: Google, Bing, Yahoo, or DuckDuckGo (a limited search service famous for its refusal to collect your data or track your searches).

- **Search Engine Suggestions.** As you type into Safari's search box, it tries to save you time in two ways. First, it sprouts a list of common search requests, based on what millions of other people have sought. This list changes with each letter you type. Second, Safari may auto-complete the address based on what you've typed so far, using suggestions from your History and bookmarks list. This switch shuts off those suggestions. (It's here primarily for the benefit of privacy hounds, who object to the fact that their search queries are processed by Apple in order to show the suggestions.)

- **Safari Suggestions.** Safari searches (Chapter 2) can find matches from the iTunes, iBooks, and App stores; from databases of local businesses, restaurants, and theaters; and from the web. Unless you turn this off.

- **Quick Website Search.** You can search *within* a site (like Amazon or Reddit or Wikipedia) using only Safari's regular search bar, as described on page 438. If, that is, this switch is on.

- **Preload Top Hit.** As you type into the search box, Safari lists websites that match. The first one is the Top Hit—and if this switch is on, Safari secretly downloads that page while you're still finishing your search. That way, if the Top Hit *is* the page you wanted, it appears almost instantly when you tap.

  But here's the thing: Safari downloads the Top Hit with *every* search—which uses up data. Which could cost you money if you're using cellular data.

General

- **Passwords, AutoFill.** Safari's AutoFill feature saves you tedious typing by filling in your passwords, name, address, and phone numbers on web forms automatically (just for the sites you want). It can even store your credit card information, which makes buying things online *much* easier and quicker.

  The AutoFill screen lists the different kinds of data that Safari can auto-fill for you: your contact info, website account names, and passwords. (Open the Passwords page to see the complete list of the passwords it's memorized; tap Edit to delete certain ones.) You can also see your credit cards. (Tap Saved Credit Cards to see or delete the memorized cards.)

- **Frequently Visited Sites.** As you know from page 434, when you have nothing open in Safari, it likes to offer a page full of icons representing sites you visit often. Turn off this switch if your privacy concerns outweigh the convenience of this feature.

- **Favorites.** As described on page 434, your Favorites in Safari are just ordinary bookmarks in an extraordinary folder. Here you can choose a *different* folder as the home of your Favorites.

- **Open Links.** When you tap a link with your finger, should the new page open in front of the current page—or behind it? Answer here.

- **Show Tab Bar.** A row of tab buttons appear in landscape orientation (Plus models only).

- **Block Pop-ups.** In general, you want this turned on. You really don't want pop-up ad windows ruining your surfing session. Now and again, though, pop-up windows are actually useful. When you're buying concert tickets, for example, a pop-up window might show the location of the seats. In that situation, you can turn this option off.

●●○○○ Verizon 🎵 **2:01 PM** ✈ ☀ 94% ▰	●●○○○ Verizon 🎵 **2:01 PM** ✈ ☀ 94% ▰
‹ Settings **Safari**	‹ Settings **Safari**
	Frequently Visited Sites ⬤
SEARCH	Favorites Favorites ›
Search Engine Google ›	Open Links In New Tab ›
Search Engine Suggestions ⬤	Block Pop-ups ⬤
Safari Suggestions ⬤	Content Blockers 1 ›
Quick Website Search On ›	
Preload Top Hit ⬤	PRIVACY & SECURITY
About Search & Privacy...	Do Not Track ⬤
	Block Cookies Allow from Websit... ›
GENERAL	Fraudulent Website Warning ⬤
Passwords ›	About Safari & Privacy...
AutoFill ›	
Frequently Visited Sites ⬤	

Privacy & Security

- **Do Not Track.** If you turn this on, then websites agree not to secretly track your activity on the web. The problem is, of course, that this program is voluntary—and the sleazy operators just ignore it.

- **Block Cookies.** You can learn all about cookies—and these options to tame them—on page 453.

- **Fraudulent Website Warning.** This option makes Safari warn you when you try to visit what it knows to be a *phishing* site. (Phishing is a common Internet scam. The bad guy builds a fake version of Amazon,

PayPal, or a bank's website—and tries to trick you into "logging in." You therefore unwittingly give up your name and password.)

- **Clear History and Website data.** Like any web browser, Safari keeps a list of websites you've visited recently to make it easier for you to visit them again: the History list. And like any browser, Safari therefore exposes your activities to any suspicious spouse or crackpot colleague. If you're nervous about that prospect, then tap Clear History to erase your tracks. This feature deletes all the cookies that websites have deposited on your "hard drive."

- **Use Cellular Data.** The Reading List feature (page 443) is wonderful. But because it requires downloading entire web pages to your phone—and then syncs them to all your other Apple gadgets—it uses a lot of data. If you fear going over your cellphone plan's monthly data allotment, then turn this off. You'll be allowed to save sites to your Reading List only when in a Wi-Fi hotspot.

- **Advanced.** Safari recognizes HTML5, a web technology that lets websites store data on your phone, for accessing even when you're not online (like your Gmail stash). In Website Data, you can see which web apps have created these databases on your phone and delete them if necessary.

  JavaScript is a programming language whose bits of code frequently liven up web pages. If you suspect some bit of code is choking Safari, however, you can turn off its ability to decode JavaScript here.

  The Web Inspector is for website programmers. You connect your phone to a Mac with a USB cable; then, in Safari on the computer, you choose Debug→iPhone→[the name of the website currently on the iPhone's screen]. You'll be able to examine errors, warnings, tips, and logs for HTML, JavaScript, and CSS—great when you're designing and debugging web pages or web apps for the iPhone.

News

If there's a new app, there must be a new Settings page for it.

Page 388 describes the new News app. Here's where you indicate whether it's allowed to bug you with Notifications about new news stories, whether it's allowed to fetch news in the background (at some cost to battery life), and whether it can fetch new news over the cellular network (at some cost to your data allowance).

And you can turn off the Story Previews (where the first couple of lines of each news story appear right in the app).

Music

The Music app looks different if you've subscribed to the $10-a-month Apple Music service, as you can read in Chapter 7. If you turn off Show Apple Music, the new tabs (For You and New) disappear. Which makes sense if you're not a subscriber, since they're doing you no good.

Use Cellular Data lets you guard against having your streaming music eat up your monthly cellular data allowance. If it's off, then you can download and play back music only over Wi-Fi. On this panel, you can adjust three iPod playback features: Sound Check, EQ, Volume Limit. See page 235. And you can sign up for iTunes Match (page 217).

Finally, there's Home Sharing. Conveniently enough, you can access your iTunes music collection, upstairs on your computer, right from your iPhone, over your home Wi-Fi network. Or at least you can if both machines are signed into the same Apple ID. Here's where you enter the Apple ID that matches your iTunes setup.

Videos

Here's what you can adjust for the Videos app:

- **Start Playing.** When you play a video you've seen before, you can have it begin either from Where Left Off or From Beginning.

- **Show iTunes Purchases.** Do you want the Videos app to show all the TV shows and movies you've ever bought from Apple—even the ones you haven't actually stored on the phone?

- **Home Sharing.** You can also access your iTunes video collection, just as described a few paragraphs ago. Same deal here.

Photos & Camera

Here's a motley collection of photo-related settings:

- **iCloud Photo Library.** If you switch this feature on, iOS will store every picture and video from your phone on your online iCloud account, so you can access them from any Apple gadget. (Keep in mind that it will eat up a lot of your iCloud storage space.)

- **My Photo Stream, iCloud Photo Sharing.** These are the master on/off switches for Photo Streams, which are among iCloud's marquee features (see page 296 and page 299).

- **Upload Burst Photos.** Recent iPhones can snap 10 photos a second when you hold your finger down on the shutter button. That's a lot of photos, which can fill up your iCloud storage fast. So Apple gives you the option to exclude them from the uploads.

- **Summarize Photos.** In the Photos app, the Years and Collections screens generally display one tiny thumbnail for every single photo. This feature is designed to make those displays more manageable by displaying fewer, but representative, thumbnails. (You won't see any difference unless you have a pretty huge collection of photos.)

- **Repeat, Shuffle.** These options work just as they do for music. Repeat makes the slideshow loop endlessly; Shuffle plays the slides in random order.

- **Grid** turns the "Rule of Thirds" grid on or off (the tic-tac-toe lines) on the camera's viewfinder screen.

- **Record Video at 60 FPS.** This option, exclusive to the iPhone 6 and 6 Plus, makes your phone shoot twice as many frames per second as normal video (60 instead of 30). The result: exceptionally smooth playback—and much bigger video sizes.

- **Keep Normal Photo.** See the Tip on page 254.

iBooks

Why, it's every setting imaginable that pertains to the iBooks ebook reading app. They're described on page 362.

Podcasts

These settings affect the Podcasts app described on page 394. They govern how often the app auto-downloads new episodes, and how many; whether it can do so using cellular data (instead of Wi-Fi); and whether you want the app to auto-delete podcasts you've already listened to.

Game Center

You can read about the Game Center on page 356. This page of preferences offers options like these:

Game Invites

More security stuff. Do you want your phone to permit invitations from other people to play games? How about people in the same room or building, inviting you to play over Wi-Fi or Bluetooth? Here are the on/off switches for Allow Invites and Nearby Players.

Game Center Profile

Here's your Game Center player name. Tap it to edit your nickname, make your Game Center listing invisible to strangers (Public Profile), or associate a new email address with your account.

Friend Recommendations

Playing games isn't much fun without friends to play against, so Game Center is happy to suggest fellow Game Center participants from your Contacts list or your Facebook account. Unless you turn off these switches.

Twitter, Facebook, Flickr, Vimeo

These pages let you enter your name and password just once, in this one place, for each of these popular web services—so that the iPhone and its apps can freely access those accounts without having to bother you.

Each of these panels also offers an Install button (facing page, left), making it quick and easy to download the official Twitter, Facebook, Flickr, and Vimeo apps.

The Twitter and Facebook options offer some additional choices:

- **Twitter.** The Update Contacts button adds your friends' Twitter account names to their cards in Contacts, saving you that tedious data entry.

- **Facebook.** Tapping Settings summons some options that, by now, should be familiar: You can give it permission to know your location when you post to Facebook; you can tell the phone how to alert you when new Facebook posts arrive (Notifications); you can limit the app's updating itself in the background; and you can prevent it from using Cellular Data. You can also limit Facebook video recordings to standard definition, to avoid massive data charges.

  The Allow These Apps items let you control which built-in apps can access your Facebook account; for example, turn off Calendar if you don't want to see your friends' Facebook birthdays on your calendar.

  Finally, Update All Contacts is the powerful button that adds photos and Facebook account names to the corresponding friends' cards in your Contacts app, as described on page 106.

••ooo Verizon 📶	4:21 PM	⊹ 100% 🔋✦	••ooo Verizon 📶	4:22 PM ⊿ ⊹ 100% 🔋•

‹ Settings   **Twitter**

Settings

🐦 **Twitter**   [INSTALL]
Twitter Inc.

American   ›

User Name @name

BSM   ›

Password Required

Bump   ›

Sign In

Doodle   ›

F. Melter Lite   ›

Create New Account

Fly Delta   ›

Twitter is a simple communication service
made up of 140-character messages called
Tweets.

Hipmunk   ›

Learn More about Twitter

iMovie   ›

JotNot Pro   ›

Nest   ›

Netflix   ›

App Preferences

At the bottom of the Settings app screen, you see a list of apps that have
installed setting screens of their own (above, right). For example, here's
where you can edit your screen name and password for the AIM chat program, change how many days' worth of news you want the NY Times
Reader to display, and so on. Each one offers an assortment of changeable
preference options.

It can get to be a very long list.

PART FIVE

Appendixes

Appendix A
Signup & Setup

Appendix B
Troubleshooting & Maintenance

A

Signup & Setup

Y ou gotta admit it: Opening up a new iPhone brings a certain excitement. There's a prospect of possibility, of new beginnings. Even if you intend to protect your iPhone with a case, there are those first few minutes when it's shiny, spotless, free of fingerprints or nicks—a gorgeous thing.

This chapter is all about getting started, whether that means buying and setting up a new iPhone, or upgrading an older model to the new iOS 9software that's described in this book.

Buying a New iPhone

Each year's new iPhone model is faster, has a better camera and screen, and comes packed with more features than the previous one. Still, "new iPhone" doesn't have to mean the iPhone 6s ($200 with a 2-year contract) or 6s Plus ($300). You can still get an iPhone 6 for $100, or the 5s free (with contract).

In any case, once you've chosen the model you want, you also have to choose which cellphone company you want to provide its service: AT&T, Verizon, T-Mobile, or Sprint. Each has something to offer.

Verizon has the best U.S. cellular coverage, and by far the most 4G LTE (high-speed Internet) areas. Most Sprint plans include unlimited Internet use, which is a rare perk these days. AT&T's high-speed Internet networks are faster than anyone else's. T-Mobile's plans cost the least in many ways (free texting and Internet when you're overseas; unlimited music and video without using up any of your data allowance; no 2-year contract; they'll pay off the early-termination fee if you switch from a rival carrier), but its phone network is the smallest.

Research the coverage where you live and work. Each company's website shows a map of its coverage.

You can buy your iPhone from a phone store (Verizon, Sprint, T-Mobile, AT&T), an Apple Store, from a retail store (RadioShack, Walmart, and so on), or from the Apple website. You can buy the phone either with or without a 2-year contract. Yes, that surprises many people—but most people still opt for the contract, because the 16-gigabyte phone's initial price is $200 that way. Without the contract, it costs $600 or more.

With a contract, the phone is locked to the cellphone company you're choosing; it works *only* with that company's network. For example, a locked AT&T phone won't work with Verizon, Sprint, T-Mobile, or any other carrier, and you can't insert the SIM card from a non-AT&T phone and expect it to work. (The exception: When you travel overseas with a Sprint or Verizon iPhone, you can insert a different country's SIM card into it for use while you're there. And if you coughed up the $600 for an unlocked phone, it works with anyone's SIM card.)

All right then: Here you are in the store, or sitting down to do some ordering online. Here are some of the decisions you'll have to make:

- **Transferring your old number.** You can bring your old cellphone or home number to your new iPhone. Your friends can keep dialing your old number—but your iPhone will ring instead of the old phone.

    It usually takes under an hour for a cellphone-number transfer to take place. During that time, you can make calls on the iPhone, but you can't receive them.

NOTE: Transferring a landline number to your iPhone can take several *days*.

- **Select your monthly calling plans.** Signing up for cellphone service involves more red tape than a government contract. In essence, you have to choose *three* plans: one for voice calls (required), one for Internet service (required), and one for text messages (optional). The variations are complicated, but a quick web search ("iPhone 6s plans compared") can help you make sense of them.

    AT&T's plans are typical. For $80 a month, you get unlimited calling and texting, plus 2 gigabytes a month of Internet use.

    Of course, who has any idea what 2 gigabytes of data is? How much of that do you eat up with email alone? How much is one YouTube video?

    As you approach your monthly limit, you'll get warnings by text message, but you can also see your data usage on your phone (see page 560). Yes, it's a pain to have to worry about data limits, but at least monitoring them is fairly easy. If you use more than your allotted amount, you're automatically billed a surcharge—for example, $10 for each additional gigabyte.

All four cell companies offer unlimited free calls to other phones from the same company. All but the cheapest plans offer unlimited calls on nights and weekends.

And all iPhone plans require an "activation fee" (ha!).

TIP: The choice you make here isn't etched in stone. You can change your plan at any time. If you have AT&T, for example, visit *www. wireless.att.com*, where you can log in with your iPhone number and make up a password. Click My Account, and then click Change Rate Plan to view your options.

As you budget for your plan, keep in mind that, as with any cellphone, you'll also be paying taxes as high as 22 percent, depending on your state. Ouch.

Setting Up a New Phone

In the olden days, you couldn't use a new iPhone at all without hooking it up to a computer. Now, though, the setup process takes place entirely on the phone's screen.

You don't need a computer to back up your phone, because iCloud backs it up. You don't need a computer to store your music and video collections, because the App Store remembers what you've bought and lets you re-download it at any time. You don't need a computer to download and install iPhone software updates, because they come straight to the phone now. You don't even need a computer to edit photos or to create mail folders; that's on the phone, too.

The first time you turn on a brand-new iPhone—or an older one that you've erased completely—the setup wizard appears. Swipe your finger where it says slide to set up. Now you're asked about 14 important questions:

- **Language; Country.** You won't get very far setting up your phone if you can't understand the instructions. So the very first step here is to tell it what language you speak. When you tap a language, you're next asked to tell the phone where in the world you live. (It proposes the country where you bought the phone. Clever, eh?)

- **Wi-Fi Networks.** Tap the name of the Wi-Fi network you want, enter the password if required, and tap Join.

  Or, if there's no Wi-Fi you can (or want to) hop onto right now, then tap Choose Cellular Connection.

- **Location Services.** The iPhone knows where you are. That's how it can pinpoint you on a map, tag the photos you take with their geographic locations, find you a nearby Mexican restaurant, and so on.

  Some people are creeped out by the phone's knowing where they are, worrying that Apple, by extension, also knows where you are. So here's your chance to turn off all the iPhone's location features. Tap either Enable Location Services or Disable Location Services.

- **Touch ID.** If you have an iPhone 5s or later, you're now invited to teach it your fingerprint, for the purposes of unlocking it without having to type a password. See page 59 for more on registering fingerprints. (You can also tap Set Up Touch ID Later. When the time comes, you can revisit this process in Settings→Touch ID & Passcode.)

- **Passcode.** Whether you opted to store a fingerprint or not, you're now asked to make up a six-digit *passcode* (password) for unlocking your phone. You'll need it whenever the phone won't accept Touch ID—for example, after you've restarted the phone.

TIP: You don't have to accept iOS 9's proposal of a six-digit passcode. Tap Passcode Options to reveal more choices, like Custom Alphanumeric Code (any password you like, any length, any characters), Custom Numeric Code (any number of digits), or 4-Digit Numeric Code (like in the old days).

- **Apps & Data.** If you've owned an iPhone before, or if you backed up this phone and then erased it, you don't have to load it up with all your apps and settings by hand. This screen offers to reload all your stuff from your most recent backup. (See Chapter 14 for details on iPhone backups.)

  Tap Restore from iCloud Backup (if your backup was on iCloud) or Restore from iTunes Backup (if your backup was on your computer).

  If you've never owned an iPhone before, you can choose Set Up as New iPhone to start fresh.

  There's even a new option here—sneaky, Apple!—called Move Data from Android. You download a companion app on your old Android phone (called Move to iOS). When you open it, the app (on Android) asks you to enter a number code that's offered by your iPhone at this stage. Then the Android phone asks what kinds of data you'd like copied to your iPhone: your Google account (email, calendar, and so on), web bookmarks, text messages, contacts, and photos (Camera Roll). When you hit Next, the transfer begins, wirelessly and automatically.

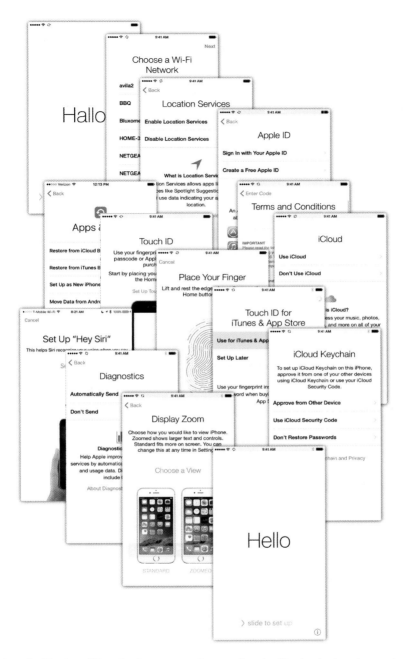

- **Apple ID.** A million features require an Apple ID—just about any transaction you make with Apple online. Buying anything from Apple, from a song to a laptop. Using iCloud (Chapter 15). Playing games against other people online. Making an appointment at an Apple Store.

If you already have an Apple ID, tap Sign In with Your Apple ID and enter it here. If not, tap Create a Free Apple ID. You'll be asked to provide your name, birthday, email address (or you can create a new iCloud email address), a password of your choice, and answers to a few security questions (you'll have to get them right if you ever forget your password). You also get to decide if you'd like the honor of receiving junk email from Apple.

(You can tap Skip This Step if you don't want an Apple ID, at least for now. You can get one later in Settings.)

- **Terms and Conditions**. On the screen full of legalese, tap Agree, and then Agree.

- **Apple Pay.** Next up: If you have an iPhone 5s or later, you're now invited to store your credit cards, for the purpose of turning on Apple Pay. The process is described on page 524.

  If you don't want to use Apple Pay, or don't want to set it up now, hit Next anyway, and then hit Set Up Later in Wallet.

- **iCloud Keychain** is a terrific feature. It stores all your web user names and passwords—and even credit card numbers—so you don't have to memorize them and type them in over and over. It's all synchronized across all your Apple machines (iPhone, iPad, Mac, and so on).

  If you take this opportunity to set it up, you're asked what you want to use as your iCloud Security Code. That's yet another four-digit passcode, which you may need someday to recover all your passwords if you have a really lousy day and lose *all* your Apple gadgets. Fortunately, the iPhone offers to use your iPhone passcode (the one you've already set up) as your iCloud Security Code, so you don't have another code to remember.

  On the next screen, you're supposed to enter a phone number—yours or that of "someone you trust"—which Apple will use as a secondary way to verify your identity if you have to recover your iCloud Keychain without having any of your Apple gadgets available.

- **Siri.** Here's your chance to set up Siri, the greatest phone advance in 15 years. In iOS 9, if you want to be able to use the "Hey Siri" hands-free mode (page 132), you're supposed to speak a few sample sentences so that Siri learns your voice. Tap Set Up Siri to do that now, or hit Turn On Siri Later if you don't want Siri at all, or want to do the setup later (in Settings→General→Siri).

- **Diagnostics.** Behind the scenes, your iPhone sends records back to Apple, including your location and what you're doing on your iPhone.

By analyzing this data en masse, Apple can figure out where the dead spots in the cellular network are, how to fix bugs, and so on. The information is anonymous—it's not associated with you. But if the very idea seems invasive, here's your chance to prevent this data from being sent.

- **App Analytics.** A related question: Is it OK for Apple to send statistics about how you use your apps to the makers of those apps?

- **Display Zoom.** On bigger-screened phones like the iPhone 6 and 6s models, you get this choice. It asks how you want to exploit the larger screen. If you choose Standard, you'll see more stuff (icons, menus, lines of text) per screenful than on smaller iPhones. If you choose Zoomed, then you'll see the same amount of stuff, but *bigger*. (The one exception: You don't get the extra buttons on the widescreen keyboard described on page 70.) You can always change your mind in Settings→Display & Brightness.

- **Welcome to iPhone.** Your phone is set up. Tap Get Started to jump to the Home screen.

> **NOTE:** A new iPhone no longer asks if you want to turn on Find My iPhone. It's turned on automatically; see page 518. It also no longer asks if you want to download the free iCloud Drive app (page 334)—but you should.

Upgrading an iPhone to iOS 9

If you bought an iPhone 6s or 6s Plus, great! iOS 9 comes on it preinstalled.

But you can also upgrade an iPhone 4s, 5, 5c, 5s, 6, or 6 Plus to this new software—in any of three ways:

- **Upgrade it wirelessly.** *Upgrading* means installing iOS 9 on top of whatever is already on your iPhone. You don't lose any data or settings.

  This is the easiest way to upgrade. You've probably already seen the little red number on your Settings app icon, and on the word "General" inside it; the phone is trying to tell you that iOS 9 is ready to download. Tap Settings→General→Software Update to see the iOS 9 logo; tap Download and Install. (You have to be on a Wi-Fi network, and it's wise to have your iPhone plugged into power.)

- **Upgrade it from iTunes.** If you wish, you can also perform the upgrade using the iTunes program on your computer. This method takes less time but, of course, requires being at your computer.

To begin, connect your iPhone and click its icon at top left (see page 497). On the Summary tab, click Check for Update, and then click Download and Update.

- **Restore it.** This is a more dramatic step, which you should choose only if you've been having problems with your phone or if, for some other reason, you would like to start completely fresh. This step backs up the phone, erases it completely, installs iOS 9, and then copies your stuff back onto the phone.

Connect the phone to your computer, open iTunes, and then click Restore iPhone.

The updating or restoring process takes awhile. You'll see the iPhone restart. When it's all over, the PC-free setup process described on the previous pages begins automatically.

> **NOTE:** Not all features work on all phones. For example, even with iOS 9, an iPhone 4s doesn't get AirDrop and some Continuity features (Chapter 16).
>
> The iPhone 4s may also be very slow with iOS 9—you've been warned.
>
> If you find your iPhone crawling, especially when you type, consider turning off Background App Refresh in Settings→General. And leave some space free; a full phone is a slow phone (page 611).
>
> If your iPhone 4s is *still* crawling along like an anesthetized slug, there's always the nuclear option: Erase it completely and load it up again. Many people report happier tidings after that extreme procedure.

Software Updates

As you're probably aware, phone software like the iPhone's is a perpetual work in progress. Apple constantly fixes bugs, adds features, and makes tweaks to extend battery life and improve other services.

Updating Directly on the Phone

One day you'll be minding your own business, and you'll see a red numbered badge appear on the Settings app's icon on the phone. Open Settings→General→Software Update to read about the new update and install it. Note, though, that unless it's plugged into a power source, your phone won't install an iOS update unless its battery is at least half full.

Install Updates from Your Computer

Maybe you're not that adventurous and you'd prefer to install your software update the old-fashioned way. No problem: Connect the iPhone to iTunes, wirelessly or not (page 497). Then click the iPhone's icon in iTunes; on the Summary pane, tap Check for Update.

Restrictions and Parental Controls

If you're issuing an iPhone to a child, or someone who acts like one, you'll be gratified to discover that iOS offers a good deal of protection. That's protection of your offspring's delicate sensibilities (it can block pornography and dirty words) and protection of your bank account (it can block purchases of music, movies, and apps without your permission).

To set this up, visit Settings→General→Restrictions. When you tap Enable Restrictions, you're asked to make up a four-digit passcode that permits only you, the all-knowing parent, to make changes to these settings. (Or you, the corporate IT administrator who's doling out iPhones to the white-collar drones.)

●●ooo Verizon 🤝	9:57 PM	✈ ✳ 90% ▰▰▰
❮ General	**Restrictions**	

Disable Restrictions

ALLOW:

🧭	Safari	⬤
📷	Camera	⬤
📹	FaceTime	⬤
🎤	Siri & Dictation	⬤
📡	AirDrop	⬤
▶	CarPlay	⬤
🎵	iTunes Store	⬤
📖	iBooks Store	⬤

●●ooo Verizon 🤝	9:57 PM	✈ ✳ 90% ▰▰▰
❮ General	**Restrictions**	

ALLOWED CONTENT:

Ratings For	United States >
Music, Podcasts & News	Expl... >
Movies	All >
TV Shows	All >
Books	All >
Apps	All >
Siri	All >
Websites	All >

PRIVACY:

Once you've changed the settings described below, the only way to change them again (when your kid turns 18, for example) is to return to the Restrictions page and correctly enter the password. That's also the only way to turn off the entire Restrictions feature (tap Disable Restrictions and correctly enter the password). To turn it back on, you have to make up a password all over again.

Once Restrictions is turned on, you can put up data blockades in a number of different categories.

Allow

For starters, you can turn off access to iPhone features that locked-down corporations might not want their employees—or parents might not want their children—to use, because they're considered either security holes, time drains, or places to spend your money: Safari (can't use the web at all), the Camera, FaceTime, Siri & Dictation, or CarPlay (Apple's specialized connection for certain car models, in which your iPhone's relevant icons appear on the car's dashboard screen).

A second list of options lets you block access to iTunes Store and the iBooks Store, and turn off the option to download Podcasts. You can stop your kid from Installing Apps or Deleting Apps, too. And In-App Purchases permits you to buy new material (game levels, book chapters, and so on) from within an app that you've already bought. In other words, even if you've shut down access to your offspring's ability to install new apps, as described above, this loophole remains.

Many of these restrictions work by *removing icons altogether* from the iPhone's Home screen: Safari, iTunes, and Camera, for example. When the switch says Off, the corresponding icon has been taken off the Home screen and can't be found even by Spotlight searches.

Allowed Content

Here you can spare your children's sensitive eyes and ears by blocking inappropriate material.

Ratings are a big deal; they determine the effectiveness of the parental controls described in this section. Since every country has its own rating schemes (for movies, TV shows, games, song lyrics, and so on), you use the Ratings For control to tell the iPhone which country's rating system you want to use.

Once that's done, you can use the Music, Podcasts & News, Movies, TV Shows, Books, and Apps controls to specify what your kid is allowed to watch, play, read, and listen to. For example, you can tap Movies and then tap PG-13; any movies rated "higher," like R or NC-17, won't play on the iPhone now. (And if your sneaky offspring try to buy these naughty songs, movies, or TV shows wirelessly from the iTunes Store, they'll discover that the Buy button is dimmed and unavailable.)

For some categories, like Music, Podcasts & News and Siri, you can turn off Explicit to prevent the iPhone from playing iTunes Store songs that contain naughty language, or speaking them.

Websites lets you shield impressionable young eyes from pornography online. It offers these settings:

- **All Websites.** No protection at all.

- **Limit Adult Content.** Apple will apply its own judgment in blocking dirty websites, using a blocked-site list that it has compiled.

  That doesn't mean you can't override Apple's wisdom, however. The Always Allow and Never Allow controls let you add the addresses of websites that you think should be OK (or should not be OK).

- **Specific Websites Only.** This is a "whitelist" feature. It means that the entire web is blocked except for the few sites listed here: safe bets like Disney, PBS Kids, Smithsonian Institution, and so on. You can add your own sites to this list, but the point is clear: This is the web with training wheels.

Privacy

These switches can prohibit the unauthorized user from making changes to the phone's privacy settings, which are described on page 570.

Allow Changes

These items (Accounts, Cellular Data Use, Background App Refresh, Volume Limit) are safeguards against your offspring fiddling with limits you've set.

Game Center

These controls let you stop your kid from playing multiplayer games (against strangers online) or adding game-playing friends to the center.

Cases and Accessories

The iPhone has inspired a torrent of accessories. Stylish cases, speakers, docks, cables—the list goes on forever.

Just be sure you're buying something that fits your phone. For example, the Lightning connector (where the charging cable connects) on the iPhone 5 and later doesn't fit any of the charging accessories that came before it—at least not without the help of Apple's $30 adapter (or the $40 adapter that has an 8-inch cable "tail").

Accessory companies have been busy introducing Lightning-compatible gear. But for now, buyer beware—or buyer stock up on $30 adapters.

So what might you add to your iPhone?

- **Cases.** It's the iPhone Paradox: People buy the thinnest, sleekest smartphone in existence—and then bury it in a bulky carrying case. There's just something so wrong about that. On the other hand, this thing is made of glass; the instinct to protect it is understandable.

  Hundreds of cases are available. If you're worried about droppage, choose a silicone rubber case; it does a better job of protecting your phone than hard plastic cases. You can also get cases with built-in battery backups, credit card slots, and even speakers.

- **Everything else.** Speaker docks. Bluetooth speakers. Headphones and earbuds, wired and cordless. Credit card readers. Car cigarette-lighter adapters. Alarm clocks. Video-out cables. Stylish styluses. Touchscreen-compatible gloves. Tripods. Panorama stands. Kickstands. Car mounts. Activity monitors. Lenses. You Google it, you'll find it. The iPhone is, without a doubt, the most accessorized phone in the world.

B

Troubleshooting & Maintenance

The iPhone is a computer, and you know what that means: Things can go wrong. This particular computer, though, is not quite like a Mac or a PC. It runs a spin-off of the OS X operating system, but that doesn't mean you can apply the same troubleshooting techniques.

Therefore, let this appendix be your guide when things go wrong.

First Rule: Install the Updates

There's an old saying: "Never buy version 1.0 of anything." In the iPhone's case, the saying could be: "Never buy version 9.0 of anything."

The very first version (or major revision) of anything has bugs, glitches, and things the programmers didn't have time to finish the way they would have liked. The iPhone is no exception.

The beauty of this phone, though, is that Apple can send it fixes, patches, and even new features through software updates. One day you'll glance at your Home screen's Settings icon, and—bam!—there'll be a badge indicating that new iPhone software is available.

So the first rule of trouble-free iPhoning is to accept these updates when they're offered. With each new software blob, Apple removes another few dozen tiny glitches.

And sure enough: Within the first few weeks of iOS 9's existence, software updates 9.0.1 and 9.1 came down the pike. And more will come.

Six Ways to Reset the Phone

The iPhone runs actual programs, and as actual programs do, they actually crash. Sometimes, the program you're working in simply vanishes and you find yourself back at the Home screen. Just reopen the program and get on with your life.

If the program you're in just doesn't seem to be working right—it's frozen or acting weird, for example—then one of these resetting techniques usually clears things right up.

NOTE: Proceed down this list in order! Start with the easy ones.

- **Exit the app.** On an iPhone, you're never aware that you're launching and exiting programs. They're always just *there*, like TV channels, when you switch to them. There's no Quit command. But if a program starts acting glitchy, you can make it quit.

  To do that, double-press the Home button to bring up the app switcher. Find the "card" that represents your balky app, and then flick it upward to quit it. Try reopening it to see if the problem has gone away.

- **Turn the phone off and on again.** If it seems something more serious has gone wrong, then hold down the Sleep switch for a few seconds. When the screen says slide to power off, confirm by swiping. The iPhone shuts off completely.

  Turn it back on by pressing the Sleep switch for a second or two.

- **Force restart the phone.** If you haven't been able to force quit the program, and you can't shut the phone off either, you might have to force a restart. To do that, hold down the Home button *and* the Sleep switch for 10 seconds. Keep holding, even if the screen goes black or you see the "power off" slider. Don't release until you see the Apple logo appear, meaning that the phone is restarting.

- **Reset the phone's settings.** Relax. This procedure doesn't erase any of your data—only the phone's settings. From the Home screen, tap Settings→General→Reset→Reset All Settings.

- **Erase the whole phone.** From the Home screen, tap Settings→General→Reset→Erase All Content and Settings. Now, *this* option zaps your stuff—*all* of it. Music, videos, email, settings, apps, all gone, and all overwritten with random 1's and 0's to make sure it's completely unrecoverable. Clearly, you're getting into last resorts here. Of course, you can then sync with your backup (iTunes or iCloud) to copy all that stuff back onto your iPhone.

- **Restore the phone.** If none of these steps solve the phone's glitchiness, it might be time for the nuclear option: erasing it completely,

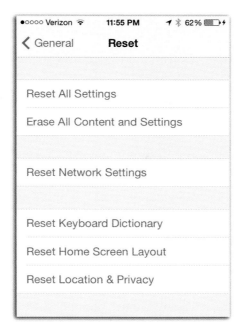

resetting both hardware and software back to a factory-fresh condition.

> **TIP:** If you're able to sync the phone with iCloud or iTunes *first*, do it! That way, you'll have a backup of all those intangible iPhone data bits: text messages, call logs, Recents list, and so on. iTunes will put it all back onto the phone the first time you sync after the restore.

If you backed up to iTunes: Connect the phone to your computer, as described in Chapter 14. In iTunes, click the iPhone icon and then, on the Summary tab, click Restore.

The first order of business: iTunes offers to make a backup of your iPhone (all of its phone settings, text messages, and so on) before proceeding. Accepting this invitation is an excellent idea. Click Back Up.

If you backed up to iCloud: You can restore your phone this way only if your iPhone is completely wiped empty. If it's not, manually erase it using iTunes first.

During the setup screens described on page 597, tap Restore from iCloud Backup. You're shown the three most recent backups; tap the one you want. The phone goes right to work downloading your settings and account information. Then it restarts and begins to download your apps; if you're in a hurry for one particular app, tap its icon to make iCloud prioritize it. At any time, you can check the restore process's status in Settings→iCloud→Storage and Backup.

When that's all over, you can get to work downloading your music (if you're an iTunes Match subscriber).

iPhone Doesn't Turn On

Usually, the problem is that the battery's dead. Just plugging it into the USB cord or USB charger doesn't bring it to life immediately, either; a completely dead iPhone doesn't wake up until it's been charging for about 10 minutes. It pops on automatically when it has enough juice to do so.

If you don't think that's the trouble, try the force-restarting trick described earlier. And if even that doesn't work, read on.

The Force Restore

If your phone gets stuck starting up at the Apple logo, or it just stays black, then something more serious may have happened. Phones, like the best of us, sometimes get confused.

The solution is the drastic, but effective, force-restore process (known to techies as the Default Firmware Update mode).

Open iTunes on your computer. Connect the iPhone with its white USB cable. Now hold down the Sleep switch and Home button simultaneously for 10 seconds—then release *only* the Sleep switch.

Keep the Home button pressed until iTunes tells you that an iPhone in Recovery mode has been detected; click OK. (If you see anything but blackness on your iPhone's screen—an Apple logo, for example—then the process didn't work. If the problem has not, in fact, gone away, then you should start again.)

iTunes tells you again that you're in Recovery mode and offers only one button: Restore iPhone. Click that, and then confirm by clicking Restore & Update. The process of reinstalling the latest, fresh copy of iOS begins.

> **TIP:** Every now and then, the cycle of backing-up-and-restoring goes amiss. You find yourself stuck at that Restore iPhone button—but you don't want to wipe it empty! There's stuff on it that hasn't been backed up!
>
> In that case, download the free program called RecBoot (for Mac) or TinyUmbrella (Mac or Windows). (You can download them from this book's "Missing CD" page at *www.missingmanuals.com*.) They have one tiny purpose in life: exiting Restore mode without erasing your phone.

Once everything's running fine, you can restore all your apps and settings from the latest backup as described on page 609.

Battery Life Is Terrible

If your battery seems to drain faster after you've installed iOS 9, maybe it's because you're *using* the phone more, checking out the cool new features.

If that's not the problem, consult the battery-saving tips on page 40.

Out of Space

It happens all the time. You couldn't imagine filling up 64 or 128 gigabytes of storage, so you saved some money by buying an iPhone with less. And now you can't even take a video or a photo, because your phone reports that it's full. You're frozen out until you have the time and expertise to delete some less important stuff.

The biggest space hogs on your phone are video files, photo files, apps, and music files. Heck, deleting just one downloaded movie or TV show could solve your storage crunch instantly.

Fortunately, iOS makes it very easy to see what's eating up your space— and to delete the fattest ones to make the most room with the least effort. The key is to visit Settings→General→Storage & iCloud Usage→Manage Storage.

The list here shows what's using up your space, biggest first; by tapping the > button, you can see the details and, in most cases, make some deletions on the spot.

Delete Photos and Recorded Videos

Unfortunately, this display shows how much space your Camera videos and photos take up, but it doesn't let you delete them. To purge your photos, the quickest method is to hook up to iTunes, import the photos, and take advantage of the option to delete the freshly imported photos from the phone (page 508).

Turning off your Photo Stream can give you back an instant gigabyte, too (page 296).

Delete "Other" Items

You know the colored graph of what's on your phone that shows up in iTunes (page 498)? Often, the biggest item here is the mysterious Other category. What is that stuff? It's caches (Internet data stored on the phone to make repeated visits faster), backups, partial downloads, and data from iOS's built-in apps—all your text messages and email, for example. Here's how you clean them out:

- **Delete the web browser cache.** The phone saves web pages into its own memory so they'll appear faster the next time you try to visit them. If you've had your iPhone awhile, those cache files can really add up. Open Settings→Safari; tap Clear History and Website Data. You may get a speed boost as a side effect.

- **Delete text messages.** In the Messages app, you can delete individual texts or entire conversations (page 167); because they frequently include photo, audio, or video files, you can reclaim a lot of space.

- **Delete email attachments**. Files downloaded with your email take up a lot of space, too. The solution is to delete the email account (Settings→Mail, Contacts, Calendar→[account name]; scroll down and tap Delete Account)—and then add it again.

  In the process, you'll vaporize all the attachment files and message caches that you've ever downloaded and opened on your phone. When you add the account back again, those files will still be online, ready to download—but only when you need them. (This trick works for most account types—just not for POP3 accounts.)

- **Delete voice memos, music files, and ebooks.** Audio files and iBooks eat up a lot of space, too. Consider purging the recordings, books, and songs you can do without (from within the Voice Memos, iBooks, and Music apps). You can re-download them later from the App, iTunes, or iBooks stores—no charge—whenever you like.

Phone and Internet Problems

How can the phone part of the iPhone go wrong? Let us count the ways:

- **Can't make calls.** First off, do you have enough cellular signal to make a call? Check your signal-strength dots. Even if you have one or two, flakiness is par for the course, although one bar in a 3G, 4G, or LTE area is much better than one bar in a slower area. Try going outside, standing near a window, or moving to a major city (kidding).

  Also, make sure airplane mode isn't turned on. Try calling somebody else to make sure the problem isn't with the number you're dialing.

  If nothing else works, try the resetting techniques described starting on page 607.

- **Can't receive calls.** If calls seem to go directly to voicemail and the phone never even rings, check to make sure Do Not Disturb isn't turned on (page 116).

- **Can't get on the Internet.** If you're not in a Wi-Fi hotspot (there's no ●●○○○ at the top of the screen) and you don't have cell service (no **E**, **O**, **3G**, **4G**, or **LTE** logo at the top of the screen), well, then, you're in a "No Service" area, or the phone thinks you are. (In the latter case, try turning the phone off and then on again.)

- **Can't send text messages.** Make sure, of course, that you've signed up for a texting plan. Also, make sure you haven't turned on Show Subject Field (page 177) and forgotten to fill out the body of the message.

Warranty and Repair

The iPhone comes with a one-year warranty and 90 days of phone tech support. If you buy an AppleCare+ contract ($100), you're covered for a second year.

If, during the coverage period, anything goes wrong that's not your fault, Apple will fix it free. In fact, AppleCare+ covers damage even if it *is* your fault, for $80 each time—even if you drop the phone or get it wet. Maximum: twice.

You can either take the phone to an Apple Store, which is often the fastest route, or call 800-APL-CARE (800-275-2273) to arrange shipping back to Apple. In general, you'll get the fixed phone back in 3 business days.

Out-of-Warranty Repairs

Once the year or two has gone by, or if you damage your iPhone in a way that's not covered by the warranty (backing your car over it comes to mind), Apple charges $200 to repair an iPhone (it usually just replaces it).

The Battery Replacement Program

Why did Apple seal the battery inside the iPhone, anyway? Everyone knows lithium-ion batteries don't last forever. After 300 or 400 charges, the iPhone battery begins to hold less charge (perhaps 80 percent of the original). After a certain point, the phone will need a new battery. How come you can't change it yourself, as on any normal cellphone?

Apple's answer: A user-replaceable battery takes up a lot more space inside the phone. It requires a plastic compartment that shields the guts of the phone from you and your fingers; it requires a removable door; and it needs springs or clips to hold the battery in place.

In any case, you can't change the battery yourself. If the phone is out of warranty, you must send it to Apple (or take it to an Apple Store) for an $85 battery-replacement job. (As an eco-bonus, Apple properly disposes of the old batteries, which consumers might not do on their own.)

What to Do About a Cracked Screen

Keeping your iPhone in a case may lower the chances of your dropping it or scratching it—but it can't prevent bad luck. An incredible number of iPhone screens meet an untimely end, even with cases on.

Apple will happily replace your phone's screen for $110 to $150, depending on the model. It'll do it the same day if you take the phone into an Apple Store, or you can mail it in and get a replacement in 3 to 5 days. (If you've bought the AppleCare+ extended-warranty service, then a replacement is $50 to $100, depending on the model.)

There are plenty of other companies that can repair a cracked screen, though. The reps from *iCracked.com*, for example, send a technician to you and perform the fix on the spot.

And then there's the do-it-yourself technique. You can buy a screen-replacement kit for about $60 online, complete with the special tools you need to open the iPhone and do the job yourself. It's a job that requires care, patience, and some dexterity (Google can help you find the step-by-steps), but it's a good option if you're technically savvy.

Where to Go from Here

At this point, the iPhone is such a phenomenon that there's no shortage of resources for getting more help, news, and tips. Here are a few examples:

- **Apple's official iPhone User Guide.** Yes, there is an actual download-able PDF user's manual. *http://support.apple.com/manuals/*

- **Apple's official iPhone help website.** Online tips, tricks, and tutorials; troubleshooting topics; downloadable PDF help documents; and, above all, an enormous, seething treasure trove of discussion boards. *www.apple.com/support/iphone/*

- **Apple's service site.** All the dates, prices, and expectations for getting your iPhone repaired. Includes details on getting a temporary replacement unit. *www.apple.com/support/iphone/service/faq/*

- **iMore blog.** News, tips, tricks, all in a blog format. *www.imore.com/*

- **iLounge.** Another great blog-format site. Available in an iPhone format so you can read it right on the device. *www.iLounge.com/*

- **MacRumors/iPhone.** Blog-format news, accessory blurbs, help discussions; iPhone wallpaper. *www.macrumors.com/iphone/*

- **iPhone Atlas.** Discussion, news, apps, how-tos. *www.iphoneatlas.com*

Index

1xRTT networks 417–418
3G networks 24, 418
  speed of 420
4G networks. *See* LTE network
4K video 265–266
30-pin connector 31

A

abbreviation expanders 73–74
AC adapter 32
accented characters 72–73
accessibility 187–212
  AssistiveTouch 201–203
  dictation 80–86
  double-tap timing 191
  grayscale screen 195
  Guided Access (kiosk mode) 208–210
  hearing assistance 206–207
  increasing screen contrast 198–199
  increasing text size 197
  LED flash on ring 207
  monaural mode 207
  phonetic feedback 190
  Reachability feature 21–22
  Reduce Motion feature 199
  Rotor 189–190
  routing calls to speakerphone 206
  Screen Curtain 189
  shortcut to features 211–212
  Speak Auto-text 196
  Sticky Keys 205
  subtitles 208
  switch control 200–201
  touchscreen accommodations 203–204
  TTY settings 581
  turning off vibration 205
  typing feedback 191
  typing in Braille 189
  typing options 190
  using phone with hearing aids 206–207
  video descriptions for the blind 208
  VoiceOver 188–191
  white-on-black mode 195–196
  zooming the screen 192–195
accessories 605–606
  AC adapter 32
  EarPods 32
  Lightning-connector compatible 606
  USB cable 32
Activation Lock 521
Add Call. *See* conference calling
address book. *See* Contacts app
address/search bar
  Quick Website Search 438
  typing web addresses 433–435
advertising
  iAds location privacy 572
  limiting tracking 573
  removing from web articles 451–452
AirDrop 49, 331–334
  between a phone and a Mac 543–544
  defined 331
  step by step 332–333
  turning off 334
  who can see you 333–334
airplane mode 43, 422–423
  controlling by voice 134
  controlling from Control Center 423
  settings 557
  vs. Do Not Disturb 116
AirPlay 244
  peer-to-peer AirPlay 244
  switching among speakers 235
AirPrint 329–330

alarm clock 350–352
  alarm labels 351
  choosing a song 351
  controlling by voice 135
  deleting or editing alarms 352
  status bar icon 25
Amazon
  music sales 494
  searching within 438
  use of cookies 453
answering calls. *See* **calling**
antennas 32
AOL mail accounts 457–458
App Analytics 601
Apple ID
  acquiring during setup 599–600
  creating for a child under 13 530
  forgotten 574
  signing out 574
  viewing account information 574
Apple Music 215–217
  Beats 1 radio 217
  features 216–217
  free trial 216
Apple Pay 524–528
  participating retailers 524
  security of 527–528
  settings 574
  setting up 524–526
  shopping with 526–528
  using online 528
Apple TV
  AirPlay 244
  Photo Stream 298
apps. *See also* **App Store**
  Apple starter set 324
  automatic updates 323, 574
  Back button 328–329
  Background App Refresh 564
  Calculator 337–338
  Calendar 339–348
  Clock 349–354
  Compass 354–356
  defined 309
  deleting 316–319
  finding settings 322
  Find My Friends 413
  Find My iPhone 518–521
  folders 319–322
  force quitting 327
  free Apple apps 412–413
  free re-downloading 522–523
  Game Center 356–359
  Google Voice 181
  Health 359–362

  how to buy 312
  iBooks 362–372
  iMovie 413
  in-app purchases 604
  iTunes Store 237–240
  iTunes U 413
  Keynote 413
  location-based 18
  location-tracking controls 571–572
  Mail 457–486
  Maps 373–387
  Music 215–233
  News 388–390
  Notes 390–394
  Numbers 412
  opening with Siri 133
  organizing 316–319
  Pages 412
  Pandora 232
  Photos 269–307
  Podcasts 394–397
  preferences settings 591
  Reflector 244
  Reminders 397–403
  running in the background 327–328
  Stocks 403–405
  storage report 564
  Suggested Apps 563–564
  suggested on Lock screen 18
  switching among 20–21
  third-party photo editors 276–277
  Tips 405–406
  turning off automatic updates 42
  updates 322–323
  Videos 240–244
  Voice Memos 406–408
  Wallet 409–410
  Weather 410–412
  WhatsApp 180
App Store. *See also* **apps**
  App Details page 312–314
  Apple starter apps 324
  auto backups 314–315
  defined 309
  file-size limit 314
  finding good apps 323–325
  in-app purchases 604
  + on price button 312
  re-downloading 314–315
  searching 311–312
  shopping from iPhone 310–315
  shopping in iTunes 315
  troubleshooting 315

app switcher 325–327
  background apps 327–329
  summon on the 6s 326
arrow notation 4
AssistiveTouch 201–203
AT&T
  data network speeds 417–418
  EDGE network 417–418
  GSM network 28
  HSPA+ network 418
  LTE network 418
  personal hotspot 426
  using the iPhone overseas 28–29
  vs. other carriers 595
attachments
  deleting 612
  opening 474–475
  photos or videos 482
  saving graphics and pictures 475
  viewing in Messages 165–166
  .zip files 475
Audible.com 496
audiobooks
  buying in iTunes Store 496
  managing in iTunes 506
audio messages 172–174
  deleting 174
  turning off 173
auto-capitalization 565
autocorrect 73–74
  make it stop replacing certain words 74
  turning off 565
AutoFill
  passwords and credit card numbers
    446–448
  settings 585
automatic app updates 323

B

Back button 328–329
  gesture 35, 227
background apps 327–328
Backspace key 64–65
Back to My Mac 514
backups 510–512
  automatic app backups 314–315
  deleting 512
  Encrypted iPhone Backup 511
  iCloud-based 517
  iCloud Drive 334–336
  preventing a backup 500
  restoring from backup 511–512
banners 56

battery
  battery usage screen 44–45
  brightness settings 567–568
  charging 39–40
  improving battery life 40–45, 611
  replacement program 614–615
  settings 570
  status bar icon 26
  turning off automatic app updates 42
  turning off Location Services 376
  using airplane mode 43
  using Bluetooth LE 185
Bcc
  defined 480
Beats 1 radio 217
black-and-white photos 272–273
blocking calls and texts 581
Bluetooth
  4.0 185
  address 562
  AirDrop 331–334
  Bluetooth LE 185
  car kits 184–185
  connecting a physical keyboard 78–79
  controlling by voice 134
  pairing 234–235
  setting up a Personal Hotspot with 426
  speakers and headphones 233–235
  status bar icon 25
  turning off to save power 43
  turning on and off 558–559
bookmarks 438–441
  creating 439–440
  defined 438
  editing 440
  favorites icons 434–435
  folders 440
  iCloud syncing 517
  in iBooks 368
  in Maps 379
Braille keyboard 189
brightness controls 567
  controlling by voice 134
  in iBooks 367
  in Maps 385
burst mode 256–257
buttons
  adding outlines 198

C

Calculator app 337–338
  memory function 338
  scientific calculator 338

Calendar app 339–348
  alerts 344–345
  alternatives to 348
  color-coded categories 347–348
  controlling by voice 139–140
  Day view 339–340
  editing and deleting events 346–347
  Exchange syncing 549–550
  Facebook integration 347–348
  iCloud syncing 516–517
  invitations 344
  limiting past events 579–580
  making an appointment 342–345
  Month view 340
  notes 345
  Outlook invitations 550–551
  Quick Actions 37
  repeating events 343
  setting default category 580
  settings 579–580
  sharing calendars in Family Sharing
      533
  showing week numbers 579
  special views in Plus model phones 341
  subscribing to online calendars 341
  time zones 579
  Travel Time settings 343
  Week view 340–341
  Year view 340
caller ID 183
  FaceTime settings 583
  hiding yours 581
  iOS 9 guessing 114
calling 95–101
  answering calls 113–114
  Blocked list 178
  Caller ID 183
  call forwarding 182
  calling plans 596–597
  call waiting 181–182
  Contacts app 101–112
  dumping calls to voicemail 15, 115
  FaceTime audio calls 126–127
  FaceTime video calls 123–126
  Favorites 96–98
  from a Mac 536–537
  from Contacts 102
  from Recents list 99–101
  keypad 112
  merging calls 121–122
  noise cancellation 207
  overseas call settings 581
  putting someone on hold 122
  Remind Me Later option 115–116
  Respond with Text option 115
  routing calls to speakerphone 206

  silencing the ring 114, 114–115
  troubleshooting 613
  two calls at once 120
  using earbuds 113–114
  while using Wi-Fi 114
camcorder. See **video camera**
Camera app 26–27, 245–307. See
      also **Photos app**
  burst mode 256–257
  exposure lock 250–251
  face detection 248
  filters 259
  flash 251–252
  focus lock 250–251
  front camera 257–258, 267
  geotagging photos 305–307
  HDR mode 254–255
  LED flash 27
  Live Photos 260–262
  macro mode 249
  opening 246
  opening from Lock screen 18
  overview 245–247
  overview of modes 247
  panoramas 262–264
  quick access to 50
  Quick Actions 37
  reviewing a photo 256
  Rule of Thirds grid 253
  screen captures 307
  self-timer 258
  setting exposure 249–250
  sharing and using photos 286–296
  Square mode 262
  still photos 248–259
  taking the shot 255–256
  True Tone flash 251
  using with FaceTime 125–126
  Video mode 264–267
  volume-key shutter 255
  white balance 248–249
  yellow box 248–249
  zooming 252–253
Camera Roll 280. See also **Photos app**
  vs. All Photos 304
capitalization
  Caps Lock 64, 565
  how to dictate 85–86
  keyboard shortcuts 64, 72
carpenter's level 355–356
carriers
  calling plans compared 596–597
  choosing while overseas 558
  compared 595
  contracts 596
  information 582

Cc
defined 480
viewing 476–477
CDMA networks 28–29
cellular data
cellular triangulation 376
for iBooks videos 372
managing 559–561
networks 24–25
on/off switches 561
signal status bar icon 24
turning off to save power 43
cellular networks 417–419
1xRTT network 417–418
3G 418
4G LTE 418
EDGE network 417–418
HSPA+ 418
settings 559–561
Wi-Fi Assist 561
character preview 565
charging 39–40
with AC adapter 39
with Lightning connector 31–32
with USB cable 32, 39
chat programs 181
children
Family Sharing 528–533
Guided Access (kiosk mode) 208–212
parental controls 603–605
Clock app 349–354
alarm clock 350–352
auto-time zone on/off 572
controlling by voice 136
opening the timer 50
Quick Actions 37
settings 565
stopwatch 352–353
timer 353–354
World Clock 349–350
Compass app 354–356
carpenter's level 355–356
orienting a map 376
settings 584
true north vs. magnetic north 354
conference calling 120–122
GSM vs. CDMA phones 120
swapping calls 120–121
configuration profiles. *See* **profiles**
Contacts app 101–112
adding contacts from email 474
adding photos 105–106
adding photos from Facebook 106
adding someone quickly 110–111
address-book groups 118
assigning relatives 106

Blocked list 178
blocking calls and texts 581
controlling by voice 136–137
defined 101
deleting someone 111
designating VIPs 465–466
editing contacts 103–111
Facebook groups 102
Favorites 96–98
groups 102
iCloud syncing 516–517
importing from Twitter 107
Import SIM Contacts 578
linking names 109–110
My Info 578
navigating list of contacts 102
personalizing fields 108
searching your company's directory
548–549
settings 578
sharing contacts 111
sort order 578
using to address email 479
vibration patterns 107–108
Continuity 535–544
calling from a Mac 536–537
Instant Hotspot feature 539–540
setting up 535–536
texting from a Mac 538–539
contrast 198–199
Control Center 47–51
AirDrop 49
airplane mode 47–48, 423
AirPlay 49
Bluetooth 48
calculator 50
camera 50
closing 51
defined 47
doesn't open on first try 50
Do Not Disturb 48
gesture to open 35
LED flashlight 50
open from Lock screen 18
playback controls 49
Rotation Lock 48–49
screen brightness 49
Timer 50
using with Siri 47–51
Wi-Fi 48, 423
cookies 453
copying 86–89
copy key 70
from one email to another 481–482
photos 282, 292
text messages 179–180

corporate features **545–554**
  about Exchange ActiveSync 545–546
  accessing SharePoint sites 552
  accessing your company's directory
    548–549
  calendar syncing 549–550
  email 547–548
  invitations 550–551
  mobile device management 546
  Outlook Web Access (OWA) 546
  perks of using 545–547
  security 546
  setting up Exchange ActiveSync
    547–550
  troubleshooting 551–552
  virtual private networking 552–554
credit cards **446–448**
  and Apple Pay 524–528
  using the camera to enter 447–448
cropping photos **274–307**

D

data speeds **24–25**
date
  setting 565
deafness. *See also* **accessibility, hearing
  assistance**
deleting
  all content and settings 566
  apps 316–319
  attachments 612
  audio messages 583
  AutoFill information in Safari 585
  Calendar events 346
  cities in Weather app 412
  email 472–473
  family member from Family Sharing 531
  Favorites 98
  favorites icons 434
  mailboxes 460
  notes 392
  "other" items 611–613
  phone backup file 512
  photos 285
  photos and videos 611
  photos from iCloud Photo Stream 303
  photos from My Photo Stream 298–299
  playlists 494
  podcasts 396
  recent calls 100
  reminders 400
  RSS feeds 443
  Safari bookmarks 440
  Safari history 442
  space-hogging apps 564

  stocks 404
  text messages 167–168, 612
  tickets from Wallet 410
  video messages 583
  VIPs 465
  voicemail messages 159–160
  web browser cache 612
diacritical marks **72–73**
dialing **95–96**
  keypad 112
  touchtones 119
  with Siri 134
dictation **80–86**
  capitalization 85–86
  correcting errors 82
  punctuation 82–84
dictionary
  definitions 89
  in iBooks 369
  resetting 69
  resetting keyboard suggestions 566
  spelling 69
  using Google as 438
dimming the screen **41, 567–568**
  shortcut 210–211
directions **381–382**
  new Transit option 382
  voice control 140
disabilities. *See* **accessibility**
DiskAid **180**
Dock **46**
Do Not Disturb **116–118**
  allowing special callers through 117–118
  controlling by voice 134
  defined 116
  in Messages 165
  repeated calls 118
  Silence option 118
  status bar icon 25
  turning on or off 117
double-tapping **35**
downloads
  automatic app updates 574
  email attachments 474–475
  over cellular network 237
dragging **33**
DuckDuckGo **437**
Dynamic Type **197**

E

earbuds
  answering calls with 113–114
  dumping calls to voicemail 115
  EarPods 32
  limiting volume 235–236

playback controls 222
Siri 131
using volume clicker as camera shutter 255
ebooks. *See also* **iBooks app**
Audible.com 496
managing in iTunes 506
EDGE network 24, 417–418
speed of 420
editing
photos 269–277
ringtones 122–123
Safari bookmarks 440
Safari Favorites page 434–435
video 268–269
voice recordings 408
email 457–486
adding senders to Contacts 474
addressing from Contacts 479
addressing groups 479, 480
Always Bcc Myself 577
ask before deleting 577
attaching photos or videos 482–483
avoiding spam 484–485
Cc and Bcc 480
collapsing messages 481–482
composing and sending 478–484
deleting batches of messages 473–474
deleting single messages 472–473
downloading 460–464
Exchange syncing 547–548
filing 468–469, 472
flagging messages 466–468
flag style 576
formatting text 483
forwarding 471–472
free accounts 457–458
free account with iCloud 521–522
gestures 468–469
Load Remote Images 577
managing accounts 485–486
marking as unread 477
message preview 485
opening attachments 474–475
POP 3 and IMAP accounts 459–460
"push" data controls 575
Quick Actions 37
QuickType suggestions 66–68
quote level (indentation) 483–484
reading 469–470
replying 470–471
reply notifications 472
saving graphics and pictures 475
searching 477–478
selecting the sending account 480
setting default account 486, 577

setting lines to show in preview 576
settings 575–577
setting up your account 457–460
sharing attachments 475
sharing contacts 111–112
showing the To/Cc label 485
signatures 484
subject line 481
suggested email groups 479
swipe gesture options 576
threading 463–464, 577
To/Cc badges 576
unified inbox 462–463
using live links 470
viewing header details 476–477
VIP list 465–466
virtual private networking 552–554
voice control 138–139
emergency calls 59
emoji keyboard 77–78
Encrypted iPhone Backup 511–512
ePub files 363–365
EQ (equalization) 235
erasing the phone 566

F

Facebook 427–428
account settings 427
alert sounds 569
app 427
calendar integration 347–348
Contacts groups 102
Game Center integration 358
importing names and photos from 106–107
posting photos to 289–290
posting with Siri 148
privacy 573
settings 590
Share button 428
sharing web links 442
face detection 248
FaceTime 123–127
audio calls 126–127
call blocking 581
capturing a screenshot 126
ending a call 126
initiating a call 124–125
muting audio or video 126
on/off switch 583
rotating the screen 125
settings 583–584
switching to back camera 125–126
video calls 123–126

Fake Calls app 325
Family Sharing 528–533
  appointments, photos, and reminders
    533
  approving purchases 531–532
  hiding your purchases 532
  locating family members 532–533
  setting up 529–531
  using 531–533
favorites
  deleting 98
  in Contacts 96–98
  in Maps app 380–381
  in News app 389
  rearranging 98
  web bookmarks 434–435
filters 259, 273–274
Find My Friends 324, 413
  controlling by voice 145
Find My iPhone 324, 413, 518–521
  Activation Lock 521
  defined 518
  displaying a message 519
  Lost Mode 519–520
  remote wipe 520
  Send Last Location 521
  tracking the phone 520
fingerprint security. See Touch ID
flagged email messages 466–468
  flag vs. orange dot 576
flash 26–27, 251–252
  as video light 267
  for rings and notifications 207
  LED flash 251
  screen flash 252
flashlight
  turning on quickly 50
Flash plug-in 429
flicking 33–34
Flickr
  posting photos to 289–290
  settings 590
FlightTrack Pro 325
Flyover and Flyover Tours 386–387
folders 319–322
  creating and editing 319–321
  creating in iTunes 321–322
  deleting 321
  moving 321
  renaming 321
fonts
  bigger or bolder text 197–198
  Dynamic Type feature 568
  in iBooks 367
force quitting apps 327
force restarting 15, 608

force restoring 610–611
Force Touch 36–39
  Peek and Pop features 38–39
  Quick Actions 36–37
front camera 257–258
  flash for 252

G

Game Center 356–359
  Facebook integration 358
  finding friends 358
  finding games 358–359
  getting started 356–357
  parental controls 605
  playing games 358–359
  points and achievements 357–358
  settings 589–590
geotagging 305–307
gestures
  backspace in Calculator 338
  customizing 469
  double-tapping 35
  dragging 33
  email 468–469
  flicking 33–34
  force-pressing 36–39
  hard-pressing 79–80
  in AssistiveTouch mode 202
  in VoiceOver 188
  magnify sections of a web page
    431–432
  pinching and spreading 34
  punctuation with one gesture 70–72
  rightward swipe 461
  rotating in Maps 375
  scroll up or down in Safari 432
  selecting text in Safari 87
  split tap 188
  swipe to go back 556
  swiping 33
  swiping from left edge 227
  swiping in from the edge 35–36
  working with photos 280, 282–284
  zooming 192–193
  zooming in Maps 374
getting online. See Internet
Gmail
  setting up account 457–458
  setting up push email for 460
  using to avoid spam 485
Google
  Google Maps 373
  Google Mobile 324–325
  Google Voice 181
  search 436

GPS. *See also* **navigation**
geotagging 305–307
how the iPhone does it 375
location-based reminders 401–402
Maps app Navigation mode 382–384
status bar icon 26
turning off to save power 42–43
graphics
fetched images in email 577
saving from Safari 446
groups
Family Sharing 528–533
for Do Not Disturb feature 118
in Contacts 102
in Mail 479, 480
GSM phones
networks 28–29
swapping calls 120
Guided Access (kiosk mode) 208–210

H

Handoff 540–543
compatible programs 541
settings 563
setting up 542–543
hashtags 428
HDR photos 254–255
headphones 233–235
headphone jacks 29–30
limiting volume 235–236
Health app 359–362
adding medical information 362
and Fitbit 360
fitness device compatibility 359–360
setting up 360–361
HealthKit. *See* **Health app**
hearing assistance 206–207
adjusting stereo mix 207
LED flash for alerts 207
mono audio 207
noise cancellation 207
subtitles 208
using phone with hearing aids 206–207
"Hey Siri" feature 132
turning off 154
hiding
Caller ID on outgoing calls 581
flagged email folder 467
microphone button 565
photos 282
purchases from Family Sharing 532
VIP email folder 466
highlighting
in iBooks 369

History list 441–442
clearing 587
erasing 442
Home button 19–22
accessibility 22, 211–212
accessing Reachability feature 21–22
activating Siri 20
app switcher 20–21
defined 19
double-click speed 206
gets sticky 202
triple-press 210–212
waking the phone 19
Home screens 45–47
background 46–47
badges 45
Dock 46
folders 319–322
icons 45
navigating 45–46
organizing your downloads 316–319
Quick Actions 36–37
Reduce Motion feature 199
resetting layout 567
restoring 319
Home Sharing
playing music from your computer 236
settings 588
HTML5 587
hyperlapse video 268

I

iBackup Viewer 180
iBooks app 362–372
adding bookmarks 368
adjusting screen brightness 367
creating collections 365–366
dictionary 369–372
downloading books 362–363
downloading cover art 365
ePub files 363–365
finding free books 364–365
free re-downloading 522–523
highlighting 369
making notes 369
organizing your library 365
PDF files 363–365
reading and turning pages 366–368
settings 372
syncing bookmarks 372
type size 367
using as audiobook reader 371
using Scrolling View 367
viewing table of contents 367
viewing white text on black 366

iCloud
    automatic app updates 574
    Back to My Mac 514
    backups 517
    defined 513–515
    email account 521–522
    Find My iPhone 518–521
    free music, video, apps storage
        522–523
    iCloud Drive 334–336, 515–516
    iCloud Photo Library 304–305
    iCloud Photo Sharing 299–304
    My Photo Stream 296–299
    Reminders syncing 397
    sharing calendars 348
    signing up 513
    storage prices 523–524
    syncing 515–518
    syncing web tabs 450–451
    viewing storage 564
    VIPs 466
iCloud Drive 334–336
    accessing 334–335
    expanding storage limit 336
    turning on 334
iCloud Keychain
    initial setup 600
iCloud Photo Library 304–305
    accessing your photos 305
iCloud Photo Sharing
    creating an album 299–300
    editing an album 303–304
    receiving an album 302
    settings 300–302
    sharing albums publicly 301
    subscriber posting 300–301
    technical requirements 299
icons 45
    adding outlines 198
    for Internet connections 419
IMAP accounts 459–460
iMessages 170–175. *See also* **Messages**
    app, text messages
    advantages 170–172
    Blocked list 178
    blocking 581
    defined 170–172
    distinguishing from text messages 172
    finding chat transcripts 180
    multimedia tricks 172–175
    on/off switch 176, 582
    photo messaging 175
    read receipts 176
    sharing contacts 111–112
iMovie for iPhone 269
in-app purchases 604

Instagram 325
    Square mode 262
Instant Hotspot 539–540
international calling 28–29
Internet 417–428
    3G network 418
    connection icons 419
    EDGE network 417–418
    faster sites for slow connections 440
    Instant Hotspot 539–540
    parental controls 603–605
    Personal Hotspot 424–427
    Safari settings 584–587
    Safari web browser 429–456
    speed 24–25
    troubleshooting 613
    Twitter and Facebook 427–428
    VoLTE 419
    Wi-Fi 419–422
invitations 550–551
iOS 9
    design 196–200
    troubleshooting 607
    updates 602–603
iPhone
    accessories 32–33
    as phone 95–127
    calling plans 596–597
    camera 245–307
    cases and accessories 605–606
    charging 39–40
    defined 1–2
    erasing 566
    finding basic stats 502–503
    finding your phone number 101
    information about 562
    keypad 112
    locking and unlocking 15
    on/off switch 14–15
    powering off 608
    pricing 595
    projecting the screen 244
    recording the screen 244
    renaming 562
    resetting 607–610
    sales statistics 1
    screen 23–26
    serial number 562
    setting up 597–601
    SIM card slot 27–29
    sources for news, tips, and tricks
        615–616
    status bar icons 24–26
    storage statistics 564
    syncing 497–501

troubleshooting 607–616
upgrading to iOS 9 601–602
used as a watch 16
using overseas 28–29
volume controls 22–23
waking 19
iPhone 4s
30-pin connector 31
antennas 32
applying filters 259
camera resolution 27
limitations with iOS 9 602
micro-SIM card 29
iPhone 5, 5s, and 5c
antennas 24, 32
camera resolution 27
LTE networks 25
screen resolution 23
iPhone 6 and 6 Plus
antennas 32
Apple Pay 524–528
display zoom options 567
expanded keyboard 70
finding the Sleep switch 14
price 595
Reachability 21–22
special calendar views 341
two-column Notes layout 392
VoLTE 419
zoom style 601
iPhone 6s
3D Touch feature 204–205
antennas 32
Apple Pay 524–528
display zoom options 567
expanded keyboard 70
finding the Sleep switch 14
Force Touch 36–39
hard-pressing 79–80
Live Photos 260–262
new way to switch apps 326
price 595
Reachability 21–22
screen flash 252
VoLTE 419
what's new 4–7
zoom style 601
iPhone 6s Plus
3D Touch feature 204–205
antennas 32
Apple Pay 524–528
display zoom options 567
expanded keyboard 70
finding the Sleep switch 14
Force Touch 36–39

hard-pressing 79–80
Live Photos 260–262
new way to switch apps 326
price 595
Reachability 21–22
screen flash 252
special calendar views 341
two-column Notes layout 392
VoLTE 419
what's new 4–7
zoom style 601
iPhoto
preventing automatic opening 509
iPod features. See **Music app, Videos app**
iTunes 489–512
creating smart playlists 504–505
downloading 33
Encrypted iPhone Backup 511
erasing the phone 608–609
getting media onto your computer 492
importing music from a CD 492
iTunes Radio 230–233
iTunes Store 237–240
On My Device options 509
organizing apps 316–317
playlists 224–227, 492–494
syncing contacts and calendars 509
syncing with iPhone 497–501
tabs 502–509
three apps in one 489–490
turning off autosyncing 500–501
upgrading the iOS 601–602
iTunes Match 217
iTunes Radio 230–233
controlling with Siri 143
creating stations 231–232
defined 230–231
Now Playing screen 232
Play More Like This 232
Siri voice commands 233
iTunes Store 237–240, 494–497
alternative music stores 494
authorizing computers 497
defined 237
free re-downloading 522–523
iTunes U 496
Not on This iPhone 239
Purchased Items list 239
Redeem button 237
ringtones 239
searching 238
settings 574
TV and movies 495–496
Wish List 232
iTunes U 324, 496

J

Java 429
JavaScript 587

K

keyboard 63–79
  abbreviation expanders 73–74
  auto-capitalization 565
  autocorrect 565
  Backspace 64–65
  Caps Lock 64, 565
  connecting a physical keyboard 78–79
  Copy, Cut, and Paste 86–89
  cursor keys 70
  installing the emoji keyboard 77–78
  international keyboards 76–77
  loupe (magnifying glass) 65–66
  numbers layout 65
  period shortcut 66
  QuickType suggestions 66–68, 565
  repeating keys 205
  resetting dictionary 566
  Return key 65
  selecting text 87
  settings 565–566
  Shift key 64
  Speak Auto-text command 196
  spelling checker on/off 565
  Sticky Keys 205
  switching among keyboards 76
  third-party 74–76
  tips and tricks 65–68
  typing shortcuts 565
  Typing Style options 190
  widescreen mode 70
Keychain 517–518
keypad 112
  inputting touchtones 119
kiosk mode. See Guided Access (kiosk
  mode)

L

language
  dictation 80–86
  for video subtitles 242
  initial setup 597
  international keyboards 76–77
  settings 565
  Siri's languages 130, 154
LED "flash on ring" 207
level 355–356
Lightning connector 31–32, 605–606
  adapter plug 31

Lightning-to-HDMI cable 31
Lightning-to-VGA cable 31
video output adapters 31
light sensor 27, 41
links
  in email 470
  link-tapping tricks 445
  options panel 434
  settings 585
  Shared Links 442–443
  sharing 455
Live Photos 260–262
  defined 260–261
  reviewing 261
  sharing 261–262
  taking 260
Location Services 42, 571–572
  how the phone knows where it is
    375–376
  initial setup 598
  location-based apps 18
  location-based reminders 401–402
  privacy settings 571
  resetting warnings 567
  Share My Location feature 571
  turn apps on and off 571–572
locking the phone 15–16
  auto-lock settings 564–565
Lock screen 15–19
  Maps navigation 16
  missed calls and texts 16–17
  notifications 16–17, 55–56
  opening camera from 246
  security 18–19
  sleep settings 564–565
  suggests an app at this time 18
  time and date 16
  unlocking with Home button 20
Lost Mode 519–520
loupe 65–66
  in Safari address bar 66
LTE network 418
  disabling 559

M

macro mode 249
Macs
  AirDrop feature 543–544
  Handoff feature 540–543
  Instant Hotspot feature 539–540
  texting from 538–539
  using to make calls 536–537
magazines. See Newsstand
magic wand button 270
magnifying glass 65–66

Mail app. *See* **email**
Maps app 373–387
  bugs and controversy 373
  cellular positioning 376
  controlling by voice 140
  defined 373–374
  favorites and recent searches 380–381
  finding friends and businesses 379–380
  finding yourself 376
  Flyover and Flyover Tours 386–387
  getting directions 381–382
  GPS 375
  Location page 378–379
  Navigation mode 382–384
  Night mode 385
  orienting yourself 354, 376
  Passenger Navigation mode 384–385
  public transit directions 382
  Quick Actions 37
  searching for locations 376–378
  settings 584
  spoken instructions volume 584
  traffic reports 385–386
  view options 374–375
  Wi-Fi positioning 375–376
merging calls 121–122
Messages app. *See* **text messages**
microphones 30
  back microphone 30
  hiding the microphone button 565
  noise cancellation 207
  second mike for noise canceling 30
micro-SIM cards 29
missed calls 99
MMS messaging 176. *See also* **text mes-**
    sages
  on/off switch 583
  saving incoming photos or videos
    179–180
mobile device management 546
Move Data from Android 598
movies
  buying or renting on iTunes 495–496
  free re-downloading 522–523
  trivia and showtimes from Siri 146–147
  Videos app 240–244
  viewing library 505
multitasking
  app switcher 20–21
  background app refresh 564
  getting online while on a call 114
music
  buying on iTunes 494–495
  creating smart playlists 504–505
  identifying songs 144
  iTunes Store 494–497

iTunes Store alternatives 494
  monaural mode 207
  Music app 215–233
  playlists 492–494
  storage 504–505
Music app 215–233. *See also* **earbuds,**
    headphones, iTunes Store, music,
    speakers
  adding album art 221
  Apple Music service 215–217
  Beats 1 217
  Connect tab 217
  controlling from earbuds 222
  controlling with Siri 143
  equalization 235
  For You tab 229
  iTunes Match 217
  iTunes Radio 230–233
  Loop button 223
  My Music tab 218–220
  New tab 229–230
  Now Playing screen 232
  options panel 219–220
  playback controls 220–224
  playback while locked 224
  playing from your computer 236
  playlists 224–227
  scrubber 221
  settings 588
  sharing songs 223
  shuffle songs 223
  Sound Check 236
  Up Next list 227–229
  volume limit 235–236
mute switch 22–23, 118–119
My Photo Stream 296–299
  defined 296
  deleting photos 298–299
  iCloud syncing 516
  on a Mac or PC 298
  on Apple TV 298
  on/off switch 516, 588
  saving photos from deletion 297–298
  turning on 297

N

nano-SIM cards 29
navigation. *See also* **GPS**
  in Maps app 382–384
  location-based reminders 401–402
  passenger mode 384–385
networks
  resetting settings 566
  speeds 24–25
  status bar icons 24–25

News app 388–390
    defined 388
    For You tab 389
    searching 389
    settings 587
    using offline 390
newspapers. *See* News app
noise cancellation 30, 207
No Service 613
Notes app 390–394
    adding formatting and photos 390–392
    compatibility with other email programs
        393–394
    controlling by voice 141–142
    defined 390
    Exchange syncing 550
    iCloud syncing 517
    navigation 392–393
    Quick Actions 37
    searching notes 392
    settings 580
    syncing notes 393–394
    viewing attachments 392–393
Notification Center 52–57
    gesture to open 35
    managing Lock screen 55–56
    Notifications tab 54
    open from Lock screen 18
    settings 561–562
    Today tab 53
notifications 51–57
    alerts 57
    answering 51
    banners 56
    customizing 55–56
    defined 51
    hiding 51
    Notification Center 52–57
    on Lock screen 16–17, 55–56
    opening 52
    responding to 51–52
    spoken 191
    three styles 56–57
    turning off 56
    turning off vibration 205
numbers layout 65

O

Ocarina 325
oleophobic screen 23
on/off switch 14–15
opening
    attachments 474–475
    camera 246
    Control Center 47

Settings app 556
    using Siri to open apps 133
optimizing iPhone storage 305
Outlook
    calendar invitations 550–551
    Outlook Web Access (OWA) 546
    setting up email account 457–458

P

pairing
    Bluetooth accessories 183–184
    Bluetooth on/off switch 558–559
    car systems 184–185
    fitness device 185
    headphones or speakers 234–235
    keyboard 78–79
    Mac 538–539
panoramas 262–264
parental controls 603–605
    blocking inappropriate material
        604–605
    blocking websites 605
    Family Sharing 528–533
    Game Center 605
    Guided Access (kiosk mode) 208–210
    in-app purchases 604
    restricting apps 604
    Safari 454
passwords
    Encrypted iPhone Backup 511
    Erase Data option 59
    forgotten Apple ID 574
    for parental controls 603
    Keychain 517–518
    letting Safari create 452–453
    memorized in Safari 585
    saving in Safari 446–448
    setting up 58–59
PDF files
    reading in iBooks 363–365
    zooming 368
Peek and Pop 38–39
    link-tapping tricks 445
peer-to-peer AirPlay 244
Personal Hotspot 424–427
    defined 424
    fee for 424
    turning off 426
    turning on 424–425
    via Bluetooth 426
    via USB cable 426
    via Wi-Fi 425
phishing
    Safari warnings 586

Phone app 95–96. *See also* **calling**
  Blocked list 178
  Quick Actions 37
phone features
  accessibility 187–212
  caller ID 114, 183
  call forwarding 182
  call waiting 181–182
  conference calling 120–122
  hiding your number on outgoing calls
    581
  merging calls 121–122
  muting 118–119
  noise cancellation 207
  speakerphone 119–120
  storage statistics 564
  tracking call time and data usage
    560–561
  Visual Voicemail 157–161
phone number
  transferring 596
  where to find 101
photos. *See also* **Photos app**
  assigning to Contacts 105–106
  attaching in Mail 482–483
  deleting 611
  sharing in Family Sharing 533
  syncing to a computer 508
  syncing to the phone 506–507
  take from Messages app 169
  texting 175
  texting recent 169
Photos app 269–307. *See also* **Camera
    app, My Photo Stream**
  adding favorites 286
  Albums tab 280–282
  assigning photos to Contacts 293–294
  auto-enhance button 270
  black-and-white photos 272–273
  color and light controls 270–273
  creating and deleting albums 287–288
  cropping and straightening 274–276
  deleting 285
  editing photos 269–277
  excluding bursts from iCloud 589
  Faces 281
  filters 259, 273–274
  Finger Browse gesture 280
  flicking, rotating, zooming, panning
    282–284
  hiding a photo 282
  iCloud Photo Library 304–305
  iCloud Photo Sharing 299–304
  moments, collections, years 278–280
  My Photo Stream 296–299
  photo orientation 255

  Recently Deleted folder 281–282
  red-eye removal 274
  saving your edits 277, 293
  searching 284–285
  selecting photos 286–287
  settings 588–589
  sharing and using photos 286–296
  slideshow controls 292
  texting photos 288–289
  using third-party editing apps 276
  wallpaper 294–296
pinching and spreading 34
  photos 282–284
playback controls 220–224
  in Control Center 49
  loop music 223
  mini-player 220
  Now Playing screen 220–224
  previous/next 222
  scrubber 221
  shuffle 223
  switching among speakers 235
  video 240–242
  volume keys and silencer 22–23
playlists 224–227, 492–494
  creating on the phone 225–226
  defined 224
  editing or deleting 227, 493–494
  Up Next list 227–229
  using 226–227
Podcasts app 394–397
  defined 394
  managing podcasts in iTunes 505–506
  playing 396–397
  settings 396
  streaming vs. downloading 395
  subscribing to series 395–396
POP3 accounts 459–460
Popular Near Me
  privacy settings 572
pop-up blocker 452, 586
printing. *See* **AirPrint**
privacy
  advertising settings 573
  blocking calls and texts 581
  by app 572
  Do Not Track 586
  hiding notifications on Lock screen 17
  hiding texts on Lock screen 179
  Location Services settings 571–572
  Private Browsing 453
  settings 570–573
  turning off search engine suggestions
    584
Private Browsing 453–454

proactive features
app icon on Lock screen 18
guessed Caller ID 114
Siri Suggestions screen 93–94
suggested email groups 479
projecting 244
pronunciation
fixing Siri's 153–154
proximity sensor 27
punctuation
dictating 82
typing shortcuts 70–71
"push" email 575
turning off to save power 42

Q

Quick Actions 36–37
QuickType keyboard 66–68
settings 565
turning off 68
Quick Website Search 438

R

radio
Beats 1 217
iTunes Radio 230–233
radio signals 24
Reachability feature 21–22
Reader mode 451–452
Reading List 443–445
reading voice 196
Read Receipts
on/off switch 582
Recents list 99–101
defined 99
deleting calls 100–101
recording the phone's screen 244
Reddit
searching 438
Redeem button 237
red-eye removal 274
Reflector app 244
region
settings 565–566
relatives
recording in Contacts 106
Reminders app
adding a new task 400
controlling by voice 140–141
creating new lists 398–399
creating reminders with Siri 397–398
default list 580–581

Details screen 400–402
iCloud syncing 517
location-based reminders 401–402
Quick Actions 37
"Remind Me About This" feature
402–403
Scheduled list 400
settings 580
sharing reminders in Family Sharing
533
timed reminders 400–401
Remind Me About This 402–403
Remind Me Later 115–116
renaming your iPhone 562
repair service 613–614
resetting
all settings 566, 608
erasing the phone 566, 608–609
force restarting 608
force restoring 610–611
location warnings 567
restoring the iPhone 608
troubleshooting steps 607–610
Wi-Fi networks 566
resolution 265–266
Respond with Text 115
editing default messages 581
restaurants 142–143
restoring the iPhone 511–512
restrictions. See **parental controls**
Retina display 23
Return key 65
ringer
settings 568–570
volume 568
ringtones
creating your own 122–123
different for each person 107
for text messages 108
from iTunes Store 239
managing in iTunes 506
settings 569–570
silencer switch 22–23
Vibrate on Ring 568
Vibrate on Silent 568
vibrate, then ring 123
vibration patterns 107–108
roaming 559
Rotation Lock 48–49
status bar icon 26
Rotor 189–190
RSS feeds 438, 442–443
Rule of Thirds grid 253

S

Safari 429–456
Back button 430
bookmarks 438–441
clearing cache 612
clearing History list 587
cookies 453
favorites icons 434–435
full-screen mode 432
graphics 446
History list 441–445
iCloud syncing 517
link-tapping tricks 445
memorized web passwords 585
memorizing contact information 447
parental controls 454
passwords list 585
password suggestions 452–453
phishing warning setting 586
pop-up blocker 586
popup blocker 452
private browsing 453–454
Quick Website Search 438
Reader mode 451–452
Reading List 443–445
Reload button 430
RSS feeds 442
saved passwords and credit cards
      446–448
search/address bar 430
search engine choice 584
searching 435–438
security 452–454
selecting text 87
settings 584–587
Stop button 430
Suggested Sites 436
switching to desktop sites 435
tabbed browsing 449–450
Top Hits 435
typing a web address 433–435
using the loupe 65–66
Web Inspector 587
zooming and scrolling 431–432
saving
email attachments 475
graphics 446
passwords and credit card info 446–
      448
photos 293
to iCloud Drive 334–336
screen 23–26
3D Touch feature 204–205
brightness settings 567–568
dimming to save power 41
how glass is made 24
increasing contrast 198–199
invert colors and grayscale 195–196
protecting 24
repairing 615
touchscreen accommodations 203–
      204
trick to dim instantly 210–212
turning off 43
turning off auto-brightness 41
turning off while using VoiceOver 189
zoom style for larger phones 601
Screen Curtain 189
screenshots 307
scrolling
in Safari 431–432
scrubber
music 221
videos 241
searching. *See also* **Spotlight**
email messages 477–478
iBooks 365
in Safari 435–438
in the Settings app 555
News app 389
photos 284–285
Quick Website Search 438
search settings 563
Siri Suggestions screen 93–94
turning off Safari suggestions 584–585
your corporate directory 548–549
security
Activation Lock 521
clearing History list 587
cookies 453
corporate concerns 546
emergency calls 59
Family Sharing 528–533
fingerprint access to apps 62
of Apple Pay 527–528
online parental controls 454
parental controls 603–605
passwords and credit cards 446–448
passwords and fingerprints 57–62
phishing warning setting 586
pop-up blocker 452, 586
private browsing 453–454
protecting SIM card 559–560
protecting the Lock screen 18–19
Safari 452–454
Send Last Location feature 521
setting up a password 58–59
setting up fingerprints 59–62
Siri 149
Touch ID 59–62
turning off Character Preview 63

selecting
  photos 286–287
  text 87
selfies. *See* **front camera**
Send Last Location 521
serial number 503
Settings 555–591
  AirDrop controls 333–334
  airplane mode 557
  app preferences 322
  Battery panel 570
  Bluetooth panel 558–559
  Carrier 558
  Cellular panel 559–561
  change with Siri 134
  Compass 584
  Control Center 47–51
  Control Center panel 562
  date and time 565
  Diagnostics & Usage 573
  Display & Brightness panel 567–568
  Do Not Disturb panel 562
  FaceTime 583–584
  Flickr and Vimeo 590
  Game Center 589–590
  General panel 562–567
  iCloud panel 573
  iTunes & App Store panel 574
  Keyboard 565
  limiting background apps 328
  Location Services 571–572
  Mail, Contacts, Calendars panel 575–580
  managing storage space 611–613
  Maps 584
  Messages 582–583
  Music 588
  News 587
  Notes 580
  Notification Center 55–56
  Notifications panel 561–562
  on/off labels 199–200
  password 58–59
  Personal Hotspot panel 561
  Phone 581–582
  Photos & Camera 588–589
  Podcasts 396, 589
  Privacy panel 570–573
  Reminders 580
  Reset screen 566–567
  resetting all settings 608
  Restrictions panel 565
  Safari 584–587
  Siri 154–155, 563
  Sounds panel 568–570
  Spotlight 563

text messages 176–178
Touch ID & Passcode panel 570
Twitter and Facebook 573, 590
Wallet & Apple Pay 574
Wallpaper panel 568
Wi-Fi panel 557–558
setting up a new phone 597–601
shake to undo 88–89, 205
shared photo streams. *See* **iCloud Photo Sharing**
SharePoint 552
sharing
  AirDrop 331–334
  bonus buttons in the Share panel 454–456
  bookmarks 434–435
  contacts 111–112
  file attachments 475
  iBooks highlighting and notes 369
  iCloud calendars 348
  iCloud Photo Sharing 299–304
  Live Photos 261–262
  music 223
  notes 392
  photos from texts 179–180
  Shared Links listing 442–443
  Share sheet 330
  to Twitter and Facebook 428
  URLs 442
  videos 290–291
  Voice Memos 407
Shift key 64
shortcuts
  abbreviation expanders 73–74
  from Lock screen to app 17
  in Settings 556
  jump to next Reading List article 444
  opening the camera quickly 246
  triple-press Home to dim the screen 210–211
  typing ".com" 430
signatures 484
silencer switch 22–23
  Vibrate on Silent setting 568
SIM card 27–29
  compatibility 596
  protecting with a PIN 559–560, 582
Siri 129–155
  alarm clock 135
  and iTunes Radio 233
  booking restaurants 142–143
  business lookups 142
  changing iPhone settings 134
  changing voice gender 154
  checking your calendar 139–140
  choice of language 563

choice of speaking voice 563
clock 136
Contacts lookup 136
controlling music 143
dialing by voice 134
dictation 80–86
driving directions 140
email 138
Facebook and Twitter commands 148
finding facts 147–148
Find My Friends 145
fixing name comprehension 153–154
funny things Siri says 150–152
gender of 131
"Hey Siri" feature 132
history of 130
how to trigger 131
identifying songs 144
in AssistiveTouch mode 201
language and accent 130, 154
making to-do lists 398
movie info 146–147
music playback 143
notes 141–142
opening apps 133
opening Settings panels 134
relationships (mom, boss, etc.) 153
Reminders 140–141
searching Twitter 149
security 149
settings 154–155
Siri Suggestions screen 93–94
sports scores 146
stock lookups 144
switching gender 563
text messages 137
timer 135–136
troubleshooting 150
using 131–132
using to change settings 47–51, 556
weather 144
web searches 145
what to say 133–149
Wolfram Alpha 147–148
Sleep switch 13–15
dumping calls to voicemail 15
sleep timer 353–354
slideshows 292
settings 589
smart playlists 504–505
smileys 77–78
SMS messages. See text messages
SoundHound 325
sounds
alarms and alerts 569–570
spam 484–485

speakerphone 30, 119–120
routing calls to 206
speakers 233–235
AirPlay 235
switching among 235
volume keys 22–23
speech 196. See also dictation, Siri,
        VoiceOver
Alex voice 189
auto-highlighting 196
choice of voice 196
dictation 80–86
iBooks reads to you 371
Speak Auto-text command 196
speaking rate 196
Speak Screen command 196
Speak Selection command 90, 196
VoiceOver app 188–191
spelling checker 68–69
dictionary 69
sports trivia 146
Spotlight 90–94
how to use 90–92
limiting scope 92–94
new location 46
personalizing 92–93
proactive search screen 93–94
Suggestions feature 91
spreading and pinching 34
Sprint
CDMA network 28
data network speeds 417–418
LTE network 418
personal hotspot 426
using the iPhone overseas 28–29
vs. other carriers 595
square photos 262
Standby mode 14
auto-lock time 564–565
waking the phone 19
status bar 24–26
airplane mode 25
battery meter 26
call forwarding 26
cell signal 24
clock 25
GPS 26
network speeds 24
network type 24–25
padlock 26
syncing 26
Teletype mode 26
VPN 26
Wi-Fi signal 25
Sticky Keys 205

Stocks app 403–405
  controlling by voice 144
  customizing portfolio 404–407
  landscape view 404
stopwatch 352–353
storage 504–505
  freeing up space 611–613
  iCloud Drive 334–336
  storage statistics 564–565
straightening photos 274–307
subject field
  in text messages 177
subtitles 208
  setting language 242
Suggested Apps 563–564
swapping calls 120–121
swiping 33, 35–36
Switch Control 200–201
syncing
  automatic 497–498
  contacts and calendars 509
  Continuity 535–544
  drag and drop 501
  ebooks and audiobooks 506
  Handoff feature 540–543
  iBooks bookmarks 372
  manually 500–501
  multiple iPhones 510
  notes 393
  overview 499–500
  photos 506–509
  Reminders to iCloud 397
  turning off autosyncing in iTunes 501
  using iTunes tabs 502
  via iCloud 515–518
  via Wi-Fi 498–499
  with Exchange ActiveSync 545–554
  with iTunes 497–501
  with multiple computers 510

T

tabbed browsing 449–451
  switching among windows 450
  syncing with iCloud 450–451
Teletype mode
  settings 581
  status bar icon 26
tethering. See Personal Hotspot
text
  hard-pressing to select 79–80
  making screen fonts bigger or bolder
    197–198
  selecting 87
  size in iBooks 367
  zoom style for larger phones 601

text messages
  addressing and sending 168–169
  audio texting 172–174
  auto-deleting 583
  auto-deleting messages 583
  Blocked list 178
  character count 177–178
  defined 162
  deleting 167–168, 612
  Do Not Disturb feature 165
  extracting from iPhone 180
  free 180–181
  Google Voice 181
  group messaging 176–177
  hiding on Lock screen 179
  iMessages 170–175, 582
  list of conversations 166–168
  marking as read 168
  MMS on/off 583
  notification settings 178–179
  preserving 180
  Quick Actions 37
  QuickType 66–68
  Read Receipts on/off 582
  receiving 162–164
  repeat alert 179
  Respond with Text option 115
  searching 167
  sending recent photos 169
  settings 176–178, 582–583
  sharing photos and videos 288–289
  Show Subject Field 177
  switch to a phone call 164–165
  texting from a Mac 538–539
  texting photos and videos 288–289
  tones for each person 108
  troubleshooting 613
  turning preview on and off 179
  video messaging 174–175
  viewing attachments 165–166
  voice control 137
  WhatsApp 180
text to speech. See speech
third-party keyboards 74–76
  installing 76
  limitations 75
threading email 463–464
time. See Clock app
time-lapse video 268
timer 50, 353–354
  controlling by voice 135
  sleep timer 353–354
time zones 579
  auto-set on/off 572
Tips app 405–406

T-Mobile
   free international texting and Wi-Fi 29
   GSM network 28
   personal hotspot 426
   using the iPhone overseas 28–29
   vs. other carriers 595
Today screen 53
to-do lists 397–403. *See also* **Reminders app**
Touch ID 59–62
   access to apps and websites 62
   adding a fingerprint 60
   initial setup 598
   renaming or deleting fingerprints 61
   troubleshooting 62
   where fingerprints are stored 61
touchtones 119
traffic reports 385–386
transferring your phone number 596
troubleshooting 607–616
   App Store 315
   battery life 611
   battery replacement 614–615
   calling problems 613
   Continuity 535–536
   cracked screen 615
   diagnostics preferences 600–601
   Diagnostics & Usage settings 573
   email problems 613
   erasing and restoring the phone 608–609
   Exchange ActiveSync 551–552
   force restarting 608
   force restoring 610–611
   installing updates 607
   Internet problems 613
   iPhone 4s sluggishness 602
   phone won't turn on 610–611
   preventing photo program from opening 508–509
   RecBoot program 610
   resetting settings 608
   resetting the phone 607–610
   restoring from backup 511–512
   restoring the phone 602
   running out of memory 611–613
   Siri 150
   text messages 613
   TinyUmbrella program 610
   Touch ID 62
   warranty and repair 613–614
   Web Inspector 587
True Tone flash 251
TV episodes 495–496
   free re-downloading 522–523
   viewing library 505

Twitter 427–428
   account settings 427
   alert sounds 569
   app 427
   defined 427
   good app for 325
   hashtags 428
   importing Contacts 107
   posting photos to 289–290
   posting with Siri 148
   privacy 573
   searching with Siri 149
   settings 590
   Share button 428
   Shared Links button 442–443
   special keyboard 428
typefaces. *See* **fonts**
typing. *See also* **keyboard**
   abbreviation expanders 73–74
   accented characters 72–73
   audio feedback 191
   in non-English languages 76–77
   punctuation 70–71
   QuickType suggestions 66–68
   resetting dictionary 69
   selecting text 87–89
   smileys 77–78
   spelling checker 68–70
   third-party keyboards 74–76
   tips and tricks 65–66
   turning shortcuts on and off 565
   Undo 88–89
   web addresses 433–435

U

UDID 503
Undo 88–89
unified inbox 462–463
   customizing 462–463
unlocking the iPhone 15–16
Update All Contacts button 106
updates 562–563, 602–603
   turning off automatic app updates 42
   why you should accept 607
upgrading
   via a restore 602
   via iTunes 601–602
   wirelessly 601
Up Next list 227–229
   defined 227–228
   using 228–229
USB cable 32

V

Verizon
CDMA network 28
data network speeds 417–418
LTE network 418
personal hotspot 426
using the iPhone overseas 28–29
vs. other carriers 595
vibrations
for incoming calls 107–108
for text messages 108
settings 568–569
vibrate, then ring 123
video calling. *See* **FaceTime**
video camera 264–267
changing focus 266
resolution 265–266
settings 588
Slo-Mo mode 267–268
taking a still photo while filming 266
Time-Lapse mode 268
zooming while recording 266
videos
attaching in Mail 482–483
deleting 611
editing 268–269
posting to YouTube and Vimeo
290–291
storage 504–505
syncing to a computer 508
syncing to the phone 506–507
texting 288–289
video messages 174–175
Videos app 240–244. *See also* **movies**
aspect ratios 243
descriptions for the blind 208
earbuds clicker 242
playback controls 240–242
scrubber 241
subtitles 208, 242
TV output 243–244
zooming 243
Vimeo
posting videos to 291
settings 590
VIPs
in email 465–466
vision assistance
audio movie descriptions 208
VoiceOver 188–191
Visual Voicemail 157–161
call details 160–161
changing password 581
defined 157
deleting 159–160

dialing in 161
dumping calls to voicemail 15
listening to deleted messages 160
recording your greeting 160
sending calls to 115
setting up 157–158
using 158–161
voice control. *See* **Siri**
voicemail. *See* **Visual Voicemail**
Voice Memos app 406–408
defined 406
editing recordings 408
making recordings 406–407
sharing 407
syncing to iTunes 406
VoiceOver 188–191
Alex voice 189
gestures 188
hints 189
Navigate Images options 191
on/off with Home button triple-click
211–212
phonetic feedback 190
Rotor 189–190
speaking rate 189
typing in Braille 189
voice recognition. *See* **dictation**
voices. *See* **speech**
VoLTE 419
volume
limit 235–236
of Maps' spoken instructions 584
of ringer 568
Sound Check 236
turning off volume keys 568
volume keys 22–23
using as camera shutter keys 255
VPN (virtual private networking)
552–554
status bar icon 26
VPN on Demand 553–554

W

waking the phone 14
Wallet app 409–410
iCloud syncing 517
settings 574
wallpaper 294–296
animated 294
turning off motion 199
warranty 613–614
battery replacement 614–615
Weather app 410–412
adding new cities 412
controlling by voice 144

web browser. *See* **Safari**
websites about the iPhone 615–616
WhatsApp 180–181
what's new in iOS 9 7–10
 Back button 328–329
 changes to "Hey Siri" 132
 Continuity over cellular airwaves 537
 Double-tap Timeout 191
 "Likely Caller ID" 114
 Move Data from Android 598
 News app 388–390
 new Share panel buttons 454–456
 proactive email groups 479
 proactive searching 93–94
 public transit directions 382
 "Remind Me About This" feature
  402–403
 revamped Notes app 390–394
 setting a SIM card PIN 559–560
 Settings app Battery panel 570
 Settings search box 555
 touchscreen accommodations 203–
  204
 trick to dim screen instantly 210–212
 turning off vibration 205
 turn off Character Preview 63
 Wi-Fi Assist 561
what's new in the 6s series 4–7
 3D Touch feature 204–205
 app switcher 326
 Force Touch 36–39
 link-tapping tricks 445
 Live Photos 260–262
 screen flash 252
white cable 32
widescreen keyboard 70
 cursor keys 70
Wi-Fi 419–422
 address 562
 airplane mode 422–423
 commercial hotspots 421–422
 controlling by voice 134
 controlling from Control Center 423
 defined 419
 finding hotspots 419
 hotspot connection data 421
 hotspot invitations 420
 initial setup 597
 Instant Hotspot feature 539–540
 list of hotspots 420–421, 557
 printing with AirPrint 329–330
 sequence of connections 420
 settings 557–558
 speed of 420
 turning off 43, 422–423
 using while on a call 114

 voice calls over the network 25
 Wi-Fi Assist 561
 Wi-Fi Positioning System 375–376
 wireless syncing with iTunes 498–499
Wikipedia
 searching 438
Windows AutoPlay
 preventing it from opening 508–509
**wireless speakers and headphones
  233–235**
Wish List (iTunes Store) 232
Wolfram Alpha 147–148
World Clock 349–350

Y

Yahoo
 setting up email account 457–458
Yelp 379
YouTube
 posting videos to 290–291

Z

.zip files 475
zooming 192–195
 camera digital zoom 252–253
 Follow Focus command 193
 gestures 192–193
 in Safari 431–432
 iPhone 6 and 6s families 567
 menu 193
 on/off with Home button triple-click
  211–212
 photos 282–284
 Show Controller command 194

THE MISSING CD

There's no
CD with this book;
you just saved $5.00.

Instead, every single web address, practice
file, and piece of downloadable software
mentioned in this book is available at
missingmanuals.com (click the Missing
CD icon). There you'll find a tidy
list of links, organized
by chapter.